Creating Programs
for the Gifted

SERVING SPECIAL POPULATIONS SERIES

BOOKS FOR THE GIFTED CHILD

CREATING PROGRAMS FOR THE GIFTED
A Guide for Teachers, Librarians, and Students

NOTES FROM A DIFFERENT DRUMMER
A Guide to Juvenile Fiction Portraying the Handicapped

SERVING PHYSICALLY DISABLED PEOPLE
An Information Handbook for All Libraries

Creating Programs for the Gifted

A Guide for Teachers, Librarians, and Students

Corinne P. Clendening
and
Ruth Ann Davies

R. R. Bowker Company
New York and London, 1980

Published by R. R. Bowker Company
1180 Avenue of the Americas, New York, N.Y. 10036
Copyright © 1980 by Xerox Corporation
All rights reserved
Printed and bound in the United States of America

Library of Congress Cataloging in Publication Data
Clendening, Corinne P.
   Creating programs for the gifted.

   (Serving special populations series)
   Bibliography: p.
   Includes index.
   1.   Gifted children—Education.   2.   School libraries.
I.   Davies, Ruth Ann, 1915–   joint author.   II.   Title.
III.   Series.
LC3993.C56   371.95′3   80-10544
ISBN 0-8352-1265-3

With loving pride and great expectations
this book is dedicated to our nieces and nephews:
Gary, Gail, Glen, Sally, and Lauren Trilli
and
Walter, Denise, and Natalie Hafner

Contents

Preface

The major thrust of this book is to provide viable answers to pertinent questions raised in the Marland Report, *Education of the Gifted and Talented* (Report to the Congress of the United States by the U.S. Commissioner of Education, 1972). The gifted and talented: Who are they? Why should we be particularly concerned about the gifted and talented? Aren't special provisions undemocratic? Can we identify the gifted and talented? Are special programs beneficial? What are the best administrative arrangements for programs? What are the necessary components of a good program? What are the educational implications of research on the gifted and talented? Part I is concerned with providing thoughtful answers to these basic and persistent questions.

Part II offers model programs designed to provide qualitatively differentiated learning experiences for the gifted and talented. These model programs have been developed highly mindful of the unequivocal specification of the Marland Report that "special programs for the gifted and talented are *essential* [and that] . . . Special grouping and special planning, carefully conceived and executed, provide opportunities for the gifted to function at proper levels of understanding and performance" (p. 39).

Careful search of the literature has revealed *not a single voice* among recognized authorities in the field of gifted education affirming the popular albeit spurious notion that "cream will always rise to the top" with regard to the gifted and talented. To the contrary, expert consensus not only affirms a differentiated program of excellence "meticulously planned from the outset," but also emphasizes that what will be taught, what will be learned, and what specific and unique teaching strategies will be employed must all be specified (*Conn-Cept VII: A Connecticut Primer on Program Development for the Gifted and Talented*, Task Force Report on Curriculum, Hartford, Conn.: Connecticut State Department of Education, 1978, pp. 4–5).

This guide, then, has been designed to provide practical, workable answers for teachers, librarians, administrators, school board members, and parents involved either in initiating new programs or in strengthening existing programs for the gifted and talented. It should also serve as a workbook for students interested in working with the gifted and talented. The hope is that it will serve as a guide and companion, a *vade mecum* on the challenging journey that lies ahead. In the words of the Chinese proverb, the most important step in a thousand-mile journey is the first step. May the journey be a success from the first step to the last!

An endeavor of this magnitude requires the cooperation of a large number of persons, only a few of whom can be mentioned here. For invaluable assistance on the local, state, and national levels, the authors wish to acknowledge their indebtedness with gratitude to the following North Hills School District teachers of the Gifted and Talented Program, who have creatively participated in designing, field testing, and implementing many of the programs highlighted in this book: Carol Doyle, Isabelle Hammerstein, Mabel Heinlein, Nancy Nahi, Patricia Olean, Shirley Pittman, Mary Sanderson, Nina Shevchik, Faye Smith, Joy Zimmerman; and Royce Rice.

The following North Hills School District (Pittsburgh, Pennsylvania) administrators also deserve mention: *Dr. Victor Morrone,* who pioneered in innovative programs for the gifted and talented in the North Hills School District; *Dr. Joshua Geller,* who, as superintendent of the North Hills School District, gave impetus, leadership, and support to the establishment of the North Hills School District Program for the Gifted and Talented; and *Robert Irvin,* principal in the North Hills School District, who serves so staunchly as administrative advisor to and advocate for the gifted program.

The following dedicated educators and scholars are also noteworthy: *Noretta Bingaman,* of the Commonwealth of Pennsylvania's Department of Education, for her expertise in gifted education generally and her wise counsel during the critically formative stages of district program development, audit, and evaluation; *Jean Gatling Farr,* program director of the Right to Education for Gifted and Talented, Bureau of Special and Compensatory Education, Pennsylvania Department of Education, and member of the Advisory Ad Hoc Panel of the Federal Office of Gifted and Talented, not only for her continuing wisdom and know-how in gifted programming on both state and federal levels, but most especially for her enduring graciousness in consenting to serve both as a consultant to this work and to the readers of this work as well; and *John Grossi,* director, Gifted and Talented Project of the Council for Exceptional Children, who has rendered great assistance to the present work and who, too, has consented to serve as a contact person for program developers wishing to consult with him.

As consultants, Jean Gatling Farr and John Grossi bring an added practical dimension to this book. They will explore with the reader avenues pertaining to program development, implementation, staffing, in-service, funding, resources, facilities, and evaluations. Farr may be contacted at her office at 500 Valley Forge Plaza, 1150 First Ave., King of Prussia, Pa. 19406 (215-265-3706). Grossi may be contacted at the CEC, 1920 Association Dr., Reston, VA 22091 (800-336-3728).

Our deepest gratitude is reserved for all the children of the North Hills School District who have brought life and delight to these programs, and especially to Brian, Kristen, and Grant, who have truly made this labor one of love.

Creating Programs
for the Gifted

Part I
Educating the Gifted and Talented

1

The Nation's Commitment to Educating the Gifted and Talented

Aren't special provisions undemocratic? If DEMOCRATIC educational practice is interpreted as the SAME education for all, the answer is yes. If we believe that democratic education means appropriate educational opportunities and the right to education in keeping with one's ability to benefit, the answer is no.

*Sidney P. Marland, U.S. Commissioner of Education**

Since the debut of the intelligence test at the beginning of the twentieth century, teachers, administrators, school boards, parents, and lastly legislators have puzzled over the dilemma of educating gifted students in a public educational program geared primarily to a philosophy of egalitarianism. Just as the Declaration of Independence and the Constitution define the rights of American citizens, so *Education of the Gifted and Talented,* the 1971 report to Congress by U.S. Commissioner of Education Sidney P. Marland, defined for the first time in the country's history the rights of gifted and talented children and youth to experience differentiated educational programs commensurate with their special capabilities. This landmark document "signaled the beginning of a broad based and sustained interest in developing appropriate educational programs for gifted and talented children."[1] (See Appendix A for the text of the Marland Report.)

The Marland Report appeared on the contemporary scene at the direct behest of the Congress of the United States. Congress had included in the Elementary and Secondary Education Amendments of 1969, Sec. 806, "Provi-

*Sidney P. Marland, Jr., *Education of the Gifted and Talented,* vol. 1, Report to the Congress of the United States by the U.S. Commissioner of Education (Washington, D.C.: Government Printing Office, 1972), p. 25.

sions related to gifted and talented children."* This amendment explicated congressional intent that gifted and talented students should benefit from federal education legislation, notably from Titles III and V of the Elementary and Secondary Education Act (ESEA). Sec. 806 directed the Commissioner of Education to conduct a study to:

1. Determine the extent to which special educational assistance programs are necessary or useful to meet the needs of gifted and talented children.
2. Show which existing Federal educational assistance programs are being used to meet the needs of gifted and talented children.
3. Evaluate how existing Federal educational assistance programs can be more effectively used to meet these needs.
4. Recommend new programs, if any, needed to meet these needs.[2]

THE MARLAND REPORT ANALYSIS

The Marland Report is the commissioner's response to the congressional mandate of Sec. 806. It provided the basic parameters essential for developing differentiated educational programs for the gifted and talented on the state and local district levels.

DEFINITION

Gifted and talented children are those identified by professionally qualified persons who by virtue of outstanding abilities, are capable of high performance. These are children who require differentiated educational programs and/or services beyond those normally provided by the regular school program in order to realize their contribution to self and society.

Children capable of high performance include those with demonstrated achievement and/or potential ability in any of the following areas, singly or in combination:

1. general intellectual ability.
2. specific academic aptitude.
3. creative or productive thinking.
4. leadership ability.
5. visual and performing arts.
6. psychomotor ability.

It can be assumed that utilization of these criteria for identification of the gifted and talented will encompass a minimum of 3 to 5 percent of the school population.[3]

IDENTIFICATION

Evidence of gifted and talented abilities may be determined by a multiplicity of ways. These procedures should include objective measures and professional evaluation measures which are essential components of identification.

Professionally qualified persons include such individuals as teachers, administrators, school psychologists, counselors, curriculum specialists, artists, musicians, and others with special training who are also qualified to appraise pupils' special competencies.[4]

---

*On January 28, 1969, the proposal was jointly introduced by Congressman Erlenborn and his colleagues in the House and by Senator Javits and his fellow senators. H.R. 4807, the Gifted and Talented Children Education Assistance Act of 1969, passed the House. Sec. 718 was incorporated in P.L. 91-230 (the ESEA amendment of 1969), which was signed into law April 13, 1970. Minor differences in definition in gifted and talented in the two versions were resolved as "children who have outstanding intellectual ability and creative talent." Sec. 806 amended Sec. 521 of the Higher Education Act of 1965 (relating to fellowships for teachers). *Education of the Gifted and Talented,* vol. 1, Report to the Congress of the United States by the U.S. Commissioner of Education (Washington, D.C.: Government Printing Office, 1972), p. 9.

DIFFERENTIATED PROGRAM CHARACTERISTICS

The advisory panel established three characteristics for a differentiated educational program:

1. A differentiated curriculum which denotes higher cognitive concepts and processes.
2. Instructional strategies which accommodate the learning styles of the gifted and talented and curriculum content.
3. Special grouping arrangements which include a variety of administrative procedures appropriate to particular children, i.e., special classes, honor classes, seminars, resource rooms, and the like.[5]

PROFILE OF THE GIFTED
AND TALENTED POPULATION

What are they like?

In general, gifted children have been found to be better adjusted and more popular than the general population, although there are definite relationships between educational opportunities and adjustment.

The gifted explore ideas and issues earlier than their peers.

Gifted pupils, even when very young, depart from self-centered concerns and values far earlier than their chronological peers.

Of all human groups, the gifted and talented are the least likely to form stereotypes.

What about their social and economic origins?

Even though the major studies have not employed detailed community searches, giftedness has been found in all walks of life.

Can we identify the gifted and talented?

Obviously, we can identify giftedness—or it identifies itself, particularly when a 2-year-old begins to read or play the piano.

Identification includes many factors: (1) age of identification, (2) screening procedures and test accuracy, (3) the identification of children from a variety of ethnic groups and cultures, and (4) tests of creativity.

Can we identify the very young gifted or talented child?

On the basis of both early and current studies, we *can* identify these children quite apart from their tendency to emerge at times on their own.

Since the gifted child is advanced beyond his age group, we may assume greater stability of intelligence than in the average or below average; young gifted children can be individually tested and accurately identified.

How accurate are screening procedures and tests?

A number of studies have shown that individual tests identify gifted children much more accurately than do group measures. *Half* of an identified gifted population remains unidentified with group tests alone.

The most highly gifted children are penalized most by group test scores; that is, the higher the ability, the greater the probability the group test will overlook such ability.

Teachers are able to nominate about half of the gifted. (Similar levels of accuracy occur when they attempt to nominate the creative.)

It has long been recognized that extreme environmental factors affect the performance of children in many areas, including intelligence. The measured intelligence of children declines when they are isolated or emotionally starved, as it does when verbal and nonverbal stimuli are lacking.

Can we identify the gifted from minorities and diverging cultures?

There is ample evidence that highly gifted children can be identified in all groups within our society.

It is reasonably well-known that with help, young children from poverty backgrounds can improve their I.Q. levels significantly.

Since the full range of human talents is represented in all the races of man and in all socio-economic levels, it is unjust and unproductive to allow social or racial background to affect the treatment of an individual.

Can we identify the creative and talented?

There are higher relationships between general intelligence and the individual tests of creativity than among the individual measures themselves. Although a few studies have supported the creativity-intelligence distinction, most have established substantial relationships between creativity and intellectual aptitude.

The trend is away from the global use of "creativity" as a psychological concept similar to intelligence. Goldberg has suggested the use of the term, "creative" be assigned to novel, reality adapted, disciplined and fully realized products, and that "divergent thinking" be used to describe new attributes of ability.

What is a good operational definition of "gifted and talented"?

Generally, the following evidence indicates special intellectual gifts or talent:

1. Consistently very superior scores on many appropriate standardized tests.
2. Judgment of teachers, pupil personnel specialists, administrators, and supervisors familiar with the abilities and potentials of the individual.
3. Demonstration of advanced skills, imaginative insight, and intense interest and involvement.
4. Judgment of specialized teachers (including art and music), pupil personnel specialists, and experts in the arts who are qualified to evaluate the pupils' demonstrated and/or potential talent.

What is a good estimate of the number of gifted and talented children?

Some people put the figure at 3 percent of the total school population while others would range as far as 15 percent to include those children with a special talent who may lack the full spectrum of "giftedness."

Even taking the very conservative estimate of 3 percent, the size of the population—1.5 million—demands attention.

EDUCATIONAL IMPLICATIONS OF RESEARCH

Gifted and talented youth are a unique population, differing markedly from their age peers in abilities, talents, interests, and psychological maturity.

Gifted and talented youth are the most versatile and complex of all human groups, possibly the most neglected of all groups with special educational needs.

Research studies on special needs of the gifted and talented demonstrate the need for special programs. Contrary to widespread belief, these students cannot ordinarily excel without assistance.

The relatively few gifted students who have had the advantage of special programs have shown remarkable improvements in self-understanding and in ability to relate well to others, as well as in improved academic and creative performance.

The programs have not produced arrogant, selfish snobs; special programs have extended a sense of reality, wholesome humility, self-respect, and respect for others.

A good program for the gifted increases their involvement and interest in learning through the reduction of the irrelevant and redundant.

Identification of the gifted and talented in different parts of the country has been piecemeal, sporadic, and sometimes nonexistent.

Many of the assumptions about giftedness and its incidence in various parts of the American society are based on inadequate data, partial information, and group tests of limited value.

The United States has been inconsistent in seeking out the gifted and talented, finding them early in their lives, and individualizing their education.

Particular. injustice has occurred through apathy toward certain minorities, although neglect of the gifted in this country is a universal, increasing problem.[6]

SUMMARY OF FINDINGS

Differential educational provisions for the gifted and talented had an extremely low priority in the competition for the federal, state, and local educational funding. Concern for program development was miniscule.

Minority and culturally different gifted and talented children were scarcely being reached.

Twenty-one states had made legislative or regulatory provisions for gifted and talented children; frequently these provisions were not mandatory and represented mere intention. Only 10 states had full-time personnel in their state educational agencies assigned to gifted education.

Contrary to popular myth, gifted and talented children were *not* succeeding on their own. In fact, the reverse was true.

Identification of the gifted and talented suffered woefully from inadequate testing, inadequate funds, and in some cases from indifference, apathy, and hostility.

Where differentiated programs for the gifted and talented had been implemented, the effects were measurable.

The federal role in providing services to the gifted and talented was for all practical purposes nonexistent.

THE COUNCIL FOR EXCEPTIONAL CHILDREN SURVEY

In October 1976, the Office of Gifted and Talented, U.S. Office of Education, commissioned the Council for Exceptional Children (CEC) to conduct a state education agency (SEA) survey, which would: (1) elicit the current existence, status, and capacity of information systems and data bases within those states as related to legislation, resources, and existence of programs and services to gifted and talented children, and (2) produce currently available data from those sources. The resultant summary of findings, *The Nation's Commitment to the Education of Gifted and Talented Children and Youth,* was published by CEC in April 1978.[7]

The Marland Report data was the benchmark from which growth as noted in the CEC Survey was measured.

Using the most conservative estimates (3%), there were at least 1,352,915 gifted and talented school-age persons in the U. S. and its territories in 1976–1977; this study found that only 437,618 gifted and talented students were *actually* receiving services.

The Marland Report stated that 21 states had legislation governing programs and services for the gifted and talented. The CEC Survey identified 33 states with actual statutes and another 10 states with written and adopted policies governing educational services for the gifted and talented; 8 states had neither statutes nor administrative policy.

Without question, the status of gifted and talented education in the U. S. in 1977 was healthier than it was in 1971–1972; all major areas surveyed reflected measurable or assumed growth.

Only 11 states have more than the equivalent of one full-time person in the State Educational Agency designated to work in gifted and talented programs. Ten states still had less than a half-time equivalent; four states had no one at all.

Despite the gains reported, the quality of services provided was unanswered; no data was forthcoming that demonstrated the appropriateness or effectiveness of the present services to the gifted and talented.

The conditions identified in the Marland Report as deterrents were found to be operative in 1977—lack of adequate funding from both Federal and state coffers, lack of trained personnel assigned to work with programs for gifted and talented, lack of sufficient training opportunities for those who want to improve their skills, lack of substantiated procedures for identifying gifted and talented children, lack of adequate information in program effectiveness, and lack of information from and to all levels of this important enterprise.

The impact on indifference and apathy on both the federal and state levels regarding the education of the gifted and talented made by the Marland Report is attested to by the findings of the CEC survey. State-level advances are notable and, indeed, encouraging and "tend to inspire an attitude of cautious optimism on the part of those who have long considered the gifted and talented as the neglected stepchildren of our educational system."[8]

Table 1 highlights milestones from 1870 to 1978 in the history of American education for the gifted and talented.

TABLE 1   MILESTONES IN THE HISTORY OF GIFTED
AND TALENTED EDUCATION

DATE	PUBLICATION OR EVENT	DESCRIPTION
1870	Francis Galton, *Hereditary Genius: An Inquiry into Its Laws and Consequences* (New York: Appleton).	Stated that mental capacities are inherited and follow certain laws of transmission; the first quantitative psychological study of giftedness.
1903	J. McK. Cattell. "A Statistical Study of Eminent Men," in *Popular Science Monthly* 62 (1903): 359–377.	Stated the belief that innate characteristics were more potent than social tradition or physical environment.
1916	Lewis M. Terman, *The Measurement of Intelligence* (Boston: Houghton).	Recommended that courses of study be designed to permit progress at a rate normal for the individual student; also recommended that teachers measure out the work for each child in proportion to the child's mental ability.
1925	Lewis M. Terman, *Genetic Studies of Genius. Mental and Physical Traits of a Thousand Gifted Children,* vol. 1 (Stanford, Calif.: Stanford University Press).	Initiated a longitudinal study of approximately 1,500 children with high IQ's; study now in progress for more than 50 years.

TABLE 1 (cont.)

DATE	PUBLICATION OR EVENT	DESCRIPTION
1926	G. Wallas, *The Art of Thought* (New York: Harcourt).	Identified four distinct stages in forming new thoughts: preparation, incubation, illumination, verification.
1931	White House Conference on Child Health and Protection, Report of the Committee on Special Classes, "Gifted Children," in *Special Education: The Handicapped and the Gifted,* Education and Training, Sec. 3 (New York: Century), pp. 537–550.	Stressed that giftedness meant "merely the child with exceptional intelligence" and did *not* refer to gifts in art, music, poetry, and other areas.
1945	*General Education in a Free Society: A Report of the Harvard Committee* (Cambridge, Mass.: Harvard University Press).	Stressed that equality of opportunity does not mean identical provision for all; rather it means access for all to those avenues of education that match their gifts and interests.
1950	The National Education Association's Educational Policies Commission, *Education of the Gifted* (Washington, D.C.: National Education Association).	Decried America's neglect of mentally superior children and the resulting shrinkage of personnel in the sciences, arts, and professions.
1950	J. P. Guilford's presidential address to the American Psychological Association (APA).	Challenged APA members to pursue research studies of creativity.
1953	A. F. Osborn, *Applied Imagination: Principles and Procedures of Creative Problem Solving* (New York: Scribner).	Recommended "brainstorming" as a means of utilizing personal interaction.
1954	Abraham Maslow, *Motivation and Personality* (New York: Harper).	Believed that the creative person is healthy and self-actualizing; that creativity involves a fundamental change in personality structure; and that this change occurs in the direction of fulfillment.
1956	Benjamin Bloom, *Taxonomy of Educational Objectives: The Classification of Educational Goals,* Handbook 1, Cognitive Domain (New York: McKay).	Grouped learning experiences in a hierarchy from the lowest to the highest mental processes; advanced the theory that knowledge is but the first step along the road to learning.
1957	Sputnik orbited by the Russians.	Generated unparalleled congressional interest in and concern for upgrading education in mathematics, science, and foreign languages.
1958	Congress passed National Defense Education Act.	Authorized federal funds for educational purposes in the form of loans and grants; provided funds for strengthening specific educational offerings in science, mathematics, and foreign languages in both public and private schools on the basis of national interest.

TABLE 1 (cont.)

DATE	PUBLICATION OR EVENT	DESCRIPTION
1958	Rockefeller Brothers Fund, *The Pursuit of Excellence: Education and the Future of America,* America at Mid-Century Series, Special Studies Project Report 5 (New York: Doubleday).	Stressed that it is the birthright of each American citizen to have his or her individuality respected; correlated the optimum development of the individual with the health of society itself, for enabling each citizen to achieve to the optimum of his or her potential is a means of society's reinvigorating itself.
1959	Irving A. Taylor, "The Nature of the Creative Process," in *Creativity: An Examination of the Creative Process,* ed. by P. Smith (New York: Hastings House).	Identified five levels or dispositions to creativity: expressive, technical, inventive, innovative, emergentive.
1959	J. P. Guilford, "Traits of Creativity," in *Creativity and Its Cultivation,* ed. by H. Anderson (New York: Harper).	Identified 120 factors of intellectual ability embodied in a three-dimensional theoretic model of intelligence, which he called the "Structure of Intellect."
1960	John C. Flanagan designed and initiated Project TALENT.	Undertook a scientific national longitudinal inventory of human talents encompassing some 440,000 students in 1,350 secondary schools in all parts of the country; planned follow-up studies for the next quarter-century to relate performance in adult life to aptitudes measured in adolescence.
1960	Report of the President's Commission on National Goals, *Goals for Americans* (Englewood Cliffs, N.J.: Prentice-Hall).	Stated that equality of opportunity for all citizens to experience an educational program uniquely reflective of the individual citizen's capabilities is the only goal worthy of a free society.
1961	John Gardner, *Excellence: Can We Be Equal and Excellent Too?* (New York: Harper).	Stated that equalitarianism is wrongly conceived when it ignores differences in native capacity and achievement; stressed the necessity of all who care about excellence in a society vigilantly striving to prevent the waste of talent.
1962	Jacob Getzels and Philip Jackson, *Creativity and Intelligence: Explorations with Gifted Students* (New York: Wiley).	Reported research that substantiated a valid distinction between creativity and the traditional concept of general intelligence.
1962	E. Paul Torrance, *Guiding Creative Talent* (Englewood Cliffs, N.J.: Prentice-Hall).	Defined creative thinking as the process of sensing gaps or disturbing, missing elements; forming ideas or hypotheses concerning them; testing these hypotheses; and communicating the results, perhaps modifying and retesting the hypotheses.
1964	David R. Krathwohl, ed., *Taxonomy of Educational Objectives: The Classification of Educational Goals,* Handbook 2, Affective Domain (New York: McKay.	Grouped educational objectives in a hierarchy from the simple to the complex, with each level demanding of the learner an ever greater sense of personal involvement, decision making, and commitment.

TABLE 1 (cont.)

DATE	PUBLICATION OR EVENT	DESCRIPTION
1968	Arnold Toynbee, "Is America Neglecting Her Creative Talents?" in *Creativity across Education,* ed. by Calvin Taylor (Ogden: University of Utah Press).	Declared "To give a fair chance to potential creativity is a matter of life and death for any society. This is all important, because the outstanding creative ability of a fairly small percentage of the population is mankind's ultimate capital asset."
1970	Congress passed P.L. 91-230.	Mandated in Sec. 806 that the U.S. Commissioner of Education conduct a study evaluating the status of education for the nation's gifted and talented children and report findings, together with recommendations, to the Congress not later than one year after the enactment of this act.
1970	Frank E. Williams, *Classroom Ideas for Encouraging Thinking and Feeling* (Buffalo, N.Y.: D. O. K. Publishers).	Provided a three-dimensional model for implementing cognitive-affective behaviors in the classroom.
1971	Sidney P. Marland, Jr., U.S. Commissioner of Education, report to Congress, *Education of the Gifted and Talented* (Washington, D.C.: Department of Health, Education, and Welfare).	Prepared report in compliance with the 1970 congressional mandate (P.L. 91-230), Sec. 806) for a status report on education of gifted and talented children; generated considerable interest on the federal, state, and local levels.
1972	U.S. Commissioner of Education Report, *Education of the Gifted and Talented,* an official document of the Committee on Labor and Public Welfare (Washington, D.C.: Government Printing Office).	Acclaimed as a landmark document in the education of gifted and talented children.
1972	ERIC Clearinghouse on Handicapped and Gifted Children established.	Operated by the Council for Exceptional Children since its inception in 1972, the Clearinghouse gathers, evaluates, abstracts, and disseminates information on all aspects of gifted and talented education.
1972	National/State Leadership Training Institute (LTI) on the Gifted and Talented established.	Created and funded through a grant authorized by the Education Professions Development Act, LTI has directed its efforts to changes at the state level, developing training programs and modules for regional offices, states, and local education agencies.
1972	U.S. Office of Education, Office of Gifted and Talented established under the Special Projects Act of P.L. 93-380.	Focused national attention on the needs of gifted and talented children; provided leadership in explaining and promoting differentiated programs for the gifted and talented on the state, regional, and local levels.
1975	Congress passed P.L. 94-142, the Education for All Handicapped Children Act.	Guaranteed that all exceptional children have available to them a free *appropriate* public education.

TABLE 1 (cont.)

DATE	PUBLICATION OR EVENT	DESCRIPTION
1978	The Council for Exceptional Children, *The Nation's Commitment to the Education of Gifted and Talented Children and Youth* (Reston, Va.: Council for Exceptional Children).	Reported findings from the 1977 survey of states and territories identifying current policies, resources, and services for the education of gifted and talented children in all 50 states and U.S. territories.
1978	Congress passed P.L. 95-561.	Provided financial assistance to state and local educational agencies, institutions of higher education, and other public and private agencies and organizations to assist such agencies, institutions, and organizations to plan, develop, operate, and improve programs designed to meet the special educational needs of gifted and talented children.

NOTES

1. Council for Exceptional Children, *The Nation's Commitment to the Education of Gifted and Talented Children and Youth: Summary of Findings from a 1977 Survey of States and Territories* (Reston, Va.: Council for Exceptional Children, 1978), p. 3.
2. Sidney P. Marland, Jr., *Education of the Gifted and Talented,* vol. 1, Report to the Congress of the United States by the U.S. Commissioner of Education (Washington, D.C.: Government Printing Office, 1972), p. 9.
3. Ibid., p. 10.
4. Ibid., p. 11.
5. Ibid.
6. Ibid., pp. 15–23.
7. Council for Exceptional Children, *The Nation's Commitment.*
8. David M. Jackson, "The Emerging National and State Concern," in *The Gifted and the Talented: Their Education and Development,* the Seventy-eighth Yearbook of the National Society for the Study of Education, pt. 1, ed. by A. Harry Passow (Chicago, Ill.: National Society for the Study of Education, 1979), p. 62.

2
The Nature of Giftedness: Characteristics and Identification

> Abilities do not appear in isolation; people who perform well on tests such as the Stanford-Binet also tend to have many other abilities and talents that do not lend themselves readily to measurement in a testing situation. The gifted as a group possess many abilities, interests, and talents which are complex and advanced beyond the ordinary.
>
> *Ruth A. Martinson**

Educators commonly define the young gifted and talented population as the upper 3 to 5 percent of school-age children and youth who are clearly superior to their peers not only in intellectual ability but also in specific academic aptitude, creative and/or productive thinking, and achievement in the visual and performing arts. No longer is intellectual giftedness the sole indicator or characteristic. According to guidelines used in South Carolina, the term creative and productive thinking refers to "those students who have advanced insight, outstanding imagination, intense interest in one or more fields of achievement, innovative or creative reasoning ability, ability in problem solving, and high attainment in orignal or creative thinking."[1]

CHARACTERISTICS

Numerous characteristics of the gifted and talented have been identified by researchers during the past 80 or more years. Lists of characteristics have been compiled by authorities in the field such as Lewis Terman, Catherine Cox, James Gallagher, E. Paul Torrance, J. P. Guilford, Joseph S. Renzulli, and Ann Isaacs as well as many others. The U.S. Office of Gifted and Talented, recognizing the need for an identification guide, commissioned the Council for

*Ruth A. Martinson, *The Identification of the Gifted and Talented* (Reston, Va.: Council for Exceptional Children, 1975), pp. 1–2.

13

Exceptional Children (CEC) to prepare a synthesis from the multiplicity of separate listings of gifted and talented characteristics. The result was the following fact sheet entitled *Characteristics of the Gifted and Talented.*[2]

CHARACTERISTICS OF THE GIFTED AND TALENTED

There are numerous lists of characteristics or distinguishing features and attributes of gifted and talented children. Teachers and parents should interpret any single list, including this one, as exemplary rather than exclusive. Few gifted children will display all of the characteristics. Understanding the characteristics of gifted and talented children will help parents and teachers sharpen their observations of these children in two distinct ways: (a) While characteristics do not necessarily define who is a gifted child, they do constitute observable behaviors that can be thought of as clues to more specific behaviors, and (b) these characteristics are signals to indicate that a particular child might warrant closer observation and could require specialized educational attention, pending a more comprehensive assessment.

GENERAL CHARACTERISTICS OF GIFTED/TALENTED CHILDREN

They typically learn to read earlier with a better comprehension of the nuances of the language. As many as half of the gifted and talented population have learned to read before entering school. They often read widely, quickly, and intensely and have large vocabularies.

They commonly learn basic skills better, more quickly, and with less practice.

They are better able to construct and handle abstractions than their age mates.

They are frequently able to pick up and interpret nonverbal cues and can draw inferences which other children have to have spelled out for them.

They take less for granted, seeking the "hows" and "whys."

They display a better ability to work independently at an earlier age and for longer periods of time than other children.

They can sustain longer periods of concentration and attention.

Their interests are often both wildly eclectic and intensely focused.

They frequently have seemingly boundless energy, which sometimes leads to a misdiagnosis of "hyperactive."

They are usually able to respond and relate well to parents, teachers, and other adults. They may prefer the company of older children and adults to that of their peers.

CREATIVE CHARACTERISTICS

They are *fluent* thinkers, able to produce a large quantity of possibilities, consequences, or related ideas.

They are *flexible* thinkers, able to use many different alternatives and approaches to problem solving.

They are *original* thinkers, seeking new, unusual, or unconventional associations and combinations among items of information. They also have an ability to see relationships among seemingly unrelated objects, ideas, or facts.

They are *elaborative* thinkers, producing new steps, ideas, responses, or other embellishments to a basic idea, situation, or problem.

They show a willingness to entertain complexity and seem to thrive in problem situations.

They are good guessers and can construct hypotheses or "what if" questions readily.

They often are aware of their own impulsiveness and the irrationality within themselves and show emotional sensitivity.

They have a high level of curiosity about objects, ideas, situations, or events.

They often display intellectual playfulness, fantasize, and imagine readily.

They can be less intellectually inhibited than their peers in expressing opinions and ideas and often exhibit spirited disagreement.

They have a sensitivity to beauty and are attracted to aesthetic dimensions.

LEARNING CHARACTERISTICS

Gifted and talented children often show keen powers of observation, exhibit a sense of the significant, and have an eye for important details.

They often read a great deal on their own, preferring books and magazines written for youngsters older than themselves.

They take great pleasure in intellectual activity.

They have well developed powers of abstraction, conceptualization, and synthesizing abilities.

They have rapid insight into cause-effect relationships.

They tend to like structure, organization, and consistency in their environments. They may resent the violation of structure and rules.

They display a questioning attitude and seek information for the sake of having it as much as for its instrumental value.

They are often skeptical, critical, and evaluative. They are quick to spot inconsistencies.

They often have a large storehouse of information regarding a variety of topics which they can recall quickly.

They show a ready grasp of underlying principles and can often make valid generalizations about events, people, or objects.

They readily perceive similarities, differences, and anomalies.

They often attack complicated material by separating it into its components and analyzing it systematically.

They have a well developed common sense.

BEHAVIORAL CHARACTERISTICS

They are willing to examine the unusual and are highly inquisitive.

Their behavior is often well organized, goal directed, and efficient with respect to tasks and problems.

They exhibit an intrinsic motivation to learn, find out, or explore and are often very persistent. "I'd rather do it myself" is a common attitude.

They enjoy learning new things and new ways of doing things.

They have a longer attention and concentration span than their peers.

They are more independent and less subject to peer pressure than their age mates. They are able to be conforming or nonconforming as the situation demands.

They have a highly developed moral and ethical sense.

They are able to integrate opposing impulses, such as constructive and destructive behavior.

They often exhibit daydreaming behavior.

They may seek to conceal their abilities so as not to "stick out."

They often have a well developed sense of self and a realistic idea about their capabilities and potential.

RESOURCES

Barbe, W. A., & Renzulli, J. S. *Psychology and education of the gifted.* (2nd ed.). New York: Halstead Press, 1975.

Delp, J., & Martinson, R. *The gifted and talented: A handbook for parents.* Ventura, CA: Office of the Superintendent of Schools, 1975.

Gallagher, J. J. *Teaching the gifted child.* (2nd ed.). Boston: Allyn and Bacon, 1975.

Ginsberg, G. *Is your child gifted?* New York: Simon and Schuster, 1976.

Kaufman, Felice. *Your gifted child and you.* Reston, VA: The Council for Exceptional Children, 1976.

Martinson, R. *The identification of the gifted and talented.* Reston, VA: The Council for Exceptional Children, 1976.

Newland, T. Ernest. *The gifted in socioeducational perspective.* Englewood Cliffs, NJ: Prentice-Hall Inc., 1976.

Prepared by Bruce Boston, Fairfax, Virginia.

IDENTIFICATION

Identification of the gifted and talented is a complex and demanding task. In the belief that talent and ability have a better chance of flourishing if they are identified early and nurtured consistently, the U.S. Office of Gifted and Talented commissioned Jean N. Nazzaro, staff member of CEC, to prepare an identification procedural guide. The resultant fact sheet, which follows, is entitled *Identification of the Gifted and Talented.*[3]

IDENTIFICATION OF THE GIFTED AND TALENTED

Because human potential can express itself across a broad spectrum of specific abilities, and because the outer limits of potential can also be reached in this same variety of contexts, the most important question to ask when identifying the gifted and talented is "gifted at what?"

In recent years educators of the gifted and talented have spurned a generalized notion of giftedness which, historically, has concentrated on particular cognitive skills such as verbal and reasoning abilities. Instead, a concept of giftedness has been advanced which looks at specific ability areas, stressing the capability of high performance in such diverse contexts as creative and productive thinking, the visual and performing arts, leadership ability, and psychomotor ability, in addition to more traditional expressions of giftedness like general intellectual ability, or in readily measurable specific abilities such as math, physics, or chemistry.

Because identifying gifts and talents other than sheer academic ability is still a relatively unrefined diagnostic skill, some school systems continue to cling to standardized ability and aptitude tests to identify *all* kinds of gifted and talented children. Other useful methods may include teacher nomination, parent interviews, peer nomination, autobiographical inventories, case studies, the evaluation of student products, auditions, and teacher observation checklists. Some more appropriate methods and steps are suggested below in regard to the six ability areas set forth by the US Office of Education as contexts in which giftedness or talent may emerge.

Screening for General Intellectual Ability

Many school systems make use of group IQ tests for their first level screening effort. Although research has shown group tests to be misleading when used as a rigid guideline, they are still one of the more effective methods of defining a group which then can be more carefully assessed on an individual basis. The Stanford-Binet Intelligence Test and The Wechsler Intelligence Scale for Children—Revised (WISC-R) are considered to be among the best instruments currently available for identifying children with high general intellectual ability on an individual basis. Additional nominations of potentially gifted youngsters should be sought from parents, peers, teachers, and librarians. Minimum IQ scores of 125 to 135 are generally required for placement in a program for the intellectually gifted. In dealing with minority, disadvantaged, and handicapped children, extreme caution is advised in relying on IQ scores since most tests have not been standardized on these populations.

PROBING FOR CREATIVE OR PRODUCTIVE THINKING

In addition to the Torrance Test of Creative Thinking, a number of nontest ways of identifying the creatively gifted have been described by E. Paul Torrance (1977). His techniques are based on the observation of children's behavior and an analysis of what they produce. Strengths in the following areas may indicate exceptional creativity:

Ability to express feelings and emotions.

Ability to improvise with commonplace materials and objects.

Articulateness in role playing, sociodrama, and story telling.

Enjoyment of and ability in visual arts, such as drawing, painting, and sculpture.

Enjoyment of and ability in creative movement, dance, and dramatics.

Enjoyment of and ability in instrumental and vocal music and music rhythm.

Use of expressive speech.

Fluency and flexibility in figural media.

Enjoyment of and skills in group activities and problem solving.

Responsiveness to the concrete.

Responsiveness to the kinesthetic.

Expressiveness of gestures and body language and the ability to interpret body language.

Humor.

Richness of imagery in informal language.

Originality of ideas in problem solving.

Problem centeredness or persistence in problem solving.

Emotional responsiveness.

Quickness of warm-up.

DISCOVERING TALENT IN VISUAL AND PERFORMING ARTS

The opinions of experts, peers, and parents should be solicited when identifying children with special talents. A biographical sketch by a parent can reveal a great deal about precocity in all areas of exceptional ability. Children who take lessons in dance, music, and art outside the school setting should be identified and their teachers asked to comment on the child's potential. Auditions may be conducted. Often a youngster's peers know more about a child's special talents than do the adults in the environment. Ask students to list classmates whom they would like to have help them with art projects, or to nominate classmates for a talent show. Arts specialists within the school system are also excellent resources for identifying talented youngsters.

DETERMINING EXCEPTIONAL LEADERSHIP ABILITY

Within a given school or community there are *emerging* leaders as well as class presidents. Leadership is not always channeled in socially acceptable ways. The child who "gets others in trouble" is still a leader, as are *con artists* and *hustlers*. The search for leadership potential should include community workers connected with churches, Scout troops, preschool centers, playgrounds, and recreation halls. The list should include young children who seem to be competing successfully with older children. The search should identify leaders of street gangs. Ask parents if their children take charge in their daily routines. Ask dance teachers, "Who innovates?" and "Who leads and who follows?" Observation by teachers is invaluable in identifying class and school leaders.

DETERMINING SPECIFIC ACADEMIC APTITUDES

While the standardized group achievement tests often used to screen for specific academic aptitudes are useful for measuring acquired knowledge, they are not designed to indicate potential. Children who are consumed by specific interests, e.g. dinosaurs, volcanoes, puzzles, or stamps, may be in the first stages of demonstrating a specific academic aptitude. Self motivation is a strong indicator of exceptional ability and early identification and nurture are essential. Parents and/ or students may be asked to fill out checklists indicating how free time is spent and what specific interests are pursued.

IDENTIFYING OUTSTANDING PSYCHOMOTOR ABILITY

Who is chosen first by other children as game leader? Who always seems to be on the winning team? Observe children on the playground. Ask parents about outside activities. At what age did the child ride a bicycle? Bat a ball? Does the youngster show special talent or interest in dance, gymnastics, swimming? Does he or she enter athletic competitions? Can the child fix things easily? Ask Little League coaches, athletic club directors, and dancing school teachers for nominations of the potentially gifted in psychomotor ability.

SUCCESSFUL PROCEDURES

A successful screening and identification program requires early identification; a continuing search; the involvement of a variety of professionals, community workers, and parents; and the use of multiple methods. Flexibility is required to discover children who are believed to have outstanding potential but who may not qualify on the basis of test scores. Some hold the mistaken belief that "talent will out." Research has shown, however, that talent and ability have a better chance of flourishing if they are identified early and nurtured consistently.

RESOURCES

Fortna, R. O., & Boston, B. O. *Testing the gifted child: An interpretation in lay language.* Reston, VA: The Council for Exceptional Children, 1976.

Maker, C. J. *Providing programs for the gifted handicapped.* Reston, VA: The Council for Exceptional Children, 1977.

Martinson, R. A. *The identification of the gifted and talented.* Reston, VA: The Council for Exceptional Children, 1975.

Torrance, E. P. *Discovery and nurturance of giftedness in the culturally different.* Reston, VA: The Council for Exceptional Children, 1977.

Prepared by Jean N. Nazzaro, The Council for Exceptional Children.

An invaluable handbook is *The Identification of the Gifted and Talented* by Ruth A. Martinson. This instructional syllabus presents a rationale for the identification of gifted students, suggests appropriate procedures, contains numerous evaluation instruments, and devotes special attention to the identification of economically and culturally disadvantaged youngsters. This is an extremely effective tool for use in programs for parents as well as in in-service programs for school personnel. The following list, taken from the handbook's contents, indicates the diversity of coverage in this basic work.[4]

Definition
The Importance of Identification
Screening and Identification
Screening Measures—Assets and Limitations
    Teacher Nomination
    Group Intelligence and Achievement Tests
    Nomination by Others
    Nomination by Peers
    Parent Nomination

STATE POLICY CONCERNING IDENTIFICATION OF THE GIFTED AND TALENTED

The methods and procedures used to identify gifted and talented students vary from state to state. The ERIC Clearinghouse on Handicapped and Gifted Children contacted the state educational agency supervisor, coordinator, or director of gifted and talented programs in states known to have excellent identification-testing procedures to determine which instruments were used in their programs.[5] Among intelligence tests, the Stanford-Binet and the Wechsler Intelligence Scale for Children—Revised (WISC-R) were used most frequently; the Stanford Achievement Test (SAT) and the California Test of Mental Maturity were also widely used. The Tennessee Self-Concept Scale was in wide use as a personality instrument and the Torrance Test of Creative Thinking was also a frequently employed screening device. The Scale for Rating Behavioral Characteristics of Superior Students, developed primarily by Joseph S. Renzulli, was widely used as a screening instrument among teachers and program directors. (The sources for purchase of these various instruments are listed at the end of this chapter.)

Selection and use of testing instruments and/or procedures require the guidance of an expert in the field. John Grossi, director of the Gifted and Talented Project, The Council for Exceptional Children (1920 Association Dr., Reston, Va. 22091, toll free tel. 800-336-3728), should be contacted for information about any phase of the gifted and talented program.

A compendium of state identification methods and procedures is presented here to facilitate the reader in pinpointing his or her own state's policy. Adapted from The Council for Exceptional Children, *The Nation's Commitment to the Education of Gifted and Talented Children and Youth: Summary of Findings from a 1977 Survey of State and Territories* (Reston, Va.: CEC, 1978).

STATE ADMINISTRATIVE POLICY: DEFINITIONS AND IDENTIFICATION

ALABAMA

DEFINITION. Gifted children are those identified by professionally qualified persons as possessing a high degree of general intellectual ability.

Talented children show unusual ability along nonacademic lines and are capable of profiting from advanced instruction and of making a career in their special field. They may or may not function within the same I.Q. range as the gifted. The common denomination for the gifted and talented is the capacity for superior achievement. These are children who require differentiated educational programs and/or services beyond those normally provided by the regular school program in order to realize their contribution to self and society. . . .

Children capable of superior achievement include those with demonstrated achievement and/or potential ability in any of the following areas, singly or in combination:

A. General intellectual ability
B. Specific academic aptitude
C. Creative or productive thinking
D. Leadership ability
E. Visual and performing arts
F. Psychomotor ability

(Gifted and Talented, general guidelines issued by Alabama State Department of Education)

IDENTIFICATION PROCEDURES. Criteria for identification of the gifted should encompass a minimum of 3 to 5 percent of the school population of 130 I.Q. or above. The school system should recognize that some children may be talented with or without functioning within the I.Q. range of the gifted.
(Gifted and Talented, general guidelines issued by Alabama State Department of Education)

ALASKA

DEFINITION. Gifted and talented children are those identified by qualified persons who, by virtue of outstanding abilities, are capable of exceptional performance. These are children who require differentiated educational programs and/or services beyond those normally provided by the regular school program in order to realize their contribution to self and society.

This definition seeks to distinguish two groups of children from their peers on the basis of exceptional performance. The two groups are the (1) intellectually gifted and (2) the talented. While intellectual superiority and talent are highly related, the relationship is less than perfect; that is, not all talented children are intellectually superior while most intellectually superior children display exceptional talents. These two groups of students can be distinguished from their normal peers on the basis of a variety of performance indicators.
(Alaska Department of Education Special Education Regulations Handbook, as amended September 1977)

IDENTIFICATION PROCEDURES. Identification of students as gifted/talented must be done through the use of *multiple performance indicators*. No single test, test score, other measurement or nomination procedures should be the determining factors. Both objective and subjective measurements must be used. While some standardized tests exist for identification of giftedness and talent, districts may adopt them or develop their own in order to meet local needs. Multiple performance indicators to identify intellectually gifted might include, but are not limited to, the following: superior score on an individual or group achievement tests; superior score on individual or group intelligence tests; superior score on aptitude tests in specific areas; pupil products such as grades, class activities, and work; such as: exceptional art work, creative writing, musical ability, "inventions," etc.; nominations from teachers, parents, peers, self, and community members.

Talented children are those who have demonstrated exceptional performance in one or more of the following areas: creative or productive thinking; leadership; visual or performing arts; manipulative skills.
(Alaska Department of Education Special Education Regulations Handbook, as amended September 1977)

ARIZONA

DEFINITION. "Gifted child" means a child of lawful school age who due to superior intellect, advanced learning ability or both is not afforded an opportunity for otherwise attainable progress and development in regular classroom instruction and who needs special instruction, special ancillary services or both to achieve at levels commensurate with his intellect and ability.

IDENTIFICATION PROCEDURES.

Screening

A gifted child shall demonstrate *achievements and/or potential ability* in one or more of the following areas:

1. Creative or productive performance within the top 3% of district students.
2. Specific academic aptitude—95% or above on standardized achievement tests in one or more subject areas.
3. General intellectual ability—I.Q. 130 or above based on an individualized testing program. . . .

A referral for evaluation is required by ARS § 15-1013 for possible placement in a special education program and this referral shall be made after consultation with the parent or guardian of the child to be evaluated.

The placement of a child in a gifted program shall be reviewed once each semester, if requested by the parent or guardian of the child or recommended by the person conducting the gifted program.

(Arizona Administrator's Guide, 1972–73)

. . . an evaluation shall include but need not be limited to:

Obtaining information regarding the developmental history and cultural background of the child. . . .

A current medical history and health status report

A current vision and hearing screening

An educational evaluation, with review of the child's academic history. . . .

To place a child in a program for the gifted, written parental permission must be obtained.

(Special Education Conditions and Standards Relating to Identification and Placement, 1976)

ARKANSAS

DEFINITION. No adopted policy.

IDENTIFICATION PROCEDURES. No adopted policy.

CALIFORNIA

DEFINITION. California's statutes governing education of gifted and talented are separate from exceptional child statutes.

. . . "Mentally gifted minor," as used in this article, means a minor enrolled in a public primary or secondary school of this state who demonstrates such general intellectual capacity as to place him within the top 2 percent of all students having achieved his school grade throughout the state or who is otherwise identified as having such general intellectual capacity but for reasons associated with cultural disadvantages has underachieved scholastically. . . .

For the purposes of this article, the general intellectual ability of a minor shall be evidenced by one or more of the following factors: (a) Achievement in schoolwork; (b) Scores on tests measuring intellectual ability and aptitude; (c) The judgments of teachers and school administrators and supervisors who are familiar with the demonstrated ability of the minor.

IDENTIFICATION PROCEDURES. The responsibility for the identification of a pupil as a mentally gifted minor . . . shall rest with the administrative head of the school district or an employee of the district designated by him. The identification shall be based upon a developmental case study made by an identification and placement committee . . . of all pertinent evidence as to a pupil's general intellectual and scholastic capacity (including but not limited to a completed screening and nominating form and a psychologist's summary and evaluation). The committee shall consist of the school principal, a classroom teacher familiar with the school work of the pupil, a credentialed school psychologist, and any other person or persons designated by the district employee responsible for making the identification . . .

a. A score at or above the 98th percentile on a full scale individual intelligence test approved by the Superintendent of Public Instruction and administered to the pupil by a person qualified to administer individual intelligence tests. The norm to be used for the score is the norm for children of the same age as the pupil tested.

b. For a pupil in grades seven through twelve, a score at or above the 98th percentile in each of two tests chosen from a list of tests approved for the purpose by the State Board of Education and administered by a qualified person to the pupil while he was enrolled in grade 7 or above and within 24 months of the date of identification.

c. The judgments of teachers, psychologists, and administrators and supervisors who are familiar with the demonstrated ability or potential of the minors. In any given district not more than five (5) percent of the pupils identified under Section 3821 as mentally gifted minors shall be identified on such judgments alone. . . .

COLORADO

DEFINITION. No adopted policy.

IDENTIFICATION PROCEDURES. No adopted policy.

CONNECTICUT

DEFINITION. "Extraordinary learning ability" is deemed to be the power to learn possessed by the top five percent of the students in a school district as chosen by the special education planning and placement team on the basis of (1) performance on relevant standardized measuring instruments or (2) demonstrated or potential academic achievement or intellectual creativity.

"Outstanding talent in the creative arts" is deemed to be that talent possessed by the top five percent of the students in a school district who have been chosen by the special education planning and placement team on the basis of demonstrated or potential achievement in music, the visual arts or the performing arts. *(Policies, Procedures and Guidelines for Gifted and Talented Programs, 1976)*

IDENTIFICATION PROCEDURES. Screening and identification criteria should be based on a study of all available evidence as to the pupil's ability and/or potential by personnel qualified to administer and interpret appropriate standardized tests; judge demonstrated ability, potential, intellectual creativity and leadership; recognize outstanding talent in the creative arts. . . .

Section 10-76 of the General Statutes requires that the screening and identification criteria for those who are gifted and talented must be approved by the State Department of Education.

Items for Consideration in Screening and Identification Criteria:
Extraordinary Learning Ability

a. Very superior scores on appropriate standardized tests. Criteria for "very superior" might be the upper two or three percent of an appropriate criterion group or scores which are at least two standard deviations above the local norms. . . .

b. Judgments of teachers, pupil personnel specialists, administrators and supervisors who are familiar with the pupil's demonstrated and potential ability.

c. Utilization of a multi-criteria approach is necessary.

d. Intense interest and involvement in a specific intellectual area.

Additional items of evidence used in the creative arts category should include:

a. Evidence of advanced skills, imaginative insight, intense interest and involvement.

   b. Judgments of outstanding talent based on appraisals of specialized teachers, pupil personnel specialists, experts in the field and/or others who are qualified to evaluate the pupil's demonstrated and potential talent.
(Policies, Procedures and Guidelines for Gifted and Talented Programs, 1976)

DELAWARE

DEFINITION. "Exceptional persons" means a handicapped person or a gifted and talented person, as defined herein.

"Free appropriate public education" means special education that is specially designed instruction including classroom instruction, instruction in physical education, home instruction, and instruction in hospitals and institutions, and related services as defined by State Board of Education Rules and Regulations and as may be required to assist a handicapped person to benefit from an education. . . .

"Gifted or talented person" means a person in the chronological age group four through twenty years inclusive, who by virtue of certain outstanding abilities is capable of a high performance in an identified field. Such an individual, identified by professionally qualified persons, may require differentiated educational programs or services beyond those normally provided by the regular school program in order to realize his or her full contribution to self and society. A person capable of high performance as herein defined included one with demonstrated achievement and/or potential ability in any of the following areas, singularly or in combination:

1. general intellectual ability
2. specific academic aptitude
3. creative or productive thinking
4. leadership ability
5. visual and performing arts ability
6. psychomotor ability

IDENTIFICATION PROCEDURES. Identification of the gifted/talented should be done as a series of steps. The first step is *screening* through the use of multiple methods; the second is *identification* and *case study*. Screening includes some or all of the following: group tests of intelligence and achievement, creativity tests, teacher nominations, parent information, pupil data, pupil products, and teacher and parent notations on traits and behavior which may or may not be positive. Identification involves individual testing and case study which should be followed by educational planning.
(State Guidelines for Developing Local Plans for the Education of Gifted and Talented Students, 1975)

DISTRICT OF COLUMBIA

DEFINITION. "Gifted and talented" means children and, where applicable, youth, who have been identified at the preschool, elementary, or secondary level as (1) possessing demonstrated or potential abilities that give evidence of high performance capability in areas such as intellectual, creative, academic or leadership ability or in the performing and visual arts; and (2) needing differentiated education or services beyond those being provided by the regular school system to the average student in order to realize these potentialities.
(Policy Statement on Education of the Gifted and Talented. Approved by the Board of Education, March, 1976)

IDENTIFICATION PROCEDURES. Being developed.

FLORIDA

DEFINITION. Gifted—one who has superior intellectual development and is capable of high performance. The mental development of a gifted student is two (2) standard deviations or more above the mean. In most tests the mean intelligence quotient is 100 and the standard deviation is 15–16.
(Regulations of the Florida State Board of Education, 6A-6)

IDENTIFICATION PROCEDURES. . . . A student is eligible for special programs for the gifted if the student demonstrates:

a. Superior intellectual development—an intelligence quotient of two (2) standard deviations or more above the mean on an individually administered standardized test of intelligence. In most tests the mean intelligence quotient is 100 and the standard deviation is 15–16. The standard error of measurement may be considered in individual cases.
b. A majority of characteristics of gifted children according to a standard scale or checklist.
c. Need for a special program.

Procedures for student evaluation. The following are the minimum evaluations required to determine a student's eligibility and educational placement: an evaluation of intellectual functioning, characteristics of the gifted, statement of nonacademic performance, and the need for a special program.

This rule shall take effect July 1, 1977.
(Regulations of the Florida State Board of Education, 6A-6)

GEORGIA

DEFINITION. Students are intellectually gifted if their potential cognitive powers, when developed, qualify them to become high-level innovators, evaluators, problem-solvers, leaders or perpetuators in the complex society in which they live. Cognitive powers as used in this definition signify the complete range of intellectual functions, sometimes referred to as intellect, intelligence or mental abilities. Included are psychological concepts such as thinking, abstract reasoning, problem-solving, creativity, verbal comprehension, numerical facility among others.
(Regulations and Procedures: Special Education Program, 1976)

IDENTIFICATION PROCEDURES. For a student to be eligible for placement in a special program he must have the potential to perform at a significantly higher level than the average student. Significantly higher level refers to performance which places a student at least 1 1/3 standard deviations above the mean of the mental ability tests administered. Placement must be decided by the local placement committee after careful review of a complete case study on the student, which includes data relative to student's cognitive abilities, special interest, psychological data, school achievement, emotional and social maturity, creative ability, and recommendation of teacher.
(Regulations and Procedures: Special Education Program, 1976)

HAWAII

DEFINITION. Being developed.

IDENTIFICATION PROCEDURES. Being developed.

IDAHO

DEFINITION. Gifted/talented refers to those students with demonstrated achievement and/or potential ability in one or more of the following areas: general intellectual; specific academic aptitude, creative or productive thinking, leadership, visual/performing arts, or psychomotor ability.
(Administrative Rules and Regulations for Special Education)

IDENTIFICATION PROCEDURES.
Minimum Assessment Procedures. In order to qualify a student for full-time placement in a program for gifted/talented, *three or more* of the following five listed methods must be used in the assessment procedure: (1) achievement test scores; (2) intelligence test results; (3) results of creativity tests; (4) nominations, observations, and recommendations of teachers and other school personnel; (5) documentation from experts in a given field (art, music, drama, etc.).

Minimum Eligibility Criteria for Placement. The student must meet *three or more* of the following criteria: (1) scores on standardized achievement tests at or above the 98th percentile in the majority of areas tested; (2) scores on an individual intelligence test at or above the 98th percentile; (3) results of creativity tests or other assessments indicating demonstrated or potential ability in areas of creative and productive thinking, advanced insight, outstanding imagination, innovation or creative reasoning ability, advanced perception of cause and effect relationships, or ability in problem-solving or abstract concepts; (4) results of nomination or documented observations by two or more persons with expertise recognized by the Child Study Team in areas of academic or non-academic endeavors, and could include demonstrated or potential ability in leadership, mechanical, motor, or manual dexterity of student assessed; (5) documentation from one or more experts recognized by the Child Study Team in a given field such as art, music, drama, speech, language (debate, oratory) or other performance areas in visual/performing arts.

In addition, there must be documentation that the student's needs cannot be provided for with regular classroom instruction on a full-time basis.

Requirements for Re-evaluation. The need for re-evaluation shall be determined annually by professional judgment of the Child Study Team. Re-evaluation should include a review of student progress toward initially-stated goals and objectives, and could include any assessments employed by the school district such as parent, teacher, and student (self) surveys or questionnaires.

(Administrative Rules and Regulations for Special Education)

ILLINOIS

DEFINITION. Gifted Children shall be defined as those children who consistently excel or show the potential to consistently excel above the average in one or more of the following areas of human endeavor to the extent they need and can profit from specially planned educational services: General Intellectual Ability . . . Specific Academic Aptitude . . . Creative Thinking . . . Leadership Ability . . . Visual and Performing Arts Ability . . . Psychomotor Ability.

(Rules and Regulations to Govern the Administration and Operation of Gifted Education Reimbursement Programs, 1976)

IDENTIFICATION PROCEDURES. The process for identifying children as gifted in one or more of the above areas of giftedness shall be determined by the LEA—[Local Educational Agency]. However, the identification process shall meet the following standards: The identification process must compare the gifted student's abilities to that of others in the LEA population; The identification process must establish criteria before the child is selected from the target population for special instructional programs or services; The identification process must establish specific cutoff points when standardized tests are used; The identification process must indicate a direct relationship between the criteria for selection and the instructional program or service provided for gifted children; The identification process must indicate that the criteria for selection have been applied equally to every child in the LEA population; The identification process must describe in detail specific criteria used for student identification or, where appropriate, attach same as a sample to the preapproval application; The identification process must use a minimum of *three* of the following identification devices in identifying gifted children in any one of the above six areas of giftedness: intelligence tests (must be used as *one* of the devices to determine giftedness in Area 1 [General Intellectual Ability] achievement tests, aptitude tests, creativity tests (must be used as *one* of the devices to determine giftedness in Area 3 [Creative Thinking], personality inventories, self-concept inventories, teacher or specialist evaluation, past school performance, other identification devices may be used when approved by the Illinois Office of Education.

(Rules and Regulations to Govern the Administration and Operation of Gifted Education Reimbursement Programs, 1976)

INDIANA

DEFINITION. "Gifted and Talented" are those children and youth whose talents, abilities and accomplishments allow them to excel or who show the potential to excel consistently in any human endeavor, and who require qualitatively differentiated educational programs and/or services in order to realize their contribution to self and society. This includes, but is not limited to:

1. the academically gifted—general intellectual ability and/or demonstrated specific academic aptitude
2. the creatively gifted—divergent, imaginative, original or productive thinking
3. the kinesthetically gifted—psychomotor talent or skills in the visual or performing arts
4. the psycho-socially gifted—leadership ability and ethical or moral development

IDENTIFICATION PROCEDURES. No adopted policy.

IOWA

DEFINITION. Gifted and talented children are those identified by professionally qualified persons who by virtue of outstanding abilities are capable of high performance. These are children who require differentiated educational programs and/or services beyond those normally provided by the regular school program in order to realize their contribution to self and society.

Children capable of high performance include those with demonstrated achievement and/or potential ability in any one of the following areas, singly or in combination: intellectual ability, creative and productive thinking, leadership ability, visual and performing arts, specific ability areas.
(Iowa Plan of Action for Gifted and Talented Students, Adopted 1974)

IDENTIFICATION PROCEDURES. Gifted and talented students with high potential shall be evidenced by two or more of the following factors in a given or specific area: Achievement in school work; scales or tests measuring intellectual ability and aptitude; scales or tests measuring creativity; scales or tests measuring leadership ability; judgments of teachers and/or counselors, school administrators, supervisors; opinions of parents and/or peers who are familiar with students' special competencies; evidence of exceptional talent; other appropriate indicators.
(Talented and Gifted Notebook issued by Iowa Department of Public Instruction, functions as general guidelines)

KANSAS

DEFINITION. Intellectually gifted individuals are those who have potential for outstanding performance by virtue of superior intellectual abilities. The intellectually gifted are those with demonstrated achievement and/or potential ability. Individuals capable of outstanding performance include both those with demonstrated achievement and those with minimal or low performance who give evidence of high potential in general intellectual ability, specific academic aptitudes, and/or creative thinking abilities.
(Kansas State Plan for Special Education, 1974)

IDENTIFICATION PROCEDURES.
Phase I: Initial Referral and Screening. The purpose of the initial referral and screening procedure is to locate and identify candidates for gifted programs subject to comprehensive evaluation and selection criteria. Appropriate screening procedures include, but are not limited to: School professional referral (e.g. by administrator, principal, teacher, psychologist, or counselor); parent referral; peer referral; self referral; referral and information from community or agency sources; group tests of intelligence; group tests of achievement.
Phase II: Comprehensive Evaluation. The comprehensive evaluation of students referred for programs for the gifted shall utilize multi-disciplinary and multi-sourced information. . . . In this phase of the identification procedure, it is recommended that use be made of as many of the following possible assessment tools as necessary to insure the inclusion of achieving, underachieving, culturally different, handicapped, and disadvantaged individuals. Examples of assessment tools useful in a comprehensive evaluation are: Individual tests of intelligence; individual tests of achievement; autobiographical inventories; tests of creative thinking

abilities; tests of critical thinking; aptitude tests; interest inventories; data from school counselors; sociometric devices; rating scales; appropriate checklists; pupil products; academic history and grades; demonstrated accomplishments; other relevant individual data.

Phase III: Final Review for Possible Placement. Student information and data compiled during the initial referral, screening and comprehensive evaluation phases shall be submitted to the district's/cooperative's placement committee for final consideration. Evidence of intellectual giftedness shall be determined by professionally qualified persons.

(Kansas State Plan for Special Education, 1974)

KENTUCKY

DEFINITION. Gifted and talented children are those who by virtue of outstanding ability are capable of high performance. These high performance children are the ones who have demonstrated achievement or potential ability in any of the following areas, singly or in combination: general intellectual ability, specific academic aptitude, creative or productive thinking, leadership ability, visual and performing arts, psychomotor ability.

IDENTIFICATION PROCEDURES. No adopted policy.

LOUISIANA

DEFINITION. Being developed.

IDENTIFICATION PROCEDURES. Being developed.

MAINE

DEFINITION. "Gifted and talented" are those identified by professionally qualified persons who, by virtue of outstanding ability, are capable of high performance. These are children who require differentiated educational programs and/or services beyond those normally provided by the regular school program in order to realize their contribution to self and society.

"Children capable of high performance" include those with demonstrated achievement and/or potential ability in any of the following areas, singly or in combination: general intellectual ability, specific academic aptitude, creative or productive thinking, leadership ability, visual and performing arts, and psychomotor ability.

(Education of the Gifted and Talented—Position Paper, Gifted and Talented Advisory Board, 1975)

IDENTIFICATION PROCEDURES. No adopted policy.

MARYLAND

DEFINITION. Maryland's statutes which govern programs for the gifted and talented are separate from statutes governing education of other exceptionalities.

For the purpose of this subtitle the gifted and talented are those elementary and secondary students who are identified by professionally qualified persons as having outstanding abilities in the areas of general intellectual capabilities or specific academic aptitudes or in the creative, visual or performing arts.

These gifted and talented students have a need for differentiated services beyond those normally provided by the regular school program in order to develop their potentialities.

IDENTIFICATION PROCEDURES. The identification of gifted and talented students includes screening and identification. The screening procedure must take place first to ensure that potentially gifted students are given the opportunity to demonstrate their talents. . . . The identification procedures and criteria will be specific to different areas of giftedness and appropriate to the various types of experiences to be offered, and determined by the amount of talent and the available resources in the area. . . .

Special consideration should be given as early as possible to culturally different and underachieving gifted and talented students. . . .

Screening for gifted and talented students should not overlook children who are in special programs for the handicapped. . . .

Maryland has detailed guidelines for screening and identification of students who demonstrate exceptional abilities in the following areas: general intellectual ability, specific academic aptitude, leadership ability, creative and productive thinking, visual and performing arts, psychomotor skills.

The guidelines for general intellectual ability and/or specific academic aptitude are below. Guidelines for other ability areas are not included due to space limitations.

Screening/Identification of Students Who Demonstrate General Intellectual Ability and/or Specific Academic Aptitude

Initial Screening

Intelligence and achievement tests.

Performance at two or more grades above grade level.

Score of 120 on a group intelligence test.

Score of 130 on an individual intelligence test.

School systems may at their own discretion wish to include students of the initial screening who do not meet the above but are strongly recommended by staff, parents, and others.

Behavior checklist.

Identification

More difficult tests of specific aptitudes (such as DAT, APT, and PTM) should be used for final selection.

Individual intelligence testing should be used for early primary students and for students whose eligibility is questioned.

Specific scores for entry into the program should be determined by each school district on the basis of available scores.

Those students who meet the intellectual criteria should be further screened for social maturity and any other disabling intellectual handicap which might inhibit performance in differentiated programs.

("Maryland Guidelines for Gifted and Talented Programs," developed by SEA but not yet approved by Board of Education)

MASSACHUSETTS

DEFINITION. No adopted policy.

IDENTIFICATION PROCEDURES. No adopted policy.

MICHIGAN

DEFINITION. The "gifted and/or academically talented" means elementary and/or secondary school students who may be considered to be (1) intellectually gifted, (2) outstanding in school achievement, and/or (3) those who have outstanding abilities in particular areas of human endeavor, including the arts and humanities.

IDENTIFICATION PROCEDURES. Being developed by SEA. Local districts must develop procedures and submit an application to receive state funds authorized under Section 47.

MINNESOTA

DEFINITION. High potential children are those who by virtue of outstanding abilities are capable of high performance. These are children whose potentialities can be realized through differentiated educational programs and/or services beyond those normally provided by the regular school program. Children capable of high performance include those with demonstrated achievement or potential ability in any of the following areas, singly or in combination: General intellectual ability;

specific academic aptitude; creative or productive thinking; leadership ability; visual and performing arts.
(Suggested Approach to the High Potential: Gifted and Talented Pupils, Approved by State Board of Education, 1976)

IDENTIFICATION PROCEDURES. School districts may use a variety of measures to identify such students. Such measures include but are not limited to one or more of the following:

1. Achievement of students at or above the 95th percentile on a standardized measure. Such measure shall not discriminate with respect to the ethnic or cultural backgrounds of pupils in Minnesota.
2. Teacher recommendations, particularly where a standardized test is not available or when available tests are, in the opinion of the school district, an inadequate measure of the pupil's ability.
3. Parent recommendations.
4. Student recommendations (either self or peer selection).
5. Demonstrated performance.

(Suggested Approach to the High Potential: Gifted and Talented Pupils, Approved by State Board of Education, 1976)

MISSISSIPPI

DEFINITION. Gifted and talented children are those identified by professionally qualified persons who, by virtue of outstanding abilities, are *capable of high performance*. These are children who require differentiated educational programs and/or services beyond those normally provided by the regular school program in order to realize their contributions to self and society.
(Policies and Operating Procedures for the Mississippi Program for Exceptional Children, 1976)

IDENTIFICATION PROCEDURES.
School's Responsibility
Complete . . . Pupil Personal Data Sheet for each student being referred.
Submit Pupil Personal Data Sheet to a Regional Screening Team for eligibility determination. The items listed below should be included; note that flexibility is allowed here because of the great variety in programs. The procedure for identification of students must be spelled out in your pilot program proposal submitted to the Special Education Section.

a. Group scholastic aptitude tests
b. Standardized achievement tests
c. Teacher recommendations and/or anecdotal records
d. Scholastic record
e. Evidence of special intellectual aptitude
f. Individual intelligence tests (required for any program with academic orientation)
g. Auditions, copies of creative work, and other supporting evidence.

The recommendation of the Local Survey Committee must be included on the Pupil Personal Data Sheet.
Eligibility for Class Placement
Prior to placement in a class for the gifted/talented, students must be screened and declared eligible for this type of program by a Regional Screening Team. The school district must have approval of its pilot program from the Special Education Section before pupils may be served.
After one year of placement in a class for the gifted/talented, students must be reassessed by the Local Survey Committee. . . .
(Policies and Operating Procedures for the Mississippi Program for Exceptional Children, 1976)

MISSOURI

DEFINITION. "Gifted children," children who exhibit precocious development of mental capacity and learning potential as determined by competent professional evaluation to the extent that continued educational growth and stimulation could best be served by an academic environment beyond that offered through a standard grade level curriculum.

IDENTIFICATION PROCEDURES. Identification and selection of students as Gifted/Talented should be determined through the use of multiple criteria: Standardized or observable tests and m˞ ˱arements; demonstrated or potential abilities as determined by qualified indi˯. ˹als; or by other valid means such as peer nominations, semantic differential tests, self-nomination, or citizen nomination. *No singular test, test score, other measurement, or nomination should be the determining factor.* . . .

Standardized tests help to identify those students who are verbally gifted and those who have unusual ability in particular academic aptitudes (science, math, reading, etc.), but there are many students whose rare and distinctive gifts in music, writing, or the arts are not revealed by tests, but rather by performance in these creative areas. These abilities can be manifest and found singly or in combinations in any of the following areas: leadership ability, a specific academic aptitude, visual and performing arts, and general intellectual ability or productive thinking. . . .

Other sources which can be used to identify Gifted/Talented students include citizens who are knowledgeable about the student, other teachers, counselors, or others whose training and expertise qualify them to appraise the special competencies of the students. Parents should be included whenever possible.
(Program Development Regulations and Guidelines Services for Gifted/Talented, Adopted by State Board of Education, 1975)

MONTANA

DEFINITION. Being developed.

IDENTIFICATION PROCEDURES. Being developed.

NEBRASKA

DEFINITION. Gifted children shall be defined as children who excel markedly in ability to think, reason, judge, invent, or create and who need special facilities and/or educational services in order to assist them to achieve more nearly their potentials for their own sakes, and for the increased contributions they may make to the community, state, and nation.
(Section 79-339, R.R.S. Supp. 1967)

Gifted/talented refers to children or students who have been identified at the elementary or secondary level as having demonstrated or potential abilities which give evidence of high performance capability in areas such as intelligence, creative thinking, academic aptitude, leadership, visual or performing arts, psychomotor ability; and in order to realize these potentialities need ˞rograms and services which will accommodate their individual differences be˞ ˞d those being provided by the school system to the typical student.
(Regulations for Approved Programs and Criteria fo˞ ˞ Classification of Gifted/ Talented Students Approved by the State Board of Ea˞.˞˞ion, 1976)

IDENTIFICATION PROCEDURES. The identification of gifted/talented students is the responsibility of the superintendent or a delegated staff member. Identification must be accomplished by the use of multiple methods (i.e. more than one) such as intelligence tests, achievement tests, aptitude tests, teacher nominations, parent nominations, peer nominations, student products, measures of creativity, records of past performance or other predictive measures embracing the following areas: general intellectual ability, specific academic aptitude, creative or productive thinking ability, leadership ability, visual or performing arts ability, psychomotor ability.

Eligibility for the program shall be determined by procedures involving one person from at least two of the following groups: Administrators, parents, students, teachers, pupil personnel specialists, counselors, qualified testers, or others who are familiar with the aptitude and potential of students.

To be eligible for approval for a program for gifted, school districts must first identify students in category (i), general intellectual ability and in category (ii), specific academic aptitude. (Students need qualify in only one category by either an I.Q. test or an achievement test.)

The criteria for eligibility in category (i), general intellectual ability, shall be a rank of 98th percentile or higher on an individual psychological test (I.Q.) approved by the State Department of Education and administered by a licensed psychologist or a person holding a Nebraska teaching or service certificate endorsed as a school psychologist or psychological assistant. (Results of I.Q. tests need only be reported to State Department of Education when a student qualifies, but testing may be repeated as many times as determined necessary and useful by the local school in order to qualify a student. I.Q. tests currently approved by the State Department of Education are: Stanford Binet, Form L-M, the Wechsler Intelligence Scale for Children—Revised, Wechsler Pre-School and Primary Scale of Intelligence, or Wechsler Adult Intelligence Scale.)

The criteria for eligibility in category (ii), specific academic aptitude, shall be annual maintenance of a 96th percentile rank or higher on a standardized achievement test. The composite score or comprehensive individual subtest scores for either reading, science, language, social studies or math may be used. If a subtest score is used to determine eligibility the subtest must relate to the special program to which the student is being assigned.

After identifying students in categories (i), general intellectual ability and (ii), specific academic aptitude, a program may identify from categories (iii), creative or productive thinking ability, (iv) leadership ability, (v) visual or performing arts ability, and (vi) psychomotor ability up to 5 percent of its total student population and not to exceed 10 percent of the total student population or 10 students, whichever number is greater, when added to the total number of students identified in categories (i), general intellectual ability and (ii), specific academic aptitude.

Gifted/talented in the areas of (iii), creative or productive thinking ability, (iv), leadership ability, (v), visual or performing arts ability and (vi), psychomotor ability may be identified by any multiple criteria designed or selected by the local program for gifted/talented. That criteria must be included in the application for initiating or continuing a program for gifted/talented and must be approved by the State Department of Education or developed in cooperation with the State Department of Education. (See Suggested Identification Methods supplement to Rule 3.)

(Regulations for Approved Programs and Criteria for the Classification of Gifted/ Talented Students Approved by the State Board of Education, 1976)

NEVADA

DEFINITION. The academically talented are those students whose level of mental development is so far advanced that they have been identified by professionally qualified personnel as those who require differentiated educational programs and/ or services beyond those normally provided by regular school programs in order to realize their contribution to self and society.

(Standards and Instructions for Administration of Exceptional Pupil Education Programs, revised 1976)

IDENTIFICATION PROCEDURES. The performance on an individual psychoeducational evaluation shall determine an intelligence quotient as measured by nationally recognized, standardized intelligence and/or achievement tests which place the child in the upper two percent of the population. In addition, an academically talented student shall manifest outstanding academic achievement and sufficient evidence of creative and productive thinking.

(Standards and Instructions for Administration of Exceptional Pupil Education Programs, revised 1976)

NEW HAMPSHIRE

DEFINITION. No adopted policy.

IDENTIFICATION PROCEDURES. No adopted policy.

NEW JERSEY

DEFINITION. Being developed.

IDENTIFICATION PROCEDURES. Being developed.

NEW MEXICO

DEFINITION. The quality of giftedness is a complex, multifaceted human dimension which takes many forms. The gifted child is a productive or potentially productive individual who is original, fluent, flexible or divergent in his behavior and is superior in intelligence and/or creativity.
(A Plan for the Delivery of Special Education Services in New Mexico: Regulations, 1976)

IDENTIFICATION PROCEDURES. Required Evaluation Data (Screening must be completed prior to referral for diagnostic evaluation.)

1. Screening
   a. hearing
   b. vision (near, far, color discrimination)
2. Case history
   a. educational
   b. family (inclusive of language dominance of the home)
   c. medical information
   On the basis of the compiled information, a decision will need to be made as to continuation or redirection of the eligibility process.
3. Educational assessment by qualified personnel
   a. individual intelligence test (one required)
      Appropriate Wechsler Intelligence Scale
      Stanford-Binet Intelligence Scale
      Leiter International Performance Scale
   b. Diagnostic supportive tests (one required though more than one may be necessary to confirm the educational diagnosis)
      Wallcock-Morgan Creativity
      Creative Ability Inventory
      Torrance Tests of Creative Thinking
      Differential Aptitude Tests
   c. Individual achievement tests (one required)
      Iowa Test of Basic Skills
      Metropolitan Achievement
      Peabody Individual Achievement Test
4. Tests recommended for additional evaluation for educational programming
   a. Goodenough-Harris Draw-a-Person Test
   b. Culture Fair Intelligence Test
   c. Ravin Progressive Matric
   d. Hiskey-Nebraska Test of Academic Aptitude
   e. Renzulli Scale for Rating Behavioral Characteristics of Superior Students

Analyzing the Data for Educational Needs

1. Local districts are encouraged to offer unique educational opportunities to all students functioning within the category of gifted. Generally the student has a superior intellect; however, consideration for special education must not be on test scores alone. A measured I.Q. (full scale) may be depressed as a result of language or cultural differences.
2. Superior skill or ability may be demonstrated in a given area as determined by standarized tests of creativity or as verified by two or more experts in the appropriate field.

(A Plan for the Delivery of Special Education Services in New Mexico: Regulations, 1976)

NEW YORK

DEFINITION. Gifted and talented children are those identified by professionally qualified persons who, by virtue of outstanding abilities, are capable of high performance. These are children *who require differentiated programs and/or services beyond those normally provided by the regular school program* in order to realize their contribution to self and society.

This broad definition must be further refined to reflect the multifaceted dimensions of their abilities and competencies. These dimensions include *demonstrated* or *potential* abilities in the areas of: general intelligence, specific academic aptitude, creative or productive thinking, leadership, the visual or performing arts, psychomotor activities.
(Position Paper No. 23: Educating the Gifted and Talented in New York State. A Statement of Policy and Proposed Action by the Regents of the University of the State of New York, 1976)

IDENTIFICATION PROCEDURES. A reliable, comprehensive screening and identification program for gifted and talented children has the following characteristics: early identification, continuing search, involvement of various professionals, use of multiple resource materials, and complete study and information on the abilities of the gifted and talented pupils.
(Position Paper No. 23: Educating the Gifted and Talented in New York State. A Statement of Policy and Proposed Action by the Regents of the University of the State of New York, 1976)

NORTH CAROLINA

DEFINITION. A child who is gifted and talented is one who falls within the upper ten percent in the total school district on intelligence tests, achievement tests, and/or scales that rate behavior characteristics. This child has academic talent and generally performs above average in his class work and/or may demonstrate a special talent in areas such as creativity, communication, leadership, decision making, forecasting and planning as indicated by the use of behavioral scales and checklists. Considerations must be given to the ethnic composition of the pupil population.
(Rules Governing Programs and Services for Children with Special Needs)

IDENTIFICATION PROCEDURES.
Required Screening or Evaluation before Placement: Educational evaluation (data collected routinely on all children) Other information. . . .

Recommended Screening or Evaluation Before Placement: Psychological evaluation (an individual intelligence test) Each LEA shall develop its procedures and have these adopted by the local Board of Education.

The LEA must establish the criteria to be met in pupil identification and what forms it will use. It is strongly suggested that the criteria include:

test data—two or more tests (use of group IQ tests is highly questionable)

performance data—demonstration of skills, grades, nominations, checklists and scales

developmental data—case studies, anecdotal records, biographical data

Forms to be used should include:

1. recommendations (or referrals) by school personnel using selected checklists to specify pupil behaviors
2. educational data—tests scores and/or stanines
3. student profile—compilation of objective and subjective data
4. school based committee evaluation and recommendation—signed and dated
5. parental permission for additional testing if applicable
6. parental permission for placement or non-placement which includes information on the right of review and program description
7. Administrative Placement Committee placement—signed and dated.

(Gifted and Talented Placement Procedures, North Carolina Department of Public Instruction)

NORTH DAKOTA

DEFINITION. "Gifted child" means a gifted and talented child identified by professional, qualified persons, who, by virtue of outstanding abilities, is capable of high performance and who requires differentiated educational programs and services beyond those normally provided by the regular school program in order to realize his contribution to self and society. (*15-59-01*)

IDENTIFICATION PROCEDURES. No adopted policy except that "any student enrolled in a program for gifted children shall have been identified by a qualified professional evaluator."
(Special Education in North Dakota, Guide 1—Laws, Regulations and Guidelines for Special Education for Exceptional Students, 1976)

OHIO

DEFINITION. Uses USOE definition plus the eligibility requirements described in "Identification Procedures."

IDENTIFICATION PROCEDURES. Any child who meets the following requirements shall be eligible for programs approved under this standard: Is of legal age; shows evidence of functioning in the upper three percent of the student population, or functioning two standard deviations above the mean on objective test instruments, or having the potential of functioning within either of these groups.

Evidence of special abilities to be determined by the use of multiple criteria including at least one item from each of the following: *Nominations*—professional nominations obtained through the use of a checklist by teachers, counselors, psychologists and/or other staff as well as individuals in specific fields from the private sector; parent, peer and/or self-nomination through the use of locally developed procedures and instrumentation. *Measures of Ability*—aptitude/creativity test instruments applicable to the type of program being developed; general ability inventories, utilized on a group or individual basis, individual and/or group intelligence tests. *Performance and/or Interests*—Standardized achievement test instruments applicable to the type of program being developed, classroom performance based on cumulative record data, normal or criterion-referenced interest inventories.

Areas of giftedness shall include the following: superior intellectual ability; specific academic aptitude; creative or productive thinking; leadership ability; visual and performing arts; psychomotor ability.

The school district shall have written criteria to determine eligibility for, and placement of, students in approved programs and services which shall include: standards adopted by the State Board of Education; a process complying with State and Federal guidelines for informing the parent(s) or guardian(s) of the program prior to placement of any student in programs for gifted/talented children; priorities to establish selection of students on the basis of individual needs.
(Program Standards for School Foundation Units for Gifted Children, 1975)

OKLAHOMA

DEFINITION. Gifted and talented children are those identified by professionally qualified persons who, by virtue of *outstanding abilities*, are *capable of high performance*. These are children who require differentiated educational programs and/or services beyond those normally provided by the regular school program in order to realize their contribution to self and society.

Children capable of high performance include those with *demonstrated achievement* and/or potential ability in any one of the following areas, singly or in combination: general intellectual ability, specific academic aptitude, creative or productive thinking, leadership ability, visual and performing arts, psychomotor ability.
(Definition and Identification of Academically Gifted Students, functions as general guidelines from SEA)

IDENTIFICATION PROCEDURES. This procedure is divided into five phases. . . .
Phase I—In-service—The selection process begins with an in-depth in-service training of all teachers and pertinent school personnel about the following: (1) goals and commitment of the program, (2) characteristics of gifted children, (3) selection criteria, (4) guidelines for program development within the school. . . .
Phase II—Data Collection— . . . about the abilities, interests, needs, experi-

ences, and motivation of students . . . for accurate identification and . . . collected through a variety of means and kept in a case study file for each student begin considered for special programs. . . .

Initial screening of students will begin with a listing of students who have scored 125+ on a group intelligence test or achieved at the 98+ percentile in any area on achievement test scores.

These criteria will provide . . . list of academically talented students which will be sent to faculty and counselors for their comments, recommendations *and additions.* . . .

Additional students will be added to this list from faculty, peer, parent, and self-nominations. . . .

Autobiographies of each student will be written in language arts classes. . . . *Teachers will evaluate the content and style of autobiographies for indication of unusual abilities among students not included in test score list as well as those already being considered.*

Academic histories on initial group to include previous grades, test scores, etc. will be compiled. . . .

Teachers will meet in teams to share and discuss the placement of students.

*Phase III—Selection Committee and Initial Screening—*All data will be considered by a selection committee composed of teachers, counselors, and administrators . . . [whose] purpose . . . is to recommend those students whose records *indicate* unusual general ability or specified academic aptitude for individual testing. . . .

Phase IV—Measurement of Abilities by Individual Intelligence Tests and Other Instruments. . . .

*Phase V—Final Selection—*Information from individual testing is sent back to the selection committee. The purpose of the committee in this phase is to recommend *students who will benefit most from a differentiated program for gifted students.*

OREGON

DEFINITION. Educationally able and gifted children means those children who have demonstrated or show potential of a very high level of academic or creative aptitude. (*ORS 343.395*)

IDENTIFICATION PROCEDURES. Being developed.

PENNSYLVANIA

DEFINITION. *Mentally Gifted/Talented—*Outstanding intellectual and/or creative ability, the development of which requires special activities or services not ordinarily provided in the regular program. Persons shall be assigned to a program for the gifted when they have an IQ score of 130 or higher. A limited number of persons with IQ scores lower than 130 may be admitted to gifted programs when other criteria in the person's profile strongly indicated gifted ability.

*Talented—*Outstanding talent as identified by a team of competent educators and professionals in the areas of art, music, dance, photographic arts or theater, the development of which requires special activities or services not ordinarily provided in the regular program. A person identified as talented shall be eligible to attend the Governor's School for the Arts.
(Section 341.1, Special Education Standards issued by The Commissioner for Basic Education, April 1977)

IDENTIFICATION PROCEDURES. Mentally gifted children of elementary and secondary school age who have been identified by multiple criteria, including teacher recommendation, academic achievement, group and individual psychological testing and interest inventories, as ranking among the top three percent of the nation's school-age population and who will benefit from individualized programs utilizing school professional personnel, professional service personnel, and community personnel to provide and encourage acceleration, enrichment, resource tutoring, independent study and leadership skills aimed at developing each child's potential to function as a productive and creative adult, are the individuals eligible for special programs for the gifted.

Whether a pupil qualifies for a class for the gifted is determined by such factors as intelligence quotient (130 or better on individual psychological test), achievement, scholastic record, aptitudes and interests and by professional recommendation and counseling interviews as determined by the guidelines issued by the Department of Education, Bureau of Special Education.

(Special Education Standards of the Pennsylvania Department of Education, 1972)

RHODE ISLAND

DEFINITION. Being developed.

IDENTIFICATION PROCEDURES. Being developed.

SOUTH CAROLINA

DEFINITION. Gifted and talented children and youth are those identified by professionals and other qualified individuals as having outstanding abilities and who are capable of high performance. These are children and youth whose abilities, talents, and potential require qualitatively differentiated educational programs and/or services beyond those normally provided by the regular school program in order to realize their contribution to self and society.

Children and youth capable of high performance include those with demonstrated achievement and/or potential ability in any of the following areas, singly or in combination: general intellectual ability; specific academic aptitude; creative or productive thinking; leadership ability; visual or performing arts; psychomotor ability.

IDENTIFICATION PROCEDURES. Identification and selection of students as gifted/talented must be determined through the use of multiple criteria: tests and measurements, standardized or observable; demonstrated or potential abilities as determined by qualified individuals or by other valid means, such as teacher nominations, peer nominations or parent questionnaires. No single tests, test score, other measurement, or nomination should be the determining factor. Interpretation of the data gathered is of the utmost importance in the identification and selection of students. Not to be overlooked are the following groups: racial and ethnic minority groups, the culturally different, the physically handicapped, the child who displays various types of classroom behavior problems.

A comprehensive assessment should include the following components:

1. Description of the student's current functioning by the classroom teachers, peers, parents, or other parties on an appropriate referral form or checklist.
2. Individual tests of intelligence or other measurements as deemed necessary by professionally qualified persons.
3. Educational assessment, including achievement level and skills, strengths and weaknesses.
4. Evaluation of communicative skills and language development.
5. Objective description of the child's social and adaptive behavior.

SOUTH DAKOTA

DEFINITION. SEA uses definition listed below with special programming limited to intellectually gifted as defined: The Gifted and Talented students are those children and youth whose abilities, talents, and potential for accomplishment are outstanding in comparison with their peer group and/or the total school population. These are persons of exceptional promise in any of several fields, including the following: general intellectual ability, specific academic aptitude, creative thinking, leadership ability, visual or performing arts ability, psychomotor development.

An intellectually gifted child is one who has been determined by the local placement committee to have superior intellectual development and is capable of high performance, including demonstrated achievement or potential ability. A

gifted child shall have an IQ of 130 or above as identified by a standardized individual test of intelligence.
(South Dakota State Plan for Gifted and Talented, 1973)

IDENTIFICATION PROCEDURES. No adopted policy.

TENNESSEE

DEFINITION. A child whose intellectual abilities and potential for accomplishment are so outstanding that they require a variety of special provisions to meet the established educational needs and who has an intelligence quotient at least two standard deviations above the norm as measured by an individual intelligence test is considered intellectually gifted.
(Rules, Regulations and Minimum Standards, Tennessee Board of Education, 1976)

IDENTIFICATION PROCEDURES. Criteria for Eligibility for Special Education Services
A child must have one or more of the following characteristics:

Capabilities that exceed those of most children of the same chronological age range.

Abilities considered consistently remarkable.

Regular school curriculum barely approximates the demands of either learning capacity or the anticipated social roles of a child with this ability.

Advanced interests and psychological maturity.

All available data (referral, screening, assessment, including certification by specialist) relevant to making recommendations for educational programming should be compiled for consideration by the multidisciplinary team (M-team). The purpose of the M-team is to recommend the appropriate educational program for the child through a careful evaluation of all data. All recommendations made by the M-team must be included in a written report which will also include specific educational objectives for the child.
(Rules, Regulations and Minimum Standards, Tennessee Board of Education, 1976)

TEXAS

DEFINITION. Gifted and talented students means students with extraordinary learning or leadership ability or outstanding talent in the creative or vocational arts whose development requires programs or services beyond the level of those ordinarily provided in regular school programs. SEA also defines gifted and talented in their State Plan as:

Those with demonstrated achievement and/or potential ability in any of the following areas, singly or in combination: general intellectual ability; specific academic aptitude; creative or productive thinking; leadership ability; visual and performing arts; psychomotor ability.

IDENTIFICATION PROCEDURES. No adopted policy.

UTAH

DEFINITION. Children and youth capable of high performance include those with demonstrated achievement and/or potential ability in any of the following areas, singly or in combination: any of the numerous intellectual abilities, special academic aptitude, creative or productive thinking; talents in visual and performing arts; and various psychomotor abilities.
(Standards and Guidelines for Gifted/Talented Programs, 1977)

IDENTIFICATION PROCEDURES. Procedures for identifying gifted and talented students should include, but not necessarily be limited to, the following features: appropriate objective evaluation instruments should be used; subjective, disciplined, judgmental evaluations by appropriate professionals should be used; annual identification procedures should be carried out.

Services—All school districts or combinations of districts are eligible to participate in the program funding through competitive proposals submitted based on the standards and guidelines below.

1. Programs designed for gifted and talented students should be integrated into the regular school program.
2. Programs designed for gifted and talented students should provide alternatives rather than additions to the regular school program.
3. Identification of gifted and talented youth in all walks of life and in all areas of the state should be given continuing attention.
4. Gifted minority and handicapped children and youth should be given specific attention. . . .
    a. Appropriate objective evaluation instruments should be used.
    b. Subjective, disciplined, judgmental evaluations by appropriate professionals should be used.
    c. Annual identification procedures should be carried out. . . .
5. . . .
6. Evaluation should be an integral part of the program and should be based upon adequate evaluative criteria. . . .
7. LEA's should be free to exercise a high degree of local option in the development of programs designed for the gifted and talented students.
8. The program should reach all children identified as gifted and talented at every grade level (including preschool) and in all curriculum areas.

(Standards and Guidelines for Gifted/Talented Programs, 1977)

VERMONT

DEFINITION. Being developed.

IDENTIFICATION PROCEDURES. No adopted policy.

VIRGINIA

DEFINITION. Gifted and talented children are those identified by professionally qualified persons who, by virtue of outstanding abilities, are capable of high performance. These are children who require differentiated educational programs and/or services beyond those normally provided by the regular school program in order to realize their contribution to self and society.

Children capable of high performance include those with demonstrated achievement and/or potential ability in any of the following areas, singly or in combination: general intellectual ability, specific academic aptitude, creative or productive thinking, leadership ability, visual and performing arts, psychomotor ability.
(Superintendents Memorandum No. 6973, 1974)

IDENTIFICATION PROCEDURES. Gifted students, generally, are among those who meet or exceed at least one of the following two measurable criteria:

1. A score on standardized tests of ability (SCAT, STEA, etc.) that falls at least two standard deviations above the mean or at least above the 95th percentile.
2. A group intelligence quotient of 120 or higher. . . .

The talented student may or may not possess the characteristics as defined for the gifted student. Generally, talented students are those who demonstrate superior aptitudes or abilities (and outstanding leadership qualities) in: manipulative skills, mechanics, expressing ideas (oral or written), music, art, drama, dance, etc.

WASHINGTON

DEFINITION. . . . a gifted student is defined as one who is identified by professionally qualified persons as having extra-ordinary intellectual and/or creative abilities which are demonstrated by high performance. Multiple criteria must be

used to make any determination about a student's superior ability. For funding purposes, students identified by the above procedures must comprise no more than 3% of the student population in Washington State.
(Biennial Budget Estimates from Superintendent of Public Instruction, 1977)

IDENTIFICATION PROCEDURES. Being developed.

WEST VIRGINIA

DEFINITION. Intellectually gifted children are those children who fall at the top one percent (1%) level in general intellectual ability as measured by the Stanford-Binet Intelligence Scale or a comparable instrument.
(Guidelines for Special Education, 1975)

IDENTIFICATION PROCEDURES. Screening data previously accumulated will be made available to the local director of special education. Screening shall be done by using one of the following tests: Slosson Intelligence Test, California Test of Mental Maturity, Otis-Lennon.

An intelligence level shall be determined by an individual examination by a qualified examiner. . . . A minimum full-scale intelligence quotient of 130 points (two or more standard deviations above the average) should be required for consideration as a candidate for the program.

The intellectual efficiency of the child should be considered as well as his level of intelligence.

The social and emotional adjustment of the child should be additional considerations.
(Guidelines for Special Education, 1975)

WISCONSIN

DEFINITION. No adopted policy.

IDENTIFICATION PROCEDURES. Being developed.

WYOMING

DEFINITION. No adopted policy.

IDENTIFICATION PROCEDURES. No adopted policy.

SOURCES FOR TESTING INSTRUMENTS

California Short-Form Test of Mental Maturity, published by CTB/McGraw-Hill, Del Monte Research Pk., Monterey, Calif. 93940. (Appropriate for use with students of all ages.)

Scales for Rating Behavioral Characteristics of Superior Students, by Joseph S. Renzulli, Linda H. Smith, Alan J. White, Carolyn M. Callahan, and Robert K. Hartman, published by Creative Learning Press, Box 320, Mansfield Center, Conn. 06250.

Stanford Achievement Test—Revised, published by Harcourt Brace Jovanovich, Inc., 757 Third Ave., New York, N.Y. 10017. (Appropriate for grades 1.5–12.)

Stanford-Binet Intelligence Test, published by Houghton Mifflin Inc., distributed by Riverside Publishing Co., 1919 S. Highland Ave., Lombard, Ill. 60148. (Appropriate for use with students of all ages.)

Tennessee Self-Concept Scale, published by Counselor Recordings and Tests, Box 6184, Acklen Sta., Nashville, Tenn. 37212. (Appropriate for students 12 years and older.)

Torrance Tests of Creative Thinking, published by Personnel Press, Inc., distributed by Ginn and Co., Box 2649, Columbus, Ohio 43216. (Appropriate for use with students of all ages.)

Wechsler Intelligence Scale for Children—Revised, published by The Psychological Corp., 304 E. 45 St., New York, N.Y. 10017. (Appropriate for use with ages 6 to 16 years, 11 months.)

NOTES

1. South Carolina Department of Education, *State Guidelines—Gifted and Talented* (Columbus, S.C.: South Carolina Department of Education, 1977–1978), sec. 2.1.
2. Bruce Boston, *Characteristics of the Gifted and Talented* (Washington, D.C.: U.S. Office of Gifted and Talented, 1979).
3. Jean N. Nazzaro, *Identification of the Gifted and Talented* (Washington, D.C.: U.S. Office of Gifted and Talented, 1979).
4. Ruth A. Martinson, *The Identification of the Gifted and Talented* (Reston, Va.: Council for Exceptional Children, 1975), pp. iii–iv.
5. Richard O. Fortna and Bruce O. Boston, *Testing the Gifted Child: An Interpretation in Lay Language* (Reston, Va.: Council for Exceptional Children, 1976).

3

The Nurture of Giftedness: Qualitatively Differentiated Programs

The class approach to teaching—that lockstep, never look to the right or to the left, keep eyes glued to the textbook, hurry to complete the text before the end of the semester approach—has been designed to move the bright, the average and the slow through the textbook at the same rate. And if the teacher can gauge the rate just right, the average can walk through the text, the slow can stumble through, and the bright, who could have run through so easily, can just stand around and wait.

*Ruth Ann Davies**

In conducting evaluation studies, I have witnessed far too many programs for the gifted that are essentially fun-and-games activities; such activities lack continuity and show little evidence of developing in a systematic fashion the mental processes that led these children to be identified as gifted.

Joseph S. Renzulli†

Providing each gifted and talented student with the opportunity to experience a quality, optimum education is a goal that does not become operational until a differentiated program translates that promise into actuality. The goal is the promise; the program is the means of goal attainment. School districts today face the challenge of designing and implementing special instructional programs that will offer the ablest students those learning experiences that are uniquely appropriate for them.

*Ruth Ann Davies, The School Library Media Program: Instructional Force for Excellence (New York: R. R. Bowker, 1979), p. 29.

†Joseph S. Renzulli, The Enrichment Triad Model: A Guide for Developing Defensible Programs for the Gifted and Talented (Mansfield Center, Conn.: Creative Learning Press, 1977), p. 6.

41

Appraising issues in education of the gifted in 1979, James Gallagher stated:

> Relatively little attention has been paid to the actual content that would make up the heart of any differentiated program, regardless of the particular learning environment in which it was delivered. . . . it is clear that the educational practitioner who must provide direct service to gifted students is essentially entering a difficult instructional situation almost totally unarmed because there are few, if any, organized curriculum resources to draw upon.[1]

The various states have provided general guidelines for curriculum development in programs for the gifted and talented (see Chapter 4). *The responsibility, however, for designing a differentiated curriculum—one denoting the higher cognitive concepts and processes, which employs instructional strategies and curriculum content to accommodate the learning styles of the gifted and talented, and providing special grouping arrangements such as special classes, honors classes, seminars, resource rooms, and the like—has been delegated to the local school district by the individual state educational agencies* (see Chapter 5).

PROGRAM DESIGN

Authorities in the field of gifted education agree that curriculum units and materials for the gifted and talented must employ the most sophisticated scientific program engineering, such as that advocated by Jerome Bruner in his monumental work *The Process of Education.*[2] Although programs for the gifted must above all else be learner centered, flexible, open-ended, and replete with options and alternatives, they must at the same time be carefully and thoughtfully designed to provide unity, continuity, balance, and harmony within the total program. Excellence in instruction begins with an overall directional plan for the sequential development of a fundamental body of knowledge. Lack of continuity and articulation in the instructional program condemns the learner to a fragmented education of disjointed bits and pieces. A blueprint of excellence clearly identifies all elements basic to the program and having identified the elements, orders them into patterns of logical, progressive sequence. An educational program of excellence is carefully structured to guard against inadequacies, for how can understanding be complete if basic structure is misplaced or missing? Recognizing the limitations of the term *differentiated programs,* Renzulli strives to safeguard the inherent quality of the program by refining that term to be *qualitatively differentiated programs*[3]—programs that are scientifically designed and carefully implemented to meet the unique educational and social growth needs of each gifted and talented student.

District Program Components

In summarizing research findings within the area of program development for the gifted and talented, Frederick Tuttle, Jr., recommends that to achieve the best program possible, program developers should proceed carefully and methodically through a series of steps, assuring satisfactory coverage of all areas that should be considered. Tuttle advocates that the following areas be explored by a district program development team comprised of teachers, administrators, curriculum specialist, pupil personnel staff, and parents:[4]

1. Need for the program in the specific school district.
2. Philosophy and objectives of the program.

3. Types of gifted to be included in the program.
4. Screening and identification criteria.
5. Professional and lay staff to work with the program.
6. Physical facilities and transportation.
7. In-service training.
8. Differentiated learning and thinking activities for the gifted individuals.
9. Administrative design.
10. Community resources.
11. Special funding.
12. Evaluation.
13. Role of parent(s).
14. Special consultative services.
15. Articulation.

The foregoing elements provide the basic framework for state guidelines and for district program design (see Chapters 4 and 5).

PROGRAM PLANNING STRATEGIES

Sandra Kaplan, in the basic handbook *Providing Programs for the Gifted and Talented,* gives background information essential for the development of district programs for these students. She equates the success of a district program with the meticulous planning of each phase of program design, structure, and implementation.[5]

> The level of acceptance, integration, and workability of a plan within an institution is directly related to the involvement of the planners and the time spent in program planning. Because the dimensions of a program are the composite result of the input, dialogue, and decision-making experiences of the team designated with the task of planning, careful consideration must be given to preparation for planning. [See Checklist 1, Planning Sequence Worksheet; Checklist 2, Planning Activities and Time Modules Worksheet; and Checklist 3, Agenda for Planning Meeting Worksheet.] Fundamental to the outcome of the planning team's effort is its perception of the task and the amount of latitude with which it can function. Presenting the planners with guidelines that clarify the organizational givens and instructional options provides them with necesssary direction. Research data, literature, and exemplary models supplied to the team insure a common understanding of the concepts underlying a program for the gifted and talented. . . . [See Part II for models for team examination.]
>
> When both the purpose and progress of the planners are communicated and when others are invited to visit or react to planning sessions, the final product will stimulate greater interest and acceptance. A program which is simply imposed upon a system is less likely to fulfill the needs of students or achieve the commitment of the system than is a program which emerges from a well-chosen, instructed, and communicative planning team.

Kaplan stresses the following points for planning:[6]

Organizing a planning team with comprehensive and diverse representation.

Outlining the boundaries and standards for the end product.

Incorporating implementation procedures with program design.

Designating a person with supervisory responsibility for planning [see Chapter 4 for job description of the supervisor].

Understanding the expectations and perceptions held for the program.

Familiarizing the team with various program options and patterns.

In a translation of Kaplan's recommendations into a step-by-step procedure, the following planning activities should take place:

CHECKLIST 1 PLANNING SEQUENCE WORKSHEET*

PHASE	TASKS	STATUS		
		Organizing	In Progress	Completed
P	Designating leadership			
L	Formulating a planning committee			
A	Reviewing the research, literature, models			
N	Assessing existent local conditions			
N	Understanding program criteria, requirements			
I	Developing philosophy, goals, objectives			
N	Defining program dimensions: prototypes,			
G	materials, personnel, evaluation			
	Formalizing a written plan			
P	Communicating and publicizing the program			
R	development			
E	Allowing for reaction and revision			
P	Obtaining formal approval and commitment			
A	Assigning roles and responsibilities			
R	Coordinating and devising forms and procedures			
I	for identification and certification of			
N	program participants			
G	Orienting students, parents, educators			
	Organizing and providing inservice			
	Developing curriculum and related materials			
	Planning evaluative procedures			

*Sandra N. Kaplan, *Providing Programs for the Gifted and Talented: A Handbook* (Reston, Va.: Council for Exceptional Children, 1975), p. 15.

CHECKLIST 2 PLANNING ACTIVITIES AND TIME MODULES WORKSHEET*

TASK	DELEGATED RESPONSIBILITIES	ANTICIPATED OUTCOMES			STRUCTURED TIME MODULES	
		Develop	Review	Approve	Beginning Date	Ending Date

*Sandra N. Kaplan, Providing Programs for the Gifted and Talented: A Handbook (Reston, Va.: Council for Exceptional Children, 1975), p. 16.

45

CHECKLIST 3   AGENDA FOR PLANNING MEETING WORKSHEET*

DATE OF MEETING_____   DATE OF NEXT MEETING_____

I. REPORT OF PROGRESS

II. ITEMS FOR ACTION

III. DISCUSSION ITEMS	RECOMMENDATIONS

IV. ASSIGNMENT	PERSON RESPONSIBLE	DUE DATE

*Sandra N. Kaplan, *Providing Programs for the Gifted and Talented: A Handbook* (Reston, Va.: Council for Exceptional Children, 1975), p. 17.

STEP 1. The superintendent of the district appoints a coordinator or supervisor of the Gifted and Talented Program and delegates both responsibility and decision-making authority to that staff member. To provide direction and impetus to the program, the superintendent then spells out his or her own commitment to the program and delineates roles and responsibilities of the coordinator, of central office staff members, of subject area coordinators, of building principals, and of faculty members (see Table 2).

STEP 2. The coordinator or supervisor of the Gifted and Talented Program appoints the Planning-Steering Committee, which is comprised of teachers from all subject areas and librarians on both the elementary and secondary levels, curriculum specialists, administrators, pupil personnel staff, representatives of the teachers' educational association, community representatives, and parents of gifted and talented students.

STEP 3. In its first meeting, the Planning-Steering Committee is briefed on the purpose and function of the committee and on the role and responsibilities of the individual committee members, and is oriented to the specifics of program design. This committee has a leadership role in anticipating the following questions, for which they must be able to supply answers:[7]

WHY is a program necessary?
The literal interpretation of the statement, "an education commensurate with each child's ability to learn" (which is part of the philosophy of general education), reinforces and explains the reason for differentiated programs for the gifted and talented. Identification of the differences and specialties among students mandates provisions which develop these characteristics. The gifted and talented represent a group of students whose learning style and thinking dimensions demand experiences which are outside the educational mainstream.

WHAT does a program provide?
A program for the gifted and talented provides multidimensional and appropriate learning experiences and environments which incorporate the academic, psychological, and social needs of these students. The implementation of administrative procedures and instructional strategies which afford intellectual acquisition, thinking practice, and self-understanding characterize a program for the gifted and talented. A program assures each student of alternatives which teach, challenge, and expand his knowledge while simultaneously stressing the development of an independent learner who can continuously question, apply, and generate information.

WHEN and WHERE will provisions for the program be made available?
The ability of the school and home to articulate and accept the logic and objectives for a program determine the readiness and subsequent time to begin the program. Identification of the preparatory steps and implementation procedures as well as the assignment of a coordinating leader, indicate the course of action to follow as well as the time needed to implement the tasks.

HOW will the provisions be put into operation?
The operation of the program is, in many cases, dependent upon an allocation of money to be spent selectively to support it. It is totally dependent on trained personnel and appropriate facilities and materials. The program can only be put into operation when students and educators know the answers to the questions you are now reading.

WHO will be responsible for implementing these provisions?
The personnel responsible for the program must be those who are adept at working with the behavioral and mental attributes of the gifted. They are staff members who can provide flexibly and humanely for the uniqueness of this group of students as well as for the diversity among its members.

TABLE 2   SCHOOL DISTRICT ROLES AND RESPONSIBILITIES*

COORDINATOR	TEACHER	STUDENT	PRINCIPAL	CENTRAL OFFICE STAFF
Design, develop, coordinate, and evaluate the program.	*Classroom:* Provide an enriched individualized program for the gifted.	Attend regular or specially scheduled programs or events.	Become knowledgeable about the unique needs of the gifted.	Provide the necessary staff to implement and support all identification, program development, material acquisition, inservice training, publicity, evaluation, and related procedures that are required to provide a qualitatively differentiated program for the gifted and talented.
Develop and implement curriculum (techniques, materials) related to enriching the total program.	Assist students in planning, organizing, and evaluating tasks.	Complete selected tasks.	Become acquainted with gifted students in the school.	
Prepare financial, statistical, and descriptive reports as needed to develop, maintain, and account for the program.	Screen, develop, and provide appropriate materials for the gifted.	Communicate and share learning experiences with peers, teachers, and parents.	Stimulate interest in and concern for the gifted.	Define and coordinate the requisite roles and responsibilities of the school board, superintendent, psychologist, psychometrist, counselor and classroom teacher.
Coordinate identification and certification procedures.	Evaluate pupil progress.	Practice decision-making skills.	Urge teachers to provide qualitatively differentiated program for the gifted in their classrooms.	
Serve as a consultant and resource to the staff, students, and parents involved with the program.	Interpret the program to parents.	Develop self-awareness and understanding.	Cooperate with district personnel in identifying the gifted and implementing programs for them.	
Participate as part of the Educational Services staff.	*Itinerant:* Support classroom teachers and building principals in their teaching relationships with the gifted and talented.	Participate in planning and evaluating learning experiences within the program.	Encourage and assist teachers in securing appropriate instructional materials for the gifted.	
Promote public relations activities at the local, county, and state levels.	Provide an enriched extension of the regular curriculum for gifted students in intra- or extra-classroom settings.		Meet regularly with parents to explain the program to them.	
	Demonstrate diverse methods of instruction appropriate for the gifted. . . .		Work cooperatively with other personnel in objectively evaluating the program.	

*Sandra N. Kaplan, *Providing Programs for the Gifted and Talented: A Handbook* (Reston, Va.: Council for Exceptional Children, 1975), p. 20.

Likewise, committee members must be prepared to offer informed rebuttal to unfounded criticisms such as:[8]

Programs for the gifted and talented reinforce the segregation of students
The definition of gifted and/or talented naturally segregates these children from others. Isolation, as differentiated in meaning from segregation, is not the aim of a program for these pupils. Segregation is the program's goal only as it applies to the separateness of learning experiences from the general curriculum but not as it applies to the separation of children from children. The reason for segregating students is far more important than the definition. The concept of segregation for status and expediency cannot be equated with segregation for learning efficiency and effectiveness. The segregation of the gifted and talented for various purposes at various times can promote the use of techniques and materials which enhance the quality of education for all children.

The utilization of individualized instruction abolishes the need for separate programs for the gifted and talented
Individualized instruction is a term which has become misused and misinterpreted. It can be identified as a method of teaching or as an organizational pattern for teaching. Regardless of its definition, individualized instruction implies the need to provide for individual differences within the context of a given administrative arrangement. In its purest form, individualized instruction should provide a separate educational program for *every* child. Even though individualized instruction accommodates the gifted and talented to a greater degree than the traditional classroom operation, it cannot replace separate programs which expose the students to learnings that exist beyond the confines of even the best individually instructed classroom. The idea that one type of provision will satisfy the needs of these gifted students is unacceptable.

Overemphasizing the gifted and talented through a special program creates an elitist population
In programs where the gifted and talented spend some portion of their school time interacting with other students, the probability of their becoming an elite group is minimized. If the students perceive participation as a reward for their intelligence and if attendance promotes status by virtue of the design and offerings of the program, then the student cannot be held responsible for flaunting or misrepresenting the group to which he belongs. Likewise, where the gifted and talented program is not seen in relationship to other programs, it presents a faulty picture of both its purpose and its participants. When students understand the reason for their participation and where opportunities are created for them to share outcomes from the program, research has shown that they relate more successfully and are well received by others.

What is good for the gifted and talented is good for all children
The premise that gifted and talented children are still children does not mean that they are like all other children. Recognition of their capacity and potential for learning characterizes them as deviating from the norm. The argument that all children should have the educational experiences, to a greater or lesser degree as it relates to their ability to learn, is one which at least gives the gifted and talented some special attention. A program tailored to the gifted and talented but applied to the average causes frustration and failure for the average; conversely, a program designed for the average and made available to the gifted and talented restricts self-fulfillment for the gifted and talented and can also cause frustration and failure for the gifted!

If classroom teachers were doing their job, there would be no need to offer a special program for the gifted and talented
In most situations, the classroom teacher is a generalist who lacks the specialized preparation needed to work with the gifted and talented. The classroom teacher with a heterogeneous population can only be expected to find alternatives for the gifted and talented and to guide them toward these alternatives. The teacher is

not a failure because she realizes her inadequacies and inability to be all things to all children.

What is offered to the gifted and talented should be commensurate with what is offered to the students in other special education programs
Research indicates the predominance of fiscal and professional support for programs for the handicapped without the same degree of support for programs for the gifted and talented. Equality of need for all special programs must be stressed without mandating equality of the type or scope of the program. The cliché that gifted are not handicapped is incorrect, for the lack of educational means for the gifted and talented results in handicapping their potential. The amount of attention and acceptance given to "special education" must include appropriation for gifted and talented programs as part of the same title.

STEP 4. Members of the Planning-Steering Committee are invited by the coordinator or supervisor of the Gifted and Talented Program to chair or serve on one of the following subcommittees:

Committee for Examination and Translation of the State Guidelines for Gifted and Talented Programs.

Committee for Research of Programs outside the District.

Committee to Develop Student Identification Criteria.

Committee to Study the Regular Curriculum and Make Recommendations for Adaptations for the Gifted and Talented Students.

Committee to Serve as Reaction Agents to Proposals for Program Design and Content.

Committee to Plan and Implement an In-service Program for Teachers and for Parents.

STEP 5. The faculty, at an all-day in-service workshop, is oriented to the basic elements of designing, structuring, and implementing the district's program for the gifted and talented.

Members of the Parents' Advisory Committee for the Education of the Gifted and Talented as well as interested school board members are invited to attend and participate in the workshop program.

In a general orientation meeting, a recognized authority in the field of gifted and talented education—if possible a staff member from the state educational agency for gifted and talented education—provides an overview of the purpose and dimensions of a district program for gifted and talented students, including:

Historical perspective.

Federal program recommendations; definition, identification criteria, program parameters, and expected outcomes.

State mandates, recommendations, due process procedures, and field services.

Exemplary programs in the county and state.

Following the formal presentation, the chief school administrator invites all teachers, administrators, board members, and parents to become coparticipants in designing, structuring, and implementing the district's program for the gifted and talented. The superintendent then invites members of the audience to ask questions concerning any phase or element of the proposed district program.

Following the discussion period, the coordinator or supervisor of the program will:

Outline the procedure for designing, structuring, and field testing the curriculum for the gifted and talented as well as the target dates for each phase of program development.

Introduce those educators—consultants from outside the district and those from within the district—who will be in charge of designing program format, contents, and procedures.

Invite each member of the audience to share ideas and suggestions with the Planning-Steering Committee and/or the program designers.

Invite teachers to enroll in the three-credit extension course, The Nature and Nurture of Creativity, which is being offered by the school district (see Example 1).

Invite each participant to obtain his or her Orientation Resource Kit and workshop schedule and program following this general meeting.

EXAMPLE 1   DESCRIPTION OF PROPOSED PROGRAM OF IN-SERVICE EDUCATION

A. Title: *The Nature and Nurture of Creativity.*
B. Statement of Need: Each Pennsylvania school district, by state mandate, must design and implement special education programs for the mentally gifted. This course here proposed has been structured to translate the Pennsylvania *Guidelines for the Operation of Special Education Programs for the Mentally Gifted* into operational plans and programs reflecting the research findings and recommendations concerning the characteristics, the capabilities, and the development-growth potential of gifted and talented children and youth.
C. Content of the Program:
   1. Description
      The primary purposes of this course are:
      a. To provide an in-depth study of the unique characteristics and developmental growth needs of the intellectually gifted and creatively talented student.
      b. To provide laboratory experiences in designing learning programs which will uniquely meet the developmental-growth needs of the intellectually gifted and creatively talented student, kindergarten through grade twelve, in the following eight subject-matter divisions: language arts, literature, social studies, mathematics, science, foreign languages, music, and art.
   2. Competencies to be developed:
      a. Teachers will build background knowledge of the research findings and recommendations concerning the unique characteristics of the intellectually gifted and the creatively talented student.
      b. Teachers will develop instructional programs providing enrichment on the horizontal level in each of the eight basic curricular areas.
      c. Teachers will develop instructional programs providing acceleration on the vertical level in each of the eight basic curricular areas.
      d. Teachers will develop and field test techniques and programs for stimulating adventurous thinking.
   3. Means of developing competencies:
      a. Teachers will become conversant with the *Guidelines* . . . developed by the Pennsylvania Bureau of Special Education.
      b. Teachers will become conversant with the research findings and recommendations of the recognized leaders in the field such as: J. J. Gallagher, J. P. Guilford, J. S. Renzulli, and E. P. Torrance.

EXAMPLE 1 (cont.)

c. Teachers will become conversant with the divergent approaches followed singly or in combination to provide instructional programs for the intellectually gifted and the creatively talented student, including: enrichment of content, acceleration of content, individualization of instruction, open-ended curriculum, goal-directed programs to develop and/or foster such diverse aspects of giftedness as creativity, critical thinking, evaluative thinking, adventurous thinking, leadership, etc.

d. Teachers will participate in laboratory sessions where program support needs and student developmental-growth needs are related to curriculum design and media mix and match.

e. Teachers will design and field test teaching-learning strategies to nurture creativity.

4. Method and criteria for evaluating competencies:

a. Teachers will rate the instructional programs they have designed by employing the "Intellectual Processes Rating Scale" to determine the degree of coverage in each program of the divisions and subdivisions of the "Taxonomy of Educational Objectives" on both the cognitive and the affective levels.

b. Teachers will submit to the class for critical evaluation and review the instructional programs they have designed for the intellectually talented and creatively talented student.

c. Teachers will field test programs they have designed to discover student reaction to content, process, media support, and learning activities.

D. Administrative Responsibility: Dr. Joshua Geller, Superintendent.

E. Who Will Teach the Program: Ruth A. Davies, Supervisor of Media Services, North Hills School District and Faculty Member of the Graduate School of Library and Information Sciences, University of Pittsburgh.

F. Resources Available: Bibliography; professional library collection; model programs for the gifted from California, Connecticut, Florida, Georgia, Illinois, Minnesota, Nebraska, New York, North Carolina, Pennsylvania, Rhode Island, and Virginia; professional consultants; media and support equipment to be provided by the North Hills School District.

G. Program Evaluation: The student will, as an individual and as a member of the class, evaluate the effectiveness of the in-service program in light of their competency attainment.

H. Participants: Approximately 25 North Hills school teachers.

I. Clock Hours: Approximately 45 hours.

J. Schedule: Program will begin April 11, 1981 and terminate June 20, 1981. Class times will be arranged at the first class meeting and will include 25 hours of laboratory experience to be scheduled on five separate Saturdays.

K. Credits: 3 credits for teachers achieving the competencies specified in Section C-2 above.

The workshop sessions are kept to a maximum of 30 participants so there will be a free exchange of ideas; each workshop will explore the identical areas being explored in the other workshops. To avoid a threatening climate, the workshop participants will be given the choice of whether to tape the workshop session. Topics discussed at the workshop sessions include:

Profile of the gifted and talented.

Procedures, instruments, and teacher involvement in student nomination for participation in the Gifted and Talented Program.

Purpose of Individualized Educational Programs (IEPs).

Teacher concerns about the proposed differentiated instructional program for the gifted and talented.

Board member concerns about the program.

Parent concerns about the program.

Principal concerns about the program.

Types and kinds of programs and the unique characteristics of each.

Following the discussion, the group will summarize its concerns and recommendations. Summaries from all the workshops are then sent to the superintendent's office for his or her study and for his or her office staff to reproduce and distribute, hopefully the next day, to the teachers, principals, and other participants in the various workshops. If tapes have been made of the various workshop sessions, they should be sent to the coordinator or supervisor of the Gifted and Talented Program for his or her study and for sharing with the members of the Planning-Steering Committee.

STEP 6. Each faculty member as a follow-up to the in-service program hopefully will examine, study, and react to the ideas contained in the Orientation Resource Kit he or she received at the general in-service meeting. These kits contain the following:

An abstract of the Marland Report, *Education of the Gifted and Talented* (see Appendix A).

State mandates and recommendations concerning the education of gifted and talented.

The U.S. Office of Gifted and Talented Fact Sheets:

Career Awareness for the Gifted and Talented (see Appendix C)

Characteristics of the Gifted and Talented (see Chapter 2)

Creative Thinking Techniques (see Appendix C)

The Culturally Diverse Gifted and Talented Child (see Appendix C)

Curriculum for the Gifted and Talented (later in this chapter)

Developing a Community Based Mentorship Program for the Gifted and Talented (see Appendix C)

Developing Individualized Education Programs (IEPs) for the Gifted and Talented (see Appendix C)

Developing Programs for the Gifted and Talented (later in this chapter)

Evaluation of Programs for the Gifted and Talented (see Appendix C)

Finding Funds for the Gifted and Talented (see Appendix C)

The Gifted and Talented Handicapped (see Appendix C)

Identification of the Gifted and Talented (see Chapter 2)

Math and Science for the Gifted and Talented Child (see Appendix C)

Parents of Gifted and Talented Children (see Appendix C)

The Preschool Gifted and Talented Child (see Appendix C)

Reading for the Gifted and Talented (see Appendix C)

What Is Creativity? (see Appendix C)

Instructional program design guides (see Tables 3, 4, and 5).

A checklist of district Gifted and Talented Committees with an invitation for the teacher to indicate interest in serving on one or more committees.

An invitation to the teacher to submit suggestions to the coordinator or supervisor of the Gifted and Talented Program to be considered for incorporation into the differentiated curriculum.

TABLE 3   DIVERSIFICATION FOR INDIVIDUALIZATION
OF INSTRUCTION*

PROBLEM	SOLUTION
Same goal for all, yet each student is a unique learner	Individualize the teaching-learning program to enable each learner to reach a common goal in a unique way

SUBPROBLEMS	SOLUTIONS
Each student in any given class differs in abilities from every other class member	Devise a variety of appropriate, significant, challenging experiences commensurate with class ability range; wide enough in latitude to challenge and satisfy both the slowest and the quickest learner
Each student in any given class differs in environmental and cultural background from every other class member	Provide learning experiences, activities, guidance, and resources that will compensate for any learner's environmental or cultural disabilities
Each student in any given class differs in progress rate from every other class member	Provide appropriate experiences, activities, guidance, and resources, so that each learner can begin on his or her own maturity level to learn at his or her own comprehension rate
Each student in any given class differs in drive from every other class member	Provide appropriate experiences, activities, guidance, and supporting resources that will create, motivate, and sustain interest in "perceiving, behaving, becoming"
Each student in any given class differs in creativity from every other class member	Provide appropriate experiences, activities, and resources that will encourage the expression and development of each learner's creative potential
Each student in any given class differs in personal goals from every other class member	Provide appropriate experiences, activities, guidance, and resources that will encourage each learner to strive for self-realization, self-fulfillment, and self-understanding
Each student in any given class differs in needs from every other class member	Provide ample opportunity for each learner to find within each school experience assurance of authentic concern for his or her developmental needs as a student, as a future citizen, and as a human being

*Ruth Ann Davies, *The School Library Media Program: Instructional Force for Excellence* (New York: R. R. Bowker, 1979), p. 92.

A bibliography listing the materials available from the district professional library on educating the gifted and talented.

Abstracts from *Creativity in the Classroom* by E. Paul Torrance: "Creative Ways of Teaching" (see Example 2) and "Creative Ways of Learning" (see Example 3).

An abstract from *Developing Creativity in the Gifted and Talented* by Carolyn M. Callahan (see Example 4).

Schedule of in-service programs with detailed description of topics to be discussed and list of the discussion leaders.

TABLE 4   ENRICHMENT: GROUPING, ACCELERATION, GUIDANCE*

Enrichment is any experience that replaces, supplements,
or extends instruction normally offered by the school.

GROUPING	ACCELERATION	GUIDANCE
Provisions that facilitate the student's access to special learning opportunities	*Activities that promote learning beyond regularly prescribed curriculum*	*Experiences that promote understanding of the self and others and explore opportunities for careers*
Cluster grouping within the regular class	Early entrance or pre-school classes	Individual conferences
Special regular classes	Double grade promotion	Group meetings
Part-time groups before, during, after school or on Saturdays	Advanced placement classes	Career and vocational counseling
Seminars	Ungraded classes	Educational counseling
Minicourses	Multi-age classes	Community programs and sponsorship
Team teaching	Tutoring	Scholarship societies
Alternative schools	Correspondence courses	Study groups
Resource room or demonstration classroom	Extra classes for extra credit	Special education classes
Itinerant or resource teacher	Credit by examination	Tutoring
Field trip and cultural events	Independent study	
Special summer programs	Continuous progress curriculum	
	Year-round school	
	Flexible scheduling	
	Block or back-to-back classes	

*Adapted from Marsha M. Correll, *Teaching the Gifted and Talented* (Bloomington, Ind.: Phi Delta Kappa Educational Foundation, © 1978), p. 25.

EXAMPLE 2   CREATIVE WAYS OF TEACHING*

What can teachers do to provide the conditions in which creative thinking abilities have a predominate role?

1. Provide opportunities for creative behavior

   Make assignments that call for original work, independent learning, self-initiated projects, and experimentation

   Ask questions that call for productive thinking

   Use curricular materials which provide progressive warm-up exercises, which permit one thing to lead to another, and activities which make creative thinking both legitimate and rewarding

   Use curricular materials which familiarize children with the nature of the creative-thinking process through the lives of eminent creative people

   Develop skills in the use of analogy

*E. Paul Torrance, *Creativity in the Classroom,* What Research Says to the Teacher Series (Washington, D.C.: National Education Association, 1977), pp. 23–27.

TABLE 5   SPECIFICATIONS FOR THE LANGUAGE ARTS*

Content Skills Units	COGNITIVE BEHAVIOR						AFFECTIVE BEHAVIOR			
	Knowledge	Comprehension	Application	Analysis	Synthesis	Evaluation	Receiving	Responding	Valuing	Attitudes
	Terminology Information Concepts	Defining Interpreting Generalizing	Inferring Predicting	Elements Relationships	Creating	Objective Subjective Criteria	Awareness Willingness Attentiveness	Compliance Willingness Satisfaction	Acceptance Preference Commitment	Positive Neutral Negative
Listening a. b. . . .										
Speaking a. b. . . .										
Reading a. b. . . .										
Writing a. b. . . .										

*From John U. Michaelis, Ruth H. Grossman, and Lloyd F. Scott, *New Designs for Elementary Curriculum and Instruction* (New York: McGraw-Hill, 1975), p. 159.

EXAMPLE 2 (cont.)

2. Develop skills for creative teaching

   Stress the skills and strategies of inquiry, creative research, and problem solving

3. Reward creative achievements

   Be respectful of the unusual questions children ask

   Be respectful of the unusual ideas and solutions of children

   Show children that their ideas have value

   Provide opportunities for and give credit for self-initiated learning

   Provide chances for children to learn, think, and discover without threats of immediate evaluation

4. Establish creative relationships with children

   Permit one thing to lead to another, to embark with the child on an unknown adventure

   Be ready to accept and respond to student inventiveness

   Create an environment which is definitely a responsive one in which the child finds encouragement, respect, and guidance

5. Facilitate creative behavior

   Give purpose to creative writing

   Provide experiences which make children more sensitive to environmental stimuli

   Develop a constructive attitude toward the information taught

   Provide adequate warm-up for creative activities

   In warming-up pupils for creative thinking, avoid giving examples or illustrations which will freeze or unduly shape their thinking

   Provide unevaluated (off-the-record) practice

   To evoke originality in thinking, make it clear that such thinking is expected and will be rewarded

EXAMPLE 3   CREATIVE WAYS OF LEARNING*

In this writer's opinion, the weight of present evidence indicates that people fundamentally prefer to learn in creative ways—by exploring, manipulating, questioning, experimenting, risking, testing, and modifying ideas. Teachers generally have insisted that it is more economical to learn by authority. Recent research suggests that many things, though not all, can be learned more effectively and economically in creative ways rather than by authority. It also appears that many individuals have an especially strong preference for learning creatively, learn a great deal if permitted to use their creative thinking abilities, and make little educational progress when we insist that they learn by authority. Such suggestions open exciting possibilities for better ways of individualizing instruction.

Learning creatively takes place in the process of sensing problems or gaps in information, making guesses or hypotheses about these deficiencies, testing these guesses, revising, and retesting them, and communicating the results. Strong human needs are involved in each stage of this process. If we sense that something is missing or untrue, tension is aroused. We are uncomfortable and want to do something to relieve the tension. This makes us want to ask questions, make guesses, or otherwise inquire. Uncertain as to whether our guesses are correct, we continue to be uncomfortable. Thus, we are driven to test our guesses, correct our errors, and modify our conclusions. Once we discover something, we want to tell someone about it.

We learn by authority when we are told what we should learn and when we accept something as true because an authority says that it is. The authority may be a classroom teacher, parent, textbook, newspaper, or reference book. Frequently it is majority opinion, the consensus of our peer group. In our democratic culture, there is a tendency to emphasize the rightness of the majority in determining the truth.

*E. Paul Torrance, *Creativity in the Classroom,* What Research Says to the Teacher Series (Washington, D.C.: National Education Association, 1977), pp. 22–23.

EXAMPLE 3 (cont.)

From these differentiations and from research evidence, it appears that learning by authority primarily brings into play on the part of the learner such abilities as recognition, memory, and logical reasoning—the abilities most frequently assessed by traditional tests of intelligence and scholastic aptitude. In contrast, creative learning involves such abilities as evaluation (especially the ability to sense problems, inconsistencies, and missing elements), divergent production (e.g., fluency, flexibility, originality, and elaboration), and redefinition.

Several well-known studies indicate that the creative thinking abilities can be important in educational achievement. It appears, however, that these abilities are less useful in classes and schools where teachers insist that children learn almost entirely by authority.

EXAMPLE 4 DEVELOPING CREATIVITY IN THE GIFTED AND TALENTED:
PRACTICAL IMPLICATIONS FOR THE TEACHER*

Research leads to some general considerations about what a teacher might do to encourage creative production by students in the classroom.

1. Provide a nonthreatening atmosphere. The classroom environment should be structured in such a way that students' ideas and opinions are respected, ridicule of new ideas is eliminated, questioning is encouraged, and questions are asked that allow students to be open and uninhibited in response.

2. Refrain from becoming the judge of the worth of all products in the classroom. An open, nonjudgmental attitude on the part of the teacher will allow more freedom for divergent production as well as the evaluative skills necessary for the complete creative process. Encourage students to develop criteria to judge both the work of peers and themselves.

3. Model creative thinking and/or introduce other individuals who are able to illustrate the creative thinking process to the students. The teacher should take care to model creative problem solving procedures on as many occasions as possible, not simply during "creativity time."

4. Attempt to integrate activities and questions that encourage divergent production and evaluation into as many content areas as possible. The necessity of illustrating transfer of these skills to all areas of thinking cannot be overestimated.

5. Make a conscious effort to remind students to be creative, to be original, to try to think of new ways to solve a problem, etc.

6. Systematically reward novel production. The use of operant conditioning to reinforce specific types of novel behavior can lead to an overall increase in creative production. For example, the reinforcement of the use of a variety of sentence structures in an essay has been shown to influence overall creative writing skill. Care should be taken to choose appropriate reinforcement. Gifted children can be expected to value rewards that are somewhat unique.

7. Provide stimuli for as many of the senses as possible. A variety of stimuli encourage the student to view the problem from a variety of perspectives and also seem to enhance the sense of openness and psychological freedom.

8. Make use of warm-up activities when moving from highly structured convergent or memory type activities into activities requiring students to engage in creative production. Such brief activities should be used to reaffirm the nonthreatening environment and are most effective if they relate to the task to be accomplished.

9. Incorporate activities into the classroom instruction that require students to generate a large number of correct responses. That is, provide open-ended questions that have no single, right answer.

10. Instruct students in the principles of brainstorming, but incorporate strategies for self evaluation of the quality of ideas. Furthermore, brainstorming activities will be most productive if tied to "real problems" or "meaningful production" rather than simple games.

11. Be a participant in the actions. Do not merely pose problems, but be an active problem solver.

*Carolyn M. Callahan, *Developing Creativity in the Gifted and Talented* (Reston, Va.: Council for Exceptional Children, 1978), pp. 71–72.

EXAMPLE 4 (cont.)

12. Encourage students to express positive self statements about their creativity and avoid negative self evaluations. Provide them with guiding statements of attitudes, approaches to problems, and orientations to the process.

13. Attempts to incorporate published material into the curriculum are dependent on the understanding and commitment of the teachers who are using the curriculum. No packaged materials are independent of the teacher's use of those materials, and the effectiveness of creativity training materials seems to be particularly influenced by the teacher's attitude and the environment of the classroom.

14. Whichever strategies are adopted for classroom use must be evaluated within the particular classroom with your particular students and teaching style. What works in one situation will not always work in others. Continual assessment of the objectives of instruction is crucial.

CONCEPTS OF IN-SERVICE PROGRAMS

A wide variety of programs for the gifted and talented have been developed within the school districts of the United States. Just as each school district is unique, so is each school within each district. Consequently, each program for the gifted and talented must also be unique. "No one type of program is best for all gifted and talented students or all schools."[9] Nevertheless, certain basic elements are common to all. The purpose, then, of a district in-service program is to promote faculty understanding of the overall dimensions and parameters of the district's particular gifted and talented program. All faculty members should become conversant with each of the following concepts. The first three concepts—program goals, basic program alternatives, and the difference between "provisions" and "programs"—are taken from Correll.[10]

1. Program goals
   a. *Superior Achievement*—Gifted and talented youngsters should have ample opportunities to realize their potential to the fullest extent possible.
   b. *Self-Directedness*—The freedom, responsibility, and capability to manage one's time is an important ingredient of self-fulfillment and productivity.
   c. *Acceptance of Responsibility*—The leadership capabilities of gifted and talented pupils imply increased responsibilities to self, home, and society.
   d. *Creative Thinking and Expression*—This goal seeks the development of creativity in a rich variety of constructive ways.
   e. *Aesthetic Awareness*—This goal focuses upon the development of positive feelings toward things of beauty and consequence.
   f. *Acceptance of Divergent Views*—This goal views tolerance for divergent thought as an aid to learning.
   g. *Pursuit of Alternative Solutions*—This focus is on development of patterns of thinking which seek alternate solutions to problems prior to action. It seeks the development of a capacity for reasoning and effective decision making.
   h. *Commitment to Inquiry*—The development of a pattern of thinking is stressed, which continually questions, probes, tests, and investigates.
   i. *Preparation for Satisfying Life-Style and Career*—The need for a gifted and talented person to enter into a career that is commensurate with his/her abilities, interests, and spiritual satisfaction is understood.

2. Basic program alternatives [see Table 4]
   a. *Enrichment of content*—enrichment is any experience that replaces, supplements, or extends instruction normally offered by the school.
   b. *Grouping*—provisions that facilitate the student's access to special learning opportunities such as:
      Cluster grouping within the regular class
      Special regular classes [see Chapter 5]
      Part-time groups before, during, after school or on Saturdays
      Seminars
      Minicourses
      Team teaching
      Alternative schools
      Resource room or demonstration classroom
      Itinerant or resource teacher
      Field learning experiences and cultural events
   c. *Acceleration*—activities that promote learning beyond regularly prescribed curriculum
      Early entrance or preschool classes
      Double grade promotion
      Math and reading levels programs on the elementary level
      Honors courses
      Advanced placement classes
      Ungraded classes
      Multi-age classes
      Tutoring
      Correspondence courses
      Extra classes for extra credit
      College courses for credit
      Early entrance to college
      Credit by examination
      Independent study
      Continuous progress curriculum
      Year-round school
      Flexible scheduling
      Block or back-to-back classes
   d. *Guidance*—experiences that promote understanding of the self and others and explore opportunities for careers
      Individual conferences
      Group meetings
      Career and vocational counseling
      Educational counseling
      Community programs and sponsorship
      Scholarship societies
      Study groups
      Special education classes
      Tutoring
3. Difference between "provisions" and "programs"
   a. *Provisions* are offered by numerous schools through enrichment or acceleration within the regular classroom.
   b. *Programs* are directed toward the systematic development of long-

range goals that are coordinated to develop the abilities and competencies of gifted pupils from the time of their identification through their
graduation.

4. Enrichment—an instructional program for the gifted and talented breaks
the restrictive bonds of course content, textbook, and classroom.
   a. *Depth of understanding* results from exploring more fully and ade-
      quately the topics, concepts, experiences, and activities introduced in
      the classroom (see Part II).
   b. *Breadth of understanding* results from idea linkage and open-ended
      learning where significant topics, concepts, experiences, and activities
      are discovered and explored (see Part II).
   c. *Relevance* in the teaching/learning program for the gifted and talented
      provides significant learning experiences that are commensurate with
      the individual student's own needs, interests, goals, abilities, and con-
      cerns as well as those experiences that are significant and directly
      related to the contemporary world—current happenings and events,
      social and political happenings, economic developments, technological
      and scientific advancements, cultural developments and achievements,
      and emerging patterns of change.

5. Cognitive and affective domains (see Table 5).
   a. *Taxonomy of Educational Objectives: Handbook I, Cognitive Domain*,
      edited by Benjamin Bloom et al. (New York: David McKay, 1956),
      classifies the educational objectives in the cognitive area in this hierar-
      chy:
      Knowledge
      Comprehension
      Application
      Synthesis
      Evaluation
      Programs for the gifted and talented stress those learning experiences
      at the upper levels of cognition (see Chapter 5 for the further deline-
      ation of the cognitive domain).
   b. *Taxonomy of Educational Objectives: Handbook II, Affective Domain*,
      edited by David R. Krathwohl et al. (New York: David McKay, 1964),
      classifies affective educational objectives in this hierarchy:
      Receiving
      Responding
      Valuing
      Organizing
      Characterization by a value or value complex
      Programs for the gifted and talented stress those learning experiences
      that involve valuing, organizing a value system, and acting consistently
      in accordance with internalized values (see Chapter 5 for further delin-
      eation of the affective domain).

6. J. P. Guilford's Structure of the Intellect Model. This teaching/learning
   model provides a structure that presents a scheme and elements for either
   developing or presenting learning experiences.[11] The idea is to use this
   model as a tool when planning programs for the gifted and talented, relating content to products and operations (see Chapter 5 for further analysis
   of Guilford's Model).

7. Frank E. Williams's Model for Implementing Cognitive-Affective Behaviors, in *Classroom Ideas for Encouraging Thinking and Feeling* (Buffalo, N.Y.: D. O. K. Publishers, 1970, p. 3). Presents the dimensions of content-teaching processes and student behavior to emphasize the strands of possibilities with the dimensions of: curriculum, teacher behavior (strategies or modes of teaching), and pupil behaviors (see Chapter 5 for further delineation of the model).

8. Curriculum Principles and Premises, from *Curriculum Change Toward the 21st Century* by Harold G. Shane (Washington, D.C.: National Education Association, 1977, pp. 59–70).

   a. The need to develop a spirit of "global community" in an increasingly interdependent world has reaffirmed an important task for education: to recognize and to respect the concepts of multiethnic, polycultural, and multilingual education in pluralistic societies both in the United States and abroad.

   b. Education has assumed new significance as a positive force for peace in a world capable of destroying itself.

   c. Learning is a lifelong process, and education, therefore, should be seen as a seamless continuum of experience from early childhood to old age.

   d. The value to the learners of their experiences obtained through education is more important than the routes they may follow in obtaining those experiences.

   e. The aspirations and abilities of the student are best served when the student's learning experiences are at least partly self-directed rather than selected entirely by teachers.

   f. Because of the impact of attitudes, comments, and actions of teachers (the "hidden curriculum" reflecting what teachers really value), greater efforts should be made to ensure that this latent curriculum becomes clear and provides wholesome input for the learner.

   g. Because the experiences of each learner are unique, teachers should expect a wide range of performance from children, youth, and adults.

   h. Good instruction is personalized rather than individualized.

   i. The opportunity for universal early childhood education should be an integral part of the structure of education in a seamless learning continuum.

   j. Adult education that exceeds mere literacy should receive worldwide emphasis.

   k. Ability, motivation, and readiness rather than certificates or diplomas should serve as the learner's prime credentials.

   l. When and where teaching and learning occur must not be bounded either by the school walls or by our preconceived ideas as to what should be learned at the once-traditional age for learning it.

   m. Persons in the field of career or occupational education should develop their programs in ways that recognize even more fully that vocational activity—the jobs held and services performed—often is sequential and will require greater versatility from members of the work force in the years ahead.

   n. Traditional patterns of home-school relations need to be reconsidered and perhaps sharply modified in recognition of changes in the family, which in many instances today is often an "affinity group" rather than the nuclear family consisting of mother, father, and children.

o. Present social trends, which are characterized by accelerating change and increasing complexity, have enhanced the need for basic communication skills such as the ability to handle the written and spoken word and to deal with number concepts.

p. Valid methods of instruction vary from one learner to another, hence the goal of equitable educational opportunity can be approached only when schooling provides—at least in some respects—experiences that are different for each student.

q. Traditional instructional methods should be expanded to include problem-solving approaches, and their emphasis on cognition and valuing should be renewed.

r. Interdisciplinary learning should be stressed and the art of comprehending and anticipating complex relationships should be fostered.

s. Good vocational or occupational education should be more thoroughly permeated by the content of a general or "liberalizing" education; conversely, it should be recognized that a sound liberal education also will be inherently vocational in the years ahead.

t. Because human differences and educational uniformity cannot be reconciled, the testing and measurement of content skills should be evaluated on an individual basis.

u. There is a need to teach the concept of alternative futures since, lacking a desirable image of tomorrow's possible worlds, one lacks purpose, goals, and the motivating spirit of community that are needed to serve as guides to action.

v. Instruction in subject matter fields should develop a deepening understanding of contemporary threats to the biosphere, include socially useful service in its maintenance, and communicate to youth the need for achieving balance or equilibrium between humans and their environment.

w. So that desirable alternative futures can be envisioned, work in the social studies should be redesigned so as to promote a grasp of human geography and of planetary cultures as they exist today.

x. In studying possible futures, the natural and physical sciences, both in content and methodology, should serve as illustrations of truth-validating inquiry.

y. In the symbolic sciences—language arts, foreign language, mathematics, linguistics, and the like—more heed should be given both to basic communication skills and to recognizing propaganda, shoddy advertising, and political double-talk.

9. Developmental skills program (see Appendix F and Appendix G).

a. Skills are the tools for productive learning, effective thinking, and intelligent action.

b. The real test of the effectiveness of the skills program will come when the student of today intelligently and creatively applies his or her skills in solving future problems.

c. Skills are thinking-learning-communicating tools essential for self-initiated and self-directed knowledge building.

    d. An effective skills program is planned for the timely integration of skills with content development.

    e. The skill should be taught functionally rather than as a separate or isolated learning experience.

    f. The skill development program must be flexible to allow skills to be taught when and as needed.

10. School library as a learning laboratory.*

    a. The educationally effective school library is a learning laboratory that provides unlimited resources for learning,† guidance in how to learn, and a climate conducive to learning (see Appendix G).

    b. The school librarian is a *teacher* whose subject is learning itself.[12]

    c. The school librarian is an invaluable member of the teaching team for the gifted and talented and is directly involved in all phases of the school's program for the gifted and talented—design, structure, implementation, and evaluation.

    d. The school librarian frequently serves in the capacity of mentor for students embarking on individualized research projects.

    e. The school librarian frequently organizes and teaches seminars (see Part II, Model 43, Revving Up for College).

    f. Since curriculum is the *planned* interaction of pupils with content, resources, and instructional processes, face-to-face communication between the teacher or teaching team and the school librarian is absolutely essential (see Chapter 5 for teacher-librarian planning procedure).

11. Pilot projects (see Chapter 5 for Pilot Project Design and Analysis Guides).

    a. The purpose of field testing each unit in the Gifted and Talented Unit is to determine the adequacy, the learner appeal, and the teachability of the unit.

    b. The *Handbook of Curriculum Evaluation,* edited by Arieh Lewy and sponsored by the International Institute for Educational Planning (New York: Longman, 1977), is a comprehensive work that provides guidance in all phases of curriculum development and assessment.

CURRICULUM DESIGN AND DEVELOPMENT

Two U.S. Office of Gifted and Talented fact sheets can well serve as a fitting review of the in-service program. They are the following *Curriculum for the Gifted and Talented*[13] and *Developing Programs for the Gifted and Talented.*[14]

CURRICULUM FOR THE GIFTED AND TALENTED

The development and implementation of a curriculum which allows gifted and talented students to develop their potential and explore new domains of knowledge should be a high priority for all school systems. Educators responsible for designing curriculum for the gifted and talented must be well grounded in the special characteristics and abilities of these students in order to devise effective and challenging learning activities.

What is a curriculum?
Simply put, curriculum is a course of study. As such, it includes both the content

---

*Abstracted from The School Librarian: Instructional Partner in the Gifted and Talented Program in Chapter 5.

†Through bibliographies of special collections, computerized data retrieval, and interlibrary loan the school library provides unlimited access to information.

to be learned and the processes which facilitate that learning. Curriculum is the medium through which learning occurs.

How does a curriculum for the gifted and talented differ from a "regular" curriculum?
Gifted and talented students, because of their special abilities, require opportunities which encourage:

The development of abstract thinking.

The sharpening of reasoning abilities.

Practice in creative problem setting and solving.

Higher cognitive processing, i.e., analysis, synthesis, and evaluation.

In the case of particular talents, educational settings which allow them a full range of expression.

Curricula for the gifted and talented often include activities which focus on interpretation of material being investigated, summative skills, creativity, divergent thinking, decision making, and independent inquiry. While instructional units for both the gifted and talented curriculum and regular curriculum can be similar, the breadth, depth, and intensity of learning activities within the gifted and talented curriculum mark it as distinctive.

What do the terms "enrichment" and "acceleration" mean in connection with a curriculum for the gifted and talented?
Enrichment programs are generally those which go beyond normal classroom activity by offering students a greater latitude of inquiry. A unit on the American Revolution, for instance, could be enriched by an exploration into the concept and historical development of revolution.

Acceleration programs generally cover the same material as a normal curriculum but at a much faster pace. This is common in math and science programs for the gifted, where two or more years of work may be covered in a year or less.

Who determines a curriculum for the gifted and talented?
Teachers are usually responsible for the design and implementation of curriculum for their gifted and talented students. Students can also share in this responsibility. It is important to emphasize that curriculum for these students should not be a predetermined route which all must follow. Curriculum is a framework for individual learning alternatives. As such, it should be flexible enough to meet the needs of both pupils and teachers.

Does a curriculum designed for the gifted and talented diminish the role of the teacher?
The major goal of a curriculum for the gifted and talented is to provide more opportunity for independent learning. The processes of learning and thinking assume a higher priority than the internalization of information. This emphasis enhances the role of the teacher as a director of learning while diminishing the teacher's role as a conduit for data.

What are some important considerations in designing a curriculum for the gifted and talented?
The most desirable curriculum is one which fits the learning modes of the students. It should allow students the opportunity both to create and consume learning as well as offer alternative activities for achieving learning objectives.

What are some curriculum alternatives for the gifted and talented?
Among the many options available, teachers and program planners may want to consider the following examples:

Subject or skill. A particular domain of knowledge or skill which provides the substance for directing the curriculum, such as scientific research skills which can be applied in many situations.

Core subject. A generalized theme or topic with broad and diverse applications to several subject areas which is used to develop and integrate learning experiences, such as the interdependence of man.

Basic question. An outline of basic questions which formulates the learning experience, such as "What is causing the energy crisis?"

Process. Particular thinking skills which are applied to selected topics or themes, such as designing a new city.

Teachers must also consider the environment in which a curriculum will be used. It should include personal, social, and cultural elements which can become learning tools. While the curriculum should have a strong theoretical foundation, it should also produce measurable outcomes.

Curricula can come in a variety of formats. Some common formats include the learning guide, the unit, the task card, the learning center, and the learning kit.

RESOURCES

For more information concerning curriculum for the gifted and talented, contact the consultant for gifted and talented education in your state department of education or write to: The Council for Exceptional Children, 1920 Association Drive, Reston, VA 22091.

Readings in the area which may be helpful are:
Fliegler, L. *Curriculum planning for the gifted.* Englewood Cliffs, NJ: Prentice-Hall, 1964.
Furlong, B. (Ed.). *Unicornucopia: A guidebook for the gifted and talented.* Tempe, AZ: Kyrene School District #28, 1977.
Kaplan, S. *Providing programs for the gifted and talented.* Reston, VA: The Council for Exceptional Children, 1975.
Patterson, J., Saino, J., & Turner, J. R. *Why doesn't an igloo melt inside?* Memphis, TN: Memphis City Public Schools, 1973.

DEVELOPING PROGRAMS FOR THE GIFTED
AND TALENTED

The success of programs for the gifted and talented student depends on sound development, efficient identification, and exemplary curriculum. Where there are a number of positive program alternatives there is no need to become locked into a single design. Consideration should be given to all available program formats before deciding which single or combination of alternatives to employ.

How do I begin?
The first step in program development is planning. Planning is usually divided into three components:

Needs analysis. Because every community represents a unique constellation of factors, an analysis of local needs should be conducted. This analysis should consider all aspects of the community and educational system to determine a realistic base for the size and scope of the program. Often, the availability of funds and physical facilities will have a bearing on the dimensions of the program. A team representing a cross section of the community should conduct this assignment.

Target group. The needs assessment may also provide important information on the target group for the program. A broadened concept of giftedness has been established by the US Commissioner of Education in the 1971 *Report to Congress on the Education of the Gifted and Talented.* This definition cites six categories of giftedness: general intellectual ability, specific academic aptitude, creative or productive thinking, leadership ability, visual and performing arts, and psychomotor ability.

Identification. Multiple criteria should be used to identify students in the target category and should include both standardized and subjective assessments. For the intellectually gifted, measures on achievement and intelligence tests are appropriate with scores falling in the upper 2 to 3 percentiles of national or local norms. High creative producers can be identified through the use of tests of creativity and creativity checklists. Judgments by professional personnel using more subjective instruments should be combined with standardized assessments of either intellectual or creative ability. Parents and other adults knowledgeable about a child's performance outside the school should be consulted. In the creative arts, potential or demonstrated ability can be assessed through the judgments of experts in the field through interviews and/or auditions. In selecting students for a gifted and talented program, the student's areas of interest, abilities, and insight should be considered.

What kind of staff should be employed?
The selection of staff is a key factor in the success of the program. Desirable characteristics for teachers of the gifted and talented student include demonstrated competency in general educational techniques such as developing individualized curriculum, utilization of innovative techniques, use of strategies which encourage high levels of thinking, extensive knowledge of their subject area(s), along with such personal characteristics as self confidence, security, understanding, and a desire to work with gifted and talented students. Though often overlooked, stamina is a highly desirable factor, too.

What objectives are appropriate for a program for the gifted and talented student?
Objectives for the program should be established at several levels of the design. These levels involve the program, the teacher, and the pupil. Defining objectives is an essential part of program development, as they often form the basis of evaluation. Program objectives relate to the target population and anticipated development. Teacher objectives integrate more general program objectives with the specific needs of the students while tapping personal teacher strengths and interests. Pupil objectives are the vehicle through which the program goals are achieved.

What program designs are commonly employed?
There are three general designs that program planners find useful:

Centralized. This is a regional concept in programing which can serve the specialized needs of the gifted and talented student from a number of different school districts. A regional resource center is usually established which offers a wide range of facilities and a staff of experts in gifted and talented education. The center can specialize in one specific area of giftedness or provide options in many academic or talent categories.

Cluster. This also features a resource center, but offers services to students from several schools within a given district or from several districts. It may serve elementary students, secondary students, or a combination of the two.

Decentralized. The decentralized design offers programing for the gifted and talented within the local school and an itinerant teacher approach is often employed. This design may incorporate several approaches to programing for the gifted and talented by making a teacher of the gifted available to consult with regular classroom teachers or to conduct demonstration lessons.

What resources exist for program planning?
All areas rich in resources. Each district should investigate those resources available for use with its program. Community resources within any area may encompass all of the natural environment and urban centers. Specialists in a number of occupations may reside in your community. Members of the local school staff may also constitute valuable human resources.

How is curriculum for the program determined?
The curriculum for a gifted and talented program is not a road map for the teacher to follow without making any detours. It is unique in every community and with every target population. However, there are some common elements upon which the curriculum should be based. It should focus on the development of skills which are beyond the scope of the regular classroom, and content should

be in the student's areas of interest. Subject matter should be studied in its appropriate context, using the techniques of the field rather than engaging in an abstract exercise. It should also focus on the conceptual themes of important ideas rather than on the mere collection of new facts. Finally, the curriculum should include options which offer the student the freedom to explore.

How are programs for the gifted and talented evaluated?
Evaluation should be conducted at each program level where objectives were established. The objectives should be written in measurable terms or should cite the instrument which will be used in the evaluation of that objective. Both cognitive and affective assessments should be made in order to view the program from several perspectives. Evaluation can be *formative,* where data is collected throughout the operation of the program in order to point out areas which may need modification, or *summative,* which takes place at the conclusion of the program to determine end results. A combination of both types has proved to be most successful.

RESOURCES

For more information concerning programing for the gifted and talented student, contact the state consultant for the gifted and talented in your state department of education or write: The Council for Exceptional Children, 1920 Association Drive, Reston, VA 22091.

Additional reading in the area which may be helpful:

Boston, Bruce O. *Gifted and talented: Developing elementary and secondary school programs.* Reston, VA: The Council for Exceptional Children, 1975.

Ellis, Arthur S., & Ratner, Ronald. *Decision-making man.* St. Charles, IL: Aron Communications, 1976.

Kaplan, Sandra N. *Providing programs for the gifted and talented.* Reston, VA: The Council for Exceptional Children, 1975.

Mager, Robert F. *Preparing instructional objectives.* Belmont, CA: Lear Siegler, Inc./Fearon Publishers, 1975.

Maker, June C. *Providing programs for the gifted-handicapped.* Reston, VA: The Council for Exceptional Children, 1977.

Martinson, Ruth A. *The identification of the gifted and talented.* Reston, VA: The Council for Exceptional Children, 1975.

Prepared by Lynne D. Niro, Hamden, Connecticut.

A VERY SPECIAL TEACHER

The teacher of the gifted and talented must be a master teacher and a very special human being. Such a teacher should certainly possess in abundance those demanding characteristics specified by the Pennsylvania *Guide for Organizing and Operating Programs for the Mentally Gifted and Talented* (see Chapter 4). A list of specifics, however, can only hint at the full dimension required of a teacher of the gifted and talented; philosophically, there is so much more that should be there. The epitome of such a teacher is perhaps best presented in the portrait painted by that much respected and beloved professor, educational psychologist, and philosopher William H. Burton:

> Teaching is not a routine or rule-of-thumb process; it is a genuine intellectual adventure. . . . Teaching demands . . . the ability to adapt boldly, to invent, to create procedures to meet the ever changing demands of a given learning situation. Teaching demands continuous, imaginative anticipation of the mental processes of others, the ability to think quickly, to phrase questions and answers so as to stimulate thinking, the ability to keep intricate and subtle learning activities organized and moving toward a desirable outcome without at the same time dominating or coercing. Teaching necessitates a broad background of technological information.

Teaching cannot possibly be done on the basis of common sense or experience alone. A surgeon could not possibly learn how to operate for appendicitis on the basis of common sense and raw experience. Engineers do not build tunnels from two sides of a mountain to meet squarely in the middle on the basis of common sense or raw trial and error. To do either of these things on the basis of common sense or experience alone would result in many deaths and in huge waste of money. These things are done successfully on the basis of lengthy, difficult professional training which includes a period of experience under guidance. Naturally, later experience and critical analysis of that experience play a large part in improving skill, but this experience and analysis are enlightened by the preparatory training in basic technology. Furthermore, there is demanded in addition the ability to make courageous adaptations of known procedures to unexpected conditions and unusual variations, and the ability to invent new procedures. So it is with teaching. A teacher can no more teach little children to read on the basis of her common sense or uncritical experience than can the surgeon operate or the engineer carry out projects. An even closer parallel can be drawn between the diagnosis of illness by the physician and the diagnosis of learning difficulty by the teacher.

How then will the actual necessary skills be developed? Largely through the resolute critical analysis of one's own experience. This analysis is possible only with teachers who see clearly that teaching is in fact dynamic instead of static, an exciting intellectual enterprise, and whose self-analysis is illuminated by adequate general and technological background. Teaching, more than most human activities, demands the use of judgment, imagination, initiative, and enthusiasm. Particularly does it demand the use of freely working, creative imagination.[15]

EXCELLENCE: MYTH OR REALITY

Any school district wishing to pay more than mere lip service to the national promise of providing all students with opportunity to experience quality, optimum education should study closely the admonition of noted historian Arnold Toynbee, as voiced in an article entitled "Is America Neglecting Her Creative Talents?":

> To give a fair chance to potential creativity is a matter of life and death for any society. This is all important because the outstanding creative ability of a fairly small percentage of the population is mankind's ultimate capital asset.[16]

Recognizing that responsibility as obligation, such a school district will provide an instructional program with special dimension for the intellectually gifted and creatively talented student, for fostering educational excellence for all certainly recognizes the right of gifted children, too, to reach their potential. Not to do so would not only break faith with America's youth, but also negate the enlightened self-interest of the nation itself. It is a paradox that the Soviet Union so many times is quicker than the United States in recognizing its own vested interest in nurturing the excellence of its gifted and talented, whether that excellence manifests itself in the promise of the arts, the sciences, or athletics. Unquestionably, the provision of such programs is costly in terms of money, personnel, time, expertise, and effort, but who in America would hazard the cost to its people of the symphony not written, the energy source not developed, or the cancer cure not discovered?

NOTES

1. James J. Gallagher, "Issues in Education for the Gifted," in *The Gifted and Talented: Their Education and Development,* the Seventy-eighth Yearbook of the Na-

tional Society for the Study of Education, ed. by A. Harry Passow, pt. 1 (Chicago, Ill.: University of Chicago Press, 1979), pp. 32–33.

2. Jerome S. Bruner, *The Process of Education* (Cambridge, Mass.: Harvard University Press, 1960).

3. Joseph S. Renzulli, *The Enrichment Triad: A Guide for Developing Defensible Programs for the Gifted and Talented* (Mansfield Center, Conn.: Creative Learning Press, 1977).

4. Frederick B. Tuttle, Jr., *Gifted and Talented Students,* What Research Says to the Teacher Series (Washington, D.C.: National Education Association, 1978), p. 20.

5. Sandra N. Kaplan, *Providing Programs for the Gifted and Talented: A Handbook* (Reston, Va.: Council for Exceptional Children, 1975), p. 12.

6. Ibid.

7. Ibid., p. 8.

8. Ibid., pp. 10–11.

9. Marsha M. Correll, *Teaching the Gifted and Talented* (Bloomington, Ind.: Phi Delta Kappa Educational Foundation, © 1978), p. 23.

10. Ibid., pp. 23–24.

11. Kaplan, *Providing Programs,* p. 82.

12. Douglas M. Knight, Foreward to *Library Services for the Nation's Needs: Toward Fulfillment of a National Policy,* by the National Advisory Commission on Libraries (Washington, D.C.: National Advisory Commission on Libraries, 1968).

13. Council for Exceptional Children, *Curriculum for the Gifted and Talented* (Washington, D.C.: U.S. Office of Gifted and Talented, 1978).

14. Lynne D. Niro, *Developing Programs for the Gifted and Talented* (Washington, D.C.: U.S. Office of Gifted and Talented, 1978).

15. William H. Burton, *The Guidance of Learning Activities: A Summary of the Principles of Teaching Based on the Growth of the Learner,* 3rd ed. (New York: Appleton-Century, 1962), pp. 267–268. © 1962. Reprinted by permission of Prentice-Hall, Inc., Englewood Cliffs, N.J.

16. Arnold J. Toynbee, "Is America Neglecting Her Creative Talents?" in *Creativity across Education,* ed. by Calvin W. Taylor (Ogden: University of Utah Press, 1968), p. 1.

4
Model State Guidelines
for District Gifted
and Talented Programs

In matters pertaining to education, each state is sovereign; therefore, it is the special responsibility of the various state departments of education to translate the Marland Report into operational guidelines. The following statement by Jean Gatling Farr, Program Director, Right to Education for Gifted and Talented, Bureau of Special and Compensatory Education, Pennsylvania Department of Education, sets a background for interpreting the Pennsylvania model state guide, which is reproduced in this chapter.

GIFTED EDUCATION IN PENNSYLVANIA

Pennsylvania has been in the forefront in gifted education since the foresight engendered with a legislative mandate in 1961 recognizing the gifted and talented as an exceptionality. Amidst the halcyon days of Sputnik concern, the mandate was strengthened in 1963 with a funding system providing excess cost reimbursement through Special Education monies. This reimbursement is predicated upon costs accrued for Special Education program delivery over and above what is the usual subsidy tuition funding provided by the Commonwealth. In 1977, monies specifically allocated within the state education budget for gifted and talented totaled approximately $18 million, or roughly 2 percent of the budget.

Though fiscal incentive was present, growth of programs during the 1960s and early 1970s was sporadic: Many good programs have survived, but just as many collapsed or failed to expand. As enrollments began to decline and school districts were imperiled with teacher layoffs, declining enrollments, and the inflationary tax dollar, efforts in gifted education became even more limited. As is often the case, the attitudinal justification for severe lessening of program operation was that gifted education was a luxury, a frill budgetary item which school districts with belt-tightening woes could ill afford. Consequently, even though the State Code specifically included the gifted within the same framework as all other Special Education categories, subject to the accompanying State Board Regulations and Special Education Standards for operation, progress was indeed slow . . . until the banner year of 1975. To the relief and delight of advocates of gifted education in Pennsylvania, as a result of federal law 93-380 and the Catherine D. suit in federal court, the State Board of Education extended Due Process Right to Education to all exceptional school-age persons, including the gifted.

Such procedures became fully effective for the gifted on July 1, 1976, granting an extension of one year for planning and initial implementation for those districts and intermediate units [IU] in which little programming then existed. Full programming, K–12 grades, thus had the impact of due process for impetus.

And impetus there has been! At times the Oklahoma Land Rush has seemed mild in comparison. The growth rate has surged from 29,000 youngsters identified and placed into programs in 1976–1977, to 52,000 for 1977–1978. However, even with the growth intensity, only two-thirds of the gifted and talented have been identified in order to receive due process Right to Education.

On September 30, 1977, new Standards for Special Education were published in order to provide necessary information for attendant legal compliance. The following are a few of the particular specifications for the gifted and talented in Pennsylvania:

I. Definition

MENTALLY GIFTED

(Exceptional persons who possess) outstanding intellectual and creative ability, the development of which requires special activities or services not ordinarily provided in the regular program. Persons shall be assigned to a program for the gifted when they have an IQ score of 130 or be admitted to gifted programs when other educational criteria in the person's profile strongly indicate gifted ability. *IQ score:* attained through individual psychological test administered by a certified school psychologist.

As stated in the *Guide for the Operation of Programs for the Mentally Gifted and Talented,* Pennsylvania Department of Education [PDE].

Identification of the mentally gifted is based upon assessment of multiple screening criteria, followed by individual intelligence testing by a certified school psychologist prior to placement.

TALENTED

Outstanding talent as identified by a team of educators and professionals competent in the areas of art, music, dance, photographic arts, or theater, the development of which requires special activities or services not ordinarily provided in the regular program. A person identified as talented shall be eligible to attend the Governor's School for the Arts.

II. Individualized Education Program

An evaluation requires the analysis and investigation necessary to develop an Individualized Education Program (IEP) appropriate for the person.

This extension of development of IEPs, intended nationally through the Education for All Handicapped Children Act (P.L. 94-142), became a vital component in gifted education as a result of its inclusion in Pennsylvania within Special Education; as an exceptionality, the gifted are accorded this right within our state. Since September 1978 any identifications must result in an IEP before placement into program.

In order to accomplish this awesome task, monies were allocated through each of the 29 Intermediate Units for IEP training and assistance to occur within all 505 school districts during the crucial initial years of implementation.

III. District Plan

It is a first-line district responsibility to provide an appropriate education for its gifted. This responsibility entails a detailed written plan, such a plan to be carefully delineated, specifying its services to the gifted and also identifying those regular education programs which may be used to implement IEPs. These district plans shall be incorporated in the Intermediate Unit Plan to be submitted to the

Pennsylvania Department of Education for approval. The programs and services, developed in accordance with a planned curriculum, shall be developed in order to provide a continuum of programs and services appropriate for the student's age and development. The Department provides guidelines describing appropriate kinds of curricula and types of service.

IV. CURRICULUM AND ORGANIZATION

The task of effectively providing for the education of gifted children and youth requires major changes in concepts and in practice. Inseparable is the demand that all pertinent objectives of differential education for the gifted be specifically defined and formulated. The implementation of these objectives calls for a transformed curriculum, as well as for

1. Modification in the typical organization and scheduling of the school day;
2. Tailored instructional materials and methods;
3. Specialized teacher preparation and specific teacher selection;
4. Education of the community for sustained cooperation, understanding, and support.

The essential challenge is to put these objectives into practice through development and use of IEPs for each child, with the periodic offering of due process to parents. As a gifted student's special education program is based upon those alternatives available and appropriate to him or her in the school district's regular education program, only after such alternatives are assessed in light of the needs of the gifted should decisions be made as to how many and which special education alternatives are necessary for IEP development. In essence, each gifted school-age person's total program must be appropriate regardless of which (special and/or regular education) implements the IEP.

The basic patterns of these programs, in regular and special education, include the following, singly or in combination:

1. Enrichment of content
2. Acceleration of content
3. Individualization of instruction
4. A modified, open-ended curriculum
5. Specific goal-directed programs to develop and/or foster such diverse aspects of giftedness as creativity, critical thinking, evaluative thinking, leadership, etc.

The organizational patterns for delivery of these services through approved Special Education programs include

1. Full-time classes
2. Part-time programs
3. Resource rooms
4. Itinerant programs
5. Regular programs with supportive services (this direction is recommended only for those gifted students who most resemble bright average students in school districts which have strong regular education alternatives in sufficient numbers and types to meet the needs of each student Guidelines).

As giftedness ranges from extraordinary to genius-level potential, the alternatives from which individual IEPs can be structured are limitless. Presently, the organizational patterns in the state are at minimum special education coverage level; itinerant and resource rooms, comprising the bulk of available opportunities, though limited in depth and scope, are sound beginnings and reflect tremendous new insights and understandings of the needs of the gifted. Of course, the variety of alternatives to be offered, the flexibility so demanded of us as we plan and schedule for the identification of the culturally disadvantaged and the gifted handicapped, the role of parents in devising IEPs . . . all of these require fresh new vistas from each of us. In Pennsylvania we feel as though we have truly just begun in providing for our gifted.

The *Guide for Organizing and Operating Programs for the Mentally Gifted and Talented* was issued by the Pennsylvania Department of Education in 1979. This guide, which was developed and revised by an ad hoc committee on gifted education in Pennsylvania, augments the *Generic Standards for the Operation of Special Education Programs and Services.* The committee, whose members were chosen for experience in and knowledge of research and for their development and implementation of programs for the gifted, was formed under the auspices of the Bureau of Special Education in July 1971, and has met monthly.

Such a guide cannot cover all situations found in any state. Instead, conclusions should be viewed as providing the best of current thinking concerning programming, as well as concurring with Pennsylvania regulations, laws, and standards. Any new programs that are developed according to this guide should only enhance program quality.

The *Guide for Organizing and Operating Programs for the Mentally Gifted and Talented* is reproduced in the following pages as a prototype of state operational guidelines to be followed by local school districts in initiating and/ or strengthening programs for the gifted and talented. The outline of contents, which precedes the actual text of the document, indicates the scope of this guide.

    I. General Statement
   II. Pupils
       A. Admissions Criteria
       B. Initial Identification/Referral of Candidates for Gifted Program
       C. Screening Based on Initial Identification/Referral
       D. Individual Psychological Testing
       E. Final Evaluation and Placement
       F. Provisions for the Culturally Deprived or Disadvantaged Gifted Student
       G. Mentally Gifted/Handicapped
       H. Talented: Governor's School for the Arts
       I. Continuance
       J. Withdrawal
  III. Educational Management
       A. Reimbursable Special Education Programs
       B. Nonreimbursable Regular Education Programs
       C. Organization
       D. Scheduling
   IV. Individualized Education Program (IEP) and Curriculum
       A. Goals
       B. Subject Area Content, Concepts, and Learning Tasks
       C. Multidisciplinary Offerings
       D. Curricula Summary
       E. IEP Development and Maintenance for the Gifted
    V. Facilities, Instructional Materials, Equipment, and Supplies
   VI. Personnel
       A. The Teacher of the Gifted
       B. In-Service
  VII. Supervision
       A. Need
       B. Supervisor
       C. Suggested Duties and Responsibilities
       D. Direct Supervision of Teachers
 VIII. Evaluation
       A. Goals of Program Evaluation
       B. Goals in IEP Evaluation
       C. Dissemination
       D. Group Meetings

I. GENERAL STATEMENT

Special provisions for gifted children and youth demonstrate the concern of citizens, legislators, and educators for giving young people of school age the opportunities they need for developing their own capabilities and talents. These provisions contribute to the fulfillment of individuals as responsible, creative human beings; to the strengthening of our democratic society; and to the improvement of our way of life.

Benefits from programs for gifted children extend to other children as well. School district personnel throughout Pennsylvania have stated that their efforts in developing and maintaining programs for gifted students have improved the total educational programs of the districts. This improvement has come about, and can continue to come about, because of careful identification of children with certain characteristics and abilities and because of the placement of these children in suitable programs.

Programs for gifted children fit into the spectrum of special programming for all children who have special learning needs. These programs are logical manifestations of our concern for individual differences, for equality of educational opportunity, and for the optimal development of each child. By recognizing and educating the gifted as a group with identifiable differences (capabilities, interests, and needs), teachers and school administrators can plan educational programs to fit the individual needs of extremely able persons and at the same time include experiences that help them develop their problem-solving and creative abilities.

School districts not only specify objectives and plan special facilities and provisions but also determine how such programs are to be evaluated. These plans include alternatives from kindergarten through grade 12 and from which an individualized educational program (IEP) for each gifted child will emerge. In-service education is a necessity—both to help teachers understand the gifted child and to enable them to motivate and facilitate the development of students' analytical, evaluative, and creative skills, as evidenced in ongoing IEPs.

The recognition of individual differences among children and the attempt to educate each child in terms of strengths and potentialities are key features of American educational practice. Evidence of the special needs of the gifted child is sometimes subtle and relatively inconspicuous. Because there is some difficulty in making necessary and desirable curricular adaptations to the special needs of gifted children, the American school, according to scholars and behavioral scientists, must give more effort to recognition and development of suitable educational provisions for the full range and diversity of the gifted child's capabilities. This effort shall result in increased productivity.

All pertinent objectives of differential education for the gifted should be especially defined and formulated. The implementation of these objectives calls for a modified curriculum as well as for:

1. A modification in the typical organization and scheduling of the school day.
2. Tailored instructional materials and methods.
3. Competencies in teacher preparation and specific teacher selection.
4. Education of the community for sustained cooperation, understanding, and support.

The challenge is to turn these objectives into practice through development and use of individualized education programs for each child, with the periodic offering of due process to parents.

For society's potential innovators, the humane consequences of knowledge need to be an integral element of learning. Social concern is the context for all studies; otherwise, gifted youth will ask, "Knowledge for what?" Any program that reflects the development of citizens who possess *only* a pragmatic view of their intellectual talent is shortsighted.

II. PUPILS

A. ADMISSIONS CRITERIA

In Pennsylvania schools, identification of the mentally gifted is based on multiple screening criteria and individual intelligence testing by certified school psychologists prior to placement. Determining which pupils are to be tested involves a thorough study of the backgrounds and records of the entire student population.* In screening school data to locate candidates for individual testing, the school staff determines potentiality in the light of such factors as:

1. Group Intelligence Test Score: Those with a group IQ score of 130 or better are likely candidates. However, if other factors show potentiality, group test IQ may be lower. A knowledge of test ceiling is helpful in estimating the value of this score as one of the screening criteria.
2. Achievement Test Scores: Standardized norms are used in most achievement tests. High ability is usually indicated by scores two grade levels above that of the pupil, or a percentile rating of about 90. Again, it is helpful for one to know the ceiling of the test to be able to judge its value as a screening criterion for the gifted.
3. School Records: Pupils with consistently high marks may be gifted, but this factor must always be studied to determine if marks are influenced by conditions other than native ability.
4. Teacher Observations: When [teachers] clearly understand the nature of giftedness, their observation of children in the classroom can yield invaluable insights. Use of checklists for recording pupil traits of the gifted and anecdotal accounts of significant pupil activities and abilities must be considered. Teachers look for these characteristics of the gifted:
    a. *High Academic Achievement*—The gifted student may show as much unevenness in subject matter abilities as do other children, but overall grade point average is usually high. He or she requires fewer detailed and repeated instructions and often anticipates them. He or she works readily with symbols, such as words and numbers, instead of direct experience and actual objects.
    b. *Advanced Vocabulary and Reading Level*—The gifted student has a large vocabulary that he or she uses easily and accurately. He or she retains what has been heard or read without much rote or drill. He or

*Special conditions such as physical handicaps, emotional disturbance, and deprived background may prevent a pupil from demonstrating the characteristics described in this chapter. Giftedness *may* be identified in such a pupil by skilled observation, and there is a rich field of potential giftedness to be explored in our schools. (Refer to II, Pupils, Secs. B, F, and G.)

she usually can read books that are two or more years in advance of the rest of the class and usually reads at an early age.

c. *Expressive Fine Arts Talent*—The gifted student's wide range of interests stems from a vivid imagination. He or she visualizes actions and things from descriptions and frequently creates original stories, plays, poetry, tunes, and sketches. He or she can use materials, words, or ideas in new ways.

d. *Wholesome Personal-Social Adjustment*—The gifted student adjusts easily to new associates and situations, is alert and keenly observant, and responds quickly. He or she possesses a keen sense of humor and incorporates suggestions from others into his or her own thinking and actions. Companions are often one or two years older, but they recognize the gifted student's superior ability in planning, organizing, and promoting. The gifted also display evidence of emotional stability in ordinary behavior.

e. *Early Physical Competence*—Gifted students are usually characterized by early physical development; they tend to be taller and heavier and to have fewer physical defects. They not only enjoy outdoor games but excel in them. They usually enjoy superior health and, as a result, have fewer absences from school due to illness. They generally possess especially good eye-hand coordination.

f. *Superior Intellectual Ability*—Gifted students exhibit superior ability in reasoning, generalizing, thinking logically, and comprehending. They can perform highly difficult mental tasks and learn more rapidly and more easily than most children. These children also have a longer concentration span, and they are keenly aware of processes in their environment.

g. *Effective Independent Work*—The gifted student displays competency for effective independent work by evaluating himself or herself and modifying his or her behavior accordingly. He or she possesses superior insight into problems, is not easily distracted, and is less prone to change his or her mind once an opinion is formed. Such students show their effectiveness by applying learning from one situation to more difficult situations.

h. *Persistent Curiosity*—The gifted student displays deep-seated interests. To gratify this insatiable curiosity he or she may enjoy using encyclopedias, dictionaries, maps, globes, and other references in addition to original source materials.

i. *Strong Creative and Inventive Power*—Gifted students possess intense intellectual curiosity, imagination, and creativity. They have unusual power to see new structures and processes and to express these visions in speaking, writing, art, music, or some other form. Their work has freshness, vitality, and uniqueness. An individual may create new ideas and substances or may invent and build new mechanical devices. He or she sometimes runs counter to tradition and continually questions the status quo, which leads him or her to do the unexpected occasionally.

j. *Special Scientific Ability*—The gifted student with this sort of talent will use the scientific method of thinking. He or she will employ sound research methods and will grasp scientific concepts quickly. He or she will be curious about the natural world, is not easily discouraged by failure of experiments or projects, and will seek causes of failures. He or she will spend much time on special individual projects, such as making a collection, constructing a radio, or making electronic computers.

k. *High Energy Level*—The gifted student is usually very energetic, undertaking and completing task after task. He or she participates in various extracurricular activities, holds leadership roles, and frequently concentrates on long-range, unattainable, and vaguely defined goals.

l. *Demonstrated Leadership Ability*—The gifted student displays ability to help a group reach its goals. He or she often will improve human relationships within a group and will achieve prominence by individual effort. He or she enters into activities with enthusiasm and is able to influence others to work toward desirable goals.

m. *Well-developed Mechanical Skills*—The gifted student who possesses mechanical ability may be identified by unusual manipulative skills and spatial ability. He or she perceives a visual pattern complete with details, similarities, and differences. He or she excels in craft projects and is interested in mechanical gadgets, devices, and machines. He or she comprehends mechanical problems and puzzles and likes to draw plans and sketches of mechanical objects.

B. INITIAL IDENTIFICATION/REFERRAL OF CANDIDATES FOR GIFTED PROGRAM

Each school district should develop a list of possible gifted students from the total school population, using criteria based on available pupil data.

This list of candidates should be developed from several of the following criteria:

1. Scores of two or more years above grade placement on nationally normed achievement tests (e.g., Metropolitan or Stanford Series, etc.).
2. School records indicating unusual ability.
3. Group intelligence scores which are part of school district pupil records.
4. High scores on teacher checklists for identifying gifted characteristics such as
    a. Local checklists, such as those developed in Bucks County and Berks County [see Checklist 6].
    b. Standardized checklists, for example: Renzulli-Hartman Scale for rating behavioral characteristics of superior students; California Checklist for Primary Grade Gifted Students; Science Research Associate List; Dade County Talented Pupil Characteristics Scale; and Bloom and Krathwohl Rating Scale for Intellectual Development Skills.
5. References or referrals from parents, peers, community agencies, etc., based on reliable data. For example:

    North Carolina Parent Nomination Forms

    Rockford, Illinois, Parent Questionnaire for Kindergarten Children

An aid in further screening is arranging the list of candidates in priority order from highest probability to lowest probability on the basis of weighted multiple criteria.

C. Screening Based on Initial Identification/Referral

Screening for giftedness can take many forms and diverse approaches. Some of the approaches to screening are:

1. After screening by a professional team (supervisor of gifted, school psychologist, guidance counselor, teacher(s) of gifted, etc.) drop the least likely candidates.
2. Further screening should include further testing by instruments designed specifically for the gifted in areas of cognition, affective domain, psychosocial adjustment, and/or creativity.
3. *Cognitive Tests for Measuring Thinking*
   a. Convergent Thinking
      Group Intelligence Tests*—if not administered in basic education and included as a referral criterion. Examples (ceiling IQ measured approximately 145):
         California Mental Maturity
         Otis-Lennon
      *In the tests listed, upper level IQ scores correlate poorly with individual psychological test scores and assessment.
   b. Divergent Thinking
      1. Creativity Tests. Examples (suggested grade level uses):
            Torrance Tests of Creative Thinking—Verbal (4–12)
            Torrance Tests of Creative Thinking—Figural (1–12)
            Guilford's Tests of Creativity—Verbal, Figural (4–6)
      2. Intellectual Maturity. An example:
            Goodenough-Harris Drawing Test—Figural
4. *Affective Tests for Measuring Feeling*
   a. Convergent Tests
      1. Character and Personality. Examples (suggested grade level uses):
            Early School Personality Questionnaire (1–3)
            Children's Personality Questionnaire (3–6)
            Jr.-Sr. High School Personality Questionnaire (6–12)
            California Tests of Personality (K–12)
      2. Self-Concept. Examples (suggested grade level uses):
            "How Do You Really Feel about Yourself?" (4–12)
            Tennessee Self-Concept Scale (5–12)
            Self-Concept as a Learner, Elementary Scale (3–12), Secondary Scale (7–12)
   b. Divergent Tests. Examples (suggested grade level uses):
            Barron Welsh Art Scale of the Welsh Figure Preference Test (1–12)
            Personality Rating Scale (K–12)
            Preschool Academic Sentiment Scale (K–1)
5. *Interests, Observations, and Social-Emotional-Adjustment Appraisals*
   Examples of teacher observations, student self-inventories, and other devices may be found in the following:
   a. Rice, Joseph P., *Developing Total Talent*, Springfield, Ill.: Charles C. Thomas, 1970. pp. 199–203, Interest-Performance-Capability Check-

list, Physical Development Instrument, Social Development Scale, Emotional Development Appraisal, Parent Inventory.
   b. Williams, Frank E., *A Total Creativity Program,* Englewood Cliffs, N.J.: Educational Technology Publications, Inc., 1972. Volume I, "Identifying and Measuring Creative Potential," and Volume III, "Teacher's Workbook" (lists and checklists of pupil thinking and feeling behaviors).
   c. Meeker, Mary N., "A Rating Scale for Identifying Creative Potential."

D. INDIVIDUAL PSYCHOLOGICAL TESTING

Selected students should then be scheduled for individual psychological testing by a certified school psychologist. Tests may include:

WPPSI. Wechsler Pre-School/Primary Scale of Intelligence (Preschool–K). Approx. ceiling IQ measured is 155. (Useful with most children in these grades. Reference to age use is in the test manuals.)

WISC-R. Wechsler Intelligence Scale for Children (K–10). Approx. ceiling IQ measured is 160.

WAIS. Wechsler Adult Intelligence Scale (10–Adult). Approx. ceiling IQ measured is 179.

Stanford-Binet Intelligence Scale (K–12). Approx. ceiling IQ measured is 165.

E. FINAL EVALUATION AND PLACEMENT

1. Individual psychological test results should be used as a final consideration for placement.
2. Placement is based on *all* screening criteria, plus an IQ score of 130 or more on an individual psychological test. Placement can be considered for exceptions to the individual psychological mental measurement score if the professional team feels that other screening criteria in the student's profile strongly indicate gifted potential.
3. If the student is eligible for gifted provisions, an IEP (individualized education program) is developed according to available program alternatives and placed in the student's profile as a basis for differential and appropriate education agreed upon through due process and parental IEP involvement.

F. PROVISIONS FOR THE CULTURALLY DEPRIVED OR DISADVANTAGED GIFTED STUDENT

Massive efforts have been directed toward overcoming the inadequacies of educational programming for the culturally disadvantaged, but relatively little attention has been devoted to disadvantaged youth who have unusually high potentials for learning and creativity. One stimulus for the present concern for the education of the disadvantaged is the belief that children from low-income, ethnic, and racial minority groups constitute one of the nation's largest unmined sources of abilities.

Culturally disadvantaged children are difficult to identify. The position may, therefore, be taken that many of these children's intellectual talents have been depressed and cannot be identified in the same way that those of children who have received enriched cultural advantages can be identified.

Research shows that the development of intellectual potential is directly related to motivational and personality variables, environmental conditions, and the instructional program.

Identification procedures, especially those involving standardized intelligence tests, may prove to discriminate against the poor and culturally different.

Therefore, the identification of gifted children and youth within disadvantaged populations is not amenable to simple solutions. Rather, it involves issues such as racial and geographic isolation, socioeconomic class, student interaction, and community control.

The priority question is, basically, how to provide for the wide range of individual differences in any school population.

The following identification procedures are suggested:

1. Make a deliberate search for disadvantaged children who exhibit above-average ratings on the usual IQ and achievement tests and identify them in their early school years. Provide them [with] highly enriched learning opportunities, such as those normally available in middle and upper socioeconomic families who emphasize verbal interactions, cause-and-effect learning, and conceptualization and generalization from experience.

2. Devise observation instruments and rating scales, which staff members may be taught to use when searching for the special qualities of social leadership, creative problem solving, independent judgment or logical thinking demonstrated by actions, not words.

Employ individual evaluations of these students by using multiple criteria and then program them according to their individual cognitive and affective needs.

3. Maintain a continuous identification-awareness process among the staff for those students who are slow to develop their strengths or who repress evidence of their ability.

4. Once children are identified as exhibiting exceptional potential, alert parents and staff to the students' needs for more complete use of their abilities. Both teachers and parents may need to enhance the self-concept of these gifted students.

5. Maintain an up-to-date file of opportunities available to disadvantaged talented and gifted youths who intend to pursue further education. Apprise the students and their parents of appropriate programming and application procedures for these opportunities and scholarships. Work with college admissions officials to realistically modify programs to fit the needs of "high risk" but strongly motivated students.

In recent years, many school systems have misinterpreted the long-overdue concern for the education of poor and minority students as meaning that programs for the disadvantaged must take precedence over provisions for the gifted. What is needed now is a clear affirmation by educators and communities that they are concerned with the development of potential of all kinds.

Since gifted and talented individuals are found in all groups, there is no need or justification for depriving students of opportunities. Nor is there any basis for not providing the disadvantaged gifted student [with] special opportunities that are essentially compensatory in nature while maintaining standards of excellence.

G. Mentally Gifted/Handicapped

Most school organizational patterns for the gifted do not include gifted handicapped children, i.e., the orthopedically handicapped, hard of hearing, deaf, visually handicapped, blind, learning disabled, and emotionally disturbed, in their screening and selection for gifted provisions. Too often the handicap is emphasized rather than the strength. At worst, there have been instances when gifted and emotionally disturbed adolescents are being taught with procedures better suited for mentally retarded youngsters.

Strength should be cultivated, particularly in the case of the deaf and/or blind child, for the distractions which intrude upon the majority of these gifted children are less evident. Numerous instances can be cited of handicapped persons who made outstanding contributions to society. If the self-image is depressed and learning opportunities are limited during school years, a valuable resource has been wasted.

Youngsters who are treated as disabled will tend to become so, while the youngster who is challenged and encouraged may take pride in his or her uniqueness and may well produce original ideas and accomplishments.

The provisions discussed in this guide should apply to the gifted handicapped through IEPs.

H. Talented: Governor's School for the Arts
1. definition

Artistically talented, school-age persons are those who consistently display creative potential at an early age and later develop skills and outstanding abilities to perceive, understand, create, perform, and respond to artistic activities; and who need differentiated education or services beyond those provided by the regular school system in order to realize their potentialities.

Five major factors distinguishing the artistically talented student are:

a.   Fluency of imagination and expression—the freedom with which the child adapts his or her ability to the diverse situation.

b.   A highly developed sensibility for spatial distribution and organization, often emphasizing rhythm and movement.

c.   An intuitive quality of imagination—the ability to bring into existence constellations or events that did not exist before.

d.   Directness of expression, which manifests itself when an experience is in tune with the child's desire to express it visually.

e.   A high degree of self-identification with subject matter and medium—an intensity of feeling for the medium.

2. philosophy and rationale

Historically, schools have dealt with the arts in a very limited way, principally as recreation or as an exposure of all students to several areas without provisions for the development of specialized abilities. Meaningful experiences in dance, theater, photography, and filmmaking are limited. In art, music, and creative writing, students are generally frustrated by time and space constraints, the lack of equipment and facilities, and limited exposure to master teachers or artists.

It is apparent to educational scholars and behavioral scientists that many artistically talented students are perceived by their peers as being "different." The students often say that they are "misunderstood" or that they feel "alone." That these students must have a time and a place where they can meet each other is of paramount importance. At such a place they can discover that they are not alone, but that other artistically talented students do exist and share the same kinds of feelings, attitudes, and anxieties. Living and working in an environment that provides for artistic freedom and encourages creative thinking and action reaffirm their positive convictions and enhance their self-images. Here they can discover that it is "okay" to be creative or talented.

Aware of the need to identify talented students and correct the imbalance of artistic opportunities in the schools, the Pennsylvania Department of Education's Bureau of Curriculum Services and Bureau of Special Education, in conjunction with the state's 29 intermediate units, have developed and sponsored the Pennsylvania Governor's School for the Arts. Each summer the school offers a unique living/learning experience to a selected number of the Commonwealth's most talented high school students in the arts, including handicapped students.

The Governor's School recognizes that highly talented students in the arts possess extraordinary potential for developing similar talents in their peers and communities. Opportunities for these students to exercise this potential for leadership are seldom provided in Pennsylvania schools. For this reason, a major part of the Governor's School is directed to classes and workshops in which the student is helped to discover his or her full potential for leading others in examining strategies which the artist/leader can employ in marshaling the talents of others, and in developing a model to be implemented in each student's school or community.

3. HISTORY

Pennsylvania has been conscious of preserving and nurturing the talent of its children for some years. In 1967–1969 the state, as the recipient of federal ESEA money, established summer arts programs for high school students at Temple University's Ambler Campus and at Westminster College.

After a four-year search for support, funding was obtained for a state-sponsored program through the state Bureau of Special Education in 1973. With special education funds distributed in the form of scholarships through the 29 intermediate units in the state, the Pennsylvania Governor's School for the Arts was established. Handicapped students were, and continue to be, funded through a federal ESEA grant.

Selection is made through application and audition. Application brochures and posters are disseminated through the intermediate units to all public, private, and parochial high schools. The intermediate units, following Governor's School guidelines, select the best of local applications. Semifinalists are then invited to attend auditions/interviews held at strategic locations throughout the state. Final judging is conducted by Governor's School department chairpersons and guest specialists in each field.

4. MAJOR GOALS OF THE GOVERNOR'S SCHOOL

a. To enable each artistically talented student to refine his or her potential through intensive and extensive learning experiences which are beyond the capability of traditional school curriculum.

b. To enable each artistically talented student to explore his or her potential for developing skills of a high order in a field of the arts other than that in which he or she has concentrated and to apply these new skills and understandings to his or her total personal and artistic development.
c. To enable each artistically talented student to realize his or her potential for creating new works of art in both individual and group situations.
d. To enable each artistically talented student to realize his or her potential for furnishing leadership for arts programming in his or her school and community.

Goals and strategies are developed specifically in music, art, drama, dance, photography and creative writing.

5. GOVERNOR'S SCHOOL PROGRAM

Participation of handicapped students is actively encouraged and each year the Governor's School hosts a number of them. Except for a staff of interpreters and mobility experts who attend to their specialized requirements, these students participate in the same programs as nonhandicapped students. In addition to their artistic growth, involvement in the school is usually their first real social experience with their nonhandicapped peers. The opportunity for nonhandicapped students to live and work with their handicapped peers is equally rewarding.

I. CONTINUANCE

All due process, Right-to-Education procedures apply for the mentally gifted (Title 22, Chap. 13, Pt. III, Sec. 13.31–13.33), as do all IEP procedures outlined in *Generic Standards*.

J. WITHDRAWAL

All due process, Right-to-Education procedures apply for the mentally gifted (Title 22, Chap. 13, Pt. III, Sec. 13.31–13.33), as do all IEP procedures outlined in *Generic Standards*.

III. EDUCATIONAL MANAGEMENT

A. REIMBURSABLE SPECIAL EDUCATION PROGRAMS

Such programs and services curricula meet all regulations and standards of special education for the gifted:

1. Program organization includes one or more of the four special education alternatives.
2. Classes, resource rooms, and itinerant programs contain only those students who are gifted according to mandates.
3. Program plan is approved by PDE.
4. Curriculum content, pace, and depth are designed specifically to meet the individual needs of the gifted.
5. Curriculum is based on recognized, researched educational theory for gifted children.

6. Curriculum goals encompass both cognitive and affective domains and involve those teaching strategies which address the higher levels of intellect: cognition, convergence, divergence, and critical analysis.
7. All program curriculum is demonstrably different from local regular education in goals, objectives, depth, breadth, pace, and instructional materials; and it emphasizes variety, creativity, and excellence through use of original sources.
8. Curriculum is constantly monitored, evaluated, and changed, when necessary, by a staff trained and experienced in gifted education and theory.

B. Nonreimbursable Regular Education Programs

The following can be applied for those gifted students whose appropriate program is to be constructed from both special and regular education alternatives:

1. Accelerated and/or enriched regular education programs which are flexible and open-ended and which can be used as part of a gifted student's IEP if so indicated by current levels of student achievement and potential.
2. Such programs should be described and approved as part of the IU/SD* special education plan.
3. Such programs might include, but are not to be limited to:
   a. Advanced placement courses†
   b. Honors courses
   c. Subject acceleration
   d. Subject enrichment
   e. Early entry to school
   f. Grade skipping
   g. Telescoped or mini-courses
   h. Independent study
4. All regular programs, and accompanying adjustment in scheduling, should be closely monitored and evaluated by a staff team with background and experience in gifted education.
5. All regular education alternatives should be a part of the IEP–due process procedure.
6. Regular curriculum should provide for guidance and counseling services commensurate with the abilities, potentials, and needs of the gifted when the IEP indicates the services are necessary.

C. Organization

Developing programs for the gifted depends upon effective communication between personnel in school districts and those in intermediate units. This leads to cooperative planning, promoting and sharing ideas and provisions, each contributing that which it can best provide.

1. Cooperation between school districts and intermediate units:
   a. Assignment of one or more persons full time to promote and supervise programming and administration provisions is recommended. If no

---

*[Intermediate Unit/School District].

†As prescribed by College Entrance Examination Board or an equivalent institution.

      such position presently exists, the superintendent or the director of special education should take the responsibility or obtain the services of a qualified person.

    b. Annual statewide or local conferences help focus attention on the needs of gifted children and youth as well as provide broad-based in-service opportunities.

    c. Organized identification of gifted pupils is an example of district–intermediate unit cooperation.

2. Planning Process
    a. The intermediate unit plan for special education provides data on the number of gifted students, the program alternatives (regular and special) available in each school district and intermediate unit, and the procedures used to identify and evaluate gifted students and programs. The school district's long-range plans also reflect these provisions.

    b. Coordination of public relations activities by the district, the intermediate unit, and the Department of Education is necessary for the dissemination of accurate information on due process, IEPs, and program plans.

    c. Keeping a resource file of community talents will contribute to program enrichment and, at the same time, encourage these individuals to actively support this type of programming.

    d. Individuals at various levels, such as members of local school boards, intermediate unit boards, advisory councils, PTAs, PAGE (formerly PASEMG), TAG, etc., may be organized to implement short-term or long-term objectives.

D. SCHEDULING

Programs for gifted children are as divergent in their concepts as the districts and intermediate units that conduct them. Scheduling of such programs is, therefore, contingent upon the structure in which the program must function. The gifted child's special program is predicated on those alternatives available to him or her in the school district's regular education program. These regular education alternatives must be explained in the intermediate unit special education plan if they are to comprise part of the program for the gifted. Only after such a survey is done and regular education alternatives have been stated should decisions be made as to how many—and which—special education alternatives are necessary to meet the individual needs of the gifted population.

1. The basic alternatives, whether regular or special education, include the following, singly or in combination:
    a. Enrichment of content
    b. Acceleration of content
    c. Individualization of instruction
    d. A modified, open-ended curriculum
    e. Specific goal-directed programs to develop and/or foster such diverse aspects of giftedness as creativity, critical thinking, evaluative thinking, leadership, etc.

2. The organizational patterns and direction of approved reimbursable special education programs may include:
    a. Itinerant programs

    b. Resource rooms
    c. Part-time programs
    d. Full-time programs
    e. Supportive services in regular education. (This direction is recommended only for those gifted students who most resemble bright average students in school districts which have strong regular education alternatives in sufficient numbers and types to meet the needs of each student.)
  3. Supportive service needs for the gifted vary widely and may include:
    a. Transportation
    b. School psychological services
    c. Appropriate guidance and counseling services on elementary and secondary levels
  4. Supplementary Regular Education
    Provisions which do not require, or are not reimbursed as, special education but can be used to fill the requirements of an IEP are:
    a. Early entry to school
    b. Grade skipping
    c. Ungraded classrooms
    d. Scholars (honors) programs
    e. Independent study
    f. Early admission to college
    g. Condensed school program (mini-courses)
    h. Community-based learning resources
    i. Advanced standing
    j. Advanced placement

The following should be adhered to:

1. The student should be involved in a special education program designed for the gifted in accordance with the organizational patterns in the *Special Education Standards.*
2. The student should be involved in a regular education program that is designed for the individual giftedness of that person and which can be met in the regular education curriculum.
3. The program should be held during the normal hours of the school day.
4. A teacher of gifted youngsters should have ample time for preparation, regular teacher contact, special arrangements, IEP development, etc.

IV. INDIVIDUALIZED EDUCATION PROGRAM (IEP) AND CURRICULUM

A. GOALS

Since gifted children have special characteristics and special demands are often placed upon them by society, the goals and objectives for gifted children as stated in IEP are important. The educational goals and objectives must be based upon the unique characteristics which the gifted child brings to the learning situation.

Because gifted children in American schools today should provide the nucleus of responsible leadership tomorrow and because society will expect much of them, their special education should prepare them adequately to discharge these responsibilities. Research indicates that:

1. Society needs creators or innovators.
2. Society needs gifted persons who translate new concepts and discoveries into useful products and institutions. They are the implementors.
3. Society needs those who know how to share and communicate ideas: writers, lecturers, teachers, etc.
4. Society needs intelligent consumers and maintainers of culture.

Gifted youngsters, at maturity, should be especially active in the first three roles. They should be prepared to be involved to a much greater degree than they are now.

If the needs of society are to be met, the school curriculum should reflect these goals for its gifted population:

a. Development of problem-solving skills.
b. Development of the ability to discern all options in making choices (decision-making competency).
c. Development of the ability to originate and enjoy culture and aesthetics, both historical and contemporary.
d. Participation in challenging vocational and avocational activities.
e. Development of the ability to work at the higher levels of Bloom's *Taxonomy* and Guilford's Structure of the Intellect.
f. Enhancement of high potential through interstimulation with mental peers.
g. Encouragement and nurture of those elements of Torrance's stages of creativity which are not specifically involved in the above items.

B. Subject Area Content, Concepts, and Learning Tasks

When subject area objectives are considered, a statement should be made regarding full-time and part-time involvement. In a full-time program, basic sequential skills, as well as enrichment, acceleration, emotional and social progress, and the enhancement of capabilities and potential, must be part of the educational fare. In a part-time program, appropriate basic sequential skills are generally taught in the regular classroom. Educational objectives for the gifted in both regular and special classrooms focus on enrichment, acceleration, emotional and social aspects of early maturity, and the enlargement of each child's potential capabilities and performance. Program goals need to be stated in light of the amount of time to be spent in each setting and as evidenced by the measured needs of the child.

Curriculum alternatives must be available to build an individualized and appropriate program (IEP) based on the child's current academic achievement, emotional maturity, social adaptation, psychomotor skills, and prevocational and vocational skills.

C. Multidisciplinary Offerings

Complexity is an important characteristic of the intellectual capability of the gifted. They often view discrete subject areas as a fragmentation of reality.

Since they usually master basic skills earlier than their peers, they are ready for multidisciplinary programs in the primary grades. These offerings should incorporate three major goals: continued maintenance of skills, enrichment through the global approach to problems, and acceleration through integrated application of knowledge.

Multidisciplinary curricular provisions include the humanities and the integrated sciences.

D. Curricula Summary

Each segment of the gifted curriculum should have enough alternatives to meet individual needs and interests. Depth, breadth, and pace of such alternatives must be geared to the potential and the performance of the individual gifted child. However, overall program quality and suitability should be regularly evaluated in terms of curriculum excellence and the goals that research has found to be applicable to the gifted.

E. IEP Development and Maintenance
for the Gifted

1. Individualized educational programs for the gifted are a part of Right to Education due process.
2. Specific guidelines on IEP procedures are found in *An Introduction to Individualized Education Program Plans in Pennsylvania, Revised, 1978.*
3. When IEPs are developed and maintained, both special and regular education programs should be delineated as necessary to an appropriate educational plan based on current potential, ability, and needs of each gifted student.
4. Prior to the writing of IEPs, group parent training conferences may be held to review and discuss program offerings. Such conferences do not waive or diminish a parent's/guardian's right to participate in the development of the IEP.
5. IEP format may be developed locally but contain the component parts stated in the special education standards.

V. FACILITIES, INSTRUCTIONAL MATERIALS, EQUIPMENT, AND SUPPLIES

1. Facilities should be appropriate to the needs of the program and have adequate space and storage.
2. Facilities may include both the school and the community.
3. Instructional materials for special education classes for the gifted should be different from those purchased for the regular curriculum.
4. Instructional materials may include, but are not restricted to, supplementary books, pamphlets, and periodicals; selected special programs (The Great Books Program); sophisticated teaching devices (computers, calculators, and TV equipment); extraordinary filmstrips, tapes, and recording consumable laboratory equipment beyond normal requirements.
5. Expenditures for special instructional materials need not be excessive.

VI. PERSONNEL

A. THE TEACHER OF THE GIFTED

Each school district, having studied its student population and defined the needs of the gifted in the school district/intermediate unit plan, should carefully select the teachers who will implement the programs. Ideally, the teaching staff for the gifted will include some persons who participated in the preliminary study of needs.

The competent teacher of the gifted possesses these qualities:

Understanding academic giftedness

Awareness of needs of the gifted arising from their developmental tasks

Ability to teach at the level of inspiration

Flexibility in classroom management

Superior intellectual ability

Broad cultural interests and enthusiasms

Skill in stimulating students' independent study and creativity

Sound mental health and the capacity to deal with groups of varied personalities, opinions, and interests

Competency in classroom teaching at the gifted child's threshold of learning

Skill in coordinating programs and services for the gifted with other aspects of the school program

Suggested background for teachers of the mentally gifted in Pennsylvania public schools:

1. Possession of an Instructional II (permanent) teaching certificate.
2. It is possible for a beginning teacher to be an excellent teacher of the gifted when he or she possesses most of the characteristics described and has a proper in-service program to help him or her understand the needs, characteristics, and curriculum of gifted children.
3. Completion of a graduate program at an accredited institution or an approved in-service program for permanent certification.
4. Either of the following plans:
   a. Twelve credit hours, selected from these 2- or 3-credit courses:
      1. Introductory courses (minimum of 2 credits):
         Psychology of exceptional children
         Growth and development of children and youth
      2. Gifted children and youth (minimum of 2 credits):
         Psychology of the gifted
         Nature and nurture of creativity
         Giftedness in handicapped students
      3. Provisions for the gifted (minimum of 6 credits):
         Directing independent study programs
         Flexible classroom management
         Guiding student research
         Methods and programs for the gifted
         New approaches to fostering learning (such as inquiry, simulation games, etc.)

4. Relevant courses (minimum of 2 credits):
   Group interaction techniques
   Interpersonal relationship skills
   Psychology of adjustment
   Psychology of adolescence
   Psychology of young children

   b. In lieu of a prescribed list of courses, the graduate school or in-service agency may award credits on the basis of demonstrated competencies. . . . This plan combines in-service and professional experience with campus study.

5. Recommendation of superintendent of school district or director of intermediate unit in which most recent service was performed.

B. IN-SERVICE

In the planning of school district or IU programs, gifted program personnel must become involved with other basic education staff members through

1. Informational meetings
2. Outside speakers and consultants
3. Workshops stressing identification and needs
4. Coordination training in processes for cooperative effort in planning and IEP development

During the school year there should be substantive in-service sessions for the teachers of the gifted. A variety of programs may include the following:

1. A planned series on specific topics
2. Curriculum
3. Methodology
4. Group dynamics
5. Teaching strategies
6. Visiting other programs
7. Attendance at appropriate state, regional, and national conferences
8. Evaluation techniques
9. Specific problems affecting the program
10. Current trends affecting gifted programs
11. Developing public relations strategies which enhance the image of the program and parent involvement.
12. PDE-approved in-service [training] for teacher certification.

All in-service [training], especially for credit (item 12), should have, as criteria, behaviorally stated, measurable statements of teacher/administrator competency or change.

VII. SUPERVISION

A. NEED

Supervision of gifted programs ranges from state level to the school level. The supervisor, though responsible for both program design and evaluation, should involve others in planning the program and developing evaluation criteria, subject to final approval by the Bureau of Special Education.

B. Supervisor

Positions of leadership in the area of the mentally gifted are relatively new. In few other educational positions is there such a close tie between regular and special education. It is a unique field, too, in that such a wide disparity exists in planning for these children.

Factors [in] choosing a supervisor:

1. Consultant-coordinator skills:
    Extensive curriculum knowledge
    Teaching experience with gifted children
    Tests-and-measurement background
    Techniques for stimulating students to think productively
    Supervisory training in helping relationship development
    Knowledge of processes to screen students
    Knowledge of administrative provisions
    Graduate study in psychology and in the education of the mentally gifted.
2. At least one half-time supervisor is suggested for state-approved programs [in] districts and a full-time supervisor for an intermediate unit program. Cooperative planning between IUs could accomplish this.
3. There should be a reasonable ratio of full-time teachers to each supervisor; the assumption is that many other areas demanding supervision, in addition to that of directing teachers (see specific duties), exist.
4. College and/or university training programs can help teachers develop the competencies they need if they eventually become supervisors of gifted programs. Supervisors should work closely with people in higher education to insure quality.

C. Suggested Duties and Responsibilities

It is recommended that the following duties and responsibilities for district and IU supervisors, plus the competencies for teacher supervision, be used in writing job descriptions, interviews, staff relationships, and the development of gifted students' individualized educational programs.

The primary responsibility of the supervisor of gifted programs is related to instruction, though it may vary to some degree depending on whether the supervisor is IU-based or district-based.

GENERAL RESPONSIBILITIES—THE SUPERVISOR

1. Implements regulations and directives of the Department of Education, Bureau of Special Education, pertaining to the gifted and talented.
2. Implements policies and guidelines pertaining to the special education program.
3. Informs the PDE's director of special education on the current status of programs and services for the mentally gifted and recommends plans to improve the program.
4. Stays knowledgeable about colleges and universities and community, state, and national organizations that provide services for the mentally gifted and that train professional workers.

SPECIFIC DUTIES—THE SUPERVISOR

1. Is a resource person for the staff and to all school personnel who serve the gifted in both special and regular education.
2. Observes and supervises the activities of the staff and keeps written evaluations of teachers to insure competency.
3. Is responsible for administrative details as inventories; the scheduling of services; requisition of equipment, supplies, and instructional materials; expense accounts; and Department of Education forms.
4. Conducts regular in-service training for the staff.
5. Recruits, interviews, and recommends applicants for positions on the staff.
6. Provides consultative services to administrators, supervisors, counselors, psychologists, teachers, and parents.
7. Serves as a team member, possibly team leader, for the development of initial and subsequent IEPs and due-process evaluations.
8. Participates in local, state, and national conferences, workshops, and seminars on the gifted to keep abreast of innovations in the field.
9. Acts as a liaison person with federal programs in the intermediate unit and with the state and district, upon request.
10. Orients new staff.
11. Arranges, with district school personnel, the scheduling needs of gifted children.
12. Helps revise the intermediate unit plan and develop district plans.
13. Sets up meetings with students' parents and orients IEP development.

D. Direct Supervision of Teachers

Direct supervision has two primary functions: maintenance of instructional quality and improvement.

The supervisor needs competencies for:

1. Regular cooperative planning of each IEP with each teacher supervised.
2. A supportive, rather than a directive, supervisory approach based on the concepts which foster self-growth of the individual in planning and accomplishing objectives.
3. A process of identification and acquisition, through in-service activity, of further teaching competencies.
4. Continuous evaluation of individual student growth in terms of demonstrated competency per IEP.
5. Acceptance and use of self-evaluation techniques by staff members.

VIII. EVALUATION

Evaluation is a two-pronged effort. One, each IEP is evaluated and updated yearly for each gifted student. Two, each gifted program, K–12, should be evaluated and updated no less than yearly. Audiences for such evaluation include:

Parents. Their first concern is the most appropriate education for their children.

Pennsylvania Educators. They are concerned with program development and educational opportunities for gifted and talented students.

Administrative Staff in the Department of Education. They are responsible for implementing policy. One of their main tasks is to assist local projects.

Secretary of Education. The secretary is ultimately responsible for making major policy decisions regarding changes in, or continuation of, programs.

Key Pennsylvania Legislators. They make funding decisions to change or continue programs.

Educators outside Pennsylvania. These include professionals in other state departments and the Office of Gifted and Talented, U.S. Department of Health, Education, and Welfare, as well as district personnel throughout the nation who are interested in innovations and their effects on gifted children.

A. GOALS OF PROGRAM EVALUATION

Evaluation includes review of the following:

1. Specific objectives and goals
2. Identification, screening, and placement
3. Organizational instructional patterns
4. Instructional materials and methods
5. Counseling
6. Growth as evidenced in IEPs
7. School-community support of the program.

Program evaluation provides monitoring of the following:

1. Methods of data collection and interpretation
2. Objectives stated in measurable terms
3. Accomplishment of goals, as related to the measurable objectives
4. The specific activities to reach the objectives

B. GOALS IN IEP EVALUATION

IEP evaluation guidelines are found in *An Introduction to Individualized Education Program Plans in Pennsylvania Revised, 1978, Guidelines for School Aged IEP Development.*

1. Evaluation plans should be made in terms of the program's specific objectives and ultimate goals.
2. Evaluation should be made from the outset of the program.
3. Evaluation should survey attitudes of both participants and nonparticipants.
4. Evaluation should be designed for longitudinal study.
5. Evaluation should include the following district and intermediate unit people:

   Administrators and supervisors, preferably those trained in gifted-child education

   Participating and nonparticipating teachers, counselors, children, parents, and lay people

   School psychologists

6. In-service training in the design and interpretation of measuring instruments should be conducted for those involved in evaluation.
7. In-service training to help teachers evaluate individual students should be provided.
8. Means should be provided for evaluating the effectiveness of the program's current curriculum offerings and instructional methods.
9. Evaluation should be conducted yearly and outcomes should be published.

C. Dissemination

Effective programs are strengthened when the administrator communicates with all those involved in the education of the gifted. Passing on information helps improve programs by:

1. Stimulating new ideas and approaches.
2. Providing guidance for the development of new programs.
3. Establishing coordination between programs for the gifted and other segments of the total school program.
4. Fostering closer ties between the home and the school.

[A table indicating effective dissemination of program information is presented at the top of the next page.]

D. Group Meetings

It is essential that regular class teachers, supervisors, and building principals know about the purposes and activities of the gifted programs. The following are useful.

Administrative meetings: The program supervisor needs to meet with all principals and other administrators in a district to explain the need for the program, overall program objectives and administrative procedures (space needed, student selection process, how parents will be contacted, role assignments for the IEP team).

Faculty meetings: Prior to student selection, all teachers in each school should be informed of their role in selection and the development and maintenance of IEPs. Qualifications of students, program objectives, instructional media, and evaluation methods should be clearly stated. Comments and questions should be encouraged, especially from teachers who have negative opinions about the program. Teachers should be invited to visit the program in operation and be told whom to notify when students have problems. Contacts with regular-class teachers should be made frequently throughout the year to answer questions, to exchange ideas and resources, and to coordinate IEP programs and pupil projects.

Parent meetings: Three types of parental involvement should be made available:

1. Individual conferences: Each parent, as a part of the IEP team, participates in discussions of objectives, activities, and progress.
2. In-service meetings to which parents are invited to hear guest speakers informed about gifted education and specialists in specific areas.

DISSEMINATION TARGET	MEDIA	ORIGINATOR	CONTENT
Program Teachers	Staff Meetings, Workshops, Newsletters, Individual IEP Conferences	Program Supervisor	New instructional materials, innovative approaches, opportunities for in-service training: meetings, workshops, conventions, etc.
Program Supervisor	Newsletters, Journals, Workshops, Individual IEP Conferences	PDE Federal Government Other Programs	Descriptions of programs, funding sources, convention and workshop dates
Administrators	Brochures, Newsletters, Periodic reports, Individual IEP Conferences	Program Supervisor PDE	Program activities, evaluation, state regulations
Regular Class Teachers	Student Newspapers, Faculty Meetings, Bulletins, Individual IEP Conferences	Program Staff Students	Program operation, on-going projects, daily activities, student progress
Parents	Student Newspapers, Brochures, Meetings, Individual IEP Conferences	Students Program Staff	Goals, on-going projects, daily activities, student progress
General Public	News Releases, Brochures	Program Staff PR Office	Program activities, special projects, awards

3. Program brochure: A brochure, distributed to all interested persons, should include brief descriptions of the special needs of the gifted child, program structure, answers to frequently asked questions about the gifted, a listing of program staff, etc. In addition, the PDE brochure "A Guide for Parents . . . Mentally Gifted Children and Youth" should be distributed upon request.

5

Model District Program for the Gifted and Talented

The public school system is a partnership program between a state and its local school districts. Educational laws passed by each state legislature and the decisions of state departments of education determine local school district instructional policies and procedures. The North Hills School District program, *Learning Unlimited: An Instructional Program for the Intellectually Gifted and Creatively Talented Secondary Student,** is presented here as a prototype of a local school district program designed and structured in compliance with the Pennsylvania document *Guide for Organizing and Operating Programs for the Mentally Gifted and Talented*, which is reproduced in Chapter 4. The contents page for *Learning Unlimited*, which follows, indicates the scope of this program.†

Introduction

Rationale: Why a Differentiated Program for the Gifted and Talented?

Who Are the Intellectually Gifted and Creatively Talented Students?

Basics Employed in Designing, Structuring, and Implementing the Program

Philosophy

What Knowledge Is of the Most Worth?

Program Requirements

Curriculum

Depth, Breadth, Relevance

*Copyright 1979 Ruth A. Davies. Prepared by Ruth A. Davies, Program Consultant; Royce A. Rice, Secondary Gifted and Talented Program Coordinator; and North Hills School District administrative staff and secondary faculty.

†Although the title of this program refers to the secondary student, the same philosophies, goals, and objectives apply to the elementary program as well.

Independent Study
Subject Area Content, Concepts, and Learning Tasks
  Language Arts
  Literature
  Social Studies
  Mathematics
  Science
  Modern Languages
  Music
  Art
The School Librarian: Instructional Partner in the Gifted and Talented Program
Librarian as Member of the GATE Teaching Team
Pilot Projects
GATE Program of Studies

INTRODUCTION

The North Hills School District's Secondary Program for the Intellectually Gifted and the Creatively Talented, *Learning Unlimited,* was initiated in September 1977. A year of in-service study and program planning preceded the actual introduction of the program. The school year 1977–1978 served as a period of bold innovation coupled with careful, thoughtful, objective evaluation; a period devoted to testing and appraising heretofore untried teaching/ learning strategies and new curricular content as well as a period devoted to rethinking and reevaluating critically the more than twenty honors, independent study, and advanced placement courses already in the North Hills secondary program. The major concern has been to gain insight and perspective by exploring the new, the untried, and the unfamiliar as well as by discovering something new, significant, and unexpected in the familiar.

The Elementary Program for the Intellectually Gifted and the Creatively Talented, which was initiated in September 1976, has served as the foundation on which the Secondary Program has been carefully built. The elementary and the secondary programs are in reality a single program, which has been designed ever to broaden, ever to deepen, ever to reinforce and extend learning through a logical progression of interlocking, cohesive, and mutually supportive learning experiences. Thus continuity, unity, balance, and harmony have been scientifically built into the program. The identical philosophy, commitment to excellence, and concern for the optimum development of each child and youth in the North Hills schools undergird and unify the entire program for the intellectually gifted and creatively talented, K–12.

RATIONALE: WHY A DIFFERENTIATED PROGRAM FOR THE GIFTED AND TALENTED?

The North Hills School District consistently endeavors to provide a quality, optimum education for each child and youth in its schools. Providing an instructional program scientifically designed to meet the unique growth potential of the intellectually gifted and the creatively talented student is, therefore, compatible with the district's commitment to provide a quality, optimum education for all students.

The North Hills School District recognizes the validity of the tenets set forth by the following educational authorities.

L. M. Terman, in his monumental work *Genetic Studies of Genius,* stressed the importance of a nation's nurturing its intellectual talent. He stated:

> It should go without saying that a nation's resources of intellectual talent are among the most precious it will ever have. The origin of genius, the natural laws of its development, and the environmental influences by which it may be affected for good or ill, are scientific problems of almost unequaled importance for human welfare.[1]

The Harvard Report, *General Education in a Free Society,* affirmed that equality in education does not mean an identical education for all. Rather, it means an educational program that recognizes and provides adequately for the vast actual differences among students. The report emphasized that

> though common aims must bind together the whole educational system, there exists no one body of knowledge, no single system of instruction equally valid for every part of it.[2]

> Within a generation the problem of how best to meet this immense range of talent and needs has grown up, like the fabled beanstalk, to overshadow virtually every other educational problem. It is in truth at the heart of any attempt to achieve education for democracy.[3]

> Equal opportunity does not mean identical provision for all. Rather it means access for all to those avenues of education which match their gifts and interests.[4]

The Rockefeller Report, *The Pursuit of Excellence,* warned that unused talent deprived the nation "of the mainspring of its vitality."[5] It urged that America recognize that

> there is no more searching or difficult problem for a free people than to identify, nurture and wisely use its own talents. Indeed, on its ability to solve this problem rests, at least in part, its fate as a free people. For a free society cannot commandeer talent; it must be true to its own vision of individual liberty. And yet at a time when we face problems of desperate gravity and complexity an undiscovered talent, a wasted skill, a misplaced ability is a threat to the capacity of a free people to survive.[6]

> Every democracy *must* encourage high individual performance. If it does not, it closes itself off from the main springs of its dynamism and talent and imagination, and the traditional democratic invitation to the individual to realize his full potentialities becomes meaningless.[7]

> By insisting that *equality* means an exactly similar exposure to education, regardless of the variations in interest and capacity of the student, we are in fact inflicting a subtle but serious form of inequality upon our young people. We are limiting the development of individual excellence in exchange for a uniformity of external treatment. . . . Because many educators reject the idea of grouping by ability, the ablest students are often exposed to educational programs whose content is too thin and whose pace is too slow to challenge their abilities.[8]

The Report of the President's Commission on National Goals, *Goals for Americans,* reiterated that the basic natural resource of the United States is its people.[9] The report stressed that

> there is no such thing as "mass education." Every use of the phrase is a denial of a vital reality; education is a wholly individual process.[10]

Our devotion to equality does not ignore the fact that individuals differ greatly in their talents and motivation. It simply asserts that each should be enabled to develop to the full, in his own style and to his own limit. . . . This means that there must be diverse programs within the educational system to take care of the diversity of individuals, and that each of these programs should be accorded respect and stature.[11]

To urge an adequate program for the gifted youngsters is not to recommend favoritism. They do not need more attention than other children—in some situations they may even need less. They need a different kind of attention.[12]

Children of high academic talent . . . should be given the opportunity to move more rapidly. There should be various forms of grouping by ability from the earliest years of school; and every effort should be made to provide enrichment for the gifted student.[13]

Arnold Toynbee, noted historian, in an article entitled "Is America Neglecting Her Creative Talents?," expressed alarm at America's failure to recognize and nurture the intellectual abilities and the creative talents of its citizens. He stated that

to give a fair chance to potential creativity is a matter of life and death for any society. This is all important because the outstanding creative ability of a fairly small percentage of the population is mankind's ultimate capital asset.[14]

The North Hills School District recognizes its responsibility to provide an instructional program with special dimension for the intellectually gifted and the creatively talented student—not to do so would be to break faith with students and parents and would, in fact, negate the promise of providing each student with the opportunity for a quality, optimum education.

WHO ARE THE INTELLECTUALLY GIFTED AND CREATIVELY TALENTED STUDENTS?

F. S. Manchester, Pennsylvania Commissioner for Basic Education, has defined the mentally gifted as follows: "Children who have outstanding intellectual and/or creative ability, the development of which requires special activities or services not ordinarily provided by local educational agencies."[15]

In the report to the Congress of the United States by the U.S. Commissioner of Education, *Education of the Gifted and Talented,* the various dimensions of giftedness are defined as follows:

Gifted and talented children are those identified by professionally qualified persons who, by virtue of outstanding abilities, are capable of high performance. These are children who require differential educational programs and services beyond those normally provided by the regular school program in order to realize their contribution to self and society.

Children capable of high performance include those with demonstrated achievement and/or potential ability in any of the following areas:

1. General intellectual ability
2. Specific academic aptitude
3. Creative or productive thinking
4. Leadership ability
5. Visual and performing arts
6. Psychomotor ability[16]

J. Renzulli and R. Hartman constructed a scale for rating behavioral characteristics of superior students.[17] Four categories of particular concern are:

Part I: Learning characteristics
Has unusually advanced vocabulary for age or grade level
Uses terms in a meaningful way
Has verbal behavior characterized by "richness" of expression, elaboration, and fluency
Is a keen and alert observer
Usually "sees more" or "gets more" out of a story, film, etc., than others
Reads a great deal on his own
Usually prefers adult-level books
Does not avoid difficult material
May show a preference for biography, autobiography, encyclopedias, and atlases

Part II: Motivational characteristics
Is easily bored with routine tasks
Strives toward perfection
Is self-critical
Is not easily satisfied with his own speed or products
Is quite concerned with right and wrong, good and bad
Often evaluates and passes judgment on events, people, and things

Part III: Creativity characteristics
Displays a great deal of curiosity about many things
Is constantly asking questions about anything and everything
Displays a keen sense of humor and sees humor in situations that may not appear humorous to others
Displays a good deal of intellectual playfulness
Fantasizes
Imagines, "I wonder what would happen if . . ."
Manipulates ideas
Is often concerned with adapting, improving, and motivating institutions, objects, and systems

Part IV: Leadership characteristics
Is self-confident with children his own age as well as adults
Seems comfortable when asked to show his work to class
Adapts readily to new situations
Is flexible in thought and action and does not seem disturbed when the normal routine is changed
Tends to dominate others when they are around
Generally directs the activities in which he is involved

The Renzulli-Hartman *Scale for Rating Behavioral Characteristics of Superior Students* is an intrinsic component of the North Hills identification-selection process.

E. Paul Torrance, recognized authority in the field of creativity, in his recent publication *Creativity in the Classroom,* defined creativity as follows:

Creativity [is] the process of sensing problems or gaps in information, forming ideas or hypotheses, testing and modifying these hypotheses, and communicating the results. . . . Under this definition, it is possible to subsume the major elements of most other definitions. The production of something new or original is included in almost all of them. Creativity is sometimes contrasted to conformity and is defined as the contribution of original ideas, a different point of view, or a new way of looking at problems; whereas, conformity is defined as doing what is expected without disturbing or causing trouble for others. Creativity has also been defined as a successful step into the unknown, getting away from the main track, breaking out of the mold, being open to experience and permitting one thing to lead to another, recombining ideas or seeing new relationships among ideas. . . .

Concepts such as curiosity, imagination, discovery, innovation, and invention are also prominent in discussions of creativity.[18]

The *Torrance Tests of Creative Thinking* are used in the North Hills School District to identify those students with a high degree of creativity. These tests measure fluency, flexibility, and originality—three areas heretofore unexplored. Different forms of the test will be given at three-year intervals to determine the degree of growth evidenced in each of the three areas of creativity.

BASICS EMPLOYED IN DESIGNING, STRUCTURING, AND IMPLEMENTING THE PROGRAM

I. *Guidelines for the Operation of Special Education Programs for the Mentally Gifted* (Pennsylvania Department of Education, 1974)
   A. Philosophy
   B. Curriculum
      Goals
      Subject area content, concepts, learning tasks
   C. Screening
   D. Scheduling
   E. Staff
      Teacher of the gifted
      In-service
      Supervision
   F. Evaluation
II. Ten Goals of Quality Education (Pennsylvania Department of Education)
III. *Becoming an Educated Person: A Statement of Philosophy and Objectives* (North Hills School District)
IV. Bloom's *Taxonomy* (Cognitive and Affective Domains)
V. Structure of Intellect Model (J. P. Guilford)
VI. A Model for Implementing Cognitive-Affective Behaviors (Frank Williams)
VII. Research findings and recommendations
   A. William Burton
   B. James Gallagher
   C. J. W. Getzels
   D. John Gowan
   E. Abraham Maslow
   F. S. J. Parnes
   G. J. S. Renzulli
   H. H. A. Smith
   I. Calvin Taylor
   J. E. Paul Torrance
   K. Frank Williams
VIII. *Process of Education* (Jerome Bruner)
   A. Identification and ordering of fundamentals
   B. Unity, continuity, balance, and harmony in design

IX. Psychology of teaching and learning
   A. Purpose
   B. Significance
   C. Motivation
   D. Climate
   E. Discovery
   F. Perceive, behave, become
   G. Inquiry process
   H. Divergent, creative, adventurous thinking
   I. Self-actualization
X. Thinking-Learning-Communicating Skills Continuum, K–12 [see Appendix F]
XI. Blueprint for teaching-team cooperation and function

PHILOSOPHY

Two basic guides have been followed in spelling out the philosophy undergirding the Program for the Intellectually Gifted and the Creatively Talented: *Guidelines for the Operation of Special Education Programs for the Mentally Gifted* and *Becoming an Educated Person.* The following philosophic tenets set forth in the Pennsylvania Department of Education (PDE) *Guidelines* are endorsed by the North Hills School District.[19]

> Differential programs for gifted children fit within the spectrum of special treatment for all children who have learning needs. These programs are logical manifestations of our concern for individual differences, for equality of educational opportunity, and for optimum development of each child. By treating and educating the gifted as a group with identifiable differences (capabilities, interests, and needs), teachers and school administrators can plan educational programs to fit the individual needs of extremely able boys and girls and at the same time include experiences to develop their problem-solving and creative abilities.
>
> *Benefits for programs for gifted children extend to other children as well.* School district personnel throughout Pennsylvania have stated that their efforts in developing and maintaining programs for gifted students have resulted in improvement of the total educational programs of the districts. This improvement has come about and can continue because of careful identification of children with certain characteristics and abilities as well as from the placement of these children in suitable programs. . . .
>
> The task of effectively providing for the education of gifted children and youth requires major changes in concepts and practice. Inseparable from this is the demand that all pertinent objectives of differential education for the gifted be specifically formulated. The implementation of these objectives calls for a transformed curriculum, as well as for (1) modification in the typical organization of the school day; (2) tailored instructional materials and methods; (3) specialized teacher preparation and specific teacher selection; and (4) education of the community for sustained cooperation, understanding, and support. None of these plans is easy to carry out, and what is even more difficult to confront is the fact that one provision alone is not enough. The essential challenge is to put these plans into practice as soon as effectively possible.
>
> We emphasize that, for society's potential innovators, the humane consequences of knowledge must be an integral element of learning. Social concern has to become the context in which all studies are couched or else gifted youth will ask, "knowledge for what?" Any enrichment program that reflects the development of citizens who possess only a pragmatic view of their talent use is short-sighted.

The North Hills School District statement of philosophy, *Becoming an Educated Person,* as indicated previously in the Rationale, pledges the North Hills to provide an instructional program of excellence for all students. The components of such a program are carefully spelled out:[20]

> Each student will develop competency in basic skills *at a level appropriate with his ability and development.* He will be able to read with understanding, express ideas effectively in writing, perform arithmetical computations, reason mathematically and logically, listen critically, speak effectively, develop perceptual skills and use learning skills.*
>
> Each student will develop the ability to understand and respond effectively to people, ideas, objects, and events in the world. He will be able to recognize, explain, evaluate, and respond to these conditions and events.
>
> An educated person is one who has knowledge of social, political, and natural events. He can identify and explain such events; he has the ability to relate these events historically and scientifically to the world in which he lives and to changing conditions. He has acquired valid criteria with which to make judgments. An educated person has the knowledge and experience to understand human similarities and differences and demonstrates respect for humanity and the dignity of the individual. He understands the relationship between [the] human being and his social, political, and natural environments and seeks intelligent use of the environment.
>
> Each student will grow toward the realization of his own intellectual, emotional, motivational, and physical potential. This goal affirms the belief that each student is a unique individual and has great potential for growth. Furthermore, it assumes that the fullest development of each student is in the best interest of a democratic society; and that the freedom to inquire, to challenge ideas and to examine alternatives, while valuing the freedom of others, is consonant with the idea of individual development and societal improvement.

WHAT KNOWLEDGE IS OF THE MOST WORTH?

To translate the foregoing philosophy into an instructional program, it is necessary to address oneself to the question raised by the Pennsylvania Department of Education, knowledge for what? To answer this question is to provide the overall philosophy directing curricular design. The North Hills School District has turned to Edgar Dale, professor at Ohio State University, for direction. Dale brought his wisdom, educational expertise, and extraordinary concern for human growth and development to bear in formulating the answer to this question. He stated:[21]

> By knowledge I mean information, skills, and attitudes incorporated into one's intellectual and emotional habits.
>
> That knowledge is of the most worth which enables a person to do the best that he can, to be fulfilled, to achieve a sense of his identity. The curriculum of the school must help students attain a sense of their individual and social worth.
>
> That knowledge is of the most worth which generates knowledge. Knowledge which can be turned into effective power has high value.
>
> That knowledge is of the most worth which contributes a sense of joy, delight, exhilaration, poignancy to the life of the learner. This requires in-depth experiences which develop a zest for life, the joy of discovery, the Eureka effect, as a continuing accompaniment to life richly lived. *This is not a call for more entertainment. Entertainment is too limited a concept. Such emphasis is often upon gratifica-*

---

*The Thinking-Learning-Communicating Skills Continuum, K–12 [see Appendix F] provides the framework for translating this promise into a viable basic skills instructional program.

tion of the senses, which constantly calls for increasing stimulation. In the end, this results in the dulling of the senses and a constant search for new ways of being bored [emphasis supplied].

In a world brimming with knowledge it is not enough to ask whether what is learned has worth. We must rather ask, "What is of most worth?" The greatest value, in my opinion, is a belief in the dignity of man. To dignify man is to honor, to exalt, to make worthy. It is easy to say this, but to translate it into reality is today's greatest challenge.

Many studies show that additional time spent on reflection, on thinking about what we have read, heard, seen or done is highly profitable. Hence the importance of that knowledge which helps us organize, classify, pattern, structure, rearrange, reconstruct, synthesize, conceptualize what we know. The able teacher helps students develop connections, interactions, relationships, patterns [see Appendix F].

The North Hills School District believes that a viable educational program— one grounded in the verities—must be adaptable, flexible, open-ended, expandable, and responsive to the interests and goals of the individual student as well as to his educational, social, and personal growth needs and capabilities.

PROGRAM REQUIREMENTS

In designing the program for the gifted and talented, each of the requirements spelled out in the Pennsylvania Department of Education *Guidelines* has been fulfilled:[22]

  I. The activity must be distinctive and different to the extent it can be described
 II. The instructional approach should be designed for children of high ability. "Distinct and different" refers to the program for gifted children as compared to the common educational program of the school
III. Programs for gifted children may take several forms. Basically these are:
   A. Enrichment or acceleration of content
   B. Independent study
   C. Individualization of instruction
   D. Curricular modifications
   E. Instructional methods designed to develop reasoning processes such as creativity, critical thinking, and evaluative thinking [see Appendix F]
 IV. Activities desired . . . include:
   A. Early admission to school or grade level
   B. Advanced placement courses
   C. Grouping across grade lines, such as placing students from various grades into one group
   D. Remedial work in skill subjects for students with low achievement but high ability
   E. Assignment of special guidance and counseling services to students with high ability
   F. Use of progammed materials
   G. Grouping of students for special purposes or special classes
   H. Organization of library or learning center, or instructional media center capabilities
   I. Selected special programs such as The Great Books Program, inquiry training, or national curriculum projects
  V. Development of other characteristics, within the individual not necessarily directed toward academic achievement, that might be supported include:
   A. Leadership potential
   B. Sensitivity to needs of others
   C. Divergent thinking ability

D. Interest in creativity activities
E. High goal orientation
F. Kinesthetic ability
G. Foresight
H. Unusual vocabulary development
I. Abstract thinking
J. Insight into problems
K. Reasoning
L. Problem solving
M. Humor and wit
N. Range of interest and curiosity

CURRICULUM

In designing the curriculum for the gifted and talented students, the definition provided by the U.S. Department of Health, Education, and Welfare has been followed:

> The *curriculum* is considered to encompass the instructional activities planned and provided for pupils by the school or school system. The curriculum, therefore, is the planned interaction of pupils with instructional *content,* instructional *resources,* and instructional *processes* for the attainment of educational objectives.[23]

The educational goals on which the program is designed are set forth in the *Guidelines* as follows:

> Educational goals and objectives should be established on the unique characteristics which the gifted child brings to the learning situation. Studies of the gifted highlight their unusual characteristics and capabilities, e.g., their ability to think abstractly and to generalize widely, their creative abilities, and their leadership performance.

> In order to meet these needs of society, the school needs to set these goals for its gifted population:
>
> a. Development of the ability to meet problem situations with problem-solving skills
> b. Development of the ability to discern all the options in making choices in society
> c. Development of the ability to originate and enjoy the cultural and aesthetic activities of man—both historical and contemporary
> d. Participation in challenging vocational and avocational activities
> e. Development of the ability to work at the higher levels of Bloom's *Taxonomy* and Guilford's Structure of the Intellect
> f. Enhancement of high potential thru inter-stimulation with their mental peers
> g. Encouragement and nurture of those elements of Torrance's stages of creativity which are not specifically involved in the above items[24]

As specified in the goals above, the program for the gifted and talented has been designed to incorporate the following basics: (1) Bloom's *Taxonomy of Educational Objectives* in both the cognitive and affective domains; (2) Guilford's Structure of the Intellect; and (3) Torrance's stages of creativity.

Bloom's *Taxonomy of Educational Objectives* (Cognitive Domain)[25]
1.0 *Knowledge:* recall of specifics, patterns, structure, or setting
    1.1 Knowledge of specifics—specific bits of information
        1.1.1 Knowledge of terminology
        1.1.2 Knowledge of specific facts
    1.2 Knowledge of ways and means of dealing with specifics—organizing

    1.2.1 Knowledge of conventions—usages, styles, forms
    1.2.2 Knowledge of trends and sequences—with respect to time
    1.2.3 Knowledge of classification and categories—classes, sets, divisions, arrangements
    1.2.4 Knowledge of criteria—judging facts, principles, opinion, criteria
    1.2.5 Knowledge of methodology—techniques, methods of inquiry
2.0 *Comprehension:* relating knowledge—knows and can use material or idea
    2.1 Translation—paraphrasing ideas
    2.2 Interpretation—reordering, rearranging
    2.3 Extrapolation—extension of trends beyond given data
3.0 *Application:* use of abstractions in concrete situations
4.0 *Analysis:* the breaking down of information into its elements
    4.1 Analysis of elements—recognizing unstated assumptions, distinguishing facts from hypotheses
    4.2 Analysis of relationships—connections and interactions between elements and parts of a communication
    4.3 Analysis of organizational principles—analyzing the structure and organization of a communication
5.0 *Synthesis:* putting together of elements and parts to form a whole
    5.1 Production of a unique communication—conveying ideas, feelings, and/or experiences
    5.2 Production of a plan, or proposed set of operations—developing a plan of work meeting task requirements
    5.3 Derivation of a set of abstract relations—classifying phenomena or moving from symbolic representations to deductions
6.0 *Evaluation:* quantitative and qualitative judgments, using standards and criteria
    6.1 Judgment in terms of internal evidence—evaluation on basis of accuracy, logic, and consistency
    6.2 Judgment in terms of external criteria—evaluation of material with reference to standards and criteria

Krathwohl, Bloom, and Massia's *Taxonomy of Educational Objectives* (Affective Domain)[26]
1.0 *Receiving:* attending
    1.1 Awareness—conscious of a situation, phenomenon, object, or state of affairs
    1.2 Willingness to receive—giving attention but neutral toward stimulus
    1.3 Controlled or selected attention—selection of stimuli to be attended to; attention controlled by learner
2.0 *Responding:* actively attending
    2.1 Acquiescence in responding—compliance or obedience
    2.2 Willingness to respond—voluntary response accompanied by learner choice and consent
    2.3 Satisfaction in response—behavior accompanied by feeling of satisfaction, pleasure, zest, or enjoyment
3.0 *Valuing:* behavior motivated by commitment to underlying value
    3.1 Acceptance of a value—consistent in response; perceived by others as holding the belief or value
    3.2 Preference for a value—sufficiently committed to the value to pursue it, to seek it out, to want it
    3.3 Commitment—certainty bordering on faith; includes loyalty to a position, group, or cause
4.0 *Organization:* organization of values into a system; determining interrelationship of values; establishment of priorities
    4.1 Conceptualization of a value—individual sees how the value relates to those already held or to new ones
    4.2 Organization of a value system—bringing together a complex of values and placing them into an ordered relationship

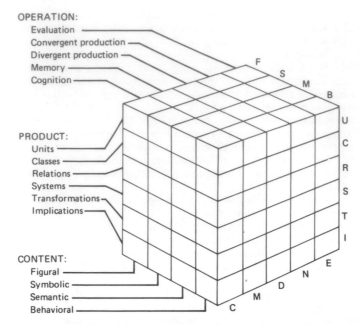

OPERATION:
Evaluation
Convergent production
Divergent production
Memory
Cognition

PRODUCT:
Units
Classes
Relations
Systems
Transformations
Implications

CONTENT:
Figural
Symbolic
Semantic
Behavioral

FIGURE 1. Guilford's Structure of the Intellect Model. From J. P. Guilford, *The Nature of Human Intelligence.* New York: McGraw-Hill, 1967, frontispiece.

5.0 *Characterization by a Value or Value Complex:* individual acts consistently in accordance with the values he has internalized
    5.1 Generalized set—persistent and consistent response at a very high level
    5.2 Characterization—demonstrates in behavior a consistent philosophy of life or set of values

Guilford's Structure of the Intellect [see Figure 1] is a three-dimensional cube consisting of intellectual *operations, products,* and *content*[27]
1.0 *Content*
    1.1 Figural—refers to material that can be distinguished by form, size, shape, color, or texture
    1.2 Symbolic—consists of figural elements which have meaning; for example, the number system, chemical formulas, map symbols
    1.3 Semantic—refers to language-based communication
    1.4 Behavioral—covers such content as the development of social skills
2.0 *Products*
    2.1 Implications—refers to the act of predicting or anticipating based on existing evidence
    2.2 Transformations—refers to extending knowledge beyond the known to new situations
    2.3 Systems—refers to organizing information in an orderly manner, showing the interrelationship of the parts to each other and to the whole itself
    2.4 Relations—refers to any bond or connection that renders one entity in any way relevant to another
    2.5 Classes—refers to a group in which all members possess at least one common characteristic
    2.6 Units—refers to a group which is a subdivision of a larger group; a single person or thing regarded as an individual but belonging to an entire group

3.0 *Operations*
    3.1 Cognition—involves discovery, recognition, comprehension, awareness, and understanding
    3.2 Memory—involves storage and retention of knowledge; the ability to recall information as needed
    3.3 Divergent production—involves scanning stored information, searching for many possible solutions; thinking in different directions, going off in new and untried ways
    3.4 Convergent production—involves redefinition, transformations, recognizing best or conventional solutions
    3.5 Evaluation—involves the ability to determine if solution fits the problem and is workable

Torrance's stages or levels of creativity[28]
1.0 *Wanting to Know*
    1.1 Asking questions
    1.2 Engaging in the absorbed search for truth
    1.3 Testing guesses
    1.4 Finding better ways of finding out
    1.5 Preparing for the use and extension of learning skills throughout life
2.0 *Digging Deeper*
    2.1 Attempting more difficult tasks
    2.2 Shunning mediocrity and the quick easy way
    2.3 Hungering for excellence and working hard to achieve it
    2.4 Keeping open the capacity for genuine affection, love, empathy, and honesty of feeling
3.0 *Looking Twice and Listening for Smells*
    3.1 Looking from different angles
    3.2 Taking a closer look
    3.3 Experiencing with all senses
    3.4 Submerging self in ideas and projects
    3.5 Enjoying working alone at times
4.0 *Listening to a Cat*
    4.1 Learning to listen and communicate with understanding
    4.2 Trying to find out what really matters to others
    4.3 Developing skills of empathy
    4.4 Expressing ideas and feelings accurately and honestly through nonverbal means
    4.5 Expressing self through creative movements, creative dramatics, visual art, and creative reading
5.0 *Crossing Out Mistakes*
    5.1 Gathering courage to attempt something difficult and important, even with the expectation of making mistakes
    5.2 Using mistakes constructively to move forward to new levels of skills and dignity
    5.3 Learning reality through direct, personal experience
6.0 *Getting Into and Out of Deep Water*
    6.1 Testing one's skills and abilities
    6.2 Testing the situation
    6.3 Testing one's resources
    6.4 Taking calculated risks
    6.5 Asking questions for which no ready answer exists
    6.6 Making choices
    6.7 Seeing defects in the existing order
    6.8 Gaining confidence in the ability to "get out of deep water"
7.0 *Having a Ball*
    7.1 Enjoying bursting forth to a new level of knowing and functioning
    7.2 Being able to laugh, play, fantasize, and loaf
    7.3 Being careful but not overcautious or fearful
    7.4 Finding fun and pleasure in work and learning

8.0 *Cutting Holes to See Through*
   8.1 Tolerating complexity
   8.2 Manipulating complexity, incompleteness, and imperfections to achieve breakthroughs and genuine innovations

In addition to the stages or levels of creativity, the following observations and recommendations of Torrance have been employed in structuring the program for the gifted and talented:[29]

Man's nature requires that he have anchors in reality, that he have structure in his environment, and that he have authorities upon which he can depend

In the education and guidance of the gifted child there is a place for:

Both creative learning and learning by authority

Both intelligence tests and tests of creative thinking

Both moral courage and social adjustment

Both the mastery of what is known and the creation of new knowledge

Both original answers and correct ones

Both conforming and nonconforming behavior

Both a responsive and a stimulating environment

Both a respect for the common humaneness and sex differences of boys and girls

Both discipline and creative behavior

The teacher of the gifted must:

Learn to value creative thinking and forge an environment which places value on creative activity so that the highly creative student will not have to exist as a miserable deviate in the shadow of his more successful peers

Find ways of assisting children to be more sensitive to environmental stimuli and to trust their own perception of reality

Permit and encourage manipulation of objects and ideas

Lead students to test systematically each new idea

Develop tolerance of new ideas

Teach the child to value his own creative thinking

Beware of forcing a set pattern

Develop a creative classroom climate

Teach skills for avoiding peer sanctions

Understand the creative process and share this understanding with pupils

Dispel the sense of awe of masterpieces

Encourage and evaluate self-initiated learning

Create "thorns in the flesh," to be sensitive to defects, to recognize the disturbing element

Create necessities for creative thinking

Provide for both active and quiet times for the production of ideas

Make available resources for working out ideas

Encourage the habit of working out the full implication of ideas

Develop constructive criticism—not just criticism

Encourage acquisition of knowledge in a variety of fields

Become more adventurous spirited

Williams's Model for Implementing Cognitive-Affective Behaviors[30] has provided guidance in structuring learning experiences that transcend factual information and stress thinking creatively and feeling creatively in both the cognitive

D1⇄D2→D3

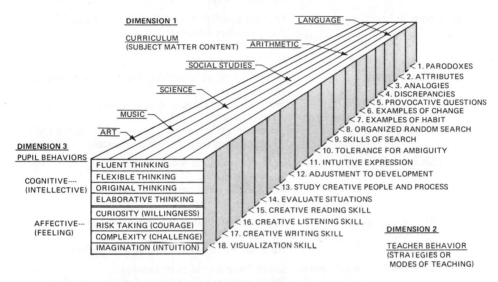

FIGURE 2. Model for Implementing Cognitive-Affective Behaviors in the Classroom. From Frank E. Williams, *Classroom Ideas for Encouraging Thinking and Feeling*. Buffalo, N.Y.: D. O. K. Publishers, 1970, frontispiece.

and the affective areas [see Figure 2]. Williams's model, similar to Guilford's Structure of the Intellect Model, has three dimensions.

DIMENSION 1: Lists the subject areas of the curriculum

1. Language
2. Arithmetic
3. Social studies
4. Science
5. Music
6. Art

DIMENSION 2: Lists 18 styles or categories of teaching strategies

1. Paradoxes:	Common notion not necessarily true in fact Self-contradictory statement or observation
2. Attributes:	Inherent properties Conventional symbols or identities Ascribing qualities
3. Analogies:	Situations of likeness Similarities between things Comparing one thing to another
4. Discrepancies:	Gaps or limitations in knowledge Missing links in information What is not known
5. Provocative questions:	Inquiry to bring forth meaning Incite knowledge exploration Summons to discovering new knowledge
6. Examples of change:	Demonstrate the dynamics of things Provide opportunities for making alterations, modifications, or substitutions

7. Examples of habit:

    Effects of habit-bound thinking
    Building sensitivity against rigidity in ideas and well-tried ways

8. Organized random search:

    Using a familiar structure to go at random to build another structure
    An example from which new approaches occur at random

9. Skills of search:

    Search for ways something has been done before (historical search)
    Search for the current status of something (descriptive search)
    Set up an experimental situation and search for what happens (experimental research)

10. Tolerance for ambiguity:

    Provide situations which puzzle, intrigue, or challenge thinking
    Pose open-ended situations which do not force closure

11. Intuitive expression:

    Feeling about things through all the senses
    Skill of expressing emotion
    Be sensitive to inward hunches or nudges

12. Adjustment to development:

    Learn from mistakes or failures
    Develop from rather than adjust to something
    Developing many options or possibilities

13. Study creative people and process:

    Analyze traits of eminently creative people
    Study processes which lead to problem-solving, invention, incubation, and insight

14. Evaluate situations:

    Deciding upon possibilities by their consequences and implications
    Check or verify ideas and guesses against the facts

15. Creative reading skill:

    Develop a mind-set for using information that is read
    Learning the skill of generating ideas by reading

16. Creative listening skill:

    Learning the skill of generating ideas by listening
    Listen for information allowing one thing to lead to another

17. Creative writing skill:

    Learning the skill of communicating ideas in writing
    Learning the skill of generating ideas through writing

18. Visualization skill:

    Expressing ideas in visual form
    Illustrating thoughts and feelings
    Describing experiences through illustrations

DIMENSION 3: Lists 8 pupil behaviors

1. *Cognitive-Intellective behaviors*
    Fluent thinking (to think of the *most*):

    Generation of a quantity
    Flow of thought
    Number of relevant responses

    Flexible thinking (to take *different* approaches):

    Variety of kinds of ideas
    Ability to shift categories
    Detours in direction of thought

Original thinking (to think in *novel* or *unique* ways):	Unusual responses Clever ideas Production away from the obvious
Elaborative thinking (to *add on* to):	Embellish upon an idea Embroider upon a simple idea or response to make it more elegant Stretch or expand upon things or ideas

2. *Affective-Feeling behaviors*

Risk taking (to have *courage* to):	Expose oneself to failure or criticisms Take a guess Function under conditions devoid of structure Defend own ideas
Complexity (to be *challenged* to):	Seek many alternatives See gaps between how things are and how they could be Bring order out of chaos Delve into intricate problems or ideas
Curiosity (to be *willing* to):	Be inquisitive and wonder Toy with an idea Be open to puzzling situations Ponder the mystery of things To follow a particular hunch just to see what will happen
Imagination (to have the *power* to):	Visualize and build mental images Dream about things that have never happened Feel intuitively Reach beyond sensual or real boundaries

Each of the above 18 strategies and each of the 8 pupil behaviors have been woven intrinsically within the curricular fabric, K–12.

In addition to Bloom, Guilford, Torrance, and Williams, these additional authorities have shaped the design, content, and structure of the Gifted and Talented Program.

Ralph Hallman has recommended that the following criteria be used when structuring curriculum for the gifted:[31]

The criterion of connectedness: *You Cannot Create Out of Nothing*

Combination of ideas

Composition of ideas

Configuration of ideas

Novel relationships

New organizations

Integration, oneness, fusion

The criterion of originality

Individuality

Novelty, newness, freshness

Unpredictability

Uniqueness

Surprise, free and spontaneous response

Not mechanical

The criterion of nonrationality (unconscious)
   Fusing images into new creations
   Producing new connections
   Plasticity of thinking
   Openness to experience
The criterion of self-actualization, a pattern of personality growth
   Personality change in the direction of fulfillment
   Connection between motivation and action or performance
   Pushing the level of aspiration upward
The criterion of openness to possibilities
   Moving from actuality toward solutions which are possible but undetermined
   Characterized by: sensitivity, tolerance of ambiguity, self-acceptance, and spontaneity

Sidney Parnes has made the following recommendations as to priorities to be established and applied in curriculum design:[32]

The importance of taking notes and keeping a record of ideas.

The value of setting deadlines and quotas for production of ideas.

The value of setting aside certain times and places for deliberate idea production.

The value of providing opportunity for deliberate practice in problem-solving on a variety of problems.

The necessity of developing a balance between the judgment and the imagination, as well as between the open awareness of the environment through all of the senses and the deep self-searching . . . into data stored in the memory cells, between the logic and the emotion, between the deliberate creative effort and the incubation, and between the individual working with the group and the individual working alone.

William Burton, Roland Kimball, and Richard Wing, in their monumental work *Education for Effective Thinking,* admonish educators to avoid the pitfalls and errors resulting from the lack of continuity and system. In the formulation of the Gifted and Talented Program, the following admonitions and recommendations have been seriously regarded and carefully applied:[33]

Creative thinkers are not developed in any line by stuffing them with subject matter.

No one ever learned to think under conditions of uncontrolled, uninhibited freedom.

Freedom, like discipline, can become an end in itself, activity for activity's sake.

The results of pointless freedom are lack of continuity and system, acceptance of fuzzy, inadequate reasons for one's beliefs, and eventually a demand for continual stimulation by new trivia.

Discipline and freedom, properly defined, are inescapable necessities in good thinking.

Discipline is the power to hold fast to the moral conviction that one must think straight, must follow facts wherever they lead, must accept conclusions which are contrary to one's emotional desires, must draw inferences which can be validated, must avoid stating fool conclusions which are not susceptible to checking, must persist through difficulties, must accept conclusions only after critical scrutiny.

Freedom is power to tackle any problem, to consider any facts or conclusions though some of them may seem absurd, to draw inferences as one sees the facts. Freedom is emancipation from whim and impulse, from bias and prejudice, which interfere with thinking.

Discipline is power to accept, to use, and to regulate freedom.

Freedom is the power to use discipline in the pursuit of one's chosen purposes and to reject irresponsible capriciousness.

Continuity, unity, balance and harmony—the benchmarks of educational excellence stressed by Jerome Bruner[34]—have been carefully built into the foundation that undergirds, supports, and unifies the Gifted and Talented Program, K–12. A continuous, unifying concern of this program is learning how to learn—mastering the skills of thinking, learning, and communicating understanding. To guarantee the adequate development of these basic skills, a detailed continuum has been articulated [see Appendix F]. The major divisions of the continuum are as follows:

PART ONE: THINKING SKILLS
  I. Thinking processes:
    A. Make effective use of perceptive thinking.
    B. Make effective use of associative thinking.
    C. Make effective use of conceptual thinking.
    D. Make effective use of problem solving.
    E. Make effective use of critical thinking.
    F. Make effective use of creative thinking.
    G. Make effective use of adventurous thinking.
  II. Thinking in the cognitive area:
    A. Make effective use of knowledge-building skills.
    B. Make effective use of comprehension skills.
    C. Make effective use of application skills.
    D. Make effective use of analysis skills.
    E. Make effective use of synthesis skills.
    F. Make effective use of evaluation skills.
  III. Thinking in the affective area:
    A. Make effective use of receiving (attending) skills.
    B. Make effective use of responding skills.
    C. Make effective use of valuing skills.
    D. Make effective use of organizing skills.
    E. Make effective use of characterizing/valuing skills.

PART TWO: LEARNING SKILLS
  I. Locating information:
    A. Make effective use of libraries.
    B. Make effective use of books.
    C. Make effective use of dictionaries.
    D. Make effective use of encyclopedias.
    E. Make effective use of other basic reference tools.
    F. Make effective use of periodicals and periodical indexes.
    G. Make effective use of newspapers and newspaper indexes.
    H. Make effective use of U.S. government documents, publications, and indexes.
    I. Make effective use of pamphlets.
    J. Make effective use of primary source materials.
    K. Make effective use of audiovisual media.

II. Acquiring information through purposeful and appreciative reading:
   A. Develop reading competence.
   B. Adjust reading rate to purpose.
   C. Read to form relationships.
   D. Read literature with perception and appreciation.
III. Acquiring information through purposeful and appreciative listening:
   A. Develop listening competence.
   B. Make effective use of critical listening.
   C. Make effective use of appreciative listening.
IV. Acquiring information through purposeful viewing and observing:
   A. Recognize that viewing is visual inspection.
   B. Recognize that observing goes beyond viewing and stresses adherence to criteria or following a scientific model.
   C. Recognize that viewing is purposeful looking and that observing is carefully and scientifically studying and interpreting what is seen.
   D. Apply critical thinking skills when "reading" visual media.
   E. "Read" visual media and employ the inquiry processes.
   F. Study teacher-constructed and commercially prepared learning guides.
   G. Organize and consolidate the ideas gained from viewing with ideas gained from other print and nonprint sources as well as from own past experience.
   H. Explore the artistic, technical, psychological, biographical, and historical components of the fine arts.
   I. Become acquainted with the great artists, past and present, and their works.
   J. "Read" the record of man's historical past.
   K. Recognize abilities essential for effective observation.
V. Constructing and interpreting surveys and opinion polls:
   A. Recognize that a survey is an investigation of things as existing or of events past.
   B. Recognize that a poll is a sampling or collection of opinions.
   C. Recognize that an opinion is an answer that is given to a question in a given situation.
   D. Recognize the basic steps employed in conducting an opinion poll.
   E. Recognize various data-collecting techniques.
   F. Analyze nationally recognized surveys.
   G. Design and field test surveys.
VI. Learning through group and social interaction:
   A. Recognize that excellence in interpersonal relationships is based on psychological maturity.
   B. Recognize the characteristics of a psychologically mature person.
   C. Perceive the characteristics of an effective group member.
   D. Recognize the purpose and function of a committee.
   E. Recognize the purpose and function of a panel.
   F. Recognize the purpose and function of a buzz group.
   G. Appreciate the value of parliamentary procedure.
VII. Organizing information:
   A. Make effective use of outlining techniques.

B. Recognize the distinguishing characteristics and mechanics of the two basic outlining systems.
C. Make effective use of note-taking techniques.

PART THREE: COMMUNICATION SKILLS
  I. Writing as a communication tool:
    A. Perceive the significance of writing.
    B. Perceive the significance of functional literacy.
    C. Perceive the hallmarks of excellence in written communication.
  II. Writing the essay:
    A. Perceive the distinguishing characteristics of the essay form.
    B. Become aware of the techniques employed in designing and structuring the essay.
  III. Writing the research paper:
    A. Recognize the purpose and value of the research paper.
    B. Study the procedure to follow as outlined in basic style manuals or research guides.
  IV. Speaking as a communication tool:
    A. Perceive that speech is a vehicle for conveying thought and emotion.
    B. Perceive that effective speaking is a learned process.
    C. Perceive the requirements for a speech of quality and effectiveness.
    D. Perceive the distinguishing characteristics of the speech designed to entertain or amuse.
    E. Perceive the distinguishing characteristics of the speech designed to inform or instruct.
    F. Perceive the distinguishing characteristics of the speech designed to stimulate or actuate through emotion.
    G. Perceive the distinguishing characteristics of the speech designed to convince or move to action.
    H. Perceive the distinguishing characteristics of debate.

A planned, sequential, developmental thinking-learning-communicating skills program is a vital component of the Gifted and Talented Program. These skills are the tools for effective thinking, productive learning, and intellectual action throughout a student's lifetime. The real test of the effectiveness of the Gifted and Talented Program will come when the student currently in the program intelligently applies the necessary skills or solves the vital problems he or she will face as an adult. "Perhaps much of what the pupil learns . . . will wear thin or become obsolete, but skills learned in school continue to be functional indefinitely . . . . Skills are the most permanent of learnings.[35]

Because skills are of vital importance, the implementation of the Skill Continuum has not been left to chance. Rather, skill introduction, reinforcement, and extension have been carefully integrated within the basic framework of the total program, K–12. The spiral design advocated by Bruner has been carefully employed. Example 5, The Introduction, Reinforcement, and Extension of Chronology and Time Line Skills, illustrates the skill progression experienced by the student as he moves from grade to grade, and from learning experience to learning experience.

EXAMPLE 5   THE INTRODUCTION, REINFORCEMENT, AND EXTENSION
OF CHRONOLOGY AND TIME LINE SKILLS

The introduction, reinforcement, and extension of each basic skill outlined in the Thinking-Learning-Communicating Skills Continuum [see Appendix F] is carefully integrated within the framework of the teaching-learning program. The goal is to enable every student to progress steadily to an ever higher level of skill competence as he or she moves from one learning experience to the next.

The following is but a limited sampling of the opportunities afforded the student to achieve mastery of chronology and time line skills.

GRADE THREE
Unit: Transportation
Skill Integration Activities:
The time line is reintroduced stressing the general sequence of transportation developments rather than a sequence of specific dates.
Resources (Child's World):

Going Places by Land: A Time Line Story, 16 picture-story cards

Going Places by Water: A Time Line Story, 16 picture-story cards

Going Places by Air: A Time Line Story, 16 picture-story cards

GRADE FOUR
Unit: Japan
Skill Integration Activities:
The concept of the time line is extended to—
1. Link and sequentialize events.
2. Highlight the interplay of people and events.
Resource:

Adventures with World Heroes by Henry Bamman et al. (Benefic Press), Natsume Kinnosuke, pp. 234–235

GRADE FIVE
Unit: The Civil War
Skill Integration Activities:
The concept of chronologies is introduced—
1. Perceiving the distinguishing characteristics of chronologies and their informational value.
2. Using chronologies to identify significant events and people.
The concept of using encyclopedias and almanacs to discover chronologies and time lines is introduced—
1. Making effective use of encyclopedias.
2. Recognizing distinguishing characteristics and informational value of almanacs.
Resources:

Arrow Book Club Time Line (Scholastic). Drawings along a time line highlight persons and events in American history beginning with the year 1420 and ending with the year 2000. This time line serves as a model to be followed when converting chronologies into time line entries.

Abraham Lincoln Life Line (Scholastic). Drawings along a time line highlight important events in the life of Abraham Lincoln. This time line serves as a model to follow when highlighting important events in a person's life.

Highlights of American History (*World Book*, vol. 20). Drawings along a multilevel zigzag time line highlight persons and events in American history beginning with the year 1600 and ending with the year 1885. This time line serves as a model to follow when developing a zigzag or spiral time line to portray an extensive period of time.

A Chronology from 2300 B.C. to 1976 A.D.: Information Please Almanac. This chronology provides a checklist of important persons and events in American history beginning with the year 1600, to be used in expanding the time line *Highlights of American History* (*World Book*, vol. 20).

EXAMPLE 5 (cont.)

GRADE SIX
Unit: The Aztecs, the Mayas, and the Incas
Skill Integration Activities:
The concept of synthesizing chronology listings into time lines is introduced—
1. Making use of synthesizing skills.
2. Recombining parts of previous experience with new material; reconstructing a new order or pattern.
Resources (Collins-World)

Chronology Chart of the Aztec World and World Events: The Aztecs . . . by Victor von Hagen

Chronology Chart of the Inca World and World Events: The Incas . . . by Victor von Hagen

Chronology Chart of the Mayan World and World Events: The Maya . . . by Victor von Hagen

These three chronologies are combined to form a three-level time line representing the important events and people in the history of the Aztecs, the Incas, and the Mayas.

GRADE SEVEN
Unit: The Prehistoric World
Skill Integration Activities:
The concept of synthesizing chronology listings into time lines is reinforced by—
1. Making use of synthesizing skills.
2. Recombining parts of previous experience with new material; reconstructing a new order or pattern.
Resources:

An Encyclopedia of World History—Ancient, Medieval, and Modern, Chronologically Arranged, ed. by William L. Langer (Houghton), pp. 3–6. Introduces the student to the prehistoric periods of history—

1. Paleolithic 4. Chalcolithic
2. Mesolithic 5. Bronze Age
3. Neolithic 6. Iron Age

Introduces the student to the concept of how centuries and years before and after Christ are reckoned.

The Road of Civilization (Richtext Press). Presents the chronological view of history beginning with the date 1,000,000 B.C. and ending with the year 1965 A.D. Introduces the use of a chronology to identify man's advancing civilization under the six headings—

1. Food 4. Science
2. Shelter 5. Transportation
3. Communication 6. Manufacturing and trade

The Geological Time Scale: Periods and Systems and Derivation of Names (Science Dictionary of the Animal World, by Michael Chinery, Watts), pp. 122–123.

Time Chart of Fossil Man (Our Human Ancestors, ed. by Frances M. Clapham, Watts). Presents in a detailed time line the history of animals and humans beginning with the date 10,000,000 B.C. and ending with the year 10,000 B.C.

GRADE EIGHT
Units: Each American History Unit
Skill Integration Activities:
The concept of chronologies is reintroduced and extended—
1. Perceiving the distinguishing characteristics of chronologies and their informational value.
2. Using chronologies to identify significant events and people.
The concept of informational retrieval as a learning tool:
1. Making effective use of basic reference tools.
2. Valuing books as carriers of knowledge—rich data banks for information retrieval.

EXAMPLE 5 (cont.)

3. Grasping, translating, inferring the intent; selecting, organizing, and expressing ideas.

Resources:

The Annals of America (Encyclopaedia Britannica Corp., 20 vols.). This 20-volume set is a chronological record of American life, action, and thought from 1492 to 1968. This comprehensive reference set is a collection of source materials of American history including laws, speeches, transcriptions of dialogues, on-the-scene reports, reminiscences and other primary sources; this is an excellent tool for identifying significant people, events, and developments to be placed on a time line begun in the first unit in eighth-grade American History and continued throughout the year.

American History Atlas by Martin Gilbert (New York: Macmillan). This atlas presents the history of America in 112 maps beginning with 50,000 B.C. and ending with 1968; this is an excellent reference tool for identifying significant people and events to be highlighted on a time line begun in the first unit in eighth-grade American History and continued throughout the year.

GRADES NINE AND TWELVE

Units: Each Advanced Placement World History and/or U.S. History Unit

Skill Integration Activities:

The concept of the time line is reinforced and extended—

1. Linking and sequentializing events.
2. Highlighting the interplay of people and events.

The concept of informational retrieval as a learning tool is reinforced:

1. Making effective use of basic reference tools.
2. Valuing books as carriers of knowledge—rich data banks for information retrieval.

Resources:

The Timetables of History by Bernard Grun (New York: Simon & Schuster). An encyclopedic reference tool presents a horizontal linkage of people and events: the range covers recorded history from its first exact date, 4241 B.C., through 1974; each double page has seven columns and the reader can scan any given year horizontally and discover what was taking place under the categories: history and politics; literature and the theater; religion, philosophy, and learning; visual arts; music; science, technology, and growth; and daily life.

Model 33, The Pros and Cons of Space Colonization [Part II], illustrates the integration of skills from both the cognitive and affective domains within the content and the process of a learning project. Likewise, this example further demonstrates the principle of teaching skills at the optimal appropriate time, i.e., when the student has need not only to learn the skill but to apply it. Throughout this learning project, the student is asked continually to make value judgments entailing effective use of critical thinking skills—not only in amassing options concerning the feasibility of space colonization but also in thoughtfully weighing and critically assessing the merits and validity of such options within the process of heated debate.

For skill learning culmination, several reinforcing and summarizing activities are provided: (1) at the beginning of twelfth grade each senior evaluates his or her skill proficiency by checking the 84-page Thinking-Learning-Communicating Skills Continuum, after which, in a scheduled conference with a faculty mentor, the student seeks prescriptive remediation for noted areas of weakness; and (2) each senior in the program builds a research procedural manual containing style sheets, research guides and models, and other scholarship tools [see Part II, Model 43, Revving Up for College].

Program continuity—a hallmark of the Gifted and Talented Program—not only emphasizes the thinking-learning-communicating skills but also embraces the planned integration of the *Ten Basic Goals of Quality Education* (EQA). Learning experiences that translate these ten goals, as specified by the Pennsylvania Department of Education, into support activities have been provided throughout the total program. The ten goals are:

1. Self-understanding
2. Understanding others
3. Basic skills
4. Interest in school and learning
5. Good citizenship
6. Good health habits
7. Creativity
8. Vocational development
9. Understanding human accomplishment
10. Preparation for a changing world

The spiral approach to building continuity, unity, and quality into the fabric of the total program embraces the deliberate recurrence of certain basic or fundamental themes, concerns, and/or frames of reference. Each of the following is an example of themes, concerns, and/or frames of reference introduced on the primary level and then reinforced and extended on subsequent levels:

1. Adventurous Thinking
2. Attitudes and Judgments
3. Career Exploration
4. Communicating Artistically, Creatively, Electronically
5. Feelings, Concerns, Commitments
6. Finding the Facts, Filtering the Facts, Facing the Facts
7. Great Books, Past and Present
8. Learning to Cope
9. Learning to Learn
10. Listening with the Inner Ear
11. Mind Boggling Phenomena
12. Observations and Impressions
13. Openness to Experience and Change
14. Perceiving, Behaving, Becoming
15. Scientific Thinking
16. Seeing with the Inner Eye
17. Self-Awareness, Self-Evaluation, Self-Actualization
18. Social Awareness, Concern, Commitment
19. They Made a Difference
20. What If . . . , Why Not?

DEPTH, BREADTH, RELEVANCE

In designing, building, and implementing the program for the gifted and the talented, depth, breadth, and relevance have been carefully structured into the content, process, and product of each learning experience. These terms—depth, breadth, and relevance—signify the following instructional dimensions:

DEPTH. Through extensive and intensive reading, viewing, and listening, facts and events are probed; ideas are linked; cause and effect relationships are explored; and answers are found to questions such as "Then what happened?" "Why did it happen?" and "What were the consequences, implications, and results?"

BREADTH. Through extensive and intensive reading, viewing, and listening, learning is extended beyond the *usual,* beyond the *commonplace,* and beyond the *prescribed* to encompass discovering that which is significant and important but unsuspected and unexplored.

RELEVANCE. Through extensive and intensive reading, viewing, and listening, learning experiences are provided that match the student's needs, interests, aspirations, and concerns. Learning experiences are also provided that are reflective of the contemporary world in which the student lives.

Subject area boundaries, traditionally restrictive and constrictive, must be removed if depth, breadth, and relevance in content, process, and product are to prevail. Therefore, a multidisciplinary, confluent approach to curriculum building must be the rule and not the exception. Depth, breadth, and relevance also prohibit the traditional one-textbook approach to knowledge building.

A look at the following examples will demonstrate the application of the foregoing principles.

THE PROS AND CONS OF SPACE COLONIZATION

DEPTH. This Learning Project provides an in-depth study of socioeconomic problems involved in federal funding of a space colonization program as well as the scientific and technological problems to be solved in establishing space colonies on a permanent basis (see Part II, Model 33).

BREADTH. This Learning Project extends the student's understanding of space colonization by introducing the theories and recommendations of Isaac Asimov, T. A. Heppenheimer, and Ray Bradbury.

RELEVANCE. This Learning Project directly reflects the students' consuming interest in space habitation as evidenced by their overwhelming endorsement of the Academy Award motion picture "Star Wars." This Learning Project brings a high degree of relevance to the question of space colonization by relating it directly to the voter revolt in California on June 6, 1978, when the electorate decisively endorsed Proposition 13 and thereby drastically curtailed California's taxing power.

THE TASADAY: A STUDY OF A PRIMITIVE CULTURE FROZEN IN TIME

DEPTH. This Individual Learning Program introduces the student to the case study method, "a gathering and organization of all relevant materials to enable an in-depth study and an analysis of a person, an event, a community, a society, or a culture." The Learning Guide, Analysis of a Culture, which accompanies this Program, highlights 31 separate and distinct categories of information to be searched for when conducting an in-depth study of a culture (see Part II, Model 30).

BREADTH. This Individual Learning Program extends the student's understanding of prehistoric societies by presenting an in-depth study of the

Tasaday, a small group of primitive people discovered in 1971 living in the Philippines on the Island of Mindanao. The Optional Learning Activities offered in this program extend the student's awareness not only of other contemporary primitive societies but especially of the four basic career fields in anthropology: ethnology, archeology, history, and paleontology.

RELEVANCE. In this Individual Learning Project the student "is invited to apply his own knowledge, observations, feelings, and value judgments when analyzing and interpreting the facts." Optional Learning Experiences invite the student to consult the Career Resource Center at the senior high school for a survey of educational requirements and career possibilities in the field of anthropology.

PROGRAM LEARNING GUIDE: "APPOMATTOX AND THE END"

DEPTH. This mini-program provides an in-depth study of the surrender of Robert E. Lee to Ulysses S. Grant on April 9, 1865. Highlighted are the text of the notes exchanged between the two military leaders; the surrender document itself; a verbatim report of the dialogue exchanged; and eyewitness accounts of the event (see Part II, Model 38).

BREADTH. In this mini-program the student extends his understanding beyond the emotions and reactions of the two chief participants to encompass those of the onlookers as well as those back home in the South and in the North.

RELEVANCE. In this mini-program the student becomes a direct participant in this dramatic, emotion-charged event as he reads the letters, diaries, and eyewitness accounts; as he listens to General Lee's Farewell to His Troops; and as he studies the photographic record of the people involved in this event.

Using several basic textbooks provokes multidimensional learning. The seventh grade employs the tribasal approach to teaching World History. The three textbooks are:

1. *Discovering Our World's History* by Dorothy Fraser and Alice Magenis (American Book) is a comprehensive recounting of man's advancing civilization period by period.
2. *The Human Adventure* by Mariah Marvin, Stephen Marvin, and Frank Cappelluti (Addison-Wesley) is a comprehensive text highlighting the social and human aspects of world history.
3. *The Rise of the West* by Ira Peck, William Johnson, and Frances Plotkin (Scholastic), coupled with its set of four support filmstrips, provides a high degree of on-the-scene perspective through student interaction projects.

Grades 8–12 likewise employ the multitext approach in a variety of subject areas. The vast majority of the learning projects for the gifted and talented are *not* textbook based but, rather, are concept based.

INDEPENDENT STUDY

Independent study reflective of the individual student's needs, interests, goals, concerns, and abilities is a necessary part of an instructional program emphasizing depth, breadth, and relevance. Two separate and distinct approaches to independent study are employed: (1) independent study within the framework of the honors courses in English, foreign languages, literature, mathematics, science, social studies, and speech arts; and (2) independent study separate and distinct from prescribed courses. These independent study programs are designed, implemented, and evaluated by the student in cooperation with a faculty mentor as the student works independently in laboratory, library, or studio.

SUBJECT AREA CONTENT, CONCEPTS, AND LEARNING TASKS

In considering subject area objectives, a statement must be made regarding full-time and part-time involvement.* With a full-time program, consideration of basic sequential skills as well as enrichment, acceleration, emotional and social progress, and the enhancement of each child's capabilities and potential must be part of the educational environment. With a part-time program, basic sequential skills are generally planned for in the regular classroom. Educational objectives in gifted classrooms focus on enrichment, moderate acceleration, emotional and social aspects of early maturity, and the enlargement of each child's potential capabilities and performance.

The following sections deal with appropriate ways of presenting and teaching content, effective strategies to enable the gifted child to learn, retain, and apply what is offered.

Unlike many curriculum guides, this is not a "cookbook" for gifted programs. It is a frame on which to build for individual growth.

LANGUAGE ARTS

An enriched language arts program should develop effective communication skills beyond basic reading, writing, and speaking abilities. Understanding is an essential element of effective communication. Insights gained through interpersonal relationships, as well as instruction, facilitate understanding in communication.

The finest endowments of individuals, communities, and nations can count for nothing if people cannot make themselves understood. Some of the primary communication goals of the gifted program are to help youngsters understand, appreciate, and utilize their language with skill, discrimination, power, and compassion. When these are accomplished, young speakers and writers are more likely to create freely, to develop self-confidence, to understand other individuals, and to take long strides toward the realization of their own potential.

A program for gifted children should be planned around their ability to learn facts quickly, superior reasoning ability, and high level of creativity.

Goals for this area should enable the gifted child to understand that:

1. Categorizing and generalizing are means of ordering relationships.
2. Figurative language is a basic way of extending meaning and explaining relationships.
3. Meaning derived through language is unique and is representative of each individual's singular experience.

*[This section is adapted from *Guidelines for the Operation of Special Education Programs for the Mentally Gifted* (Harrisburg, Pa.: Pennsylvania Department of Public Instruction, 1974), pp. 5–17.]

The child needs to experience activities that encourage independent thinking, planning, and problem solving: (1) associating and interrelating concepts; (2) evaluating facts and arguments critically; (3) creating new ideas and originating new lines of thought; (4) reasoning through complex problems; (5) understanding other situations, other times, and other people, as well as his or her own environmental surroundings.

Academic experiences should be calculated to stimulate learners to progress from learning to thinking, from convergent to divergent production and knowledge. Tasks that produce cognition, memory, and convergent thinking—such as the acquisition and storage of facts, spelling, phonics, sight reading, vocabulary, word skills, the application of correct solutions—are often too limited. The pupils should have at least equal time for divergent and evaluative thinking—those skills requiring creative solutions, critical thinking skills, and decision making.

Creative products in language arts are less easily accomplished in grades one through three if they depend on a working command of communication tools. Yet these are the years when many or most children are quite open-minded and well motivated. In a society that places a high degree of approval on conformity, it is not an easy task to help each child recognize and accept himself or herself so that he or she may dare to become a unique individual.

The study of English can be expanded advantageously to include all forms of communication. Electronic media communication skills, currently almost the exclusive province of advertising specialists and entertainers, should become an arena students examine with care and interest. In examining all forms of verbal and nonverbal communication, students should be asked to: (1) determine what message they receive from film, television, or radio, and (2) invent techniques for projecting similar messages. In a communications laboratory, for instance, the learner will "do" communication rather than read about it. Textbooks will give way to primary source material. The total environment will be a "master textbook" and the entire society will be recognized as educational. This premise means a change in teaching style as well as change in content.

Teaching strategies should provide for active participation in interpersonal relationships using communication skills. Drama, role playing, and creative writing are examples of vehicles that may be used effectively in this area. Confidence in language usage among the gifted must be developed concurrently with language skills in order to provide for productive usage that will benefit both the child and society.

The teacher role shifts from authoritarian to consultative, a teacher becomes one who asks questions rather than gives "facts," one who provokes thinking and promotes excitement rather than administers lectures and tests. Teachers who were educated in traditional techniques need to retool if they are to be effective in reaching gifted children living in the media-oriented world of the present. While equipment and supplies can be expensive for optimum communication laboratory strategies, subject matter relevancy and child involvement with teacher can be implemented even with limited resources.

LITERATURE

For the average child, learning is expected to accumulate; for the gifted, it is expected to accelerate. In few areas can an instructional program be as flexible and supportive of that role as can literature. It can serve as a high-speed vehicle to realms far beyond the ones the child has known.

The gifted can be delighted by the meaning, by the way the author has chosen to express this meaning, and by the realization that literature can be used as a time-space machine to link the individual with other times, other countries, and other languages. Selections of materials should be made on the basis of ideas rather than vocabulary.

Discussions of similarities and differences encourage pupils to crystallize their own ideas, to perceive relationships, and to develop generalizations, transformations, and implications—all of which are the intellectual abilities that underlie critical thinking.

The study of literature can and should encourage divergent thinking. Here, creative writing, as analyzed in discussion and in the comparison of styles, language, or structure, may teach evaluation skills.

It is desirable to engage children in studies of mythology, fables, folktales, biography, drama, and stories, as well as various elements of prose and poetry, so that all can learn about cultural values held by mankind in a cross section of countries. The child secures a better understanding of universal ideas, of himself or herself, and of different writing skills and techniques. Intellectual abilities are developed as teachers help pupils to think independently, critically, and creatively, while these young people assess, compare, and evaluate different forms of literature and the work of different authors. Gifted learners find that biographies are a broad, interesting source of information about people, their motives, their values, and their accomplishments.

In the wide field of prose, gifted young learners are made familiar with the elements of narrative form, setting, plot, character, time, and voice. In the challenging land of poetry, they become familiar with sound, meter, stanza, alliteration, and imagery.

The literature curriculum may well focus on the thematic approach, which enables teachers to provide an arena for youth-adult communication. In this approach, one of the structures recommended identifies main theme, such as heroism, temptation (the Faust figure), and situational ethics (Prometheus).

Also noted are stress application, analysis, synthesis, and evaluation activities. For example, a study of some of the stories with a Faust theme can help young people to examine their own temptation problems without violating their personal privacy. Study of the Faust theme will provide skills in making objective evaluations and using strategies.

Gifted learners can use to good advantage an inquiry process or discovery approach as they study various units of literature. The importance of the teacher's work with the gifted student lies not in what he or she can give the learner but what the learner can accomplish on his or her own. Students should be involved in processes of defining, question asking, data gathering, observing, classifying, generalizing, and verifying.

The language that forms the basis for studies of literature is an open structure; its instability requires an eclectic and pragmatic approach. The eclectic view will allow for selecting documents from different systems of thought and will accommodate the numerous attitudes of the students in any given classroom situation. The pragmatic view allows for individualization of language tasks that are most effective for the student who may be gifted in symbolic and figural dimensions rather than semantic ones. Four organizational approaches are recommended: history and chronology, genre, text analysis, and theme. The historical survey permits the students to follow the development of a literary tradition and to study authors and their periods in their proper perspective. A study of representative periods helps students to understand that literature is not written in isolation. A study of genre provides a means for making explicit the differences and similarities among the various forms. Text analysis offers rich opportunities to analyze and synthesize structure, style, and meaning by examining the internal relationships of a literary work.

A study of semantics and critical thinking will include inductive and deductive logic, propaganda devices, identification of the levels of diction, areas of dialects, and the tools for improving and correcting composition.

Note—A word of caution must be interjected at this point: Delight in reading and an abiding interest in and appreciation of literature are constant aims and persistent concerns of the North Hills School District's reading and literature programs. Because "the book report has probably done more to destroy the love of reading and the joy of books than any other single educational practice," and because the clinical, post-mortem approach to the analysis of literature has created attitudes of dislike and even contempt for reading and literature, these practices are to be avoided in the GATE program.

SOCIAL STUDIES

Gifted students should develop much of their potential as participating members of society through the social studies program. They seldom blossom under a traditional lecture approach. The gifted should take an active part in the study of man and society; should learn about values, the importance of values, and the reaction of others to their own decision making; and should test their opinions, ideas, and skills among peers, older children, and adults.

The fundamental thrust in this subject area should be to make the social studies relevant to the gifted learner—relevant to his or her developing social skills through active participation and purposeful study. Ample allowance should be made in the program for problem solving. Details of problem-solving situations proceed from setting a goal, through appraising the situation, through the generation of ideas, to productive solutions and confirmation or rejection of the process.

While the spiral development of concepts and ideas is accepted, divergent thinking, organization, and analysis can be promoted through free and controlled discussion. Creativity should be stressed at all levels of curriculum development.

Gifted students should examine questions relating to interpersonal relationships, intercultural relationships, and international relationships as presented in a behavioral science inquiry. With this model in the program, students begin to perceive themselves as productive thinkers with responsibility to themselves and to society. They should become aware of the significance of evaluating the validity of information in terms of its initial source and the ever-changing quality of factual information in the social sciences. Gifted students should begin to examine the discrepancies between information they discover and that coming from another. Experience in observing these discrepancies can develop within the pupil a spirit of inquiry that can motivate future learning.

Major goals of the social studies must include the development of human potential through process goals, personal goals, and situational goals. The student perceives the reasons for specific assignments; is able to communicate abstract ideas and analyze complex theories, concepts, and broad generalizations; uses specific data; and evaluates the reliability of sources.

When gifted students are involved in special research projects, such projects should demonstrate clearly that inductive reasoning, deductive reasoning, and divergent thinking are in evidence. The gifted student must learn to use the strategy of decision making: (1) identifying a problem; (2) collecting the evidence; and (3) making a relevant decision based on the evidence. The capacity to reason reflectively and constructively concerning the problems of humankind and the world should be the major goal of instruction in the social sciences.

Four subgoals in both the cognitive and the affective realms are essential if the major goal is to be achieved: (1) depth and precision of understanding on the part of the students in the handling of concepts and ideas rather than mere additions to a store of facts; (2) the ability to think abstractly, critically, and reflectively with social science data; (3) a set of values and attitudes that assures that the individual respects facts and attitudes of others; and (4) acceptance of the responsibility to contribute, either as leader or follower, to group action toward orderly solutions to social problems.

MATHEMATICS

Mathematical programs for gifted children should provide learning experiences that stimulate and sustain their interest, ability, and imagination. There are four basic premises involved in all mathematical programs for gifted children: (1) the gifted can learn to enjoy mathematics; (2) all teachers differ in their ability to think quantitatively; (3) all gifted children differ in their ability to think quantitatively; and (4) all teachers differ in their degree of mathematical interest.

Mathematical programs at the primary and intermediate levels must be influenced by the need for the tangible, the abstract, the real, and the relevant. Mathematics requires sequence and continuity for understanding; therefore, instruction should relate the order and discipline inherent in mathematical content areas to concurrent learning experiences in other subjects. The program as a whole should emphasize and promote a desire for complexities beyond the requirements of the standard curriculum.

The intellectual processes of cognition and comprehension, knowledge or memory, divergent and convergent application, analysis and synthesis, and evaluation as well as creativity must be considered indispensable to the mathematics program.

Teaching generalizations and problem solving becomes particularly necessary in later school years where curriculum design must be based on cognitive and instructional styles as well as on mathematical content.

Mathematics is a consistent discipline at all levels with its components rooted in both content and process. Mathematics, therefore, must be studied in a meaningful and structured manner, but should be adjusted to the student's rate of learning, to his or her ability to make abstractions, and to his or her need for application of a given mathematical concept. Thus, patterns of instructional grouping should use teaching strategies sensitive to the needs and abilities of the gifted student.

SCIENCE

Science programs for the gifted emphasize basic concepts, fundamental principles, and key modes of inquiry. Stress must be placed on independent study and higher-level intellectual activities. Provision for independent work should begin in the primary grades and reach its optimum during the high school years.

Primary students can be tentatively recognized as gifted participants in science activities. These children are best identified by their continued interest in and inquisitiveness regarding science. Identification during the intermediate grades will be much more positive. Here, a strong emphasis may be placed on independent study and research, with the student's moving into the foreground and the teacher's role becoming that of consultant.

In the past two decades, a considerable amount of attention has been directed to the development of science programs at all levels, and there are available a variety of curriculum materials (K–12) from which to choose in implementing programs that meet local needs. National studies, financed by national foundations and governmental grants, eventuated in curricular programs that are available for classroom use. Available for elementary science programs are:

SAPA. Science as Process Approach, originating from action by the AASA

ESS. Elementary Science Study, providing maximum opportunity for individualization

SCIS. Science Curriculum Improvement Study

Available for secondary science programs are:

BSCS. Biology Programs

PSSC. Physics Programs

Project Physics. Harvard

Chem Study

All of these are available through major educational publishers.

Teaching strategies that help gifted students to achieve optimum participation in science incorporate their high intelligence, broad range of interests, superior study skills, and latent drive. The teacher's responsibility is to establish a learning situation with such characteristics as:

1. *A variety of information sources.* School and community libraries should be readily available, with provisions for students to have ready access to materials not usually used by their age peers.
2. *Mastery of essential study and research techniques.* If we are to help a student explore strong interest areas, we must help him or her to acquire the techniques for study and research that enable him or her to make a meaningful and valid exploration. Quite often this means that younger students need guidance in these skills at an earlier age than we ordinarily provide such training.
3. *Teaching in depth.* For the gifted student we should provide challenging situations that require the use of technical vocabulary and sophisticated research techniques.

4. *Exploration of the frontiers of knowledge.* In any area of science one soon reaches horizons with only conjecture of what lies beyond. For the gifted this can be a challenging moment and the teacher can seize on this opportunity for encouraging the development of creative thinking and ensuring sound procedural techniques in pursuing creative science explorations.
5. *Critical thinking.* Science knowledge is never static and the consistent questioning of accepted principles is what has given us our ever-expanding knowledge of the universe. The teacher can encourage and stimulate the kind of thinking that moves our understanding and insight into new dimensions, revising or discarding old concepts.
6. *Community resources.* Science is a curriculum area where community resources must be integrated into the ongoing learning processes.

It is difficult for the school today to offer students an adequate understanding of the world of science, which is characterized by ever-accelerated change. New theories and processes provide a myriad of scientific concepts with which the school classroom and laboratory are not always equipped to deal. Schools must turn to the industrial and research facilities in the community to help students and teachers gain insight into science as a vital factor in contemporary life.

MODERN LANGUAGES

Some experience with and some degree of skill in using a modern foreign language are indispensable elements in the education of the gifted. The international responsibilities of our nation make it imperative that our gifted citizens have a responsible proficiency in the use of at least one modern foreign language.

Generally the stress of specific foreign language courses for the gifted should center on development of major concepts, skills, principles, and content objectives, implemented by flexible teaching that enhances the child's potential for language achievement.

Since language study is best begun very early, the academically talented pupil should have an opportunity to begin a modern foreign language in the elementary school, whenever the proper conditions for such study exist and qualified instruction is available. At this age, the pupil learns language automatically as behavior, and not as a rational process. Such programs offer rich possibilities for the future of modern language study.

Recent developments in the national life and the world situation indicate a need for mastery of languages of the Near East, Russia, India, China, Japan, and Africa. These should augment the traditional offerings of western European languages (see Part II, Model 28, Russian Culture and Language).

Whenever it is possible under local conditions, it is highly desirable to create a special group or groups of students particularly talented in language study. The methods and materials used in this special group should be different, in order to facilitate better quality of result, greater depth and enrichment, more flexibility, and added individual responsibility. At the advanced level, students who show high potential should have an opportunity to follow special study plans, which may be similar to the Advanced Placement Program. Even in small schools, where separate sections are not feasible, the talented pupil should be served by encouraging individual initiative and progress.

MUSIC

Gifted learners need to be involved in playing, singing, creating, analyzing, and listening, to make music aesthetically important in their lives. Performance experiences provide natural and direct opportunities for involvement with real musical content.

Musical programs for the gifted should contain the seed of innovation. Children should be encouraged to explore new dimensions of artistic expression; new instruments and tonal effects; new combinations of rhythm, music, art, words, dance, and drama. New ways of learning should feature multimedia programming with individual control of pacing, and should encourage self-directed projects. Gifted children should be aware of traditional concepts and free to challenge them—including notation system—and to experiment with new and divergent ways to produce, organize, and record sounds that express fresh and original ideas in keeping with the times in which they live.

All students should be exposed to music, with reference not only to the art itself, but also to its genuine contribution to the full development of the person. Music is far from being vague or imprecise. It embodies certain elements of movement—rhythm, tempo, pitch, accent, dynamic shaping, tone quality— that give music a precise shape. The real goal in music education is to expand perception of this language, giving students the tools to make their own discoveries at whatever level they approach music.

The following content should be regarded as essential to a music program for gifted students; facts are of value only as they contribute to concept formation, the ability to draw valid generalizations, and the development of needed musical skills. The content for a music program should provide for:

Awareness of musical expression through rhythm, motion, and symmetry.

Musical projection through sequencing and articulation.

Consultation of relevant research and its implications for innovation.

Development of listener interest through musical principles and appreciation.

Development of aesthetic judgment.

Understanding of the cultural and historical value in music.

Development of musical concepts—ideas about abstract qualities of music that lead to an ability to generalize and categorize, or focus on and pursue a single abstraction, developing creative products, personal or social in their value.

Development of skills in performance, reading, listening, conducting, and other areas of applied music is of vital importance.

Creation of original products.

The development of musical concepts, ideas about abstract qualities of music that lead to an ability to generalize and categorize, should have a high priority. It must be remembered that the most important concepts are those concerned with basic properties of music and that the development of skills in performance, reading, listening, conducting, and other areas of applied music is of vital importance. However, not every student needs to acquire the same degree of proficiency in *all* skills.

ART

Art is a universal expression of experience and feeling emanating from talent trained in perception. The quality of art education can help save us from being locked into a static environment.

As in other subject areas, some children and youth are talented in one or more of the arts, and not necessarily at the expense of abilities in science or other disciplines. Quality instruction in art is particularly sensitive because of its personal dimension in the way it is linked to the young person's relatively fragile self-concept.

Art is an integral part of the human environment. Appreciation and historical significance of artists and art forms contribute to an imaginative and stimulating art program. Performance without preparation in these aesthetic values results in talent energy lacking direction and purpose.

The artistically talented need art training in depth as well as in breadth. Creativity has only recently assumed a special emphasis in general education, and yet creativity has been a fundamental aim of art education for decades. Art activity of itself does not ensure creative activity on the part of the students. Guidance by a teacher who is a talented and practicing artist will emphasize the creative rather than the conforming tradition of art.

Several important aims and enterprises need to be given close attention in the study and practice of art. These include observing and interpreting art and nature; gaining a mature knowledge of the arts, both past and present; developing self-understanding and strengthening one's self-image; and striving to maintain democratic conditions for people and ideas in art. The emphasis of a basic art course for the talented youth should include skill development in a variety of media, self-development through an individualized approach to the analysis and practice of art, and a personally relatable knowledge of art and the humanities.

In the scheduling of art classes, it must be remembered that creative assignments and projects are not likely to be completed satisfactorily within a prescribed amount of time, because individual differences are reflected to a greater extent in this educational area than in many others.

In the creative process the exploratory search for answers, the incubation of ideas, the conscious rethinking, and the closure on a final solution are frequent steps that a well-directed art project will bring out. Academically gifted students are noted for their high intellectual potential, but great variances in abilities and temperament exist among them. The uniqueness of the product of art, the artist himself or herself, and the process of art make this subject especially adaptable and challenging to the higher intellectual skills of the gifted.

THE SCHOOL LIBRARIAN: INSTRUCTIONAL PARTNER IN THE GIFTED AND TALENTED PROGRAM

[The following statement is taken from *The Pennsylvania Guide for School Library Media Specialists* (Pennsylvania School Librarians Association, 1978), pp. 84–85.]

The educationally effective school library is a learning laboratory which provides resources for learning, guidance in how to learn, and a climate and an environment conducive to learning. The school librarian is a teacher whose subject is learning itself. Because the librarian is a teacher of all students he or she is involved directly in all phases of the school's program for the intellectually gifted and creatively talented student—design, structure, implementation, and evaluation.

Educational experts recognize that excursions into learning by the gifted and talented student—inquiry, discovery, challenge, acceleration—mandate the scientifically planned and synchronized use of library resources and the individualized guidance of the school librarian. For example:

> Nowhere in the school is there to be found a more promising situation for the academically gifted . . . than in the library. (Cleary, Florence D. *Blueprints for Better Reading,* 2nd ed. New York: H. W. Wilson, 1972, p. 155.)

> The quality and availability of materials . . . will be major factors in whether or not the program [for the gifted] is successful. (Burns, Paul C., et al. *The Language Arts in Childhood Education,* 2nd ed. Chicago: Rand McNally, 1971, pp. 386–388.)

> The extent to which a successful library program will substantially improve the total reading program cannot be overestimated. Children who can choose from a wide range of carefully selected books, and who receive instruction in library and reference skills from a trained teacher-librarian, are likely to become more interested and capable readers. (Austin, Mary C., et al. *The First R: The Harvard Report on Reading in Elementary Schools.* New York: Macmillan, 1963, p. 232.)

> Because learning is an individual process, emphasis on learning produces a trend toward more individualized instruction. Ideally the laboratory and the library become centers of learning. (Conner, Forrest P., and William J. Ellena, eds. *Curriculum Handbook for School Administrators.* Washington, D.C.: American Association of School Administrators, 1967, pp. 257–258.)

> The resources of the library should be used continually to enrich the work in mathematics. The library is the heart of an enrichment program for the superior learner with special interest in mathematics. (Grossnickle, Foster E., et al. *Discovering Meanings in Elementary Mathematics,* 5th ed. New York: Holt, 1968, p. 440.)

> Studies have shown how closely good school libraries in elementary and secondary schools are related to academic achievement, to remaining in high school, and to going on to college. Project Talent, a research study covering almost half a million high school students, reports that the quality of the school library is, in fact, among the four most important factors closely associated with such measurements of student performance as staying in school, achievements, and going to college. (Keppel, Francis. *The Necessary Revolution in American Education.* New York: Harper and Row, 1966, pp. 132–133.)

> The scope of knowledge has become too vast to be covered extensively within the boundaries of classroom instruction, superior though that instruction might be. Through the school library, these boundaries can be extended immeasurably in all areas of knowledge and in all forms of creative expression, and the means provided to meet and to stimulate the many interests, appreciations, and curiosities of youth. . . . The extent to which many children and young people of today will be creative, informed, knowledgeable, and within their own years, wise, will be shaped by the boundaries of the content of the library resources available within their schools. (American Association of School Librarians. *Standards for School Library Programs.* Chicago: American Library Association, 1960, pp. 3–4.)

Critical, creative, and adventurous thinking (basic goals of the gifted and talented program) require appropriate raw materials for the fashioning of thought. "A creative idea can hardly be born if there is no rich medium in which it can grow."

(Kagan, Jerome, ed. *Creativity and Learning*. Boston: Beacon Press, n.d., p. viii.) Likewise, "Pupils do not learn to think critically by thinking critical thoughts about nothing in particular." (Carpenter, Helen McCracken, ed. *Skill Development in the Social Studies,* Thirty-third Yearbook. Washington, D.C.: National Council for the Social Studies, 1963, p. 33.)

LIBRARIAN AS MEMBER OF THE GATE TEACHING TEAM

The cooperation of the teacher and the librarian in planning for the effective and efficient use of library media, equipment, facilities, and staff is the keystone of a media support program.* Since curriculum is the *planned interaction* of students with content, resources, and instructional processes, face-to-face communication between teacher and/or teaching team and the librarian is absolutely essential to the success of the Gifted and Talented Program. The procedure that is recommended for the planned integration of the library support program with the gifted and talented teaching/learning program is as follows.

I. The teacher and the librarian in a scheduled conference determine the development and support needs of the unit or teaching plan by identifying
   A. Unit goals
   B. Behavioral objectives
   C. Special class, group, and individual student needs, interests, goals, abilities, progress rates, and concerns
   D. Specific topics, concepts, skills, and attitudes, to be introduced, reinforced, and extended
II. The teacher and the librarian analyze the basic components of the unit or teaching plan that require the direct support of instructional media by
   A. Identifying specific topics in the *cognitive area* under the following headings
      1. What persons?   4. What events?
      2. What places?   5. What concepts?
      3. What things?   6. What fundamentals?
   B. Identifying specific topics in the *affective area*
      1. What attitudes?   3. What value judgments?
      2. What appreciations?   4. What self-perceptions?
   C. Identifying specific thinking-learning-communicating skills
      1. Listening   9. Making assumptions
      2. Recalling   10. Analyzing
      3. Observing   11. Criticizing
      4. Outlining   12. Problem solving
      5. Comparing   13. Interpreting
      6. Summarizing   14. Synthesizing
      7. Classifying   15. Communicating
      8. Generalizing
   D. Identifying specific possibilities for tie-ins with previous learnings
   E. Identifying culminating activities
   F. Identifying evaluation procedures and techniques

*Adapted from *The School Library Media Program: Instructional Force for Excellence* (New York: R. R. Bowker, 1979), pp. 89–91.

III. The teacher and the librarian share the responsibility for
    A. Determining how each topic can best be developed
    B. Determining which experiences will be required of
       1. The entire class
       2. Special groups
       3. Individual students
    C. Designing strategies for
       1. Introduction of unit
       2. Linking ideas
       3. Stimulating creativity
       4. Encouraging group interaction
       5. Stimulating divergent thinking
       6. Sustaining interest
       7. Encouraging student self-evaluation of progress
    D. Designing appropriate learning guides
    E. Designing optional and/or branching experiences and activities
    F. Determining which learning experiences can best occur
       1. In the classroom
       2. In the library media center
       3. In the large-group instruction room
       4. In the seminar rooms
       5. In other areas of the school
       6. In the community
    G. Giving consideration to the following
       1. How can understanding be facilitated?
       2. How can learning be developed logically?
       3. How can learning be individualized?
       4. How can failure be avoided?
       5. How can boredom and frustration be minimized?
       6. How can interest be motivated, sustained, and rewarded?
       7. How can creativity be stimulated?
       8. How can previous learnings be reinforced and extended?
       9. How can relevancy be assured?
       10. How can open-ended learning be encouraged?
       11. How can learning be extended into other curricular and cocurricular areas?
       12. How can alternative enrichment experiences be provided?
IV. The librarian builds a media support program to match the developmental needs of the teacher's unit or plan by
    A. Searching for appropriate media
    B. Determining media usage sequences and patterns
    C. Designing optional learning experiences
    D. Designing and producing or planning to have the students produce media to meet special needs
    E. Assembling and grouping media
 V. The teacher and the librarian share the responsibility for implementing the library media support plan
    A. The teacher preschedules class, group, and individual student
       1. Use of the library media center
       2. Use of other school facilities

    3. Field trips and laboratory experiences
    4. Culminating activities
  B. The students work in the library media center
    1. The librarian serves as teacher, consultant, and mentor
      a. Orienting the class to new tools, new techniques, and procedures
      b. Working directly with groups and individuals
      c. Encouraging students to explore beyond the prescribed learning experiences
    2. The students in conference with the teacher determine program adjustment and modification
VI. The teacher and the librarian determine the effectiveness of the media support program as evidenced in this unit
  A. The librarian, at the invitation of the teacher, participates in the culminating activities
  B. The librarian solicits suggestions and criticisms from the students
  C. The teacher shares with the librarian his or her evaluation of the effectiveness of the unit
    1. Identifying learning experiences and activities that were successful
    2. Identifying learning experiences and activities that were less than successful and need to be deleted or modified
    3. Identifying areas of student interest that emerged during the teaching of the unit and are to become part of the unit when next taught
    4. Suggesting possible changes in content, process, and media usage when unit is next taught
  D. The librarian makes an anecdotal record of changes to be made in the content of the unit and in the procedure
    1. Files the unit outline, work sheets, bibliographies, learning guides, and anecdotal report in the library media center's curriculum file under the teacher's name
    2. Adds to the "To Be Purchased List" the added copies of titles needed for this unit
    3. Adds to the "Areas and Topics Needing Additional Materials List" those areas and topics not adequately covered in the existing collection.

PILOT PROJECTS

It is recommended practice that each new instructional program be field-tested as a pilot project before being put into use throughout the system. The purpose of the pilot project is to determine the adequacy, quality, effectiveness, learner appeal, and teachability of the program. The International Institute for Educational Planning, in its *Handbook of Curriculum Evaluation,* advocates the field testing of instructional programs in order "to determine in some detail what needs to be revised as well as why and where the revision is needed."[36]

The North Hills School District field-tests new programs via the pilot project method. Figure 3, Pilot Projects; Example 6, Pilot Project Design and Analysis Guide; and Checklist 4, Learning Project Evaluation Report, outline the procedures involved in field-testing a proposed instructional program.

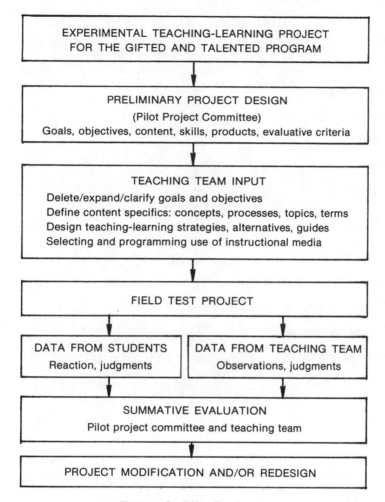

FIGURE 3. Pilot Projects.

EXAMPLE 6   PILOT PROJECT DESIGN AND ANALYSIS GUIDE

Project Title _____

Teachers Involved _____

School _____ Grade Levels _____

Number of Students Involved _____

Number of Class Periods Required _____

Project Began _____ Project Ended _____

Project Goals:

Project Objectives:

Project Content:
    Concepts—

      Persons—

      Places—

      Things—

EXAMPLE 6 (cont.)

Events—

Processes—

Terminology—

Skills—

Attitudes—

Appreciations—

Judgments—

Teaching-Learning Strategies:
Orientation procedures—

Motivational procedures—

Group interaction procedures—

Divergent thinking experiences—

Culminating activities—

Teaching-Learning Guides:

Field Experiences:

Instructional Media:
Print—

Nonprint—

Resource People:

Project Evaluation:
Student Reactions—

Teacher Observations—

Teacher Concerns and Reservations—

Teacher Recommendations—

Teacher's Signature _____ Date _____

CHECKLIST 4   LEARNING PROJECT EVALUATION REPORT

Teacher _____   Date _____
Learning Project _____   Grade(s) _____
Date Project Introduced _____   Date Project Concluded _____

	Low				High
1. How adequate is the title of this project? Comment:	1	2	3	4	5
2. How significant is this project? Comment:	1	2	3	4	5
3. Are the objectives attainable? Comment:	1	2	3	4	5
4. Do the learning activities match the spectrum of student interest? Comment:	1	2	3	4	5
5. Do the students bring to this project adequate background knowledge? Comment:	1	2	3	4	5
6. Are the suggested teaching strategies effective? Comment:	1	2	3	4	5
7. How adequate are the instructional media? Comment:	1	2	3	4	5
8. How did the students rate this project? Comment:	1	2	3	4	5
9. How do you rate this project? Comment:	1	2	3	4	5

GATE PROGRAM OF STUDIES

ELEMENTARY LEVEL (K–6)

1. Provision is made within the regular language arts, science, social studies, art, music, and physical education classes to enrich and individualize class learning experiences to accommodate the special competences and performance levels of the gifted and talented children. Approximately half of the elementary gifted student's time is spent in regular classes.
2. Accelerated learning programs are offered in separate differentiated programs:
   a. *Mathematics level program.* Approximately 5 hours a week of the elementary gifted student's time is spent in a cross-grade, multilevel math program.
   b. *Reading levels program.* Approximately 8 hours of the primary-level gifted student's time is spent in a cross-grade, multilevel reading program. Approximately five hours of the middle-grade level gifted student's time is spent in a cross-grade, multilevel reading program.

  c. *Differentiated GATE (Gifted and Talented Enrichment) Program.* Approximately two hours a week of the elementary gifted student's time is spent in a block-time two-hour session. Approximately one hour a week of the fifth- and sixth-grade gifted student's time is spent learning the Russian language.
  d. Independent study with a tutor or mentor is provided on all levels, K–6.

SECONDARY LEVEL (JR. HIGH SCHOOL)

1. The junior high school program for the gifted and talented offers three basic types of enrichment/acceleration learning experiences
  a. *Honors Courses*
     English
     Foreign languages
     Mathematics
     Science
     Social studies
  b. *Independent Study* (under the guidance of tutor or mentor)
  c. *Seminars*

SECONDARY LEVEL (SR. HIGH SCHOOL)

The senior high school program for the gifted and talented offers the following options:

1. *Advanced Placement Courses*
American History	French
Biology	German
Calculus	Latin
Chemistry	Physics
Composition	Spanish
English	Studio Art

2. *Honors Courses*
Advanced Composition	Creative Writing
American Studies	English Literature
American Values	Language Skills for College
College Mathematics—Liberal Arts	Research Skills for College
College Mathematics—Science and Engineering	World Cultures
Contemporary Literature	World Literature

3. *Independent Study*
American History	Government and Politics
Anthropology	Graphic Arts
Archaeology	Journalism
Art	Mathematics
Careers	Music
Economics	Photography
Electronic Communication	Science and Technology
English	Social Problems
European History	Studio Art
Filmmaking	Theater
Foreign Languages	

4. *Foreign Exchange Study Programs*
5. *College Courses*
6. *Early Admission to College*

SPECIAL FACILITIES

Career Resource Center

Computer Center

GATE Resource Center* (see Checklist 5, Resource Kits Available from the GATE Resource Center)

Instructional Materials Center†

Learning Laboratories‡

   Humanities

   Science/Math

Libraries

   Elementary: each of the 9 elementary schools, K–6

   Jr. High: each of the 2 junior high schools, 8–9

   Intermediate High: grades 9–10

   Sr. High: grades 11–12

Planetarium

Seminar rooms/Conference rooms/Viewing-listening-taping-typing rooms

Television Production Studio

CHECKLIST 5   RESOURCE KITS AVAILABLE FROM THE GATE RESOURCE CENTER

Kit No.	Title and Grade Level
1	I Am Me (K–1)
2	Meet My Friends, Nathaniel Benchley and Arnold Lobel (K–1)
3	Meet My Friends, Stan and Jan Berenstain (K–2)
4	Meet My Friend, Paul Galdone (K–2) (2 boxes)
5	Meet My Friends, Russell and Lillian Hoban (K–1)
6	Meet My Friend, Brian Wildsmith (K–1) (2 boxes)

*The GATE Resource Center provides resource kits for each GATE teaching/learning unit, K–6. These resource kits include all of the print (books, pamphlets, laboratory guides, museum learning guides, etc.) and nonprint (filmstrips, cassettes, disc recordings, art prints, study prints, maps, charts, graphs, slides, motion pictures, videotapes, etc.) media basic for the comprehensive *introduction* of the unit to the GATE students. Since open-ended learning and idea linkage are hallmarks of the GATE Program, no prepackaged resource kit could possibly foresee the myriad resources that will be essential for matching student interest and for providing adequate topic development. The school library, therefore, is the GATE learning laboratory, which provides the depth, breadth, and relevance essential for actualizing the promise of "learning unlimited." [The contents of resource kits are listed for a number of the programs included in Part II, Instructional Programs for the Gifted and Talented.]

†The district instructional materials center, in addition to providing a wealth of curriculum support media, provides a data terminal linkup with the Northland Public Library computer. This dial-access system provides instant retrieval of the Northland Library holdings by author, illustrator, title, and subject.

‡The Humanities Learning Laboratory and the Science/Math Learning Laboratory provide specialized media collections, basic reference tools, career resources, typewriters with math and/or science symbols, and work-study areas. A subject coordinator or teaching specialist is available for consultation and guidance in each center.

CHECKLIST 5 (cont.)

Kit No.	Title and Grade Level
7	Meet My Friend, Don Freeman (K–1)
8	Stories for Joining In (K–1)
9	Exploring with Color (K–1) (3 boxes)
10	I Can Read about Ghosts and Other Scary Things (1–2) (2 boxes)
11	Your Neighborhood: Workers and Friends (1–2) (11 boxes)
12	The Circus (K–3) (2 boxes)
13	Dinosaurs (K–3) (2 boxes)
14	Planning the Menu for Cinderella's Party (2–3) (3 boxes)
15	The Seasons of the Year (2–3)
16	Aesop's Fables (2–4)
17	Fun with Words (3) (2 boxes)
18	Meet My Friend, Edna Miller (2–3)
19	Meet My Friend, Janusz Grabianski (2–3)
20	The Why and How of the Calendar (2–3)
21	American Tall Tales (3–4) (2 boxes)
22	Indians of North America—Eastern United States (2–3) (4 boxes)
23	Indians of North America—Western United States (2–3) (6 boxes)
24	Best Loved Fairy Tales from Europe (3–4) (2 boxes)
25	A Walk About in Australia (3–4)
26	Alaska (3–4)
27	Cold Lands (3–4)
28	The Vikings (3–4)
29	Getting to Know the Japanese (3–4) (4 boxes)
30	Japanese Realia (3–12)
31	Volcanoes (4–6)
32	Hawaii (3–4) (3 boxes)
33	Meet Marguerite Henry, Newberry Award Winner (3–5) (3 boxes)
34	Reading Poetry for Fun (K–4)
35	Learning about Reptiles and Amphibians (4–6)
36	Learning about Insects and Spiders (4–6)
37	Becoming Acquainted with Old Glory (5–6) (2 boxes)
38	Threatened Western Wildlife (5–6) (2 boxes)
39	Westward Ho! The Wagons (5) (13 boxes)
40	Midwest and the Plains (5) (2 boxes)
41	Colonial America (5) (3 boxes)
42	Colonial America: Revolutionary War (5) (3 boxes)
43	The Northeast (5) (5 boxes)
44	The South: The Civil War (5) (4 boxes)
45	The South: Everglades (5) (3 boxes)
46	The South: Literature and Music (5) (3 boxes)
47	The South: Slavery (5) (2 boxes)
48	California and the West (5) (5 boxes)
49	Women Who Have Made a Difference (5–8) (4 boxes)
50	Seeing with the Inner Eye (5–8)
51	Greek and Roman Mythology (5–8) (2 boxes)
52	The Miracle of Plants (5–8) (3 boxes)
53	Stories to Blow Your Cool (5–6) (2 boxes)
54	Exploring the Ocean World (6–8) (3 boxes)
55	Poetry: Serious and Otherwise (5–8)
56	Mind Boggling Phenomena (5–8) (2 boxes)
57	The Wizardry of Words (6–8) (2 boxes)
58	The History of Transportation (5–8) (3 boxes)
59	Canada (6)
60	The Caribbean (6)
61	Mexico (6) (6 boxes)
62	If I Had Lived during the Middle Ages (6–8) (2 boxes)
63	An Anthropologist Studies Rain Forest Cultures (6–8) (2 boxes)
64	Learning about Ecology (6–8) (2 boxes)

CHECKLIST 5 (cont.)

Kit No.	Title and Grade Level
65	The Wonderful World of Plants (2–3) (3 boxes)
66	Arty Things to Do—Cartooning (3–6)
67	The Wonderful World of Animals (2–3) (3 boxes)
68	Communication (3) (2 boxes)
69	Dreams of Freedom: Ethnic Minorities (5–8) (3 boxes)
70	Folk Tales, Legends, and Myths (3–5)
S1*	Getting to Know Me (K–1)
S2	How Can I Find Out? (K–1)
S3	Getting Along in School (K–1)
S4	Read and Reason (K–1)
S5	Sing Along, Play Along (K–1)
S6	Laugh with Us (K–1)
S7	Tales of Winnie the Witch (K–1)
S8	Listen to Learn (K–1)
S9	How to Grow Book Worms (K–3)
S10	Visit a Country: Hear Its Stories (K–3)
S11	Charlotte's Web (3–5)
S12	Davy Crockett (5)
S13	First Man Down the Colorado; and High Flying Spy (5)
S14	Legacy of the Incas (6)
S15	Museum Replica: Rosetta Stone (3–12)
S16	Show Me a Poem (3–5)
S17	Civilizations of Early America (5–8)
S18	Exploring Wilderness Trails (5–8)
S19	Literature for Children: Animals, Distant Lands, Fairy Tales, Humor (4–6)
S20	Literature for Children: Poetry (4–6)
S21	Beverly Cleary Interview (3–6)
S22	Clyde Bulla Interview (3–6)
S23	Doris Gates Interview (3–6)
S24	Zilpha Snyder Interview (3–6)
S25	Theodore Taylor Interview (3–6)
S26	How to Write Poetry (4–6)
S27	Write Yourself a Fairy Tale (3–4)
S28	Jean Craighead George Interview (3–6)
S29	Scott O'Dell Interview (3–6)
S30	Sid Fleischman Interview (3–6)
S31	Richard Chase Interview (3–6)
S32	Call It Courage (4–6)
S33	John Philip Sousa Band in Concert (4–8)
S34	Door in the Wall (6)
S35	I, Juan de Pareja (6–8)
S36	Julie of the Wolves (4–8)
S37	The Loner (4–6)
S38	An Ever Hungrier World (6–8)
S39	Old Ramon (5–8)
S40	Sing Down the Moon (3–5)
S41	Bambi (3–4)
S42	Ben and Me (3–4)

*Single concept resource kit

IDENTIFICATION FORMS USED IN THE GATE PROGRAM OF STUDIES

[Checklist 6, Intellectual Processes Rating Scale; Checklist 7, Criteria for Identification of the Mentally Gifted Student (Grades 1–12); Checklist 8, A Student Looks at Himself/Herself; and Checklist 9, Teacher Evaluation, are presented below.]

CHECKLIST 6   INTELLECTUAL PROCESSES RATING SCALE*

Name _____ Birth date _____ Grade _____

Teacher _____ District _____ Date _____

Rate each statement by putting an X on the appropriate line after the statement. The lines are numbered 1 to 5 and represent the degree to which you have noticed the described intellectual process. The bases for making a judgment are given as follows.

INTELLECTUAL PROCESSES:†

1. You have not noticed this process.
2. You have noticed this process to a slight degree.
3. You have noticed this process to a considerable degree.
4. You have noticed this process to a large degree.
5. You have noticed this process to a very large degree.

	Rating Scale				
Item to Be Evaluated	1	2	3	4	5
1. Cognition (the process of discovery, rediscovery, recognition, comprehension, and understanding)	—	—	—	—	—
2. Memory (the retention of information in any form accumulated through in-school and out-of-school experiences)	—	—	—	—	—
3. Convergent production (the production of information from given information where the emphasis is upon achieving conventionally accepted or best outcomes)	—	—	—	—	—
4. Divergent production (the production of information from given information where the emphasis is upon a variety of ideas from the same source)	—	—	—	—	—
5. Evaluation (to reach decisions or make judgments concerning the goodness—correctness, suitability, adequacy, desirability—of information in terms of criteria of identity consistency and goal satisfaction	—	—	—	—	—
Subtotals (number of X's in each column):	—	—	—	—	—
Total for all columns:					_____

INTELLECTUAL ABILITIES AND SKILLS‡

1. You have not noticed this intellectual ability and skill.
2. You have noticed this intellectual ability and skill to a slight degree.
3. You have noticed this intellectual ability and skill to a considerable degree.
4. You have noticed this intellectual ability and skill to a large degree.
5. You have noticed this intellectual ability and skill to a very large degree.

*This composite rating scale is taken from part of the Berks Elementary Enrichment Program, Inter. Unit #14, Reading, Pa.

†This part is adapted from J. P. Guilford and P. R. Merrifield, "The Structure of Intellect Model: Its Uses and Implications," *Reports from the Psychological Laboratory,* no. 24. Los Angeles: University of Southern California, April 1960.

‡This part is adapted from Benjamin S. Bloom and D. R. Krathwohl, *Taxonomy of Educational Objectives* (New York: David McKay Co., Inc., 1956, 1964), and "Test-Item Folio No. 1" and Sec. III Appendices, *Questions and Problems in Science* (Princeton, N.J.: Educational Testing Service, 1956).

CHECKLIST 6 (cont.)

Item to Be Evaluated	Rating Scale				
	1	2	3	4	5
1. *Knowledge* is finding in a task or problem the appropriate signals, cues, and clues which will bring out stored knowledge.	—	—	—	—	—
a. Knowledge of specifics (to recall specific and isolable bits of information—very low level of abstraction)	—	—	—	—	—
b. Knowledge of terminology (to know the referents most appropriate to a given use of specific verbal and nonverbal symbols)	—	—	—	—	—
c. Knowledge of specific facts (to know dates, events, places, and the like, with precision or approximation)	—	—	—	—	—
d. Knowledge of ways and means of dealing with specifics (to be aware of organizing, studying, judging, and criticizing patterns of organization)	—	—	—	—	—
e. Knowledge of conventions (to be conscious of the characteristic way of treating and presenting ideas and phenomena)	—	—	—	—	—
f. Knowledge of trends and sequences (to know the processes, direction, and movements of phenomena with respect to time)	—	—	—	—	—
g. Knowledge of classifications and categories (to know of the fundamental classes, sets, divisions, and arrangements of a purpose, a problem, and the like)	—	—	—	—	—
h. Knowledge of criteria (to be aware of the criteria by which facts, principles, opinions, and conduct are tested or judged)	—	—	—	—	—
i. Knowledge of methodology (to be aware of the methods of inquiry, techniques, and procedures employed in investigating phenomena)	—	—	—	—	—
j. Knowledge of the universals and abstractions in a field (to know the major ideas, schemes, and patterns by which phenomena and ideas are organized—highest form of abstraction and complexity)	—	—	—	—	—
k. Knowledge of principles and generalizations (to recognize the abstractions which are of value in explaining, describing, predicting, or determining the most relevant action or direction to be taken)	—	—	—	—	—
l. Knowledge of theories and structures (to know the body of principles and generalizations together with their interrelations which present a clear, rounded, and systematic view of a complex field—most abstract formulations)	—	—	—	—	—
2. *Comprehension* is knowing what is being communicated and using the idea even though not perceiving the fullest implications.	—	—	—	—	—
a. Translation (to paraphrase, to render, or to alter the form of the original communication with accuracy)	—	—	—	—	—

CHECKLIST 6 (cont.)

Item to Be Evaluated	Rating Scale				
	1	2	3	4	5
b. Interpretation (to explain or summarize the communication by reorganization or rearrangement)	—	—	—	—	—
c. Extrapolations (to extend the given data to determine implications, consequences, corollaries, effects, and the like in accordance with the original communication)	—	—	—	—	—
3. *Analysis* is breaking down a communication into its elements or parts to clarify the hierarchy or the relation of ideas.	—	—	—	—	—
a. Analysis of elements (to distinguish between facts and hypotheses and to recognize unstated assumptions)	—	—	—	—	—
b. Analysis of relationships (to recognize the connections and interactions between elements and parts of a communication)	—	—	—	—	—
c. Analysis of organizational principles (to recognize the form, pattern, and structure, both explicit and implicit, which make the communication a unit)	—	—	—	—	—
4. *Synthesis* is putting together elements and parts into a whole pattern or structure not clearly there before.	—	—	—	—	—
a. Production of a unique communication (to communicate ideas, feelings, and experiences of others)	—	—	—	—	—
b. Production of a plan or proposed set of operations (to develop a plan of work or a proposal of a plan of operations that satisfies the requirements of the task)	—	—	—	—	—
c. Derivation of a set of abstract relations (to develop a set of abstract relations either to classify or explain phenomena, or to deduce propositions or relations from a set of basic propositions or symbolic representatives)	—	—	—	—	—
5. *Evaluation* is judging the value of purposes, ideas, methods, and the like, involving criteria as well as standards of appraisal.	—	—	—	—	—
a. Judgments in terms of internal evidence (to evaluate the accuracy of a communication by the logical relationships evident in it)	—	2	—	4	—
b. Judgments in terms of external criteria (to evaluate the material with reference to selected or remembered criteria)	—	—	—	—	—
Subtotals (number of X's in each column):	—	—	—	—	—

Total for all columns: _____

Section Totals: Knowledge_____; Comprehension_____; Analysis_____;
Synthesis_____; Evaluation_____

Final Total: _____

CHECKLIST 7   CRITERIA FOR IDENTIFICATION OF THE MENTALLY GIFTED STUDENT
(GRADES 1–12)

Student _____   Grade _____

Teacher(s) _____   Date _____

_____

In nominating a student for participation in the Gifted and Talented Enrichment Program, please indicate the degree to which you have observed the following characteristics in the student.*

Characteristics to Be Evaluated	Slight	Moderate	Marked
1. *High Academic Achievement.* The gifted student shows as much unevenness in subject matter abilities as do other children, but his overall grade point average is usually high. He requires less detailed and fewer repeated instructions, often anticipating them. He works readily with symbols, such as words and numbers, in place of direct experience and the actual objects.	—	—	—
2. *Advanced Vocabulary and Reading Level.* The gifted student has a large vocabulary that he uses easily and accurately. He retains what he has heard or read without much rote or drill. He can read books that are one or two years in advance of the rest of the class. He usually reads at an early age.	—	—	—
3. *Expressive Fine Arts Talent.* The gifted student's wide range of interests stems from his vivid imagination. He is able to solve problems in aesthetic fields and can visualize actions and things from descriptions. He frequently creates original stories, plays, poetry, tunes, and sketches. He can use materials, words, or ideas in new ways.	—	—	—
4. *Wholesome Personal-Social Adjustment.* The gifted student adjusts easily to new associates and situations. He is alert, keenly observant, and responds quickly. He possesses a keen sense of humor and incorporates suggestions from others into his own thinking and actions. His companions are often one or two years older, but they recognize his superior ability in planning, organizing, and promoting. He also displays evidence of emotional stability in ordinary behavior.	—	—	—
5. *Early Physical Competence.* The gifted student is usually characterized by his early physical development. He has a tendency to be taller, heavier, and has fewer physical defects. Not only does he enjoy outdoor games preferred by average children, but tends to excel in these games. He usually enjoys superior health and, as a result, has fewer absences from school due to illness. He also possesses especially good eye-hand coordination.	—	—	—

*Pennsylvania Department of Education, *Guidelines for the Operation of Special Education Programs for the Mentally Gifted,* 1974, pp. 18–20.

CHECKLIST 7 (cont.)

Characteristics to Be Evaluated	Slight	Moderate	Marked
6. *Superior Intellectual Ability.* The gifted student exhibits superior ability in reasoning, generalizing, thinking logically, and comprehension. He is able to perform highly difficult mental tasks and to learn more rapidly and more easily than most children. This child also has a longer concentration span and is keenly aware of the processes of his environment.	—	—	—
7. *Effective Independent Work.* The gifted student displays his competence for effective independent work by evaluating himself and modifying his behavior accordingly. He possesses superior insight into problems, is not easily influenced, and is less prone to change his mind once an opinion is formed. His effectiveness is also displayed by applying learning from one situation to more difficult situations.	—	—	—
8. *Persistent Curiosity.* The gifted student displays a deep-seated interest in some subject or field. In an attempt to gratify this insatiable curiosity he may also enjoy using encyclopedias, dictionaries, maps, globes, and other references.	—	—	—
9. *Strong Creative and Incentive Power.* The gifted student possesses high-powered intellectual curiosity, imagination, and creativity. He has unusual power to see new structures and processes and to express his visions in speaking, writing, art, music, or some other form. His work has freshness, vitality, and uniqueness. An individual may create new ideas and substances or he may invent and build new mechanical devices. He sometimes runs counter to tradition and is continually questioning the status quo. He may do the unexpected.	—	—	—
10. *Special Scientific Ability.* The gifted student with scientific talent will use the scientific method of thinking. He will enjoy scientific research methods and will grasp scientific concepts in short periods of time. He will display a curiosity about the natural world. He is not easily discouraged by failure or experiments or projects and will seek causes and reasons for things. He will spend much time on special projects of his own such as making a collection, construction of a radio, and making electronic computers.	—	—	—
11. *High Energy Level.* The gifted student displays a high level of energy. He keeps active by undertaking and completing task after task. He participates in various extracurricular activities, holding leadership roles in many, and frequently concentrates on long-range, unattainable, and poorly defined goals.	—	—	—
12. *Demonstrated Leadership Ability.* The gifted student displays an ability to help a group reach its goals. He often will improve human relationships within a group and will achieve prominence by individual effort. He enters into activities with enthusiasm and is able to influence others to work toward desirable or undesirable goals. He can take charge of the group.	—	—	—

CHECKLIST 7 (cont.)

Characteristics to Be Evaluated	Slight	Moderate	Marked
13. *Well-Developed Mechanical Skills.* The gifted student who possesses mechanical ability may be identified by unusual manipulative skills and spatial ability. He excels on craft projects and is interested in mechanical gadgets, devices, and machines. He comprehends mechanical problems and puzzles and likes to draw plans and sketches of mechanical objects.	—	—	—

Comments _____

_____

_____

_____

_____

CHECKLIST 8 A STUDENT LOOKS AT HIMSELF/HERSELF

Please show whether you agree or disagree with each of the statements by marking one of the spaces.

	Strongly Agree	Agree	Disagree	Strongly Disagree
1. I am a good athlete.	—	—	—	—
2. I am a good student.	—	—	—	—
3. I am popular with other students.	—	—	—	—
4. I am one who understands and accepts other people.	—	—	—	—
5. I am very sociable and know how to get along with people.	—	—	—	—
6. Other people recognize that I am an intelligent person.	—	—	—	—
7. I am warm and understanding.	—	—	—	—
8. I am easy to get along with.	—	—	—	—
9. I enjoy working with scientific and mechanical things.	—	—	—	—
10. I enjoy abstract or mathematical problems.	—	—	—	—
11. I am one who likes to work independently on special projects.	—	—	—	—
12. I enjoy debating or discussing an idea.	—	—	—	—
13. I enjoy "losing myself" in a good book or in imagination.	—	—	—	—
14. I have a good sense of humor.	—	—	—	—
15. My work is often quite original.	—	—	—	—
16. I am able to come up with a large number of ideas or solutions to problems.	—	—	—	—

CHECKLIST 8 (cont.)

	Strongly Agree	Agree	Disagree	Strongly Disagree
17. I am able to take charge of planning a project.	—	—	—	—
18. I don't mind being different from other students.	—	—	—	—
19. I like to study subjects that are challenging or difficult.	—	—	—	—
20. I often use music, art, or drama to express my feelings.	—	—	—	—
21. I don't like to accept what someone else says without challenging it.	—	—	—	—
22. I feel strongly about things and often express my feelings even if I think others will disagree.	—	—	—	—
23. I spend more time than I would need to on assignments because I enjoy the learning.	—	—	—	—

24. Here are six areas of talent. In which area do you see yourself as being most talented? Rank them as you see them applying to your abilities. (1) First talent area, (2) Second talent area, etc.

_____General intellectual ability

_____Specific academic aptitude (in one subject area, such as science, math)

_____Creative thinking

_____Leadership ability

_____Visual and performing arts

_____Psychomotor ability (such as mechanical skills or athletic ability)

CLASS SUMMARY SHEET GIFTED AND TALENTED

Teacher _____   Date _____

School _____   Grade _____

Talent Areas

Student's Name	Intellectual	Academic (specify)	Leadership	Creative Thinking	Visual Perform. Arts	Psycho-motor
_____						
_____						
_____						
_____						
_____						
_____						
_____						
_____						
_____						

CHECKLIST 9   TEACHER EVALUATION

This evaluation list of personal qualities that each pupil possesses should help us in formulating individual programs.

Name _____   School _____

Which of these characteristics have you observed in this pupil?

_____ Uses vocabulary beyond age level

_____ Learns processes rapidly

_____ Memorizes quickly

_____ Perceives abstract ideas readily

_____ Sees elements of a problem clearly

_____ Can generalize from given facts

_____ Has great curiosity about nature of man and universe

_____ Follows complex directions easily

_____ Shows resourcefulness in use of materials

_____ Has high degree of self-criticism

_____ Possesses unusual imagination

_____ Reacts quickly in most situations

_____ Has greater than average concentration and attention span

_____ Demonstrates initiative in planning with a group

_____ Organizes personal tasks effectively

_____ Is a rapid reader

_____ Spends considerable time reading

_____ Reading covers a wide range of subjects

_____ Retains easily what he has read

_____ Makes frequent and effective use of the library

_____ Sets up personal reading programs

_____ Shows interest in science

_____ Likes to write creatively

_____ Talks easily before a group

_____ Possesses manual dexterity

_____ Demonstrates good taste in matters of art

_____ Pursues hobbies with keen interest

NOTES

1. L. M. Terman, *Genetic Studies of Genius,* vol. 1, *Mental and Physical Traits of a Thousand Gifted Children* (Stanford, Calif.: Stanford University Press, 1925), p. vii.
2. *General Education in a Free Society: A Report of the Harvard Committee* (Cambridge, Mass.: Harvard University Press, 1945), p. 79.
3. Ibid., p. 81.
4. Ibid., p. 86.
5. Excerpts from *The Pursuit of Excellence: Manpower and Education,* which appeared in *Prospect for America.* Copyright © 1958, 1959, 1960, 1961 by Rockefeller Brothers Fund, Inc. Reprinted by permission of Doubleday & Company, Inc., p. 35.
6. Ibid.
7. Ibid.
8. Ibid.
9. *Goals for Americans,* © 1960 by the American Assembly Columbia University. Reprinted by permission of Prentice-Hall, Inc., Englewood Cliffs, N.J., p. 53.
10. Ibid., p. 56.
11. Ibid., p. 81.
12. Ibid., pp. 84–85.
13. Ibid.
14. Arnold Toynbee, "Is America Neglecting Her Creative Talents?" in *Creativity across Education,* ed. by Calvin Taylor (Ogden: University of Utah Press, 1968), p. 1.
15. *Guidelines for the Operation of Special Education Programs for the Mentally Gifted* (Harrisburg, Pa.: Pennsylvania Department of Public Instruction, 1974), p. 8.

16. U.S. Commissioner of Education, *Education of the Gifted and Talented: A Report to the Congress of the United States* (Washington, D.C.: U.S. Department of Health, Education, and Welfare, 1972).
17. Joseph S. Renzulli and Robert K. Hartman, "Scale for Rating Behavioral Characteristics of Superior Students," in *Exceptional Children*, November 1971, pp. 243–247.
18. E. Paul Torrance, *Creativity in the Classroom*, What Research Says to the Teacher Series (Washington, D.C.: National Education Association, 1977), p. 6.
19. *Guidelines for the Operation of Special Education Programs*, pp. 1–2.
20. *Becoming an Educated Person* (Pittsburgh, Pa.: North Hills School District, 1975).
21. Edgar Dale, *Building a Learning Environment* (Bloomington, Ind.: Phi Delta Kappa, 1972), pp. 41–50.
22. *Guidelines for the Operation of Special Education Programs*, pp. 42–45.
23. John F. Putnam and W. Dale Chismore, eds., *Standard Terminology for Curriculum and Instruction in Local and State School Systems* (Washington, D.C.: U.S. Department of Health, Education, and Welfare, 1970), p. 3.
24. *Guidelines for the Operation of Special Education Programs*, pp. 4–6.
25. Benjamin S. Bloom et al., eds., *Taxonomy of Educational Objectives: The Classification of Educational Goals*, Handbook I: *Cognitive Domain*. Copyright © 1956 by Longman Inc. Reprinted with permission of Longman Inc., New York.
26. David R. Krathwohl et al., *Taxonomy of Educational Objectives: The Classification of Educational Goals*, Handbook II *Affective Domain*. Copyright © 1964 by Longman Inc. Reprinted with permission of Longman Inc., New York.
27. J. P. Guilford, *The Nature of Human Intelligence* (New York: McGraw-Hill, 1967), frontispiece.
28. E. Paul Torrance, "What It Means to Become Human," in *To Nurture Humaneness: Commitment for the 70's*, ed. by Mary-Margaret Scobey and Grace Graham (Washington, D.C.: Association for Supervision and Curriculum Development, National Education Association, 1970), pp. 3–7.
29. E. Paul Torrance, "Toward the More Humane Education of Gifted Children," in *Creativity: Its Educational Implications*, comp. by John Curtis Gowan et al. (New York: John Wiley, 1967), pp. 53–70.
30. Frank E. Williams, *Classroom Ideas for Encouraging Thinking and Feeling* (Buffalo, N.Y.: D. O. K. Publishers, 1970).
31. Ralph J. Hallman, "The Necessary and Sufficient Conditions of Creativity," in *Creativity*, pp. 16–17. Reprinted with permission of the *Journal of Humanistic Psychology*, Spring 1963.
32. Sidney J. Parnes, "Education and Creativity," in *Creativity*, p. 36.
33. William Burton, Roland Kimball, and Richard Wing, *Education for Effective Thinking* (New York: Appleton-Century-Crofts, 1960).
34. Jerome S. Bruner, *The Process of Education* (Cambridge, Mass.: Harvard University Press, 1960).
35. Helen McCracken Carpenter, ed., *Skill Development in Social Studies*, Thirty-third Yearbook (Washington, D.C.: National Council for the Social Studies, 1963), p. 33.
36. Arieh Lewy, ed., *Handbook of Curriculum Evaluation*, International Institute for Educational Planning (New York: UNESCO distributed by Longman, 1977), p. 85.

6

Prometheus Unbound, or Realizing Great Expectations

All this world is heavy with the promise of greater things, and a day will come, one day in the unending succession of days, when beings who are now latent in our thoughts and hidden in our loins, shall stand upon this earth as one stands upon a footstool and shall laugh and reach out their hands amidst the stars.

*H. G. Wells**

Surely we can greatly extend both the reach and the grasp of our brilliant youths, or what's an education for?

Julian C. Stanley†

Undeniably important as the preceding chapters have demonstrated *theoretical construct* to be in the success of an educational program for the gifted and talented, the personalization of a learner-centered environment is even more strategic in actualizing the potential of gifted children and youth. Perhaps the most effective way to illustrate this assertion is to share—just before the actual model programs are presented in Part II of this book and from the experiential vantage point of a teacher of the gifted—an anecdotal focus of just how the realization of great expectations is taking place in one elementary gifted and talented program particularly at the primary level.

The reason for selecting this elementary/primary focus is both pedagogical and pragmatic. *Pedagogically,* the teacher implements—and Brian, Kristen, and Grant enthusiastically pursue—a gifted program that endorses Renzulli's belief that an important part of all programs for the gifted should focus on "the *systematic* development of the cognitive and affective processes which brought these children to our attention in the first place."[1] *Pragmatically,* the success of

---

*H. G. Wells, "The Discovery of the Future," in *Smithsonian Treasury of Science* (New York: Simon and Schuster, 1960), pp. 1171–1193.

†Julian C. Stanley, "Concern for Intellectually Talented Youths: How It Originated and Fluctuated," *Journal of Clinical Psychology* 5, no. 3 (1976): 41.

these youngsters in assimilating concepts indicative of the higher register of Bloom's Taxonomy presents the highest validity for gifted education programs at the elementary level, while at the same time evoking the most eloquent defense against revocation or curtailment of such elementary programs as the first expedient in times of budget crunch, reduction in staff, or vested-interest budget battles. At such crisis times and in one way or another, elementary programs seem always first to be sacrificed, and elementary gifted programs promise to be no exception to the rule.

Third-graders Brian, Kristen, and Grant entered the GATE Program during first grade. Happy, healthy, loved, and loving, these attractive children closely resemble their chronological peer group in most ways. Aside from qualification for the program, the most important factor that these children identified as gifted share is, as Gallagher has succinctly observed elsewhere, "the ability to absorb abstract concepts, to organize them more effectively, and to apply them more appropriately than does the average youngster."[2] Thus far in their "undergraduate" careers, these children have been blessed both with a home life supportive of learning and with experienced, responsive classroom teachers who shun a stifling lockstep regimen.

Each week these children are personally welcomed into the GATE room for a two-hour session, where an unambiguously positive and nonthreatening learning environment is a constant. Within the parameters of respect both for individuals and for the merit of ideas, intellectual playfulness mingles with scholarly camaraderie. Risk taking in thinking and communicating new thoughts, testing new ideas, and trying new techniques are constantly aided and abetted for there is no fear of failure here. Honest self-evaluation of effort, progress, and product—there is no grading system other than personal, positive "crits"—is far more productive and exacting. The children have learned early that the only sin is *not* to try and that recognizing and admitting to a mistake is just becoming that moment wiser than you were the moment before.

The children exhibit an infectious zest for learning and a remarkable tolerance for arduous tasks. Even more intriguing is a burgeoning self-awareness of their own learning progress and learning needs, which actually invites as "lifelong learning skills" the introductory principles of some very large concepts. As second-graders they quickly grasped the rudiments of "brainstorming," became avid practitioners, and jumped at the opportunity to teach others. As beginning third-graders, they are now refining that skill (see Checklist 10, Questions to Stimulate Thinking during Brainstorming). Another thread running welcome and unfettered through the tapestry of their GATE learning experience is the concept of "know thyself." Through the production of a *Mostly Me* book, they are discovering the strengths, weaknesses, and other characteristics that make each one of them a unique human being. Lest there be too much preoccupation with self, Kristen, Grant, and Brian, by writing letters and designing greeting cards and remembrance tokens at birthday and holiday times, are discovering both the responsibility and joy of "lighting up" another's life through their interaction with an elderly pen pals club.

In preparation for studying "Our Wonderful World of Plants" (see Part II, Model 7) and "Our Wonderful World of Animals" (see Part II, Model 6), the children ventured into the concepts of identification, differentiation, and classification. Concurrently, they have become aware of the synergistic effect and are quick to reap the benefits from using it.

CHECKLIST 10 QUESTIONS TO STIMULATE THINKING DURING BRAINSTORMING*

Other Uses
  Can it be put to other uses as is?
  Can it be put to other uses if it is modified?

Adaptation
  What else is like it?
  What other ideas does it suggest?
  What could you copy?
  Whom could you imitate?

Modification
  What new twist could be made?
  Can you change the color, size, shape, motion, sound, form, or odor?

Magnification
  What could be added?
  Can you add more time, strength, height, length, thickness, or value?
  Can you duplicate or exaggerate it?

Minification
  Can you make it smaller, shorter, lighter, or lower?
  Can you divide it up or omit certain parts?

Substitution
  Who else can do it?
  What can be used instead?
  Can other ingredients or materials be used?
  Can you use another source of power, another place, or another process?
  Can you use another tone of voice?

Rearrangement
  Can you interchange parts?
  Can you use a different plan, pattern, or sequence?
  Can you change the schedule or rearrange cause and effect?

Reversibility
  Can you turn it backward or upside down?
  Can you reverse roles or do the opposite?
  Can you blend things together?
  Can you combine purposes?

Transformation
  Can you change its form in any way?
  Can you burn it, punch a hole in it, paint it?

---

*Carolyn M. Callahan, *Developing Creativity in the Gifted and Talented* (Reston, Va.: Council for Exceptional Children, 1978), pp. 30–31.

Field learning experiences provide a stimulating change of pace for these children. In general, however, such experiences truly enhance a child's depth, breadth, and relevance of learning—rather than being a mere recreational diversion—*only* when they meet the following three criteria: they must be validly related to the learning project at hand, the purpose of the field learning experience must be introduced and fully prepared for well in advance of the trip, and there must be some meaningful production thereafter. The following describes what took place in the third-grade GATE sessions before, during, and after a field learning experience to Phipps Conservatory. (This is the culminating activity recommended in "Our Wonderful World of Plants," but it lends itself equally well as an initial orientation strategy.)

In GATE sessions prior to the visit to Phipps Conservatory, the students were thoroughly oriented to the skills and techniques of observation, note-taking, and especially the recording of personal reactions; the purpose of a conservatory; the work of a botanist and a horticulturalist; and the possibilities for exploration of the plant world within their very own community.

The big day finally arrived. Armed with clipboards, ball-point pens, and full understanding that each child was perfectly free to react to and record only that which was personally significant, Brian, Kristen, and Grant enthusiastically took copious notes of anything that intrigued them as they scampered through a two-hour exploration of the conservatory. How seriously, how joyously, and how individualistically they worked—recording botanical names, noting changes in temperature among the various exhibit rooms, and involuntarily "oh-ing" and "ah-ing" as the aesthetic experience of beauty overwhelmed them.

The remaining criterion for a successful field learning experience—meaningful production thereafter—was implemented at the children's first GATE session following the trip. The task set before them was to write an account of their visit to Phipps by organizing and making use of their notes gathered at the conservatory. These accounts would be considered for publication in the annual edition of the *Gater Gazette*.

At this time the teacher employed the following teaching-learning technique, which she has frequently found useful in vaulting children's quicksilver fluency of thought over the barrier imposed by the sheer physical laboriousness of second- and third-grade handwriting. After organizing notes, each child dashes off a penciled rough draft of what he or she wants to say and then dictates it aloud to the teacher, who simultaneously types it, immediately producing a double-spaced copy for the heady amazement of the child. Each child, being delighted at the volume he or she has produced, rushes off to correct and "think up more" so as to occasion a return engagement with the typewriter. And then the pleasure of reading the work aloud! Using this technique, first Kristen, then Grant, and then Brian produced the following first draft accounts, each of which far better exemplifies the child's individuality than could any description.

After preparation of her handwritten copy, Kristen dictated the following report to the teacher.

PHIPPS CONSERVATORY DOES IT AGAIN

Finally, we were at Phipps Conservatory. We went in and everybody had to go to the bathroom. First, we were in the Oriental Room and put a quarter in the wishing well. We looked at the Bonsai trees and then we looked at the white pine and the Taxus plant. We saw palm trees. We went into the cactus room and saw Agaue Victory, Reguen, Jumping Cactus, Golden Barrel Cactus, Heat of Flame. The Century Plant is very big. We saw pretty flowers. Then we got to the Palm Room. We saw the Oil Palm, Sugar Palm. We saw a lot of statues. Finally, we got to the English Room. There were pretty plants and flowers there.

There were many things to see like the Circus Room. There were poodles made out of flowers and a ball made out of flowers, too, that were dyed with colors. I learned many experiences. I liked it very much. I learned alot.

After preparation of his handwritten copy, Grant dictated the following to the teacher.

PHIPPS IS NO GIP!!!

We went to Phipps Conservatory. We were going slower than the teachers. "That," I never thought I would see.

Kristen asked me to pitch a quarter in a fountain some twenty feet away. We had a great time in the Oriental Room. Huge hanging baskets of flowers.

Flowers and More Flowers

I was getting tired, but it's worth it. Man! I never knew this place was so big. It's beautiful.

We're out now. Miss Davies bought us all a wafle plant. Miss Davies and Miss Clendening treated us all to lunch at McDonalds.

Thoughts While At The Conservatory By Grant

Beautiful flower arrangements

Intense beauty everywhere

Bonsai* was beautiful

Perfect

God made intense beauty. It still lives.

Work is worth it, if this is the result.

The quietness of nothingness is forever.

The Lord loves plants.

Desert Room: The Desert Room was unbelievably hot! They had a huge African plant. They had a tiny little cactus from Mexico. Kristen was about ready to take off her shirt she was so hot. There was sand everywhere I looked. We walked, walked, and walked, and walked and walked.

Oriental Room: It had a pleasant temperature. There were lots of hanging baskets. Kristen got cold (I don't believe her!).

Bonsai: Small trees everywhere. Kristen wrote til we left practically (Gee Whiz).

Flower Show: There were flowers everywhere. This time Kristen looked!!! These were poodles made out of flowers.

After preparation of his handwritten copy, Brian dictated the following report to the teacher.

PHIPPS CONSERVATORY KOOL KIDS

We GATE Dudes were on a field trip. It was fascinating. We learned about Osage Oranges. A botanical name is a true name of a tree or flower. Dr. George Washington Carver invented uses for the peanut. Miss Clendening said: "I hope that some day perhaps Brian or Kristen or Grant may discover a use for the Osage Orange that will benefit all mankind." Grant said: "Beauty was made by God and can never be destroyed." I say that, too.

We saw trees made so small that a twenty-year-old tree is only about ten inches tall! It was important to keep it hot in some rooms and cold in others because flowers like different climates in order to keep living. Grant said that he would like to invent a space cruiser made out of flowers on the inside and tropical tree bark on the outside. We saw a University on the way. We picked Osage Oranges. Osage Oranges have a liquid that they send out on cuts. Just like medicine on us. Grant said to pitch a quarter in the wishing well in the English Room. Grant loved the tunnels. They were in the tropical room. There was nothing but cactus in the desert room.

My mother and I had most of the cactuses that they had there. There were plants in the Oriental Room that looked like vines! The circus room was nice. It was beautiful. It was greatly designed. We saw the Autumn Flower Show.

*Japanese art of keeping trees under a foot tall.

Miss Davies took (It was ugly, bad looking and made the room look bad and made the people mad) paper off the floor and put it in the trash can. The rooms (only some of them) had Greek statues.

The one room was greatly designed into shapes.

The Conservatory had had a terrible disaster, Miss Davies said. She said that where the tunnels Grant loved was all destroyed because the rain and hail and snow broke the windows and killed the flowers.

The windows are built stronger now. The flower show had all different kinds of flowers. There were flowers from all over the world. They were from Paris, Germany, and alot of other places. There was a whole lot of little trees from Japan.

Miss Davies said that we were visiting the whole world by looking at the flowers and trees. It seemed like we walked a mile or more. It was so big! The outside looked like it was all glass and no flowers or trees. The inside looked like no glass and all flowers and trees.

There were flowers that were colored in dye. Then they were put together like balls, seals, and poodles and put in the Circus Room. Whoever thought of making them was brilliant! The way all the people had to go was to stay to the left on the walks and then you would see everything.

And it worked! We were all over the place. THE END.

Below is the teacher's reaction to the closure production by the children following their field learning experience.

TEACHER'S ANECDOTAL RECORD ENTRY

One of my most exciting teaching experiences—this day! These beginning third-graders are marvelous. They find the invitation "to dictate" after a written preparation an irresistible fantastic enticement. They worked like "beavers"—spending 2 1/4 hours working first on their written drafts, dictating to teacher, revising to add additional thoughts, dictating again, and then reading proudly (with expression!) their work to the group. Brian became so involved with his writing that he continued well into the lunch period. Grant and Kristen worked twenty minutes into lunch period and said they wished they could stay longer.

Each of the several times I have tried this technique with the children it has been excitingly successful. It's really thrilling to see the children be fluent and excited about writing, especially when they sense the need of or embellishment potential of supplying quotation marks, dashes, parenthetical elements, and of course generous exclamation marks. It's truly amazing just how accurate these third-graders are in their use of punctuation mechanics. Dictating aloud seems to increase their sensitivity to punctuation mechanics as a real help to them in carrying across what they really want to tell.

As can be detected from the foregoing, these children are attuned to beauty, but each one has responded in his or her own fashion. Thus it is throughout their participation in the total program: Each one brings forth his or her individuality whether it is in selection of particular topic to study, mode of learning, or closure production. All are excellent readers and read consistently on their own time; each has a healthy sense of humor; and each one is unique.

Grant is excellent at analyzing, organizing, and giving clear directions, and at this point in life expects "to explore space someday with a small brave crew," as he neatly turns the phrase.

Kristen, although meticulous about spelling and cursive writing, prefers to express her feelings and thoughts with the beauty of line, color, and design and adores nothing so much as her two dogs and gymnastics classes.

Brian's *joie de vivre* is contagious and he seeks to share it with all, whether by a holiday rhyme or a cheerfully endearing letter. Brian, who confesses to keeping a secret journal at home in addition to the one at GATE, is a reflective thinker who continually dredges up and brings to current problems thoughts and knowledge previously encountered.

The children have responded well to journal keeping, one of the tenets of the Elementary GATE Program K–6, and enjoy reviewing past entries with great amusement. They are very pleased when certain entries are adjudged appropriate for publication in the annual *Gater Gazette,* as were the following two entries.

DRAT, RATS AND FOO!*

Tuesday, the 6th of March. I was looking forward to going on the GATE field trip. I ran in and jumped on my mother's bed, trying to convince her that I was over my sickness, but it didn't work. I thought I would go so I had saved my film. Instead, another day of TV will do! And more of that terrible medicine! The rest of the day was worse than the medicine (which is so gooey that you have to mix it with water to drink it). The only fun I had all day was drawing Peanuts characters from the newspapers—which is certainly not as much fun as a GATE Field trip!

The process of transferring characters from newspapers and comics strips onto paper is done like this:

1. Find comic character in newspaper that you wish to copy.
2. Unfold comic strip and take out any part inside.
3. Place comic strip character and drawing paper on top and place total Parcel against window.
4. Position character where you want him or her on your drawing paper.
5. Get black pencil and trace over outlines and all designs on shirts or pants of character—stay at window to do step 4 and step 5.
6. Color in character however you like, but make sure you use the same kind of colored pencils. DO NOT USE MARKERS BECAUSE THEY MESS UP!
7. REMINDER: You can make any characters from any comic strip or comic book and make your own different pictures or strips,

FOR INSTANCE, you can make Dick Tracy talk to
Charlie Brown!

GRANT, Grade 2

THE SECOND GRADE GATE YEAR
AND THE GREATEST OF THEM ALL!

The first day in GATE I was a little scared but I found I could live with it. I have fun with the other people in my GATE class working together. I designed a title page featuring a pteranodon's head as the lower case letter "a." Brainstorming is fun. GATE stands for "Gifted and Talented Education." We wrote a letter to Mrs. Farr for the first time. Mickey Mouse is 50 years old this year! We had a contest for a pumpkin in October. I am a reporter for GATE. We learned how to write a story by using, "Who," "When," "What," "Where," and "Why" on our five fingers. That's all for today. I will get in my car and drive away.—Oh I forgot—I'm looking forward toward next year. I hope it won't run away like this year, and hope it will stay. The End by Brian†
†I love volcanos shooting in the air in which I call dinosaur land. I have Invasion of the Dinosaurs every Christmas instead of train robbers attack the train—under the Christmas tree, that is.

BRIAN, Grade 2

*This production and the one that follows it were accomplished by the writing/dictating/rewriting technique previously described.

It is true that children such as Grant, Kristen, and Brian need and benefit from special programs for the gifted and talented, but their need and benefit are secondary to society's need and benefit from bringing to fruition children such as these. Getzels and Dillon remind us that

> the conditions of modern life demand not only high intellectual ability in the traditional fields of learning, but also giftedness in all fields of human aspiration, the social as well as the technological, the artistic as well as the scientific, the humanistic as well as the economic.[3]

It is equally true that society will bring these children to fruition only if its schools provide programs predicated on the verity that "human beings are fragile, and the human condition is easily mutilated or destroyed by human institutions in which it is possible for individuals to become lost or forgotten."[4]

Although programs for the gifted and talented must be carefully designed and structured, they must also be directly responsive to the needs, interests, goals, and concerns of each individual student, not only as a learner but—especially— as a human being. It is imperative that children who qualify for the Gifted and Talented Program be identified as early as possible and that the school district nurture and help actualize their promise not only as learners, not only as creative thinkers, not only as citizens, but, above all, as fine human beings. The program for the gifted and talented *must* be concerned with the intellectual, artistic, and spiritual values by which people live and by which their judgments are made and their purposes defined. The program *must* help each student to answer the all-important question of how to achieve, strengthen, and preserve a genuinely free society in which men and women are authentic persons who are masters rather than slaves of the forces that shape their world.*

The students themselves must clearly perceive that it is mete and right to march to a different drumbeat just so long as one keeps in tune with his or her fellow human beings and in step with one's own best self. For knowledge alone is not enough; knowledge plus skills is not enough; knowledge coupled with integrity and wisdom is not enough; and knowledge joined with compassion is not enough. Only when all five—knowledge, skills, integrity, wisdom, and compassion—are blended so that each supports the other do we have the kind of person who exemplifies the ideal of personal excellence.

REQUISITES UNDERGIRDING A PROGRAM FOR THE GIFTED AND TALENTED

To assure the quality and safeguard the integrity of the program for the gifted and talented, value judgments must be made. Each of the basic requisites listed below must be consistently respected and unwaveringly adhered to:

1. That the elementary and secondary programs for the gifted and talented in reality be a single, seamless, ongoing program that has been carefully designed ever to broaden, ever to deepen, ever to reinforce and extend learning through a logical progression of significant interlocking, cohesive, and mutually supportive learning experiences.

---

*The desired ends and purposes of education as identified by the Commission on Instructional Technology in *To Improve Learning: An Evaluation of Instructional Technology,* ed. by Sidney G. Tickton (New York: R. R. Bowker, 1971), vol. 1, p. 15.

2. That the elementary and secondary GATE teachers plan and work cooperatively as team teachers.
3. That at the beginning of each school year, monthly staff meetings be scheduled so that the GATE teachers can plan and coordinate their work as a team; can cooperatively design and structure learning projects; can evaluate teaching strategies, instructional programs, student achievement and reaction, field experiences, and instructional media; can compile bibliographies for learning projects and learning stations; can determine program implementation and development progress; can determine program support needs; and can share individual GATE teacher concerns.
4. That participation in the GATE program should never be cause for student frustration or despair; participation in the program should be occasion for developing to the fullest one's own capabilities and interests in a climate characterized by teacher/learner mutual respect, shared concerns, and delight in the teaching/learning enterprise.
5. That autonomy and flexibility in choice of learning projects, methodology, media selection and usage, field experiences, activities, and focus of interest are guaranteed each student as well as each teacher.
6. That the school district provide adequate professional and paraprofessional staff, adequate budget, adequate facilities, adequate instructional media and equipment, and continuing, unwavering support from the administrative staff.

NOTES

1. Joseph S. Renzulli, *The Enrichment Triad Model: A Guide for Developing Defensible Programs for the Gifted and Talented* (Mansfield Center, Conn.: Creative Learning Press, 1977), p. 6.
2. James J. Gallagher, *Teaching the Gifted Child,* 2nd ed. (Boston: Allyn and Bacon, 1975), p. 19.
3. J. W. Getzels and J. T. Dillon, "The Nature of Giftedness and the Education of the Gifted," in *Second Handbook of Research on Teaching,* A Project of the American Educational Research Association, ed. by Robert M. W. Travers (Chicago: Rand McNally, 1973), p. 689.
4. Betty Atwell Wright et al., *Elementary School Curriculum: Better Teaching Now* (New York: Macmillan, 1971), p. 21.

Part II

Instructional Programs for the Gifted and Talented

7

Model Programs, Grades K–12

Unless otherwise specified, each model in this section is a component of the North Hills School District Program for the Gifted and Talented. These models incorporate in their design Bloom's and Krathwohl's objectives and the strategies of Guilford, Torrance, Williams, Hallman, Parnes, and Burton (see Chapter 5). Each model has been field-tested in actual teaching/learning situations. Grade indication is not definitive, but, rather, is an indication of where within the North Hills Program this unit has been taught.

Each model has been designed to provide myriad topics that the students "might like to explore at greater depths and higher levels of involvement."* The content of each unit is of greater scope than any class, group, or individual student could possibly master. This has been done by design—*individualization begins with informed choices among significant options.*

Teaching strategies indicate the method of presentation that has been employed in generating interest, stimulating thinking, and facilitating student interaction with content. Content is what is to be learned; teaching strategies are instructional management devices designed to effect learning.

Questions concerning any of these models should be addressed to: Corinne P. Clendening, Coordinator of the Elementary GATE Program, North Hills School District, 200 McIntyre Rd., Pittsburgh, Pa. 15237, tel. 412-367-6229.

*Joseph S. Renzulli, *The Enrichment Triad: A Guide for Developing Defensible Programs for the Gifted and Talented* (Mansfield Center, Conn.: Creative Learning Press, 1977), p. 17.

MODEL 1   ORIENTATION TO THE GATE PROGRAM (K–1)

Theme: I Am Me—And I Want To Be

Grade: K–1

Teaching Goal: To provide learning experiences that will encourage the gifted student to discover delight and challenge in learning and in becoming acquainted with himself or herself as a creative, responsive, and loving human being.

Teaching Objectives:

This project has been designed and structured to provide these basic understandings:

Because you are a human being you can think.

You can think about your family, your friends, your neighborhood, and your community.

You can think about things and places.

You can read and make friends with books, with authors, and with illustrators.

You can dream about where you would like to go, what you would like to do, and what you would like to be.

You can be kind, thoughtful, and helpful.

You can learn about yourself and the world in which you live.

You can be happy and you can help make others happy.

This project has been designed and structured to foster and develop these attitudes and appreciations:

You are responsible for what you do and what you say.

Happiness is part of sharing and caring.

We all need each other.

Learning to learn is exciting and lots of fun.

Reading is a delightful way to make friends.

Words are fascinating to discover and use.

The world of plants, animals, and sounds is beautiful.

Teaching Strategies:

No time limitations are imposed on this project. Number of students in the GATE group coupled with student interest and delight is the factor determining the duration of this project whether it be two weeks, two months, or longer.

Learning to learn with pure enjoyment and delight is the major concern determining whether any or all of the experiences outlined here are to be offered to the group or to any individual in the group.

Procedural Outline:

   I. The motion picture, *I Am Me—And I Want to Be* (Sandler Films) is presented and the following concepts are discussed:

     A. Everyone is different.

        Size—who is the tallest in the GATE group? Smallest?

        Family—how many brothers and/or sisters? Aunts? Uncles? Cousins?

        Favorite foods—candy, ice cream, pies, cakes, sandwiches, pizza, etc.

        Favorite television programs

        Favorite comic strip

        Favorite colors

        Favorite sports and/or games

        Favorite pastime

        Favorite person or persons

        Favorite pets

MODEL 1 (cont.)

B. Variety can be exciting.

The GATE program is going to provide a wide variety of learning experiences.

Each person in the GATE group is important.

Each person in the GATE group will share in making suggestions and in deciding exciting things to do.

C. Happiness begins with liking yourself.

What kind of person do you like best?

What kind of person do you like least?

What makes you happy?

What makes you sad?

Are you ever afraid?

Are you ever brave?

Do you do thoughtful things?

What kind of person do you want to be?

II. The self-concept filmstrips series *Getting to Know Me* (SVE) is presented and discussed. The filmstrips are:
A. *People Are Like Rainbows*

We are all alike in some ways and we are all different in some ways.

Differences are as acceptable as likenesses; neither is the basis for loving and being loved.

Differences add another dimension to our experiences.

Each person's behavior affects others.

People are like rainbows; all the different colors make the rainbow beautiful.

All the different kinds of people and different ways of living make the world an interesting place.

B. *A Boat Named George*

To be able to work cooperatively with others, one must appreciate one's own worth and appreciate the worth of others.

It is fun to share ideas and to work cooperatively with others.

Even hard work is easier when shared with a friend.

C. *Listen, Jimmy!*

To be liked, to feel liked, one must like and feel for others.

Bragging and boasting don't win friends.

Listening to others carefully is a good habit to develop.

D. *Strike Three! You're In!*

Participation brings respect, friendship, and a feeling of personal worth.

Being part of a team is a good feeling.

You cannot expect to be best in everything.

Each person does some things very well.

III. The motion picture *Names, Names, Names and Why We Need Them* (Sandler Films) is presented and discussed, and the following questions are explored:
A. What boys' names are your favorites?
B. What girls' names are your favorites?
C. Do you have a nickname? How did you get the nickname?
D. What pet names are your favorites? Why?
E. If you were to write a story, what names would you give the people in your story?

MODEL 1 (cont.)

F. What does the word *signature* mean?

IV. The book *Books Are Fun* by Geri Schobert is read and discussed.

A. Why does everyone want to read?

B. "Children read books in school to learn many new things," for example:

"Books for Beginning Readers" series.

"I Can Read about History" series.

"I Can Read about Science" series.

"I Want to Be" series.

C. It is fun to organize a book club and share what you have read with the other club members.

Naming the book club should be one of the first club activities.

Keeping a careful record of what you have read is a good habit to develop.

Telling stories to kindergarten children would be a worthwhile activity.

D. The author of a book is talking to you.

An author can be your friend; you can share many delightful reading experiences together.

During this year in the GATE Program, you will become acquainted with many authors and their stories.

E. The illustrator of a book is talking to you.

An illustrator can be your friend; you can share many picture conversations together.

During this year in the GATE Program, you will become acquainted with many illustrators and their pictures.

F. Many stories have delighted children for many long years.

The television program "Once Upon a Classic" presents stories that have delighted children in many lands for a very long time.

Ask your grandmother and your grandfather to tell you some of the stories they learned when they were children.

Did you know that Peter Rabbit is more than 75 years old?

The Tale of Peter Rabbit was written by Beatrix Potter.

Beatrix Potter is a wonderful friend to get acquainted with.

Did you know that Peter Rabbit had a cousin? His name was Benjamin Bunny.

Did you know that children all over the world know and dearly love Beatrix Potter and her stories?

Here are the little books written and illustrated by our new friend Beatrix Potter:

Appley Dapply's Nursery Rhymes	*The Tale of Mr. Tod*
Cecily Parsley's Nursery Rhymes	*The Tale of Mrs. Tiggy-Winkle*
Ginger and Pickles	*The Tale of Mrs. Tittlemouse*
The Pie and the Patty Pan	*The Tale of Peter Rabbit*
The Roly-Poly Cookie	*The Tale of Pigling Bland*
The Tailor of Gloucester	*The Tale of Squirrel Nutkin*
The Tale of Benjamin Bunny	*The Tale of the Flopsy Bunnies*
The Tale of Jemima Puddle-Duck	*The Tale of Timmy Tiptoes*
The Tale of Johnny Town-Mouse	*The Tale of Tom Kitten*
The Tale of Little Pig Robinson	*The Tale of Two Bad Mice*
The Tale of Mr. Jeremy Fisher	

MODEL 1 (cont.)

Are Beatrix Potter's illustrations an important part of the stories? Try an experiment to prove whether the illustrations help tell the story. Choose a story by Beatrix Potter which the GATE group hasn't heard or seen before; tell this story without using the book. Then tell the story using the illustrations in the book or a filmstrip that reproduces the book illustrations. Which way does the group think is the "best" way—with or without the illustrations?

The following filmstrips (SVE) are "authentic reproductions" of Beatrix Potter's books:

The Tale of Peter Rabbit   *The Tale of Two Bad Mice*

The Tale of Squirrel Nutkin   *The Tale of Mrs. Tiggy-Winkle*

The Tale of Benjamin Bunny   *The Tailor of Gloucester*

The Tale of Jeremy Fisher

V. Sharing is an important part of caring.
   A. Many learning experiences you will have this year as part of the GATE Program you can share with your classmates or other children in the school, in your family, or in the community.
   B. Think of all the ways you can share what you have enjoyed doing, seeing, hearing, making, and imagining in GATE.

   How could you share these experiences?

   How could you arrange with your classroom teacher to share these experiences with your class?

   How could you arrange with the kindergarten teacher to share stories and other activities with the kindergarten children?

   C. Holidays are happy times if someone cares and shares.

   Make a list of holidays.

   For each holiday, make a list of things you could do to bring happiness to others.

   After each holiday has been celebrated, add to the list the additional things you did to make someone happy.

VI. The next learning activity in GATE is 'Becoming the Best Me."
   A. Think of all the ways you could become a "better me."
   B. Remember all the ways you have been a "better me" through sharing and caring.
   C. Remember that each day you are a brand new "ME"!

MODEL 2   BECOMING THE BEST ME

Learning Project: Becoming the Best Me
Grade: K–1
Project Goal: To provide learning experiences that will deepen the students' self-perception, will give insight into what is and what is not desirable behavior, and will provide thought-provoking ideas that will help the students make value judgments.
Teaching Objectives:

To widen, deepen, and extend the concepts of self introduced in the learning project I Am Me—And I Want to Be.

To increase the students' awareness that learning can be fun.

To provide opportunities for the students to work cooperatively as productive members of a group.

To provide opportunities for the GATE students to develop a feeling of responsibility for one's own behavior.

MODEL 2 (cont.)

To provide opportunities for the GATE students to share with their classmates and schoolmates when and where possible.

Teaching Strategies and Methods:

No time limitations are imposed on this project. Student interest is the main factor that determines whether this GATE project lasts two weeks, two months, or longer.

A basic part of this project is for the students to appraise their own actions with honesty and to want to become the best persons possible.

Procedural Outline:

I. Orientation to this project.
   A. The group discusses the question 'Why do we have schools?"

   Do we need to be able to read?

   Do we need to be able to write?

   Do we need to be able to add and subtract?

   Does what we want to be as a grown-up require our going to school?

   B. Why do we have a GATE program?

   Will the GATE program help us become better students?

   Will the GATE program help us become better human beings?

   Will the GATE program help us know ourselves better?

   Is getting along in school important?

II. *Getting Along in School* is a filmstrip set that has a serious message told in a delightful way.
   A. The filmstrip *Being on Time* is viewed and discussed.

   What routines are important?

   How can we be responsible for establishing good habits?

   Are we responsible for helping others be on time?

   Is being on time a way of being courteous and dependable?

   B. The filmstrip *Doing Things for Yourself* is viewed and discussed.

   What does it mean to be self-reliant?

   Why is obeying rules part of being self-reliant?

   What can you do for yourself this year that you couldn't do a year ago?

   How can you help others in your classroom and on the playground be more self-reliant?

   C. The filmstrip *Taking Care of Things* is viewed and discussed.

   What is meant by taking personal responsibility?

   What is meant by careful use of materials?

   Should a careless person have a pet?

   Make a list of things you should do to take care of a pet.

   Are rules necessary to see that things in school and at home are properly cared for?

   D. The filmstrip *Working with Others* is viewed and discussed.

   Can you accomplish more in a shorter time working with others?

   Make a list of things you have done that required the help of others.

   Do grown-ups need the help of other grown-ups? Of children?

   Do teachers need the help of other teachers? Of children?

   How can you share ideas?

   What is the difference between sharing ideas and being bossy?

MODEL 2 (cont.)

Can the GATE students in this group work well together?

E. The filmstrip *How Quiet Helps* is viewed and discussed.

Use a tape recorder to discover how much unnecessary noise there is in your classroom, in the hall, in the library.

What is the difference between unnecessary and necessary noise?

What is noise pollution?

Is it really selfish to be noisy?

Does the story *Noisy Nancy Norris* have a message for us?

F. The filmstrip *Listening and Following Directions* is viewed and discussed.

Are the three basic rules important for grown-ups as well as children?

Listen to, or read carefully, all the directions before starting.

Ask questions if you don't understand.

Follow each step in order.

Make a list of things your mother does that require her to read and follow directions.

Make a list of things your father does that require him to follow directions.

Make a list of things you and your family do that might require you or your parents to ask for directions.

III. The filmstrip series *Read and Reason* tells much more about getting along at school, at home, and in the community.
A. Rather than have the viewing of these filmstrips be by the entire group, each one is the responsibility of one GATE student to view, to present to the group, and to lead the discussion.
B. The six filmstrip titles are:

I Can Do Everything	*The Shopping Trip*
I Was Just Going To	*Sticks and Stones*
Lost and Found	*Who Says So?*

C. If the classroom teacher wishes, the GATE students can share these filmstrips with the class.

The GATE students, in preparing for the presentation to the class, will be relating what they have learned about being responsible, about sharing ideas, about being self-reliant, and about doing the best job possible.

IV. If the interest of the GATE students remains high, a number of significant learning experiences can be shared with the kindergarten.
A. The filmstrip set *Sing Along, Play Along* presents four traditional singing games with additional verses. The four games are:

The Farmer in the Dell	Row, Row, Row Your Boat
London Bridge	The Mulberry Bush

B. The new verses introduce new activities, which require following directions.

Introducing the kindergarten children to the new verses and new activities will give the GATE students a real experience in teaching children to follow directions.

V. If the interest of the GATE students remains high, the following filmstrip sets will offer further opportunities for the students to share with kindergarten children and their own classmates a number of viewing and listening experiences.

A. The filmstrip set *Laugh with Us* includes the following four filmstrips:

Children in the Water	*The Dog Who Thought He Was a Boy*
The Curious Cow	*The Zoo That Moved*

MODEL 2 (cont.)

B. The filmstrip set *Tales of Winnie the Witch* includes the following six filmstrips:

The Accident and Derring-Do	*The Lake Murkwood Monster*
Bossy, Boring Maurice the Beast	*Lucifer and Bully Balderdash*
The Glut's Peanut Butter Pie	*The Magic Words*

Resource Kit:
  FILMSTRIPS

Getting Along in School (Coronet—6 filmstrips, 3 records, 1 teaching guide)

Being on Time	*Listening and Following Directions*
Doing Things for Yourself	*Taking Care of Things*
How Quiet Helps	*Working with Others*

Laugh with Us (New York Times—4 filmstrips, 2 records)

Children in the Water	*The Dog Who Thought He Was a Boy*
The Curious Cow	*The Zoo That Moved*

Read and Reason (New York Times—6 filmstrips, 3 records, 1 teaching guide)

I Can Do Everything	*The Shopping Trip*
I Was Just Going To	*Sticks and Stones*
Lost and Found	*Who Says So?*

Sing Along, Play Along (New York Times—4 filmstrips, 2 records, 1 teaching guide)

The Farmer in the Dell	*The Mulberry Bush*
London Bridge	*Row, Row, Row Your Boat*

Tales of Winnie the Witch (SVE—6 filmstrips, 6 records, 6 teaching guides)

The Accident and Derring-Do	*The Lake Murkwood Monster*
Bossy, Boring Maurice the Beast	*Lucifer and Bully Balderdash*
The Glut's Peanut Butter-Pie	*The Magic Words*

MODEL 3   MEET MY FRIEND, PAUL GALDONE

Learning Project: Meet My Friend, Paul Galdone
Grade: K–1
Project Goal: To provide learning experiences that will introduce the gifted students to
  Paul Galdone as illustrator and as storyteller extraordinary.
Teaching Objectives:
  · This project has been designed and structured to provide these basic understand-
  ings:

Many stories have been enjoyed by our parents, our grandparents, and our great
grandparents, and by us today.

Pictures are to be "read" for they, too, tell a story.

Storybook friends live in our memory.

Storytelling is lots of fun.

This project has been designed and structured to foster and develop these attitudes
and appreciations:

Reading is a wonderful adventure.

Illustrations are fascinating and delightful.

Paul Galdone's illustrations tickle our funny bone for they make us laugh.

Each illustrator "tells" a story in a different way.

Belonging to the Busy Bee Book Club is a real adventure.

MODEL 3 (cont.)

Procedural Outline:
  I. Group orientation to and overview of this project.
    A. A list is made of the students' favorite stories.
    B. As many different illustrated editions as possible are gathered of each story listed.

        The students examine each book and select the illustrated editions they like best.

        The students study the title page to discover the name of the illustrator of each book.

        The students then group the various books illustrated by Paul Galdone.

        Each student selects the Paul Galdone illustrated books he or she wishes to read.

    C. Filmstrips (Weston Woods) of the following Galdone stories are previewed by individual students:

        The House That Jack Built

        The Little Red Hen

        Old Mother Hubbard and Her Dog

        The Old Woman and Her Pig

    D. The use of filmstrips to make storytelling more effective is discussed.

        Individual students demonstrate how best to use a filmstrip for storytelling.

        Storytelling techniques are explored and practiced.

    E. The dramatization of stories by a group is discussed.

        The need to speak distinctly is stressed.

        The need to speak so the words can be visualized is stressed.

        The use of appropriate gestures is demonstrated.

        The use of props is explored and then demonstrated.

        The necessity of knowing the dialogue is fulfilling the individual's obligation to the group.

  II. The fun of sharing what is read is explored.
    A. Book clubs are one form of sharing enjoyment of reading.

        The Busy Bee Book Club is introduced.

        Membership materials are introduced.

        The value of keeping a careful record of what is read is discussed.

        Various possibilities of club programs are discussed.

        How the Busy Bee Book Club could be of service to the school, the home, and the community is explored.

    B. A videotape of one or more of Galdone's stories is made.
    C. The group writes a news item for the GATE newspaper highlighting Paul Galdone and his books.

Resource Kit (Grade 1):
  BOOKS (all illustrated by Paul Galdone)

    Androcles and the Lion (McGraw-Hill)

    Benjie Goes into Business by Patricia Martin (Putnam)

    The Gingerbread Boy (Seabury)

    Henny Penny (Seabury)

    Hereafterthis (McGraw-Hill)

    The History of Little Tom Tucker (McGraw-Hill)

MODEL 3 (cont.)

The History of Mother Twaddle and the Marvelous Achievements of Her Son Jack (Seabury)

The Horse, the Fox, and the Lion (Seabury)

The Lady Who Saw the Good Side of Everything (Seabury)

The Life of Jack Sprat, His Wife, and His Cat (McGraw-Hill)

The Little Red Hen (Seabury)

The Little Red Hen (Scholastic)

Little Red Riding Hood (McGraw-Hill)

Little Tuppen (Seabury)

The Monkey and the Crocodile (Seabury)

The Moving Adventures of Old Dame Trot and Her Comical Cat (Seabury)

Obedient Jack, An Old Tale (Watts)

Old Mother Hubbard and Her Dog (McGraw-Hill)

The Old Woman and Her Pig (McGraw-Hill)

Puss in Boots (Seabury)

Three Aesop Fox Fables (Seabury)

The Three Bears (Seabury)

The Three Bears (Scholastic)

Three Billy Goats Gruff (Seabury)

Three Little Pigs (Seabury)

Three Little Pigs (Scholastic)

Tom, Tom the Piper's Son (McGraw-Hill)

The Town Mouse and the Country Mouse (McGraw-Hill)

FILMSTRIPS (Weston Woods—1 filmstrip, 1 record, 1 teaching guide)

The House That Jack Built

The Little Red Hen

Old Mother Hubbard and Her Dog

The Old Woman and Her Pig

MODEL 4   LISTEN TO LEARN

Learning Project: Listen to Learn

Grade: 2

Project Goal: To provide listening experiences that will enable the students to develop a greater degree of self-perception as thinking, reasoning, responding, loving, concerned human beings.

Teaching Objectives:

To deepen, widen, and reinforce the concept of self introduced in the first-grade learning experiences: I Am Me—And I Want to Be, and Becoming the Best Me.

To sharpen the students' perceptive listening skills.

To provide mind-stretching, adventurous thinking experiences.

Teaching Strategies and Methods:

No time limitations are imposed on this project. Student interest is the main factor that determines whether this GATE project lasts two weeks, two months, or longer.

A basic part of orientation to this project is for the students to learn how to listen with accuracy, with imagination, with challenge, with delight, and with curiosity.

MODEL 4 (cont.)

Procedural Outline:

I. Orientation to this project.

  A. What is listening?

     Is listening the same as hearing?

     If you are listening to a baseball game on TV, do you really listen to what is being said—even in the same room?

     Listening is thinking with the ears in tune.

  B. The group plays the game Simon Says.

     This is a game that is used in a number of training sessions for adults—even adults have to learn to listen.

     After the group has played the game several times, give the game a new twist, have the leader demonstrate an entirely different action from the spoken command; see if the children were listening accurately.

  C. The group plays the game The Curious Traveler.

     The teacher tells the group that each student will be a curious traveler.

     All the students have to do is to follow the directions the leader gives.

     The leader at the beginning is the teacher; after the students have played the game several times, then a student serves as a leader. The student leader can be as imaginative as he or she wishes in giving directions.

     Typical directions given by the leader follow:

       The traveler stands up (students stand).

       The traveler faces the windows (students turn facing windows).

       The traveler faces the front of the room.

       The traveler turns toward the back of the room.

       The traveler bows his (her) head.

       The traveler raises his (her) left arm.

       The traveler raises his (her) right arm.

       The traveler lowers his (her) right arm.

       The traveler raises his (her) right arm.

       The traveler lowers both arms.

       The traveler sits down.

     After the students play this game several times, the tempo can be speeded up. The students can figure out a variety of ways to trap their fellow students into making wrong moves.

  D. A variety of other games is listed in *Listening Games: Building Listening Skills With Instructional Games* by Guy Wagner, Max Hosier, and Mildred Blackman (Macmillan: Teachers Publishing).

II. The students are introduced to the set of cassettes The One and Only, Very Special You (Eye Gate).

  A. This set has been designed to develop the skill of listening and thinking.

     As you listen you must visualize in your mind what the spoken words mean.

     Each tape tells you something important about yourself; listen, think, and become better acquainted with yourself.

  B. The group listens to the first tape, I Can't Do It.

     Following the listening session, the students are called upon to retell the story in exact sequence as presented on the tape.

     The group discusses the philosophy of being afraid to try something for fear of failure.

MODEL 4 (cont.)

No one can succeed at everything.

You never know what you can or cannot do until you try.

In summary the students recall the poem recited by the witch:

Maybe you can and maybe you can't
You'll never know unless you try.
But, 'til you decide you can,
You'll never find the reason why.

C. The group listens to the second tape, Mistakes.

Following the listening session, the students are again asked to recall carefully the exact sequence of happenings.

What were the words that tipped you off to the fact that this story was being told by the family dog?

Are mistakes caused? How was each of the mistakes in this story the direct result of hurrying?

The group discusses the philosophy expressed by Sam when he said, "Now look. Everybody makes mistakes once in awhile. If people were afraid to make mistakes, no one would ever try anything new! Sure, making mistakes isn't much fun, but you can learn from your mistakes."

D. The group listens to the third tape, Trying New Things.

Following the listening session, the students recall the exact sequence of events.

The group discusses the cautious behavior of Blinker, the smallest raccoon.

It takes courage to try something new. But trying new things is one of the ways to find out about the world and to find out about yourself.

How do you know whether you can ride a bike, swim, solve a problem in arithmetic, draw a map, or do a dozen other things if you don't try?

E. The group compares the three tapes, I Can't Do It, Mistakes, and Trying New Things.

The group votes on which tape each student liked the best.

The group discusses why each student has chosen the one tape rather than the other two.

The group makes a list of what has been important in each of the tapes.

Each student writes in his or her "My Daily Journal," what I have learned about myself.

The group thinks of various ways these stories could be shared with their classmates.

Paperbag masks.	Mural.
Finger puppets.	Videotaped play.

III. The group decides whether to continue listening to this series.
   A. The titles of the remaining tapes are read:

Making Decisions	Being Helpful
Being a Good Friend	Eating Healthy Meals
He's Different, She's Different	Snacks—Good and Bad
How I Feel	Keeping Clean
How They Feel	Brushing Teeth
Manners	It Belongs to Someone
Telling the Truth	Stealing
Being Neat	Safe Places

MODEL 4 (cont.)

Dangerous Things	Living Things
To and from School	Things You Have
Getting Lost	

B. If the group elects to continue listening to the tapes, the question is asked, "Does it make any difference in what order we listen to these tapes?"

Have the students listen to the tape Making Decisions.

The group is led to draw the conclusion that this tape continues the discussion presented in the first three tapes.

Each tape presents a single idea—each side is important for it gives information that helps us see the new idea more clearly.

C. If the group votes to continue listening to this series of tapes, every opportunity should be given to have the students see that:

Sharing is caring.

Each person is responsible for his or her own behavior.

"You Can Be Better Than You Are."

NOTE: As a summary to this learning project, the group can learn to sing this song with sincerity.

Resource Kit:
BOOK
   Listening Games by Guy Walker et al. (Collier Macmillan)
CASSETTES

The One and Only, Very Special You (Eye Gate—12 cassettes, 12 teaching guides)

Being a Good Friend	Living Things
Being Helpful	Making Decisions
Being Neat	Making Mistakes
Dangerous Things	Manners
Eating Healthy Meals	Safe Places
Getting Lost	Snacks—Good and Bad
He's Different, She's Different	Stealing
How I Feel	Telling the Truth
How They Feel	Things You Have
I Can't Do It	To and from School
It Belongs to Someone	Trying New Things
Keeping Clean	Your Teeth

MODEL 5   PLANNING THE MENU FOR CINDERELLA'S PARTY

Learning Project: Planning the Menu for Cinderella's Party
Grade: 2–3
Project Goals

To provide learning experiences that will introduce the gifted student to the skill of reading and analyzing information.

To provide learning experiences that will acquaint the gifted student with a wide sampling of Walt Disney stories and characters.

To provide learning experiences that will entice the gifted student to try his or her hand at cooking.

MODEL 5 (cont.)

Procedural Outline:
I. Orientation:
   A. The GATE group reads *Cinderella's Castle* by Walt Disney Productions.
   B. Following the group reading of the book, the GATE students recall as many of the characters as possible.
   C. A list is compiled of the characters the group has remembered.
   D. The group rereads *Cinderella's Castle* and adds the names of the characters the group has failed to recall—the list of characters in order of their appearance in the story are:

Snow White	Alice in Wonderland
The Seven Dwarfs	White Rabbit
Tinkerbell	Mad Hatter
Wendy	Queen of Hearts
Michael	Jiminy Cricket
John	Cleo the Goldfish
Peter Pan	Geppeto
Dumbo	Pinocchio
Bambi	Cinderella's Godmother
Thumper	The Prince

II. The GATE students set out to discover the names of the Seven Dwarfs using:
   A. *Walt Disney's Snow White and the Seven Dwarfs*

      The book

      The sound filmstrip

      The recording

   B. *Snow White and Other Stories from Grimm* (the students discover that in the original story written by the Brothers Grimm, the dwarfs did not have individual names).
III. Using *Walt Disney's Mickey Mouse Cookbook* the students can discover the favorite recipes of the friends who are coming to Cinderella's party.
   A. Each student is responsible for several friends listed above.
   B. After the student discovers the recipe associated with his or her Disney character, he or she copies the recipe on a special card.
   C. The group compiles a recipe book to share with classmates, family, and friends.
IV. As part of the Bookworm Reading Club activities, two different kinds of books will be explored (see Model 6 for information pertaining to the Bookworm Reading Club):
   B. Cookbooks with special appeal for children, such as:

      The Lip-Smakin', Joke-Crackin' Cookbook for Kids by Spring Asher (Golden Press)

      Little Witch's Black Magic Cookbook by Linda Glovach (Prentice-Hall)

      The Pooh Cook Book by Virginia Ellison (Dutton)

Resource Kit:
   BOOKS

   Cinderella's Castle by Walt Disney Productions (Golden Press)

   The Mickey Mouse Make-It Book by Walt Disney Productions (Random House)

   Walt Disney's Alice in Wonderland illus. by Walt Disney Studio (Golden Press)

   Walt Disney's Bambi illus. by Walt Disney Studio (Golden Press)

   Walt Disney's Cinderella illus. by Walt Disney Studio (Golden Press)

   Walt Disney's Mickey Mouse Cookbook by Walt Disney Productions (Golden Press)

MODEL 5 (cont.)

Walt Disney's Mother Goose illus. by Walt Disney Studio (Golden Press)

Walt Disney's Peter Pan illus. by Walt Disney Studio (Golden Press)

Walt Disney's Snow White and the Seven Dwarfs by Walt Disney Productions (Random House)

Walt Disney's Snow White and the Seven Dwarfs illus. by Walt Disney Studio (Golden Press)

Walt Disney Presents Winnie-the-Pooh and Eeyore's Birthday illus. by Walt Disney Studio (Golden Press)

Walt Disney Presents Winnie-the-Pooh: A Tight Squeeze illus. by Walt Disney Studio (Golden Press)

RECORDS (Walt Disney Productions)

Walt Disney's Story of Alice in Wonderland

Walt Disney's Story of Bambi

Walt Disney's Story of Dumbo

FILMSTRIPS (Walt Disney Educational Materials)

Bambi

Snow White and the Seven Dwarfs

Winnie-the-Pooh and the Honey Tree

MODEL 6   OUR WONDERFUL WORLD OF ANIMALS

Learning Project: Our Wonderful World of Animals

Grade: 2–3

Project Goal: To quicken within the student an insatiable curiosity about the mysteries of animal behavior and to foster an enduring compassionate concern for the welfare of all animals.

Teaching Objectives:

This project has been designed and structured to provide opportunities for the students:

To explore animal behavior—adaptations, life cycles and styles, and habitats—with scientific accuracy, wonder, challenge, and delight.

To share with fellow GATE students and with classmates what has been learned about animal behavior.

To explore career opportunities in the fields of animal study and care.

To become acquainted with Aileen Fisher as a naturalist and as an author.

To perceive the difference between fact and fantasy.

To discover the variety and kinds of books shelved in school library in the 500s and 600s dealing with animals.

To read, to view, to listen, to think, and to communicate thought accurately and effectively with wonder and delight.

Teaching Strategies and Methods:

No time limitations are imposed on this project. Number of students in the GATE group coupled with student interest is the factor determining the duration of the project, whether it be two weeks, two months, or longer.

A basic part of the orientation to this project is to explore with the students the advantage to be gained by sharing not only with fellow GATE students but with their classmates what they have learned about the wonderful world of animals.

After group orientation to the project, each student is encouraged to explore as widely as he or she wishes.

MODEL 6 (cont.)

Procedural Outline:
  I. Group orientation to the project.
    A. The students explore the meaning of the project title "The Wonderful World of Animals."
      1. *Wonderful:* causing wonder; marvelous; remarkable.
      2. *World:* all of certain parts, people, or things of the earth.
    B. The students apply the two definitions and make a list of examples such as:
      1. *Wonderful*
          Using the card catalog, discover the titles of books beginning with the word WONDERFUL. For example:

          The Wonderful Egg by Dahlov Ipcar

          Wonderful Flight to the Mushroom Planet by Eleanor Cameron

          Wonderful Wizard of Oz by Frank Baum

          Wonderful World of Cats by Beth Brown

          Wonderful World of Dogs by Beth Brown

          Wonderful World of Horses by Ned Hoopes

      2. *World*
          Using the card catalog, discover the titles of books beginning with the word WORLD. For example:

          World of Christopher Robin by A. A. Milne

          World of Pooh by A. A. Milne

          World of the Ant by David Costello

          World of the Opossum by James Keefe

          World of the Prairie by David Costello

    C. The students pool their impressions of the television program "The Wild, Wild World of Animals."
      1. What kinds of animal programs have they seen?
      2. What kinds of information about an animal does "The Wild, Wild World of Animals" provide?
    D. The students compile a list of kinds of information they would like to discover about animals ("The Ways of Animals" list).
      1. This list will be used as a guide throughout this project.
      2. The list will be expanded by the students to reflect new kinds of insight gained during this project.
 II. Exploring the multimedia kit "The Ways of Animals" (Bowmar Nature Series)
    A. Before the kit is opened, the students speculate as to the meaning of the title "The Ways of Animals."
    B. Upon opening the kit, the students discover 10 books, 10 filmstrips, and 10 cassettes.
    C. The students discover that Aileen Fisher is the author of each of the following 10 books:

    1. *Animal Disguises*   7. *Now That Days Are Colder*
    2. *Animal Houses*   8. *Sleepy Heads*
    3. *Animal Jackets*   9. *Tail Twisters*
    4. *Filling the Bill*   10. *"You Don't Look Like Your Mother,"*
    5. *Going Places*   *Said the Robin to the Fawn*
    6. *No Accounting for Tastes*

    D. The students discover that a sound filmstrip matches each of the books in the kit.
III. The students as a group read the book *Animal Disguises,* and then see the matching filmstrip.
    A. The students share their ideas gained from the book and filmstrip.
      1. An animal can blend into its surroundings so well that it "may cause you to blink or trick you to think it isn't there at all."

MODEL 6 (cont.)

2. An animal's color and shape can help protect it from its enemies.
3. When an animal's color or shape blends with its surroundings, we say the animal is camouflaged.
4. Some animals have colorings that mimic the appearance of animals its enemies avoid. This kind of protection is called mimicry.

B. The students begin a science word list.
   1. The words *camouflage* and *mimicry* are listed and the students define the meaning of each of the terms.
   2. The students will each take responsibility for discovering important new science words in the remaining nine books by Aileen Fisher and in the accompanying filmstrips.

C. Each student selects one or more of the books to read and then shares with the GATE group.
   1. In preparation, the group reviews the list "The Ways of Animals" previously compiled.

      Each student is responsible for identifying the specific "ways" found in the Aileen Fisher book he or she has read.

      Each student is responsible for adding to the list new "ways" he or she has discovered.

   2. Each student, upon completion of the book, previews and studies the matching filmstrip.

      Important concepts are identified.

      New words are listed and defined.

      In preparation for sharing the filmstrip with the GATE group each student is encouraged to search out other media: books, pictures, filmstrips, and/or slides.

IV. If the classroom teacher wishes, the GATE students will share their understanding of "The Ways of Animals" with the class.
   A. When scheduled to do so by the classroom teacher, each student will show a filmstrip and provide the explanation.
      1. Prior to projecting the filmstrip, the student will introduce new terms.
      2. Following the presentation, the student will answer questions, mention other sources of information, and offer to help the class members locate materials.
   B. If the classroom teacher wishes, the GATE students will organize and maintain a learning center, "The Ways of Animals," in the classroom.

V. The GATE students as individuals pursue their exploration of animal behavior.
   A. Using a life science concept learning guide, the students will categorize the information under the following headings:

1. Food	8. Change
2. Shelter	9. Dependency
3. Coverings	10. Interdependency
4. Rest	11. Adaptations
5. Protection	12. Does this animal live in or near our
6. Movement	community?
7. Growth	

   B. If the classroom teacher wishes, the GATE students will continue to share with their classmates new information gained.

VI. The GATE students search out other books written by Aileen Fisher.
   A. By checking the card catalog in the school library, they discover the following:
      1. *Cricket in a Thicket*
      2. *Going Barefoot*
      3. *In the Woods, in the Meadow, in the Sky*
      4. *Listen, Rabbit*
      5. *Where Does Everyone Go?*

MODEL 6 (cont.)

B. As part of the Reading Club (Bookworms) activities, the students read and discuss Aileen Fisher
   1. As a naturalist
   2. As a poet
   3. As an author
   NOTE: If the students have not been introduced to the sound filmstrip set "How to Grow Bookworms" (Eye Gate), several of the filmstrips can be introduced here. For example:
   Why We Read
   How to Share Our Reading
   The Bookworm bookmarks, book title summary chart, reading record booklet, and membership pins (Library Products)* can also be introduced at this time.
C. If the classroom teacher wishes, the GATE students can share with their classmates, either in the library or the classroom, the Wonderful World of Aileen Fisher.

VII. As a culminating activity, the students explore a number of avenues under the heading "What more do we need to know?"
   A. Does the *Childcraft* reference set have additional information?
      1. Volume 5 is entitled *About Animals*—the contents lists the following:

	page
The Animal Kingdom	4
It's a Mammal	28
It's a Bird	50
It's a Fish	68
It's a Reptile	82
It's an Amphibian	98
Many-Legged Creatures	110
The World of the Sea	130
The Hidden World	148
Staying Alive	158
Animal Ways	172
The Animals' World	190
Living Together	214
Animals of Long Ago	214
People and Animals	232
Domestic Animals	256
Vanishing Animals	294
Favorite Animals	304
Hard Words	322

      2. *Childcraft Annuals*
         About Animals—1971
         Animals in Danger—1974
   B. Does the Compton's *Precyclopedia* reference set have additional information?
      1. Volume 1 contains the following:

Animals—Can You See It?	74–79
The Special Long Sleep	80–83
A Tale About Tails	84–87
How to Catch a Giraffe	88–91
Animal Partners	92–97
Insect Castle Builders	98–103

      2. Volume 12 contains the following:

Choosing a Pet	74–81
The Pets in the Dream	82–83
Which Dog?	84–85

*Library Products, Box 130, Sturgis, Mich. 49091, tel. 616-651-5076.

MODEL 6 (cont.)

C. Does *Disney's Wonderful World of Knowledge* reference set have additional information? (Attention is called to the joining of the two words, *Wonderful* and *World* in the title of this set.)
1. Volume 1 contains the following:

Animals—In Jungles and Forests	9–33
Animals—Beasts of the Open Country	34–53
With Water, Ice, and Snow	55–69
A Mountain Peak Is Home	71–79
Life at the Poles	81–91
They Live in Water but Need Air	93–99
They Who See Best in the Dark	101–105
The Animals Who Live with Us	107–122

2. Volume 6 contains the following:

Birds in Flight	9–59
Amphibians and Reptiles	61–77
Fish: A World of Blue Light	79–99
Insects	101–123

3. Volume 12 contains the following:

Man's Best Friends	39–59

D. What career opportunities are there in the field of working with and/or taking care of animals?
1. The filmstrip series *Working with Animals* (Troll) introduces a number of careers in the care and training of animals. The following sound filmstrips explain the skills, duties, and environment of each career:

Animal Careers for You

Canine Control Officer

Pet Shop Worker

Veterinarian and Aides

Park Naturalist

Humane Educator

2. The following books introduce a variety of careers working with animals:

Animal Doctors by Carla Greene

At the Pet Hospital by Jane Hefflefinger

Careers in Animal Care by Christopher Benson

Careers in Conservation by Christopher Benson

I Know an Animal Doctor by Ckika Iritani

I Want to Be a Zoo Keeper by Carla Greene

I Want to Be an Animal Doctor by Carla Greene

What Can She Be? A Veterinarian by Gloria Goldreich

3. Interviewing community friends who work with animals is a good way to find out about careers working with animals.

How do you prepare for an interview?

How do you schedule an interview?

What questions do you ask?

How do you thank a person for his or her time?

How can you share the information with your fellow GATE group or with your classmates?

E. What agencies protect animals from neglect and/or cruelty?
1. If you want to locate information on animal care in the yellow pages of the telephone book, under what headings would you look?

Using the yellow pages index, see if you can discover people and agencies that care for and protect animals.

MODEL 6 (cont.)

Two headings give information: "Animal Hospitals" and "Animal Shelters."

2. Check the animal hospitals and see how many you can find that are located near where you live.
3. Check the animal shelters list; carefully write the name of the shelter, the address, and the telephone number on an index card.
4. Make a list of questions to ask the person in charge of each shelter.

Be sure to ask how the agency gets money to support its work.

Be sure to ask if the agency has booklets that will explain its work.

Be sure to ask if the agency will send someone from the agency to talk to the GATE group, and/or your class, and/or your school.

5. How can you help protect animals from neglect and cruelty?

Could you sponsor a "Be Kind to Animals" week?

What could you do to teach and to demonstrate kindness?

How could you get your parents, friends, and neighbors to take part in your special "Be Kind to Animals" week?

VIII. Field experiences for the GATE students to participate in and, if the classroom teacher wishes, to share with their classmates.
   A visit to:

   The aviary
   An animal hospital
   A pet shop
   The zoo

IX. Discovering the wonderful world of animals in:
   A. Books of fiction and fantasy such as:
      1. *Freddy the Detective* by Walter Brooks
      2. *Once a Mouse* and *Puss in Boots* by Marcia Brown
      3. *Old Mother West Wind* by Thornton Burgess
      4. *Tough Enough* by Ruth and Latrobe Carroll
      5. *Happy Lion* by Louise Fatio
      6. *Walter the Lazy Mouse* by Marjorie Flack
      7. *How to Read a Rabbit* by Jean Fritz
      8. *Dr. Dolittle* by Hugh Lofting
      9. *Winnie-the-Pooh* by A. A. Milne
      10. *Little Raccoon and the Thing in the Pool* by Lilian Moore
      11. *Marshmallow* by Clare Newberry
      12. *The Tale of Peter Rabbit* by Beatrix Potter
      13. *Curious George* by Hans Rey
      14. *Cricket in Times Square* by George Selden
      15. *Emilie* by Tomi Ungerer
      16. *Charlotte's Web* by E. B. White
   B. Poetry such as:
      1. *I Went to the Animal Fair* by William Cole
      2. *Listen, Rabbit* by Aileen Fisher
      3. *Animal Antics in Limerick Land* and *Poetry for Bird Watchers* by Leland Jacobs
      4. *Little Raccoon and Poems from the Woods* by Lilian Moore
   C. Songs such as :
      1. "Frog Went A-Courtin' "
      2. "Here Comes Peter Cottontail"
      3. "Old Dog Tray"
      4. "Rudolph the Red-Nosed Reindeer"
      5. "Talk to the Animals"
      6. "Who's Afraid of the Big Bad Wolf?"

MODEL 6 (cont.)

    D. Story prints such as:
        1. "The Baby Show" by Margaret Ross
        2. "Bedtime" by Margaret Ross
        3. "Benjamin Bunny" by Beatrix Potter
        4. "Goodnight Time" by Molly Brett
        5. "Jemima Puddle-Duck" by Beatrix Potter
        6. "Mickey Mouse" by Walt Disney
            NOTE: Many of the Disney animal characters are to be found in the 12-volume reference set *Disney's Wonderful World of Knowledge.*
        7. "Peter Rabbit" by Beatrix Potter
        8. "The Village Shop" by Margaret Ross
    E. Study prints such as (SVE)
        1. "Farm and Ranch Animals"
        2. "Pets"
        3. "Zoo Animals"
X. Special reinforcing activities for the GATE students and, if the classroom teacher wishes, for their classmates.
    A. Study the book *Which Is Which?* by Solveig Russell and learn how to tell the difference between:
        1. Butterflies and moths
        2. Arabian and Bactrian camels
        3. Bees and wasps
        4. Land snails and slugs
        5. African and Indian elephants
        6. Monkeys and apes
        7. Toads and frogs
        8. Beavers and muskrats
        9. Alligators and crocodiles
      10. Seals and sea lions
    B. Make a list of the strange things that animals, birds, fish, insects, and reptiles do. Have a contest to see who in the GATE group or in the class can identify the animal, bird, fish, insect, or reptile you are describing. The following books by Leonora Hornblow will help you start your list of strange things:
        1. *Animals Do the Strangest Things*
        2. *Birds Do the Strangest Things*
        3. *Fish Do the Strangest Things*
        4. *Insects Do the Strangest Things*
        5. *Reptiles Do the Strangest Things*
    C. Make bird feeders and bird shelters to help your feathered friends over the winter. The following book has a number of suggestions: *Bird Feeders and Shelters You Can Make* by Ted Pettit.
    D. Form a committee to discover animal programs to be presented on television. This committee will be responsible for alerting the GATE group and, if the classroom teacher wishes, the class each Monday as to the scheduled animal program during that week.

THE WAYS OF ANIMALS

Student _____ Date _____

The Name of the Animal I Learned about Is _____
This Is What I Learned about the Behavior of This Animal:

    Food _____

    _____

    _____

MODEL 6 (cont.)

Shelter _____

_____

_____

Coverings _____

_____

_____

Rest _____

_____

_____

Protection _____

_____

_____

Movement _____

_____

_____

Growth _____

_____

_____

Change _____

_____

_____

Dependency _____

_____

_____

Interdependency _____

_____

_____

Adaptation _____

_____

_____

Does this animal live in our community? _____

MODEL 7   OUR WONDERFUL WORLD OF PLANTS

Learning Project: Our Wonderful World of Plants

Grade: 2–3

Project Goal: To quicken within the student an insatiable curiosity about the mysteries of the world of plants and an abiding appreciation of the beauty and order of the world of plants.

Teaching Objectives:

This project has been designed and structured to provide opportunities for the students:

To explore the world of plants—varieties, characteristics, life cycles, adaptations and habitats—with scientific accuracy, wonder, challenge, and delight.

To share with fellow GATE students and with classmates what has been learned about the ways of plants.

To explore career opportunities in the fields of plant study, propagation, and care.

MODEL 7 (cont.)

To become acquainted with Millicent Selsam as a naturalist and as an author of science books for children.

To discover the variety and kinds of books dealing with plants that are available in the school media center.

To summarize what has been learned in the previous unit, Our Wonderful World of Animals, together with what has been learned in this unit, Our Wonderful World of Plants, by organizing a student nature guide.

To read, to view, to listen, to think, and to communicate thought accurately, effectively, and creatively.

Teaching Strategies and Methods:

No time limitations are imposed on this project. Number of students in the GATE group coupled with student interest is the factor determining the duration of the project, whether it be two weeks, two months, or longer.

A basic part of the orientation to this project is to explore with the students the advantage to be gained by sharing not only with fellow GATE students but with their classmates what they have learned about the wonderful world of plants.

After group orientation to the project, each student is encouraged to explore as widely as he or she wishes.

Procedural Outline:

   I. Group orientation to the project.
     A. The students view the sound filmstrip *The Bears' Nature Guide: Almost Everything Small Bears and Kids Need to Know about . . . the Animals, the Plants, the Earth Itself* (Random House).
       1. This serves as a review of the learnings gained from the unit Our Wonderful World of Animals.
       2. It serves, also, as an introduction to the world of plants.
     B. The students read the book *The Bears' Nature Guide,* and explore the possibility of each student's making a nature guide to record his or her own observations and thoughts about the world of nature.
  II. As an introduction to the unit, the students read *A First Look at the World of Plants* by Millicent E. Selsam and Joyce Hunt (Walker).
     A. The students become acquainted with the joint authors.
     B. Checking the card catalog in the school library, the students discover the following books by Selsam and/or Hunt:
       1. *A First Look at Flowers*
       2. *A First Look at Leaves*
       3. *Mimosa, the Sensitive Plant*
       4. *Popcorn*
       5. *The Tomato and Other Fruit Vegetables*
       6. *Vegetables from Stems and Leaves*
     C. Reading the above books introduces the students to the following concepts:
       1. Any living thing that is not an animal is a plant.
       2. Some plants have roots, stems, and leaves; some do not.
       3. Some plants have flowers; some do not.
       4. Some plants are green; some are not.
       5. Some plants are so small that they can only be seen under a microscope.
       6. Bacteria are the tiniest plants in the world; each plant is a single cell.
       7. Bacteria get their food from other plants and animals.
       8. Algae are almost as small as bacteria; chlorophyll makes algae and other plants green.
       9. Liverworts and mosses are called bryophytes; they have no real roots, stems, or leaves.
     10. Fungi are not green like algae, liverworts, and mosses; they have no roots, stems, or leaves.

MODEL 7 (cont.)

11. Mushrooms are a common type of fungus.
12. Puffballs are fungi that are round like balls.
13. Molds are the fungi you see growing on bread, fruit, cheese, and some-times leather.
14. Ferns have real roots, stems, and leaves; they form new plants from spores just as mosses and fungi do.
15. Gymnosperms have roots, stems, and leaves like ferns; they produce seeds instead of spores.
16. Angiosperms are flowering plants; their seeds have a covering called a fruit.
17. To tell angiosperms apart you have to look at the leaves, the flowers, and the fruits.
18. Any part of a plant that has seeds in it is called a fruit.
   D. The students summarize what they have learned in their *Nature Guide.*
III. The students explore the multimedia kit "The Ways of Plants" (Bowmar Nature Series).
   A. Upon opening the kit, the students discover 10 books, 10 filmstrips, and 10 cassettes.
   B. The students discover that Aileen Fisher is the author of each of the 10 books in the kit, just as she had been the author of the 10 books in the kit "The Ways of Animals."
   C. The titles of the 10 books in the kit are:
      1. *Now That Spring Is Here*   6. *Petals Yellow and Petals Red*
      2. *Mysteries in the Garden*   7. *Swords and Daggers*
      3. *And a Sunflower Grew*   8. *Prize Performance*
      4. *Seeds on the Go*   9. *A Tree with a Thousand Uses*
      5. *Plant Magic*   10. *As the Leaves Fall Down*
   D. In preparation for exploring the contents of the kit "The Ways of Plants," the students discuss what the "ways" of plants might include.
      1. They define the following terms:
         Biology: the study of living things.
         Zoology: the study of animals and animal life.
         Botany: the study of plants and plant life.
         Biologist: a person who is an expert in the field of biology.
         Botanist: a person who is an expert in the field of botany.
         Zoologist: a person who is an expert in the field of zoology.
      2. Each student in this learning project will have the opportunity to discover how botanists think and act.
      3. In searching out information on the "ways" of plants, the students, in order to write plant *biographies,* will use the following as guides:
         The name of the plant.
         Where the plant lives.
         Description of the plant: roots, stems, flowers, leaves, seeds.
         Conditions favorable to the plant's growth.
         Interesting facts about the plant.
         Whether or not this plant grows in the community.
         Whether or not this plant is beneficial to mankind.
         Whether or not this plant is beneficial to animals.
IV. Each student selects one or more of the books from the kit to read and then prepares to introduce the book to the group.
   A. Upon completion of the book and the viewing of the matching filmstrip, the student, in conference with the school library media specialist, will identify and then select additional materials—books, filmstrips, study prints, charts, and slides—to share with the group.
   B. He or she will lead group discussion following his or her presentation.
   C. The group will add to their *Nature Guide* new and interesting information they have gained.
   D. If the classroom teacher wishes, the student will share this information with the class.

MODEL 7 (cont.)

V. Following the presentation and discussion of the concepts obtained from reading the books and viewing the filmstrips contained in the Bowmar kit "The Ways of Plants," the following culminating activities will follow:

A. The group will write a letter to Aileen Fisher sharing with her their thoughts and feelings about her nature study books.

B. The group will view the 8mm motion picture *Basic Needs of Plants* (Encyclopaedia Britannica), which reemphasizes many of the concepts encountered in this learning project, including:
  1. Experiments showing why plants must have minerals, water, light, and air to thrive.
  2. The scientific method of observing, testing and retesting, and drawing conclusions.

C. The group will add to their *Nature Guide* additional information of significance to them.

D. The students will work in the library media center exploring topics either of their own invention or ones they have chosen from the following list:
  1. Amazing plant facts
  2. Balance in nature
  3. Banyan trees
  4. Bees, flowers, and pollination
  5. Contributions of Johnny "Appleseed" Chapman
  6. Contributions of Luther Burbank
  7. Contributions of George Washington Carver
  8. Flowerpot gardens
  9. Food from plants
  10. Giants of the plant world
  11. House plants
  12. How plants move
  13. Insect-eating plants
  14. The origin and importance of Arbor Day
  15. Plant experiments
  16. Plants as pets
  17. Plants that cure
  18. Plants that give off light
  19. Plants that give us beverages, candy, and chewing gum
  20. State flowers, trees, birds, mammals, insects, and fish
  21. Strangler fig
  22. Textiles from plants
  23. Trees in our community
  24. Tropical flowers
  25. Tropical fruits
  26. Unusual seeds
  27. What does a conservationist do?
  28. What does a farmer do?
  29. What does a florist do?
  30. What does a forester do?
  31. What does a naturalist do?
  32. What does a plant experimenter do?
  33. What is a terrarium and how do you make one?
  34. The wonderful world of flowers
  35. The wonderful world of trees

VI. A scout master from the community will explain scouting and a scout's concern for safeguarding the plants and animals of the woodlands.

A. The purpose of having a scout earn a merit badge is explored.

B. The list of merit badge subjects is distributed (see Checklist A at the end of this model).

C. The value of using a field guide such as the scouts' *Field Guide* is explored.

D. The concept of wild-flower conservation is developed and ways of safeguard-

MODEL 7 (cont.)

ing wild flowers are discussed; planting wild flowers in home gardens is explored as a positive measure to beautify the community and safeguard rare wild flowers (see Checklist B at the end of this model).

    E. Scouts from the junior and/or senior high school will share with the group safety tips to be observed when exploring in wooded areas.

VII. A florist from the community will explore with the group the best way to care for home plants.

    A. How to prepare and care for a terrarium will be demonstrated.

    B. How to keep a schedule for watering and feeding plants will be explained.

    C. The preparation and work of a florist will be discussed.

VIII. The art teacher explores with the students the relationship of nature to art.

    A. Introduces the concept of nature as an art motif evidenced in:

Advertising	Jewelry
Calendars	Paintings
Gift wrapping	Textiles
Greeting cards	Wallpaper
Household furnishings	

    B. Introduces the concept of collecting and painting from nature.

        1. John Hawkinson, artist and illustrator, has published two books (Albert Whitman), which present a variety of techniques to be used in printing and painting from nature:

          Collect, Print, and Paint from Nature
          More to Collect and Paint from Nature

        2. Hawkinson encourages gathering specimens, examining them closely, and then experimenting artistically with reproducing them.

        3. Hawkinson says:

          In this world we live in we are surrounded by the grace and beauty of nature. The leaves, flowers, moss and ferns in a beech-maple forest, for example, all have their individual patterns which mold together to make a larger design in nature.

          By bringing home leaves and other specimens from the woods and fields and by making prints or paintings with them, you become aware of their shape and beauty. And by placing them in different designs, as you paint, you create your personal impression of the trip you took. (From *Collect, Print, and Paint from Nature,* by John Hawkinson. Copyright © 1963 by Albert Whitman & Company, p. 2.)

IX. A field learning experience in North Park conducted by the park naturalist includes:

    A. The scientific approach to specimen collecting.

    B. Poisonous plants to avoid.

    C. Endangered plants NOT to touch.

    D. Using field guides to identify plants.

    E. The training and work of a naturalist.

X. The students in a series of laboratory sessions with the art teacher and/or the GATE teacher create their painted impressions of the plants gathered.

XI. A laboratory session is held in the school library; the librarian introduces:

    A. The various series of field guides available for student use and loan:

      The Golden Field Guides (Golden Press)

      The Grosset All-Color Guides (Grosset and Dunlap)

      The Peterson Field Guides (Houghton Mifflin)

    B. The learning station "The Miracle of Plants" that has been set up for the GATE students to use in continuing their self-elected study of plants the rest of the school year (see Checklist C at the end of this model).

XII. As a culminating activity, the students have a guided tour of Phipps Conservatory (see Chapter 6 for student reaction to the tour).

MODEL 7 (cont.)
CHECKLIST A: MERIT BADGE SUBJECTS*

American Business
American Heritage
Animal Science
Archery
Architecture
Art
Astronomy
Athletics
Atomic Energy
Aviation
Basketry
Beekeeping
Bird Study
Bookbinding
Botany
Bugling (See Music)
Camping
Canoeing
Chemistry
Citizenship in the Community
Citizenship in the Nation
Citizenship in the World
Coin Collecting
Communications
Computers
Consumer Buying
Cooking
Cycling
Dentistry
Dog Care
Drafting
Electricity
Electronics
Emergency Preparedness
Energy
Engineering
Environmental Science
Farm Arrangements
Farm Mechanics
Farm Records

Fingerprinting
Firemanship
First Aid
Fish and Wildlife Management
Fishing
Forestry
Gardening
Genealogy
General Science
Geology
Golf
Hiking
Home Repairs
Horsemanship
Indian Lore
Insect Life
Journalism
Landscaping Architecture
Law
Leatherwork
Lifesaving
Machinery
Mammals
Masonry
Metals Engineering
Metalwork
Model Design and Building
Motorboating
Music
Nature
Oceanography
Orienteering
Painting
Personal Fitness
Personal Management
Pets
Photography
Pigeon Raising
Pioneering

Plant Science
Plumbing
Pottery
Printing
Public Health
Public Speaking
Pulp and Paper
Rabbit Raising
Radio
Railroading
Reading
Reptile Study
Rifle and Shotgun Shooting
Rowing
Safety
Salesmanship
Scholarship
Sculpture
Signaling
Skating
Skiing
Small-Boat Sailing
Soil and Water Conservation
Space Exploration
Sports
Stamp Collecting
Surveying
Swimming
Textile
Theater
Traffic Safety
Truck Transportation
Veterinary Science
Water Skiing
Weather
Wilderness Survival
Wood Carving
Woodwork

CHECKLIST B: WILDFLOWER SOURCES

Information on wild flowers can be obtained from the sources listed below. In some cases, there may be a nominal charge.

ALGROVE
Box 459H
Wilmington, MA 01887

CLASSICAL ARTIFACTS
Aladdin House Ltd.
Dept. N-10D
648 Ninth Ave.
New York, N.Y. 10036

CONLEY'S GARDEN CENTER
Boothbay Harbor, ME
04538

*Taken from the *Boy Scout Handbook,* available from the Boy Scouts of America, North Brunswick, N.J. 08902.

MODEL 7 (cont.)

DIETRICK GARDENS
Rte. 2
Dexter, MI 48130

GARDENS OF THE BLUE RIDGE
Ashford, McDowell
County, NC 28603

GRIFFEY'S NURSERY
Rte. 3, Box 17A
Marshall, NC 28753

JAMIESON VALLEY GARDENS
Rte. 3-B
Spokane, WA 99203

LESLIE'S WILDFLOWER
NURSERY
30 Summer St.
Methuen, MA 01844

LOUNSBERRY GARDENS
Box 135
Oakford, IL 62673

MIDWEST WILDFLOWERS
Box 664B
Rockton, IL 61072

MINCEMOYERS
RD 5, Box 397-H
Jackson, NJ 08527

ORCHID GARDENS
Rte. 3
Grand Rapids, MN 55744

PINEDALE GREENHOUSE
Mineral Bluff, GA 30559

PLAIN AND FANCY
Milford, NH 03055

PUTNEY NURSERY, INC.
Box H
Putney, VT 05346

REFORESTATION, INC.
Box 8146
Dept. GJ
Spokane, WA 99203

SAVAGE FARM NURSERY
Box 125 AK
McMinnville, TN 37110

VAN BOURGONDIEN
BROTHERS
Box A, 245 Farmingdale
Rd, Rte. 109
Babylon, NY 11702

VICK'S WILDGARDENS, INC.
Box 115
Gladwyne, PA 19035

WESTON NURSERIES
E. Main St., Rte. 135
Hopkinton, MA 01748

WOODLAND ACRES NURSERY
Dept. 4972
Crivitz, WI 54114

CHECKLIST C: LIBRARY LEARNING STATION—THE MIRACLE OF PLANTS

BOOKS

Ask Any Vegetable by Reinhart Eshmeyer (Prentice-Hall)

Botany by M. K. Hage, Jr., and Vere DeVault (Steck-Vaughn)

Carnivorous Plants by John F. Waters (Watts)

Easy to Grow Vegetables by Robert Gambino (Harvey House)

Farming in Boxes by Peter Stevenson (Scribner)

From Seed to Salad by Hannah L. Johnson (Lothrop)

Growing: Green Thumbs and Dirty Hands Creative Activities series (Childrens Press)

Growing Plants from Fruits and Vegetables by Jane Sholinsky (Scholastic)

The Herb and Spice Book for Kids by Alice Siegel and Margo McLoone (Holt)

House Plants Indoors/Outdoors by the editorial staff of Ortho Books (Ortho Books)

How to Grow a Jelly Glass Farm by Kathy Mandry and Joe Toto (Pantheon)

Kids Outdoor Gardening by Aileen Paul (Doubleday)

Living Things That Poison, Itch, and Sting by Phyllis S. Busch (Walker)

Peanuts by Franklin Watts (Childrens Press)

Peas, Beans, and Licorice by Olive L. Earle (Morrow)

Plant Science by Boy Scouts of America (Boy Scouts)

Plants for Pets by D. X. Fenten (Lippincott)

Plants That Eat Insects: A Look at Carniverous Plants by Anabel Dean (Lerner)

Plants That Heal By Millicent Selsam (Morrow)

Plants That Move by Millicent Selsam (Morrow)

Plants We Eat by Millicent Selsam (Morrow)

Play with Leaves and Flowers by Millicent Selsam (Morrow)

Play with Plants by Millicent Selsam (Morrow)

Play with Seeds by Millicent Selsam (Morrow)

MODEL 7 (cont.)

Poison Plants by Alan Eshleman (Houghton Mifflin)

Projects With Plants by Seymour Simon (Watts)

Science Dictionary of the Plant World by Michael Chinery (Watts)

What's in the Names of Flowers?, rev. ed., by Peter Limburg (Coward)

FILMSTRIPS:

How to Make a Terrarium (Troll)

Investigating Parts of a Flower (Herbert Budek)

Life Cycle of a Plant (Herbert Budek)

The Role of Flowers and Fruits (SVE—2 filmstrips, 1 record, 1 teacher's guide)

Flowers: Their Parts and Functions

Fruits: Their Growth and Classification

The Seed Plants (Coronet—8 filmstrips, 4 records, 1 teaching guide)

How Flowers Make Seeds

How They Sprout and Grow

Leaves and Their Work

The Major Kinds

Roots and Stems

Seeds and Their Dispersal

Their Adaptations

Their Uses

MODEL 8   COMMUNICATION

Grade: 3

Unit: Communication*

Project Goals:

To preplan with the classroom teacher to bring greater depth, breadth, relevance, and challenge to the classroom-based instructional program and then to translate that plan into substantive and significant learning experiences, which the GATE students, upon completion, will share with the class.

To provide the opportunity for the student to explore widely, to discover challenge and delight in learning how to learn, and to enjoy working with others.

Possible Enrichment Topics:

1. Abbreviations	16. Clocks
2. Advertising	17. Coat of arms
3. Alphabet	18. Codes
4. Atlantic cable	19. Coins and paper money
5. Banners	20. Colophons
6. Bells	21. Computers
7. Body language	22. Dewey decimal classification
8. Books	23. Filmstrips
9. Braille	24. Flags
10. Bulletin boards	25. Graphs and charts
11. Bumper stickers	26. Greeting cards
12. Calendars	27. Hieroglyphics
13. Card catalogs	28. Labels
14. Cartoons	29. Libraries
15. Cattle brands	30. License plates

*Model 9, Fun with Words, is an in-depth linguistics study that the GATE students pursue as part of this unit.

MODEL 8 (cont.)

31. Lighthouses
32. Logos
33. Magazines
34. Maps
35. Messages without words
36. Morse code
37. Motion pictures
38. Museums
39. Newspapers
40. Paper, ink, pen, pencil
41. Phonograph
42. Photography
43. Pictures/illustrations
44. Postal service and stamps
45. Posters
46. Printing
47. Radio (AM, FM, CB, HAM)
48. Reference books
49. Satellites
50. Secret messages
51. Sign language
52. Skywriting
53. Smoke signals
54. Songs
55. Statistics
56. Study prints
57. Sun dials
58. Symbols
59. Talking books
60. Telegraph
61. Telephone
62. Television
63. Totem poles
64. Trademarks
65. Transparencies/transvisions
66. Typewriter
67. Videotape
68. Alexander Graham Bell
69. Louis Braille
70. Grace Darling
71. George Eastman
72. Thomas Edison
73. Helen Keller
74. Guglielmo Marconi
75. Samuel F. B. Morse
76. Christopher Sholes

MODEL 9   FUN WITH WORDS

Grade: 3

Project Goal: To provide learning experiences that will introduce the students to words—
their meaning, their power, their beauty.

Teaching Objectives:

This project has been designed to provide these basic understandings:

Skill is the ability to do something well.

Skill with words is the ability to use words well.

The dictionary and the thesaurus are two important tools to be used in acquiring skill with words.

The fictional character Amelia Bedelia uses the *literal* meaning of words.

Some words have relatives called synonyms, antonyms, homonyms, and homographs.

Building one's vocabulary is a lifelong process.

Working crossword puzzles is an effective way to build knowledge of words.

This project has been designed to foster these attitudes and appreciations:

Appreciation of the multiple meaning of words.

Appreciation of the many opportunities to use words creatively.

Appreciation of the beauty of word usage in poetry and song.

Delight in discovering new words.

Delight in experimenting with words.

Delight in playing word games.

Delight in reading about Amelia Bedelia and her many mixed-up word adventures.

Delight in reading other books written by Peggy Parish.

Teaching Strategies:

No time limits are imposed on this project. Number of students in the group coupled with student interest is the factor determining the duration of the project whether it be two weeks, two months, or longer.

MODEL 9 (cont.)

A basic part of group orientation to the project is to provide opportunities for the students to explore the synergistic effect of sharing knowledge gained and then to determine appropriate methods and procedures for pooling information.

Partial Procedural Outline:

I. Group orientation to the project

   A. The adventures of the literal-minded maid Amelia Bedelia are enjoyed by the group.

      1. The *Amelia Bedelia* series of books written by Peggy Parish (Harper) is read and discussed by the group.
Amelia Bedelia
Come Back, Amelia Bedelia
Good Work, Amelia Bedelia
Play Ball, Amelia Bedelia
Teach Us, Amelia Bedelia
Thank You, Amelia Bedelia

      2. The *Amelia Bedelia* series of filmstrips (New York Times) is enjoyed by the group.
Amelia Bedelia
Come Back, Amelia Bedelia
Play Ball, Amelia Bedelia
Thank You, Amelia Bedelia

   B. *The First Book of Language and How to Use It* by Mauree Applegate (Watts) serves as an introduction to the study of words.

      1. You have a built-in motion picture projector in your mind.

         This projector takes up no room, runs silently, and is very easy to operate.

         This projector shows on the screen of your mind what you see, what you hear, and what you imagine.

      2. Words can make pictures in the mind of the listener and the reader.

      3. In order to help people understand what you mean, you must know how words work.

   C. The dictionary and the thesaurus are two "word banks."

      1. The dictionary gives the following information about words:
Meaning
Correct spelling
Pronunciation
Synonyms
Antonyms
Part of speech
Sometimes a picture or an illustration

      2. Locating a word in the dictionary and studying it does *not* mean it is yours.
A word becomes part of your vocabulary when you use it easily.
Most adults have a vocabulary of at least 10,000 words.
President Wilson had about 60,000 words in his vocabulary.

      3. During this school year, each student is going to keep a list of new words he has discovered.

      4. Using the Scott, Foresman *Beginning Dictionary,* discover how a dictionary can help you.
Read the section entitled, "Using this dictionary."
Can you teach yourself:
How to find a word.
How to find a meaning.
How to use the pronunciations.
How to use this dictionary for spelling and writing.
The parts of a dictionary entry.

      5. A thesaurus is a treasury or storehouse of words arranged in categories.

MODEL 9 (cont.)

Using a variety of words increases your word power.

Using the Scott, Foresman thesaurus *In Other Words: A Beginning Thesaurus*, discover how a thesaurus can help you replace "tired" words.

Read the "Self-Help Introduction."

> Using *In Other Words . . . A Thesaurus Exercise Book,* test your ability to use this reference tool.

D. A pun is a play on words.
  1. Using *Pun Fun* by Ennis Rees (Hale), select several puns you enjoy.
  2. Using other books of puns, which you will find in your school library, select those you particularly enjoy; perhaps you and your friends will compile a notebook of puns to share with your classmates.
E. Many poems use words that rhyme.
  1. Why do you think that TV commercials use rhyming words to sell a product?
  2. Rhymes, games, and chants are not only part of your childhood, but they were part of your parents', your grandparents', and your great-grandparents' childhood.
  3. The book *Did You Feed My Cow?* by Margaret Taylor (Harcourt) contains a number of rhymes and chants that have been popular for a number of years.

     > Borrow *Did You Feed My Cow?* from the school library and take it home to share with your parents, grandparents, and other relatives; perhaps you will be surprised to discover the number of rhymes and chants they will know.

     Try your hand at making up a rhyme or a chant.
  4. Frequently when asked to write in a friend's autograph book, a person will write a poem.

     > The following books (Scholastic) contain a number of poems that have been written in autograph books:
     > *Remember Me When This You See* by Lillian Morrison
     > *Yours Till Niagara Falls* by Lillian Morrison
  5. The following poetry books (Garrard) are fun to explore:

     Animal Antics in Limerick Land selected by Leland Jacobs
     Arithmetic in Verse and Rhyme selected by Allan and Leland Jacobs
     Catch Your Breath: A Book of Shivery Poems selected by Lilian Moore
     Funny Bone Ticklers in Verse and Rhyme selected by Leland Jacobs
     Funny Folks in Limerick Land selected by Leland Jacobs
     Poetry for Bird Watchers selected by Leland Jacobs
     Poetry for Chuckles and Grins selected by Leland Jacobs
     Poetry of Witches, Elves, and Goblins selected by Leland Jacobs
     Poetry on Wheels selected by Lee Hopkins
     Sports and Games in Verse and Rhyme selected by Allan and Leland Jacobs
F. Dr. Seuss, in his stories, makes up many nonsense words; see how many nonsense words you can discover in the following books (Random House):

  Bartholomew and the Oobleck
  Horton Hears a Who
  How the Grinch Stole Christmas
  I Had Trouble in Getting to Solla Sollew
  The Lorax
  McElligot's Pool

MODEL 9 (cont.)

Sneetches and Other Stories

There's a Wocket in My Pocket!

Thidwick: The Big-Hearted Moose

  II. Individual students will work at their own rate and proceed to explore the world of words in each subsequent learning project.

    A. Each child will keep the form "New Words I Have Discovered" up to date throughout the school year.

    B. Spelling bees and definition bees will be held periodically.

Resource Kit:

  BOOKS

    Antonyms: Hot and Cold and Other Words That Are Different as Night and Day by Joan Hanson (Lerner)

    The Charlie Brown Dictionary by Charles Schulz (Random House)

    Homographs: Bow and Bow and Other Words That Look the Same but Sound as Different as Sow and Sow by Joan Hanson (Lerner)

    Homonyms: Hair and Hare and Other Words That Sound the Same but Look Different as Bear and Bare by Joan Hanson (Lerner)

    If You Talked to a Boar by Michael Sage (Lippincott)

    In Other Words: A Beginning Thesaurus by W. Cabell Greet et al. (Scott, Foresman)

    Let's Find Out About Names by Valerie Pitt (Watts)

    Let's Find Out About Words by Cathleen FitzGerald (Watts)

    More Antonyms: Wild and Tame and Other Words That Are as Different in Meaning as Work and Play by Joan Hanson (Lerner)

    More Homonyms: Steak and Stake and Other Words That Sound the Same but Look as Different as Chili and Chilly by Joan Hanson (Lerner)

    More Synonyms: Shout and Yell and Other Words That Mean the Same Thing but Look and Sound as Different as Loud and Noisy by Joan Hanson (Lerner)

    What Can You Do with a Word? by Jay Williams (Collier)

    Words Inside Words by Michael Sage (Lippincott)

    Would You Put Your Money in a Sand Bank? (Fun with Words) by Harold Longman (Rand McNally)

  STUDENT TABLET

    New Words I Discovered (Educational Reading Service)

  POSTER

    Welcome to the City of Mispelled Words (Scholastic)

MODEL 10 LITERATURE ENRICHMENT UNIT: "CALL IT COURAGE"

Grade: 4

Unit: Literature

    1. Introduce the entire book from which the reading selection has been taken.

      Call It Courage by Armstrong Sperry. Macmillan paperback.*

    2. Introduce biographical material about the author. Armstrong Sperry.

      Something about the Author, Gale Research, vol. 1, pp. 204–205.

    3. Introduce material explaining how the book came to be written.

      The Story behind Modern Books by Elizabeth Montgomery, pp. 136–141.

    4. Introduce the story in the following formats:

      FILMSTRIPS

        Adventure (Pied Piper—sound filmstrip)

        Call It Courage (Miller-Brody—sound filmstrip)

*This unit is typical of the enrichment experiences that provide depth, breadth, and relevance for students in an accelerated reading levels program.

MODEL 10 (cont.)

RECORDING
    Call It Courage (Miller-Brody—record or cassette)

5. Introduce other books written by Armstrong Sperry.

FICTION	NONFICTION
Black Falcon	*All about the Jungle*
Danger to Windward	*Amazon: River Sea of Brazil*
Hull-Down for Action	
Lost Lagoon	
Rain Forest	
Storm Canvas	

6. Introduce media paralleling the theme "Courage to Survive."
PRINT
    Adventure in Survival by Maurice Bean
    Escape by Sigurd Senje
    Firestorm by Maurine Gee
    Island of the Blue Dolphins by Scott O'Dell
    Jon the Unlucky by Elizabeth Coatsworth
    Julie of the Wolves by Jean George
    Landslide by Veronique Day
    A Long Vacation by Jules Verne
    Strange Intruder by Arthur Catherall
    Three without Fear by Robert DuSoe
    Two on an Island by Bianca Bradbury
    The Village That Slept by Monique De Ladebat
    White Water, Still Water by J. Allan Bosworth
    Wild Venture by James Johnson
    Zeb by Lonzo Anderson
NONPRINT
    River Boy. 2 filmstrips with recording (Educational Enrichment Materials)

7. Introduce media that further develop topics mentioned in *Call It Courage.*
Newbery Medal
Bookmarks—Children's Book Council
Posters
The John Newbery Medal. (Treasure Trove Library Binders, dist. by Weise-Winkler
    Bindery).
Your Newbery Friends (Miller-Brody)

8. Introduce the Carnegie Hero Fund Commission. Established April 15, 1904, by
Andrew Carnegie to recognize acts of selfless heroism performed in the United
States and Canada. Medals of bronze, silver, and gold are awarded.

The book *Rescue! True Stories of Heroism* by L. B. Taylor, Jr. (Watts) relates many
of the dramatic episodes that young medal winners have been a part of.

MODEL 11   ROMAN NUMERALS

Subject: Mathematics
Grade: 4
Topic: Learning to Use Roman Numerals
Subtopic 1: How did the Romans write their numbers 1 through 1,000?

Sources:
The Story of Numbers by Patricia Lauber (Random House), pp. 46–53

The New Book of Knowledge, vol. 16 (Grolier)

The Reader's Digest Almanac (Reader's Digest), check the index for Roman numerals

The World Almanac (Doubleday), check the index for Roman numerals

MODEL 11 (cont.)

Subtopic 2: How did the Romans add numbers?

Source:
The Day the Numbers Disappeared by Leonard Simon (McGraw-Hill), p. 37

Subtopic 3: How did the Romans subtract numbers?

Source:
The Day the Numbers Disappeared by Leonard Simon (McGraw-Hill), p. 37

Subtopic 4: How did the Romans multiply numbers?

Source:
The How and Why Wonder Book of Mathematics by Esther Highland (Grosset and Dunlap), p. 31

Optional activity 1: Review what you have learned about Roman numerals by using the Cyclo-teacher* with the following:
Cycle M46—sides 1 and 2
Cycle M47—sides 1 and 2
Cycle M48—sides 1 and 2

Optional activity 2: Prepare a transparency or a poster showing Roman numerals for:

1	100	4,000	25,000	1,000,000
10	1,000	5,000	50,000	5,000,000
50	2,000	10,000	100,000	10,000,000

Source:
The World Book, vol. 16 (Field Enterprises)

Optional activity 3: Make a series of flash cards to be used in testing your class's ability to interpret Roman numerals.

Optional activity 4: Place on transparencies problems in addition, subtraction, and multiplication using Roman numerals you wish to present to your class.

Optional activity 5: The Statue of Liberty holds in her left hand a tablet on which the date July IV, MDCCLXXVI, is written. Can you translate that date into arabic numerals? Do you know why this date is significant?

MODEL 12   GREAT BOOKS, PAST AND PRESENT

Learning Experience: Great Books, Past and Present
Grades: 4, 5, 6
Teaching Goal: To provide delightfully challenging excursions into the realm of the literary greats—past and present.
Teaching Objectives:
This project has been designed and structured to provide opportunity for the GATE student:

To explore the literature of the past and present with openness, keen anticipation, and delight.

To form a wide acquaintanceship and a lasting friendship with authors and illustrators who have made their mark in the literary world.

To enjoy and savor the imaginary happenings of fiction.

To perceive and to value the impact of human beings on the course of events as portrayed in biography, history, and legend.

---

*The Cyclo-teacher is a self-instructional teaching machine with programmed cycles for each of the disciplines on the elementary and junior high school level. This machine and its accompanying cycles are only sold by Field Educational Publications, Inc., 609 Mission St., San Francisco, Calif. 94105.

MODEL 12 (cont.)

To sample widely from the literary smorgasbord of adventure, biography, drama, fantasy, history, mystery, poetry, and science fiction.

To develop the lifelong habit of reading for pure enjoyment.

This project has been designed and structured to foster and develop these appreciations and attitudes:

Reading is a delightfully rewarding form of recreation.

A discriminating reader willingly explores beyond the "known."

Insight into human nature and social problems is a rich dividend accrued from reading both fiction and nonfiction.

Reading is a springboard for adventurous thinking.

The appeal of quality literature is universal and timeless.

Reading is not only thought provoking but emotion evoking.

A love of reading is a common characteristic shared by men and women who have achieved lasting recognition.

Teaching Strategies and Methods:

The Great Books theme is introduced as a basic part of the GATE Orientation Project.

This is a yearlong learning experience.

The major thrust of this continuous learning experience is to provide delightful and challenging excursions into the realm of quality literature.

The emphasis is on pure enjoyment.

Formal book reports have NO place in this learning project.

Great books are highlighted when timely as a regular part of each GATE learning project.

Limitless opportunities are given for each GATE student to explore widely as many types and kinds of literature as possible.

Students are encouraged, but not required, to relate literature to creative writing by experimenting with a variety of literary genres.

All the resources of the junior and senior high schools are available so that each student can read in any area that has special appeal.

Procedural Outline:

I. This learning experience is introduced during the GATE Orientation Project.

    A. It is particularly timely to introduce this theme when the students are being taught to keep a daily journal.

    B. The following can well serve as models:

My Journals and Sketchbooks by Robinson Crusoe (Harcourt)

This edition, translated from the French, was copyrighted in 1974.

It is based on the classic *Robinson Crusoe* by Daniel Defoe, first published in 1719.

A classic is a book that has lasting and universal appeal.

Robinson Crusoe has been read and enjoyed for over 260 years and has been translated into each of the major languages of the world.

The Story Behind Great Books by Elizabeth Montgomery provides insight into why and how this book was written.

It is based on the experiences of Alexander Selkirk.

Defoe asked himself:

"What would a man do, all alone?"

"How would he live?"

"How would he keep from loosing his mind?"

MODEL 12 (cont.)

Elizabeth Montgomery has written two other literary histories:

The Story Behind Great Stories

The Story Behind Modern Books

The Henry Reed series by Keith Robertson uses the journal approach in telling a story; the series includes:

Henry Reed, Inc.

Henry Reed's Baby-Sitting Service

Henry Reed's Big Show

Henry Reed's Journey

Gertrude Kloppenberg, Private and its sequel, *Gertrude Kloppenberg, Two,* by Ruth Hooker are written as journals.

II. The class discusses the reason for certain books having lasting and universal appeal.
- A. A list of titles is made of those books recognized as classics.

    The card catalog is checked to discover which titles are available in the school library.

    Arrangements are made to obtain those titles not in the library from the junior and/or senior high libraries.

    Using the three literary histories by Elizabeth Montgomery, students compile a list of additional titles worthy of being read.

    Each student takes the responsibility for compiling a list of classics recommended by his or her parents, relatives, and friends.

- B. The Newbery Award and the Newbery Honor books are contemporary books of quality having the promise of becoming classics of the future.

    John Newbery was a bookseller in eighteenth-century England.

    The Children's Services Division of the American Library Association elects the award winners.

    The bronze medal is awarded for the "most distinguished contribution to American literature for children."

    The silver medal is awarded for honor books.

- C. Many of the Newbery Award and Honor books are great favorites of North Hills students.

    A number of these titles fit right into the regular instructional program:

    Fourth grade—

    Cold Lands: *Julie of the Wolves* by Jean George; *Mr. Popper's Penguins* by Richard and Florence Atwater

    Hawaii: *Call It Courage* by Armstrong Sperry

    Japan: *The Cat Who Went to Heaven* by Elizabeth Coatsworth

    Fifth grade—

    Explorers: *The King's Fifth* by Scott O'Dell

    Colonial: *The Matchlock Gun* by Walter Edmonds; *The Witch of Black Bird Pond* by Elizabeth Speare

    Northeast: *Invincible Louisa* by Cornelia Meigs; *Miracles on Maple Hill* by Virginia Sorenson; *Misty of Chincoteague* by Marguerite Henry; *Onion John* by Joseph Krumgold

    South: *Across Five Aprils* by Irene Hunt; *Amos Fortune* by Elizabeth Yates; *Perilous Road* by William Steele; *Rifles for Watie* by Harold Keith; *Sounder* by William Armstrong

    Midwest: *Caddie Woodlawn* by Carol Brink

MODEL 12 (cont.)

California and the West: *And Now Miguel* by Joseph Krumgold; *Black Pearl* by Scott O'Dell; *Blue Willow* by Doris Gates; *The Loner* by Ester Weir; *Mocassin Trail* by Eloise McGraw; *Sing Down the Moon* by Scott O'Dell

Sixth grade—

Canada: *Incident on Hawk's Hill* by Allan Eckert

South America: *Chucaro: Wild Pony of the Pampa* by Francis Kalnay; *The Magic Ball and Other Tales* by Charles Finger

If I Had Lived in the Middle Ages: *The Door in the Wall* by Marguerite de Angeli

Pirates: *The Dark Frigate* by Charles Hawes

D. The GATE students can take the responsibility for sharing with their classmates the classics, the Newbery Award and Honor books, and other books they have enjoyed.

Post on class bulletin board and/or announce over the intercom television programs such as "Once Upon a Classic."

Organize a literary club open to all students who are interested.

Make bookmarks highlighting favorite books, authors, illustrators.

Present a classroom or assembly program such as "Meet the Newbery Author(s)."

Present a filmstrip literary program for your class or literary club.

Make dioramas to advertise favorite books.

Prepare a dramatization of a book.

Videotape a scene from one of the classics or literary award books.

Write a book review for the school or district GATE newspaper.

Earn a scout merit badge for literature study.

Prepare bibliographies of print and nonprint media popularizing an author or a literary type or theme such as "courage."

MODEL 13   MIND-BOGGLING PHENOMENA

Grades: 4–6
Goal: To entice the GATE student to explore the realm of phenomenal happenings and to discover that truth is stranger than fiction.
Teaching Objectives:

To introduce the students to the function of The Center for Short-lived Phenomena.

To introduce the students to a wide variety of sudden, unexpected, and hard-to-believe phenomena.

Teaching Strategies and Methods:

After the GATE class is introduced to the meaning of phenomena and the types and kinds of resources available, each student will independently pursue his or her own interests in this area.

A special shelf in the library will be designated "Mind-Boggling Phenomena," and this collection of print and nonprint media will be constantly changing and expanding.

Procedural Outline:
  I. Group orientation to and overview of this learning activity.
    A. Definition of the term *phenomena* from context.
      1. *It's Still a Mystery* by Lee Gebhart and Walter Wagner

      The word *phenomena* is found on pp. 40, 48, 67, 69, 73, 82, 95.

MODEL 13 (cont.)

2. *Guinness Book of Phenomenal Happenings* by Norris McWhirter and Ross McWhirter (Sterling)

In the Introduction, p. 5, the student can discover from context the meaning of phenomena.

The Guinness World Records Exhibit Hall, located in the Empire State Building in New York City, is a treasure trove of information on phenomenal happenings (see p. 1)

B. The singular form *phenomenon* is discovered by checking the *World Book Encyclopedia Dictionary*.

C. The filmstrip series *Strange Phenomena* (SVE) is viewed and discussed.
   1. The Loch Ness Monster
   2. Unusual Science Facts
   3. ESP
   4. Mind over Matter
   5. ESP in Men and Animals
   6. Precognition

D. The Center for Short-lived Phenomena* is introduced.
   1. *Unbelievable . . . but True* by James Cornell presents the following facts:

   The center was established in 1968 to gather information about all major biological, geophysical, and astrophysical events.

   Headquarters is in Cambridge, Mass.

   Each year the center's hot line reports almost 200 events.

   Thirty-two documented stories from the center's files.

   2. *Strange, Sudden, and Unexpected!* by James Cornell presents 39 events on file at the center.

E. Students volunteer to establish and conduct a Center for the Study of Phenomena.
   1. A director will be elected.
   2. Sixth-grade GATE students, who wish to, can contract to serve as contributing board members:

   Be responsible for setting up the center.

   Be responsible for introducing the purpose of the center to the fourth- and fifth-grade GATE students.

   Be responsible for searching out materials for the special library collection "Mind-Boggling Phenomena."

   Be responsible for compiling a list of phenomena to be researched.

   Be responsible for compiling a record of information gathered.

II. The students proceed to explore on their own.
   A. The director of the Center for the Study of Phenomena and his or her staff will schedule and conduct meetings at their discretion.
   B. As a culminating activity, the director of each center will meet and develop a plan for sharing information gained.
      1. If there is sufficient interest, a meeting of all participants in the project—all schools, all students who participated in the project—will be held.
      2. If there is sufficient interest, the articles judged best by a jury selected by the directors will be published in May.

Resource Kit:

BOOKS (Scholastic)

Strange but True: 22 Amazing Stories by David Duncan

Strange Sudden and Unexpected! by James Cornell, Jr.

Unbelievable . . . but True! by James Cornell

FILMSTRIPS

Myths? Monsters? Mysteries? (SVE—6 filmstrips, 6 records)

*138 Mt. Auburn St., Cambridge, Mass. 02138, tel. 617-492-3310.

MODEL 13 (cont.)

The Abominable Snowman—Myth or Monster?

Atlantis—Where Are You?

Reincarnation—Have We Lived Before?

Sasquatch—Fact or Fiction?

UFO's—Are We Being Watched?

Witchcraft—An Evil to Fear?

Psychic Phenomena (SVE—4 filmstrips, 4 cassettes, 1 teaching guide)

Dreams and Telepathy

Ghosts, Spirits and Haunted Houses

Psychic Seeing, Hearing and Sensing

Science and Seance

Strange Phenomena (SVE—6 filmstrips, 3 cassettes, 1 teaching guide)

ESP

ESP in Animals and Men

The Loch Ness Monster

Mind over Matter

Precognition

Unusual Science Facts

MEDIA KIT

Strange Phenomena (SVE—10 copies)

Nature and Science

The Mind

Monsters

MODEL 14   ORIENTATION TO THE GATE PROGRAM (GRADE 5)

Grade: 5

Procedural Outline:

    I. Purpose of the GATE Program.

        A. Provide unlimited opportunities for the student to explore far beyond textbook, course of study, and classroom.

            The textbook is limited by size to presenting only skeletal information.

            Depth and breadth of understanding require that the student bring form and substance to the textbook outline.

            Example: Analyze the first chapter in the social studies textbook currently being studied and list under the following headings those topics introduced or mentioned but not adequately covered:

Persons	Concepts
Places	Attitudes
Things	Appreciations
Events	

            Search out print and nonprint media to match the developmental needs of each of the above topics; gather all these materials together as evidence of the informational limitations of the textbook.

            Multiply the numbers of material required to support the first chapter in the textbook by the total number of chapters as an estimate of the support needs of the textbook.

MODEL **14** (cont.)

The multimedia approach to knowledge building and extending mandates that the school library serve as a learning laboratory where students come to work intensely and creatively with the ideas contained in:

Books	Recordings
Pamphlets	Slides
Periodicals	Motion Pictures
Documents	Art prints
Filmstrips	Videotapes

B. Provide unlimited opportunities for the student to think adventurously and creatively.

Adventurous thinking—Daring to think bold, new thoughts; projecting beyond the facts to fashion creative, yet plausible, answers to tantalizing questions such as "What if . . . ?" "What would happen if . . . ?" "Do you suppose . . . ?" "Is there a possibility . . . ?"

Creativity—The power to develop to the fullest all abilities, those that are known and those that are hidden; to be all that one can be. The magic of creativity is to form new ideas, to invent, to discover.

C. Provide unlimited opportunities for the student to identify and then solve problems for which there are no easy or ready-made solutions.

Example: Who really discovered America?
What are the dimensions of personal excellence?
Are we the masters of our fate?

Social progress has been achieved by those who have thought creatively, adventurously, selflessly, and courageously.

The group views and then discusses the motion picture *Sequoyah* (Walt Disney Educational Media)

Selflessness in service to his fellowman was Sequoyah's major characteristic.

At the cost of great sacrifice and suffering—even though he was lame he walked endless miles to study various Indian languages—he singlehandedly invented the "talking leaves."

This motion picture is one of a series entitled *They Made the Difference.*

During this school year each student will compile a list of people who have made a significant contribution to civilization.

As a culminating activity, each student will have the opportunity to nominate candidates for election to the GATE Hall of Fame.

Clara Ingram Judson, author of 14 biographies for young people, envisioned America as a "tapestry woven of threads of many colors:

"People stand in the foreground of this tapestry, woven boldy against the rich background of natural resources and beauty.

"The crosswise threads are the masses of people, who have come from many lands in search of a better life—these are the people whose work and sacrifices have forged a mighty nation.

"The vertical threads give strength and shape to the pattern—these threads represent the leaders of our country, the men and women in government, industry, science, education, social work, and the arts who have guided America's destiny.

"Around this tapestry, holding it firmly, are the beliefs Americans share:
Faith in government by the people.
Devotion to freedom.
Belief in education.
And the conviction that each individual is important.

MODEL 14 (cont.)

"People, leaders, ideals—these are the tapestry that is America.

"And the tapestry is not finished. Youth must soon take over the weaving. If their part is to be worthy of what has gone before, youth must remember that each generation's freedom must be earned . . . by building even higher aspirations for the future" (*Andrew Carnegie* by Clara Ingram Judson, Follett, pp. 5–7).

D. Provide unlimited opportunities for the student to explore the world of art, music, and literature.

To be open and responsive to artistic experiences both as a direct participant or creator and as an appreciative reactor.

To become acquainted with the great artists, musicians, and writers, past and present.

E. Provide unlimited opportunities for the student to develop and practive mature thinking/learning skills.

Organizing and recording ideas in a notebook.

Maintaining a daily journal.

Being responsible for long-range assignments.

Developing stick-to-itiveness.

Evaluating critically and objectively one's own achievements.

F. Provide unlimited opportunities for the student to grow in self-awareness, self-discipline, self-respect, and in concern for achieving the highest level of personal excellence.

Exploring in depth a variety of careers.

Developing an understanding of socioeconomic problems.

Perceiving one's own potential for intellectual, social, artistic, and economic achievement.

Perceiving that in a democracy each individual is the shaper of his or her own destiny.

Accepting the responsibility that accompanies serving in a leadership capacity.

II. Design of the GATE Program.
   A. Myriad opportunities will be provided for the student to serve in the capacity of resource consultant to his or her classmates.
   In social studies for each unit the student will select a consultant role such as:

Agriculturalist	Geologist
Artist	Historian
Biographer	Humanitarian
Book reviewer	Inventor
Dietitian	Musician
Doctor	Naturalist
Educator	Sociologist
Folklorist	Statistician
Geographer	Travel agent

In social studies, English, and science, the student will have the option of previewing nonprint media and then presenting them to the class.
   B. Myriad opportunities for each student to pursue in depth his or her own special interests will be provided.

The Experience and Interest Inventory will be completed by each student and an interest profile identified.

MODEL 14 (cont.)

C. Myriad opportunities will be provided for the student to work as a productive, cooperative member of a learning group or team.

Each student will serve in a variety of capacities:

Originator of group activities.

Captain of the learning team.

Participant of the team under the direction of another.

D. Myriad opportunities for each student to participate in learning experiences on the building, district, and community levels will be provided.
Typical multilevel experiences:

Planning and/or participating in assemblies.

Writing articles for a newspaper.

School

District

Northland Public Library

Making announcements over the intercom.

Developing and carrying out social service activities.

Decorating the school for holidays and other special occasions.

Dramatizing stories or telling stories to the primary grades.

Planning and/or participating in field learning experiences.

Planning and/or participating in district-wide GATE activities.

Organizing and/or directing a variety of recreational activities such as:

Chess tournaments	Square dancing
Spell-downs	Christmas caroling

MODEL 15 BECOMING ACQUAINTED WITH OLD GLORY

Grade: 5
Learning Project: Becoming Acquainted with Old Glory
Project Goal: To provide learning experiences that will encourage the student to discover a new dimension to his or her identity as an American citizen.
Teaching Objectives:

To provide learning experiences that will enable the student to discover and to cherish his or her heritage as an American citizen.

To provide learning experiences that will quicken student interest in American history.

To provide learning experiences that will widen the student's knowledge of the dramatic events in which the American flag has played a dominant role.

To provide learning experiences that will encourage the student to think independently and creatively.

To provide learning experiences that will encourage the student to find satisfaction and challenge in group participation.

Teaching Strategies and Methods: ,

This learning project was requested by the GATE students following an incident reported in the newspapers and over the radio and highlighted on television. A steelworker at the Jones and Laughlin steel mill in Pittsburgh had used a large American flag to cover his new automobile and protect it from the mill dust. A very few minutes after the steelworker had left his car in the company parking lot, the police stations, the radio stations, the television stations, and the newspapers began to get calls from irate citizens demanding that the flag immediately be removed from the car and that the steelworker, who had desecrated the flag, be arrested. A very angry crowd

MODEL 15 (cont.)

formed near the parking lot and threatened the security guards. Finally, the steel-worker was located in the mill and came out to remove the flag. When informed by the police that he was guilty of violating the 1968 federal law specifying a penalty for desecrating the flag, the man maintained that he meant no disrespect to the flag and that he had no idea that it was unlawful to use the flag in this manner.

The GATE students were very concerned about the man's considering the flag as a "thing" rather than as a symbol of their nation. They agreed that whether or not he was aware of the 1968 federal penalty act, he had been insensitive to say the least.

At the conclusion of the discussion, one of the students said, "I bet many people do not know the history of the flag and the rules to follow regarding the flag."

Another student said, "I myself would like to know a great deal more about the flag. For instance, why is it called 'Old Glory'? What do you say we spend some time learning about the flag and then let's have an assembly so that all the students in the school will learn how to show respect to the flag?"

The group voted to follow through on this suggestion and built the following background knowledge.

Content Outline:
- I. What is the flag?
  - A. A flag is a symbol that stands for a nation's basic ideas and purposes.
  - B. Every nation in the world has a national flag as its chief emblem.
  - C. The U.S. flag symbolizes the union of fifty states and over 200,000,000 people.
  - D. It symbolizes to all the American way of life.
  - E. It is our flag; it belongs to all of us.
- II. How our flag was born.
  - A. Each American colony had its own flag.
  - B. At the beginning of the Revolutionary War there were dozens of flags, some from the colonies and some from various towns.
  - C. On June 14, 1777, the Continental Congress passed the resolution:

    Resolved: that the flag of the United States be made of thirteen stripes, alternate red and white; that the union be thirteen stars, white in a blue field representing a new constellation

  - D. Flag Day is celebrated on June 14 because of the adoption of the resolution on that day.
  - E. Betsy Ross was commissioned by General George Washington to design a flag according to the description given by the Continental Congress resolution.
- III. What the colors mean:
  - A. Red symbolizes hardiness and courage.
  - B. White symbolizes purity and innocence.
  - C. Blue symbolizes vigilance and justice.
  - D. George Washington explained the symbolism of the flag by saying: "We take the stars and blue union from Heaven; the red from our Mother Country, separating it by white stripes, thus showing we have separated from her; and the white stripes shall go down to posterity representing liberty."
- IV. When to display the flag:
  - A. During the day

    From sunrise to sunset on buildings and stationary poles outside.

    On any day when the weather is good, unless an all-weather flag is used.

  - B. Usually lowered at night.

    May be displayed 24 hours a day providing it is properly illuminated during darkness.
- V. The Star Spangled Banner
  - A. Francis Scott Key wrote the poem in gratitude that the flag was still flying over Fort McHenry after being bombarded by the British in 1814.

MODEL 15 (cont.)

    B. "The Star-Spangled Banner" had fifteen stars and fifteen stripes and is on display at the Smithsonian Institution.

VI. How the flag came to be called "Old Glory."

    A. William Driver, during the Civil War, was loyal to the Union, even though his state, Tennessee, seceded.

    B. When the Civil War ended, William Driver said, "Thank God I have lived to raise Old Glory over the capitol of Tennessee."

VII. The Pledge of Allegiance.

    A. Authorship is disputed.

        Francis Bellamy

        James B. Upham

    B. Adopted by Congress, 1942

    C. Words "under God" added, 1954.

VIII. How to display and respect the flag.

    A. Rules for displaying the flag.

    B. Military color guard.

IX. Love and respect for the flag.

    A. In art.

    B. In poetry.

    C. In music.

Culminating Activity: The School Assembly (see Checklist D at the end of this model).

    I. High school band.

      A. Medley of Sousa marches.

      B. Star Spangled Banner.

    II. Marine and scout color guard.

    III. Pledge of Allegiance.

    IV. History of the American flag.

    V. Americans who have loved the flag.

      A. Francis Scott Key

      B. Barbara Fritchie

      C. John Philip Sousa

      D. John Glenn

      E. Neil Armstrong

    VI. The flag code.

    VII. Songs.

      A. There Are Many Flags.

      B. World Anthem.

Resource Kit:

  BOOKS

    The American Flag by Thomas Parrish (Simon and Schuster)

    Flags by Mary Irving (Golden Press)

    Flags of American History by David Crouthers (Hammond)

    Let's Hear It for America: Symbols, Songs, and Celebrations ed. by Bennett Wayne (Garrard)

    The Story of Old Glory by Albert Mayer (Childrens Press)

    The Story of Our Flag by Carl Glick and Ollie Rodgers (Putnam)

    The Story of the Star Spangled Banner by Natalie Miller (Childrens Press)

    The Story of the United States Flag by Wyatt Blassingame (Garrard)

    You and Your Flag, Scriptographic booklet (Channing L. Bete)

  CHART

    How to Display and Respect the Flag of the United States (U.S. Navy Recruiting Service)

  FILMSTRIPS

    The American Flag (Eye Gate—2 filmstrips, 1 cassette)

MODEL 15 (cont.)

Birth of the American Flag

Growth of the American Flag

Francis Scott Key (Encyclopaedia Britannica)

The United States Flag (SVE—2 filmstrips, 1 record, 2 teaching guides)

MOVIE

What Does Our Flag Mean? (Coronet)

CHECKLIST D   ASSEMBLY PLANNING GUIDE

School:
Date:
Time:
Grades:
Topic or Theme:
Length of Program:
Participants:
  Students—

  Teachers—

  Principal—

  Guests—

  Stage Crew/Projectionists/Technicians—

  Ushers—

Publicity:
  In-School—
    Bulletin announcements
    Public address announcements
    Homeroom announcements
    Posters
    School newspaper
    Others
  Community—
    Parent Teachers' Organizations and Mothers' Clubs
    Community Action Committee
    Kiwanis
    Rotary
    American Legion
    Veterans of Foreign Wars
    Chamber of Commerce
    Cable TV
    News Record
    Pittsburgh Press
    Post Gazette
    Others
Program Introduction:
  By Whom—

  Length of Introduction—

  What Is to Be Said?
    Explain the purpose of the assembly
    Establish rapport with the audience
    Stimulate interest

MODEL 15 (cont.)

Introducing a Speaker
 Briefly sketch speaker's background
 Welcome the speaker on behalf of the students, faculty, principal
Thanking the Speaker
 Briefly indicate appreciation
Equipment Needed:
 ( ) Filmstrip Projector
 ( ) Motion Picture Projector
 ( ) Projection Screen
 ( ) Public Address System
 ( ) Record Player
 ( ) Slide Projector
 ( ) Videotape-Television Camera
 ( ) Other Equipment

MODEL 16 COLONIAL AMERICA

Grade: 5
Unit: Colonial America
Project Goals:

 To preplan with the classroom teacher to bring greater depth, breadth, relevance, and challenge to the classroom-based instructional program and then to translate that plan into exciting substantive and significant learning experiences, which the GATE students upon completion will share with the class.

 To provide the opportunity for the student to perceive and appreciate his or her unique heritage as an American.

Possible Research Topics:

 Colonial Americans at work

Architects	Printers
Cabinetmakers	Schoolmasters
Doctors	Shipbuilders
Farmers	Shoemakers
Glassmakers	Silversmiths
Hatters	Tanners
Papermakers	Weavers
Peddlers	Wigmakers
Potters	

 Colonial Americans at home

Dress	Kinds of food and drink
Favorite recipes	The kitchen
Flower gardens	Lighting and heating the home
Girls' occupations	Preparing and serving meals
Homes	Textiles and handweaving
Household tasks	

 Colonial Americans at church

Religious beliefs	Sermons
Power of the church	Sunday Restrictions

 Colonial Americans at school

Curriculum	Discipline
Dame schools	Hornbooks

MODEL 16 (cont.)

Colonial Americans at play

> Husking bees   Spelling bees
> Quilting parties

Colonial travel, transportation, and taverns

> Boats, canoes, dugouts   Packhorses
> Coaches   Saddle horses
> Covered bridges   Toll roads
> Ferries   Wagons
> Milestones

An ordinary, a victualing, a cookshop, or tavern

> Dining rooms   Guest rooms
> Drink   Kitchen
> Food   Signboard

Colonial servants and laborers

> Apprentices   Slaves
> Indentured servants

Colonial laws, courts, punishments

> Ducking stools   Stocks
> Hangings   Trial of British soldiers following Boston Massacre
> Laws passed at town meetings   Trial of Peter Zenger
> Salem witch trials   Whipping posts

The American Revolution

> Campaigns   Memorable events
> Causes   Outcomes
> Leaders

Colonial Williamsburg: Today and yesterday

Skill Integration

> Biography as a source of historical background information (see Checklist E, Biography Summary, at the end of this model).
>
> Historical novels as a source of historical background information (see Checklist F, Historical Novel Summary, at the end of this model).

CHECKLIST E: BIOGRAPHY SUMMARY

Unit: Colonial America   Pupil_____

I read the following biography:

Title _____ Author _____

This is the story of _____ who lived in the colony or colonies

of _____ during the period:

_____
1620   '30   '40   '50   '60   '70   '80   '90 1700 '10   '20   '30   '40   '50   '60   '70

MODEL 16 (cont.)

While reading this biography I learned these facts about colonial manners and customs:

Concerning food, I discovered
The various kinds of foods commonly eaten. For example:

How foods were prepared. For example:

How foods were stored. For example:

Other facts such as:

Concerning homes, I discovered
What colonial houses looked like. For example:

The number and size of rooms. For example:

The various pieces of furniture commonly used. For example:

Concerning household chores, I discovered
The typical chores performed by the women of the family. For example:

The typical chores performed by the men of the family. For example:

The typical chores performed by the children of the family. For example:

Other facts such as:

Concerning clothing, I discovered
The kinds of garments worn and how they were made. For example:

Concerning schools, I discovered
How colonial schools differed from our schools today. For example:

Concerning occupations, I discovered
The following occupations that were new to me:

Other facts such as:

Concerning animals, I discovered
The following mentioned:

CHECKLIST F: HISTORICAL NOVEL SUMMARY

Student _____ Date _____

I have read the following historical novel:

Title _____ Author _____

This novel portrayed life during the period _____

The setting of this novel was _____

The plot of this novel was _____
_____
_____

In analyzing the historical significance of this novel, the following facts are noteworthy:
Concerning Food—
Kinds of food commonly eaten:

MODEL 16 (cont.)

How foods were prepared, preserved and stored:

Other interesting facts about food, such as:

Concerning Family Living—
  The role of the father:

  The role of the mother:

  The role of children:

  Other interesting facts about family living, such as:

Concerning the Manners and Customs of the People—

Concerning Religion—

Concerning Law and Order—

Concerning Socioeconomic Problems—

Concerning Occupations—

Concerning Education—

Concerning Games, Sports, Recreation—

Concerning Transportation and Communication—

Other Noteworthy Background Information—

Would you have enjoyed living in the time and place portrayed in this novel? Elaborate on your answer.

MODEL 17   LAW AND JUSTICE CASE STUDY

Grade: 5
Unit: California and the West
Case Study: How a citizen can become directly involved in the lawmaking process on the state and federal levels.
Purpose: To provide a significant, relevant, and appealing learning experience that will dramatize the citizen's role in lawmaking.
Procedural Outline:
  I. A group of students will read *Mustang: Wild Spirit of the West* by Marguerite Henry (Rand McNally). This biography of Annie Johnston will serve as a case study of how a citizen led the legislative fight to protect the wild mustang from extinction.
  A. Following the reading of the biography, the group will share with the class the understandings it has gained concerning the following concepts:
    1. In a democracy elected representatives are answerable to the voters.
       Evidence:

       "The everyday people are lawmakers." p. 115

       "We must trust the people, the everyday people, Annie, THEY are the lawmakers." p. 117.

       "Mr. Baring is not just a name in the paper or picture on a poster. He's a friend. MY FRIEND! My very own voice in Washington."

    2. Public opinion is a powerful influence on lawmakers.
       Evidence:

       "It might be YOUR letter to YOUR Congressman that will help save the mustang." p. 169.

MODEL 17 (cont.)

"Write to your Congressman. . . . Ask your friends to write, too. Let's unite in outrage, unite as Americans until the lawmakers are swamped with a sea of mail." pp. 178–179

"Letters from the People" pages. p. 126

3. Newspaper editorials are effective in influencing lawmakers.
   Evidence:

   "Passenger pigeons used to darken the heavens with their numbers. They and the buffalo were slaughtered by the millions. For what? For blood money, that's what! The American people will never recover from the shame of it." Lucius Beebe's editorial in the *Enterprise*. p. 126.

4. Making money prompts some businessmen to argue against protecting America's natural resources.
   Evidence:

   "What have the wild horses done to deserve butchery and mass extinction? The mustangers who make a living at it are savages. They enjoy being filth at 5 cents a pound for live horseflesh!" p. 127.

   "We at the *Enterprise* demand passage of the mustang bill. The only opposition it can possibly provoke is greed, brutality, and a total contempt for wildlife." p. 127.

5. In America even the children can be heard in the state and federal legislatures.
   Evidence:

   "The Power of Children" pp. 166–179

6. The statue of Justice is frequently portrayed as a woman who is blindfolded and holds a sword in one hand and a scale in the other.
   Evidence:

   "Without justice and fairness we are hopelessly lost." p. 202

   "Compassion is mightier than money." p. 168

B. The group wil reenact for the class the congressional hearing on H.R. 2725 at which Mrs. Annie Johnston gave testimony. pp. 197–218
C. The class as a culminating activity will summarize their learning by defining and discussing the following terms:

1. "blood money"
2. congressional committees
3. congressional hearings
4. evidence: historical
   pictorial
   statistical
5. justice vs. injustice
6. "Letters to the Editor" column
7. newspaper editorials
8. petitions
9. public opinion
10. role of the district attorney and judge
11. testimony
12. witnesses

II. Reinforcement and extension of the basic concepts presented in the case study.
   A. Other citizens have successfully influenced state and federal legislators to pass laws protecting American wildlife and natural resources.
      1. Scotty Philip was instrumental in getting H.R. 13542 passed in 1906, which set aside 3,500 acres of public land for a buffalo pasture.

      By 1900 only a few hundred buffalo existed. It was estimated that by 1910 they would have disappeared entirely.
      It has been estimated that in the period from 1800 to 1900, the buffalo population had been reduced from 40,000,000 to only a few hundred.
      Scotty Philip gathered together a small herd and cared for them. Because he cared he alerted his friends in Congress to the plight of the buffalo, and largely through his efforts the buffalo was saved from extinction.

   SOURCE: *The Buffalo King: The Story of Scotty Philip* by Nancy Veglahn (Scribner)

MODEL 17 (cont.)

2. John Muir led the fight to create national parks to preserve America's forests and natural wonders.

Through articles and speeches he told the nation that the lumber industry was destroying a priceless heritage.

His first two articles in the national magazine *Century*, "Treasures of the Yosemite" and "Features of the Proposed Yosemite National Park," published in 1890, created a furious debate between those who wanted to safeguard the forests and the miners, loggers, and herdsmen who wanted to exploit the forests for profit.

Muir became a target of a newspaper smear campaign (see *John Muir: Prophet among the Glaciers* by Robert Silverberg, pp. 197–198).

As a result of Muir's talks with President Theodore Roosevelt, 148,000,000 acres of national forests were created and the number of national parks was doubled.

SOURCE: *John Muir: Protector of the Wilds* by Madge Haines and Leslie Morrill (Abingdon)

John Muir: Father of Our National Parks by Charles Norman (Messner)

John Muir: Prophet among the Glaciers by Robert Silverberg (Putnam)

B. Annie Johnston organized the International Society for the Protection of Mustangs and Burros to help her gain public support in her battle to save the mustang.
   1. In 1974 a group of slaughter houses in Idaho began a series of aerial roundups of wild horses to be processed as pet food.
   2. Currently petitions are being circulated by the International Society for the Protection of Mustangs and Burros, 140 Greenstone Dr., Reno, Nev. 89502

   The class, if interested, should write to this society asking for official petitions to stop this slaughter and also for current information about the plight of the mustang and burro.

C. The Animal Protection Institute of America, Box 22505, Sacramento, Calif. 95882, is actively engaged in an educational and legislative program to prevent cruelty to animals.
   1. The class, if interested, should write to this society and ask for information concerning its program.
   2. If, when the information is received, the students wish to become involved in the society's work, they can take the responsibility for circulating petitions and sending them to the society's headquarters.

MODEL 18   THE SOUTH

Grade: 5
Unit: The South
Project Goals:

To preplan with the classroom teacher to bring greater depth, breadth, relevance, and challenge to the classroom-based instructional program and then to translate that plan into exciting substantive and significant learning experiences, which the GATE students on completion will share with the class.

To provide the opportunity for the students to perceive history, culture, economics, arts, science and invention, sociology, law, and education as potential life careers.

Possible Research Topics:
Agriculturalist

George Washington Carver   Citrus Industry
and plant experimentation   Cotton

MODEL 18 (cont.)

Frozen juices

Peanuts

Biographer

Mary McLeod Bethune

Sonia Bleeker

Jimmy Carter

Jefferson Davis

Emma Edmonds

Elizabeth Freeman

Barbara Fritchie

Rose Greenhow

Book reviewer

Zachery Ball, author

Robert Burch, author

Peter Burchard, author and illustrator

Vera and Bill Cleaver, joint authors

Dietitian

Southern cooking

Doctor

Ephraim McDowell

Educator

Mary McLeod Bethune

Booker T. Washington

Folklorist

Richard Chase

Joel Chandler Harris

Geologist

Caves

Gemstones

Historian

Civil War

Slavery

Humanitarian

Mary McLeod Bethune

Booker T. Washington

Inventor

Wright Brothers

Musician

Louis Armstrong

William C. Hardy

Naturalist

The Everglades

Statistician

Oxford Economics Atlas

Tobacco

Stonewall Jackson

Martin Luther King, Jr.

Robert E. Lee

Osceola

Sequoia

Sojourner Truth

Booker T. Washington

Jean Fritz, author

Jean George, author and naturalist

Irene Hunt, author

MODEL 18 (cont.)

Travel agent

  Disney World

  Everglades

Resource Kits:

LEARNING PROJECT: THE SOUTH—THE EVERGLADES

  BOOKS

    The American Alligator: Its Life in the Wild by Edward Ricciuti (Harper)

    Bayou Backwaters by Allan Eckert (Doubleday)

    Everglades National Park by Ruth Radlauer (Childrens Press)

    Everglades Wildguide by Jean George (National Park Service, U.S. Department of the Interior)

    The First Book of Swamps and Marshes by Frances Smith (Watts)

    Florida—Tourbook (American Automobile Association)

    Iron-Tail by George Sand (Scribner)

    The Moon of the Alligators by Jean George (Crowell)

    The Mystery of the Everglades by Ada and Frank Graham (Random House)

    Who Needs Alligators? by Patricia Lauber (Garrard)

    World Within a World: Everglades by Ted Lewin (Dodd)

  FILMSTRIPS

    Everglades—Ecology (Outdoor Pictures—1 filmstrip, 1 cassette)

    Everglades—Wildlife (Outdoor Pictures—1 filmstrip, 1 cassette)

    The Everglades—Florida (Imperial Film)

  MULTIMEDIA KIT

    Meet the Newbery Author: Jean Craighead George (Miller-Brody—3 filmstrips, 2 records, 4 books)

      Books

        Gull Number 737

        Julie of the Wolves

        My Side of the Mountain

        The Summer of the Falcon

      Filmstrips

        Julie of the Wolves, pts. 1 and 2

        Meet the Newbery Author: Jean Craighead George

  POSTER

    Everglades (National Park Service, U.S. Department of the Interior)

LEARNING PROJECT: THE SOUTH—THE CIVIL WAR

  BOOKS

    America's Abraham Lincoln by May McNeer (Houghton)

    The Civil War by Robert Jordan (National Geographic Society)

    The First Book of the Civil War by Dorothy Levenson (Watts)

    The First Book of Civil War Land Battles by Trevor Depuy (Watts)

    Gettysburg by MacKinlay Kantor (Random House)

    Harriet Beecher Stowe: Woman Crusader by Jean Rouverol (Putnam)

    The How and Why Wonder Book of the Civil War by Earl Miers (Grosset and Dunlap)

    Civil War Weapons by C. B. Colby (Coward)

MODEL 18 (cont.)

Long Knife: The Story of the Fighting U.S. Cavalry of the 1860 Frontier by Glen Dines (Macmillan)

Mr. Lincoln's Inaugural Journey by Mary Phelan (Crowell)

Old Abe: The Eagle Hero by Patrick Young (Prentice-Hall)

The Road to Fort Sumter by Leroy Hayman (Crowell)

Robert E. Lee: Soldier of the South by Jean Rikhoff (Putnam)

The Stolen Train by Robert Ashley (Scholastic)

The Story of Fort Sumter by Eugenia Burney (Childrens Press)

The Story of the Gettysburg Address by Kenneth Richards (Childrens Press)

The Vicksburg Veteran by F. N. Monjo (Simon and Schuster)

War Eagle: The Story of a Civil War Mascot by Edmund Lindop (Little, Brown)

William Tecumseh Sherman by Charles Graves (Garrard)

Willie and the Yank adapted by Stuart Ludlum (Scholastic)

FILMSTRIPS

The Civil War (SVE—4 filmstrips, 2 records, 4 teaching guides)

America's Trial and Agony

Darkest Hours . . . Then Peace

High Tide of Valor

A Nation Divided

High Flying Spy (Walt Disney Educational Media—2 filmstrips, 2 records)

MULTIMEDIA KIT (Miller-Brody)

Across Five Aprils (2 filmstrips, 1 record, 3 books)

Rifles for Watie (2 filmstrips, 1 record, 4 books)

RECORDS

Abe Lincoln: From Log Cabin to White House (Enrichment Records)

Clara Barton, Founder of the American Red Cross (Enrichment Records)

The Civil War Era (SVE—2 records, 1 teaching guide)

LEARNING PROJECT: THE SOUTH—LITERATURE AND MUSIC

BOOKS

Brer Rabbit and Brer Fox retold by Jane Shaw (Collins)

Grandfather Tales collected and retold by Richard Chase (Houghton)

Jack and the Three Sillies told by Richard Chase (Houghton)

The Jack Tales ed. by Richard Chase (Scholastic)

Queenie Peavy by Robert Burch (Scholastic)

Skinny by Robert Burch (Viking)

Sounder by William Armstrong (Harper)

Tales from Near-Side and Far by May Justus (Garrard)

William C. Handy: Father of the Blues by Elizabeth Montgomery (Garrard)

FILMSTRIPS

Jack and the Robbers (Pied Piper—1 filmstrip, 1 record, 1 teaching guide)

Tall Tales in American Folklore (Walt Disney Educational Media—3 filmstrips, 3 records, 3 teaching guides)

Brer Rabbit Meets the Tar Baby

Brer Rabbit Runs Away

Brer Rabbit's Laughing Place

MODEL 18 (cont.)

LEARNING PROJECT: THE SOUTH—SLAVERY
BOOKS

Black Crusaders for Freedom ed. by Bennett Wayne (Garrard)

Blacks in America: 1619–1790 by Florence Jackson and J. B. Jackson (Watts)

Blacks in America: 1791–1861 by Florence Jackson (Watts)

Blacks in America: 1861–1877 by Florence Jackson (Watts)

By Secret Railway by Enid Meadowcroft (Scholastic)

Charlotte Forten by Esther Douty (Garrard)

Early America: 1492–1812 by William Katz, Minorities in American History, vol. 1 (Watts)

Human Cargo: The Story of the Atlantic Slave Trade by Anne White (Garrard)

The Long Bondage by James McCague (Garrard)

The Man Who Bought Himself: The Story of Peter Still by Peggy Mann and Vivian Siegal (Macmillan)

Mary McLeod Bethune by Emma Sterne (Knopf)

Mumbet: The Story of Elizabeth Freeman by Harold Felton (Dodd)

Navajo Slave by Lynne Gessner (Harvey House)

North to Liberty: The Story of the Underground Railroad by Anne White (Garrard)

Profiles in Black and White: Stories of Men and Women Who Fought Against Slavery by Elizabeth Chittenden (Scribner)

The Progress of the Afro-American by John Patrick (Benefic)

The Road to Freedom, 1815–1900 by James McCague (Garrard)

The Slave Dancer by Paula Fox (Dell)

Slavery in the United States by Leonard Ingraham (Watts)

Slavery to Civil War: 1812–1865 by William Katz, Minorities in American History, vol. 2 (Watts)

Sojourner Truth, A Self-Made Woman by Victoria Ortiz (Lippincott)

To Be a Slave by Julius Lester (Dell)

FILMSTRIPS (Troll)

Mary McLeod Bethune

Frederick Douglass

Harriet Tubman

MOVIE

Slavery and Slave Resistance (Coronet)

MODEL 19   WESTWARD HO! THE WAGONS

Learning Project: Westward Ho! The Wagons
Grade: 5
Project Goals:

To provide learning experiences that will enable the GATE student to perceive and value American history in general, and the Westward Movement in particular, as an ongoing heroic drama with the happenings of the past setting the stage for the happenings of the present and the future.

To introduce the GATE student to the inquiry method and to the mysteries of adventurous, creative thinking.

Teaching Objectives:

This project has been designed and structured to provide these basic understandings:

MODEL 19 (cont.)

The Westward Movement in American History is more than recorded events: it is men and women and young people doing things—making choices; deciding what is important and what is not; taking a stand for what they believe; venturing into the unknown; being courageous despite overwhelming odds; facing trouble and uncertainty; often succeeding but sometimes failing.

Life, liberty, and the pursuit of happiness—and all other basic human rights—have been painfully and slowly won at the cost of great human suffering and sacrifice.

Reading biographies is an exciting way to relive the historic happenings of the past, for people are the shapers of history.

All societies and all human beings are interdependent; no society and no human being can long survive as an island unto itself.

This project has been designed and structured to foster and develop these attitudes and appreciations:

Appreciation of the rich heritage each American inherits from the past; the perception that contemporary man stands on the shoulders of those who have gone before.

Appreciation of the fact that America has been shaped by many kinds of people from many walks of life; perception that destiny is no respecter of race, color, or creed.

Appreciation of the fact that, while many great and famous people helped build America, countless others—pioneer men, women, and young people whose names go unrecorded, unnoted, and unsung—were the means and the force that carried civilization from the Atlantic to the Pacific.

Appreciation of the continuity and interrelatedness of history; the perception that history is an unrolling tapestry of human events.

Appreciation of the human attributes of greatness; perception of the necessity of critically and objectively evaluating the personal quality of those seeking leadership positions in the school, the community, the state, and the nation.

Appreciation of biography as a rich source of insight into the past; perception of the human dimension of history as expressed by Thomas Carlyle, "The history of the world is but the biography of great men."

Appreciation that "legend" makes history larger than life; perception that in legend the line between fact and fiction is all too often obliterated.

Appreciation of historical novels as an effective means of vicariously experiencing the happenings of the past.

Appreciation of the necessity and the value of reading between and beyond the lines.

Appreciation of the value to be accrued from successful group endeavors.

Appreciation of the high degree of satisfaction to be attained by completing a challenging assignment.

Teaching Strategies and Methods:

No time limitations are imposed on this project. Number of students involved coupled with student interest is the factor that determines the duration of each GATE project whether it be two weeks, two months, or longer.

A basic part of group orientation to this project is to provide opportunities for the students to explore the synergistic effect to be derived from sharing knowledge.

Each student, after orientation to the purpose, scope, and dimension of this project, will draw up and sign a performance contract specifying the special area of knowledge-building for which he or she will be responsible.

Procedural Outline:
 I. Group orientation to and overview of this project

MODEL 19 (cont.)

A. Definition of basic terms
   1. *Adventurous thinking:* Daring to think bold, new thoughts; projecting beyond the facts to fashion creative, yet plausible, answers to tantalizing questions such as "What if . . .?" "What would happen if . . .?" "Do you suppose . . .?" "Is there a possibility . . .?"
   2. *Creativity:* The power to develop to the fullest all abilities, those that are known and those that are hidden; to be all that one can be. The magic of creativity is to form new ideas, to invent, to discover.
   3. *Frontier:* The farthest part of a settled country; where the wilds begin.
   4. *Pioneer:* A person who settles in a part of the country that has not been occupied before except by primitive tribes.
B. Discussion of the value of learning about America's past
   1. William Jay Jacobs, American historian, in his book *Search for Freedom: America and Its People* (Encino, Calif.: Benziger Bruce & Glencoe, 1973, pp. 9–10, 18–19), explains the value of the past in the light of the present and the future as follows:

   "What is the past?

   "The past is what happened yesterday. And it is what happened all the yesterdays before that . . .

   "The past is things that men have built . . .

   "The past is the different tools and machines that men have used to make all those buildings . . .

   "The past is art . . .

   "The past is music . . .

   "The past is everything that has ever interested human beings . . .

   "The past is feelings . . .

   "The past is ideas . . .

   "The past is events . . .

   "The past is all these things, and many more. But most of all, the past is people.

   "Who built America? Certainly, great men built the American nation. . . . But they were not alone. They are only part of the story.

   "Many men and women whose names nobody remembers also built the American nation: the pioneer woman tending her fire in a wilderness cabin; the storm-tossed New England fisherman; the Negro slave, his back bent with work in a Southern cotton field.

   "Who built America? The Pony Express riders—most of them teenagers . . . ; the farmer harvesting his crop alone in a Kansas wheat field; the Mississippi River steamboat pilot guiding his sternwheeler through treacherous currents.

   "Who built America? The steelworker feeding coal to a fiery furnace in Pittsburgh for pennies a day; . . . the country doctor faithfully making calls . . . ; the immigrant peddler wandering through the West. . . .

   "America was built by many people. Most of them were ordinary people—carpenters and mechanics and lawyers and truckdrivers and housewives and students and railroad workers. Ordinary people.

   "And you? What about you?

   "Someday America will be yours. You will inherit it. And the decisions about what kind of country it will be—those choices will be yours.

   "America is forever new. It is always being built. And you are its future builders."

   2. The purpose of this project is to help you answer the question "Who built America in the past, and what will I be able to contribute to America's present and America's future?"

MODEL 19 (cont.)

3. People make the difference.

During this project, each student will compile a list of people who have influenced American history in either a positive or a negative way.

C. Exploration of the process of adventurous, creative thinking.

1. What is creativity?

Latin root word *creare* meaning to make.

Greek root word *krainen* meaning to fulfill—a promise, a prophecy, or oneself.

The magic of creativity is to form new ideas, to invent, to discover.

Creativity includes the ability to wonder, to be surprised and puzzled, to see what others have seen and to respond differently.

2. Four steps in creative thought.

Preparation—gathering facts and seeking answers.

   Facts are the raw materials from which creative thought is fashioned.

Incubation—the mind works with the facts and ideas.

Inspiration—a sudden solution or a unique idea.

Verification—testing the solution or idea.

3. Imagination is the mind's eye.

Imagination is the ability to form in the mind a picture or idea of something that is not present.

Such pictures are like the images in a kaleidoscope.

We use imagination to recreate the past, to wonder about unfamiliar people or places, and to toy with ideas about the future.

4. Creative power is a hidden treasure.

Margaret Mead, the anthropologist, estimated that man uses but 6 percent of his creative potential.

Can you develop creativity? Psychologists say "yes."

Practice improves creativity.

Highly creative people invent new responses when solving problems—they experiment with what might have been.

Creative thinking looks for a number of ideas, for variety and originality.

D. At the conclusion of this project, the student will be given the challenge of creatively imagining what his or her life could have been, if he or she had been a pioneer trailblazer.

II. The group begins to build its knowledge of westward migration in American history.

A. The students read the *World Book* reprint "Pioneer Life."

1. Attention is called to the fact that the article was critically reviewed by Robert G. Athearn, professor of history at the University of Colorado.

The significance of a "signed article" is discussed.

2. The necessity of following through on the two cross references—"Western Frontier Life" and "Westward Movement"—is stressed.

3. The transvision map reprint from the *World Book* is used throughout the reading of the reprint "Pioneer Life in America" and of the reprints "Western Frontier Life" and "Westward Migration."

Maps are invaluable in visualizing both time and place.

4. Using the main and subheadings of the reprint "Pioneer Life," the following outline is developed:

a. Pioneer life in America

(1) Conquering the wilderness

(2) Establishing the frontier

b. Moving westward

(1) Crossing the Appalachians

(2) How people traveled

(3) Trails of the pioneers

MODEL 19 (cont.)

    c. A pioneer settlement
      (1) A pioneer home
      (2) Education and religion
      (3) Law and order
      (4) Social activities
      (5) Indian attacks
    d. Crossing the Plains
      (1) The wagon train
      (2) Life on the trail

B. The group views and then discusses the motion picture *Daniel Boone* (Coronet).
  1. The value of using a motion picture is explored.
  2. The significance of the term *film literacy* is introduced and discussed.
  3. Professor John Michaelis, University of California, believes that motion pictures are very important when studying history because:

> "Processes, people, the world of nature, various types of activities, and significant events can be seen in action in a realistic setting.
>
> "Contemporary affairs, past events, and faraway places can be brought into the classroom.
>
> "Processes that cannot be visualized in any other way can be seen in action on the screen.
>
> "A broad sweep of events may be seen with various relationships highlighted, as in films showing the development of inventions, the growth of institutions, or the contributions of great men and women."[*]

  4. The group reacts to Michaelis's appraisal of the value of motion pictures.

C. The group views, discusses, and then evaluates the educational effectiveness of the following motion pictures (Coronet):
  1. *Folksongs of the Western Movement, 1787–1853*
  2. *Pioneer Journey across the Appalachians*
  3. *Pioneer Living: Education and Recreation*
  4. *Pioneer Living: The Home*
  5. *Pioneer Living: Preparing Foods*
  6. *Travel in America in the 1840s*

D. Each student reads the historical novel *Young Pioneers* by Rose Wilder Lane (Bantam Books).
  1. The students discover that the author of this novel is the daughter of Laura Ingalls Wilder.
  2. The students read other novels portraying the westward movement.
  3. The students discuss the value of historical novels as an effective means of vicariously reliving the past.

E. The students read the article "Western Frontier Life" and develop the following outline:
  1. Life on the frontier
    a. The people
    b. Food
    c. Clothing
    d. Amusements
    e. Religion
    f. Frontier towns
    g. Life in the country
  2. Transportation and communication
  3. Law and order
    a. Crime
    b. Law enforcement
    c. Indian fighting

---

[*]John U. Michaelis. *Social Studies for Children in a Democracy: Recent Trends and Developments,* 5th ed. (Englewood Cliffs, N.J.: Prentice-Hall, 1972), p. 481.

MODEL 19 (cont.)

4. An American tradition
   a. Literature
   b. Music
   c. Art
   d. Entertainment
III. Each student selects a topic or topics from the above outline to research.
   A. The concept of "film literacy" is reintroduced and the students select appropriate sound filmstrips from the following bibliography:
      1. *The Cowboy: Tough Man on a Mustang* (American Pageant)
      2. *Gold and Dreams of Gold* (SVE)

         Gold Towns of the Old West

         Ghost Towns—What Happened

         How Gold Is Mined

         A Modern-Day Prospector Named George

      3. *The Gunslingers* (American Pageant)
      4. *Pathfinders Westward* (SVE)

         Daniel Boone's Wilderness

         Rivers and Roads to the Mississippi

         Lewis and Clark Expedition, pts. I and II

         First Trails into the West

         The Mountain Men

      5. *Pioneer Women and Belles of the Wild West* (Teaching Resources)
      6. *Settling the West* (SVE)

         The Trail Blazers

         The Miners

         Wagon Trains to Railroads

         The Cattlemen

         The Farmers

         Growth of Towns and Cities

      7. *Stories from the Old West* (SVE)

         El Camino Real

         Vaquero! Vaquero!

         The Comanches: Greatest Horsemen of the West

         The Pony Express Rider

         Iron Horse, Golden Spike

         Pawnee: The Buffalo Pony

      8. *The West: The Way It Was* (American Pageant)
      9. *Westward Migration* (SVE)

         Into the Southwest

         The Oregon Country

         The Gold Rush

         Three Routes to Eldorado

   B. The students check the U.S. Landmark series to discover titles appropriate for their topic.
      1. Attention is directed to the Landmark colophon.
         An emblematic or ornamental device used to identify a publishing house or a series of books.
      2. Recommendation is made that the students check the biographical note about the author that is found in the back of the book.

MODEL 19 (cont.)

Is the author qualified by training and experience to be recognized as an authority?

3. Attention is directed to the list of series titles found at the back of each book in the series.

IV. As a culminating activity the students as a group nominate candidates for a Hall of Fame of American Frontiersmen.

A. A "Who's Who in the Westward Movement" serves as a summary of names highlighted in American historical annals.

B. Students nominate their candidates and defend each candidate's claim to fame.

C. The students, based on their observations of the westward movement and their appraisal of the human drama of the period, discuss the validity of the statement "truth is stranger than fiction."

V. The group views and then discusses the motion picture *Westward Ho! The Wagons* (Disney Studios)

A. Does this motion picture give a valid picture of the times?

B. Was this motion picture biased in its portrayal of either the white man or the Indians?

C. Who was your favorite character in the motion picture?   *

D. If you had been the director of *Westward Ho! The Wagons* what changes, if any, would you have made?

E. What insight into human nature did you gain from viewing this motion picture?

F. If you had been a pioneer trailblazer, what adventures might you have had?

WHO'S WHO IN THE WESTWARD MOVEMENT

Teacher's Answer Key

Please place in the parentheses (   ) before each name the number of the phrase which best describes that person.

Persons	*Descriptive Phrases*
(17) Grizzly Adams	1. Adventurer and explorer; a mountain named for him
(10) Stephen Austin	2. Apache warrior
(34) Sam Bass	3. Author of *Ox-Team Days on the Oregon Trail;* lived to be 98
(9) Charles Bent	4. Blazed the Wilderness Trail
(4) Daniel Boone	5. California mission priest
(19) Jemima Boone	6. Designed hunting knife; killed at the Battle of the Alamo
(6) Jim Bowie	7. Discovered the Great Salt Lake
(7) Jim Bridger	8. Discovered Yellowstone
(38) Kit Carson	9. Established a fort and trading post on the Santa Fe Trail
(29) George Catlin	10. Father of Texas
(22) John Chapman	11. Father of the Wild West Show
(11) Bill Cody	12. Founder of the Church of the Latter-Day Saints
(21) Sam Colt	13. Frontier doctor
(8) John Colter	14. Frontier peace officer; nicknamed "Wild Bill"
(15) Davy Crockett	15. Frontier legendary hero; killed defending the Alamo
(32) Abigail Scott Duniway	16. Gold discovered at his mill in California
(39) Wyatt Earp	17. Hermit in the Sierras; tamed and trained bears

MODEL 19 (cont.)

(33) Escalante

(23) Mike Fink

(31) John Charles Fremont

(2) Geronimo

(18) Josiah Gregg

(14) Bill Hickok

(37) Sam Houston

(27) Andrew Jackson

(35) Mary Layola

(13) Ephraim McDowell

(3) Ezra Meeker

(40) Annie Oakley

(1) Zebulon Pike

(28) John Wesley Powell

(30) Frederic Remington

(20) Sacajawea

(5) Junipero Serra

(36) Sitting Bull

(12) Joseph Smith

(24) Jedediah Smith

(16) John Sutter

(26) Narcissa Whitman

(25) Brigham Young

18. Historian of the Santa Fe Trail
19. Indian captive
20. Indian guide for the Lewis and Clark Expedition
21. Inventor of the six-shooter
22. Johnny Appleseed
23. Keelboatman, marksman, fighter, teller of "tall tales"
24. Led first wagon train over Oregon Trail
25. Led Mormons over Oregon Trail to Great Salt Lake
26. Missionary to Oregon Indians
27. "Old Hickory"
28. One-armed explorer of the Colorado River
29. Painted Indian portraits now in the Smithsonian Institution
30. Painted western frontier scenes
31. "The Pathfinder"
32. Pioneer suffragette
33. Priest explorer of Colorado, Utah, and Arizona
34. Robin Hood of Texas
35. Roman Catholic nun, missionary to the Oregon Indians
36. Sioux warrior
37. Tallest Texan; hero of the Battle of San Jacinto
38. Trapper and scout; explored Death Valley
39. U.S. marshall; "Lion of Tombstone"
40. Woman sharpshooter

Resource Kit:
  BOOKS

American Cattle Trails by Marian Place (Holt)

Bent's Fort: Crossroads of the Great West by Wyatt Blassingame (Garrard)

Buffalo Land by William Berry (Macmillan)

Bull Wagon by Glen Dines (Macmillan)

Cumberland Gap and Trails West by Edith McCall, Frontiers of America series (Childrens Press)

Dog Soldiers by Glen Dines and Raymond Price (Macmillan)

Famous Pioneers by Franklin Folsom (Harvey House)

  Daniel Boone, pp. 15–26
  Escalante, pp. 29–36
  John Ledyard, pp. 9–45
  Lewis and Clark, pp. 49–59
  George Catlin, pp. 63–70
  Rebecca Wright, pp. 73–77
  John Colter, pp. 81–86
  Zebulon M. Pike, pp. 89–96
  Edwin James, pp. 99–106
  Davy Crockett, pp. 109–114
  Jim Bridger, pp. 125–132
  Jed Smith, pp. 135–136
  Joe Meek, pp. 139–143

MODEL 19 (cont.)

William Bent, pp. 145–148
Marcus and Narcissa Whitman, pp. 151–155
Kit Carson, pp. 159–166
John C. Fremont, pp. 169–174
The Donner Party, pp. 177–183
Brigham Young, pp. 185–191
William Downie, pp. 199–209
Charlie Siringo, pp. 221–227
John Wesley Powell, pp. 231–243

First Wagons to California by Michael Chester, Sagas of California series (Putnam)

Flatboat Days on Frontier Rivers by James McCague (Garrard)

Forts in the Wilderness by Edith McCall, Frontiers of America series (Childrens Press)

Frontier Leaders and Pioneers by Dorothy Heiderstadt (McKay)

Daniel Boone, pp. 5–12
George Rogers Clark, pp. 13–21
Meriwether Lewis and William Clark, pp. 22–32
Zeb Pike, pp. 33–39
Johnny Appleseed, pp. 41–45
John James Audubon, pp. 47–54
Jim Bowie, pp. 56–61
Sam Houston, pp. 63–68
Sam Colt, pp. 70–75
George Catlin, pp. 77–85
Jim Bridger, pp. 88–94
Jed Smith, pp. 96–101
Josiah Gregg, pp. 103–108
William Holmes McGuffey, pp. 110–115
John Charles Fremont, pp. 117–123
Brigham Young, pp. 125–132
Francis Parkman, pp. 134–139
William Worrall Mayo, pp. 141–148
John Muir, pp. 150–157
Ezra Meeker, pp. 159–164

Frontier Living by Edwin Tunis (World)

Ghost Towns of the West by Olive Burt (Messner)

Gold Rush Adventures by Edith McCall, Frontiers of America series (Childrens Press)

Heroes of the Western Outposts by Edith McCall, Frontiers of America series (Childrens Press)

Heroines of the Early West by Nancy Ross (Random House)

The How and Why Wonder Book of Winning the West by Felix Sutton (Grosset)

Hunters Blaze the Trails by Edith McCall, Frontiers of America series (Childrens Press)

Indian Pony by Glen Dines (Macmillan)

Journal of One Davey Wyatt by Donald Honig (Watts)

Log Fort Adventures by Edith McCall, Frontiers of America series (Childrens Press)

Men Who Won the West by Franklin Folsom (Scholastic)

Mountain Men of the Early West by Olive Burt (Hawthorn)

Over the Mormon Trail by Helen Jones, Frontiers of America series (Childrens Press)

Palace Wagon Family: A True Story of the Donner Party by Margaret Sutton (Knopf)

MODEL 19 (cont.)

Pioneer Showfolk by Edith McCall, Frontiers of America series (Childrens Press)

Pioneer Traders by Edith McCall, Frontiers of America series (Childrens Press)

Saddles and Sabers: Black Men of the Old West by LaVere Anderson (Garrard)

Silver and Lead by Ralph Moody (Macmillan)

Stagecoach Days and Stagecoach Kings by Virginia Voight (Garrard)

Stalwart Men of Early Texas by Edith McCall, Frontiers of America series (Childrens Press)

Steamboats to the West by Edith McCall, Frontiers of America series (Childrens Press)

Sutter's Fort: Empire of the Sacramento by William and Celia Luce (Garrard)

To California by Covered Wagon by George Stewart (Random House)

Trails West and Men Who Made Them by Edith Dorian and W. N. Wilson (McGraw-Hill)

Wagons Ho! by Trevor Cole (Whitman)

Wagons Over the Mountains by Edith McCall, Frontiers of America series (Childrens Press)

When Cowboys Rode the Chisholm Trail by James McCague (Garrard)

When Mountain Men Trapped Beaver by Richard Glendinning (Garrard)

When Pioneers Pushed West to Oregon by Elizabeth Montgomery (Garrard)

When Wagon Trains Rolled to Santa Fe by Erick Berry (Garrard)

Wild and Woolly West by Earl Miers (Rand-McNally)

Winning the West by Harold McCracken (Doubleday)

Women of the West by Dorothy Levenson (Watts)

FILMSTRIPS

The Cowboy: Tough Man on a Mustang (Media systems—1 filmstrip, 1 record, 1 script)

Gold and Dreams of Gold (SVE—4 filmstrips, 2 cassettes, 4 teaching guides)

    Gold Towns of the Old West

    Ghost Towns—What Happened?

    How Gold Is Mined

    A Modern-Day Prospector Named George

The Gunslingers (American Pageant—1 filmstrip, 1 record, 1 script)

Heroes and Heroines of the Great West (Eye Gate—8 filmstrips, 4 cassettes)

    The Great Indian Chiefs of the Plains

    The Great Indian Chiefs of the Southwest

    The Horseback Generals

    The Kings of the Mines and Railroads

    The Legendary Cowgirls and Civilizers

    The Pathfinders

    The Scouts, Lawmen and Outlaws

    The Story of Explorers

Pathfinders Westward (SVE—6 filmstrips, 3 records, 6 teaching guides)

    Daniel Boone's Wilderness Trail

    First Trails into the West

    Lewis and Clark Expedition, pts. 1 and 2

    The Mountain Men -

    Rivers and Roads to the Mississippi

MODEL 19 (cont.)

Pioneer Women and Belles of the Wild West (Teaching Resources—1 filmstrip, 1 record, 1 teaching guide)

Pioneers of America (Eye Gate—10 filmstrips, 5 cassettes)

  Life of the Settlers

  Miners and 49ers

  Pioneer Craftsmen

  Pioneer Folk Art

  Pioneer Farming

  Pioneer Government and Law

  Pioneer Transportation and Communication

  Tradesmen and Cattlemen

  Trappers—The Mountain Men

  Western Expansion—A Vivid Portrayal of the Kind of Men and Women Who Conquered the Wilderness

Settling the West (Coronet—6 filmstrips, 3 records, 1 teaching guide)

  The Cattlemen

  The Farmers

  Growth of Towns and Cities

  The Miners

  The Trail Blazers

  Wagon Trains to Railroads

Settling the West (Outdoor Pictures—1 filmstrip, 1 cassette)

Stories from the Old West (SVE—6 filmstrips, 3 records, 6 teaching guides)

  The Comanches: Greatest Horsemen of the West

  El Camino Real

  Iron Horse, Golden Spike

  Pawnee: The Buffalo Pony

  The Pony Express Rider

  Vaquero! Vaquero!

The West: The Way It Was (American Pageant—1 filmstrip, 1 record, 1 script)

Westward Migration (SVE—4 filmstrips, 2 records, 4 teaching guides)

  The Gold Rush

  Into the Southwest

  The Oregon Country

  Three Routes to Eldorado

RECORDING

  Folksongs of the Frontier (Capitol)

MODEL 20 THE WHITE MEN DOOM AND THEN SAVE THE BUFFALO

Subject: Social Studies

Grade: 5

Unit: Midwest and the Great Plains

Topic: The White Men Doom and Then Save the Buffalo

Subtopic 1: When the first explorers came to the North American continent, there were as many as 60 million buffalo roaming free. During the period from 1800 to 1900, the

MODEL 20 (cont.)

buffalo population was reduced from 40 million to less than 800 animals. Can you discover the chain of events that caused the buffalo to be threatened with extinction?
SOURCES:
Mason, George. *The Wildlife of North America.* pp. 22–23.

Barker, Will. *Wildlife in America's History.* pp. 21–28.

McClung, Robert. *Shag, Last of the Plains Buffalo.*

Subtopic 2: Dr. Hungerford devoted the first chapter in his book *Ecology, the Circle of Life* to the wanton destruction of the American buffalo. Do you think this first chapter has a special message for us concerning our obligation to safeguard our natural resources? What is the significance of "The Great Plains Chain"?
SOURCE:
Hungerford, Harold R. *Ecology, the Circle of Life.* pp. 7–14.

Subtopic 3: What contribution did Scotty Philip and William Temple Hornaday make toward preventing the total obliteration of the American buffalo?
SOURCE:
Veglahn, Nancy. *The Buffalo King: The Story of Scotty Philip.* Chapters 11, 16, and 17.

Subtopic 4: Can you discover what a wildlife sanctuary is and how it differs from a wildlife refuge? Do you consider wildlife sanctuaries and refuges to be ecologically important?
SOURCE:
Harrison, C. W. *The First Book of Wildlife Sanctuaries.* pp. 1–2.

Optional topic 1: Each year, the U.S. Department of the Interior sells buffalo to reduce the size of a herd that has grown too large for the available public range. Can you discover the current purchase price of a buffalo being offered for sale by the Department of the interior?
SOURCE:
Harrison, C. W. *The First Book of Wildlife Sanctuaries.* p. 40.

Optional topic 2: Because the Plains Indians depended on the buffalo to supply their basic needs, they called the buffalo "The Giver of Life." Can you discover the many uses the Plains Indians made of the buffalo?
SOURCES:
Hofsinde, Robert. *The Indian and the Buffalo.* pp. 29–53.

Rounds, Glen. *Buffalo Harvest.* pp. 14–15.

American Bison, Studyprint No. 2, in the Audio Visual Enterprises Set "Wild Animals, Their Role in American History."

Optional activities:
Prepare a transparency or a poster identifying the many products the Plains Indians derived from the buffalo. If you would enjoy learning the Indian Buffalo Dance, the following sources will help you:
SOURCES:
Powers, William. *Here Is Your Hobby . . . Indian Dancing and Costumes.* Chapter XVI.

Hofmann, Charles. *American Indians Sing.*
NOTE: Music for the Buffalo Dance is available on the recording you will find in the slipcover attached to the inside of the back cover of the book.

The Indians were bewildered when the buffalo disappeared from the plains. Can you discover how the disappearance of the buffalo affected the Indians?
SOURCE:
Bleeker, Sonia. *The Sioux Indians.* pp. 139–155.

MODEL 21   CREATIVE WRITING

Optional Learning Experience: Creative Writing
Grades: 5–6
Goal: To provide opportunities for the GATE students to explore and practice the art of creative writing and the techniques of the craft.
Teaching Objectives:

To acquaint the student with the basic elements of creative writing.

To acquaint the student with the basic techniques for organizing ideas.

To develop student awareness of the power of words.

To acquaint the student with the structural elements of narrative writing.

To acquaint the student with the characteristics of a variety of literary forms.

To encourage the student to experiment with various forms of creative writing.

Teaching Strategies and Methods:

After a brief orientation from the GATE teacher, each student will proceed to build his or her knowledge of creative writing, progressing at his or her own rate, and following his or her own line of interest.

Procedural Outline:
  I. Student orientation to this project will be based on the reading and analysis of *The First Book of Creative Writing* by Julia Mahon (Watts) giving special attention to:
     A. What is creative writing?
     B. Why creative writing?
     C. Creativity in school assignments
     D. The four basic elements in writing
        1. Plotting
        2. Bringing characters to life
        3. Setting
        4. Style
     E. The importance of grammar
     F. Choosing words
     G. How to do research
        1. Using the library
        2. The noteworthy notebook
 II. Viewing the following motion pictures will sharpen the student's understanding of the four basic elements of narrative writing:
     A. *Reading Stories: Plots and Themes* (Coronet) stresses:
        1. That the action of a story is its plot.
        2. That the theme is the author's feeling about his or her story, characters, or life itself.
        3. How the theme is revealed through the plot rather than stated directly.
     B. *Reading Stories: Characters and Settings* (Coronet) stresses:
        1. Techniques used to describe characters.
        2. How settings affect characters.
        3. That through settings we can experience different times and places.
        4. That characters mean more if we recognize ourselves in them.
III. As a warm-up exercise, the student views the motion picture *Let's Make Up a Story* (Coronet)
     A. With imagination you can be anyone, go anywhere, do anything.
     B. First, you need a location or setting for your story.
     C. Then, you need something for the characters to do, a plot.
     D. Finally, you need an ending.
IV. The student proceeds to explore and experiment with creative writing.
     A. The GATE teacher serves as consultant and/or critic upon request.
     B. No student is required to submit for teacher criticism any of his or her writings.
     C. If the student wishes, his or her writing can be shared with selected students from the GATE group or with the entire group.

MODEL 21 (cont.)

D. If the student wishes, his or her writings can be entered in competition with those submitted from students in the district GATE Program.
  1. A jury of teachers and parents will judge the writings by category, for example:
       Fable
       Fairy tale
       Play
       Poetry
       Short story
  2. Those writings judged best in each category will be published in a GATE Creative Writing Anthology.

Resource Kit:
  BOOK

  The First Book of Creative Writing by Julia Mahon (Watts)

  FILMSTRIPS (Pied Piper—20 filmstrips, 20 recordings, reaction guides)

  Building Word Power

   Picture Words

   Figures of Speech

   Action Words

   Sensory Description

  Content

   Being the Thing

   Creating Fables

   Creating Just So Stories

   Creating a Picture Book

  Narrative Writing

   Elements of a Story

   Beginnings and Endings

   Conflict

   Character

  Organizing Ideas

   Kinds of Sentences

   Paragraphs

   More Than One Paragraph

   Outlines

  Practical Writing

   Giving Directions

   Interviewing

   News Reporting

   Taking a Stand

  How to Write Poetry (Educational Dimensions—4 filmstrips, 4 cassettes)

   Meanings

   Sounds

   Imagery

   Rhythm

  Write Yourself a Fairy Tale (Educational Dimensions—2 filmstrips, 2 cassettes)

   Write Yourself a Fairy Tale pt. 1, pt. 2

MODEL 21 (cont.)

Writing Short Stories (Coronet—4 filmstrips, 2 recordings)

  The Creative Writer

  The Plot

  The Characters

  The Dialogue

MOTION PICTURES (Coronet)

  Let's Make Up a Story

  Reading Stories: Characters and Settings

  Reading Stories: Plots and Themes

MODEL 22   ORIENTATION TO THE GATE PROGRAM (GRADE 6)

Grade: 6

Project Goals:

  To orient the students to the purpose, scope, and value of the sixth-grade GATE Program.

  To sharpen and refine the students' ability to think creatively.

  To extend the students' awareness that the GATE Program is an effective means of self-discovery and self-realization.

Teaching Objectives:

  This project has been designed and structured to provide learning experiences that will enable the student:

    To explore the concept of self-actualization.

    To experiment with creative and adventurous thinking.

    To discover new dimensions, greater satisfaction, and challenge in learning to learn.

    To perceive and value the contributions others have made as a result of creative, adventurous thinking.

    To perceive and value the school library as a laboratory for self-discovery and self-actualization.

Teaching Strategies and Methods:

  No time limits are imposed on this project. Number of students and student interest are the two factors that determine the duration of this GATE project and subsequent projects whether the time be two weeks, two months, or longer.

  A basic part of orienting the students to the GATE Program is to provide an overview of possible group and individual learning experiences. Administering the Interest Inventory and identifying areas of individual student interest can serve as an effective means of individualizing GATE learning experiences.

  Each student should be encouraged to explore areas of special interest and to suggest individual and/or group learning experiences.

Procedural Outline:

  I. Group orientation to and overview of the GATE Program.

    A. Why a GATE Program?

      1. The GATE Program will provide challenging learning experiences that will stretch the mind and quicken the imagination.

        The Russian language and culture will be studied throughout the school year.

        A number of challenging individual and group learning experiences will be offered, including the following:

MODEL 22 (cont.)

If I Had Lived during the Middle Ages: An Experiment in Adventurous Thinking

The Wizardry of Words

Pirates—Real and Imaginary

Historical Novels: Zestfully Reliving the Past

Great Books—Past and Present

They Made the Difference

Arty Things to Do: Cartooning, Drawing, Painting

Crafty Things to Do: Ceramics, Puppetry, Model Building, Photography, Carving, Mosaics, Macrame, Needlework, Cookery, Batik

Chillers and Thrillers

Mind-Boggling Phenomena

Interest Zingers and Zappers

Laughs, Chuckles, and Guffaws

Tantalizing Puzzles

Wonderful World of Science

2. The GATE Program will provide opportunities to bring greater depth and breadth to units being studied in the classroom.

Depth and breadth require a wealth of appropriate learning resources and a learning laboratory where the student can work with ideas creatively and intensely.

The GATE students will have the opportunity to serve as research consultants to the class for each social studies unit, assuming one of the following roles:

Agriculturalist	Dietician	Historian
Anthropologist	Economist	Musician
Archaeologist	Educator	Naturalist
Artist	Folklorist	Sociologist
Biographer	Geographer	Statistician
Book reviewer	Geologist	Travel agent

3. The GATE Program will provide opportunities for each student to learn how to think and to act creatively.

Creativity is the power to develop to the fullest all of one's abilities; to see what others have seen and to respond differently; to form new ideas, to invent, and to discover.

Margaret Mead, the anthropologist, estimated that most human beings use only 6 percent of their creative potential.

A constant goal of the GATE Program is to enable each student to achieve his or her highest level of creativity.

B. An excellent introduction to learning how to think creatively is found in *Creativity and Imagination* by Jacolyn Mott (Creative Education). (See Model 27, The Wizardry of Words, a unit based on Chapter 8 in this book.)

1. The magic of the mind is learning to think and to act creatively.

2. Psychologists believe that creativity occurs in four steps:

First, preparation:

This is a time of action—gathering facts, seeking answers.

A time of experimenting with ideas—a period of trial and error.

Hard work paves the way for success.

MODEL 22 (cont.)

Second, incubation:

> The mind considers and organizes ideas gathered during preparation.
>
> The mind combines and compares new ideas with facts and ideas already known.

Third, inspiration:

> Inspiration is a sudden solution to a problem.
>
> Examples of inspiration have occurred in every area of creativity.

Fourth, verification:

> Testing the solution to determine if it is true.
>
> If the idea fizzles, creative process begins again.

3. The desire to create would die without imagination.

> Imagination is the ability to form in the mind a picture or idea.
>
> Such mental pictures or ideas are like kaleidoscopic or teleidoscopic images or designs.
>
> We employ imagination: to recreate the past; to wonder about unfamiliar people or places; and to toy with ideas about the future.
>
> Vicarious experience is an experience that is felt or enjoyed through imagined participation in the experience of others.
>
> Vicarious imagination helps us understand and sympathize with other people.
>
> Vicarious imagination helps people solve problems—role playing is an example of vicarious imagination.
>
> Vicarious imagination makes the reader of a story or the audience watching a play become involved in the plot.

4. Everyone has creative potential that can be developed.

> All have seeds of creativity that, if nurtured, will grow.
>
> Practice improves creativity.
>
> > *The Book of Think (Or How to Solve a Problem Twice Your Size)* by Marilyn Burns (Little, Brown) provides numerous creative thinking experiences.

5. There is growing evidence that intelligence tests identify only a part of mental ability.

> Creativity and imagination are a vital part of each person's mental potential.

6. The first step in developing creativity is to wonder why.

> Serendipity is the ability to make unexpected discoveries by accident—such an ability is basic to creativity.
>
> > Examples of serendipity:
> >
> > > Vulcanization of rubber.
> > >
> > > Discovery of penicillin.
> > >
> > > Discovery of X-rays.
>
> Many discoveries are made as the result of painstaking research.
>
> > Examples of discoveries resulting from painstaking, exhaustive research:
> >
> > > Radium.
> > >
> > > Incandescent light bulb.
> > >
> > > Vaccine for polio.

MODEL 22 (cont.)

Creative people see with a wonder that blows away the clouds of habit, tradition, and prejudice.

II. Curiosity is the heart of creativity.
  A. Creative people project beyond what is to what might be.
    1. *New Trail Blazers of Technology* by Harland Manchester (Scribner) tells about ten twentieth-century inventors whose work has had great impact on modern-day life.

      Each of these men has made a difference in contemporary life.

      These creative men are the inventors of the Xerox copier, cable TV, the Polaroid camera, the Wankel engine, hovercraft, the transistor, masers and lasers, and FM radio.

      At age 14 Frederick Cottrell invented an air pollution precipitator.

        "Cot sees ahead into that field which most of us do not see. He has to have an army behind him to rake up the things he uncovers." p. 22.

    2. Leonardo da Vinci, who will be introduced in the learning project, If I Had Lived during the Middle Ages, was curious about all manner of things.

      His contributions include his work as:

Anatomist	Engineer	Naturalist
Architect	Inventor	Painter
Author	Mathematician	Philosopher
Caricaturist	Musician	Sculptor

    3. Benjamin Franklin and Thomas Jefferson were geniuses driven by insatiable curiosity.

      Research the lives of Franklin and Jefferson.

      Make a list of their accomplishments and compare with those of Leonardo da Vinci.

      Would you nominate either or both of these men to the Hall of Fame for Great Americans?

      Did Franklin and Jefferson really make a difference?

  B. A special sixth-grade ongoing GATE project is to discover men and women whom you would nominate for membership in a Hall of Fame for Creative Thinkers.

III. We all perceive differently.
  A. Perception is the meaning or mental picture that results when sensations (signals from our senses) combine with our storehouse of experiences and emotions.
    1. The tapestry of patterns supplied by the senses is different for each person.
    2. No two people perceive alike.
    3. Interest motivates perception.
    4. The North Hills School District Interest Inventory is designed to identify each student's major interests and concerns (see Appendix B).
      NOTE: Administer the inventory at this point in the orientation program. Have the GATE students compile their own interest profiles, and share their interests and concerns with the other GATE students in their GATE group.
  B. Perception is selective.
    1. The mind automatically screens sights, sounds, information.
    2. The mind files away in the memory bank information that seems to be important.
IV. Openness to experience is the launching pad for creativity.
  A. The sense of wonder, like a talent, grows with practice.

MODEL 22 (cont.)

   B. Look beyond the familiar.
   C. To marvel is the beginning of knowledge.
   D. To quest for the unknown is to go beyond the mundane, to give wings to the imagination.
   E. To ask yourself the question "What if . . . " is the first step in creative thinking.

V. Notetaking helps organize ideas and helps preserve fleeting thoughts.
   A. The geniuses of the world have commonly been notemakers.
      1. Leonardo da Vinci's notebooks are available for study.
      2. Thomas Edison was a conscientious notetaker.
   B. A well-organized notebook plus conscientious notemaking are the hallmarks of mature, creative thinkers.
   C. Keeping a journal of what you have done and specifying what needs to be done is recommended by experts in the field of developing creativity.
      1. The form My Journal, at end of this model, is designed to provide a framework for self-analysis and self-directed knowledge building.
      2. Rereading the journal at the end of the first semester is not only an effective way to review what has been accomplished but also an effective means of self-evaluation—has the student measured up to scratch? Likewise, rereading the journal at the end of the school year is both an excellent review of the sixth-grade GATE Program and an excellent basis for judging personal growth and development.

VI. A constant goal throughout the sixth grade is to have the GATE students translate the acronym TARGET into a way of learning how to learn.

<u>T</u>hinking

<u>A</u>pplying

<u>R</u>eacting

<u>G</u>rowing

<u>E</u>xploring

<u>T</u>otal learning

MY JOURNAL

Student _____ Date _____

What I did today—
  Topic I explored:

  Materials I used:

  What I learned:

  What I need to do next:

How I feel about what I did today—

MODEL 23   BOOK ILLUSTRATORS AND THEIR ART

Unit: Book Illustrators and Their Art
Subject: Humanities Interdisciplinary Unit
Grade: 6
Goal: To provide a culminating experience that will quicken student awareness of and interest in book illustrators and their art.
Objectives:
      1. To provide opportunity for the students to explore book illustration as an art form.

MODEL 23 (cont.)

2. To provide opportunity for the students to become reacquainted with illustrated books they have previously enjoyed.

3. To provide opportunity for the students to experiment with book illustrations.

Teaching Procedure:

1. Students are introduced to the unit.
   A. The filmstrip *Enjoying Illustrations* (Pied Piper) is viewed by the class.
      1. Students learn some of the ways illustrations contribute to the enjoyment of books.
      2. Students are asked to list at least three different ways illustrators can treat the same subject. .
      3. Students are encouraged to make illustrations expressing emotion, mood, and character.
   B. The motion picture *Robert McCloskey* (Weston Woods) is shown.
      1. Students meet Robert McCloskey and visit his studio.
      2. Students discover that craftsmanship must go hand-in-hand with inspiration.

II. Students are introduced to Randolph Caldecott.
   A. Students learn that he was an English Artist and illustrator who lived 1846–1886.
   B. Students learn that he is best known for his series of 16 children's picture books (Warne), which includes:
      1. *Frog He Would A' Wooing Go*
      2. *House That Jack Built*
      3. *Sing a Song of Sixpence*
      4. *Three Jovial Huntsmen*
      FILMSTRIPS (Weston Woods—sound)
      1. *Hey Diddle Diddle*
      2. *Sing a Song of Sixpence*
   C. Students learn that the Caldecott Medal is awarded each year to the illustrator voted as being the best. They examine:
      1. Caldecott Medal filmstrips (Weston Woods)
      2. Caldecott Medal posters (Horn Book)

III. Students are introduced to Leslie Brooke
   A. Students learn that he was an English artist and illustrator, a contemporary of Randolph Caldecott.
   B. Students discover that he created a series of books (Warne) called the *Johnny Crow* books, which includes:
      1. *Johnny Crow's Garden*
      2. *Johnny Crow's New Garden*
      3. *Johnny Crow's Party*
      FILMSTRIPS (Spoken Arts—sound)
      1. *Johnny Crow's Garden*
      2. *Johnny Crow's New Garden*
      3. *Johnny Crow's Party*
      4. *The Tailor and the Crow*
   C. Students learn that he had illustrated some of the traditional English nursery stories (Warne).
      1. *Story of the Three Bears*
      2. *Story of the Three Little Pigs*
      3. *This Little Pig Went to Market*

IV. Students are introduced to Kate Greenaway.
   A. Students learn that she was a poet and illustrator and was a contemporary of both Caldecott and Brooke.
   B. Students learn that she is best known for her books decorated with flowers, fruits, merry children, and landscapes, such as:
      1. *A—Apple Pie* (Warne)
      2. *The Kate Greenaway Treasury* (Collins-World)
      3. *The Language of Flowers* (Warne)

MODEL 23 (cont.)

4. *Marigold Garden* (Warne)
5. *Mother Goose* (Warne)
6. *Under the Window* (Warne)
FILMSTRIPS (Spoken Arts—sound)
1. *Marigold Garden*
2. *Under the Window*
3. *Kate Greenaway's Games*
4. *The Pied Piper of Hamelin* (from Robert Browning's poem)

V. Students are introduced to E. H. Shepard as the illustrator who created the World of Pooh
  A. The motion picture *Mr. Shepard and Mr. Milne* (Weston Woods) is viewed.
  B. The following books illustrated by Shepard are examined and discussed:
    1. *Christopher Robin Book of Verse* (Dutton)
    2. *Christopher Robin Story Book* (Dutton)
    3. *Hans Andersen's Fairy Tales* (Walck)
    4. *House at Pooh Corner* (Dutton)
    5. *Now We Are Six* (Dutton)
    6. *The Pooh Cook Book* (Dutton)
    7. *The Pooh Get-Well Book: Recipes and Activities to Help You Recover from Wheezles and Sneezles* (Dutton)
    8. *The Pooh Party Book* (Dutton)
    9. *Pooh's Song Book* (Dutton)
    10. *Pooh's Story Book* (Dutton)
    11. *Reluctant Dragon* (Holiday)
    12. *When We Were Very Young* (Dutton)
    13. *Wind in the Willows* (Scribner)
    14. *Winnie the Pooh* (Dutton)
  C. The following audiovisual materials are available for student examination:
    ART PRINTS
    1. *Pooh: His Art Gallery* (Dutton)
    2. *Pooh Posters* (Weston Woods)
    REALIA—Stuffed animals (Sears Roebuck)
    1. Eeyore
    2. Kanga
    3. Owl
    4. Piglet
    5. Pooh
    6. Rabbit
    7. Tigger
    REALIA—Figurines (Beswick)
    1. Christopher Robin
    2. Eeyore
    3. Kanga
    4. Owl
    5. Piglet
    6. Pooh
    7. Rabbit
    8. Tigger

VI. Students are introduced to the following illustrators and the books they have illustrated; they are encouraged to analyze, compare, and contrast the various styles of illustration:
  A. Joan Anglund, illustrator of:
    1. *A Child's Book of Old Nursery Rhymes* (Atheneum)
    2. *Christmas Is a Time of Giving* (Harcourt)
    3. *Cup of Sun: A Book of Poems* (Harcourt)
    4. *Do You Love Someone?* (Harcourt)
    5. *A Friend Is Someone Who Likes You* (Harcourt)
    6. *Goodbye, Yesterday* (Atheneum)

MODEL 23 (cont.)

    7. *In a Pumpkin Shell: A Mother Goose ABC* (Harcourt)
    8. *Look out the Window* (Harcourt)
    9. *Nibble Nibble Mousekin: A Tale of Hansel and Gretel* (Harcourt)
   10. *Pocketful of Proverbs* (Harcourt)
   11. *Spring Is a New Beginning* (Harcourt)
   12. *What Color Is Love?* (Harcourt)
   13. *A Year Is Round* (Harcourt)
ART PRINTS
    1. *Packet of Pictures* (Harcourt)
REALIA
    1. Anglund Plates—Months of the Year (Dekor Shop, Walter, West Germany)
B. James Daugherty, illustrator of:
    1. *Abe Lincoln Grows Up* (Harcourt)
    2. *Andy and the Lion* (Viking)
    3. *Daniel Boone* (Viking)
    4. *Landing of the Pilgrims* (Random House)
    5. *Of Courage Unlimited* (Viking)
    6. *Poor Richard* (Viking)
    7. *Rainbow Book of American History* (World)
FILMSTRIPS (Weston Woods—sound)
    1. *Andy and the Lion*
    2. *The Loudest Noise in the World*
MOTION PICTURE
    1. *James Daugherty* (Weston Woods)
C. Disney Studios (Golden Press), illustrators of:
    1. *Alice in Wonderland*
    2. *Bambi*
    3. *Ben and Me*
    4. *Brementown Musicians*
    5. *Cinderella*
    6. *The Little Red Hen*
    7. *Mary Poppins*
    8. *Peter Pan*
    9. *Pinocchio*
   10. *Snow White*
   11. *Three Little Pigs*
   12. *Uncle Remus Stories*
   13. *Winnie the Pooh and His Friends*
   14. *Winnie the Pooh and the Blustery Day*
   15. *Winnie the Pooh and the Honey Tree*
FILMSTRIPS (Walt Disney Educational Media—sound)
    1. *Alice in Wonderland*
    2. *Bambi*
    3. *Ben and Me*
    4. *Cinderella*
    5. *Mary Poppins*
    6. *Peter Pan*
    7. *Pinocchio*
    8. *Snow White*
    9. *Three Little Pigs*
   10. *Winnie the Pooh and the Blustery Day*
   11. *Winnie the Pooh and the Honey Tree*
   12. *Winnie the Pooh and Tigger*
MOTION PICTURES (Walt Disney Educational Media)
    1. *Ben and Me*
    2. *The Many Adventures of Winnie the Pooh*
D. Katherine Evans (Whitman), illustrator of:
    1. *The Boy Who Cried Wolf*

MODEL 23 (cont.)

    2. *A Bundle of Sticks*
    3. *A Camel in the Tent*
    4. *The Maid and Her Pail of Milky*
    5. *The Man, the Boy, and the Donkey*
   FILMSTRIPS (Educational Enrichment Materials—sound)
    1. *A Bundle of Sticks*
    2. *A Camel in the Tent*
    3. *The Maid and Her Pail of Milk*
    4. *The Man, the Boy, and the Donkey*
E. Gyo Fujikawa (Grosset), illustrator of:
    1. *Child's Book of Poems*
    2. *A Child's Garden of Verses*
    3. *Fairy Tales and Fables*
    4. *Mother Goose*
   ART PRINTS
    1. *Portfolio of Fujikawa Reproductions* (Grosset)
F. Paul Galdone, illustrator of:
    1. *Androcles and the Lion* (McGraw)
    2. *Barbara Fritchie* (Crowell)
    3. *Blind Men and the Elephant* (McGraw)
    4. *Cinderella* (McGraw)
    5. *First Seven Days* (Crowell)
    6. *The Frog Prince* (McGraw)
    7. *Gingerbread Boy* (Seabury)
    8. *The Hare and the Tortoise* (McGraw)
    9. *Henny Penny* (Seabury)
   10. *Hereafterthis* (McGraw)
   11. *The History of Little Tom Tucker* (McGraw)
   12. *The Horse, the Fox, and the Lion* (Seabury)
   13. *The House That Jack Built* (McGraw)
   14. *The Life of Jack Sprat, His Wife and His Cat* (McGraw)
   15. *The Little Red Hen* (Seabury)
   16. *Little Tuppen* (Seabury)
   17. *The Magic Porridge Pot* (Seabury)
   18. *The Monkey and the Crocodile* (Seabury)
   19. *The Moving Adventures of Old Dame Trot and Her Comical Cat* (McGraw)
   20. *Obedient Jack* (Watts)
   21. *Old Mother Hubbard and Her Dog* (McGraw)
   22. *The Old Woman and Her Pig* (McGraw)
   23. *Puss in Boots* (Seabury)
   24. *Three Aesop Fox Fables* (Seabury)
   25. *The Three Bears* (Seabury)
   26. *The Three Billy Goats Gruff* (Seabury)
   27. *The Three Little Pigs* (Seabury)
   28. *The Three Wishes* (McGraw)
   29. *Tom, Tom the Piper's Son* (McGraw)
   30. *The Town Mouse and the Country Mouse* (McGraw)
   31. *The Wise Fool* (Pantheon)
   FILMSTRIPS (Weston Woods—sound)
    1. *The House That Jack Built*
    2. *Old Mother Hubbard and Her Dog*
    3. *The Old Woman and Her Pig*
   MOTION PICTURES (McGraw)
    1. *Old Mother Hubbard and Her Dog*
    2. *The Old Woman and Her Pig*
G. Janusz Grabianski, illustrator of:
    1. *Andersen's Fairy Tales* (Hawthorn)

MODEL 23 (cont.)

    2. *Androcles and the Lion* (Watts)
    3. *Big Book of Animal Fables* (Watts)
    4. *Big Book of Animal Stories* (Watts)
    5. *Big Book of Pets* (Watts)
    6. *Big Book of Wild Animals* (Watts)
    7. *Grabianski's Birds* (Watts)
    8. *Grabianski's Cats* (Watts)
    9. *Grabianski's Dogs* (Watts)
  10. *Grabianski's Horses* (Watts)
  11. *Grabianski's Wild Animals* (Watts)
  12. *Grimm's Fairy Tales* (Hawthorn)
  13. *Ten Tales from Shakespeare* (Watts)
ART PRINTS
    1. *Grabianski's Portfolio* (Watts)
H. Ezra Keats, illustrator of:
    1. *Brave Riders* (Crowell)
    2. *Danny Dunn and the Anti-Gravity Paint* (McGraw)
    3. *Danny Dunn and the Homework Machine* (McGraw)
    4. *Danny Dunn and the Weather Machine* (McGraw)
    5. *Danny Dunn on a Desert Island* (McGraw)
    6. *The Egyptians Knew* (McGraw)
    7. *The Eskimos Knew* (McGraw)
    8. *Grasses* (Walck)
    9. *Hi, Cat* (Macmillan)
  10. *The Indians Knew* (McGraw)
  11. *John Henry: An American Legend* (Pantheon)
  12. *The Pilgrims Knew* (McGraw)
  13. *The Snowy Day* (Viking)
  14. *Wonder Tales of Dogs and Cats* (Doubleday)
FILMSTRIPS (sound)
    1. *John Henry: An American Legend* (Guidance Associates)
    2. *The Snowy Day* (Weston Woods)
MOTION PICTURES
    1. *Ezra Jack Keats* (Weston Woods)
    2. *John Henry* (Holt)
    3. *The Snowy Day* (Weston Woods)
POSTERS
    1. At Home (Macmillan)
    2. At School (Macmillan)
    3. In the Community (Macmillan)
    4. The Snowy Day (Horn Book)
I. Edna Miller (Prentice-Hall), illustrator of:
    1. *Mousekin Finds a Friend*
    2. *Mousekin Takes a Trip*
    3. *Mousekin's Christmas Eve*
    4. *Mousekin's Family*
    5. *Mousekin's Golden House*
    6. *Mousekin's Woodland Birthday*
    7. *Mousekin's Woodland Sleepers*
FILMSTRIPS (Educational Enrichment Materials—sound)
    1. *Mousekin Finds a Friend*
    2. *Mousekin's Christmas Eve*
    3. *Mousekin's Family*
    4. *Mousekin's Golden House*
J. Beatrix Potter (Warne), illustrator of:
    1. *Appley Dapply's Nursery Rhymes*
    2. *Letters to Children*
    3. *Roly Poly Pudding*

MODEL 23 (cont.)

4. *The Sly Old Cat*
5. *The Story of a Fierce Bad Rabbit*
6. *The Tailor of Gloucester*
7. *The Tale of Benjamin Bunny*
8. *The Tale of Jemima Puddle-Duck*
9. *The Tale of Johnny Townmouse*
10. *The Tale of Little Pig Robinson*
11. *The Tale of Mister Jeremy Fisher*
12. *The Tale of Mister Todd*
13. *The Tale of Mrs. Tiggy-Winkle*
14. *The Tale of Mrs. Tittlemouse*
15. *The Tale of Peter Rabbit*
16. *The Tale of Pigling Bland*
17. *The Tale of Squirrel Nutkin*
18. *The Tale of the Flopsy Bunnies*
19. *The Tale of Timmy Tiptoes*
20. *The Tale of Tom Kitten*
21. *The Tale of Two Bad Mice*

BIOGRAPHY OF BEATRIX POTTER

1. *The Art of Beatrix Potter* with an Appreciation by Anne Carroll Moore (Warne)
2. *Nothing Is Impossible: The Story of Beatrix Potter* by Dorothy Aldis (Atheneum)

CRAFT BOOKS

1. *Needlepoint Designs after Illustrations by Beatrix Potter* by Rita Weiss (Dover)
2. *Toys from the Tales of Beatrix Potter* by Margaret Hutchings (Warne)

CRAFT PROJECTS

1. *Plaster Molds* supplied by Activa Products, Inc. (582 Market St., San Francisco, Calif. 94104)

Benjamin Bunny	Mrs. Tiggy-Winkle
Hunca Munca	Peter Rabbit
Jemima Puddle-Duck	Tom Kitten
Jeremy Fisher	Tom Thumb

ART PRINTS (Warne)

1. *Benjamin Bunny*
2. *Peter Rabbit*
3. *Squirrel Nutkin*
4. *A Mural: The Tale of Peter Rabbit*

FILMSTRIPS (sound)

1. *The Tailor of Gloucester* (Spoken Arts)
2. *The Tale of Benjamin Bunny* (Spoken Arts)
3. *The Tale of Benjamin Bunny* (Weston Woods)
4. *The Tale of Mr. Jeremy Fisher* (Spoken Arts)
5. *The Tale of Mrs. Tiggy-Winkle* (Spoken Arts)
6. *The Tale of Peter Rabbit* (Spoken Arts)
7. *The Tale of Peter Rabbit* (Weston Woods)
8. *The Tale of Squirrel Nutkin* (Spoken Arts)
9. *The Tale of Two Bad Mice* (Spoken Arts)

REALIA—Figurines (Beswick)

1. Benjamin Bunny
2. Benjamin Bunny's Father
3. Flopsy, Mopsy, and Cotton-Tail
4. Hunca Munca
5. Jemima Puddle-Duck
6. Lady Mouse
7. Peter Rabbit
8. Poorly Peter Rabbit

MODEL 23 (cont.)

9. Squirrel Nutkin
10. Tailor of Gloucester

K. Norman Rockwell, illustrator of:
1. *Norman Rockwell: A Sixty Year Retrospective* ed. by Thomas S. Buechner (Abrams)
2. *Norman Rockwell Illustrator* by Arthur L. Guptill (Watson-Guptill)
3. *The Norman Rockwell Storybook* (Simon and Schuster)
4. *Norman Rockwell's Americana ABC* (Abrams)
5. *Tom Sawyer* (Heritage)

ART PRINTS
1. *Boys and Dog on a Raft* (Becky Thatcher Gift Shop, Hannibal, Mo. 63857)
2. *Boys Smoking a Pipe* (Becky Thatcher Gift Shop)
3. *Boys Walking Girl Home from School* (Becky Thatcher Gift Shop)
4. *The Four Seasons* (New York Graphics)
5. *Rockwell's Americans* (Scholastic)

L. Arthur Rackham, illustrator of:
1. *Cinderella* (Lippincott)
2. *Once Upon a Time: The Fairy-Tale World of Arthur Rackham* (Viking)
3. *Sleeping Beauty* (Lippincott)

M. Tasha Tudor, illustrator of:
1. *Around the Year* (Walck)
2. *Child's Garden of Verses* (Walck)
3. *Fairy Tales from Hans Christian Andersen* (Walck)
4. *First Delights: A Book about the Five Senses* (Platt)
5. *Little Princess* (Lippincott)
6. *Little Women* (World)
7. *Secret Garden* (Lippincott)
8. *Wind in the Willows* (World)
9. *Wings from the Wind: An Anthology of Poetry* (Lippincott)

ART PRINTS
1. Various illustrations available on request (Walck)
2. Original illustrations and reproductions (The Dutch Inn Gift Shop, 211 N. Water St., Mill Hall, Pa. 17751)

GREETING CARDS (The Dutch Inn Gift Shop)
1. Christmas Scenes
2. Family Gatherings
3. Flowers and Garlands

N. Edwin Tunis (World), illustrator of:
1. *Colonial Craftsmen and the Beginnings of American Industry*
2. *Colonial Living*
3. *Frontier Living*
4. *Indians*
5. *Oars, Sails and Steam*
6. *Shaw's Fortune: The Picture Story of a Colonial Plantation*
7. *Weapons*
8. *Wheels*

O. Brian Wildsmith (Watts), illustrator of:
1. *Brian Wildsmith's Birds*
2. *Brian Wildsmith's Circus*
3. *Brian Wildsmith's Fishes*
4. *Brian Wildsmith's the Twelve Days of Christmas*
5. *Brian Wildsmith's Wild Animals*
6. *Child's Garden of Verses*
7. *The Hare and the Tortoise*
8. *The Lion and the Rat*
9. *The Miller, the Boy and the Donkey*
10. *The Owl and the Woodpecker*

MODEL 23 (cont.)

  11. *Oxford Book of Poetry for Children*
  12. *The Rich Man and the Shoe-maker*
  FILMSTRIPS (Weston Woods)
   1. *Brian Wildsmith's Birds*
   2. *Brian Wildsmith's Wild Animals*
   3. *The North Wind and the Sun*
   4. *The Rich Man and the Shoe-maker*
  ART PRINTS (Watts)
   1. *A Brian Wildsmith Portfolio*
   2. *Brian Wildsmith's Animal Portfolio*
 P. Newell C. Wyeth (Scribner), illustrator of:
   1. *Boy's King Arthur*
   2. *The Deerslayer*
   3. *Drums*
   4. *Mysterious Island*
   5. *Robin Hood*
   6. *Robinson Crusoe*
   7. *Treasure Island*
   8. *Westward Ho*

VII. Students are given the opportunity to examine and compare various illustrated editions of the same title, for example:
 A. *Child's Garden of Verses* as illustrated by:
   1. Gyo Fujikawa (Grosset)
   2. Tasha Tudor (Walck)
   3. Brian Wildsmith (Watts)
 B. *Little Women* as illustrated by:
   1. Barbara Cooney (Crowell)
   2. Betty Fraser (Macmillan)
   3. Tasha Tudor (World)
 C. *The Man, the Boy and the Donkey* or *The Miller, His Son and Their Donkey* as illustrated by:
   1. Roger Duvoisin (McGraw-Hill)
   2. Katherine Evans (Albert Whitman)
   3. Brian Wildsmith (Watts)
 D. *Mother Goose* as illustrated by:
   1. Gyo Fujikawa (Grosset)
   2. Kate Greenaway (World)
   3. Tasha Tudor (Walck)
   4. Brian Wildsmith (Watts)
 E. *Robinson Crusoe* as illustrated by:
   1. Roger Duvoisin (World)
   2. Lynd Ward (Grosset)
   3. Newell C. Wyeth (Scribner)
 F. *Story of the Three Pigs* as illustrated by:
   1. Leslie Brooke (Warne)
   2. William Pene DuBois (Viking)
   3. Disney Studios (Walt Disney Productions)
   4. Paul Galdone (Seabury)
   5. William Stobbs (McGraw-Hill)
 G. *Winnie-the-Pooh* as illustrated by:
   1. Disney Studios (Walt Disney Productions)
   2. E. H. Shepard (Dutton)

VIII. Students are given the opportunity to become acquainted with illustrated books from foreign countries; for example, these illustrated children's books from Japan:
 A. *Hansel and Gretel,* illus. by Yoshitaro Isaka (Gakken Publishing, imported by Japan Publications Trading Co., 1255 Howard St., San Francisco, Calif. 94103)
 B. *How the Withered Trees Blossomed,* illus. by Yasuo Segawa (Kodansha, Ltd.,

MODEL 23 (cont.)

imported by Lippincott). NOTE: This book is printed in Japanese style—it is to be read from back to front; the text is in Japanese calligraphy as well as in English.
   C. *The Nutcracker,* illus. by Fumiko Hori (Gakken Publishing, imported by Japan Publications Trading Co.)
   D. *The Sorcerer's Apprentice,* illus. by Ryo Hei Yauagihara (Gakken Publishing, imported by Japan Publications Trading Co.)
   E. *William Tell,* illustrated by Hiroshi Mizusawa (Gakken Publishing, imported by Japan Publications Trading Co.)
 IX. Students are encouraged to try their hand at story illustration, or one or more of the following activities:
   A. Designing book jackets.
   B. Designing bookplates and/or bookmarks.
   C. Designing greeting cards with a storybook motif.
   D. Designing needlework patterns of storybook characters.

MODEL 24   IF I HAD LIVED DURING THE MIDDLE AGES

Learning Project: If I Had Lived during the Middle Ages: An Experiment in Adventurous Thinking
Grade: 6
Project Goals:
   To provide learning experiences that will enable the gifted student to perceive and enjoy history as an ongoing heroic drama with the happenings of the past setting the stage for the happenings of the present and the future.

   To introduce the gifted student to the inquiry method and to the mysteries of adventurous, creative thinking.
Teaching Objectives:
   This project has been designed and structured to provide these basic understandings:
   History is the recorded memory of the past, the source to be consulted when searching for the answers to the eternal questions:
      "Who is man?"
      "What has he achieved?"
      "Why has he sometimes failed?"
      "What might he become?"
      "What could my role be in the drama of history yet to be written?"
   Positive human characteristics such as courage, bravery, idealism, honesty, integrity, patriotism, empathy, and selflessness and each of their negative counterparts have had dynamic impact on historical events.

   All societies and all human beings are interdependent; no society and no human being can survive as an island unto itself.

   Life, liberty, and the pursuit of happiness—and all other basic human rights—have been painfully and slowly won at the cost of great human suffering and sacrifice.

   Biography is a rich source of insight into the human dimension of history.

   The acronym TARGET (the major goal of the GATE Program) stands for:
   <u>T</u>hinking

   <u>A</u>pplying

   <u>R</u>eacting

   <u>G</u>rowing

   <u>E</u>xploring

   <u>T</u>otal learning

MODEL 24 (cont.)

This project has been designed and structured to foster and develop these attitudes and appreciations:

Appreciation of man's historical heritage from the past; the perception that contemporary man stands on the shoulders of those who have gone before.

Appreciation of the continuity and interrelatedness of history; the perception of history as an ongoing, unrolling tapestry of human events.

Appreciation of the fact that the basic human rights, which are taken for granted in the United States, were undreamed of during the Middle Ages and are still unobtained in many contemporary societies.

Perception of the human attributes of greatness and of the necessity of critically evaluating the personal quality of those seeking leadership positions in the schools, the community, the state, and the nation.

Perception of the ideas behind the statement "A thing of beauty is a joy forever."

Perception of the value of biography as stated by Thomas Carlyle, "The history of the world is but the biography of great men."

Appreciation of the necessity and value of reading between and beyond the lines and of questing beyond the obvious.

Appreciation of the value to be accrued from successful group endeavors.

Appreciation of the high degree of satisfaction to be attained by completing a challenging assignment.

Teaching Strategies and Methods:

No time limitations are imposed on this project. Number of students involved coupled with student interest is the factor that determines the duration of each GATE project whether it be two weeks, two months, or longer.

A basic part of group orientation to this project is to provide opportunities for the students to explore the synergistic effect to be derived from sharing knowledge.

Each student, after orientation to the purpose, scope, and dimension of this project, will draw up and sign a performance contract specifying the special area of knowledge-building for which he or she will be responsible.

Procedural Outline:

1. Group orientation to and overview of this project.
   A. Definition of basic terms:
      1. *Adventurous thinking:* Daring to think bold, new thoughts; projecting beyond the facts to fashion creative, yet plausible, answers to tantalizing questions such as "What if . . . ?" "What would have happened if . . . ?" "Do you suppose . . . ?" "Is there a possibility that . . . ?"
      2. *Middle Ages:* The period of European History between ancient and modern times, c. 500 A.D. to 1500 A.D. This period is also referred to as the Medieval period.
   B. Discussion of the project subtitle: An Experiment in Adventurous Thinking.
      1. The group views the motion picture *Leonardo da Vinci* (Walt Disney Educational Media).

         Discusses the fact that this motion picture is one of a series entitled "They Made the Difference" and observes:

         "The history of the world is but the biography of great men"—Thomas Carlyle.

         "What is the past?

            "The past is what happened yesterday. And it is what happened all the yesterdays before that . . .

            "The past is things that men have built . . .

            "The past is the different tools and machines that men have used to make all those buildings . . .

MODEL 24 (cont.)

"The past is art . . .

"The past is music . . .

"The past is everything that has ever interested human beings . . .

"The past is feelings . . .

"The past is ideas . . .

"The past is events . . .

"The past is all these things, and many more. But most of all, the past is people"—William Jay Jacobs, *Search for Freedom: America and Its People* (Benziger, 1973), pp. 9–10.

During this project, each student will compile a list of people who have influenced history in either a positive or a negative manner.

2. The group extends its knowledge of Leonardo da Vinci:

Explores his contribution as an adventurous thinker, citing as examples his work as:

Anatomist	Mathematician
Architect	Musician
Author	Naturalist
Caricaturist	Painter
Engineer	Philosopher
Inventor	Sculptor

3. The group explores the process of adventurous thinking.

Thinking requires ideas with which to work.

Leonardo da Vinci kept notebooks on his ideas, observations, and conclusions.

Adventurous thinking takes the information acquired through the inquiry process and shapes that information into unique patterns of thought.

Roget's *International Thesaurus* lists the following synonyms for the word *inquiry:*

Search	Check
Test	Analysis
Survey	Diagnosis
Review	Question
Contemplation	Query
Investigation	Problem
Probe	Issue
Exploration	

The basic steps in problem solving are:

Recognizing that a problem exists.

Defining and delimiting the problem.

Formulating hypotheses concerning the problem.

Gathering data and drawing conclusions.

Testing the conclusions and noting the consequences of the conclusions.

After building background knowledge of life during the Middle Ages, each student will adventurously answer the question "What would my life have been like if I had lived during the Middle Ages?"

II. The group begins to build its knowledge of life during the Middle Ages by reading and then discussing each of the following basic sources:

MODEL 24 (cont.)

A. *Living in a Castle* by R. J. Unstead (Addison-Wesley)
   Use the Table of Contents as an overview of a subject; for example, this book's Table of Contents lists the following topics:

Living in a castle	Morning at Wentworth Castle
Wentworth Castle	At the castle
The Great Hall	The daily round
The hall and the solar	Everyday tasks
The people of the household	Manners and clothes
Food and drink	The lady of the household
Meat, fish, and vegetables	Dinner at the castle
Spice and herbs	Table manners: two courses
Sugar, wine, and ale	Work and play

B. *Living in a Medieval City* by R. J. Unstead (Addison-Wesley)
   Use of the Table of Contents as an overview of a subject; for example, this book's Table of Contents lists the following topics:

Fifteenth-century Florence	Shops and banks
The people	About the city
Clothes	Crime
The poor	Schooling
Craftsmen and artists	Girls
Houses	Amusements
Work	

C. *Living in a Medieval Village* by R. J. Unstead (Addison-Wesley)
   Use of the Table of Contents as an overview of a subject; for example, this book's Table of Contents lists the following topics:

Benfield	Village craftsmen
The villagers	The cottars
The land	Two poor widows
Cultivating the land	Hay-making
John Middleditch—villein	Hay-making customs
John's cottage	Summer tasks
A villein's duties	Harvest time
The reeve	Poaching
Officials of the manor	The Manor Court
The priest	Festivals

D. *Living in a Crusader Land* by R. J. Unstead (Addison-Wesley)
   Use of the Table of Contents as an overview of a subject; for example, this book's Table of Contents lists the following topics:

Crusading	Fighting the infidel
Why men went on crusades	Founding the Crusader States
Preaching the crusade	How the Crusaders ruled Outremer
The People's Crusade	Christians and Moslems
Preparing for the crusade	Life in Outremer
The way to the East	The military orders
To Jerusalem!	Crusader castles
The mailed knight	The Italian merchants
The infantry	The end of Outremer
New methods of war	

MODEL 24 (cont.)

III. Individual students take the responsibility for searching the Table of Contents of one or more of the following sources to discover additional topics not mentioned above:

A. *The Age of Chivalry* by the editors of the *National Geographic* (National Geographic Society)
B. *Cathedral: The Story of Its Construction* by David Macaulay (Houghton Mifflin)
C. *Chivalry and the Mailed Knight* by Walter Buehr (Putnam)
D. *The Crusaders* by Walter Buehr (Putnam)
E. *Everyday Life in Medieval Times* by Marjorie Rowling (Putnam)
F. *Knights, Castles and Feudal Life* by Walter Buehr (Putnam)
G. *Knights in Armor* by Shirley Glubok (Harper and Row)
H. *Knights of the Crusades* by the editors of *Horizon* Magazine (Harper and Row)
I. *Life in the Middle Ages* by Jay Williams (Random House)
J. *Life on a Medieval Barony* by William Davis (Harper and Row)
K. *Made in the Middle Ages* by Christine Price (Dutton)
L. *Master Builders of the Middle Ages* by the editors of *Horizon* Magazine (Harper and Row)
M. *Medieval Days and Ways* by Gertrude Hartman (Macmillan)
N. *The Medieval Establishment* by Geoffrey Hindley (Putnam)
O. *Warrior Knights* by the editors of Time-Life Books (Little)
P. *The West in the Middle Ages* by Anne Bailey and Seymour Reit (Golden Press)
Q. *When Knights Were Bold* by Eva Tappan (Houghton Mifflin)

IV. Individual students will contract for researching a topic or topics selected from the list compiled above.

A. A typical list of research topics follows:

Alchemy	Hold goods were sold
Astrology	Illuminated manuscripts
Bestiaries	Jewels and enamels
Caravans and cargoes	Jousts and tournaments
Castles	Knights—training and weapons
Cathedrals	Law and justice
Chivalry	Medicine, disease, pestilence
Cloth and clothing	Merchant guilds
Craftsmen and their guilds	Monks and monasteries
Crime and punishment	Music
Crusades	Peasants Revolt
Daily life in a castle	Plays
Daily life in a town	Religion
Daily life on a manor	Religious art
Fairs	Schools
Falconry	Science and technology
Farms and farming	Scribes and books
Feudal society	Stained glass
Food and feasting	Standards of living and social classes
Furniture	Tapestries
Games, sport, and recreation	Troubadours and minstrels
Heraldry	Women's role
Holy Grail	

MODEL 24 (cont.)

Famous People:

King Alfred	John Gutenberg
King Arthur	Saint Joan of Arc
Roger Bacon	Marco Polo
Saint Bernard	Mohammed
Charlemagne	Peter the Hermit
Chaucer	King Richard the Lionhearted
Eleanor of Aquitaine	William of Normandy
Saint Francis	

B. In addition to researching histories and biographies, the students will be encouraged to read the literature of the Middle Ages and contemporary historical novels to gain insight into the manners and customs of the period. For example:

Adam of the Road by Elizabeth Gray (Viking)

The Book of Hugh Flower by Lorna Beers (Harper)

The Boy's King Arthur by Sidney Lanier (Scribner)

Chanticleer and the Fox retold by Barbara Cooney (Crowell)

Connecticut Yankee in King Arthur's Court by Samuel Clemens (Dodd)

The Door in the Wall by Marguerite DeAngeli (Doubleday)

Heroic Deeds of Beowulf by Gladys Schmitt (Random House)

Hidden Treasure of Glaston by Eleanore Jewett (Viking)

Men of Sherwood by D. E. Cooke (Holt)

Merry Adventures of Robin Hood by Howard Pyle (Scribner)

The Sleepers by Jane Curry (Harcourt)

V. Individual students work at their own rate and proceed to develop their special areas of information.
   A. Each student will search out his own materials.
   B. Each student will determine which alternative learning route to travel.
   C. Each student will determine when he has completed his assignment adequately.
   D. The GATE teacher will be available for consultation and guidance upon student request.

VI. The group will weave together the information they have gained from their individual research.
   A. Following the group discussion of individual research, each student will summarize this understanding of the socioeconomic problems of the Middle Ages by comparing the standard of living of the various social classes during the Middle Ages.
      The following definition will serve as a springboard:
      Standard of living: A level of subsistence of a social class with reference to the adequacy of necessities and comforts in daily life.
   B. The group will then contrast the standard of living during the Middle Ages with the standard of living in the United States today.
      The concept of life expectancy will be introduced and discussed.

VII. As a culminating activity the group will view the motion picture *A Connecticut Yankee in King Arthur's Court* and then write their reactions.
   A. Following the viewing of the motion picture, each student will summarize the insight and understanding he has gained by writing his own imaginative projection into the Middle Ages using the project title "If I Had Lived during the Middle Ages" as the launching pad.
   B. The group will, on hearing the imaginative essay of each student, vote to select the best one.

MODEL 25   MEXICO—ITS HISTORY, ITS LAND, AND ITS PEOPLE

Enrichment/Acceleration Topics
Grade: 6
Unit: Mexico: Its History, Its Land, and Its People
Project Goals:
   To bring greater depth, breadth, and relevance to the study of Mexico.

   To provide opportunity for the student to understand, to appreciate, and to respect the Mexican people—their history, their culture, their literature, their manners and customs, their arts, their music, their government, and their social and economic problems.
Possible Research Topics:

1. Acapulco	48. Folklore and Legends
2. Adobe	49. Geographic Features
3. Agriculture	50. Government and Politics
4. Alamo	51. Guadalajara
5. Aleman, Miguel	52. Guadalupe Shrine
6. Anguiano, Lupe	53. Health and Medicine
7. Animals	54. Hidalgo, Father Miguel
8. Archeological Discoveries	55. History
9. Architecture	56. Houston, Sam
10. Artists	57. Indians
11. Arts	58. Ines, Juana
12. Aztecs	59. Inventions
13. Banking and Currency	60. Iturbide, Augustin de
14. Bartolome, Friar	61. Itzcoatl
15. Borda, Jose de la	62. Josefa, Dona
16. Border Patrol	63. Juarez, Benito
17. Callen, Plutarco	64. Lakes
18. Cardenas, Lazaro	65. Languages
19. Carlota, Empress	66. Law and Justice
20. Castellanos, Julio	67. Libraries
21. Cathedrals	68. Literature
22. Ceramics	69. Lorenzo, Agustin
23. Chavez, Carlos	70. Machu Picchu
24. Chicanos	71. Madero, Francisco
25. Chicle	72. Manners and Customs
26. Cities	73. Markets
27. Clothing	74. Maximilian, Emperor
28. Commerce and Industry	75. Mayas
29. Communications	76. Mestizos
30. Cooking	77. Mexican-Americans
31. Cortes, Hernando	78. Mexican War
32. Covarrubias, Miguel	79. Mexico City
33. Cowboys	80. Minerals
34. Crafts	81. Montezuma
35. Cuauhtemoc	82. Morelos, Jose
36. Cuernavaca	83. Museums
37. Dance	84. Music
38. Diaz, Porfirio	85. Narcotics
39. Drama and the Theater	86. National Anthem
40. Education	87. Natural Resources
41. Engineering	88. Obregon, Alvaro
42. Exports and Imports	89. Orozco, Jose
43. Family Life	90. Pan American Highway
44. Fiestas and Holidays	91. Paseo de la Reforma
45. Fishing	92. Petroleum
46. Flag	93. Plants
47. Floating Gardens	94. Posada

MODEL 25 (cont.)

95. Pueblo
96. Pyramid in Yucatan
97. Recreation and Sports
98. Relations between Mexico and the United States
99. Religion
100. Rivera, Diego
101. Santa Anna, Antonio Lopez de
102. Science and Technology
103. Sierra Madre
104. Stamps
105. Standard of Living
106. Status of Women
107. Student Exchange Program
108. Tarascans

109. Taxco
110. Textiles
111. Toltecs
112. Transportation
113. UNICEF in Mexico
114. United Nations Membership
115. University City
116. Veracruz
117. Villa, "Pancho"
118. Village Life
119. Volcanoes
120. "Wetbacks"
121. Yucatan
122. Zapata, Emiliano

MODEL 26   SEEING WITH THE INNER EYE

Learning Station: Seeing with the Inner Eye
Grade: 6
Teaching Goal: To introduce the GATE student to the art of seeing with the inner eye.
Teaching Objectives:

This project has been designed to provide these understandings:

Looking is a gift, but seeing is an art, a hard-learned craft.

A master of insight has a special way of looking beyond reality.

Practiced eyes can look beneath the surface.

Your mind's eye puts sense, sight, and imagination together.

Whimsy is seeing in a fanciful way.

Fantasy in literature and art employs nonrational phenomena; it has its own vision of reality; it gives full play to imagination and adventurous thinking.

This project has been designed to develop these attitudes and appreciations:

If you have seven-league imagination, no leap is too mighty and no height too lofty.

Using the magical eye inside one's head opens unlimited opportunities to view beyond reality.

Experimenting creatively with color, shapes, patterns, and designs is a challenging and satisfying experience.

Adults enjoy high-quality visual presentations of fantasy settings, plots, and characters.

Dreams and flights of fancy can be painted realistically in words and pictures.

Teaching Strategies and Methods:

The theme, seeing with the inner eye, is introduced to the GATE class. Student interest will determine student exploration. No time limit is imposed.

Procedural Outline:
   I. Class introduction to the learning station theme.
      A. Seeing beneath the surface.
         1. Jan Adkins, in his book *Inside: Seeing beneath the Surface,* explains how one can see with the inner eye.

            With your eyes you see part of what is before you; most of your seeing is done inside your head.

            What you see with your eyes is automatically identified by your brain.

            You have a third eye that can tell you how things are built, how they work, and how they look below the surface.

MODEL 26 (cont.)

Your third eye is a powerful, magical eye—it is a creative source of insight.

Your third eye enables you to imagine beyond time, space, and place.

2. Annette and Talus Taylor have written and illustrated a series of books that enable the reader to look beneath the surface:

The Adventures of the Three Colors

Animal Hide-and-Seek

Inside and Outside

The Magic of Color

3. The Japanese artist Mitsumasa Anno, in his book *Topsy-Turvies,* provides a number of pictures to stretch the imagination and to answer pictorially the questions:

Can a ceiling be a floor and a roof be a wall at the same time?

Can you hang a picture on the floor?

Can a stairway take you *up* from a higher place to a lower one?

4. Carol Grafton, in her book *Shapes and Colors,* demonstrates how to produce three-dimensional illusions.

5. Sid Sackson, in his book *Beyond Tic Tac Toe,* has created seven games involving both color and visual illusion.

6. Muncie Hendler, in his book *Infinite Design and Coloring Book,* presents 46 designs involving color and imagination.

B. Seeing with the inner eye enables an artist to create pictures of imaginary times, places, people, and events (see Model 23, Book Illustrators and Their Art).

1. Fantasy in motion pictures began in 1937 when the Walt Disney Studios released the full-length animated feature film *Snow White and the Seven Dwarfs.*

2. In 1940, Disney produced *Fantasia,* which is recognized today as a bona fide cinema fantasy classic.

3. The *Black Cauldron* by Lloyd Alexander, the second book in the Chronicles of Prydain; release date by the Disney Studios, 1984.

4. The motion pictures *Star Wars* and *Star Trek* have broken movie attendance records; they, too, have been acclaimed cinema fantasy classics.

5. High-quality fantasy art books made their appearance in great numbers during the late seventies; *Gnomes,* illustrated by Rien Poortvliet and published by Abrams in 1977, hit the national best-seller list just three weeks after publication. Even though it cost $17.50, it had sold 700,000 copies by 1979.

6. *Once upon a Time: Some Contemporary Illustrators of Fantasy* provides examples of the fantasy artwork of the following recognized experts in the field:

Wayne Anderson	Ken Laidlaw
Nicola Bailey	Alan Lee
Frank Bellamy	Chris McEwan
Reg Cartwright	James Marsh
Pauline Ellison	Tony Meeuwissen
Brian Froud	Owen Wood

7. *The Hobbit,* written and illustrated by J. R. R. Tolkien, is a masterpiece of seeing with the inner eye. The Abrams edition of *The Hobbit* contains over 230 full-color plates and costs $35.

C. Seeing with the inner eye enables the student of history to visualize what living in another historical period would be like.

MODEL 26 (cont.)

The Encyclopaedia Britannica Corporation has devised a means of helping today's students visualize how the ancient Greeks and Romans lived. They have developed the technique of placing acetate reconstructions over photographs of ruins of ancient Greece and ancient Rome, showing how these places looked in ancient times. The three sets are:

Historical Reconstructions of Ancient Greece (10 study prints)

The Fortifications of Ancient Aegosthena

Corinth: The Agora

Aegina: The Temple of Aphaea

Delphi: The Temple of Apollo

Mycenae: The Treasure of Altreus

Knossis: The Palace of Minos

Delos: The House of Cleopatra

Athens: The Acropolis—General View

Athens: The Parthenon and Erechtheum

Athens: The Parthenon—Interior View

Historical Reconstruction of Pompeii (4 study prints)

The House of the Faun

The Pistrinum (bakery)

The Theater

The Temple of Apollo

Historical Reconstructions of Rome (7 study prints)

Picture Map of the Roman Forum

The Roman Forum: Partial View A

The Roman Forum: Partial View B

The Circus Maximus

The Colosseum

The Basilica of Maxentius

The Mausoleum of Hadrian

II. In addition to the books in the GATE Learning Station, there is a special media collection on reserve in the senior high school library labeled *Seeing with the Inner Eye.* This special collection has been gathered by the senior high school librarian for the use of the elementary GATE students.

Resource Kit:

BOOKS

The Adventures of the Three Colors by Annette and Talus Taylor (World)

Animal Hide-and-Seek by Annette and Talus Taylor (World)

Beyond Tic Tac Toe by Sid Sackson (Pantheon)

Fairies by Brian Froud and Alan Lee (Abrams)

Gnomes by Wil Huygen, illus. by Rien Pootvliet (Abrams)

The Hobbit by J. R. R. Tolkien (Abrams)

Infinite Design and Coloring Book by Muncie Hendler (Dover)

Inside and Outside by Annette and Talus Taylor (World)

Inside: Seeing beneath the Surface by Jan Adkins (Walker)

An Invitation to the Butterfly Ball by Jane Yolen (Parents Press)

The Magic of Color by Annette and Talus Taylor (World)

MODEL 26 (cont.)

Once upon a Time: Some Contemporary Illustrators of Fantasy by David Larkin (Bantam Books)

Shapes and Colors: Cutouts for Creative Geometric Designs by Carol Grafton (Dover)

Topsy-Turvies: Pictures to Stretch the Imagination by Mitsumasa Anno (Weatherhill)

STUDY PRINTS (Encyclopaedia Britannica)

Historical Reconstructions of Ancient Greece (10 study prints)

Historical Reconstructions of Pompeii (4 study prints)

Historical Reconstructions of Rome (7 study prints)

MODEL 27   THE WIZARDRY OF WORDS

Learning Project: The Wizardry of Words
Grade: 6
Project Goal: To provide learning experiences that will enable the gifted student to understand, appreciate, and value his or her language heritage—its history, symbol system, structure, power, diversity, and beauty.
Teaching Objectives:

This project has been designed and structured to provide these basic understandings:

The history of language is an integral part of the history of civilization.

Language is a social tool or organism—the product of the society that employs it.

Language is not a fixed, immutable, circumscribed object but is an ever-growing, ever-changing body of facts and habits.

Many different languages have evolved from one parent language.

American English possesses qualities peculiar unto itself, for while it has maintained much of the mother tongue it reflects unique facets of America's culture, literature, and social history.

American culture is not homogeneous; therefore, certain linguistic features are peculiar to certain regions and are not general to others.

This project has been designed and structured to foster and develop these attitudes and appreciations:

Appreciation of human linguistic heritage from the past.

Appreciation of the complex nature of language.

Appreciation of the value of utilizing dictionaries—general and special—as power tools for effective self-expression.

Respect for and interest in linguistic differences among diverse cultures.

Curiosity as to how certain words and expressions have originated.

Appreciation of the power and beauty of the written and the spoken word.

Delight in experimenting with language—its moods, colors, flavor, pattern, variety, and power.

Appreciation of the value to be accrued from successful group cooperative enterprises.

Appreciation of the high degree of satisfaction attained from successfully completing a challenging assignment.

Teaching Strategies and Methods:

No time limitations are imposed on this project. Number of students in the GATE group coupled with student interest is the factor determining the duration of the project whether it be two weeks, two months, or longer.

MODEL 27 (cont.)

A basic part of group orientation to the project is to provide opportunities for the students to explore the synergistic effect of sharing knowledge gained and then to determine appropriate methods and procedures for pooling information.

Each student, after orientation to the purpose, scope, and dimension of the project, will draw up and sign a contract specifying the particular area of knowledge building he or she will be responsible for completing.

Following the completion of the project, each student will assess his or her degree of accomplishment by checking the form Achievement-Growth Evaluation at the end of this model.

Procedural Outline:

  1. Group orientation to and overview of this project.

    A. Definition of basic terms serves as a unifying experience.

      1. *Linguistics:* the science of language; comparative study of language structures and the study of the history and historical relationship of languages.

      2. *Semantics:* the branch of linguistics that involves the scientific study of word meanings, especially their development and alteration.

    B. Group reads and discusses Chapter 8, The Wizardry of Words, in *Creativity and Imagination* by Jacolyn A. Mott (Creative Education), stressing the following:

      Creating with words

      "Writing maketh an exact man"

      Wordmaking

      Hidden meanings

      Fossil phrases

      Expressing yourself in uncommon ways

      Twists of language

      The wonder of words

    C. Group shares understanding gained from reading *What's Behind the Word?* by Sam and Beryl Epstein (Scholastic).

      1. The group uses the Table of Contents as an outline to be followed in building understanding (an excellent example of utilizing the Table of Contents as an orientation tool).

      2. The group begins its understanding of linguistics by analyzing information gained under three main headings:

        Our language begins

          If there were no words

          Every word has a history

          Families of languages

          The beginnings of English

          English grows

          English keeps changing

          English comes to the New World

            From the Indians

            From the French

            From the Dutch

            From the Spanish

        The written word

          How writing began

          Picture writing

          The alphabet is born

MODEL 27 (cont.)

From written words to printed words

Words borrowed from all over the world

Modern English grows

New words from old

Words from names of famous people

Stuck-together words

Words that sound like what they mean

Tricks with words

D. The group reads *The Magic of Words* (Childcraft 1975 Annual) and adds additional subtopics to the list derived from *What's Behind the Word?*

E. Individual students contract for the area or areas of in-depth knowledge building for which they will be responsible.

II. Individual students work at their own rate and proceed to develop their special areas of information.

A. Each student will search out his own materials.

B. Each student will determine which alternative learning road to travel.

C. Each student will determine when the assignment has been completed.

D. The GATE teacher will be available for consultation and guidance upon student request.

III. The group will summarize this project by weaving in, where appropriate, insight and information each has gained.

A. The group will view the following motion pictures (Coronet):

1. *Discovering Language: The Alphabet Story*
2. *Discovering Language: How English Borrowed Words*
3. *Discovering Language: How English Changes in America*
4. *Discovering Language: How Words Are Made*
5. *Discovering Language: How Words Get New Meanings*
6. *Discovering Language: Varieties of English*

B. Following the viewing of each motion picture, the students will contribute what each has discovered through individualized study.

C. When all six motion pictures have been presented and discussed, the group will identify significant topics that have not been adequately developed or have been omitted entirely.

1. Individual students will volunteer to search out the overlooked or incomplete topics.
2. These students will then share with the group the information needed to complete the project.

ACHIEVEMENT-GROWTH EVALUATION

Student_____ Date _____

Learning Project_____ Grade _____

My Self-Appraisal:

I worked consistently_____ or sporadically_____

I put forth maximum effort_____ or minimum effort_____

I learned a great deal_____ or not so much as I could have learned_____

I completed my work on time_____ or I did not complete my work on time_____

I worked well with other students during this project_____

or I did not work well with other students during this project_____

The most important things I learned from this project were: _____

_____

_____

_____

_____

_____

_____

_____

In evaluating my achievement and growth during this project, I would rate myself as follows:

Excellent_____   Good_____   Fair_____   Poor_____

MODEL 28   RUSSIAN CULTURE AND LANGUAGE

Learning Project: Russian Culture and Language
Grade: 6
Project Goals:

Students will experience a stimulating learning environment encompassing freedom to learn, guidance in learning, and a richness of learning materials uniquely supportive of the learning tasks at hand, all of which will enable the students, individually and collectively, to build a growing awareness of and a *discriminating* respect and appreciation for the people—their language, heritage, and culture—of the Union of Soviet Socialist Republics in general and for Russia in particular.

Students will experience a *positive emotional climate* within a stimulating learning environment. Although individual evaluation of students will be continuously employed as a teaching/learning reinforcement technique, no grades per se will be given in an effort to promote a less threatening atmosphere. Nevertheless, students will be challenged to work diligently, encouraged to take pride in genuine accomplishment, and experience delight and personal satisfaction with their progress.

Students will develop a lifelong interest in—if not study of—that part of the world known as the Soviet Union.

Teaching Objectives:

Students will learn by the audio-lingual method to listen, to hear, and to speak basic Russian with comprehension to the degree that student capability, interest, and time limitation permit.

Students will master the Cyrillic alphabet as the basic decoding key for unlocking the fundamental literacy skills of reading and writing the Russian language.

Students will learn to read and write basic Russian with comprehension, to the degree that student capability, interest, and time limitation permit.

Students will delve into Russian history, arts, and culture as deeply as their interests carry them not only within the context of Russian language study but also through the rich media of biography, history, recordings, filmstrips, graphics, artifacts, etc.

Students will be encouraged, if they so desire, to share their accomplishment, progress, and proficiency in their study of Russian Culture and Language with classmates and parents in planned performances and/or impromptu demonstrations.

Procedural Outline:
    I. Group orientation to and overview of this learning activity
        A. Self-introduction of teacher in Russian language and presentation of teacher's name card to students.
        B. Students complete Interest Inventory:

MODEL 28 (cont.)

1. Indicating areas of special emphasis for independent study:

Architect	Historian
Artist	Musician
Biographer	Statistician
Cartographer	Travel Agent
Folklorist	Other

2. Serving as Research Consultant in above interest areas for class—synergistic effect of sharing particular knowledge building with entire class thereby increasing total class knowledge building and promoting most efficient management of time in seminar style of class.
3. Indicating reason(s) why students wish to study Russian.

C. Ground rules for conduct of Russian class:
   1. Russian is a very difficult and demanding course of study; therefore, students may choose one of two alternative ways of class participation:
      a. *Active Participation*—student participates actively in each class session by listening attentively whenever *each* person speaks, by speaking valiantly, by writing carefully, and by fully participating whenever and in whatever manner directed; thereby earning for the student his recognized place at the class table.
      b. *Associate Participation*—student elects planned quiet, independent study elsewhere in the library other than at the class table—working with a wealth of appropriate learning support resources dealing with Russian culture such as:

Books	Recordings
Pamphlets	Slides
Periodicals	Maps
Newspapers	Study prints
Filmstrips	Art prints

   2. The decision as to type of class participation is a serious one:
      a. Reasons for presenting alternative types of class participation:

      To maximize each student's learning progress and to maximize the total class learning experience.

      To insure that no one is embarrassed.

      b. A decision must be made within the first three class sessions.
      c. A decision for associate participation is *final and irrevocable* inasmuch as the active members of the class table will make rapid progess and must not be hindered by nonparticipating class members.
      d. If at any time an active participant recognizes that the work at the class table has progressed beyond his or her capability, he or she may quietly change his or her status to associate participation.
   3. Although Russian is difficult, any student who seriously tries and who is not afraid of hard work *will succeed*—even the children in Russia can speak Russian!
      a. One secret for learning Russian: Listen attentively each time each person speaks and seize every opportunity to repeat what is said—
         "Repetition is the mother of learning."—Old Russian Proverb
      b. Each student will be assured the courtesy of silence and attentiveness when he or she speaks. No one is ever to be embarrassed by discourtesy.
      c. The more one learns, the easier it is to learn more; and the more fun it becomes!
   4. At each class session students will work in their journals; in addition to specified items, students are encouraged to jot down additional notes

MODEL 28 (cont.)

pertaining to the class and learning project in any manner they desire.

    a. Journals will be examined from time to time to assess progress.

    b. An appropriate reward will be awarded at the end of the school year to the student who has kept the finest journal in regard to Russian class.

5. Individual student volunteers will keep the class informed about current newspaper and magazine articles, and posted on upcoming radio programs, motion pictures, and television programs dealing with Russia.

D. Vocabulary terms for class frame of reference:

  1. *Russian:*

    a. as an adjective—of or having to do with Russia (the Soviet Union), its people, or their language.

    b. as a noun—a native or inhabitant of Russia, especially a member of the dominant Slavic people of the Soviet Union.

    c. as a noun—the East Slavic language of Russia, the most widely used of the Slavic languages.

  2. *Language:* the speech of one nation or race; tongue.

  3. *Cyrillic Alphabet:* an old Slavic alphabet based on the Greek, invented by St. Cyril, a ninth century apostle to the Slavs; in modified form, it is still used in Russia, Bulgaria, and other Slavic countries.

  4. *Culture:* The concepts, habits, skills, art, instruments, institutions, etc., of a given people in a given period; civilization: Russian culture will be presented not only directly through the study of the Russian language, but also through rich and abundant media resources.

E. Why study Russian? Because.*

  1. Russian is one of the three most important languages in the world today.

  2. Russian is the governmental and administrative language of the peoples of the Soviet Union—over 200,000,000 people—and one-sixth of the globe in area.

  3. Russian is now, with English and German, an essential language for those interested in any branch of science and technology, e.g., space exploration.

  4. The Soviet Union publishes an immense body of literature relating to many subjects.

  5. A knowledge of the Russian language is steadily spreading to countries whose languages are rarely known by English-speaking people. Russian is becoming an increasingly important "travel-language."

  6. To "understand the Russians," it is essential to know their language—the key to their psychology and the hope for resolving the cold war and promoting world peace.

  7. Russian is a language with a great literature. Gogol, Tolstoy, and Dostoevski are among the greatest novelists in world literature.

  8. A study of Russian—a highly inflected language—provides challenge and training for the intelligence and memory at least equal to that provided by Latin and Greek. And Russian is very much alive.

  9. Russian is a very beautiful and fascinating language.

  10. Russian is worth learning because it presents ways of thinking and living quite different from our own.

F. Introduction of and demonstration to illustrate the "differentness" of the Russian alphabet:

  1. Demonstrate how without knowing Latin, French, or Spanish, it is possible for a student to find the word for "friend"—*amicus, ami,* and *amigo*—in the respective Latin, French, and Spanish dictionaries.

  2. Demonstrate that it is impossible to locate the Russian word for friend—друг—in like manner in a Russian dictionary, without first learning an entirely new alphabet.

*Adapted from "Why Learn Russian?" (p. xv) in *Russian for Beginners* by Charles Duff and Dmitri Makaroff (Barnes and Noble). Copyright © 1962 by Charles Duff and Dmitri Makaroff. Reprinted by permission of Harper & Row, Publishers, Inc.

MODEL 28 (cont.)

G. Introduction to Russian vocabulary acquisition:
  1. Students nominate and discuss *"the most important word* in any language" and "the *most important words* in any language."
  2. Teacher's candidate for *"the most important word* in any language": God—Бог

     "Mother Russia" attitude toward God

     "Communist/Soviet" attitude toward God

  3. Presentation of a "Mystery Word" vocabulary card for bread: хлеб

     Explain importance of black bread to Russian people.

     The Ukraine as "The Breadbasket of Russia."

     Provide sample of Russian Black Bread for students.

II. Russian Language Study
  A. The Cyrillic alphabet/the Russian alphabet:

Printed	Printed
А а	Р р
Б б	С с
В в	Т т
Г г	У у
Д д	Ф ф
Е е	Х х
Ё ё	Ц ц
Ж ж	Ч ч
З з	Ш ш
И и	Щ щ
Й й	ъ
К к	Ы ы
Л л	Ь ь
М м	Э э
Н н	Ю ю
О о	Я я
П п	

  1. Comparison of Cyrillic alphabet with the Roman alphabet.
  2. St. Cyril and St. Methodius as originators of Cyrillic alphabet.
  3. Derivation from Greek alphabet as vehicle to Christianize and convert the pagan Russians to the Russian Orthodox Religion via Byzantine Constantinople.

Rome	—"1st"
Constantinople	—"2nd Rome"
Moscow	—"3rd Rome"

  4. Cyrillic alphabet has 33 characters, which can be divided into 3 broad categories:

     Characters similar in sound and sight to Roman alphabet—easy task.

Characters entirely new and different from Roman alphabet—more difficult task.

Characters that look the same as Roman alphabet but symbolize different sounds—most difficult task.

5. The major part of each of the first learning sessions will be devoted to learning the letters of the Cyrillic alphabet until students:

Know the name of and how to sound each Cyrillic symbol.

Know how to write each Cyrillic symbol in script.

Know entire Cyrillic alphabet in sequence.

Recognize each Cyrillic symbol in print.

B. Essential "working" conversation for class work on Cyrillic alphabet and for vocabulary building (student facility with the following procedure grows developmentally with each class session):

1. Teacher presents each new Cyrillic letter orally and visually, with children repeating afterward. Using model alphabet cards, children practice writing the letter in pencil in their journals. As each child becomes confident, he engages in the following conversational exchange with teacher and then makes a model letter card with a black marker pen to keep for himself or herself. After children have acquired the alphabet, they will make vocabulary word cards for themselves in this same fashion. Until that time vocabulary word cards will be provided for the students at each session.

2. Conversation:

Teacher: Class, write please with pencil, "A" for two minutes; and, then, you know what to say.

Класс, пиши́те пожа́луйста, "А" карандашо́м на две мину́тый; и тогда́ вы зна́ете что говори́ть.

Student: Miss Clendening, please give me a white card.

Госпожа Кленде́нинг, да́йте мне пожа́луйста бе́лую ка́рту.

Teacher: John, why do you want a white card?

Ива́н, почему́ вы хоти́те бе́лую ка́рту?

Student: I want a white card because I want to write "A" with a pen.

Я хочу́ бе́лую ка́рту потому́ что я хочу́ писа́ть "А" перо́м.

Teacher: Very well, here is a white card.

О́чень хорошо́, вот бе́лая ка́рта.

Student: Thank you, Miss Clendening.

Спаси́бо, Госпожа́ Кленде́нинг.

Teacher: You're welcome, John.

Пожа́луйста, Иван.

C. Basic principles of grammar, phonetics, syntax, and spelling (gently presented through developmental usage):

1. Absence of articles.
2. Absence of linking verbs—is and are.
3. Negatives and abundance of double negatives.
4. Interrogatives—use of voice inflection, word order.
5. Imperatives—use of voice inflection, word order.
6. Principle of gender

Masculine, feminine, neuter

MODEL 28 (cont.)

Animate and inanimate nouns

Agreement between nouns, adjectives, verbs

7. Principle of a highly inflected language—varying endings for verbs, nouns, adjectives.
8. Special construction to show possession.
9. One major stress per word in pronounciation.
10. Absence of Western capitalization, i.e., days of week; months of year.

D. Calling the class roll:

Teacher: John, are you here today?

Ива́н, вы здесь сего́дня?

Student: Yes, I am here today.

Да, я здесь сего́дня.

Teacher: Michael, are you here today?

Михайл, вы здесь сего́дня?

Student: No, he is not here today.

Нет, он не здесь сего́дня.

Teacher: Barbara, are you here today?

Варва́ра, вы здесь сего́дня?

Student: No, she is not here today.

Нет, она не здесь сего́дня.

E. What is the date today?

Teacher: Class, what is the date today?

Кла́сс, како́е сего́дня число́?

Class: Today is October 1, 1977.

Сего́дня октя́брь оди́н, ты́сяча девятьсо́т се́мьдесят се́мь.

F. Polite expressions (representative)—

Hello: Здра́вствуйте

Good morning: До́брое у́тро

Good day/afternoon: До́брый день

Good evening: До́брый ве́чер

Good night: Споко́йной но́чи

How are you?: Как вы пожива́ете?

Very well, thank you, and you?: О́чень хорошо́, спаси́бо, и вы?

I have a head cold: У меня́ е́сть насморк

Please: Пожа́луйста

Thank you: Спаси́бо

Thank you very much: Большо́е спаси́бо

You're welcome: Пожа́луйста

It's nothing: Ничего́

G. Russian names:

1. In Russia people usually have three names, i.e.,

MODEL 28 (cont.)

The first (Christian) name: и́мя

The patronymic from the father's name: о́тчество

The family name (surname):   фами́лия

2. What is your name and surname?   Как ва́ше и́мя и фами́лия?
3. Students are introduced to a list of Russian first names.

Alexander: Алекса́ндр

Alexis: Алексе́й

Boris: Бори́с

Barbara: Варва́ра

Catherine: Екатери́на

Helen: Еле́на

Elizabeth: Елизаве́та

4. If there is a Russian equivalent, student assumes Russian name.
5. If there is no Russian equivalent, student either transliterates his English name into Russian, or selects a Russian name of his own preference.

H. Conversation about the weather:

What kind of weather is it today?

Кака́я сего́дня пого́да?

It is very pleasant.

Сего́дня о́чень хоро́шая пого́да. О́чень прия́тно.

It is very bad.

О́чень пло́хо.

It is unpleasant.

Неприя́тно.

It is very cold.

О́чень хо́лодно.

It is very hot.

О́чень жа́рко.

It is very warm.

О́чень тепло́.

It is raining.

Идёт дождь.

It is snowing.

Идёт снег.

There is a strong wind.

Си́льный ве́тер.

I. Cognates for vocabulary building:
1. Those lovely words that look (after you know the alphabet) and sound alike and have like meanings in two or more languages because they have the same origin.
2. Those words whose illustration and example are easier to understand than their explanation.

MODEL 28 (cont.)

3. Introduction of students, by way of sampling, to "the sweetest cognate they will ever meet": Chocolate— шокола́д.
4. Cognates are those wonderful words that provide such a marvelous, easy way to acquire vocabulary in a foreign language. Examples,

Aviation: Авиа́ция
Doctor: До́ктор
Fact: Фа́кт
Football: Футбо́л
Idea: Иде́я
Opera: О́пера

J. "Mystery Word" device for vocabulary building:
1. Toward the close of each class session, the teacher says, "Now it is time for the mystery word."
2. Teacher presents to each student a mystery word card representing something to eat or to drink. After spelling out and pronouncing the word with assistance from the teacher, the students try to guess, from clues supplied by the teacher, the English meaning of the word before turning over the card to check.
3. Utilizing Pavlov's principle, the teacher reinforces the students' learning of the new word by supplying to each student a sample of the new food or drink represented by the mystery word. *However, the students must earn the treat by individually engaging in the following conversation with the teacher.*

Teacher: Because you are such good students, I have a little gift for you. If you want cheese, you know what to say.

Потому́ что вы о́чень хоро́шие студе́нты, у меня́ есть вам ма́ленький пода́рок. Е́сли вы хоти́те сы́р, вы зна́ете что говори́ть.

Student: Miss Clendening, please give me cheese.

Госпожа́ Кленде́нинг, пожа́луйста, да́йте мне сыр.

Teacher: Why do you want cheese, John?

Почему́ вы хоти́те сыр, Иван?

Student: I want cheese because I like cheese.

Я хочу́ сыр потому́ что сыр мне нра́вится.

Teacher: Very well, here is the cheese.

О́чень хорошо́, вот сыр.

Student: Thank you very much.

Вольшо́е спаси́бо.

Teacher: You're welcome.

Пожа́луйста.

K. What is this? Who is this? (Question format for vocabulary building):
1. What is this? Что э́то?

This is a *cat.* Это ко́шка.

2. Who is this? Кто это?

This is the teacher. Это учи́тель.

L. Idiomatic construction to show possession (used as vocabulary-building game):
1. The idiomatic "possession" construction: I have a cat. У меня́ есть ко́шка.

with all the nouns and/or nouns plus adjectives that students can think of is utilized as a game in which students vie with one another to total the most points.

  2. Similarly, the class as a team then vies with classes in other schools to determine the winning school.

  M. Thematic approach to continued vocabulary building and conversation building through selection from thematic groups of words such as the following:

  Colors

  Days of the Week, Months, Seasons

  Family

  Food

  Holidays

  Household Furnishings

  Numerals

III. Avenues for venturing into the Russian heritage and culture

  A. History

  "Mother Russia"—"Holy Russia"

  "Russia under the Czars"

  Symbol: "The two-headed eagle" was for nearly four centuries the symbol of czarist Russia

  House of Romanov

  Russian Revolution

  U.S.S.R. = C.C.C.P.

  Symbol: "The hammer and sickle"

  Sixteen constituent republics

  Russia today

  B. Geography

  Next-door neighbor to United States via Alaska

  One-sixth of all the land there is

  More than twice as big as China or the United States

  Almost every kind of country in Russia:

  Tundra; forests; chernozem; steppes; mountains, great rivers, huge lakes

  All weather extremes

  Rich natural resources

  C. Communism (Democratic Socialism) contrasted with American Democracy

  D. Manners, customs, and other interesting things about the Russian people

  Baptism, marriage, death

  Housewarming

  Russian winter

  Russian springtime

  Dress

  Currency: kopecks and rubles

  Troika

  Collective farms

  E. Russian foods and cooking

  Caviar

  Black bread

MODEL 28 (cont.)

    Borscht

    Vodka

F. Religion and art

    Orthodox Eastern Church—Russian Orthodox Church

    Old Believers

    Icons

    Easter eggs

    Famous churches

G. Holidays and festivals

    Russian Orthodox Christmas

    Russian Orthodox Easter

    Soviet Holidays

      May Day

      Harvest Holidays

      New Year's

H. Architecture

    Byzantine influence

    Onion-top spires

    Use of wood

    Use of color

    Sitka, Alaska

I. Literature

    Count Leo Tolstoy (Tales)

    Afanasyev—Russian folktales and fairy tales

    Russian proverbs

J. Music and dancing

    Cossack war dances

    Bolshoi Ballet

    Tchaikovsky

      Swan Lake ballet

      Nutcracker ballet

      Sleeping Beauty ballet

    Rimsky-Korsakov, *The Flight of the Bumble Bee*

    Prokofiev, *Peter and the Wolf*

    Moussorgsky, *Pictures at an Exhibition*

    Khachaturian, "Sabre Dance" from *Gayne Ballet Suite*

K. Fascinating people to read about

    Ivan the Terrible

    The Tartars of the Golden Horde

    Peter the Great

    Catherine the Great

    Nicholas and Alexandra

    The Romanovs

    Rasputin

Cossacks

Potemkin

Pugachev

Lenin

Stalin

Khruschev

Brezhnev and other contemporary Russians

L. Field trip experiences

Dr. Avinoff's drawings at the Carnegie Museum.

Russian Room: Nationality Rooms in the Cathedral of Learning, University of Pittsburgh, especially at Christmastime.

St. Alexander Nevsky Church in the North Hills.

Russians in the North Hills community.

MODEL 29   THE SCIENTIFIC METHOD IN THEORY AND APPLICATION

Mini-unit: The Scientific Method in Theory and Application (revised)

Subject: Honors Science

Grade: 7

Goal: To enable the student to understand, to utilize, and to appreciate the scientific method of problem solving.

Teaching Objectives:

To provide learning experiences that will enable the student to discover how scientists, by solving problems, have changed our way of living.

To provide opportunities for the student to question, observe, compare, formulate hypotheses, experiment, employ inductive and deductive reasoning, draw conclusions, and organize and communicate findings.

To provide opportunities for the student to work as an individual, as a member of a small group, and as a member of the total class.

Procedure (the unit is reproduced here only in part):

I. A committee of students, "the teaching committee," shares with the classroom teacher and the library media specialist the responsibility for planning and for teaching this unit.

A. One week prior to the introduction of this unit to the class, the teaching committee, all of whom have volunteered for this job, work in the library media center under the guidance of the library media specialist making tentative plans for the introduction, the development, and the culmination of this unit.

1. The library media specialist explains the role of the teaching committee.

2. Committee members volunteer to be responsible for special assignments such as:

Introducing the unit to the class.

Identifying and explaining basic terminology.

Previewing, selecting, and presenting to the class both print and non-print media.

Designing and producing transparencies.

Leading class discussions.

Coordinating the work of the separate committees as well as individual students.

II. Class is introduced to the unit in the library media center.

A. The library media specialist explains the purpose of the procedure for studying this unit.

MODEL 29 (cont.)

B. Members of the teaching committee introduce basic terminology and concepts such as:
   1. Science is a special way man investigates the natural world in which he lives.
   2. Science is usable and classified information.
C. Chairman of the teaching committee asks for volunteers to be responsible for finding the answers to the following:
   1. What is science?
   2. When did man develop science?
   3. Can science help man solve problems?
   4. What is superstition?
   5. What is scientific evidence?
   6. What is fact? What is a concept?
   7. What is inductive reasoning?
   8. What is deductive reasoning?
   9. What is a hypothesis? How does a scientist arrive at a hypothesis?
   10. What is research?
   11. What is the difference between science and technology?
III. The class works in the library media center building background knowledge.
   A. The science teacher and the library media specialist work with individuals and groups as requested.
   B. The teaching committee makes arrangements for students to preview motion pictures, filmstrips, etc.
IV. A member of the teaching committee presents the motion picture *The Nature of Science: Obtaining Facts* (Coronet) and leads the discussion following the presentation of the film.
   A. Class discusses the following:
   1. How scientific facts are proven.
   2. Is astrology a science?
   3. Why are people superstitious?
   4. Why do newspapers and magazines include horoscopes?
   5. Does advertising on TV and in newspapers and magazines capitalize on human gullibility?
   6. The Romans had a saying,"Let the buyer beware"; does this slogan apply today?
   B. The five steps basic to applying the scientific method are reviewed and examples of how each step is of equal importance are given.
   1. Observation—curiosity, imagination, perseverance, accuracy, and patience are essential.
      a. Luther Burbank, as a child, used his power of observation to begin his search for improving food-giving plants.
      b. Ephraim McDowell, pioneer surgeon, based his belief that abdominal surgery would not be fatal on his observation that human tissue in the human extremities was capable of regeneration and healing.
   2. Hypothesis—making a guess about the unknown based on available facts.
      a. William Harvey, who discovered how blood is circulated, first observed that the valves in an animal heart and in a human heart were like little doors that were one-way openings. He asked himself why these doors would not permit blood to flow back and forth in the veins; searching for the answer to this question caused him to discover how blood is pumped from one side of the heart, through the lungs, through the arteries, to all parts of the body, and finally back to the heart again.
      b. Thomas Edison, one of the greatest inventors the world has ever known, made countless scientific breakthroughs because of his uncanny ability to make educated guesses based on observable facts.
   3. Experiment—testing the hypothesis.
      a. Pierre and Marie Curie, discoverers of radium, laboriously isolated one gram of radium salts from eight tons of pitchblende and determined

MODEL 29 (cont.)

the atomic weights and properties of radium and polonium. They refused to patent their processes or otherwise to profit commercially
from their discovery.

b. George Washington Carver, agricultural chemist, experimented with
agricultural products trying to discover new uses for common crops
such as peanuts, sweet potatoes, soybeans, and cotton. Through his
efforts hundreds of new uses were discovered for food crops and new
revenue sources were opened to the farmer; chemurgy, the branch of
chemistry dealing with the use of farm and forest products for purposes
other than food and clothing, came into being. Carver refused to patent
any discovery and made all of his discoveries free for the taking.

4. Theory—the hypothesis is proven to be correct by experimentation.

a. Charles Darwin, English naturalist, through the scientific method,
proved the theory of evolution in both plants and animals.

b. Thomas Malthus, an English minister, advanced the theory that living
beings multiply at such a rate that the world cannot possibly supply
enough food for them all and that it is, therefore, necessary for large
numbers of animals to die—and people, too, through disease and
wars—to keep the world population in balance.

5. Proof—the ability of the theory to stand up under any test that anyone at
all can think up.

a. Statistical proof of the effectiveness of miracle drugs validates the claim
that penicillin can destroy or sharply check the growth of various harmful bacteria such as staphylococci, gonococci, and pneumococci.

b. The population explosion, which now has reached the alarming pro-
portion of doubling each 35 years, gives credence to the theory of
Thomas Malthus, advanced in 1798 in "An Essay on the Principle of
Population."

C. The following devices are employed to test student power of observation.

1. A student is sent from the room and the class attempts to describe in
detail what he or she is wearing.

2. After viewing the photograph "Animal Camouflage," which is projected via
the opaque projector, the class lists all of the animals they are able to
recall; they are also asked to describe the environmental details of the
picture.

3. A tray containing 20 common articles is passed from student to student;
each student tries to list the 20 articles five minutes after viewing the tray.

V. The class views the motion picture *Galileo* (Coronet), and a member of the
teaching committee generates discussion by asking the following questions:

A. What were the causes that forced Galileo to retract his statement that the
earth moves around the sun? Should he or should he not have retracted his
statement?

B. Jonathan Swift, a seventeenth-century satirist, once made the statement,
"When a true genius appears in the world, you may know him by this sign,
that the dunces are all in confederacy against him." Is this human failing
evidenced in the trial of Galileo?

C. Michael Servetus, a Spaniard, was condemned as a heretic and burned at
the stake in 1553 because he presented arguments against Aristotle's ideas
that only heavenly matter could move in a circle and that everything else had
a beginning and an end. What is a heretic? Why were heretics accused of
being in league with the devil? What was the Spanish Inquisition? Is this not a
good example of the contrast between supposition and scientific evidence?

VI. The class views the motion picture *Health Heroes* (Coronet), and a member of
the teaching committee introduces each of the five students responsible for
further elaboration on contributions of the five scientists—Pasteur, Lister, Jenner,
Leeuwenhoek, Koch—depicted in the motion picture.

VII. Under the leadership of a member of the teaching committee the class discusses
the concept of the scientist as a human being. The following topics are developed and explored:

MODEL 29 (cont.)

A. What are the characteristics of a scientist?

B. What is the concept of open-mindedness?

C. What competencies must a scientist have?

D. Can a scientist ever stop learning?

E. A scientist can suggest better ways of doing things but he or she cannot force people to accept his or her recommendations.

F. What are the career possibilities in the field of science and technology?

G. True scientists rate their efforts in terms of bettering society rather than achieving financial gain for themselves.

VIII. The class discusses evidence in today's world that human beings still refuse to think scientifically. A member of the teaching committee introduces the theme of human indifference to scientific truth by providing a demonstration:

A. Members of the class vote whether or not filter-tipped cigarettes trap all of the nicotine in a cigarette.

B. Using the mechanical smoker, a student demonstrates that a large amount of nicotine is still trapped in the lungs when a filter-tipped cigarette is smoked.

C. The January 1979 *Report of the U.S. Surgeon General on the Harmful Effects of Tobacco Smoking* is studied.

1. Smokers are at least 20 times as likely to succumb to lung cancer as nonsmokers.

2. Cigarette smokers are from 6 to 10 times as likely to die of cancer of the larynx as nonsmokers.

D. The 1979 statistical analysis of heart attack death ratios released by the American Cancer Society is studied.

1. Mortality rate from coronary heart disease among men 40–49 years old was 5.51 times as great for heavy smokers as for nonsmokers.

2. Mortality rate from coronary heart disease among women 40–49 years old was 3.31 times as great for heavy smokers as for nonsmokers.

IX. As a culminating activity students each write a paragraph explaining why they believe the scientist of their choice has made the most significant contribution to man's scientific knowledge.

A. Each student shares with the class his or her reasons for selecting the scientist he or she considers to have made the most significant contribution to man's advancing civilization.

B. On a time line, the class records each scientist nominated as worthy of a Nobel Prize for science.

MODEL 30 THE TASADAY: A STUDY OF A PRIMITIVE CULTURE FROZEN IN TIME

Subject: Honors History

Grade: 7

Learning Project: Primitive Man

Individual Learning Program: *The Tasaday: A Study of a Primitive Culture Frozen in Time*

Case Study: In 1971, in the Philippines on the Island of Mindanao, a small group of primitive people was discovered deep in the heart of the unexplored rain forest. When these people, the Tasaday, were found, it was discovered they were living in a way our ancestors lived more than 50,000 years ago. They had no metal and knew nothing about farming or hunting—natural caves providing their only shelter. Yet, strangely enough, in view of the constant threat of war in our world today, these primitive people lived in total harmony with their environment and with each other—there were no words in their vocabulary for enemies, war, or weapons.

Analyzing a Case Study:

A case study is the gathering and organization of all relevant materials to enable an in-depth study and an analysis of a person, an event, a community, a society, or a culture. The reader of the case study is invited to apply his or her own knowledge, observations, feelings, and value judgments when analyzing and interpreting the facts.

In analyzing the culture of the Tasaday, use the Learning Guide: Analysis of a Culture [see later].

MODEL 30 (cont.)

Build Background Knowledge and Understanding by:

Reading and analyzing the following sources:

The Gentle Tasaday by John Nance (Harcourt Brace)

"The Tasaday: Stone Age Cavemen of Mindanao" by Kenneth MacLeish (*National Geographic*, Aug. 1972, pp. 219–249)

Viewing and analyzing the documentary sound filmstrip set:

The Tasaday: Stone Age People in a Space Age World (Associated Press; dist. Pathescope Educational Media)

Part 1—*The Cave People*

Part 2—*Civilization—Curse or Blessing?*

Optional Learning Experiences:

Compare and contrast the culture of the Tasaday of the Philippines with that of the aborigines of Australia:

The Aborigines by B. C. Ross-Larson (Creative Educational Society)

Boomerang Hunter by Jim Kjelgaard (Holiday House)

An ethnologist is a scientist who studies the similarities and differences among cultures. You can gain insight into the methods and procedures employed by an ethnologist by viewing the following sound filmstrip from the set entitled "Anthropologists at Work":

The Ethnologist (Globe Filmstrips)

An anthropologist is a scientist who studies people, their behavior, and social groups. In the field of anthropology there are four major areas of specialization:

Ethnology: the branch of anthropology dealing with the study of the similarities and differences among cultures.

Archeology: the branch of anthropology dealing with the study of prehistoric artifacts and the people who left them.

History: the branch of anthropology dealing with the use of historical restoration techniques and archeological methods in the search for understanding of the total way of life of a people.

Paleontology: the branch of anthropology dealing with the study of bone remains of people and animals.

You can gain insight into the methods and procedures employed by the specialists in each of the above fields by viewing the following sound filmstrips (Globe Filmstrips):

The Archeologist

The Historian

The Paleontologist

Continue throughout this school year to build your in-depth understanding of the work of these anthropologists as you explore the civilizations of ancient peoples such as the Egyptians, Babylonians, Assyrians, Chaldeans, Israelites, Phoenicians, Greeks, Carthaginians, and Romans.

For a survey of educational requirements and career possibilities in the field of anthropology consult the Career Resource Center at the Senior High School.

LEARNING GUIDE ANALYSIS OF A CULTURE

Student _____

Facts—

Location:

MODEL 30 (cont.)

Population:

Time span:

Arts and crafts:

Ceremonies and rituals:

Clothing:

Communication:

Currency:

Education:

Food:

Government:

Health and medicine:

Laws:

Literature:

Manners and customs:

Mobility:

Mores:

Music and dance:

Place of children:

Place of the elderly:

Place of men:

Place of women:

Records:

Religion:

Shelter:

Social and economic problems:

Superstitions:

Traditions:

Transportation:

Values:

Weapons:

Your Observations and Impressions:

Your Feelings and Concerns:

Your Attitudes and Judgments:

MODEL 31   BECOMING AN EYEWITNESS TO HISTORY: INTERPRETING PRIMARY SOURCES

Subject: Honors U.S. History
Grade: 8
Skill Development Activities: Making effective use of primary source materials
Teaching Goals: To provide learning experiences that will enable the student to uncover, process, and interpret data encoded in primary source materials (see Appendix F: Thinking-Learning-Communicating Skills Continuum, K–12).
Teaching Strategies and Procedures:

I. Class orientation to learning to interpret primary source materials.

   A. What is history?

> It is somewhat unfortunate that the word *history* should be used in several different senses. In its origin (Greek) it meant learning by inquiry. The historian was a searcher after knowledge, an investigator. But by a subtle transformation the term came to be applied to the record or narrative of what had been learned by investigation: and in this sense it passed over into the Latin *historia* and into modern speech (Allen Johnson, in *The Historian and Historical Evidence*, 1926).

> The history of the world is but the biography of great men (Thomas Carlyle, in *Heroes and Hero-Worship*, 1841).

> Human history is in essence a history of ideas (H. G. Wells, in *Outline of History*, 1920).

> Our custom of taking records and preserving them is the main barrier that separates us from the scatter-brained races of monkey. For it is the extension of memory that permits us to draw upon experience and which allows us to establish a common pool of wisdom. Knowledge of things said and done . . . is a knowledge which not merely sees us through the trivial decisions of the moment, but also stands by in the far more important times of personal or public crisis (Sherman Kent, in *Writing History*, 1941).

> Civilization can only develop if past and present learning, history, artifacts, and traditions of a group of individuals can be preserved and stored in such form that it can be communicated from one generationn to the next even as it grows larger (Jacques Costeau, in *Ocean World of Jacques Costeau*, 1975).

   B. Through this course in American history, the student will be a historian, a searcher after knowledge, an investigator.

   C. The student will have the opportunity to interpret primary source materials by:

Mastering the essentials of historical method.

Determining the authenticity and significance of primary source materials.
a. Who is the authority?
b. What is his or her background?
c. What is the purpose of the material?
d. When and under what circumstances was the information recorded?
e. Was the information written from memory or was it a direct account of what happened?
f. Is there corroboration of the facts from other sources?
g. Is the authority objective in the treatment of the material?
h. Is the material pertinent?
i. Is there mention in this source of other documents, people, or events that should be researched?

Validating and utilizing information gained from written or printed sources.

a. Account books	g. Diaries
b. Bills of sale	h. Eyewitness accounts
c. Charters	i. Handbills
d. Cookbooks	j. Handbooks
e. Court records	k. Indenture papers
f. Deeds	l. Journals

MODEL 31 (cont.)

m. Legislative records
n. Letters
o. Memoirs
p. Military records
q. Newspapers

r. Pamphlets
s. Periodicals
t. Speeches
u. Tax records

Validating and utilizing information gained from disc and tape recordings.

a. Debates
b. Hearings
c. Interviews
d. Newscasts

e. Plays
f. Poems
g. Songs
h. Speeches

Utilizing information gained from artifacts, realia, and museum holdings.

a. Banners
b. Buildings
c. Buttons
d. Cemeteries
e. Ceramics
f. Clothing
g. Currency
h. Flags
i. Household furnishings
j. Jewelry
k. Machines

l. Musical instruments
m. Paintings
n. Photographs
o. Religious articles
p. Sculptures
q. Stamps
r. Textiles
s. Tools
t. Vehicles
u. Weapons

D. The student will learn to employ more than 40 thinking skills while interpreting evidence found in primary source materials (see Checklist G, Thinking Skills Developed Through the Use of Primary Source Materials), at the end of this model.

II. Primary sources: Repositories and collections ·
A. The Library of Congress is probably the world's largest library.

Its holdings include more than 73 million items.

Its resources contain information on virtually every subject known to man.

It includes all forms of communication from papyrus to microform.

It grows at the rate of 7,000 new items every working day.

Its collections stretch along 350 miles of book shelves.

It contains 32 million manuscripts, including the papers of 23 American presidents.

It contains the world's largest cartographic collection numbering $3\frac{1}{2}$ million maps and atlases.

It contains 4 million pieces of music from classical to rock.

It contains 8 million prints and photographs, including the pictures of Matthew Brady and *Look* magazine.

It contains half a million sound recordings rich in American folklore, poetry, oral history, and music.

It contains a quarter of a million reels of motion pictures.

It contains 3 million microforms.

The Library of Congress is open every day except Christmas Day and New Year's Day.

The Information Counter of the Library of Congress offers a number of publications, recordings, facsimiles, and posters for sale.

The Library of Congress makes its vast resources available for use in the Library; there are 16 reading rooms each with a card catalog, reference collection, and librarian.

The Library of Congress offers a number of special services:

MODEL 31 (cont.)

Interlibrary loan of books and other materials to public and university libraries.

Photoduplicating Service of photographs, photostats, facsimile prints, and microfilms of research materials.

The Library of Congress compiles the National Union Catalog, a register of all the world's books published since 1454 and held in more than 1,100 North American libraries; many large public and university libraries have this catalog.

The Library of Congress offers computerized informational retrieval services to regional libraries; this service is being rapidly developed throughout the nation.

B. The National Archives is a document depository second only to the Library of Congress.

The *Harvard Guide to American History,* ed. by Oscar Handlin (Belknap Press of Harvard University), provides a comprehensive introduction to the holdings and services of the National Archives.

C. The publications of the U.S. Government are indexed and sold by the U.S. Superintendent of Documents, Government Printing Office (see Appendix G, Basic Reference Tools).

III. Primary sources: Reference tools (see Appendix G).

A. *Annals of America,* ed. by Mortimer J. Adler (Encyclopaedia Britannica), 20 vols., provides access to more than 2,200 primary sources: laws, speeches, diaries, journals, transcriptions of dialogues, on-the-scene reports, and reminiscences.

B. *Congress Investigates: A Documentary History 1792–1974,* ed. by Arthur M. Schlesinger, Jr., and Roger Burns (R. R. Bowker), 5 vols., provides access to the original documents in 29 of the most important investigations conducted by Congress.

C. *Documents Illustrative of the Formation of the Union of the United States,* published by the Superintendent of Documents (Government Printing Office), reprints the basic documents as well as the notes and papers of Alexander Hamilton, James Madison, Rufus King, and others.

D. *Makers of America* (Encyclopaedia Britannica), 10 vols., provides access to 731 primary sources describing the activities of minority groups.

E. The *Harvard Guide to American History* identifies other basic reference sources of primary source materials for each major period of U.S. history.

MODEL CHECKLIST G: THINKING SKILLS DEVELOPED
THROUGH THE USE OF PRIMARY SOURCE MATERIALS

_____ Analyzing and evaluating evidence

_____ Anticipating outcomes

_____ Applying historical method

_____ Appraising validity of arguments

_____ Appraising validity of evidence

_____ Arranging facts, events, and ideas in sequence

_____ Associating similar ideas and experiences

_____ Classifying or categorizing ideas

_____ Comparing or contrasting ideas

_____ Detecting inconsistencies

_____ Determining adequacy of evidence

_____ Determining validity of statements

MODEL 31 (cont.)

_____ Differentiating between inductive and deductive reasoning

_____ Differentiating between objective and subjective reasoning

_____ Discovering causal relationships

_____ Discovering hidden meanings

_____ Discovering thought and action patterns

_____ Distinguishing between fact and fiction

_____ Distinguishing between fact and opinion

_____ Distinguishing between fact and propaganda

_____ Drawing inferences and making generalizations

_____ Drawing valid conclusions

_____ Establishing sequence patterns

_____ Evaluating and reacting to ideas in the light of the author's purpose

_____ Evaluating attitudes and motives

_____ Evaluating authenticity of sources

_____ Evaluating definitive statements

_____ Evaluating reliability of sources

_____ Evaluating summary statements

_____ Expressing ideas

_____ Finding evidence to prove or disprove a generalization

_____ Formulating hypotheses

_____ Identifying bias

_____ Identifying main and subordinate themes or ideas

_____ Interpreting idiomatic and figurative language

_____ Interpreting implied ideas

_____ Judging reasonableness and relevancy of testimony

_____ Judging writer's and speaker's competence and integrity

_____ Making insightful judgments

_____ Organizing ideas around key questions

_____ Organizing ideas in logical patterns

_____ Organizing information in systematic order

_____ Perceiving relationships

_____ Predicting outcomes

_____ Questioning immutability of the printed word and of statistics

_____ Reaching tentative conclusions

_____ Recognizing emotional coloration

_____ Recognizing propaganda and its purpose in a given context

_____ Relating the past to the present in the study of change and continuity

_____ Seeking for association between various episodes

_____ Selecting evidence pertinent to an argument

_____ Suspending judgment where a conclusion is not warranted

_____ Synthesizing findings into an accurate and readable account

_____ Understanding abstract concepts

MODEL 32   MATHEMATICS AS A COMMUNICATION TOOL

Subjects: Mathematics, Social Studies, and Science
Grade: 8
Unit: Mathematics as a Communication Tool
Goal: To provide opportunity for the students to learn to use mathematical skills as a means of communication.
Objectives:

To provide opportunity for the students to discover the impact value of statistical information presented in graph, chart, and table form.

To provide opportunity for the students to bring a high degree of relevance to their study of science and social studies.

To provide opportunity for the students to become conversant with sources of current statistical information.

To provide opportunity for the students to become conversant with opinion polls as an effective means of judging opinions and attitudes.

Topics:
1. Ecology
    Air pollution
    Energy consumption
    Sources of energy consumed in the United States
    Noise pollution
    Solid wastes generated in the United States
    Sources of solid wastes generated in the United States
    Water pollution
    Sources of water pollution in the United States
2. Education
    Attainment by age, race, and sex
    Attainment by ethnic groups
    Enrollment in schools by age and sex
    Income by years of schooling
3. Labor
    Employed persons by major occupational groups and sex
    Employment and unemployment in the United States
    U.S. labor force earnings
4. Law enforcement
    Business losses due to crime by type of crime
    Full-time police department employees
    Index of crime
    Riot and civil disorder losses, United States
    Salary scales of police patrolmen and patrolwomen
    Total arrests by age, by sex, by crime
    World crime statistics
5. Narcotics
    Active narcotics addicts in selected cities
    Addiction in the United States
6. Population*
    Birth rate in the United States, 1900–to date
    Death rates in the United States, 1900–to date
    Growth in the United States, 1610–to date
    Immigration to and emigration from the United States
    Life expectancy rates by race, age, and sex, United States
    Life expectancy rates by race, age, and sex in foreign countries
    Marriage and divorce in the United States, 1900–to date
    World population doubling times

*For latest census data contact Chief of the Bureau of Public Information, Washington, D.C. 20233, tel. 301-763-7273.

MODEL 32 (cont.)

7. Public opinion
   American way of life: politics, patriotism, isolation
   The climate of the high school
   Counseling and educational needs of adolescents
   Drugs and narcotics
   Evaluation of educational attitudes
   People problems: population, prejudice, poverty, peace
   Vocational plans and prejudices of adolescents
   What is wrong and right with today's youth

MODEL 33   THE PROS AND CONS OF SPACE COLONIZATION

Subject: Honors Science

Grade: 9

Goal: To provide an in-depth study of space; its physical properties, its technological advancements, and its human and social implications.

Teaching Objectives:

To provide learning experiences that will enable the students:

To use science concepts, process skills, and values in making everyday decisions.

To distinguish between scientific evidence and personal opinion.

To identify the relationship between fact and theory.

To understand the interrelationships among science, technology, and other facets of society, including social and economic development.

To recognize the limitations as well as the usefulness of science and technology in advancing human welfare.

To recognize that science cannot be divorced from the critical realities of contemporary life and society.

To equate the cost of scientific and technological advancement within the context of the future benefits to society.

Teaching Strategies:

This is an eight-week unit designed to provide an opportunity for the students to assess the human and economic implications as well as the technical feasibility of space settlements.

The basic reference tool to be employed in building background information is the 185-page National Aeronautics and Space Administration (NASA) report *Space Settlements: A Design Study* (Washington, D.C.: 1977).

Space Settlements: A Design Study was a report that grew out of a ten-week program in engineering system design held at Stanford University and the Ames Research Center of NASA. The purpose of this study program was to construct a picture of how people might permanently sustain life in space on a large scale and then to answer the question "Is it feasible to do so?"

The students will study the report and then will make a value judgment as to the social and the scientific-technological feasibility of space colonization.

Teaching Procedure:

I. Student orientation to and overview of the unit.

The class is introduced to the NASA report *Space Settlements: A Design Study*

The Foreword,* written by James C. Fletcher (Oct. 1, 1976), NASA administrator, is read and discussed (see copy that follows).

*National Aeronautics and Space Administration, *Space Settlements: A Design Study* (Washington, D.C.: NASA, 1977), p. v.

MODEL 33 (cont.)

The question, "What is feasible?" can be finally answered only by future historians. If in the 14th and 15th Centuries when new technology first made transoceanic voyages possible, European rulers had inquired what they should do with this new capability, no man could have been long-headed enough to perceive all the possibilities, nor persuasive enough to communicate his vision to others. We now realize that technology is but a part of any broad stride taken by man. A perception of advantage to be gained, resolve, organization, and a continuity of effort—some of the elements that must combine with technology to effect a major human advance—is indeed vital.

Space exploration, an active pursuit for less than two decades, has already displayed an extraordinary power to alter our viewpoints and stretch our minds. The concept of spacecraft Earth, a sphere of finite resources and ominous pollution, became pervasive and powerful at the same time we first received good photographs of our planetary home. The study summarized in this volume is another mind-stretcher . . . settlement in space is not an authorized program, and no man can now say if or when such a dazzling venture may be formally undertaken. But by their efforts to put numbers on an idea, to assess the human and economic implications as well as technical feasibility, the participants in this effort have provided us with a vision that will engage our imagination and stretch our minds.

The Preface* is read and discussed (see copy that follows).

The following report grew out of a 10-week program in engineering systems design held at Stanford University and the Ames Research Center of the National Aeronautics and Space Administration [NASA] during the summer of 1975. This program, sponsored jointly by NASA and the American Society for Engineering Education [ASEE], brought together nineteen professors of engineering, physical science, social science, and architecture, three volunteers, six students, a technical director, and two codirectors. This group worked for ten weeks to construct a convincing picture of how people might permanently sustain life in space on a large scale.

This report, like the design itself, is intended to be as technologically complete and sound as it could be made in ten weeks, but it is also meant for a readership beyond that of the aerospace community. Because the idea of colonizing space has awakened strong public interest, the report is written to be understood by the educated public and specialists in other fields. It also includes considerable background material. A table of units and conversion factors is included to aid the reader in interpreting the units of the metric system used in the report.

The goal of the summer study was to design a system for the colonization of space. The study group was largely self-organized; it specified important subsidiary goals, set up work groups, and elected its project managers and committee heads. There were three project managers; each served for three weeks during which he assigned tasks, coordinated activities, and developed the outline of the final report. As a consequence of this organization, the report represents as nearly as is possible the views of the entire study group. The conclusions and recommendations are the responsibility of the participants and should not be ascribed to any of the sponsoring organizations; NASA, ASEE, or Stanford University.

An effort of the magnitude of this design study could not have been possible without major contributions by many individuals. The codirectors, Richard Johnson of NASA and William Verplank of Stanford, made available to and guided participants in the use of the resources of the Ames Research Center and Stanford University. Their continuing helpfulness and timely assistance were important contributions to the successful conclusion of the project.

*Ibid., p. vii.

MODEL 33 (cont.)

The technical director, Gerard K. O'Neill of Princeton University, made essential contributions by providing information based on his notes and calculations from six years of prior work on space colonization and by carefully reviewing the technical aspects of the study.

So many able and interesting visitors contributed to the study participants' understanding of the problem of designing a workable system for colonizing space that it is not feasible to thank them all here. Nevertheless, it is appropriate to acknowledge those from whom the study group drew especially heavily in the final design. In particular Roger Arno, Gene Austin, John Billingham, Philip Chapman, Hubert P. Davis, Jerry Driggers, Peter Glaser, Albert Hibbs, Arthur Kantrowitz, Ken Nishioka, Jesco von Putkammer, and Gordon Woodcock are thanked for their help and ideas.

The assistance of Eric Burgess, who made major contributions to the editorial work, is also gratefully acknowledged.

The class will function as a group of scientists and engineers who are reviewing and evaluating the report of the Stanford—Ames Research Center symposium.

After intensive study of the evidence, the class will then debate the pros and cons of space colonization.

II. Topics to be explored in class and pursued as independent research include:

The colonization of space

The overall system
Design goals
The history of an idea

Physical properties of space

The topography of space
Solar radiation
Matter in space
Meteoroids and space habitats
Ionizing radiation in space

Human needs in space

Weightlessness
Atmosphere
Food and water
Combined environmental stress
Environmental design to reduce stress
Small size and isolation
Design criteria
Psychological and cultural considerations
Space requirements of various community activities

Choosing among alternatives

The shape of the habitat
Shielding
What if criteria change?
Fabrication techniques
The people in the colony
Life support
Satellite solar power stations
Where the colony should be located
Mining, transport, and processing in space
The transport system
Material properties for design
Parameters of habitability
Mass as a measure of structural cost

MODEL 33 (cont.)

The plasma core shield
Structures by vacuum vapor fabrication
Interior building materials and components
Population distribution and trends
Satellite Solar Power Stations (SSPS)
Processing of metals
Glass processing
The Lunar Gas Gun Mass Driver
Passive catchers
Space transportation systems
Impact of earth launch vehicles on the ozone layer

A tour of the colony

Earth to low earth orbit
The habitat at L_5
Production at L_5
The lunar base
The mass catcher at L_5
Home to earth
Structures design concept for a shell structure
Structural systems for housing
Agriculture
Productivity
Mass shielding
The mass driver
The mass catcher
Trajectories from the moon to L_2
Rotary pellet launcher
Impact upon lunar atmosphere
Chevron shields

Building the colony and making it prosper

Preparatory work
Materials and supplies
Transportation and construction
Estimating costs and time
Production of energy in space as a potential economic justification for space colonization
Space colonization cost parametrics
Lunar SSPS power
The Flyback F-1
Methods for estimating cost and time for SSPS and more colonies
Electricity benefits
Composite variables for SSPS and additional colonies
Environmental impact of microwave power transmission

View of the future

Benefits not related to energy
Research in deep space
Rocket engines for deep space
Transport
The asteroidal resources
New methods of construction
Habitat design
Automation and productivity
Limits to growth
Some economic considerations

Recommendations and conclusions

Recommendations for research and development in critical subsystems

MODEL 33 (cont.)

Recommendations for space ventures
Conclusions

III. The students prepare to debate the pros and cons of space colonization in the immediate future by considering the following:

Isaac Asimov writing in the *National Geographic* (July 1976) stated that "we can build space colonies . . . in the near future [which] would fulfill functions that are now fulfilled by cities on the surface of the earth."

T. A. Heppenheimer, in his book *Colonies in Space* (Stackpole), states:

Colonies in space is the next giant step for mankind, evolutionary in its impact—thousands of people living and working in attractive, earthlike space communities and eventually solving the world's energy problems. This is not fantasy, not just a vague outline of future possibilities.

Thousands of prominent individuals—scientists, industrialists, writers and editors, members of Congress—are now aware of this all-but-inevitable exciting human reality that can start becoming fact before the end of the twentieth century.

Space is mankind's new frontier. Serious and careful studies have shown that large space colonies can be built soon.

Ray Bradbury, in the introduction to *Colonies in Space,* attempts to discredit the shortsightedness of those who question spending billions on space colonization so long as poverty and want torture and enslave millions here on earth.

The U.S. Congress is vested by the U.S. Constitution with the power "to lay and collect taxes, duties, imposts and excises, to pay the debts and provide for the common defense and general welfare." In establishing the hierarchy of need, Congress must make value judgments. The question must be asked, in the light of the Constitution, which needs (defense, social, economic, etc.) are of the greatest import. On what bases should value judgments be made? The complexity of today's society precludes simplistic answers.

An informed citizen who is functionally literate must be competent to relate the lessons of history to the human quest for understanding and for solving contemporary problems. For example:

Excessive taxation was a contributing factor to the decline and eventual fall of the Roman Empire.

Excessive taxation was a contributing factor in precipitating the American Revolution.

Excessive taxation—property tax collection per person increased 111 percent in the ten-year period 1966–1976—has led to a nationwide taxpayers' revolt with the first shot being fired in California on June 6, 1978, when the California voters, by a two-to-one margin, amended the state constitution to slash property taxes by 57 percent and to erect high barriers against major increases in state and local levies for years to come.

Following the revolt of the California voters on June 6, 1978, President Carter (*U.S. News & World Report,* June 19, 1978) stated: "The people of California have reflected a strong national dissatisfaction with taxes that unfairly burden middle-income taxpayers and demonstrate their impatience with the steadily increasing cost of government."

In the light of the evidence from the past, namely, that governments topple when taxes become oppressive, and in the light of contemporary evidence of taxpayer revolt, is it logical to "buy" Heppenheimer's prediction that space colonization will be subsidized by tax dollars before the end of the twentieth century?

An informed citizen who is functionally literate must be competent to make value judgments based on the effective use of critical thinking skills.

Defining the problem.

MODEL 33 (cont.)

Developing a tentative answer, hypothesizing.

  Examining and classifying available data.

  Seeking relationships, drawing logical inferences.

  Stating the hypothesis.

Testing the tentative answer.

  Arranging evidence.

  Analyzing evidence.

Developing a conclusion.

  Finding meaningful patterns or relationships.

  Stating the conclusion.

Applying the conclusion.

  Testing against new evidence.

  Generalizing the results.

When preparing, presenting, and reacting to a debate, critical thinking skills are brought into play.

MODEL 34   EXCHANGING THE MELTING POT FOR AN ETHNIC KALEIDOSCOPE*

Seminar

Grades: 10, 11, 12

Goal: To provide learning experiences that will enable the student to perceive the uniquely differing contributions made to the American national heritage by each ethnic group.

Teaching Objectives:

To encourage the student to be open to experiences of all cultures making up the rich fabric of our nation.

To encourage the student to discover that the demands of the future require a pluralistic vision not only of our country but of the entire human community, and to recognize that the future is now.

To encourage the student to realize that awareness of one's own ethnic-cultural heritage is a positive first step in building respect for one's own as well as for other peoples' ethnic/cultural backgrounds.

To encourage the student to perceive cultural pluralism as much more than an attempt to placate racial and ethnic minorities, and as a concept aiming toward a heightened sense of wholeness and well-being of the entire society based on the unique strength of each of its parts.

To encourage the student to perceive the concept of the "melting pot" as tending to obliterate ethnic/cultural diversity, as opposed to the exciting concept of the kaleidoscope as delineating each particle clearly and contributing to the beauty of the whole.†

To encourage the student to read, view, listen, and exchange ideas in an unbiased, constructively critical, analytical, and scholarly manner.

Teaching Strategies:

The seminar, which is designed for individual student in-depth study and small group interaction, is a semester course of approximately 85 days and is limited to no more than 15 students.

*For background information pertaining to multiethnic-polycultural education (the U.S. Congressional Ethnic Heritage Studies Program Act, the National Education Association's multiethnic curriculum guides, the National Council for the Social Studies Multiethnic Education Program Evaluation Checklist, and the Cardinal Premises for Educational Change) see *The School Library Media Program: Instructional Force for Excellence* by Ruth Ann Davies, 3rd ed. (New York: Bowker, 1979), pp. 24, 220–221, 279–86.

†Theodore Bikel, "U.S. Supports Arts in 'a Miserly Fashion,'" *U.S. News & World Report,* May 7, 1979, p. 81.

MODEL 34 (cont.)

It is a multigrade seminar designed for students from grades 10, 11, and 12. While individual study is the rule, cooperative pooling of information and leadership by merit of ideas are common practices.

Acceptance in the seminar is of a contractual nature; each seminar participant will "pull his or her weight."

No textbook is employed in this seminar. *Ethnic American Minorities: A Guide to Media and Materials* edited by Harry A. Johnson (Bowker) serves as a basic guide to the problems and challenges, history and traditions, and the past and future of the various ethnic groups in America as well as a basic resource for identifying both print and nonprint media pertaining to all aspects of ethnic cultures.

Overall Course Design:
1. A tentative schedule is prepared and duplicated for distribution to students at the first seminar meeting.
2. Specific ethnic cultures are pinpointed for introduction, exploration, and discussion on the schedule.
3. Each participant in the seminar will be required to: prepare an oral mini-lecture on at least two different ethnic groups and a midsemester and a final semester summation paper on a topic or topics of personal concern regarding the ideas exchanged in the seminar.

Tentative Schedule:
Day 1: Orientation to the seminar.
    Getting acquainted with the course and with each other.

        Handout 1: The Tentative Schedule.

        Handout 2: Photocopy of the contents of *Ethnic American Minorities: A Guide to Media and Materials* edited by Harry A. Johnson.

        Handout 3: Teacher's schedule of conference times available for student consultation.

        Handout 4: Definition of *ethnic group:* An ethnic group is a body of people who can be distinguished from the general population of a society by their shared values, traditions, aspirations, and other aspects of a unique social and cultural heritage that is passed on from generation to the next (*Roots of America: A Multiethnic Curriculum Resource Guide . . . ,* developed by New Jersey Education Association and the National Education Association Ethnic Heritage Projects, Washington, D.C.: National Education Association, 1975, p. 19).

        Definition of terms by each seminar participant is required. This terminology list will be included in the handbook each student is to maintain throughout the course.

Day 2: The motion picture *Who Are the People of America,* 2nd ed. (Coronet), is viewed and discussed.

Day 3: The first motion picture in the Minority Series (Coronet) is viewed and discussed: *Minorities: What Is a Minority?*

Day 4: Independent study.

Day 5: Independent study.

Day 6: Group discussion of the difference between the "melting pot" and the "kaleidoscope" concepts.

Day 7: The motion picture *Immigrants in Chains* (Films, Inc.) is viewed and discussed. This is but one title from the series of five films *The Americans: A Nation of Immigrants* based on John F. Kennedy's book of the same title.

The students compile a list of topics they believe should be researched to build background knowledge of the Afro-American. A group leader is chosen to coordinate the individual students' selection and presentation of information on these topics.

MODEL 34 (cont.)

A period of two weeks will be spent working independently and/or in small groups.

Day 8: Independent study.

Day 9: Independent study.

Day 10: Independent study.

Day 11: Independent study.

Day 12: Independent study.

Day 13: Independent study.

Day 14: Independent study.

Day 15: Independent study.

Day 16: Independent study.

Day 17: Group pooling of knowledge and discussion.

Day 18: Group pooling of knowledge and discussion.

Day 19: Afro-American guest speaker.

Day 20: The motion picture *The Autobiography of Miss Jane Pittman* (McGraw-Hill Films) is presented and continued the next two days.

Day 21: *The Autobiography of Miss Jane Pittman* is continued.

Day 22: *The Autobiography of Miss Jane Pittman* is concluded and discussed.

Day 23: Students who have made a depth study of primary source materials such as *Time of Trial, Time of Hope* edited by Milton Meltzer and August Meler (Doubleday) and *In Their Own Words: A History of the American Negro* edited by Milton Meltzer, three volumes: 1619–1865; 1865–1916; 1916–1966 (Crowell) share with the seminar happenings paralleling or substantiating the happenings depicted in *The Autobiography of Miss Jane Pittman.*

Day 24: The motion picture *The Chinese Americans: The Early Immigrants* (Handel Film Corp.) is viewed and discussed.

Day 25: The motion picture *The Japanese American* (Handel Film Corp.) is viewed and discussed.

Day 26: The motion picture *Trouble with Chinatown* (NBCTV) is viewed and discussed.

Day 27: The students compile a list of topics they believe should be researched to build background knowledge of Asian-Americans.

A group leader is chosen to coordinate the individual students' selection and presentation of information on these topics.

A period of eight days will be spent working independently and/or in small groups.

Day 28: Independent study.

Day 29: Independent study.

Day 30: Independent study.

Day 31: Independent study.

Day 32: Independent study.

Day 33: Independent study.

Day 34: Independent study

Day 35: Independent study.

Day 36: The topic "Relocation of Japanese-Americans: Right Or Wrong" will be discussed. Students who have researched primary source materials on the internment of the Japanese-Americans following Pearl Harbor will share their findings with the seminar.

MODEL 34 (cont.)

Day 37: Students who have chosen to present mini-lectures on either Afro-Americans or Asian-Americans will be scheduled to do so beginning today and continuing for the next three days.

Day 38: Student mini-lectures.

Day 39: Student mini-lectures.

Day 40: Student mini-lectures. Midsemester paper is due on this day.

Day 41: The first part of the documentary film *Indian American* (Cathedral Films) is viewed.

Day 42: The last reel of the documentary film *Indian American* is viewed and discussed.

The students compile a list of topics they believe should be researched to build background knowledge of the Native Indian American.

A group leader is chosen to coordinate the individual students' selection and presentation of information on these topics.

A period of 10 days will be spent working independently and/or in small groups.

Day 43: Independent study.

Day 44: Independent study.

Day 45: Independent study.

Day 46: Independent study.

Day 47: Independent study.

Day 48: Independent study.

Day 49: Independent study.

Day 50: Independent study.

Day 51: Independent study.

Day 52: Independent study.

Day 53: Native Indian American guest speaker.

Day 54: The motion picture *The Indian Speaks* (National Film Board of Canada) is viewed and discussed.

Students who have made a depth study of primary source materials such as *I have Spoken: American History through the Voices of the Indians* edited by Virginia Armstrong (Swallow Press) and *This Country Was Ours: A Documentary History of the American Indian* edited by Virgil J. Vogel (Harper) share with the seminar evidence they have discovered substantiating the Indians' claim of injustice.

Day 55: The motion picture *Minorities: From Europe* (Coronet) is viewed and discussed.

Day 56: The motion picture *Who Needs You?* (Greaves) is viewed and discussed.

The students compile a list of topics they believe should be researched to build background knowledge of European-Americans and Spanish-speaking Americans.

A group leader is chosen to coordinate the individual students' selection and presentation of information on these topics.

A period of 10 days will be spent working independently and/or in small groups.

Day 57: Independent study.

Day 58: Independent study.

Day 59: Independent study.

Day 60: Independent study.

MODEL 34 (cont.)

Day 61: Independent study.

Day 62: Independent study.

Day 63: Independent study.

Day 64: Independent study.

Day 65: Independent study.

Day 66: Independent study.

Day 67: Representative from the U.S. Bureau of Immigration is guest speaker.

Day 68: The motion picture *Ellis Island* (The Americans: A Nation of Immigrants series) (Films, Inc.) is viewed and discussed.

Day 69: The Broadway play *West Side Story* is read and discussed.

Day 70: *West Side Story* continued.

Day 71: *West Side Story* continued.

Day 72: Students who have prepared mini-lectures on either Spanish-speaking Americans or European-Americans will be scheduled to deliver them today and continuing for the next four days.

Day 73: Student mini-lectures.

Day 74: Student mini-lectures.

Day 75: Student mini-lectures.

Day 76: Student mini-lectures.

Day 77: The motion picture *Prejudice: Causes, Consequences, Cures* (Films, Inc.) is viewed and discussed.

Day 78: The motion picture *No Man Is an Island* (Dana Productions) is viewed and discussed (see Model 35).

Day 79: The motion picture *Minorities: Patterns of Change* (Coronet) is viewed and discussed.

Day 80: The videotape *America's Kaleidoscope of Ethnic Minorities,* written and produced by seminar students, is viewed and discussed.

Day 81: The students present and then discuss their final summation papers.

Day 82: The students present and then discuss their final summation papers.

Day 83: The students present and then discuss their final summation papers.

Day 84: The students present and then discuss their final summation papers.

Day 85: The students summarize their learnings and concerns by discussing the topic "What of the Future?"

The seminar teacher discusses with the students the possibility of their electing to pursue their interest in ethnic culture as an independent study project during the next semester.

MODEL 35   PROGRAMMED LEARNING GUIDE: "NO MAN IS AN ISLAND"

Subject: English
Grade: 10, 11, 12
Unit: Seventeenth-Century English Literature
Topic: "No Man Is an Island" by John Donne
Introduction:

John Donne set forth a philosophy that has been unending in its influence on human thought since it was first stated in seventeenth-century England. Donne wrote: "No man is an sland, intire of itselfe; every man is a peece of the Continent, a part of the Maine . . . any man's death diminishes me, because I am involved in Mankinde; and therefore never send to know for whom the bell tolls; it tolls for thee."

MODEL 35 (cont.)

The purpose of this learning guide is twofold:
1. To acquaint you with John Donne as a human being as well as a poet, philosopher, and minister.
2. To provide opportunities for you to explore further the philosophy that no man is an island.

The following media are on reserve in the library:

Grace to a Wittey Sinner: A Life of Donne by Edward Le Comte.

Take Heed of Loving Me by Elizabeth Vining. A fictionalized biography of Donne.

"There Are No Islands Anymore" by Edna St. Vincent Millay. A poem written at the beginning of World War II pleading that the United States lay aside neutrality and keep England and France from being defeated by Germany.

The Growing Human Family by Minoo Masani. Chapter 12, "No Man Is an Island," sets forth the plea for one world.

For Whom the Bell Tolls by Ernest Hemingway, A novel of the Spanish Civil War.

The motion picture *No Man Is an Island* (Coronet).

The recording No Man Is an Island (Listening Library). Orson Welles reads nine great speeches that express Man's dependence on Man.

The Declaration of Interdependence (see Checklist H at the end of this model).

Check the following to discover information:

Indexicon (Harvard Classics)

    Topic: John Donne

Essay and General Literature Index

    Topics: Alienation

            Brotherhood of man

            John Donne

Readers' Guide to Periodical Literature

    Topics: Alienation

            Brotherhood of man

            John Donne

No Man Is an Island: An Inquiry into Alienation by the Center for Humanities. A sound-slide learning program including: 160 slides in two Kodak Carousel cartridges; two cassette tapes or recordings; and a learning guide.

CHECKLIST H: THE DECLARATION OF INTERDEPENDENCE*

Human progress having reached a high level through respect for the liberty and dignity of men, it has become desirable to re-affirm these evident truths:

That differences of race, color and creed are natural, and that diverse groups, institutions, and ideas are stimulating factors in the development of men;

That to promote harmony in diversity is a responsible task of religion and statesmanship;

That since no individual can express the whole truth, it is essential to treat with understanding and good will those whose views differ from our own;

That by the testimony of history intolerance is the door to violence, brutality, and dictatorship; and

That the realization of human interdependence and solidarity is the best guard of civilization.

*Will Durant and Ariel Durant, *A Dual Autobiography,* © 1977, p. 237. Reprinted by permission of Simon and Schuster.

Therefore, we solemnly resolve, and invite everyone to join in united action,

To uphold and promote human fellowship through mutual consideration and respect;

To champion human dignity and decency, and to safeguard these without distinction of race or color or creed;

To strive in concert with others to discourage all animosities arising from these differences, and to unite all groups in the fair play of civilized life.

Rooted in freedom, children of the same Divine Father, sharing everywhere a common human blood, we declare again that all men are brothers, and that mutual tolerance is the price of liberty.

MODEL 36   THE AMERICAN DECADES: A HUMANITIES APPROACH
TO AMERICAN CIVILIZATION*

Subject: American Civilization
Grade: 12
Introduction:

It would be naive to suggest that there is no successful interdisciplinary teaching being done in American schools today, whether by individuals or by teams. I have observed excellent programs, which pursue studies of humanities materials, usually Western civilization materials. Their concern for the important question of "What is Man?" contributes to the students' awareness of themselves, their human environment, and their relationship to the rest of humanity. These courses are vital in any American high school.

The program set forth in this book has a similar involvement with human experience; but while the others often span—in one course—centuries of materials, our concern is intense involvement with familiar American materials. Our use of the American decades means that students involve themselves not only with books, paintings, and music, but also with photographs, radio recordings, films, buildings, and people— parents, grandparents, neighbors, the community. It involves a whole range of experiences—oral history, genealogy, community interaction—which should develop an immediate concern for generational communication, a very live and active American humanism.

The multifaceted study of a decade builds upon itself, relates the parts to the whole, and continually suggests further curricular flexibility. Our program also accentuates detachment. If Einstein was right when he said that education is what is left after all the facts of school are forgotten, then it would seem that method is what we also want. A study of a decade is not just a study of facts, an immersion in rote memory. We teachers must always remind the students that this experience is useful to them long after they have forgotten the name of a novel or a painting. The ultimate goal must be clear: The students will have a methodology for understanding themselves and the American landscape for the rest of their lives.

Indeed, before the students even investigate a past decade, they must begin with their American value system, the theoretical basis for the "why's" that they will be asking throughout the course, if not throughout their lives. By examining American values, past and present, and how these values are transmitted, the students will better understand themselves and their friends and relatives. They will make that discovery as did one of our students: "I think more about everyday things." This thinking about everyday things is what we are after: the methodology of an American, both outsider and insider, exploring himself and his society.

The following pages develop a workable and flexible design for reaching these two goals in a high school classroom, though the material is highly adaptable for commu-

*This course is based on the National Council of Teachers of English publication *Teaching the Decades: A Humanities Approach to American Civilization* by Brooke Workman (Urbana, Ill.: National Council of Teachers of English, 1975).

MODEL 36 (cont.)

nity colleges and for four-year colleges interested in developing introductory courses in interdisciplinary studies. The immediate design is for one semester of any three American eras—the 1920s, the 1930s, or the time from 1945 to 1960. (The World War II era was excluded because its central focus is the global war, a subject well taught in American history courses, yet one which can be reviewed in relation to the 1930s and to 1945–60.) The design consists of usable daily lesson plans with flexible additions and alternatives. It is complete with guides and handouts of value to both teachers and students as catalysts for questions, discussion, and activities. There are guides for small grouping, projects, oral history, genealogy, and evaluation. There are subject matter guides and assignments. The appendix offers alternate course outlines for those who wish to pursue American Humanities in a trimester or full-year program. The bibliography includes information for obtaining books, recordings, films, and other course materials [all material not included here].

Admittedly, this course design seems, at first glance, to be aimed at schools with excellent financial and cultural resources. But careful study of the lessons, the alternatives, and the bibliography should reveal that American Humanities works for everyone because it deals with artifacts and people, with primary sources all around us. The resources—public libraries, local buildings, TV and radio, newspapers, relics in attics, and the community itself—are waiting for students and teachers. Lively sessions, rich with firsthand recollections, have resulted from inviting older citizens to talk and answer students' questions about facets of life in a past decade. Tape-recorded or transcribed from notes, such material can become part of a permanent classroom collection.

Studying a specific era, a decade, by the interdisciplinary approach is an intensive method of understanding American civilization and its values. But no matter which decade is investigated, the study should always be considered as an exercise in methodology, an introduction to a method which students can apply to any period of the past or to that future which comes long after they have left high school.

The subject matter is and should be fascinating. Certainly the events of the 1920s, the 1930s, and the 1945–60 period are rich with excitement. Certainly, this intense study will make students feel more comfortable, more knowledgeable, about the decade of their choice than they might become through other high school courses. Students will have more time to reflect and learn names and faces which were better known by their parents, grandparents, and great-grandparents. This understanding, this sharing, is very valuable, because students will grow to understand that people much like themselves were molded by circumstances and events. Certainly, the subject matter will be of value in other courses, though it should be stressed that American Humanities is not in competition with these other courses.

The focus must be made clear: the study of one decade is a means to understanding American life in its totality. Students should see their roles as insiders and outsiders who can appreciate and objectively evaluate American culture.

The semester course which follows is, in fact, three courses, which can be expanded into two or three trimesters or into a two-semester course. There are also suggestions for future seminars and courses, as well as an indirect suggestion for other American Humanities interdisciplinary courses, other decade or thematic courses. No matter what the course, the concern is for learning a methodology.

The lessons are designed to develop the American Humanities method. Each lesson sets a daily or long-range American Humanities goal; each lesson describes procedures and alternatives for reaching each goal, which, in turn, should relate to previous goals in the total piecing together of the American Humanities puzzle.

Two concepts underlie our program: (1) Students should gain an understanding of themselves and their society by intense examination of familiar American materials which span various disciplines. (2) The methodology for understanding these materials, involvement and detachment, should provide the basis for future inquiry. An American should be able to appreciate and to analyze the fabric of American life in its parts and in its totality.

MODEL 36 (cont.)

Students and teachers and courses should be evaluated. All of us want to know "how we're doing." Most of us need some kind of evaluation to remind us if we have reached our objectives, if we are growing in skill and understanding of the course. All of us seem to thrive on positive evaluation and fear negative criticism. And all of us, I think, need to have some experience with self-evaluation.

This American Humanities program is predicated on the belief that varieties of evaluation benefit everyone—student evaluation of instructor, instructor evaluation of student, student evaluation of student, and periodic self-evaluation and course evaluation. But it is not necessarily based on any one system—behavioral objectives, a bell-shaped grading curve, the use of traditional objective tests and uniform letter grades. It seems to me that these are matters of choice for each school, each teacher, each department, each group of students—all continually evaluating with the system they find most effective and comfortable.

But I will suggest a system of evaluation which has been used with American Humanities, a system noted in the lesson plans but not designed as an ultimate answer to evaluation.

On the first day, the students are told that some educational heresies are going to be committed in the course: no tests, except a final take-home which is described on the course overview sheet; the final test will not be over facts but over the method of the course; conventional letter grades will not be given. Instead, students will be graded H, S, and U, for highly satisfactory, satisfactory, or unsatisfactory work, on the basis of teacher and student observer evaluations (though, as later noted, many students may wish the A through F grades for term projects) and nine-week self-evaluations. His H, S, or U will be the final grade, unless the instructor calls for a conference to discuss his disagreement with the student's choice. Such a conference could be called for a variety of reasons: (1) The instructor might feel the student grade is too low or too high. (2) The conference will be an in-depth discussion of the grade and perhaps an occasion for bargaining. Past experience indicates that few problems arise with self-evaluation and the conference system, probably because it is a positive system of evaluation, useful to everyone concerned.

Students are also told that they will keep class folders for assignments and for evaluation sheets containing records of each assignment. These folders will assist the student at self-evaluation time.

The assignments range from written work, oral presentation, and small group efforts to a semester project which is an important instrument for self- and course evaluation. The projects test the student's total understanding of the methodology. The students should be reassured that the projects will be the outgrowth of careful planning, class instruction in research and writing, a step-by-step system from proposal to final outline, and considerable time for research and student-teacher conferences. The projects are usually considered one of the most valuable and enjoyable parts of the course, since they are the product of student interest and choice, whether they be term papers or multimedia presentations. In fact, the project is one for which students have wished a more elaborate grading system than *H, S,* and *U.* It seems that even the teacher comments—often considerable—on the papers and in the folders are just not enough.

Whatever the methods of measurement and evaluation, the spirit of American Humanities should be positive and cooperative. Each lesson, each assignment, each experience, should give individual and mutual satisfaction to everyone involved in the course, the satisfaction of increased understanding of oneself and one's American civilization.

Ultimately, this course deals with questions which seek answers. Basic questions, basic answers: What are American values? Why did Americans believe or enjoy or create this during the decade? Do we believe and enjoy and continue to create this now? What does the artifact say about Americans, then and now? How do these ideas and artifacts relate to each other? What does the total relationship mean? In sum, what does it mean to be an American human being?

MODEL 36 (cont.)

AMERICAN HUMANITIES: TENTATIVE SCHEDULE, 1920s*

The Idea of Culture

1. Orientation
2. Meeting Each Other
3. Culture and Values in Children's Literature
4. Dominant Values and the Top Ten of TV
5. Heroes, Heroines, and Consensus Seeking
6. Other Cultures and Culture Shock
7. Film: *The Humanities Approach*
8. Theories of American Civilization
9. Artifact Day
10. Artifact Day

History: The Decade, 1920s

11. Orientation: Terms and Tentative Schedule
12. Read *Only Yesterday:* Chapters 1, 5, 6, 8, 10, and pages 266–70, 284–89
13. Film: *The Golden Twenties*
14. Filmstrip-Record or Documentary Records
15. Formation of History Small Groups and Activity Committees (e.g., Handbook, Artifacts, Bulletin Board, Radio)
16. Reading, Research, Small-Group Procedures
17. History Small Group 1
18. History Small Group 2
19. History Small Group 3
20. History Small Group 4
21. Class Consensus on History; Orientation to Oral History, Genealogy
22. Open Day
23. Oral History Presentations
24. Oral History Presentations
25. Oral History and Genealogy Presentations
26. Orientation: Term Projects

Popular Culture—Radio, Films, Best Sellers

27. Radio Recordings
28. Radio Recordings
29. Decade Films
30. Decade Films
31. Decade Films
32. Orientation: Best Sellers
33. Reading; Proposals Due; First Conferences
34. Reading; First Conferences
35. Reading; First Conferences

36. *Ragged Dick*
37. *The Great Gatsby*
38. *The Man Nobody Knows*
39. *Babbitt* or *Main Street*
40. Self-Evaluation Day

Architecture and Painting as Artifacts

41. Architecture
42. Frank Lloyd Wright and American Architecture
43. Film: *Frank Lloyd Wright*
44. Orientation: Painting as Art and Artifact
45. The Armory Show
46. Study of Decade Paintings
47. Study of Decade Paintings
48. Study of Decade Paintings
49. Student Teaching of Paintings
50. Student Teaching of Paintings
51. Film on Decade Artist
52. Student Teaching
53. Field Trip: Art Gallery
54. Student Teaching
55. Student Teaching

Poetry and Plays as Artifacts

56. Orientation: Poetry as Artifact
57. Preparation for Small Groups
58. Small Group 1: Poetry
59. Small Group 2: Poetry
60. Small Group 3: Poetry
61. Orientation: Plays as Artifacts
62. Readings and Rehearsal; Resource Person
63. Reading and Rehearsal
64. *The Hairy Ape*
65. *They Knew What They Wanted*
66. *Porgy*
67. Small Group One-Act Presentation
68. Project Final Outline Due; Discussion of Final Project
69. Second Conferences
70. Second Conferences

Dancing and Music as Cultural Exemplars

71. Dancing
72. Dancing
73. Orientation: Music as Cultural Expression
74. Formation of Music Committees
75. Committee Planning Day
76. Music Committee Presentation
77. Music Committee Presentation
78. Music Committee Presentation
79. Music Committee Presentation

*From Brooke Workman, *Teaching the Decades: A Humanities Approach to American Civilization* (Urbana, Ill.: National Council of Teachers of English, 1975), pp. 5–6.

MODEL 36 (cont.)

Conclusion

80. Term Papers Due
81. Student Project Presentations
82. Student Project Presentations
83. Student Project Presentations
84. Student Project Presentations
85. Student Project Presentations
86. Discussion and Selection of Final Test Artifacts
87. Writing the Final Test
88. Writing the Final Test
89. Return of Term Papers; Discussion
90. Self-Evaluation; Course Evaluation

Final Test

During the last week of American Humanities, you will select a large envelope containing artifacts. You are to imagine that you are living in the distant future—say 3000 A.D.—and on another planet. You have discovered a new planet on your travels, a barren planet on which you find a time capsule containing this envelope. After you return to your home planet, your anthropology society asks that you present a paper in which you describe the artifacts, theorize as to their meaning, and expand upon your analysis by suggesting what you think this barren planet once had for a culture. You are able to translate language, though you will only know what the artifacts say in themselves. Your report will be from three to five pages.

AMERICAN HUMANITIES: NAMES AND TERMS OF THE 1920s*

Gertrude Ederle	Four Horsemen	W. C. Fields
Douglas Fairbanks	Emile Coué	Tom Mix
The Galloping Ghost	Floyd Collins	Erich von Stroheim
KDKA	Enrico Caruso	*The Great Gatsby*
The Jazz Singer	Peaches and Daddy	*The Saturday Evening Post*
flapper	Eugene Debs	bobbed hair
Volstead Act	The Red Scare	Charlie Chaplin
F. Scott Fitzgerald	normalcy	John Marin
Monkey Trial	Calvin Coolidge	Bing Crosby
Man O' War	*Rhapsody in Blue*	Bix Beiderbecke
Aimee Semple McPherson	Charles Lindbergh	Fats Waller
H. L. Mencken	Jazz Age	Blind Lemon Jefferson
Sinclair Lewis	speakeasies	Frank Lloyd Wright
Will Rogers	Billy Sunday	Bobby Franks
flivver	Clarence Darrow	Laurel and Hardy
George Herman Ruth	Paul Whiteman	Gertrude Stein
The Sheik	*Main Street*	Ernest Hemingway
Spirit of St. Louis	Bruce Barton	Charleston
Teapot Dome	*The Waste Land*	Harlem Renaissance
Sacco and Vanzetti	"Avalon"	George Bellows
Eugene O'Neill	*This Side of Paradise*	*The Smart Set*
Florenz Ziegfeld	Hal Roach	*What Price Glory?*
Rudolph Valentino	Harry Houdini	Edna St. Vincent Millay
St. Valentine's Day Massacre	Dorothy Dix	Bobby Jones
Rudy Vallee	Carl Sandburg	Henry Ford
Gene Tunney	*Babbitt*	Knute Rockne
Al Smith	KKK	bathtub gin
Al Capone	Jimmy Walker	marathon dancing
bootleggers	Warren Harding	Herbert Hoover
Black Six Scandal	Louis Armstrong	Miss America
Black Thursday	Mah Jongg	skyscrapers
Clara Bow	Tin Lizzie	knickers
Jack Dempsey	Al Jolson	Freud
	Buster Keaton	

*From Brooke Workman, *Teaching the Decades: A Humanities Approach to American Civilization* (Urbana, Ill.: National Council of Teachers of English, 1975), p. 34.

MODEL 37:   THE CRUCIBLE

Subject: Honors English–Social Studies

Unit: *The Crucible* by Arthur Miller

Grade: 11

Goal: To provide opportunity for the students who have just completed an in-depth study of the McCarthy Era to compare the witch hunt of the 1950s with the Salem Witch Trials of 1692.

Teaching objectives:

1. The students will build their knowledge of the Salem Witch Trials by reading primary source materials.
2. The students will build their knowledge of the McCarthy hearings trials by reading primary source materials and by viewing videotapes of actual Senate hearings.
3. The students after reading *The Crucible* will analyze the main characters of the play and try to discover why intolerance and superstition travel in tandem.
4. The students will compare the mob hysteria of the Colonial Period with that of the United States during the McCarthy hearings.

Teaching procedure:

1. The play *The Crucible* is read in paperback format (Bantam Books).
2. The students, following the reading of the play, are given two weeks to build their understanding of both the McCarthy hearings and the Salem Witch Trials by working in the library media center where material such as the following is available:

PRINTED RESOURCES: Salem Witchcraft

Annals of Witchcraft in New England and Elsewhere in the United States from Their First Settlement: Drawn Up from Unpublished and Other Well Authenticated Records of the Alleged Operations of Witches and Their Instigator, the Devil (Somerset)

The Devil in Massachusetts: A Modern Inquiry into the Salem Witch Trials by Marion Starkey (Doubleday)

The Devil's Shadow: The Story of Witchcraft in Massachusetts by Clifford Alderman (Messner)

Mirror for Witches by Esther Forbes (Houghton Mifflin)

New England's Place in the History of Witchcraft by George Burr, facsimile ed. (Books for Libraries)

Records of Salem Witchcraft, copies from the original documents, 2 vols., American History, Politics and Law series (Da Capo)

Tituba of Salem Village by Ann Petry (Crowell)

Witchcraft at Salem by Chadwick Hanson (Braziller)

Witchcraft of Salem Village by Shirley Jackson (Random House)

NONPRINT RESOURCES: Salem Witchcraft

The Crucible (recording—Spoken Arts)

The Witchcraft of Salem Village (recording—Enrichment Records)

PRINTED RESOURCES: McCarthy hearings

Congressional Record, 1952–1953

Day of Shame by Charles E. Potter (Coward)

Freedom in Jeopardy: The McCarthy Years by Burt Hirschfeld, Milestones in History series (Messner)

Joe McCarthy and McCarthyism: The Hate That Taunts America by Roberta Feuerlicht (McGraw-Hill)

See It Now ed. by Edward ·R. Murrow and Fred W. Friendly (Simon and Schuster)

Senator Joe McCarthy by Richard Rovere (Harcourt)

The Time of the Toad: A Study of Inquisition in America by Dalton Trumbo (Harper)

NONPRINT RESOURCES: McCarthy hearings

McCarthy Senate Hearings (University Microfilm)

MODEL 38:   PROGRAMMED LEARNING GUIDE: "APPOMATTOX AND THE END"

Subject: Honors American History

Grade: 11

Topic: Appomattox and the End

Subtopic 1: As the battered, once-proud Army of Northern Virginia neared final, crushing defeat, what were some of the reactions of those on both sides who participated in these grim days?

Sources:

Eisenschiml, Otto. *Eyewitness: The Civil War as We Lived It,* chapter 20, "The Curtain Falls," pp. 666–688.

Bradford, Ned, ed. *Battles and Leaders of the Civil War,* pp. 601–607.

Subtopic 2: To set the scene, read a brief description of the bitter fighting waged up to the day of the surrender.

Sources:

Fuller, J. F. C. *Grant and Lee: A Study in Personality and Generalship,* pp. 234–241.

Dupuy, R. Ernest. *The Compact History of the Civil War,* pp. 408–413.

Subtopic 3: What degree of destruction at Petersburg and Richmond immediately preceded Lee's surrender? How would this influence Lee's decision?

Sources:

Ellis, Keith. *The American Civil War,* Putnam Pictorial Sources series, pp. 44–45.

"The Civil War (From Gettysburg to Appomattox)," Study Prints 6–10.

Subtopic 4: An exchange of notes, under a flag of truce, between the opposing commanders preceded their historic meeting on April 9, 1865. What was the tone of these notes, and what reactions were expressed by officers on either side?

Sources:

The Way to Appomattox, vol. 4 of *Battles and Leaders of the Civil War,* pp. 729–747.

Henry, Robert Selph. *The Story of the Confederacy,* pp. 459–464.

Subtopic 5: How are these events reported in secondary sources?

Sources:

Catton, Bruce. *This Hallowed Ground: The Story of the Union Side of the Civil War,* pp. 385–390.

Dupuy, R. Ernest. *The Compact History of the Civil War,* pp. 408–418.

Randall, J. G. *The Divided Union,* pp. 525–529.

Subtopic 6: Read Grant's account of Lee's surrender. What attitudes toward General Lee and toward the defeated Confederacy does he impart?

Source:

Davie, Emily, comp. *Profile of America: An Autobiography of the U.S.A.,* pp. 282–286.

Subtopic 7: To the victor goes the privilege of dictating the terms of surrender to the vanquished. In what way would you characterize the terms Grant dictated? His attitude toward the defeated army?

Sources:

The Way to Appomattox, pp. 729–746.

American History in Sound (Disc recording; listen to Record 2, Side 1, Band 1)

Subtopic 8: On the day following the signing of the surrender, General Lee bade farewell to his troops. How did his address come to be written? How would you characterize it?

Sources:

The Way to Appomattox, p. 747.

American History in Sound (Disc recording; Record 2, Side 1. End of Band 1)

Subtopic 9: Most students of U.S. history are familiar with the course of events in Ulysses S. Grant's life after the tragic conflict, but what became of General Robert E. Lee?

MODEL 38 (cont.)

Sources:

Peattie, Donald Culross. *Parade with Banners.* Read the chapter titled "Lee's Greatest Victory," pp. 147–155.

Carmer, Carl. *Cavalcade of America.* Read "President Robert E. Lee," pp. 130–133.

Optional activity 1: Review what you have learned by reading pp. 582–589, and viewing the splendid illustrations in American Heritage, *The American Heritage Picture History of the Civil War.*

Optional activity 2: Prepare a report of your findings to share with your classmates. View the filmstrip E-19, *The Road to Appomattox.* Decide whether or not you would like to use the filmstrip to illustrate your report. If you decide yes, would you show the entire strip or select certain frames?

Optional activity 3: Much is made of the contrasting impressions the two leaders made at the McLean Farm House. Read the parts in Fuller's *Grant & Lee: A Study in Personality and Generalship,* in which the author analyzes the personalities of the two men. With the insights you have already gained and with Fuller's analysis, prepare a comparison of the two men.

Optional activity 4: If you are interested in a different perspective for understanding the final, tragic, confused, and haunting moments of the Civil War, you might enjoy the diary of a Southern woman who witnessed, at first hand, the collapse of the Confederacy. Her account is bitter. Can you find human reasons for that bitterness?

Source:
Le Conte, Emma. *When the World Ended: The Diary of Emma Le Conte.*

Optional activity 5: At the end of the war, both Grant and Lee, giants of warfare, spoke eloquently on behalf of peace. Read the April 22, 1865, issue of *Harper's Weekly* (on microfilm), specifically, the article on p. 243, which discusses what the attitude of its Northern readers should be in regard to the defeated Lee and the cause he represented. What does this augur for the future and the making of the peace? Examine other issues for more evidence.

Optional activity 6: If you wish a deeper understanding of Robert E. Lee, the man, try Douglas Southall Freeman's *Lee of Virginia.* Freeman's four-volume life of Robert E. Lee won a Pulitzer Prize. This book was written expressly for young adults and shows the same devotion that made his earlier work a classic.

Optional activity 7: View the motion picture *U. S. Grant: I Remember Appomattox* (Coronet). In this film, Grant said, "Sometimes, because of circumstances, a man never lives out the life he was meant for." Do you think this statement is a perceptive commentary on Grant's own career as general and as president? This film showed the surrender at Appomattox through the eyes of Grant. Write the narrative for a film sequel showing the events of the day from the viewpoint of Robert E. Lee.

MODEL 39: AMERICAN ENGLISH: INHERITED, MANUFACTURED, AND FRACTURED

Subject: Honors English

Grade: 12

Unit: American English: Inherited, Manufactured, and Fractured

Goal: This unit will provide opportunities for the student to understand, appreciate, and value American English as the product of American society and as a reflection of the culture, folkways, and characteristic psychology of the American people.

Teaching Objectives:

1. This unit has been designed to develop these basic understandings:

   Language is a social tool or social organism—the product of the society that employs it.

   Language is not a fixed, immutable, circumscribed object but is an ever-changing body of facts and habits.

MODEL 39 (cont.)

The use of language depends in large part on such factors as home environment, education, occupation, recreation, and political and social involvement.

Speech is but one mode of communication; nonverbal language is also a basic communications skill.

American English possesses certain qualities peculiar to itself for while it has maintained much of the mother tongue it reflects unique facets of American cultural and social history and development.

American culture is pluralistic and far from homogeneous; therefore, certain linguistic features are peculiar to certain regions and are not general to others.

Recognizing propaganda, shoddy advertising, and political double-talk is a basic competency essential for functional literacy.*

2. This unit has been designed to develop these attitudes and appreciations:

Appreciation for the student's language heritage and the complex nature of language—its symbol system, structure, history, power, diversity, and beauty.

Respect for and interest in linguistic differences among diverse cultures.

Curiosity as to why linguistic differences exist.

Satisfaction and challenge in word exploration and study.

Appreciation that to be literate in a world rich in the symbols of language means to be able to communicate ideas clearly and to analyze and *enjoy* what is seen, heard, and read.†

Teaching Procedure:

1. This unit will be offered as a six-week elective course.
2. This unit will employ the following teaching/learning strategies and methods:

Each student will share responsibility for building background knowledge in depth, leading class discussions, participating in dramatizations, and in designing and conducting opinion polls.

After class orientation to the unit, each student will have unlimited time to work in the high school library to build his or her knowledge in an area of specialization.

Procedural Outline:

1. The class will be oriented to the study of American English by viewing and discussing the sound filmstrip series *Language and Its Mysteries* (Centron Educational Films).

The following concepts will be stressed:

Language is uniquely human.

Language is a learned social tool.

Languages come in families.

The story of language is the story of human activity.

2. The class will view the following motion pictures (Coronet) and then will synthesize understandings gained to date:‡

The English Language: How It Changes

The English Language: Patterns of Usage

3. The class will read and discuss *Making Sense: Exploring Semantics and Critical Thinking* by Robert R. Potter, 2nd ed. (Globe). The following topics will be stressed:

*Harold G. Shane, *Curriculum Change Toward the 21st Century* (Washington, D.C.: National Education Association, 1977), Premise XXVIII, p. 68.
†Ibid.
‡These two Coronet motion pictures reinforce and extend the concepts presented in the Coronet series "Discovering Language" introduced previously in the sixth-grade unit "The Wizardry of Words" (see Model 27). This is an illustration of Harold G. Shane's concept of the "seamless curriculum."

MODEL 39 (cont.)

Making Sense is a book about words. It is about how we use words, and how words *use* us.

Not until people understand how words use them can they use words to communicate effectively. And not until people communicate more effectively can they solve the problems that face the world today.

Gobbledygook, long common in government and law, is now spreading to the mass media. It is a good example of verbal pollution.

Words are related to thought. Thought is related to behavior, and behavior is related to everything in the world around us.

An *operational definition* tells *what to do* to experience the thing defined.

Alfred Korzybski in *Science and Sanity* (International Nonaristotelian Library Publishing Co., dist. by Institute of General Semantics) stated that too many people mistake the events in their own nervous system for events in the outside world.

Our feelings and emotions color the words we use.

Words are rascals. This is the rule of semantics. The meaning of a word is not entirely contained in the word itself. Meaning depends on context, on when and where the word is used.

Semantic reaction refers to the total response of the whole organism—mental, emotional, physical.

Semanticists are people from all walks of life who have a common interest in language, thought, and behavior.

The two nonprofit organizations serving as headquarters for semantic inquiry and education are:

Institute of General Semantics, Lakeville, Conn. 06039

International Society for General Semantics, Box 2469, San Francisco, Calif. 94126

4. Following class orientation experiences, each student will work in the library completing his or her independent linguistics research project and will, at the conclusion of the research, share with the class the knowledge he or she has gained. The research topics and activities offered for student consideration include the following:

Using these three dictionaries, the *Oxford English Dictionary, The Random House Dictionary of the English Language,* and *Webster's Third New International Dictionary of the English Language,* compare the definitions for the following linguistic terms:

American English	Nonverbal communication
Black English	Parole
Langue	Phatic language
Lexicon	Regional dialects
Linguistics	Social dialects
Nonstandard English	Standard English

Discover Professor Henry Higgins's theory concerning English dialects.

Sources: *My Fair Lady* by Alan Lerner and Frederick Lowe (New American Library)

   My Fair Lady (Columbia Masterworks Recording)

Discover the six dialect areas in the United States.

Sources: *American Speaking* (National Council of Teachers of English Recording)

MODEL 39 (cont.)

Dialects and Dialect Learning Kit (National Council of Teachers of English)

Discover the meaning and the psychological use of "doublespeak." What is the significance of the National Council of Teachers of English Doublespeak Award?

Sources: *Double-Speak in America* by Mario Pei (Hawthorn)

Weasel Words: The Art of Saying What You Don't Mean by Mario Pei (Harper)

Words in Sheep's Clothing by Mario Pei (Hawthorn)

Discovering the stories behind people's names.

Sources: *First Names First* by Leslie Alan Dunkling (Universe Books)

New Dictionary of American Family Names by Elsdon Smith (Harper)

What's in a Name by Favius Friedman (Scholastic)

Discover the stories behind place names.

Sources: *Our Language: The Story of the Words We Use* by Eloise Lambert (Lippincott)

Place Words by Bill Severn (Washburn)

Words on the Map by Isaac Asimov (Houghton)

Word Origins and Their Romantic Stories by Wilfred Funk (Funk and Wagnalls)

Discover the word histories of scientific terms.

Sources: *More Words of Science* by Isaac Asimov (Houghton)

Naming Living Things by Sarah Riedman (Rand McNally)

Word Origins and Their Romantic Stories by Wilfred Funk (Funk and Wagnalls)

Words of Science by Isaac Asimov (Houghton)

Discover stories of curious word origins.

Sources: *A Hog on Ice and Other Curious Expressions* by Charles Funk (Harper)

Horsefeathers and Other Curious Words by Charles Funk (Harper)

Thereby Hangs a Tale: Stories of Curious Word Origins by Charles Funk (Harper)

What's Behind the Word? by Harold Longman (Coward)

What's in a Word by Harold Longman (Coward)

Discover word histories for your favorite sport.

Sources: *Baseball Language: A Running Press Glossary* by Richard Scholl (Running Press)

Sports Lingo: A Dictionary of the Language of Sports by Harvey Frommer (Atheneum)

Discover the meaning of the word *slang*, and why slang plays an important part in the American English scene; an excellent source of information is found in the Introduction, Foreword and/or Preface of the following:

Sources: *Dictionary of Slang and Unconventional English* by Eric Partridge (Macmillan)

New Dictionary of Americanisms by Sylvia Clapin (Gale)

Our Language: The Story of the Words We Use by Eloise Lambert (Lothrop)

Slang Today and Yesterday by Eric Partridge (Routledge and Kegan Paul)

MODEL 39 (cont.)

Discover why Mario Pei refers to "pidgin English" as "the adult, international, and interracial version of hyporcorism."

Sources: *Book of Pidgin English* by John J. Murphy (Smith & Patterson)

The Many Hues of English by Mario Pei (Knopf)

Our Language: The Story of the Words We Use by Eloise Lambert (Lothrop)

Discover how Clarence L. Barnhart and his research staff select new words for inclusion in a dictionary of new English words; check the *World Book Year Book* for each year subsequent to the publication of *The Barnhart Dictionary of New English since 1963* (Harper and Row) to discover the new words contained in the Year Books' "Dictionary Supplement."

Sources: *The Barnhart Dictionary of New English since 1963* ed. by Clarence L. Barnhart (Harper)

World Book Year Book, 1974–to date (Field Enterprises)

Discover what is meant by "P. D. English" and why it has continued as a distinctive cultural dialect for over two hundred years.

Sources: *Hex Marks the Spot in the Pennsylvania Dutch Country* by Ann Hark (Lippincott)

Pennsylvania Dutch by Fredric Klees (Macmillan)

Pennsylvania Dutch Cook Book by J. George Frederick (Peter Smith)

Traditionally Pennsylvania Dutch by Edward C. Smith and Virginia Thompson (Hastings House)

MODEL 40 CONTEMPORARY AMERICAN CULTURE*

Subject: Honors American History
Grade: 12
Interdisciplinary unit. This is the equivalent of from six to eight week's work in four subjects (English, Social Studies, Art, and Music) and requires a time block of three class periods per day. Activities are designed to cross subject lines while providing an abundance of work in basic skills (note the activities requiring writing). In a completely interdisciplinary program similar units in the sciences (Math and Science) and electives would be occurring concurrently with the attached unit.

A school year consists of from four to six units each in Humanities, Sciences, and Electives, or an equivalent of from twelve to eighteen units of learning.

UNIT I. CONTEMPORARY AMERICAN CULTURE

OVERALL UNIT OBJECTIVE

An understanding and comprehension of the character, direction, and concerns of Contemporary American cultures.

CONTRIBUTORY OBJECTIVE NO. 1

An understanding and working knowledge of the components of a culture.

Activities

1. Establish and post on a bulletin board a working definition of the word *culture*.
2. Prepare and display a collage showing component parts or portions of a culture (consider S.A., C.A., U.S., and Can.).

*Contemporary American Cultures, *The Humanities Horizon,* A Britannica Newsletter published by Instructional Services Division, Encyclopaedia Britannica Educational Corp. 5, no. 2 (March 1972): 5–10. Used with permission of Bud Moore, Director of Language Arts, West Orange Public School, N.J.

MODEL 40 (cont.)

3. Prepare and present a medley of songs showing components of a culture.
4. Read *The Outsiders*.
   (A) Choose one scene, write a script, and present a dramatization designed to show some components of American culture.
   (B) Write a thoughtful, well-organized paper contrasting one particular aspect of Pony Boy's culture with a similar aspect of your culture.
5. Make up your own unique language, spoken by the members of a special "culture." Make rules for usage, and carry out some conversations in your invented language. Write a paper explaining some of the problems you encountered in developing a language, and point out some qualities necessary to an effective language.
6. Compose and post on the bulletin board one illustrated list showing the "free" things in life and another showing those things in life which require money. Show in your illustrations how important money is to a contented and happy life in America.

CONTRIBUTORY OBJECTIVE NO. 2

An understanding and appreciation of the role of the arts in contemporary American cultures.

Activities

1. Prepare and present a multimedia presentation showing your concept of contemporary American culture.
2. Collect examples of music, literature, art, film, and sculpture whose purpose is to convey social criticism. Display and comment on your examples to others.
3. Collect examples of music, literature, art, film and sculpture whose purpose is primarily commercial. Display and comment on your examples to the class.
4. Collect and bring to class examples of music, literature, art, film and sculpture that bear no recognizable relationship to contemporary American life and explain to the group your reasons for selecting these examples.
5. Create a work of music or literature or art that is a personal social comment on contemporary American culture. Display your commentary and have your audience evaluate its effectiveness.
6. Read and report on an American contemporary novel which deals with protest. Create a bulletin board or mobile to be a part of your report.
7. Using art as propaganda, try to create sympathy for or feeling against a particular subject. Explain in a carefully written paper, how you tried to accomplish this and what your results were.
8. View several TV commercials and determine what makes them works of art. Using your conclusions create 2 TV commercials, one which you regard as a work of art, and one which you do not regard as a work of art. Display these to the class.
9. Keep a log of TV shows you watch for one week and divide them into categories according to their purpose. Then tabulate the number of hours devoted to each category, and form some conclusions concerning the role of television in your life. Write a brief report on your findings.
10. Prepare an artistic presentation centered around the theme of drugs in contemporary American culture. Be sure your presentation makes a specific comment that others can understand. Have your audience state what they believe the comment to be.
11. Create and present a skit that reveals a personal opinion or interest or feeling.
12. Create a collage that exemplifies art as either a celebration of life, or an escape from reality, or as a purely aesthetic experience. Display the collage on a bulletin board.
13. Invite a number of artists, writers, composers, etc., to talk to the class regarding their concepts of how and why man creates. Then write a paper, make a film, or give a multimedia presentation concerning the results of these talks.
14. Take photographs of slides showing the role of art in industrial design. Present and explain these to the class.
15. Find and display one single-frame cartoon that makes a social or political statement. In a sentence or two indicate the significance of the statement made. Mount the cartoon and statement on colored paper ready for a bulletin board display.

MODEL 40 (cont.)

16. Invite a resource person in to discuss and/or demonstrate the role of dance in contemporary American culture. Try to prepare your own dance to express a particular emotion or reaction.

17. See a contemporary American play and if possible, communicate with the professionals who are involved in the production of the play. Write a report to be shared with the class detailing some of their observations concerning the role of the theatre in contemporary American society.

18. Construct a photographic exhibit centered around a theme relevant to contemporary American culture. Display your exhibit in a prominent place.

19. Create or display examples of art that comment on or involve the role of technology in contemporary American society. Write a brief explanation to go with each exhibit.

20. Prepare a wall display showing contemporary use and treatment of the American flag. Consider the following areas: fashion, politics, advertising, art, etc. Draw some written conclusions about the significance of your display, and share these with your classmates.

21. Create a display showing and explaining official proper and/or legal ways of displaying the American flag. Put up this display in a conspicuous location.

22. Write a carefully constructed theme, after viewing the displays of activities 19 and 20, explaining your point of view about contemporary uses of the American flag.

23. Wear or bring something to school that indicates the influence of a culture other than that of the U.S. Explain this influence.

24. Demonstrate or display examples of contemporary American folk art. In a paper explain the role of the examples displayed in contemporary American culture.

25. Visit a local art show and select one particular work of art. Write a paper detailing your concept of the artist's purpose in creating the work.

26. Assume that you are a member of an ethnic group other than your own. Write a poem or short story (or any other short piece) expressing your identity.

27. Following a survey of contemporary American poetry, select and analyze one contemporary American poem which expresses a particular aspect of American culture.

28. Invite a city planner to discuss with the class the nature of city planning. Then draw up and display your own general plan for an effective city.

29. Collect and present to the class 2 examples of technological art. Give some personal reactions to these in your presentation. What do you feel the artist is trying to express in each case?

30. Write three letters to the editor representing three contrasting points of view regarding the role of rock music festivals as a social force. Display copies of your letters on the bulletin board.

31. Examine censorship of the arts in the U.S. today, and prepare both sides of a debate on this topic. You will be selected to represent one side only. Hold a classroom debate, and ask the audience to write short papers judging the effectiveness of the debate.

32. Collect, display, demonstrate or create examples of art used as propaganda. With each, provide an explanation of what it is to accomplish.

33. Bring in two reproductions of American art, one to represent idealism, the other realism. Be able to defend your choice in a debate entitled, "Realism or Idealism in American Art?"

CONTRIBUTORY OBJECTIVE NO. 3

An awareness of the nature of social organization within contemporary American cultures.

Activities

1. Watch five family situation TV programs. Compare and contrast the situations of American families.
   As an individual assignment, prepare a report indicating your findings.
   As a group assignment, present a panel discussion of your findings.

2. Prepare a TV tape or dramatic presentation showing your views of a contemporary family situation. List those characteristics you plan to emphasize. Show your tape or

presentation to a group and have them determine how effectively you emphasized the intended characteristics.

3. Prepare a report on the changing role of the family in American culture.
4. Through a multimedia collage, indicate the fragmentation of American culture into various social organizations. (Use a variety of these organizations.) Determine how many organizations your viewers can list, and record your effectiveness.
5. Collect and perform pop music that reflects the aims and/or character of various social organizations in U.S. culture. Have your audience list the aims or characteristics which they observe. Compare these lists with your purpose and determine your effectiveness.

CONTRIBUTORY OBJECTIVE NO. 4: COMMUNICATION

Insight into the role of media and communication in determining the values and nature (pattern-character) of American cultures.

Activities

1. Watch several family situation programs and several commercials. Compare and contrast the family situations presented in each. Consider each program and its commercial. Prepare a means of evaluating your findings and prepare a research paper presenting your results.
2. Watch 3 separate TV programs at varying times of the day. Consider the nature of the programs and the nature of the commercials. Prepare a chart, and illustrate your findings.
3. In a written paragraph, compare and contrast the reporting of a news article in a newspaper and TV news show.
4. Using your knowledge of the impact of media, start a fad; document the process you used, and the results of your project. Post your results on the bulletin board.
5. View the film *Communications Explosion*. Prepare a visual display of your own interpretations of the effect of this explosion on your contemporary society.
6. Hold a bumper sticker contest to promote an idea, value, or change within the school community. Record the results of your efforts and post them on a bulletin board.
7. Create a visual display illustrating different sides of the ecology problem. Show how corporations, citizens, groups, government, etc., use mass media to get across their side of the issue.
8. Examine the case of the Pentagon Papers. Show in a visual display how this case illustrates a problem of communication and the free press in a free society.
9. Use graphics to "sell something" to your classmates—a product of your own invention, or an idea or value. Record your effectiveness.
10. View carefully some commercials and make a chart showing what feelings or values are associated with each product or service being promoted.
11. Invite some persons to discuss with students the responsibilities and potential of different media in light of social problems. Record the results of this discussion in an essay.

CONTRIBUTORY OBJECTIVE NO. 5

An awareness and understanding of the American Dream, its dimensions, its realization, and its cultural significance.

Activities

1. Establish and post on a bulletin board a working definition of the "American Dream."
2. Extract from particular historical documents statements that you think reflect the American Dream. Describe 3 instances in which these ideals have and 3 instances in which these ideals have not been realized. Use an illustrated chart for displaying your descriptions.
3. Assume that you are a candidate for political office. Your platform is the American Dream. From the speeches and/or writings of one or more of the following persons extract what you believe to be their version of the American Dream and construct a political speech based on their ideas. Present this speech to the class:

MODEL 40 (cont.)

Martin Luther King	Eldridge Cleaver
Ronald Reagan	Ogden Reid
Richard Ottinger	Shirley Chisholm
George Wallace	Lester Maddox

You may add to this list any political figure of similar stature.

4. Invite a legislator from the national or state level to discuss with students problems involved in the realization of the American Dream. Plan and display a course of action to remedy some of these problems.

5. Prepare and present a large-group presentation showing how contemporary popular music reflects concern with the American Dream.

6. Compose a series of songs to be collected under the title "The American Dream Is Alive and Well and Living in Rye Town." Present this to your classmates as a series of ballads or in a hootenanny.

7. Collect and/or create a series of political cartoons depicting how various groups in American society feel about the American Dream and its reality. Share these with your classmates.

8. Prepare and present skits that reveal how various groups have either realized or not realized the American Dream. Examples of these groups might include the American Indian, urban blacks, suburban commuters, the successful industrialists, sports figures, movie stars, migrant workers, the elderly, the urban poor, Puerto Ricans, the rural poor, etc.

9. Collect or create cartoons showing types of individuals who are striving or not striving for the American Dream. Make a visual display that includes explanations of each individual's attitude.

10. Extract and perform excerpts from *Man of La Mancha* and *How to Succeed in Business without Really Trying* which illustrate a particular interpretation of the American Dream. Explain in a short paper what aspects you were trying to depict.

11. Visit places involved in manufacturing or handling things commonly identified with the American Dream. Examples—Fisher Body Plant, Macy's, Con. Ed, IBM, Reader's Digest, General Foods, Kennedy Airport, Chase Manhattan Bank, NBC Studios, etc. Using a medium such as poetry, photography, painting, collage, etc. create your personal impression of this experience and display it in a prominent place.

12. Interview several immigrants regarding: what did they expect to find in America, who shared their expectations, what did they find, what regrets or appreciations do they now have, how do they now feel about the American Dream. Ask them to cite specific experiences. Write a creative paper or narration illuminating or featuring these experiences.

13. Invite some Senior Citizens to your class to discuss their observations and experiences regarding the "American Dream." Write an analysis of similarities and differences in their experiences.

14. View and report on several TV commercials that reflect the contemporary view of the American Dream. Write an analysis of the similarities and differences they present.

15. Bring in examples of board games that reflect aspects of the American Dream. Show this through a class demonstration. Design and make your own game that reflects this and have your classmates play your game.

16. Collect and bring to class examples of pop art that are reflections of the American Dream. Display them and discuss them with the class.

17. Invite community leaders to class to discuss local manifestations of the American Dream. Prepare a list of things that you can do to further your realization of the American Dream.

18. Make a collage that makes a personal comment on the role of the American Dream in your life. Display it in a prominent place.

19. Read a biography of a prominent person and write a report concerning the role of the American Dream in that person's life.

20. Compose and conduct a questionnaire to be given to local residents concerning the role of the American Dream in contemporary family life. Compile the results; create and display a chart and a collage illustrating your findings.

MODEL 40 (cont.)

21. Read the concluding paragraphs of *The Great Gatsby* and George Babbitt's speech to the Rotary Club from the novel *Babbitt*. Write a report detailing the different visions of the American Dream described in each novel.
22. Read several statements of several leaders of the Women's Liberation Movement and present a speech or speeches designed to show their viewpoint on women's share in the American Dream.
23. View several TV soap operas and game shows and report to the class on the view of the American Dream presented by these programs.
24. Read *Death of a Salesman* and report on the differing views of the American Dream represented by the characters of Ben, Willie, Biff, and Dave Singleman.
25. Based on your observations of contemporary culture, write a paper giving your views on the status of the American Dream today.
26. Play the simulation game "Ghetto." Write a short paper describing and accounting for your character's success or lack of success in improving the quality of his or her life.

CONTRIBUTORY OBJECTIVE NO. 6

An understanding of the role of environment in contemporary American culture.

Activities

1. Arrive at a working definition of *environment*. Consider as many different kinds of environment as you can. Post your results in a prominent place.
2. Examine the following series of environments:
   A square inch of earth.
   A room in your house.
   Two minutes of riding in a car.
   One minute of attendance at a pop concert or school dance.
   Two mintues of silence.
   Write a report including the equipment you used for observations, the methods utilized, your observations, and a general statement based on your examination.
3. Theatrically create contrasting environments (physical, psychological, and philosophical). Share your creations with your classmates.
4. Create various physical environments and exhibit these to the class.
5. Describe in a talk or in writing man's relationship to nature as illustrated through a personal camping experience.
6. Write a paper or prepare a collage exploring the role of environment in man's ability to live comfortably. Possible environments to consider are the urban ghetto, suburban development, rural farm, etc.
7. Place yourself in an environment totally different from the one that you are now in. Write a paper answering the following: What things do you notice that are different? What effect do they have on you? How would you go about adjusting to them?
8. Make a visual display of an emotional environment here, in a large city, in a rural area, and so on. Then superimpose this emotional environment on a natural environment. Record your results in a well-written narrative.
9. Find or create examples of art that reflects the environment in which it was created and examples of art that uses the natural environment. Display these examples.
10. Find and present to the class music that draws on the natural environment for inspiration or content. You may also use graphics.
11. Every man relates to his environment. Examine several works of literature and in a written report show how this is treated.
12. Collect pictures and writings that show how man has found beauty in different environments. Display them on a bulletin board.
13. Explore the tensions in schools today, and show how these combine to form an emotional environment. Express your findings in a creative work.
14. Create a discotheque that is organized around a particular theme. Invite the rest of the class to experience the environment you created and to comment on the effect of this environment on them.

MODEL 40 (cont.)

15. Consider the human body as a physical environment, and through a graphic or written presentation show how modern American life affects this environment.
16. From a survey of newspaper and magazine ads, determine which environments Americans are most concerned with, and describe your conclusions in a written report.
17. Examine 2 characters from contemporary American literature. In a self-revealing monologue show how each character is affected by his own psychological environment.
18. In a presentation of your own design, show how the creation of a teenage environment is affecting the American culture today.
19. Invite a resource person from the field of psychology to discuss the interaction of environment and personality. Compile notes on this presentation and list significant points for public display.

CONTRIBUTORY OBJECTIVE NO. 7

An understanding and appreciation of contemporary American values, what they are, how they are expressed, and the role they play in determining contemporary life.

Activities

1. Establish a working definition of *values*. Post this definition in a place where it can constantly be referred to by students and teachers working in this unit.
2. What values are expressed in contemporary art, music, dance, literature, history, architecture, philosophy? Devise a means for finding out and for sharing the results of your exploration of these media.
3. What classical works of art, music, dance, literature, history, architecture and philosophy are important in the contemporary American cultures? Devise a means of finding out. Share your findings with other students.
4. Read some contemporary novels and decide what values are important in them. Write a paper discussing the values of major characters in relation to contemporary American culture.
5. Look carefully at contemporary poetry and songs. Choose a particular work, and explain in a brief presentation what values are expressed and how you feel about these values.
6. Examine a variety of contemporary newspapers and magazines to learn what concerns are most important in contemporary American culture. Create and present a sharing experience using what you learn.
7. Identify one specific value you believe should be changed in some way, i.e., propagated, strengthened, lessened, etc. Devise and carry out a specific plan for changing or strengthening this value, and establish a means of evaluating your effectiveness.
8. Identify one value you feel very strongly about. Discover what you believe to be your most effective way of expressing this value. Solicit the views of six other people who will evaluate the effectiveness of your expression. Try to get some people who will agree with you and some who will disagree. Write a brief paper telling what you learned about effective expression. Consider whether the value you sought to express has changed any during this activity, or whether your attitude toward and interest in it have changed.
9. List categories (religious, social, economic, etc.). Do values in one category sometimes conflict with values in another? In what ways might they agree? Prepare a statement or chart on categories of values and polarization of values.
10. Make a careful study of the toy departments in one or more fairly large stores. Find out: What main categories of toys for children are represented? Which categories have the largest stock? Most variety? Largest displays? Highest prices? Which categories of toys sell the best? Which toys are poor sellers? Which are most popular with boys and girls of various ages? Combine all your information into an interesting and informative report that shows how American toys for children reflect the values of contemporary American cultures. Write a paper compiling your results.
11. Collect a variety of statements, both contemporary and traditional, which deal with "what an American should believe in." Identify them by source, author, and date of

MODEL 40 (cont.)

origin. Arrange and display these statements or excerpts to show how they are related to each other and to contemporary issues.

12. Invite to class some resource persons from the community to discuss with you how values are formed and how they play a role in people's everyday behavior. Consider a psychologist, clergyman, advertising person, lawyer, and others. Display on a bulletin board a list of the values and the roles they play.

13. Examine some popularly known magazine and TV advertisements to see what values are most often appealed to in an effort to sell particular products. List for each product or type of product what kind of person the ads are aimed at, for example, Ultra-Brite toothpaste, Marlboro cigarettes, Fab detergent. Which ads seem to you to be most honest? Which are selling things which may prove harmful? What devices are employed in order to make the product seem very desirable? After you feel you understand something about advertising techniques, create some ads of your own in order to demonstrate how ads are related to people's values. Are these techniques ever employed in other fields? Prepare a demonstration for the class to convey your findings.

14. Watch and analyze carefully several popular TV programs, paying special attention to the following: Who or what, according to the program, is good, acceptable, or worthwhile? Specifically how does the program create a value-impression in you, the viewer? What kind of person would this program appeal to most? Least? What advertisers pay for this program? What is the relationship between types of programs and types of advertisers? Draw together some generalizations from your study and present them to the class.

15. Look carefully at a TV program schedule for a week and determine what kinds of programs are most often scheduled for prime time, what kinds of programs are most represented in the schedule, least represented, not represented. Take a poll of students and other groups to determine their favorite TV programs. What generalizations can you make about values represented and emphasized? Share these with the class graphically and verbally.

16. Design and make an appropriate flag for the New American Revolution. Explain the meaning of its colors, shape, symbols, etc.

17. Collect and perform or play several examples of modern popular songs that reflect a change in values from the 1950s through today. Extra possibility: Write and perform a pop song that you feel reflects the direction of American values in the future.

CONTRIBUTORY OBJECTIVE NO. 8

A comprehension of the forces that may polarize and/or unite various segments of American society today.

Activities

1. Bring to class examples of publications that are aimed at specific segments of society. Write a paper identifying the segment of society to which each publication appeals and the ways in which it appeals to that segment.

2. View six television programs, and prepare a chart showing which programs foster cultural interrelationships and which ignore them.

3. Compile a list of words that tend to polarize or unite segments of society. Explain what groups would react to which words in what way, and display your lists and explanations on a bulletin board.

4. Invite into your classroom theologians to discuss the qualities of, similarities, etc., of various religions. Make and display a chart summarizing the main points of the discussion.

5. Read *The Outsiders* or other books with a similar theme and explore in a group discussion the types of socioeconomic polarization that are described. Write a summary of your reactions to this discussion and submit it to your teacher.

6. You are a student of the Ridge Street School. Write a paragraph expressing your observations about what polarizing and uniting forces are at work in your school. Post your paragraph on a bulletin board.

7. You are a member of a family. Write a paragraph expressing your observations about

MODEL 40 (cont.)

what polarizing and uniting forces are at work in your family. Display a collection of these paragraphs on a bulletin board.

8. You are a member of a community. Write a paragraph expressing your observations about what polarizing and uniting forces are at work in your community. Display a collection of these paragraphs on a bulletin board.

9. Compose and conduct a questionnaire designed to display the differing points of view of American adolescents, young adults, parents and grandparents on the Vietnam war, civil liberties, student dissent, drugs, or any other contemporary problem. Correlate and post the results of the questionnaire.

10. Using the results of the preceding questionnaire, and drawing upon your own personal experience, write and submit a paper expressing your views on the "generation gap."

11. A person from another country asks you, "What is an American?" In a paper, answer the question. Post your paper on a bulletin board.

12. In 10 short statements, answer the personal question "Who am I?" Prepare and exhibit a graphic display based upon your statements.

13. View a film or demonstrate a folk dance that reflects a particular culture. Write a paper describing what you observed.

14. View a film that illustrates the ethnic complexity of New York City and prepare a report reflecting this complexity.

15. Attempt to discern whether immigration regulations tend to polarize segments of American society. List any regulations which you feel do this, and discuss the ways in which they do this. Create a display which expresses your observations.

16. Take a field trip to specific areas which illustrate particular aspects or backgrounds of culture. Record your observations and write a general narrative showing what you learned.

CONTRIBUTORY OBJECTIVE NO. 9

An awareness of the many different life styles which exist within the American cultures.

Activities

1. Prepare and exhibit a collage of pictorial representations of life styles as depicted in the "slick" magazines.

2. Prepare a diary of a specific member of a social or cultural group quite different from your own. Consider groups in Canada and South America. Consider time cycles, clothes, fads, fashions, food. Share your diary with the class.

3. Trade ideas of foods and dress through various cultures or groups. Then illustrate by a chart or demonstration the relation of geography to food and dress.

4. Consider and show through presentation, creation or performance examples of the relative role of the arts in various cultural groups.

5. Study and learn various forms of shelter and housing indigenous to various cultural groups. Prepare and display various examples of housing.

6. Establish a model housing contest. Each model or drawing made must reflect the particular life style of a particular cultural group. Be sure an explanation accompanies each entry.

7. Prepare a model community including housing. Through maps or diagrams, depict this community.

MODEL 41   IN SEARCH OF ERNEST HEMINGWAY*

Subject: Honors American Literature
Grade: 12
Seminar: In Search of Ernest Hemingway

*This model is abstracted from Brooke Workman, *In Search of Ernest Hemingway: A Model for Teaching a Literature Seminar* (Urbana, Ill.: National Council of Teachers of English, 1979).

MODEL 41 (cont.)

INTRODUCTION: THE SEMINAR METHOD

This handbook is designed to be used every day for a semester and includes a schedule, lesson plans, material for reproduction and distribution, and a serviceable Hemingway bibliography. It is based not only on a theory about how students improve basic writing skills and acquire new reading habits, but also on four years of experience with high school students at West High School in Iowa City, Iowa. Through trial and error, from student suggestions and papers, with the discovery of new materials, the handbook evolved.

This handbook, then, is the result of my own search, not so much for Ernest Hemingway or any other author, but for a vital teaching method. I wanted my students to enjoy literature and to develop their critical reading skills in a way that no survey course would allow. From personal experience I knew that the in-depth exploration of a single author could provide an opening wedge to all of literature. Microcosm, macrocosm, if you will. So I designed a course in which in-depth analysis was shared by a group of students. Eventually this course design led to a major discovery: I had found a vital method not only for the teaching of *literature* but also for the teaching of *writing*.

THE OVERALL DESIGN OF THE COURSE

A good handbook, however pragmatic, must be flexible if it is to meet the requirements of different schools, students, teachers. This particular handbook grew out of a trimester elective for fifteen students, some very gifted in reading and writing, some merely interested in literature and self-improvement. The only prerequisite for the seminar was an American literature survey course. Students in the first seminars chose an author from all of American literature; later ones often asked to repeat an author who they had heard was exciting to study: Ernest Hemingway. Each seminar met for fifty days, and each student wrote seven position papers. Five of these were graded by the instructor and two were graded by the group. Final grades were based on the seven papers, on contributions to discussion and evaluation, and on growth. Classroom dynamics varied; the fifty-five minutes could be charged with volatile interaction or marked by quiet, thoughtful study. Always the spirit was cooperative. The seminar was great fun to teach.

Admittedly, the fifty class days were busy, so much so that the schedule included here has been revised to cover ninety class periods or an eighteen-week semester. This expanded format allows time to explore areas that could not be fully covered during a trimester—follow-up discussions, reference to critical opinion, in-class reading and writing time. Then, too, the schedule needs flexibility to allow for normal interruptions—assemblies, special events, snow days. Some instructors may want to include resource persons, telephone interviews, an eighth paper, conferences with individual students, and formal testing. Finally, seminars are not just for the gifted, though the gifted enjoy the structure and content of such a course. More time is required to improve the skills of slower readers, less competent writers.

Having taught for twenty years, I am well aware of two hazards in teaching any course: work load and boredom. Let me begin by saying that this course is not a case study of Ernest Hemingway meant to be taught by a Hemingway expert or even a teacher who has taken a graduate seminar on Hemingway. The reading assignments pose no real burden since time is built into the schedule for much of the reading of the required short story and three novels. Since the instructor is not expected to be an expert, he or she joins the seminar in much of the discovery process. As for reading and correcting student papers, time is also built into the schedule for that, plus the bonus of Defense Day evaluations of two papers by the entire seminar. And while I believe that teachers should stress to administrators that the seminar is a writing course, one that works best with fifteen students, I have tried to open up the semester schedule to make the design feasible for larger classes. Thus, I do not see the instructional load of this course to be any more burdensome than, for example, an American literature survey course.

I have found little boredom in a course that explores an attractive writer through a variety of experiences. Following the logic of chronology, so important in suggesting the development of major themes, I first selected a short story ("Indian Camp") that would define the Hemingway material. Its brevity allowed time for the in-class oral reading of additional stories, for a discussion of what makes a position paper, and for an introduction to Defense Day. Perhaps even more significantly, there was time to develop rapport within the seminar. The next two assignments dealt with longer works, *The Sun Also Rises* and *A Farewell to Arms,* two novels which invited comparison with each other and with the earlier stories. By the fourth paper, students had begun to see the autobiographical nature of the writing and were ready to deal with Hemingway the man and writer. This assignment required individual research which allowed students to take even more personal positions than they had been able to take based on in-common readings. The fifth assignment, based on a reading of choice, also encouraged individuality by offering students the opportunity to present works that others may not have read. *The Old Man and the Sea,* the sixth assignment, again brought the class together in a common and important final reading. The seventh paper had its own special delights: no reading but a good deal of reflection (if students chose summation) or creativity (if students tried imitation or parody). This sequence of seven writing assignments, reinforced by resource materials such as films, provided an antidote to boredom for students and teacher alike.

While the content has its appeal, the real vitality of the seminar design came from the position papers and the Defense Days. In fact, it was here I discovered that I was teaching a vital writing course. It soon became obvious that students were not only learning about the writing of Ernest Hemingway, but also about their own writing. The interaction of the seven written assignments made its impact, though no student ever referred to the seminar as a "writing course."

Each of the three-to-five-page, typed assignments was defined as a "position paper" because students were asked to limit their analysis to a single focus. This position was to be organized, supported by concrete detail, and mechanically sound. Since the readings were chronological, students were encouraged to build their papers upon each other, to use comparison and contrast. Writing goals were sequential, ranging from concern with proofreading and clarity to the more complex skills of documentation and synthesis. A model student paper for each of the seven assignments is included in the text.

Defense Day offered a dramatic focus for each assignment. While the instructor provided an audience for all of the position papers, two papers were read and evaluated by the entire seminar. In addition, there was an element of surprise since students did not know which papers would be chosen for a given Defense Day until all had been handed in and copies of the papers to be analyzed were made. When Defense Day arrived, two students shared their papers with the class. With the instructor acting as a classroom manager, not evaluator, members of the seminar used three criteria to respond to each paper: (1) clarity of position, (2) organization and support, and (3) mechanics. Together students arrived at a consensus grade for each paper.

Obviously, Defense Day is a time of tension. For the student facing a peer audience, there are the questions that all writers must face: Will they understand my position? Is my position supported by concrete detail? Is it mechanically sound—at least sound enough to satisfy my readers? Will I be able to respond to their questions and criticisms? What will be the final assessment? Since each student appears on two Defense Days, there is the natural concern that the second be as good as, if not better than, the first.

But Defense Day has its rewards. Since everyone comes up for Defense Day, everyone both evaluates and is evaluated. Thus, the spirit of Defense Day becomes one of cooperation. Students work together to help each other become better writers; they learn from each other as well as from the instructor. With each Defense Day, students acquire more experience in discussing and implementing the criteria of good writing. The evaluation of the Defense Day papers and of their own papers, which are returned by the instructor at the end of the day, prepares student writers for future writing assignments. Indeed, one of the major goals of the writing design becomes obvious: The Next Paper. And finally, each student has a better understanding of his or her own writing. The search for Ernest Hemingway inevitably leads home.

But this handbook is only a beginning. While it details assignments and suggests a number of concrete ways to exploit Hemingway material, its essential design can be applied to the study of other authors. I have explored four other authors in similar seminars. I chose each because I thought that author would be fun, not because I was an expert on that literary figure. And it was fun to teach F. Scott Fitzgerald (though one should never begin with *This Side of Paradise*), John Steinbeck (though *The Grapes of Wrath* is long), William Saroyan (though some of my students thought Bill must not be too bright

MODEL 41 (cont.)

with his always cosmic optimism), and J. D. Salinger (though he has resisted biographers and interviewers). Since teachers know their own interests and audiences, I will not go beyond suggesting these four writers. I do know that I would have great difficulty taking high school students through the likes of William Faulkner and Henry James. I do know that I am presently considering Richard Wright and Mark Twain. I also think that the design would work well with short story writers, science fiction writers, playwrights, and even poets.

WRITING ASSIGNMENTS

While the papers and discussions build upon themselves, the instructor may wish to emphasize a sequence of writing skills. For example, when writing assignments are made or during Defense Day, the instructor may want to announce concrete goals for writing improvement. The following developmental sequence for the seven position papers has been useful:

Paper I: "Indian Camp"
1. Following format directions is important for the initial paper: 3–5 pages, typed manuscript form.
2. The idea of a single clear position is essential for the first paper.

Paper II: *The Sun Also Rises*
1. Emphasize the use of concrete examples from the book. Ask students to use at least one direct quotation from the novel to document the position and to give "flavor" to the material.
2. Stress introductions and conclusions. What the reader reads first and last is essential in the psychology of writing.
3. Reiterate the need for careful proofreading.

Paper III: *A Farewell to Arms*
1. Stress transitions between sentences and paragraphs. Does the paper flow logically? Do connectives help to unify it? Does the organization serve to clarify the single position? Does the introduction suggest the body of the paper? Does the position find its final definition in the conclusion?
2. Encourage students to work on sentence variety. Are the sentences appealing—not all simple or compound sentences, not all beginning with the subject-verb pattern ("Catherine felt," "She said . . . ").
3. Urge students to purchase a paperback copy of *Roget's Thesaurus*. Instruct them on its use with a class copy.

Paper IV: Profile of Ernest Hemingway
1. Encourage students to use both biographical and literary material in formulating a position.
2. Discuss the need for footnotes and bibliography and provide a style sheet of correct forms. You may also wish to discuss how to edit a direct quotation, how to build a smooth transition from the text to the direct quotation, when to single space direct quotations and when to incorporate them into the double-spaced text.
3. It might be interesting to discuss teacher and student "pet peeves" regarding style. For example, some people detest "a lot" in papers, while others believe that the first-person 'I' has no place in formal writing.

Paper V: Student Choice
1. A clear plot summary and precise character descriptions are essential for a successful choice paper because many Defense Day evaluators will not have read the work under consideration.
2. Encourage students to relate previous in-common readings to the work of their choice. Comparison and contrast are useful techniques, especially for college-bound students.
3. An amusing aside: ask students if they are beginning to write like Ernest Hemingway. Unconscious imitation is one of the "hazards" of studying an author in depth.

Paper VI: *The Old Man and the Sea*
1. Since tone is so important in this novel, you may wish to discuss how style affects the mood of student papers. If a student has a serious theme about the poetic nature of a work, like this one, he or she may use serious and poetic techniques, such as similes, metaphors, symbols.

MODEL 41 (cont.)

2. Since Hemingway was absorbed by matters of style, you might suggest special writing techniques, e.g., (1) repetition, such as nearly repeating a line or using the same beginning for two sentences in a row; (2) variation, such as using a tight, short sentence to follow a long one—to catch the eye, to summarize, to punctuate.
3. Insist on careful proofreading and a minimum number of mechanical errors.

Paper VII: Summing Up

1. Encourage students to use ideas from their previous papers and those of other students. This assignment is a lesson in synthesis.
2. If you intend to encourage humor or parody in the final assignment, a review of these approaches is in order.
3. Students should be reminded of the oral nature of the final assignment. All final papers are read aloud and will not be available for prior study as in previous Defense Day situations. Ask students, therefore, to read their papers aloud to themselves until they are satisfied, not only with their reading, but also with their writing—especially word choice and cadence.

DEFENSE DAY

Successful Defense Days depend on the clarity with which the assignment was given. Discussions of how to narrow an idea to a single position should prevent papers with a lack of focus. The student model of a *typed* three-to-five-page paper and the caution that papers will be reproduced throughout the seminar should ensure satisfactory form.

The primary goal of Defense Day is to reinforce in positive ways the defender, as well as the entire seminar. Defense Day is not Destruction Day. Evaluation and grading should be supportive for future writers and defenders. It is a day of sharing, learning, and allaying fears. It is therefore important that you select good models, especially for the first defense: papers with careful typing for acceptable reproduction, papers of the specified length with a clear position and good writing. You need not choose the two best papers (or four, if your class is large and you run two consecutive Defense Days), but your choices should generally be strong papers. Conflicting viewpoints, if equally well written, can be very stimulating for the first discussion.

After you have selected the Defense Day papers, make copies for each student in the class. The copies (with or without the student's name) should be distributed during the class period before Defense Day (see Handout 1: Tentative Schedule) so that students have time to read and annotate them. Advance distribution also generates interest since students often discuss the papers among themselves before Defense Day. Keep the original papers; you will note the results of the Defense Day evaluation on each one before returning it to the author.

Defense Day begins with calm and some humor. Remind the class that it is difficult to go first, to set an example; it is also difficult to evaluate each other. Remind the present defenders that they have the delight of finishing first and subsequent opportunities to evaluate papers. Remind the class that everyone is trying to learn from each other, to improve, to enjoy studying the author chosen by the seminar. (Note: students should bring not only the defense papers to class, but also the works under discussion for possible reference.)

Two papers work well in a normal class period of approximately fifty minutes. Asking each defender to read his or her paper aloud gives everyone a chance to re-read the paper, to hear how the author emphasizes the ideas, and to make final notations. After the oral reading, the discussion should focus on three evaluative criteria: clarity of position, adequacy of supporting evidence and logical development, and mechanics. Discussing and grading a paper takes a full twenty-five minutes.

Criterion one: clarity of position. After the defender has read the paper, ask a seminar member to state the position of that paper. Summarize what the student has said to confirm that you and the class understand his or her understanding of the paper's position. Now call on another seminar member to see if he or she agrees with the interpretation of the first student. If disagreement arises, however slight, call on other members until a consensus position emerges. Of course, some students may feel that no consensus is possible or that the position of the paper is unclear.

Finally, return to the defender and ask if he or she agrees with the interpretation of a given student or with the class consensus. The defender should be allowed to reflect on his or her position and to clarify that position to those who found it unclear.

Criterion two: organization and support. After the definition of the position, consider how the author organized and supported that position. The instructor, the defender, and the seminar should review the basic outline of the paper (Introduction, Body, Conclusion); the procedure for developing a single focus; and the concrete use of plot, characters, and quotations to support generalizations. Basic questions can be asked: Is the position clear because it is logical? Is it clear because it is supported by direct reference and quotation? Does the paper stay on target or is it sidetracked by irrelevancies or the overemphasis of a minor point? Does the introduction suggest the position? Does the conclusion restate it? Is the title well chosen?

After the organization and supporting detail have been clarified, seminar members should be encouraged to react again to the position. Even if they disagree with the position, they should ask themselves whether or not it is well defended. If the position is well defended, why do some members of the seminar continue to disagree with it? This discussion is often lively, and students should be reminded that during the next class period there will be time to pursue these positions, as well as to learn what critics have said about them.

Criterion three: mechanics. Finally, seminar members should react to the paper's mechanics, page by page. Do errors distract the reader from the paper's content? Do the mechanical problems stem from poor proofreading or are they obvious errors in spelling, capitalization, usage, paragraphing? What about style—awkward sentences, imprecise or inadequate word choices, inappropriate tone, insensitivity to nuance? While this critical examination should not become an exercise in nitpicking, seminar members and especially the instructor should make clear that the clarity of a paper's position is heavily dependent on the writer's skill with mechanics.

While some instructors prefer to evaluate student papers themselves, the papers chosen for Defense Day should be graded by the group. Defense Day has its own surprises, delights, and tensions, but it should also have a cooperative spirit. One successful technique is to return to the student who originally tried to state the paper's position. That student first posed the immediate problem of clarity. Ask that student to suggest a grade and to justify it. Then move to other students, asking for grades and justifications, reminding them that the discussion has emphasized clarity of position, overall organization, adequacy of supporting evidence, and mechanics. Almost always, a consensus emerges, though the seminar may want the instructor to add his or her grade. If possible, avoid adding your grade because it tends to weigh too heavily and may make students suspicious that their opinions are secondary.

Obviously, peer grading creates tensions. Classroom friends (and enemies) find it difficult to be objective. You may feel that consensus grades are sometimes too high. The grades given at Defense Day should not, however, be seen as a diminution of "standards," for the total learning experience of Defense Day is more important than any single grade. And, as a matter of fact, my experience with four years of Defense Days indicates that students are not only generally fair but usually assign grades that are very close to my private evaluation. The seminar should never lose *its* focus: the next paper, the student wanting to write that paper and to make it even better than the last paper.

After the completion of two defense papers (or four if Defense Day is extended to two days), return graded papers to all students. They will need them for open discussion at the next class period. In addition, return the original papers of the defenders with your comments, a summary of the comments made by the seminar during the discussion, and the consensus grade.

ADAPTING THE SEMINAR TO OTHER AUTHORS

The Hemingway seminar concretizes a *process* of reading, discussion, writing, and evaluation that can be transferred to other authors, other seminars. The process, established with the first paper and repeated and reinforced throughout the semester, follows these steps:

1. Orientation: providing literary, historical, and biographical background to students
2. Reading source materials orally and individually, class discussion, audio-visual materials, and mini-lectures

MODEL 41 (cont.)

3. Choosing a paper topic: teacher suggestions and papers written by students from previous seminars
4. Writing, revising, and proofreading the paper
5. Evaluation: Defense Day and Follow-up

Although the process remains relatively constant, the content of the seminar itself may change. While Ernest Hemingway is an excellent choice, the seminar can be built around other literary figures. Selecting an author and the specific works to be considered is, of course, important since students must "live" with that author for eighteen weeks.

How, then, should the author be determined?

First, there are practical considerations. Ideally you might wish to have students use the first days of the course to select an author, but this tactic will create practical problems of time (and budget!) for ordering or otherwise securing books. Some instructors are willing to assemble materials through libraries, used book stores, and student copies, but many teachers want the security of books ordered in advance. Even when the practical problems of student selection can be overcome, the method has its hazards. Students usually have not read most of the materials and may be disappointed in or thwarted by their own choice. For example, they may blithely disregard your warning that authors like William Faulkner, Henry James, or even Saul Bellow pose problems—length, level of difficulty—for many high school students.

Second, you may have a favorite author and feel inclined to settle on that writer for the seminar. Such motivation is not necessarily sinister, for your own background and preferences can go a long way in creating a successful seminar. Certainly you may find teenage students less than enchanted with your choice of author, but this method of selection is a good risk, especially if you keep teenage interests in mind. And it does solve the practical problem of advance book orders.

Third, you may wish to rely on the experience of others—other teachers in the school or the following list of authors and titles previously taught at West High School. All were successful seminars, although Steinbeck and Salinger were probably more appealing to teenagers than Fitzgerald and Saroyan.

I have included below the seven writing assignments for each of the four authors I have used in alternate versions of the Hemingway seminar.

F. Scott Fitzgerald
  Paper I: "The Rich Boy" (1926)
  Paper II: *This Side of Paradise* (1920)
  Paper III: *The Great Gatsby* (1925)
  Paper IV: Profile
  Paper V: "Babylon Revisited" (1930)
  Paper VI: Student Choice
  Paper VII: Summation

William Saroyan
  Paper I: "The Daring Young Man on the Flying Trapeze" (1934)
  Paper II: *The Time of Your Life* (1939)
  Paper III: "The Pomegranate Trees" (1940)
  Paper IV: *The Human Comedy* (1943)
  Paper V: Profile
  Paper VI: Student Choice
  Paper VII: Summation

John Steinbeck
  Paper I: "The Harness" (1938)
  Paper II: *Tortilla Flat* (1935)
  Paper III: *Of Mice and Men* (1937)
  Paper IV: *The Grapes of Wrath* (1939)
  Paper V: Profile
  Paper VI: Student Choice
  Paper VII: Summation

J. D. Salinger
  Paper I: "A Perfect Day for Bananafish" (1948)
  Paper II: *The Catcher in the Rye* (1951)
  Paper III: "Teddy" (1953)
  Paper IV: *Franny and Zooey* (1961)
  Paper V: Profile
  Paper VI: Student Choice
  Paper VII: Summation

However you select an author, you will be wise to maintain the chronological presentation, to offer student choices, to require papers on both short and long works, and to schedule a profile paper near the middle of the course when students are becoming increasingly interested in the writer and the autobiographical nature of his or her works.

But enough. You have the Map of the Territory. It works. And you and your students should make good company in your search for Ernest Hemingway and other American writers. The trip will be memorable, more than snapshots and color slides. How I envy you in your first exploration!

MODEL 41 (cont.)

ORIENTATION TO THE SEMINAR,* DAYS 1–2

DAY 1: GETTING ACQUAINTED WITH THE COURSE AND EACH OTHER

GOALS

1. To acquaint students with the nature of the seminar and to introduce them to its method and content.
2. To help students get to know each other.

MATERIALS

1. Handout 1: Tentative Schedule.
2. After you have taught the seminar, use evaluations from former students (see Day 90) to interest beginning students.

PROCEDURE

1. Using Handout 1 as a guide, offer an overview of the course, noting particularly how writing and reading activities are correlated. Point out the variety in the course, the value of studying an author in depth, the fact that the course offers an opportunity to improve writing skills as well as opportunities for individual exploration and group discussion.
2. Stress that you genuinely want to know the students and to have them know each other. Everyone will be working together in the course.
3. Pair off students who do not know each other or who know each other only slightly. Find a partner for yourself. Ask each student to interview his or her partner without taking notes, asking questions that each partner would like answered—family, job, favorite food, sports, music, travel, plans for the future.
4. After five or ten minutes, ask each student to introduce his or her partner to the seminar by summarizing the answers to the interview questions. Now the class has taken its first step toward becoming a genuine seminar. These introductions may lead to friendships, and they will certainly help to establish the understanding and cooperation needed in later discussions, especially the evaluations on Defense Day.

ADDITIONAL SUGGESTION

A classroom bulletin board on Ernest Hemingway helps to develop interest: photographs, magazine clippings, a sample position paper (one from this handbook or from a previous seminar), maps (Illinois, Michigan, Florida, Idaho, France, Italy, Cuba, Spain). Perhaps some students have visited the geographical settings of Hemingway's life and literature and have materials to contribute to an evolving bulletin board.

DAY 2: INTRODUCING HEMINGWAY AND THE POSITION PAPER

GOALS

1. To preview Hemingway's life and work.
2. To introduce the Position Paper.

MATERIALS

1. Handout 2: The Hemingway Chronology [not included in this book].
2. Handout 3: The Position Paper.

PROCEDURE

1. Referring to Handout 2: The Hemingway Chronology, discuss the idea that the seminar will be one of discovery, of learning how Hemingway's ideas and writing developed. The first of the seven position papers focuses on the Nick Adams stories of the 1920s. In particular, the paper will formulate a position about "Indian Camp," an early short

*Brooke Workman, *In Search of Ernest Hemingway: A Model for Teaching a Literature Seminar* (Urbana, Ill.: National Council of Teachers of English, 1979). pp. 1–6.

MODEL 41 (cont.)

story that was written in Paris after World War I and appeared in a small book, *In Our Time.*

2. Note that Hemingway's life carried him from his boyhood home in Oak Park, a suburb of Chicago, to a summer home near Petoskey in upper Michigan, the setting for "Indian Camp." The family enjoyed the change of scenery and fishing (a life-long enthusiasm of the author), and Dr. Hemingway carried on his medical practice there by treating the local Ojibway Indians. Go on to observe that Hemingway moved out into the world after he graduated from high school: a cub reporter in Kansas City, World War I service in Italy, newspaper work in Toronto, expatriate life in Paris in the 1920s, trips throughout his life to Spain, Key West, Africa, Cuba, and Ketchum, Idaho.

3. Distribute Handout 3: The Position Paper and discuss the nature of a position paper. Stress the requirements of length and format (typed, double-spaced, one side, unlined paper) since clear, complete copies must be distributed for Defense Day. At this point, do not dwell on evaluation procedures since a positive attitude toward writing does not begin with apprehension about grades. Remind students that typing is required by most college teachers and that it is wise to improve their typing now. Tell them that you will provide position papers, written by high school juniors and seniors for them to examine; assure them that they will be given considerable class time for reading and writing. Useful background material and even suggestions for topics will be given as specific papers are assigned.

ADDITIONAL SUGGESTION

Some students may already have read books by or about Hemingway. Encourage them to share their initial impressions.

HANDOUT 1: TENTATIVE SCHEDULE FOR SEMINAR IN AMERICAN LITERATURE— ERNEST HEMINGWAY

ORIENTATION TO THE SEMINAR

Day 1.   Getting acquainted with the course and each other

Day 2.   Introducing Hemingway and the Position Paper

Paper I: "Indian Camp" (1925)

Day 3.   Reading aloud and discussion of "Up in Michigan" (1923) and "The Doctor and the Doctor's Wife" (1925)

ASSIGNMENT: Position Paper on "Indian Camp"

Due: _____

Day 4.   Reading aloud and discussion of "The End of Something" (1925)

Day 5.   Reading aloud and discussion of "Three Day Blow" (1925)

Day 6.   Suggestions for Position Paper on "Indian Camp" and in-class writing

Day 7.   Reading aloud and discussion of "Ten Indians" (1927)

Day 8.   In-class writing

Day 9.   Reading aloud and discussion of "The Battler" (1925)

Position Paper on "Indian Camp" due

Day 10.   Film: *My Old Man* (story published 1923)

Paper II: "The Sun Also Rises" (1926)

Day 11.   Introduction to *The Sun Also Rises:* begin reading

ASSIGNMENT: Position Paper on *The Sun Also Rises*

Due: _____

Day 12.   Reading

Day 13.   Discussion: Life in Paris in the 1920s

Day 14.   Reading

MODEL 41 (cont.)

Day 15.   Reading

Day 16.   Reading and/or distribution of Defense Day papers

Day 17.   Defense Day: "Indian Camp"

Day 18.   Follow-up discussion: students and critics

Day 19.   Film: *Hemingway's Spain: "The Sun Also Rises"*

Day 20.   Reading

Day 21.   Suggestions for Position Paper on *The Sun Also Rises* and reading or writing

Day 22.   Film: *Hemingway's Spain: "Death in the Afternoon"*

Day 23.   Reading aloud and discussion of "The Big Two-Hearted River" (1925)

Day 24.   Reading aloud and discussion of "The Big Two-Hearted River"

Day 25.   In-class writing and proofreading

Day 26.   Reading aloud and discussion of "In Another Country" (1927)

           Position Paper on *The Sun Also Rises* due

Paper III: "A Farewell to Arms" (1929)

Day 27.   Introduction to *A Farewell to Arms;* begin reading

           ASSIGNMENT: Position Paper on *A Farewell to Arms*

           Due: _____

Day 28.   Reading

Day 29.   Reading

Day 30.   Reading aloud and discussion of "Now I Lay Me" (1927) and "A Very Short Story" (1927)

Day 31.   Suggestions for Position Paper on *A Farewell to Arms* and in-class reading

Day 32.   Discussion: World War I and Hemingway, Dr. Hemingway's suicide, Key West

Day 33.   Reading; distribution of papers for Defense Day

Day 34.   Defense Day: *The Sun Also Rises*

Day 35.   Follow-up discussion: students and critics

Day 36.   Reading

Day 37.   Reading aloud and discussion of "Soldier's Home" (1925)

Day 38.   Reading

Day 39.   Reading and writing

Day 40.   Writing

Day 41.   Writing and proofreading

Day 42.   Reading aloud and discussion of "Fathers and Sons" (1933)

           Position Paper on *A Farewell to Arms* due

Paper IV: A Profile of Ernest Hemingway

Day 43.   Review of the Hemingway biography and introduction to Profile Paper

           ASSIGNMENT: Profile Paper developed from 100 pages of reading in Hemingway's biographers

           Due: _____

Day 44.   Film: *Hemingway*

Day 45.   Reading and research for Anecdote Day

Day 46.   Reading and research for Anecdote Day

Day 47.   Anecdote Day

Day 48.   Anecdote Day

Day 49.   Reading; distribution of papers for Defense Day

MODEL 41 (cont.)

Day 50.   Defense Day: *A Farewell to Arms*

Day 51.   Follow-up discussion: students and critics

Day 52.   Reading aloud and discussion of "A Clean Well-Lighted Place" (1933)

Day 53.   Reading

Day 54.   Reading, research, and writing

Day 55.   Writing

Day 56.   Writing and proofreading

Day 57.   Reading aloud and discussion of "A Day's Wait" (1933) and "The Old Man at the Bridge" (1938)

          Profile Paper on Ernest Hemingway due

Paper V: Your Choice

Day 58.   Consideration of reading choices for Paper V

          ASSIGNMENT: Position Paper on Hemingway

          Due: _____

Day 59.   Reading

Day 60.   Reading

Day 61.   Reading

Day 62.   Reading: Distribution of papers for Defense Day

Day 63.   Defense Day: Profile Paper

Day 64.   Defense Day: Profile Paper

Day 65.   Follow-up discussion: students and critics

Day 66.   Reading and writing

Day 67.   Writing

Day 68.   Writing and proofreading

Day 69.   Reading aloud and discussion of "On the Blue Water" (1936)

          Your Choice Paper due

Paper VI: "The Old Man and the Sea" (1952)

Day 70.   Introduction to *The Old Man and the Sea;* begin reading

          ASSIGNMENT: Position Paper on *The Old Man and the Sea*

          Due: _____

Day 71.   Reading

Day 72.   Discussion: Hemingway and the Nobel Prize

Day 73.   Suggestions for Position Paper on *The Old Man and the Sea* and reading

Day 74.   Reading, writing, and distribution of papers for Defense Day

Day 75.   Defense Day: Your Choice papers

Day 76.   Follow-up discussion: students and critics

Day 77.   Writing

Day 78.   Writing and proofreading

Day 79.   Previewing the Summation Paper

          Position Paper on *The Old Man and the Sea* due

Paper VII: Summing Up

Day 80.   Reading, rereading, research, and writing

          ASSIGNMENT: Summation Paper and/or Humorous Paper on Hemingway and His Work

          Due: _____

MODEL 41 (cont.)

Day 81.   Writing

Day 82.   Writing and distribution of papers for Defense Day

Day 83.   Defense Day: *The Old Man and the Sea*

Day 84.   Follow-up discussion: students and critics

Day 85.   Writing and proofreading

Day 86.   Reading aloud of final papers

Day 87.   Reading aloud of final papers

Day 88.   Reading aloud by instructor

Day 89.   Final discussion

Day 90.   Evaluation of seminar

HANDOUT 3: THE POSITION PAPER*

1. The position paper is just that: you adopt a single position about what you have read, a narrowed focus that can be developed by using concrete examples from the reading or from supplements to the reading. The position is *your* position.
2. The position paper must be three to five typed pages. The papers must be typed because at least two papers will be chosen from each assignment, reproduced, and evaluated during Defense Day by members of the seminar.
3. The possibilities for positions are nearly unlimited. You may want to develop an important quotation from a work, an important symbol, a character or a comparison of two characters, the author's style, his or her ideas about love, death, maturity, society, nature, money. You may wish to explore the author's use of names, choice of title, brand of humor. Suggestions for positions will be given with each assignment.
4. The paper must be your best writing. It will always be read by the instructor. At least two of your papers will be discussed and evaluated by the entire seminar.
5. Do not use the title of the work for your paper. Instead, your title should suggest or reflect your position.
6. Present your position logically and support it with concrete material—quotations and examples from what you have read as well as your own observations about life and literature. Don't neglect the plot or ignore the names of the characters, yet assume that your reader is your seminar classmate, who is also familiar with the work.
7. Writing good papers is hard work. It requires a clear outline. Your paper needs sharp first and last sentences, transitions between solidly developed paragraphs, varied sentences—not all beginning with pronouns, not all simple or compound constructions. It requires your sharpest and most mature language. Good writing is correct writing: don't lose your reader by failing to proofread. Read your paper aloud before typing the final draft. Finally, a good paper uses psychology: work hard on introductions and conclusions—the first and last things that the reader reads.
8. Do not rely on critics. While there will be student position papers for you to examine, take your own position.
9. Do not be afraid to adopt a position that seems "way out," fanciful, outrageous. If you have a strong position, one that may be challenged in the seminar discussion, just be sure that you have the material to defend it.
10. The writing of seven position papers is a cumulative experience. Each paper builds upon its predecessors, so do not hesitate to refer to previous papers or ideas—yours or those of other classmates. Through your own writing and by studying the works of other students, you will make discoveries about your reading and writing. New ideas will come to you. You will become aware of your own style as you consider the writing of others, especially Hemingway. And, while each paper will not necessarily be better than the last, your final production will speak for itself. You will be impressed!

*Brooke Workman, *In Search of Ernest Hemingway: A Model for Teaching a Literature Seminar* (Urbana, Ill.: National Council of Teachers of English, 1979), p. 9.

MODEL 42   MURDER, MISCHIEF, AND MAYHEM:
A PROCESS FOR CREATIVE RESEARCH PAPERS

Subject: Honors English
Grade: 12
Unit: Writing Research Papers

(W. Keith Hraus in *Murder, Mischief, and Mayhem: A Process for Creative Research Papers* [Urbana, Ill.: National Council of Teachers of English, 1978] presents an innovative approach to teaching research paper procedures and techniques to college freshmen. Two sections from this excellent handbook are included here for teacher enticement. The handbook itself must be read from cover to cover for the teacher who would try this approach to understand adequately the techniques and procedures involved.)

This book is not meant to be simply another style manual for writing college research papers. There are plenty of those around and I don't really believe another one is needed. Rather, this text works under the assumption that freshman research and research papers can be interesting, an idea so heretical I'm almost afraid to advance it. Historically, the freshman research paper was never designed to be worthwhile or interesting in itself; it was, and alas still is in many cases, a trial balloon, a stepping stone, an exercise, a preparation for graduate school and beyond. At its zenith it is a means for scholars and scientists to communicate about original investigations, but at any lower level it is a dry run. In graduate school the research paper is written to prove that one can investigate and organize material just like a full-fledged member of the profession; in college it is to prove one is ready for graduate school (or as "practice for your other courses"); and on the high school level it is taught because "students will have to write research papers in college." (Perhaps for this reason English has come to be called a "service course.") It even results in a strange kind of praise for the exercise. When high schools ask former students what work in English has proved the most valuable, the research paper is invariably at the top of the list. Students without the high school experience are often in the position described by this bewildered freshman.

My first day of class, I was told to hand in a 15-page analysis of two books at the end of the week. I got an F of course; the professor said the writing was *adequate* and the content *all right,* but the form was *all wrong.* I didn't know what he was talking about until a friend told me how to do footnotes and bibliographies. (Geraldine Allen, "What College Students Wish They'd Had in Senior English," *English Journal* 53 [1961]: 607.)

So high schools teach the research paper as part of the college survival kit, and colleges see it as a survival kit for graduate school, and graduate schools hold that it is preparation for the time when a person undertakes original research. Thus, the high school research paper is really designed as training for laboratory research, although no one seems to see it that way. The stand taken in this book is that research can be interesting in its own right, that real research is indeed possible for freshmen, and that skills learned in doing a research paper can have immediate application.

Actually, the method presented here was developed out of the frustration I felt after reading a stack of badly done freshman research papers on *Moby Dick.* My papers were of the classic scissors-and-paste type with quotations lamely held together with weak transitional sentences interrupted by bad attempts at paraphrase. Or worse, I could tell that one book in the bibliography accounted for 90 percent of the paper, or still worse, the book wasn't *in* the bibliography. Or much worse, it probably came from the *Moby Dick* cheater sold by my friendly college bookstore.

The papers themselves were dull—"lacks a clear focus," "the transition is weak between sentences," "the style is too informal," "single space quotations over five lines,"—really dull. Of course, I had a few good papers, but even they tended to be dull. It took me weeks to mark them, and I had to make up little correction games to force myself through the reading: "Today I'll read only papers in red plastic folders." But then I stumbled upon a clue.

I devised a series of library exercises to acquaint students with general reference works such as the *New York Times Index, The Readers Guide, Book Review Digest,* etc. Not that

I really planned to have my class use these sources in writing their papers, but I found that most freshmen have rarely used any reference other than *The Readers' Guide* and have a deeply rooted fear of a college library. My goal was to give them practical exposure to standard indexes and reference materials, acquaint them with our library's rapidly expanding micro-resources, and I suspect, salve my guilt in the course by teaching skills which might be useful in further college work.

The first exercise directed students to look up the *New York Times* on the day they were born and write a brief paragraph about what happened. Standard enough. They learned to use the microfilm machines and maybe noticed we carry the *Times* back to its first issue in 1851. Exercise two was designed to introduce the *Times Index* and the question was: "What were the circumstances surrounding the death of the following person?" And then each student was given a different name and date.

For years one of the fun books around our house has been a picture account of "the roaring twenties" which features close-ups of assorted gangsters riddled with bullets somewhere on Chicago's South Side. So for this question I lifted the obituary information on some of Capone's finest, put it on 3″ × 5″ cards (what else!), and dealt the cards out to the class, appropriately, face down. When the assignments were turned in, a number of students mentioned how interesting the story was surrounding their case, how strange that era must have been, and how different the account read compared to a "modern" newspaper story. We spent a few minutes in class joking about some of the mores of the 1920 gangster world they had uncovered, e.g., gold coffins, funeral processions through the "territory," the man's rivals uttering B movie eulogies. It was obvious this had been fun . . . for both of us. Looking up the review in *Book Review Digest* had been a chore, but the other was fun. Naturally, we forgot about all this when we turned to our "serious" project and everyone did his dull, badly done paper on *Moby Dick*. For the last time.

Before the next term began I spent a weekend in the library at the *Times Index* pulling out each volume, flipping to the "Murder" listings and noting the best cases dating from 1851. The kind of case I was looking for had to have certain qualities. First, it had to be a big enough case to allow students to pick and choose from the available material, to select from a mass of information the key elements, facts, details, and quotations needed to construct a paper of about two thousand words. Second, I wanted cases that extended over a period of years in which new developments kept appearing and confusing the issue. This paper was going to be a legitimate test of a student's ability to research and organize scattered and chaotic materials. Third, I tried to pick cases that seemed to touch on some aspect of the American mind and character, that revealed a national or local attitude or strange custom of the time. For instance, one choice was the 1897 case of William Guldensuppe whose dismembered body was found over a course of three weeks, except for the head. His "remains," sans head, were put together and he was given an open casket funeral attended by thousands of curious viewers. Or again falling back on the gangster crimes, I selected the 1929 shooting of Red Cassidy in the Hotsy-Totsy Club in New York. Simply from the entries in the *Index* one can sense the flavor of the period, of gangland rivalries, police corruption, missing witnesses turning up in the East River.

Fourth, I picked only cases that looked interesting, somewhat bizarre, fun to read about and research . . . and to correct. No run-of-the-mill muggings, no domestic manslaughter cases, no same-day-confession crimes. I tried to find twenty-five "classics"—boy meets girl, boy accused of killing girl, boy released for lack of evidence, town lynches boy upon release, etc. But usually I had no idea how the crime turned out or really what it was all about, and no case was selected if it was so famous there were books about it (exit Leo Frank and Lizzie Borden). For all practical purposes, this was to be "original" research, or as close as one could get in a second term freshman course.

From the outset I knew I had scored with my fourth objective. The kids were really fascinated with their projects, and although some of their cases were often as complicated as *Moby Dick*, few people had trouble "understanding" what was going on. The greatest difficulty was organizing the material and putting it into a readable format. I found almost everyone had situations where facts were misstated, jumbled, or conflicting. In some cases the newswriting style was as foreign to students as an article in a scholarly journal. Students constantly had to look up archaic terms and *sic* seemed to be needed in almost every quotation. At first some people felt snowed under with material until they realized the

MODEL 42 (cont.)

importance of the proper selection of information; by degrees they began to realize that a story entitled "Police Continue Search for Killer" would offer little that was new and was hardly worth reading. (I was reminded of the typical comment I had heard on literary papers: "Every book says the same thing about *Moby Dick,* so what should I do?")

The papers themselves turned out to be the best I had ever received. They showed real hustle in the library and actual work in rewriting. A number of people found stories in papers other than the *Times,* and a few people discovered magazine articles concerning their murders. A couple of students had referred to encyclopedias or history books for general background material. To the best of my knowledge no paper was plagiarized, a fact I attribute to the students' interest in their topics (and, possibly, the fact that most of the news stories weren't written well enough to bother copying). There were no scissors-and-paste jobs; this may have been due to the built-in "narrative" structure and chrono-logical progression of the cases. And most important of all, I enjoyed reading the papers . . . even the single-spaced quotations over five lines.

Since then I have refined and expanded the project somewhat. Recent topics have dealt with political scandals, espionage cases, biographies of minor "historical" figures, trea-sure hunts, and bare-knuckle prize-fights. Some of my best papers have been on Indian "uprisings," in which students were amazed to read contemporary accounts of "gallant horse soldiers dispatching copper-colored wretches" (Ute Indian War—1879), or how a group of Mormons used Indians to wipe out a wagon train of immigrants (Mountain Mead-ow Massacre—1857). I now allow students to pick their own topics or "areas" if they wish and I have a few takers; however, famous crimes is still the most popular category.

With this approach students often encounter unusual research problems, including strange terminology no longer in use. One student came across the term "arsenic eater" in his case and eventually discovered it was a practice for girls in the late 1800s to eat small amounts of arsenic to lighten their complexions. Also, news stories often contradict each other because in an era of sensational journalism each reporter tried to write the most revealing story possible using essentially the same facts. This forces students to be very evaluative in their research.

The research papers in this volume are the result of this kind of investigation. They were all written by students in freshman English Composition at Shippensburg State College and represent a small sample of the cases students in this class have researched in past years. A few of the murder cases are unsolved, and although they were sometimes more difficult to work with, students found them fascinating because it allowed them to formulate theories about what happened. (In fact, some of the solutions to murders are so ingenious, I'm convinced they've found the answer!) But even in those cases that are solved, I encourage students to write conclusions that are evaluative or speculative.

I chose these cases for inclusion as examples of well-constructed research papers, but at the same time I tried to pick papers that are simply interesting to read by themselves. None of these "historical footnotes" has ever appeared in formal print and have generally been forgotten by time. I impress upon students the need for good quotations, statements that reflect the "temper of the times," and I think many of these papers fit that criterion. I have corrected the obvious typos and added a few marks of punctuation for the sake of clarity, but for all practical purposes, these papers are exactly as the students handed them in.

I should add that this approach is not a panacea and that not all my attempts are successful. Like everyone else, I receive papers that need a good proofreading or that lack continuity. A few people are unable to see the forest through the trees, and they spend pages recapping the predictable outcome of new trials and further appeals. A few times I was responsible for picking bad topics. Either they were too dull (Boston Police Strike) or else I tried to make the project too "literary" and it sank under its own weight. (One failure occurred when I assigned the story of the death of Floyd Collins in the Kentucky cave and asked the student to relate it to Robert Penn Warren's novel based on the episode. The paper might have worked for a senior English major, but for a freshman elementary student it was a disaster.)

At the end of the book I have included an annotated list of over 100 research topics that have resulted in superior papers for me, the cream of about 500 cases I have assigned in the last five years, along with some basic guidelines for assigning the topics. All of these

MODEL 42 (cont.)

assignments are workable and have enough material available to allow students to construct a research paper of about ten pages or more. Sometimes students can trace magazine articles written when the incident occurred, and a few cases are cited in books. Still, every attempt has been made to stay away from those cases which for all practical purposes have been "done" by other writers and prove nothing when students "rewrite" them.

Instructors who like this approach may wish to pick up *The Hutchinson Guide to Writing Research Papers* by Helene Hutchinson (Glencoe Press) and *Perception and Persuasion* by Raymond Paul and Pellegrino Goione (Crowell). These texts deal with the research paper in unusual ways and may suggest other ideas you can use. In any case, I hope this book gives you some fresh ideas so you'll never again be forced to read a dull and predictable research paper pasted together from critical books, or culled from a single "work." I really believe that once having tried this method you'll never go back to the *Moby Dick* casebook.

GUIDELINES FOR RESEARCHING AND WRITING ABOUT A NEWSPAPER CASE

Researching popular topics through contemporary newspapers presents its own unique problems (and rewards). Teachers need to be especially aware of two of these problems. The first is that students are in complete command of their topic. No one else in the school (probably even the country) has more information than they do. In a sense, they will become the world's expert on a piece of historical minutia. This is as it should be, but at times it is difficult to provide specific help in the same way one could if the topic were on, say, *Moby Dick*. Still, most students will be able to handle the research on their own. Just warn them that newspapers often cover a story only when it's "hot." Later stories may fill in missing pieces, or students may find that details initially considered important fade as more bizarre elements enter the case.

The second unique aspect of this assignment is that these kinds of topics, although encased in a chronological format, are not neatly organized like a literary assignment. There are false leads, surprising revelations, characters who appear and disappear—in short, it is a real research problem rather than a manufactured topic. It is probably best to tell students to wade through it the first time as though the case were a Faulkner novel, and then begin to assimilate the important material into a streamlined account. The process of understanding the topic, choosing salient facts, selecting striking quotations, and putting everything in readable form is what writing a research paper is all about. Footnotes and bibliography, although important, are all mechanical items that come during the final writing.

LIBRARY RESEARCH EXERCISES

For many students a library can be a scary place. All those books, people working so quietly—everybody seems to know what they're doing and they all look so confident. Most students have been to the library before and can use the card catalog, and with a little luck they can find the book they're after (if it hasn't been lost or stolen or checked out by a faculty member for the past two years). But it's a frustrating experience because they know there's material there that would help them with a paper if only they could stumble across it. When it comes to indexes and micromaterials the situation is often frightening because most students have never used these and perhaps don't knew they exist. I have found that a library tour which concentrates almsot exclusively on these items is worth the time. Even the process of physically putting a reel of microfilm on the machine is not too mundane a maneuver; students can see how to adjust the focus and then correctly reshelve the material. College librarians seem eager to help with this, and they become "willing accomplices" when students investigate their cases.

At the conclusion of the tour I pass out a brief research exercise sheet designed to force students into using the indexes and microfilm machines that have just been examined. The three items should average out to a page and a half and take about forty-five minutes to complete.

MODEL 42 (cont.)

1. What happened on the day you were born? or Write a brief paragraph on what happened in the world on this date in the year _____. (Deal especially with "curiosities," the sociology of the times, and advertisements.)

These questions force students to actually put a reel of the *New York Times* on a microfilm machine and use it. When writing about the day of their birth, students should touch on world news, sports, movies playing at the time, and want ads. Currently I use the latter question, giving each student a different year in the nineteenth century. Then, by using the current month and day, I ask for a brief paragraph on the "temper of the times." Ask them to explain what the quality of life was like on, say, September 4, 1883. Impress upon them to stay away from floods, world news, etc., but instead concentrate on the "passions" and "oddities" of the day. How did people live? What did they wear? What strange news stories appeared? Most students find this fascinating and the results are often interesting to read.

Sample Response

On January 19, 1882, there seemed to be as many disasters in the news as there are today. There were quite a few fires, ship wrecks, murders, and a freight train was demolished while "running over 30 miles an hour."

Opera houses were popular entertainment in the North, as were "lynching parties" in the South. For 25¢ one could use toboggan trails or play polo, and for $1.50 one could have an orchestra seat at Augustin Daly's Broadway comedy *Railroad of Love*. Curling, a game played on ice with large rounded stones, and playing the zither, a flat stringed instrument, were both popular pastimes. A tour in the tropical seas was $5 a day on Atlas Lines' "comfortable passenger steamers."

On this day the *New York Times* offered two positions for females: one as a laundress and the other as a chambermaid. More jobs were advertised for men, but they didn't show any improvement—mostly butlers and office boys. Immigrants offered their services as cooks, governesses, nurses, coachmen, and grooms. Most applicants were not so much interested in salary as in a good home. Religion, race, and sobriety were always mentioned in ads.

Obituaries listed ten children who died at about the age of one year. There were three suicides, one because of "unrequited love." Duffy's Pure Malt Whiskey claimed it could cure the common cold, while Bromo Effervescent Caffeine simply stated it "cures all."

The article I found the most fascinating was entitled "Breaking Stone for a Kiss." The story concerned a man arrested for kissing a strange woman on the cheek. He was charged with assault and sentenced to six months at hard labor.

Betsy Banham

2. Write a brief account of the Harvard/Yale game in the year _____. (How the game was played, the cheers, the dress styles, etc.)

This requires students to use the *New York Times Index* for the first time. It works well using any year since the 1880s. Ask students to include the score, the heroes, how the game of football was played at that time, and what people wore. (This was a social event as much as anything else and often received front page coverage.) In a few of the years no game was played, but there is usually an explanation given and this, or an alternate game, can substitute. Most students will be surprised at how much football has changed and how descriptive the accounts are, e.g., "Haskell was laid out with an unlucky blow in the face, from which blood streamed." Team cheers are often quoted and they also prove interesting. (My favorite is "breck-akek-kek, co-ax, co-ax! whoo-up, whoo-up, paraballo '92'.")

Sample Response

Harvard and Yale did not play each other from 1894 to 1896, so I chose the Yale/Carlisle game that was played on October 25, 1896. Yale was a football power and Carlisle was a team with good size but without much knowledge of the game. Yale was expected to run away with the contest but didn't.

According to the *New York Times* account of the game, Carlisle outplayed Yale but was the victim of a "wrong decision" on the part of referee W. O. Hickcock. In the second half, with Yale leading 12–6, Carlisle running back Seneca broke a few tackles and scampered 37 yards for a touchdown. The 5,000 spectators cheered wildly (they were pro-Carlisle) and men waved their hats in the air, pretty girls clapped their hands and above the din could be heard the shrill Indian cry of "hi, hi, Carlisle, hi, hi!" But their joy was short-lived as Hickcock called the play back because he thought Yale had stopped Seneca near the line of scimmage. An argument erupted and Carlisle threatened to walk off the field if the TD didn't count. The referee persisted and the game eventually continued after some heated discussion. Yale won, but the real winners were Carlisle. After the game the fans rushed the field, hoisted the Carlisle players on their shoulders and carried them off amid a wave of cheering.

Chris Williams

3. Pick one movie made in the year _____ and tell what the critics thought about it. (Try to pick a title that sounds particularly corny.)

The third item is designed to show students how to use the *Readers' Guide to Periodical Literature* and then look up a magazine article from it. I begin with the year 1930, and by assigning different years I ask students to select a movie that sounds unusual and particularly corny. *(Bonzo Goes to College, Superman in the Volcano, Gog).* I then ask for a synopsis of one or two magazines' reviews of the film. In order to complete this assignment students must use the *Readers' Guide,* the library's circular file of catalogued periodicals, and magazine articles in a bound volume or on microfilm.

Sample Response

Time magazine described the 1946 film *Smoky* as "the story of a long, beautiful, rather intense friendship between Fred MacMurray and a horse." (Nowadays, such a description would lead to just one conclusion—rated X.) Actually, *Newsweek* called *Smoky* "a natural for youngsters and horse lovers . . . it makes a pleasant

---

RESEARCH PAPER FACT SHEET

Name _____

Working Title of Paper:
1. Period of time encompassed by topic. (Give exact date of first story and the year and month of conclusion.)

2. Categories under which topic is indexed.

3. Periodical Sources. (List articles in magazines, books, and all newspaper editorials on case.)

4. Locale where events took place. (Use an atlas if needed—try to find a local map if possible.)

5. People involved. (List major figures in case—victim, killer, detectives, etc.)

6. The amount of material on my topic is (A) enormous (B) very great (C) adequate (D) somewhat less than adequate (E) meager.

evening even for the nonequestrian moviegoer." In the film, Smoky, who has the distinction of playing both himself and the title role, is a beautiful black stallion who is adored by everyone—everyone, that is, except the villain (Bruce Cabot). There's the usual boy/girl thing between MacMurray and Anne Baxter, but it never really gets very far and *Time* stated that "the important relationship is between Cowpuncher MacMurray and stallion." Burl Ives made his film debut here and sang "Streets of Laredo," "Down in the Valley," and "Blue Tail Fly." Both *Time* and *Newsweek* treated the new film enthusiastically, pershaps because the crux of the story was about a horse—a nice shiny black horse who doesn't smoke, drink, or watch television. As *Newsweek* said, "the human beings do a nice job, but Smoky steals the show."

Bill Calaman

This general format can be used for assignments in *Book Review Digest, Education Index, Essay and General Literature Index,* and *PMLA Bibliographies,* but they are not as interesting nor are they really needed for researching murder cases. At a different point in the course I do ask students to look up one issue of *Popular Mechanics* (dating from 1902) and report on one of the more bizarre inventions of the day. These reports on electric chairs to cure seasickness, spikes to keep boys off the rears of cars, and automatic music page turners are usually fascinating. By this time students are quite familiar with the library's reference section and are able to begin research papers that use these kinds of resources.

PREPARATION AND RESEARCH

GAINING PERSPECTIVE

Now that students have had some research experience in the library, I am ready to introduce the project and assign the topics. For the most part I just shuffle the case cards and deal them out, but occasionally I take requests or attempt to match special cases to certain students. At the outset of the course I ask each student to indicate personal interests (sports, crime, Indians, historical era, etc.) as well as home town and college major. Sometimes I am able to assign a student a home town case, or one that fits a specific interest, but this is rather rare.

Upon receiving their cards, the students begin to immerse themselves in the time period. I tell them to "think 1878," for example, and they must write a brief page on what life was like in their year. What concerned people? What did they wear? Who was important? What entertainment existed? (This is like question one in the previous assignment but now students will probably do a better job.) In many instances, this information can be used in the introduction to the paper, especially if the murder case reflects dated mores or customs of the era. In the Frank T. Young case, the murder occurs in a Hanson Cab, but the girl with this topic had no idea what a Hanson Cab was so she had to look it up before she could continue her paper. Red Cassidy's murder in 1929 seems right out of the movies, and it was necessary for the student to read books on the gangland period to put it into perspective. This background research sets the scene for detailed investigation later. A brief perusal of scattered newspapers during that year usually suffices, but enterprising students will find books of popular history to read. (About a week into their research, I ask them who the President was during the period they are researching. Some are chagrined when they don't know.)

Next, students must ascertain the general layout and circumstances of their cases as best they can by using the *New York Times Index.* I ask them not to go to the papers themselves, but to scan the headings in the *Index* and fill in certain information on a "research paper fact sheet" (see sample). Item one establishes the dates a case begins and ends, essential in ascertaining the scope of a case. Most of the cases continue for a period of years, and because of frequent changes in the *Index's* format, it is easy to miss items without careful research. (In the middle nineteenth century a number of years appear in the same *Index;* in the 1920s each year is divided into six-month periods; and in the 1930s the *Index* is in two volumes alphabetically divided.) The headings usually give students an idea of what the case is all about and when the topic ends, but once into the case, some are surprised to discover that an article may appear many years later.

Item two alerts students to the headings under which their topic is indexed. Major

MODEL 42 (cont.)

headings often change as the case progresses; early years are subject oriented under "Editorials," "Political," "War," and "Miscellaneous."

Item three requires a list of periodical sources, and sends students to the *Readers' Guide to Periodical Literature* (or to *Poole's Index* if the case is before 1890). About a fourth of the topics are the subject of magazine articles or are cited in books. (Any case that resulted in a trial of some kind has a good chance of being reported in magazines, if only by a short notice.) Some students, willing to settle for newspaper articles alone, become easily discouraged when trying to use the archaic format in *Poole's Index* (which lists magazine articles from 1802–1906). They should be encouraged to use this and other references, and warned to check as far as ten years beyond their case's conclusion for material. Students are also asked to note any editorials on their case, as they are must reading.

Usually the major headings (e.g., "murder") are all that are needed here, but sometimes articles are cited by key names in the case. *The International Index to Periodicals* (beginning in 1907 but changing in 1965 to the *Social Science and Humanities Index*) is a helpful tool. Other reference books that may include material and are worth checking are *Index to Legal Periodicals* and *Psychoanalysis, Psychiatry, and Law*. Later, students may need to use *A Dictionary of the Underworld* by Eric Partridge, the *Encyclopedia of Crimes and Criminals*, and the *Dictionary of Criminology* to look up special terms. The remaining items on the fact sheet are self-explanatory. After students hand this in, class discussion about their cases usually generates enthusiasm for getting started, and it is sometimes difficult to keep students from moving ahead before they are ready.

RESEARCH WITH THE ACCENT ON THE LAST SYLLABLE

Before students can begin reading and notetaking, they must decide what they will read. I ask them to go back to the *New York Times Index* and select the stories they plan to read. Because nearly every case has a great deal of material, it is necessary for students to screen the articles carefully. Some students do this better than others, of course, but rough guidelines can be employed. If a head reads "Police Continue Search for Killer," it can be assumed that nothing new will be revealed and the article is hardly worth reading. Trials drag on, and something like "Coroner Testifies Today" can probably be left out. Appeals, jury selection, stays of execution—any item that doesn't indicate in the headline that the case is developing significantly (especially retrials with predictable outcomes) can usually be deleted. But there are no hard and fast rules. The William McClintock murder requires a close reading of something like sixty articles—almost the entire case—while the Sir Roger Charles Tichborne fiasco has over 200 stories, but only about thirty-five key items need to be read. As a general rule, the more the person reads the better off he or she is and the greater the chances for a good paper. But students tell me they take other classes besides mine (I sometimes forget that) and must fit their research into available time. When students become lost because they have selected too few articles, they can always backtrack and pick up missed stories.

As the students screen their articles, they are required to copy the essential information for finding them. (I suggest that each student buy a spiral notebook to keep this and other research material in. The chronological nature of the cases lends itself to the notebook, or note cards, procedure.) A typical *Index* entry under "Murders" might be: "Logan, (Mrs.) M; body found; Mrs. L. B. Judson admits burying it; she and husband arraigned, Los Angeles, D 23, 15:7." Among other things, students learn the story is in the *New York Times* of December 23 (they should also jot down the year—1944 in this case); I tell them to forget the column number (the last figure) because they will quickly spot the case on the page. And I warn them to be very careful to get the page number correct (page 15 in this sample). Almost every student will notice mistakes between dates and page numbers from the *New York Times Index* and the papers themselves, and this proves exasperating enough without copying the pages incorrectly to begin with. Students will encounter juicy sounding stories listed in the *Index* that simply don't exist; or they will find them on the wrong pages; or they will stumble across them in papers printed a month later along with stories that were never indexed. It is also important to be on the lookout for mistakes in the day to day unraveling of a case. Names will be spelled several ways, facts will be reversed, people shot in opening stories turn out to be hanged in later accounts. . . . In

MODEL 42 (cont.)

short, there are as many mistakes in nineteenth-century papers as there are in news stories today. This forces students to be careful researchers—one of the project goals. *And most important of all, I warn students, upon threat of death or failure, not to write in the* Index. The assigned students are usually the only ones dealing with the case in the history of the school, so tell them any underlined items are like leaving fingerprints.

The first week of this project is a key period because, in a sense, students are constructing their bibliographies. Care must be taken that all pages of any given story are included and that the important sources are recorded for future reading. I request a minimum of twenty-five sources, but thirty is better, and some run to forty or more. The key is that they include the necessary stories to construct a ten to twelve page paper.

WORDS OF CAUTION

As students begin reading and taking notes, the key item to stress is that they be as accurate as possible. News stories in papers from earlier periods read far differently than modern accounts. It seems no one ever died without a reporter hovering near to record a melodramatic statement, and every event is "the most dastardly crime every perpetrated in this fair city." Autopsies are reprinted, reporters have no qualms about accusing suspects, and editors always seem incensed about justice (or the lack of it). Racism is blatant, violence is quick, and sex is only hinted at. Students will be dumbstruck over some of the attitudes, and the "language" of the stories makes for some interesting class discussions. In a sense, more is told in these stories, but the chronological sequence of events is sometimes inaccurate in order to concentrate on the sensational material. Caution students to be skeptical, read between the lines, and actually research words they don't understand. Sex crimes are a case in point, for the crime is often explained in coded terms. (When it is reported that an "outrage" was committed, it means the girl was raped.) Psychiatrists are called "alienists," the Tombs is the name for the New York City detention center, "arsenic eating" was the practice of swallowing arsenic to impart a light complexion for cosmetic purposes, "white slavers" seem to lurk everywhere—it was the best of times, the worst of times. *All stories need to be taken with a grain of salt* and all sources evaluated in the same way modern scholars investigate conclusions arrived at by earlier researchers.

Remind students that important details, such as physical descriptions, are often given when a story breaks, but are never repeated. On the other hand, newspapers will give vast coverage to items that ultimately are of little importance simply because there is nothing else to report. (In the Anna Aumuller case, abundant space was devoted to stories about the kind of rock found with the body, a dead-end clue that was never mentioned again after an arrest was made.) In a sense, the student must provide an exact, step-by-step reconstruction of what happened, even filling in gaps with logical hypotheses if needed.

If a case goes to trial, the coverage tends to be daily, with long stretches of dialogue that simply lay the groundwork for future evidence. In these cases, students can scan the material very quickly. In fact, there are times when twenty stories can be reduced to a single line, such as: "After a long trial Albert Fish was convicted and sentenced to death."

A better method of dealing with trial material is to tell students to take courtroom testimony and use it elsewhere in the paper. During the trial, facts about the crime itself will come out that can be used in the introduction to the paper. Thus, rather than repeat the case or use the trial as the focal point, it is often possible to treat the trial as a single source of information. (This is especially true where biographical material on the victim or murderer is brought out.)

At the same time students are researching indexed stories or articles, they should be alert for material that was never cited, especially letters-to-the-editor. Cases that capture public attention often bring community reactions which range from the violent to the bizarre, and sometimes they reveal attitudes not reflected in news stories themselves. A quick glance at editorial pages is worth the effort, and a keen eye almost always results in a find of uncatalogued material. (The *New York Times* indexing for the early years is particularly "incomplete.")

Finally, it is important to warn students never to assume their case is over. People rarely stay in prison for life, or they make news while in prison, or at times they escape from prison. I ask that everyone go at least five years beyond the "last" story in the *New York*

MODEL 42 (cont.)

Times Index to be sure nothing new occurs that should be reported, and sometimes even that is not far enough. Magazine articles appear that recap the case and add further information some twenty years later, while unsolved cases are mentioned in the news every time a similar crime takes place. Harry Thaw, who killed Stanford White in 1906, was later convicted of assaulting a young boy and finally died in 1947, at which time the papers reviewed his life. It is worth remembering, too, that any event touching on Patty Hearst will make news the rest of her life.

This may be the point at which the traditional cautions about plagiarism should be mentioned. Tell students you don't want to read the old newspaper stories, but want to see their account—written in a modern style—of what happened. Occasionally I do receive research papers taken word for word from the newspapers, but the "style" shows every time. When a boxer is "thrown against the hempen strands," or a man "succumbed to a wound by his unregenerated cohort," it's pretty obvious that the student didn't write it. Most people will be forced to reshape the material because it is so badly written in the newspapers or the language is so out of date. Those rare papers that are plagiarized usually have tense and language problems so pronounced that they fail on the basis of style alone. (A preliminary check of any rough draft material, followed, if necessary, by a mild inquiry, is usually enough to deter this practice.)

ALTERNATE SOURCES

In the course of five years I have had freshman students do some amazing pieces of research, including visiting the scenes of crimes, writing descendants in the cases for information, checking trial transcripts in law libraries, and calling people once involved in the story. (In one instance I was queried by the FBI because a student tried to check out his case through an agent at the Washington office; they thought perhaps I knew something about a 1939 kidnapping that was still open on their records.) Early in the research process, I distribute a suggested format for a letter requesting information (see sample). I have found that about ten percent of any given class are able to take advantage of it.

For the most part, however, students stick to college library resources. Yet even here more is available than just the *New York Times*. I now require students to find stories in other papers and compare the accounts to decide on the accuracy of certain points. Although the *Times* is the only paper with an index to stories, it is quite easy to check exact days in other papers when a particular case is "hot." The *Philadelphia Inquirer, Chicago Tribune, New Orleans Times Picayune, Los Angeles Times, St. Louis Post Dispatch,* and many local papers all printed before the age of wire services will have revealing stories containing different information. If the library carries *Frank Leslie's Illustrated Newspaper* (1855–1922), this will give much more sensationalized accounts of cases than the *New York Times,* and students will find interesting material here. I encourage students to write letters to small town editors where a case occurred, and many times the college library can locate obscure material through interlibrary loan. The student working on the 1922 Daniel Kaber murder, for instance, was sent a complete file of all the stories from the *Cleveland Plain Dealer,* while the editor of the *Hartford Courant* provided valuable assistance to a girl investigating the 1878 Mary Stannard Case. (One item was a copy of a poem that circulated at the time which concludes: "Now all young ladies a warning take/Whether you're great or small/If you would not like to be cut in pieces/And pickled in alcohol.") These kinds of exercises not only result in better student papers, but make freshmen feel they are really involved in original research.

WRITING THE PAPER

The initial time spent on research and notetaking will vary according to the student, the case involved, and the procedure used. If the student has a particularly complicated case, or it extends for a number of years, it can take as long as two weeks just to assimilate all the materials and choose what will be read. For the average student, however, one week is enough to compile a tentative list of news articles and periodical sources to be read. (Usually the list has to be expanded once the reading is underway.)

As soon as the reading is begun students probably need two to three weeks (again depending on their case) to cover all the materials, take notes, and perhaps construct a

MODEL 42 (cont.)

Name
Address
City, State

Dear _____

As a term paper assignment in one of my college courses I am researching the
_____ murder which occurred on _____. To date
I have read all of the accounts of this case in the *New York Times* and am attempting to find other sources that might be available.

I would like to inquire if you might have material about this subject or opinions on
the case that might not generally be known. Because your paper once reported
these events (or because your family was once connected with some of these
events) I thought I would write you for information. Any information you could supply
would be greatly appreciated.

Sincerely,

Name
Address
City, State

rough draft. During the period students are reading the microfilmed copies of the *New
York Times* and other papers, class time will probably be spent on bibliographical format.
Footnoting and footnote form are important considerations, and sample newspaper footnotes can be gone over in class. The footnotes on the papers . . . generally follow the MLA
format, but there are so many variations in form I hesitate to advance a definitive style. Any
standard research guide works, and I leave it to teachers to decide among MLA, Turabian,
Campbell, etc.

INTRODUCTIONS

Although a variety of introductions can be used, the typical or standard introduction for a
paper of this kind is one that follows the old newspaper dictate of who, what, when, where.
Because most of the research papers will follow a chronological approach, it is easy for
students to begin with the first date and then explain the circumstances of the case: "On
January 23, 1879, the body of Diane Gott was discovered in an abandoned house on the
outskirts of Toledo, Ohio." This simple opening sentence is enough to explain the case's
background and also whet the reader's appetite. . . .

But even this kind of opening can be improved upon by most students with the addition
of a sentence or two at the end of the introduction that puts the case into larger perspective or hints at how it will all end. The paper on Jacob Rosenzweig, for instance, has an
introduction that begins with the girl's death but then moves quickly into the problem of
abortion in the nineteenth century. The introductions to the papers on Laura Fair and
William Kemmler both have a kind of esthetic distance to them, evoked through the use of
a quotation in the last line of the introduction. Perhaps the best kind of introduction is one
which deals entirely with general background, the milieu, the temper of the times. The
Major Cofran paper begins by explaining the state of postwar Germany; the Red Cassidy
introduction sketches the era of Prohibition; the paper on the Bannock War first reviews
previous Indian conflicts. This kind of introduction tends to be much smoother than just a
terse recital of the facts.

Instructors might wish to pass out copies of newsstand detective magazines as samples
of how cases can be introduced. They tend to be overly dramatic (even somewhat laugh-
able for sophisticated readers), but Professor Gene Collier of East Central University in
Oklahoma finds that these openings show "pizzazz and sparkle . . . and reassure the

MODEL 42 (cont.)

student writer that he can cause the reader to want more." At times students must be cautioned to "ease up" on their introductions and even tone down the material. Otherwise the result ends up like the following introduction I received a few years ago: "On October 14, 1911, the future of Avis Linnell was drastically changed. There was to be no future for she died in her room."

THE SEARCH FOR GOOD QUOTATIONS

Quotations can make or break a paper, so by the second week I ask students to hand in two quotations they plan to use in their final report. These are read in class and commented on, and students soon get an idea of what works and what doesn't. Anything in the nature of an opinion, theory, or conclusion by the police or the newspaper should be considered as a possible quotation, and a statement that reflects the mores or attitudes of the period is a must. Quotations that act as a brief summary of events, relate important pieces of information, give the "flavor" of the situation, are dramatic, racist, ironic, or satiric, or are simply so stunning that the student marvels to himself, "I don't believe anyone would say that!" should be considered. I think many of the papers . . . exhibit good choices of quotations, but here are a few that other students have used:

> "There were many who fancied that the murder was the work of negroes, and this fancy was based upon the rumor that Mrs. Hull had been outraged before she was murdered." (Jane Hull Case, 1879)

> Mrs. Hull was buried on Saturday, June 14, 1879. Throngs of people gathered outside the house and "some of them stuck so close it was evident they would consider it an honor if the hearse had run over them." Even a few days after the burial children would come to stare at the house, yet "police made no effort to drive them away, but let them drink their fill of sensation in such little drops as they could get." (Jane Hull Case, 1879)

> "The fact that so much unnecessary violence had been used, evidently after the girl's life had been ended by the cut across the throat, suggested to many that a negro, brutal always to the last degree in such cases, was the perpetrator of the crime." (Rahway Mystery, 1887)

Class time is also spent on explaining how quotations should be used in the papers. Quotations within quotations, ellipsis marks, brackets, and punctuation marks are studied through the use of a handbook, and I urge students to replace "said" with terms such as "remarked, exclaimed, replied, declared, reported," etc. Almost every quotation needs to be worked on in some way and *sic* is used much more often with this project than in more formal papers. Because of the narrative aspect of these kinds of papers, I suggest to students that they employ their own words in the middle of quotations.

> "The plain fact is that there was no excuse whatsoever for the brutality of the police," reported a *New York Times* editorial. "If there were a spark of decency or self-respect in the minds of the police commissioners, the offenders would be sharply pursued and severely disciplined."

> "The life of one white man is worth more," stated Miss Meeker, "than all the Indians from the beginning of their creation."

These forms make the papers more readable and add a slightly creative aspect.

Further admonitions might include the warning that extremely long quotations should be avoided (people seldom read them), and that it is not a good idea to use back-to-back quotations or a long series of quotations interspersed with the author's words. A rough guideline I use is that quotations should average no more than two per page, with only two long, indented quotations in the paper.

PUTTING THE PAPER TOGETHER

One of the major advantages of these kinds of topics for beginning writers is that an organizational framework is built in; events, for the most part, proceed chronologically. Still, many of these cases are confusing, and students should be cautioned that all items must be made clear to the reader. Time jumps from one event to another need to be

MODEL 42 (cont.)

pointed out, and dates (including the year) should be mentioned throughout the paper. Sentences such as the following can be employed:

"Two months later, on December 17, 1899, the case was reopened. . . ."

"It was not until the spring of 1900 that the suspect was apprehended."

"After nearly a year of appeals, Smith was executed on February 23, 1901."

These devices aid the reader with the sequence of events and retain the narrative aspect of the case.

Whenever possible, a person's title, or relationship to the case, should be cited to help readers identify the personalities involved. Most of the topics have a myriad of people coming and going throughout the narrative, so to make a key figure stand out (as well as to avoid repetitiveness) it is better to refer to Mr. Smith one time, the grocer another, and then call him "the suspect" in the following line.

Also, witnesses tend to repeat the same facts in newspaper accounts, and it is best if students pick just one person's story to recount rather than report essentially the same testimony from several people. I further urge students to "personalize" their papers whenever possible by including physical descriptions of people and the locale.

On a winter afternoon in 1917, pretty eighteen-year-old Beth Pomerantz left her Pittsburgh, Pennsylvania, home saying she was going to a repair shop a few blocks away to have her skates sharpened. The neighborhood near her house was frequented by many retired men who in their youth had worked in the grimy steel mills on the outskirts of the city.

Many times these details do not appear until much later in the story (often during the trial), but they can be easily incorporated in earlier parts of the paper. As mentioned before, trial material, if there is a trial, tends to be long and somewhat dry. At times whole accounts can be skimmed, especially if the information is predictable. Simply because there is more of it than other kinds of news should not seduce the student into using it in a wholesale manner.

WHAT TO DOCUMENT

The decision of what to footnote is a constant problem in this and other kinds of papers. Helping students distinguish what is "general information" is something that is seldom clear until graduate school I'm afraid, but again a rough guideline can be employed. As a rule anything that is constantly repeated, or *would be generally known by readers of the time,* is not footnoted. Details—dates, specific facts, exact terms—and of course all quotations require footnotes. Actually, a good deal of the writing here will be in the form of transitional sentences and background information and thus will not require a footnote. I urge students to footnote in terms of the individual sentence rather than attempt an all-inclusive footnote at the end of a paragraph.

Content footnotes are often required to define terms and include peripheral material. I require at least one content footnote, and many of these are as interesting as items included in the body of the paper. Also, content footnotes can be used to help explain vast shifts in time between events in a case. Bibliographies are somewhat easier to construct, but to avoid padding I ask that they be called "Working Bibliographies" and only stories *actually consulted and used* be included. (I require a minimum of twenty-five sources.)

CONSTRUCTING CONCLUSIONS

Because these kinds of topics are often open-ended, I ask students to devote the last two pages to their own views of the case. Was justice done? What mistakes were made? Did they find the right man? In short, as the world's expert on this case, each student must present an opinion on what happened. In unsolved cases I ask students to construct a solution, and these are often ingenious and convincing. In fact, I'm sure some of my students have solved some nineteenth-century murders (just as Edgar Allan Poe claimed he did)! Perhaps because we live in an age that believes in conspiracy, I get a great number of solutions that reflect this trend, but actually any summary that shows thought receives praise. During the last two weeks of the course I have each student give a brief oral report on his or her case, and at that time conclusions usually come under attack and

MODEL 42 (cont.)

A TEN POINT RESEARCH PAPER CHECKLIST FOR STUDENTS

1. Footnotes are numbered correctly and all commas are correct. *Dates and page numbes are accurate.* At least *one* content footnote should appear. At least one source besides the *New York Times* should be used if at all possible.
2. The bibliography is correct—reverse indentation, periods after titles, newspapers underlined, alphabetical order, etc.
3. Quotations are accurate and introduced by verbs other than "said." Where possible your own words are fused within quotations and colons and semicolons are used where needed. Brackets, ellipses, and *sic* are used to make quotations more "streamlined."
4. The date of your case is mentioned at various points in the paper, not just your introduction.
5. Attempts have been made to include the physical description of people, their position, background, etc. The paper has a "personal" touch.
6. No "you's" or "I's" in the body of the paper. The paper is written in the past tense.
7. The paper is written in your words, your own style—rather than just changing a few words from the *New York Times;* the paper is a complete rewriting.
8. The paper is well organized and easy for a reader to follow without becoming lost in a mass of detail.
9. The last two pages set forth your own analysis of the case.
10. Final copy is in a folder, has been proofread carefully, and a carbon copy is included.

---

require a good defense. I have found that the other students seem particularly interested in this phase of the course, and it's the only experience I can remember when students actually listen to their colleagues deliver an oral report. Professor Chris Madigan of Virginia Commonwealth University has his students play defense or prosecuting attorney in an oral presentation/summation to the rest of the class or jury. He reports that he is pleased with some of the questions classmates ask, although the student usually has no trouble getting the verdict desired.

THE FINAL CHECK

About a week before papers are due, I hand out "A Ten Point Research Paper Checklist for Students" (see sample). The "points" stress the form of the paper—footnotes, bibliography, quotations, etc., and for the most part are a review of material that has been covered previously. Going over these details before handing the paper in usually reduces the number of careless and "nit-picking" errors that so often blemish an otherwise good paper. Most students, having spent a good deal of time and energy on these papers, are eager to make the final product as perfect as possible.

MISCHIEF AND MAYHEM

Some of my better student papers have been on shipwrecks, treasure hunts, Indian "uprisings," sports event, and assorted scandals. In general these are handled in the same way, but there are usually more magazine articles available. In the 1860s "Indians" are indexed in the "War" section, while in the 1870s the subject is placed under "Political." (Rather interesting in itself.) Although there are a few "happy ending" Indian stories, most of the cases recount how "hardy miners dispatched heathen savages," and most students will be amazed to read about attitudes held during this period. In many ways these topics are more intriguing than murders, allowing students to be more creative in their papers. I have found that journalism students in particular like these kinds of topics and handle them as they could a feature story. After all, not all murders are interesting after a certain point, and I am reminded of the comment from the student who worked on a dismemberment case and complained that after they found the parts of the body, the "case was pretty cut and dried."

MODEL 42 (cont.)

I have also tried other approaches. One term I simply concentrated on one period in history—the 1920s. Our class "text" was Frederick Lewis Allen's *Only Yesterday,* and every student investigated a strange event during that wild period. (It seemed that for awhile I was awash, as it were, in bootleg alcohol.) On another occasion I simply asked for a history of what life was like in our area in a particular year in the nineteenth century. By using our microfilm files of old weekly county newspapers, students compiled some bizarre local histories—a kind of freaky *Foxfire.* Some students have written on their family histories, researched prior inhabitants of old houses, and taken events reported in the *London Times* from the eighteenth century to produce a kind of "Bicentennial Minutes" format about concerns of the time. Sports is another treasure trove of material, and a paper on the 1922 Princeton football season, for instance, works well as the "amazing Princeton princes go undefeated, untied, and undoubted."

I always keep a copy of each paper done and my office bulges with as many files as any big city police department. And although I never planned on it, I've become an expert on American murders since 1851, something that makes me more popular at cocktail parties. My point here is that this procedure for dealing with freshman research papers has a number of advantages, I think, and for those interested in trying it, I guarantee you'll never again be forced to read another dull and predictable paper. And this is a claim I have never found on the back of a college text on research paper writing.

MODEL 43   REVVING UP FOR COLLEGE

Elective Mini-Course
Grade: 12
Theme: Revving Up for College
Goal: To provide the student with the opportunity to evaluate, reinforce, sharpen, and extend his or her thinking-learning-communicating skills.
Teaching Strategies and Procedures:

After class orientation to the course—its purpose, scope, sequence, and schedule—each student will work independently on areas of skill development uniquely reflective or his or her competency level; all students will compile their own *Practical Scholar's Handbook for Lifelong Learning* and master the techniques of composing a resumé, a vita, and a letter of application.

Orientation to the course includes the students' taking the *National Test of Library Skills* (Larlin Corp.) as a quick review of basic reference skills, a pinpointing of areas of weakness, and an example of the kind of reference skill test given by many colleges and universities.

The scope of the course includes: diagnosis of the student's level of competence in each area of the thinking-learning-communicating skills continuum (see Appendix F, Thinking-Learning-Communicating Skills Continuum, K–12) and building to strength all areas indicating less than mastery; identification of basic reference tools needing further exploration (see Appendix G, Basic Reference Tools) and the systematic study of those tools; the review of the decimal system of outlining; the introduction or review of the Library of Congress classification system; the comparison of basic style manuals most commonly used in colleges and universities; and mastering the techniques of composing a resumé, a vita, and a letter of application.

From the first to the last day of the course, the students will compile their own vade mecum, *The Practical Scholar's Handbook for Lifelong Learning.* The basic Table of Contents will include:

Personal Plan Book: Dates, Meetings, Special Events, Appointments, Assignments, etc.

Thinking-Learning-Communicating Skills Continuum, K–12 (see Appendix F)

Basic Reference Tools (see Appendix G)

Learning Guides and Style Sheets (see Figure 4, Cybernetic-Decisional Model of Social Change, as an example).

MODEL 43 (cont.)

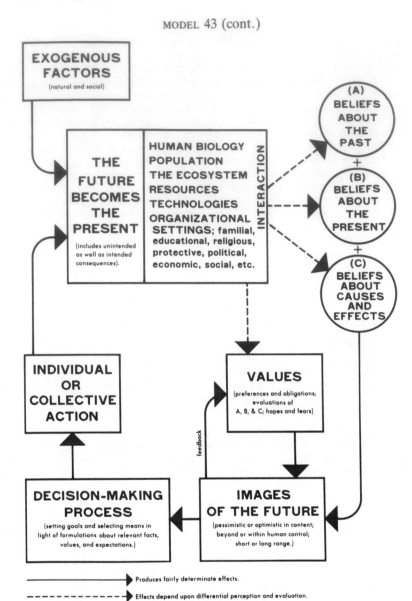

FIGURE 4. Cybernetic-Decisional Model of Social Change. From *The Sociology of the Future* by Wendell Bell and James A. Mau, editors. © 1971 by Russell Sage Foundation, New York. Reprinted by permission.

Research Guides
   How to Do Research
   Rules of Thumb for Researchers
   Checklist for Rewriting
   How to Use the *Readers' Guide*
   LC Classification Outline
Style Manuals: Contents Analysis
   A Handbook for Scholars by Mary-Claire van Leunen

MODEL 43 (cont.)

A Manual of Style . . . by the University of Chicago Press

MLA Handbook for Writers of Research Papers, Theses, and Dissertations by the Modern Language Association

The Modern Researcher by Jacques Barzun and Henry F. Graff

Student's Guide for Writing College Papers by Kate L. Turabian

Writing Research Papers by James Lester

Model Resumé

Model Vita

Model Letter of Application

8

Independent Study

The operations and goals in independent study, outlined in Table 6, illustrate how study facilitates the introduction, reinforcement, and extension of basic inquiry skills (see Appendix F). Independent study provides the opportunity for gifted students to investigate at firsthand real topics and/or problems of personal interest and concern. Gifted students need to master both the input and process phases of investigative activity specified by Renzulli (see Table 7). In independent study, the major responsibility of the teacher or mentor is to assist the student in identifying, refining, and focusing the problem (see Example 7, Management Plan for Individual or Small-Group Investigation) and to assist the student in learning how to apply the input-process procedures as the student proceeds with his or her investigation.

TABLE 6 OPERATIONS AND GOALS IN INDEPENDENT STUDY*

OPERATIONS	GOALS
Searching: The development of techniques and the introduction to materials that develop learning-to-learn skills. Example: Students using journal articles and interviews to glean important information.	Access to an array of persons, ideas, materials, experiences, and environments and the ability to evaluate the validity of information.
Assimilating: The process of "digesting" acquired information. Example: Students hypothesize solutions and make inferences.	Experiences at various levels of conceptualization including memory, translation, interpretation, application, analyses, synthesis, and evaluation.
Reporting: The expression of learned information or skills in some formalized outcome. Example: Students present information from a comparative study in a research paper.	Applying acquired information to the real-life world.

*Adapted from California State Department of Education, *Principles, Objectives, and Curricula for Programs in the Education of Mentally Gifted Minors* (Sacramento, Calif.: California State Department of Education, 1971), pp. 55–59.

TABLE 7   INPUT AND PROCESS PHASES OF INVESTIGATIVE ACTIVITY*

INPUT PHASE	PROCESS PHASE

A. The Input Operation
  1. The Identification of Information Sources
  2. The Acquisition of:
    a. Raw Data
    b. Summarized or Categorized Data
    c. Conclusions, Generalization, Principles, Laws, Facts
    d. Opinions
  3. The Use of Personal (Existing) Knowledge
B. The Input Procedures
  1. Empirical (Firsthand Experiences)
    a. Observing: Listening, Looking, Counting, Sketching, Note-taking, Charting
    b. Experimenting
    c. Interviewing
    d. Using Questionnaires
  2. Normative or Authoritative
    a. Reading
    b. Listening
  3. Aesthetic
    a. Sensing
    b. Feeling
    c. Valuing
C. The Input Sources
  1. Reference Books
  2. Non-Book Reference Material
  3. People
  4. The Environment in General
	A. The Manipulative Processes of Inquiry
	  1. Comparing and Verifying Sources of Data
	  2. Establishing Connections between Data
	  3. Recognizing Bias in Informational Sources
	  4. Classifying Data
	  5. Categorizing Data according to Function
	  6. Identifying Strong and Weak Arguments, Conclusions, etc.
	  7. Distinguishing Fact from Opinion
	  8. Recognizing
	  9. Establishing the Credibility of a Data Source
	  10. Discovering Trends, Patterns, Uniformities, and Discrepancies in Data
	B. The Creative/Productive Processes
	  1. Designing Experiments
	  2. Constructing Data-Gathering Devices
	  3. Analyzing Data and Drawing Conclusions
	  4. Perceiving Possible Solutions
	  5. Making Probability Statements
	  6. Stating Generalizations
	  7. Redefining Problems
	  8. Planning and Organizing
	  9. Creating Testable Hypotheses
	  10. Making Valid Inferences and Tracing Logical Implications
	  11. Specifying Evaluative Criteria
	  12. Evaluating according to Internal Criteria
	  13. Evaluating according to External Criteria
	  14. Building Theories and Models

*Adapted from Joseph S. Renzulli, *The Enrichment Triad Model: A Guide for Developing Defensible Programs for the Gifted and Talented* (Mansfield Center, Conn.: Creative Learning Press, 1977), pp. 66 and 67.

REPRESENTATIVE RESEARCH TOPICS

Topics are listed alphabetically, each one followed by an orientation source or sources.

Alternate Sources of Energy: A Feasibility Study
    The Energy Conservation Papers, ed. by Robert Williams, Energy Policy Project of the Ford Foundation (Ballinger)

America's Cities: Perspectives, Problems, and Prognosis
    Cities by Dwight W. Hoover, Bibliographic Guides for Contemporary Collection series (Bowker)

EXAMPLE 7   MANAGEMENT PLAN FOR INDIVIDUAL
OR SMALL-GROUP INVESTIGATION*

Name _____   School _____

Grade _____   Teacher _____

General Area(s) of Study _____

Specific Area of Study _____

Brief Description of the Problem to Be Investigated. What do I hope to find out? _____

Intended Audiences
Which individuals or groups would be most interested in the findings? List the organized groups (clubs, societies, teams) at the local, regional, state, and national levels. What are the names and addresses of contact persons in these groups?

Intended Product(s) and Outlets
What form(s) will the final product take? How, when, and where will I communicate the results of my investigation to an appropriate audience(s)? What outlet vehicles (journals, conferences, art shows, etc.) are typically used by professionals in this field?

Methodological Resources
List the names and addresses of persons who might provide assistance in attacking this problem. List the How-To-Do-It books that are available in this area of study. List other resources (films, collections, exhibits, etc.). Special equipment (e.g., camera, transit, tape recorder, questionnaire, etc.).

Necessary Information
What types of data will be needed to solve the problem? If raw data, how can it be gathered and classified? If already categorized data, where is it stored?

*Joseph S. Renzulli, *The Enrichment Triad Model: A Guide for Developing Defensible Programs for the Gifted and Talented* (Mansfield Center, Conn.: Creative Learning Press, 1977), p. 71.

America's Hidden Epidemic: Child Abuse
Somewhere a Child Is Crying: The Battered Child by Vincent J. Fontana (Macmillan)

Archaeological Discoveries in America
Digging Up America's Past (National Geographic—5 filmstrips, 5 discs or cassettes)

Arranging a Medley of George Gershwin's Tunes

Civilization as a Human Invention
What Does It Mean To Be Human? (240 slides in 3 carousel cartridges, 3 discs or 3 cassettes)

Cybernetic Problems in Bionics
The Sociology of the Future, ed. by Wendell Bell and James A. Mau (Russell Sage Foundation) see Figure 4; *Cybernetic Problems in Bionics,* ed. by H. L. Oestreicher and D. R. Moore (Gordon).

Designing and Producing a Nonnarrative Motion Picture
Exploring the Film by William Kuhns and Robert Stanley (Pflaum/Standard);
Fog (Encyclopaedia Britannica—16 mm motion picture)

Exploring Man's Last and Widest Frontier: The Space Shuttle Program
Space Settlements: A Design Study (National Aeronautics and Space Administration)

Feeding the World's Hungry People: Alternate Food Sources
Future Food: Alternate Protein for the Year 2000 by Barbara Ford (Morrow)

Holography: How Lasers Create Three-Dimensional Images
Advances in Holography, ed. by Nabil H. Farhat, 3 vols. (Dekker)

Lessons from History
A Dual Autobiography by Will and Ariel Durant (Simon and Schuster); *The
Lessons of History* by Will and Ariel Durant (Simon and Schuster)

Media: Its Impact and Meaning
Understanding Media: The Extensions of Man by Marshall McLuhan (New
American Library)

Progressivism, Muckraking, and the Anguish of Change
Progressivism and Muckraking by Louis Filler, Bibliographic Guides for
Contemporary Collections series (Bowker)

Science Fiction: The Best from the Past and the Present
Anatomy of Wonder: Science Fiction by Neil Barron, Bibliographical Guides
for Contemporary Collections series (Bowker)

Solar Cells: Magical Sources of Energy
Solar Cells, ed. by Charles E. Backus (Institute of Electrical and Electronics
Engineers)

Theories of Plate Tectonics
The Evolving Continents by Brian F. Windley (Wiley)

The Treasures of Tutankamen: Evidence of the Manners, Customs, and Beliefs
of the People of Egypt 3300 Years Ago
The Tomb of Tut-Ankh-Amen by Howard Carter and A. C. Mace, 3 vols.
(Cooper Square)

Trends in Censorship
Banned Books 387 B.C. to 1978 A.D. by Chandler B. Grannis, 4th ed.
(Bowker)

Underwater Archaeological Exploration
Archaeology beneath the Sea by George F. Bass (Harper)

Women and the "Equal Rights" Amendment
Women and the "Equal Rights" Amendment, Senate Subcommittee Hearings . . . ed. by Catharine Stimpson in conjunction with the Congressional
Information Service (Bowker)

Writing an Episode for Inclusion in a Sequel to the Television Program "Backstairs at the White House"
Forty-Two Years in the White House by Irwin H. Hoover (Greenwood);
Upstairs at the White House: My Life with the First Ladies by J. B. West
(Warner Paperback Library)

9
Advanced Placement Course Descriptions

In this chapter are descriptions of advanced placement courses—art, biology, chemistry, English (language and composition and composition and literature), French, German, history (American and European), Latin (Vergil and Catullus—Horace), mathematics (calculus), music (theory, and listening and literature), physics, and Spanish. All these course descriptions have been adapted from and are reprinted with permission from *Advanced Placement Course Descriptions,* May 1980. Copyright © 1979 by College Entrance Examination Board, New York. Course descriptions are revised regularly. Descriptions are available ($4 each; $25 for the set of 12) from College Board Publication Orders, Box 2815, Princeton, NJ 08541. For further information on advanced placement courses see Appendix E.

ADVANCED PLACEMENT: ART

STUDIO ART AND HISTORY OF ART

In art three Advanced Placement course descriptions and evaluations are offered: (1) Studio Art—General Portfolio, (2) Studio Art—Drawing Portfolio, and (3) a course in the History of Art. The two Studio Art portfolios are designed for students who are seriously interested in the practice of art. Students who plan to attend art schools or universities that require a general art course as the freshman-level requirement in that field should select the general portfolio offering. On the other hand, those who plan to attend art schools or universities that require a year of drawing rather than or in addition to a general art course at the freshman level should select the drawing portfolio. Studio Art students will be able to submit only one of the portfolio offerings in a given year; it is possible, however, that certain students may wish to submit one of each of the Studio Art offerings in successive years.

The History of Art course description is designed to introduce students to the understanding and enjoyment of works of art made by others. It is possible for students to present themselves as candidates in both Studio Art and History of Art. The descriptions of the two Studio Art portfolios appear immediately below, followed by the description of the History of Art course.

STUDIO ART: GENERAL PORTFOLIO

Since no standard, universally valid studio art course can or should exist, the Development Committee in Advanced Placement Studio Art has chosen to suggest guidelines for creating an environment for the study of art rather than to delineate a specific course. Maximum freedom is allowed not only in the structuring of courses but also in the interpreting of submission requirements for evaluation. Thus, the responsibility of creating an environment (a course) in art and in preparing the work submitted to the evaluators rests heavily upon the participating teachers and students.

COURSE DESCRIPTION: GENERAL PORTFOLIO

The Development Committee in Studio Art has had the counsel of both school and college teachers in defining the scope of work equivalent to that of introductory college courses in studio art. Because art courses vary from college to college, the guidelines provided for work in AP Studio Art do not describe the program of any particular institution, but they do reflect the coverage and level typical of good introductory college courses.

Such courses reflect three major concerns that are constants in the teaching of art: (1) a sense of quality in a student's work; (2) a personal preoccupation in depth on the part of the student with a particular mode of working, thinking, and stating; and (3) the student's need for a variety of experiences in the formal, technical, and expressive means of the artist. Advanced Placement work should reflect these three areas of concern: quality, concentration, and breadth.

Just as there is no standard introductory college course, so there can be no standard Advanced Placement Studio Art course in the secondary schools. Teachers are encouraged to give the course the shape that they feel their particular situation suggests. Therefore, the Development Committee in Advanced Placement Studio Art chooses to provide guidelines rather than a precise course description.

The Advanced Placement Program in Studio Art is intended for the highly motivated student interested in the serious study of art. Such a student may have had previous training in art, but such training is not a prerequisite for entering the program any more than it is for entering the introductory course in college. Students should, however, be made aware that Advanced Placement work involves significantly more time than the typical high school course and that the program is not for the casually interested.

The quest for quality of both production and experience in the Advanced Placement Program in Studio Art makes active demands not only on the student, but also on the teacher and, indeed, the school itself. Classes should be small enough so that teachers and students can work in close cooperation; extended time blocks should be allotted for instruction; and the teachers' other responsibilities should be reduced to reflect the greater demands of the program. The introductory college course usually meets for three two-period sessions a week, and such a schedule is preferable to the five one-hour sessions a week typical of high school. Although the course is designed as a one-year program, some schools may prefer to schedule the course in biweekly two-hour sessions and extend it over a two-year period. In such cases, the most recently published description of the evaluation should be consulted at the beginning of the second year of the course so that any changes in the evaluation materials required can be taken into account long before the materials are to be submitted.

It is recognized that the student will need to work outside the classroom, as well as in it, and beyond scheduled periods. Students should be considered responsible enough to leave the art room or school if an assignment requires them to do so, and homework, such as maintaining a sketchbook or a journal, would seem to be a necessary component of instruction. Museums and galleries should be considered extensions of school, and class time allotted accordingly. In addition, art books, slides, and reproductions can provide important examples for the serious study of art.

HISTORY OF ART
PURPOSE

The Advanced Placement Program in the History of Art is designed to introduce students to the understanding and enjoyment of works of art. It develops students' ability to examine works of art intelligently, acquainting them with the major forms of artistic expression in their own time and engendering an understanding of art from other times and cultures. In achieving this goal, the course attempts to qualify students for credit and advanced placement in American colleges. As part of this overall goal, the Examiners wish to encourage personal initiative in the design and teaching of courses at individual schools. Advantage should be taken of local resources and attention paid to the interests and needs of individual students.

COURSE

The description that follows is not meant to prescribe a model course but rather to indicate the coverage and character most commonly encountered in introductory college courses in the history of art. For the purpose of permitting advanced standing at most colleges, the course should deal chiefly with Western art from 1400 to the present. As a result of the trend in schools away from studying the history and culture of antiquity and the Middle Ages, the art survey course is one of the last means by which students can be exposed to these parts of our heritage. For this reason we urge teachers to give not less than one-third of the course to the study of ancient and medieval art. Far Eastern, African, pre-Columbian, and other artistic traditions might well be included in an Advanced Placement course, and an opportunity is given in the individual studies section of the examination for the student to concentrate on art from any culture. It is certainly hoped that the course will stimulate an interest in and understanding of the entire world of art and that reference to historical analogies and prototypes will be made in order to relate works ranging widely in time and space. However, Western art, principally from the Renaissance to the present, is the material which all versions of the Advanced Placement course should have in common.

Teachers need not feel constrained to deal with the course materials in chronological order; rather, they are encouraged to organize the course in whatever manner best serves the cause of learning.

SOME SUGGESTED THEMES

In order to encourage the study of meaningful contexts and to avoid the rote memorization of isolated names, dates, and stylistic labels, the Examiners have drawn up a *list of possible themes*. The list is meant simply to suggest the types and varieties of themes with which an Advanced Placement student should be familiar.

GENERAL

The Idea of "Progress" in Art: Is Progress a Defensible Historical Concept?

"Fine" versus "Applied" Art

The Role of the Artist in Society

Artistic Individualism versus Anonymity

ANTIQUITY—MIDDLE AGES

The Beginnings of Art in Caves, Temples, and Tombs

The Evolution of the Nude and the Humanizing of the Gods in Greek Art

Greece's Debt to Ancient Egypt and Mesopotamia

The Emergence of the Classical Ideal in Fifth-Century Greece

Form and Function in Ancient Architecture: Structures, Materials, and Use

Roman Art and Architecture in the Service of the Emperor and the Public: City Planning, Forums, Markets, Baths, Theaters, etc.

The Portrait in Antiquity: Egypt, Mesopotamia, Greece, and Rome

The House of God: Temple, Basilica, Cathedral

The Sacred Image, Pagan and Christian: The Sources and Subject Matter of Early Christian Art

The "Barbarian" Contribution to Medieval Art: The Art of the Celtic and Germanic Tribes

The Rise of the Gothic Style: Its Religious, Social, and Political Background

The Art of the Medieval Book

The Rebirth of Cities (1200–1500): The Development of Urban Architecture—City Halls, Guild Halls, Public Squares, Cathedrals, etc.

1400—PRESENT

The Concept of the Renaissance: The New Attitude toward Antiquity

The Idea of the Beautiful in the Renaissance

The Emergence of the Concept of Artistic Genius in the Renaissance

The Organization of Space: The Scientific and Expressive Aspects of Perspective, Both Renaissance and Baroque

The Artist as Story Teller (1400—1850)

Palaces, Villas, and Their Settings

Symbolism and Realism in Fifteenth-Century Northern Art

The Artist's Education: Workshops, Academies, Art Schools, and the Self-Taught Artist

The Development of Landscape, Portraiture, Still Life, and Genre from the Twelfth to the Eighteenth Century

The Impact of Patronage and the Art Market on Art

The Effect of Reformation and Counter-Reformation on the Form and Subject Matter of the Arts

The Artist as a Critic of the Social and Political Order from the Eighteenth Century to the Present

The Character of Romantic Thought and Its Expression in Art

The Influence of and Alternatives to Impressionism

The Interrelationship of Photography and the Other Visual Arts

The Emergence of the Concept of Self-Expression

Artistic Movements and Manifestos Since 1800: The Accelerating Pace of Change and the Coexistence of Conflicting Tendencies

The Influence of Non-Western Art on Modern Painting and Sculpture

The Beginnings of Abstract Art

The Influence of the Machine, Technology, and Scientific Theory on Art and Architecture

The Modern City: Architectural Design and Urban Planning

The Art of Fantasy between the Two World Wars (Dada and Surrealism)

The Changing Image of the American Landscape and City

The European Heritage of the Architecture of American Government Buildings

Art in the United States Immediately Following the Second World War: Abstract Expressionism and the Reactions to It since 1960

The Changing Size and Shape of the Painting's Surface since 1950

Art and Popular Culture since 1960

The Search for Cultural Identity through Art: Mexican, Afro-American, American Indian Art, etc.

Conceptual Art: Concentration on the Idea or Concept of Art in Opposition to a Physical Presentation

The Breakdown of Conventional Boundaries in the Arts: Mixed Media, Assemblage, Happenings, Environments, etc.

ADVANCED PLACEMENT: BIOLOGY
COURSE

The College Board recently asked departmental chairmen at the 100 colleges and universities regularly receiving the most Advanced Placement candidates in biology to describe their introductory programs in that field. A majority of the 70 respondents reported that they offer more than a single course in introductory biology. In almost all the responding institutions, however, whether they have single or multiple introductory offerings, freshmen who intend to pursue further studies in the department are most frequently enrolled in courses called "general biology." The Advanced Placement course description in biology, on the whole, places emphasis upon the principal topics covered in such introductory biology courses.

An Advanced Placement biology course in the secondary school should, therefore, seek to meet the objectives of such general biology courses at the college level. It should, for instance, have the equivalent of three class meetings and three laboratory hours a week for thirty weeks.

The aim of the course should be to achieve the following:

1. Knowledge of the facts, principles, and processes of biology.

2. Understanding of the means by which biological information is collected, how it is interpreted, and how one formulates hypotheses from available data and makes further predictions.

3. Understanding that science is a human endeavor with social consequences.

POSSIBLE COURSE EMPHASES

Introductory college biology courses differ widely in content. Each course represents an attempt to meet the needs, interests, and abilities of a particular group of students. Moreover, the emphasis of a course will vary from year to year depending on the qualifications of the instructor and the advances being made in research. Since there is no one specific college course on which to pattern an Advanced Placement biology course, an outline is given in the following pages. The outline is not intended as a syllabus, but as a guide to the secondary school teacher who should feel free to choose emphases and order of presentation of topics within the major framework of the outline.*

For purpose of study, the biological sciences may be divided into three broad areas: the molecular and cellular, the organismal, and the populational. The outline given is organized on this basis and the examination gives about equal emphasis to each of the three content areas.

Since a thorough presentation of biology involves the use of concepts learned in chemistry, students taking an advanced course in biology should first complete a course in chemistry.

College-level textbooks should be used in an advanced biology course.

I. *Molecular and Cellular Biology*
   A. Basic chemistry
      1. Atoms and isotopes
      2. Chemical bonds
      3. Chemical reactions and equilibria
      4. Energetics: free energy change and entropy
      5. Chemical composition of organisms
         a. Principal elements in organisms
         b. Properties of water
         c. Chemical structure of important organic substances
            (1) Carbohydrates, lipids, proteins, organic acids, and nucleic acids

*For representative outlines of courses, refer to the College Board publication *Beginning an Advanced Placement Biology Course.*

(2) Evidence for the α-helix structure of protein and the double-helix model of DNA

B. Cells
  1. Historical development of the cell concept
  2. Cell ultrastructure
     a. Role and limitations of biochemistry, centrifugation, and microscopy (light and electron) in understanding cells
     b. Structure and function of cell organelles
     c. Cell (plasma) membrane and its properties
     d. Viruses
     e. Comparison of prokaryotic and eukaryotic cells

C. Enzymes
  1. Enzyme-substrate complex
  2. Role of coenzymes, inorganic cofactors, prosthetic groups, and vitamins
  3. Factors affecting the rate and/or direction of enzyme reactions; competitive and noncompetitive inhibition

D. Energy transformations
  1. Aerobic and anaerobic respiration
     a. Chemical structure and function of ATP
     b. Pathways of aerobic respiration
        (1) Krebs cycle
        (2) Cytochrome (electron) transport system
     c. Pathways of anaerobic respiration
        (1) Glycolysis
        (2) Fermentation
     d. Sites of respiratory enzymes
     e. Factors affecting the rate of respiration
  2. Photosynthesis
     a. Historical developments
     b. Factors affecting the rate of photosynthesis
     c. Role of pigments and plastids
     d. Absorption spectra and action spectra
     e. Nature and interrelation of light and dark reactions
     f. Comparison between respiration and photosynthesis

E. Cell division
  1. Structure of chromosomes
  2. Mitosis and meiosis in plants and animals
  3. Cytokinesis in plants and animals; control of cell division

F. Chemical nature of the gene
  1. Watson-Crick model of nucleic acids
  2. Self-copying of DNA molecule
  3. Genetic code and chemical nature of mutation
  4. Control of protein synthesis: transcription and translation
  5. Gene regulation: structural and regulatory genes
  6. Principles of transformation and transduction

G. The origin of life
  1. Modern theories
  2. Experimental evidence

II. *Organismal Biology*
  A. Structure and function in plants with emphasis on angiosperms
     1. Root, stem, leaf, flower, seed, and fruit
     2. Water and mineral absorption and transport
     3. Food translocation and storage
  B. Plant reproduction and development
     1. Alternation of generation of fern, pine, and flowering plants
     2. Gamete formation and germination
     3. Seed structure and germination
     4. Growth and development including hormonal control: auxins, kinins, gibberellins, and other phytohormones
     5. Tropism and photoperiodicity
     6. Experimental analysis of plant development
  C. Structure and function in animals with emphasis on vertebrates
     1. Major systems: digestive, respiratory, circulatory, excretory, skeletal, muscular, and nervous
     2. Homeostatic mechanisms
        a. Neural controls in homeostasis
        b. Hormonal controls in homeostasis
     3. Hormones in reproduction
        a. Hormonal control of gamete production
        b. Hormonal control of uterine changes in mammals
  D. Animal reproduction and development
     1. Gamete formation and fertilization
     2. Cleavage, gastrulation, and germ-layer formation
     3. Differentiation of organ systems
     4. Experimental analysis of vertebrate development
     5. Extraembryonic membranes of vertebrates
     6. Formation and function of the mammalian placenta
     7. Pattern of circulation in a human embryo and the changes occurring at birth
  E. Principles of heredity
     1. History of early experiments in heredity
     2. Mendelian inheritance: dominance, segregation, independent assortment
     3. Probability
     4. Chromosomal basis of inheritance
        a. Sex determination
        b. Chromosomal abnormalities: Klinefelter's syndrome, Down's syndrome, Turner's syndrome, and others
     5. Linkage
     6. Sex-linked, sex-influenced, and sex-limited inheritance
     7. Polygenic inheritance: height and skin color
     8. Multiple alleles, human blood groups

III. *Populational Biology*
  A. Principles of ecology
     1. Energy flow and productivity in ecosystems
        a. First and second laws of thermodynamics
        b. Food chains and webs

      c. Trophic levels and pyramids
      d. Magnitude, rates, efficiency
   2. Biogeochemical cycles, such as nitrogen, carbon, and phosphorus
   3. Population growth and regulation in organisms
   4. Community structure, growth, and regulation
      a. Structure and diversity of ecological communities; major biomes
      b. Succession and climax communities
   5. Habitat
      a. Abiotic factors: chemical (e.g., pH, minerals) and physical (e.g., temperature, moisture)
      b. Biotic factors: competition, predation, mutualism, commensalism, and parasitism
   6. Concept of niche

B. Principles of evolution
   1. History of evolutionary concepts: Lamarckian and Darwinian theories
   2. Modern concept of natural selection
      a. Mutation
      b. Hardy-Weinberg equilibrium
      c. Factors affecting Hardy-Weinberg equilibrium
   3. Speciation
      a. Genetic changes in populations
      b. Role of geographic barriers
      c. Reproductive isolating mechanisms
   4. Adaptive radiation
   5. Evolutionary diversity
      a. Major features of plant and animal evolution
      b. Concepts of homology and analogy
      c. Convergence
      d. Extinction
   6. Concepts of balanced polymorphism and genetic drift
   7. Classification of living organisms
      a. Systems of classification
      b. Significance of classification scheme
   8. Evolutionary history of man

C. Principles of behavior
   1. Stereotyped and learned behavior
   2. Biorhythms
   3. Societies: ants, bees, birds, and primates
   4. Social behavior
      a. Communication and signals
      b. Dominance hierarchy
      c. Territoriality
      d. Aggression
      e. Courtship and parental behavior

D. Social biology
   1. Problem of human population growth
      a. Age structure and composition
      b. Birth and fertility rates
      c. Theory of demographic transition

2. Man's intervening role in nature
   a. Resources and their management
   b. Pollution: air, water, soil, pesticide, herbicide, radioactive, and thermal
   c. Economic aspects of algae and fungi
   d. Technology and its environmental implications
3. Implications of biomedical progress
   a. Control of human reproduction
   b. Genetic engineering and genetic counseling

ADVANCED PLACEMENT: CHEMISTRY

COURSE

The Advanced Placement chemistry course is designed to be the equivalent of the general chemistry course usually taken during the first college year. For some students, this course enables them to undertake, as freshmen, second-year work in the chemistry sequence at their institutions or to register in courses in other fields where general chemistry is a prerequisite. For other students, the Advanced Placement chemistry course fulfills the laboratory science requirement and frees time for other courses.

Advanced Placement chemistry should meet the objectives of a good general chemistry course. Students in such a course should attain a depth of understanding of fundamentals and a reasonable competence in dealing with chemical problems. The course should contribute to the development of the students' abilities to think clearly and to express their ideas, orally and in writing, with clarity and logic. The college course in general chemistry differs qualitatively from the usual first secondary school course in chemistry with respect to the kind of textbook used, the topics covered, the emphasis on chemical calculations and the mathematical formulation of principles, and the kind of laboratory work done by students. Quantitative differences appear in the number of topics treated, the time spent on the course by students, and the nature and the variety of experiments done in the laboratory.

The Advanced Placement chemistry course is designed to be taken only after the successful completion of a first course in high school chemistry. The advanced work in chemistry should not displace any other part of the student's science curriculum. It is highly desirable that a student have a course in secondary school physics and a four-year college preparatory program in mathematics. The physics course can well precede the college-level chemistry.

TIME

As in the equivalent college course, students in an Advanced Placement chemistry course should spend each week approximately 150 minutes in the classroom and 180 minutes in the laboratory, the latter preferably in not more than two sessions. Time devoted to class and laboratory demonstrations should not be counted as part of the laboratory period. It is assumed that the student will spend approximately six hours a week in unsupervised individual study.

TOPICS

The importance of the theoretical aspects of chemistry has brought about an increasing emphasis on these aspects of the content of general chemistry courses. Topics such as the structure of matter, kinetic theory of gases, chemical equilibria, chemical kinetics, and the basic concepts of thermodynamics are now being presented in considerable depth. Consequently, if the objectives of a college-level general chemistry course are to be achieved, the teaching must be done by a teacher who has completed an undergraduate major program in chemistry including at least a year's work in physical chemistry. Teachers with such training are best able to present a course with adequate breadth and depth and to develop the student's ability to reason with the fundamental facts of the science. Because of the nature of the Advanced Placement course, the teacher needs time for extra preparation both for class and laboratory and should have a teaching load that is lighter than normal.

Chemistry is broad enough to permit flexibility in its teaching, and college teachers exercise considerable freedom in methods and arrangements of topics in the effort to reach the objectives of their courses. Accordingly, there is no desire to impose greater uniformity on the secondary schools than now exists in the colleges. Therefore, the following list of topics for an Advanced Placement course is intended to be a guide to the level and breadth of treatment expected rather than to be a syllabus.

I. *Structure of Matter*
  A. Atomic theory and atomic structure
    1. Evidence for the atomic theory
    2. Atomic weights; determination by chemical and physical means
    3. Atomic number and mass number; isotopes and mass spectroscopy
    4. Electron energy levels: atomic spectra, quantum numbers, atomic orbitals
    5. Periodic relationships including, for example, atomic radii, ionization energies, electron affinities, oxidation states
  B. Chemical bonding
    1. Binding forces
      a. Types: ionic, covalent, metallic, hydrogen bonding, van der Waals
      b. Relationships to states, structure, and properties of matter
      c. Polarity of bonds, electronegativities
    2. Geometry of molecules, ions, and coordination complexes; structural isomerism; dipole moments of molecules; relation of properties to structure
    3. Molecular models
      a. Valence bond theory: hybridization of orbitals, resonance, sigma and pi bonds
      b. Other models, e.g., molecular orbital
  C. Nuclear chemistry: radioactivity and chemical applications

II. *States of Matter*
  A. Gases
    1. Laws of ideal gases; equation of state for an ideal gas
    2. Kinetic-molecular theory
      a. Interpretation of ideal gas laws on the basis of this theory
      b. Avogadro's hypothesis and the mole concept
      c. Dependence of kinetic energy of molecules on temperature: Boltzmann distribution

          d. Deviations from ideal gas laws

B. Liquids and solids
1. Liquids and solids from the kinetic-molecular viewpoint
2. Phase diagrams of one-component systems
3. Changes of state, critical phenomena

C. Solutions
1. Types of solutions and factors affecting solubility
2. Methods of expressing concentration (The use of normalities is not tested.)
3. Colligative properties, e.g., Raoult's law
4. Effect of interionic attraction on colligative properties and solubility

D. Colloidal and macromolecular dispersions: classifications; industrial and ecological applications

III. *Reactions*

A. Reaction types
1. Formation and cleavage of covalent bonds
    a. Acid-base reactions; concepts of Arrhenius, Brönsted-Lowry, and Lewis; amphoterism
    b. Reactions involving coordination complexes; amphoterism
2. Precipitation reactions
3. Oxidation-reduction reactions
    a. Oxidation number
    b. The role of the electron in oxidation-reduction
    c. Electrochemistry; electrolytic cells; standard half-cell potentials: prediction of the direction of redox reactions, effect of concentration changes

B. Equations and stoichiometry
1. Ionic and molecular species present in chemical systems: net ionic equations
2. Balancing of equations including those for redox reactions
3. Weight and volume relations with emphasis on the mole concept

C. Equilibrium
1. Concept of dynamic equilibrium, physical and chemical; LeChatelier's principle; equilibrium constants; deviations from ideality
2. Quantitative treatment
    a. Equilibrium constants for gaseous reactions: K_c, K_p
    b. Equilibrium constants for reactions in solution
        (1) Constants for acids and bases; pK; pH
        (2) Solubility product constants and their application to precipitation and the solution of precipitates
        (3) Constants for complex ions
        (4) Common ion effect; buffers

D. Kinetics
1. Concept of rate reaction
2. Order of reaction and rate constant; their determination from experimental data
3. Effect of temperature change on rates
4. Energy of activation; the role of catalysts
5. The relationship between the rate-determining step and a mechanism

E. Thermodynamics
1. State functions
2. First law: heat of formation; heat of reaction, change in enthalpy, Hess's law; heat capacity; heats of vaporization and fusion
3. Second law: free energy of formation; free energy of reaction; dependence of change in free energy on enthalpy and entropy changes
4. Relationship of change in free energy to equilibrium constants and electrode potentials

IV. *Descriptive Chemistry*

The accumulation of specific facts of chemistry, begun in the elementary course, is necessarily continued in the Advanced Placement course. Such facts are essential to enable students to comprehend the development of principles and concepts, to demonstrate applications of principle, to relate fact to theory and properties to structure, and to develop an understanding of systematic nomenclature, which facilitates communication. The descriptive facts should not be isolated from the principles being studied but must be taught throughout the course to illustrate and illuminate the principles.

A. Relationships in the periodic table: horizontal, vertical, and diagonal
B. Chemistry of nonmetals: halogens, hydrogen, oxygen, sulfur, nitrogen, phosphorus
C. Chemistry of metals: alkali metals, alkaline earth metals, aluminum, transition elements, tin, lead
D. Physical and chemical properties of compounds of carbon (organic chemistry): These provide applications of bonding, bond angles, orbitals, isomerism (including cis-trans and optical), unsaturation, aromaticity, and inductive effects and can be included under the topic of chemical bonding. These topics can be part of a separate unit that would also include homology and functional groups.

CHEMICAL CALCULATIONS

The following list summarizes types of problems either explicitly or implicitly included in the preceding material. Attention should be given to significant figures, precision of measured values, and the use of logarithmic and exponential equations.

A. Percentage composition
B. Empirical and molecular formulas from experimental data
C. Molecular weights from gas density, freezing-point, and boiling-point measurements
D. Gas laws, including the ideal gas law, Dalton's law, and Graham's law
E. Stoichiometric relations using the concept of the mole; titration calculations
F. Mole fractions; molar and molal solutions
G. Faraday's law of electrolysis
H. Equilibrium constants and their applications including their use for simultaneous equilibria
I. Standard electrode potentials and their use; Nernst equation
J. Thermodynamic and thermochemical calculations
K. Kinetics calculations

ADVANCED PLACEMENT: ENGLISH

Language and Composition
and Composition and Literature

The Advanced Placement Program offers two course descriptions and two examinations in English: AP English Language and Composition and AP English Composition and Literature. Their purpose is to identify students who have attained the reading and writing skills generally expected of those who have completed first-year college courses in composition or in composition and literature. A description of each course appears on the following pages. After each course description, sample sets of multiple-choice and essay questions for each of the examinations are presented [not included].

The courses share a common goal—to develop the students' awareness of language and to develop skills in critical reading and effective writing—but they differ essentially in content and focus. Briefly stated, the Language and Composition course stresses training in the reading and analysis of discursive prose and the writing of expository essays, whereas the Composition and Literature course concentrates on the reading and analysis of literary works and the writing of critical essays. These courses are intended to be representative of the two types of introductory English courses commonly offered in American universities and colleges, the one preparing students to use and respond to written English in a variety of contexts, the other preparing them for more specialized studies in English and American literature. They are meant to be parallel, not sequential offerings; each is presented as a suitable basis for a year's credit in English. Since both courses include and build upon skills in writing expository prose, students will ordinarily wish to take one of the examinations but not both, depending on their preparation.

To prepare for either of the Advanced Placement Examinations in English, students will, ideally, work with a teacher in a small class or a tutorial session; some may, however, study independently to supplement the work of a conventional course. In an AP English class, the teacher serves as discussion leader, critic, and scholar, helping the members of the class assume much of the responsibility for their own learning. Outside of class, the teacher confers with students to assist them with their reading, writing, and rewriting.

In developing Advanced Placement courses in English, the teacher should be guided by the descriptions below and by the detailed information in the booklets *Beginning an Advanced Placement Course in English Language and Composition* and *Beginning an Advanced Placement Course in English Composition and Literature.*

These publications have been prepared by the AP English Development Committee to assist teachers who wish to start Advanced Placement courses in English. They may be ordered from College Board Publication Orders, Box 2815, Princeton, N.J. 08541.

LANGUAGE AND COMPOSITION

Although an Advanced Placement course in English Language and Composition may be organized and taught in a variety of ways, it should reflect an awareness of the most useful theories of language and composition available to the teacher and suitable for the students. Whatever the shape of the course, it should encourage students to develop an individual style adaptable to different occasions for writing in college.

The course will include both the reading and analysis of discursive prose and the study of the process of writing—from the discovery of the topic to the preliminary drafts to the final edited draft. Students should study examples of prose from various fields and periods that will serve as models of effective styles, and the course should offer a variety of writing assignments calling for the use of different styles or tones. Through such study and practice, students gain an understanding of the principles of effective writing and become effective writers themselves.

The organized study of the structures of sentences, paragraphs, and larger discursive patterns introduces students to the semantic, structural, and rhetorical resources of the language. They learn to recognize and work with:

kinds and levels of diction, from the casual to the formal

varieties of sentence structures

logical and functional relationships of sentences within paragraphs and of paragraphs within essays

modes of discourse (narration, description, analysis)

aims of discourse (information, persuasion, and expression)

various rhetorical strategies (the logical, emotional, and ethical appeals, for example)

appropriate relationships among author, audience, and subject

Throughout this study the focus will be on both the surface features of the text and on the underlying assumptions that inform it.

Since students will study the rhetorical effects of kinds of diction and sentence patterns, the course assumes a basic knowledge of the syntactic structures and semantic components of language. Such study should neither narrowly prescribe one dialect for all occasions nor irresponsibly allow any dialect for a particular occasion. Beyond its own intrinsic humanistic value, that study, like the course itself, will help students to discover the rich resources of language and to claim them as their own.

COMPOSITION AND LITERATURE

In an AP course in English Composition and Literature, students are involved in both the study and practice of writing and the study of literature. They should learn to use the characteristic modes of discourse and to recognize the assumptions underlying various rhetorical strategies. Through speaking, listening, and reading, but chiefly through the experience of their own writing, students become more aware of the resources of language: connotation, metaphor, irony, syntax, and tone.

Writing assignments should focus on the critical analysis of literature. But assignments might also include exercises in exposition, argument, personal narrative, and the writing of stories, poems, or plays. Although much of the writing will be about literature, speaking and writing about different kinds of experiences should further develop the students' sense of how style, subject, and audience are related. The desired goals are the honest and effective use of language and the organization of ideas in a clear, coherent, and persuasive way.

In an Advanced Placement course in English Composition and Literature, students are engaged in the careful reading of literary works. Through such study, students sharpen their awareness of language and their understanding of the writer's craft. They develop critical standards for the independent appreciation of any literary work, and they increase their sensitivity to literature as shared experience. To achieve these goals, students study the individual work, its language, characters, action, and themes. They consider its structure, meaning, and value, and its relationship to contemporary experience as well as to the times in which it was written.

Students should study intensively a few representative works from several genres and periods and should concentrate on the study of challenging works of recognized literary merit, worthy of scrutiny for their complexity and richness in thought and language. Readings in translation may be included, but most of the assigned reading should be in texts originally written in English since a course should stress close attention to an author's own language and style.

ADVANCED PLACEMENT: FRENCH

French Language and French Literature

The Advanced Placement Program offers two separate, parallel courses: French Language and French Literature. Each is intended for qualified students in the final stages of their secondary school training who are interested in completing studies comparable in content and in difficulty to a full-year course in Advanced French Composition and Conversation at the third-year college level or to an Introduction to French Literature also at level 3.

Students are free to take both examinations if they so desire. Both examinations presume a minimum of one academic year's course work in advanced language or introductory literature; some secondary schools find that a two-year Advanced Placement Program is more satisfactory. The description of the French Language program appears immediately below; the description of the French Literature program follows it.

FRENCH LANGUAGE

The Advanced Placement Program in French Language is intended for those who have chosen to develop their proficiency in French without emphasis on knowledge of the literature. Students who enroll should already have a good command of the grammar and considerable competence in listening, reading, speaking, and writing. Although these qualifications may be attained in a variety of ways, it is assumed that most students will be in the final stages of their secondary school training and will have had substantial course work in the language. To ensure that the Advanced Placement French Language Examination is maintained at its intended level, a validity study has been carried out to establish the comparability of performance of college students completing a third-year French Language course in their institutions and Advanced Placement candidates.* The results of the comparison between these two groups strongly bear out the contention of the French Advanced Placement Develop-

*Reprints of "How Valid Is the French Advanced Placement Language Examination?" *French Review,* May 1975, are available from College Board Publication Orders, Box 2815, Princeton, N.J. 08541.

ment Committee that successful performance on the examination is equivalent to the performance of students who have completed six semesters of college French Language courses.

COURSE

A school's course in AP French Language,* emphasizing the use of language for active communication, has the following objectives:

A. Ability to understand spoken French in both formal and conversational situations.

B. The development of a vocabulary sufficiently ample for reading of newspaper and magazine articles, contemporary literature, and other nontechnical writings without dependence on a dictionary.

C. Ability to express ideas accurately and resourcefully both orally and in writing with reasonable fluency.

Course content can probably best reflect intellectual interests shared by the students and teacher (the arts, current events, literature, sports, etc.). Materials might well include recordings, films, newspapers, and magazines.

The course seeks to develop the language skills that are useful in themselves and can be applied to various activities and disciplines rather than to master any specific body of subject matter. The need for extensive training in the organization and writing of compositions must not be overlooked.

FRENCH LITERATURE

The Advanced Placement Program in French Literature consists of: (1) a *course* designed to provide well-motivated students with an intellectual challenge through the advanced study of French literature and language, and (2) an *examination* that measures achievement in that course.

COURSE

The objectives of a school's course† in AP French Literature are:

A. Proficiency in the fundamental language skills to a degree that enables the students
    1. to read with comprehension, at sight, prose and verse passages of moderate difficulty and mature content;
    2. to understand a lecture on a literary topic delivered by a native speaker of French;
    3. to express, orally and in writing, critical opinions and judgments phrased in correct French.
B. Sufficient knowledge to read critically and to discuss perceptively representative works of French literature. The program is not to be construed as a formal survey of literary history. However, students should be aware of the cultural context of works read and should also possess the basic vocabulary of literary criticism and analysis.

*To assist the teacher a booklet entitled *Beginning an Advanced Placement French Language Course* has been prepared and can be obtained from College Board Publication Orders, Box 2815, Princeton, N.J. 08541.

†Ibid.

ADVANCED PLACEMENT: GERMAN

GERMAN LANGUAGE AND GERMAN LITERATURE

The Advanced Placement Program offers two separate, parallel course descriptions and examinations in German: German Language and German Literature. Each is intended for qualified students in the final stages of their secondary school training who are interested in completing studies comparable in content and in difficulty to a full-year course in Advanced German Language at the third-year college level or to an Introduction to German Literature, also at level 3. Students are free to take both of these examinations if they wish, thus demonstrating achievement at the college third-year level in both language and literature. Each examination presumes a minimum of one academic year's course work in advanced language or introductory literature; some secondary schools find that a two-year Advanced Placement German sequence is more satisfactory. The description of the German Language program appears immediately below; the description of the German Literature program follows it.

GERMAN LANGUAGE

The Advanced Placement Program in German Language is intended for those who have chosen to develop their proficiency in German without special emphasis on knowledge of literature. Students who enroll should already have a good command of grammar and considerable competence in listening, reading, and writing. Although these qualifications may be obtained in a variety of ways, it is assumed that most students will be in the final stages of their secondary school training and will have had substantial course work in the language.

COURSE

A school's course in AP German Language, emphasizing use of the language for active communication, has as its objective the development of the following skills:

A. Using vocabulary, grammar, and syntax with a high degree of proficiency.
B. Understanding spoken German in both formal and conversational situations.
C. Reading newspaper and magazine articles, contemporary fiction, and nontechnical writings without the use of a dictionary.
D. Expressing ideas orally and in writing accurately and fluently.

Course content will reflect intellectual interests shared by the students and teacher (the arts, current events, literature, sports, etc.). Materials might well include recordings, films, newspapers, and magazines.

The course seeks to develop language skills that are useful in themselves and that can be applied to various activities and disciplines rather than to cover any specific body of subject matter. The need for extensive training in the organization and writing of compositions must not be overlooked.

GERMAN LITERATURE

A four-year instructional sequence is generally required to achieve the aims set forth in this course description, but a number of variations are possible. For example: (1) Advanced Placement students may receive special training within or outside the regular third- and/or fourth-year course; (2) qualified students may be permitted to bypass one or two semesters, thus reaching the fourth-year course after only two or two-and-a-half years of study; (3) if more than two sections of second- and third-year German exist, a special section may be established for able, interested students to cover the work of second- and third-year German in one year; or (4) where no provisions can be made for a fourth-year course, students may be prepared for the Advanced Placement Examination through individual tutoring.

All these approaches have proved successful, but it should be borne in mind that an Advanced Placement course can only be as good as the foundation on which it rests. The Development Committee feels strongly that any school embarking upon an Advanced Placement program in German literature should thoroughly examine the content of its basic courses. Academic excellence should be the main goal, even in beginning German classes. Good results in an introductory literature course are possible only when there has been sound achievement in the acquisition of language skills.

The course description that follows stresses a balance of linguistic and literary achievement. Candidates should have the linguistic training equivalent to the first two years of a strong college German course and the experience of applying this linguistic achievement to the work done in a third-year (i.e., level 3) college introductory course in German literature. Candidates are not required to have the training equivalent to a third-year college course in German composition and conversation as described and tested in AP German Language.

COURSE

Candidates in Advanced Placement German Literature are expected to have completed the equivalent of a one-year college Introduction to German Literature. Such a course assumes a good command of the German language and the ability to read German literature of moderate difficulty. More specifically, candidates should have proficiency in the fundamental *language skills* to a degree that enables them to:

1. Read at sight poetry, prose, and drama of moderate difficulty.
2. Understand a simple German lecture on a cultural topic.
3. Write a German narrative.

Furthermore, students should have proficiency in *reading literature* to a degree that enables them to:

1. Read with comprehension and understanding poetry, prose, and drama of moderate difficulty.
2. Write in English (or German, if the candidate prefers) an analysis and interpretation of a literary passage.
3. Demonstrate their sensitivity to techniques used in literary German.

ADVANCED PLACEMENT: HISTORY

AMERICAN HISTORY AND EUROPEAN HISTORY

The Advanced Placement Program offers two separate courses and examinations in history: American History and European History. Each is intended for qualified students who wish to complete studies in secondary school equivalent to college introductory courses in these fields. Students are free to take either or both examinations, as they prefer. Each examination presumes at least one academic year's college-level preparation, descriptions of which are set forth in this booklet. The description of Advanced Placement American History is presented first; the description of Advanced Placement European History follows it.

AMERICAN HISTORY: PURPOSE

The Advanced Placement Program in American History is designed to provide students with the analytic skills and factual knowledge necessary to deal critically with the problems and materials in American history. The Program prepares students for intermediate and advanced college courses by making demands upon them equivalent to those of full-year introductory materials—their relevance to a given interpretive problem, their reliability, and their importance—and to weigh the evidence and interpretations presented in historical scholarship. An Advanced Placement American History course should thus develop the skills necessary to arrive at conclusions on the basis of an informed judgment, and to present ideas clearly and persuasively in essay format.

COURSE

Most Advanced Placement courses are designed to give students a grounding in the chronology of American history and in major interpretive questions that derive from the study of selected themes. One common approach is to conduct a survey course in which a textbook, with supplementary readings in the form of documents, essays, or books on special themes, provides chronological and thematic coverage. A second approach is the close examination of a series of problems or topics through specialized writings by historians and through supplementary readings. In the latter type of course, the teacher can devote one segment of the course to a survey by using a concise text or interpretive history. Whichever approach is used, students need to have access to materials that can provide them with an overview of American history that helps them establish the context and significance of specialized interpretive problems.

Although there is little to be gained by rote memorization of names and dates on an encyclopedic basis, a student must be able to draw upon a reservoir of systematic factual knowledge in order to exercise analytic skills intelligently. Striking a balance between obtaining a command of systematic factual knowledge and analyzing that knowledge critically is a demanding but crucial task in the design of a successful AP course in history.

Some Advanced Placement courses stress political history and foreign affairs, others economic and social development, still others literary and cultural history. Most Advanced Placement courses deal with the colonial period, the American Revolution, the Jacksonian period, the Civil War and Reconstruction, Populism and Progressivism, the New Deal, and international affairs and domestic change in the post-1945 period. Moreover, most Advanced Placement courses seek to give students a factual basis for interpreting the following problems: the character of colonial society; British relations with the Atlantic colonies in North America; the motivations and character of American expansionism; the content of the Constitution and its amendments, and their interpretations by the Supreme Court; the growth of political parties; the changing role of government in American life, including both its early history and the emergence of regulatory and welfare-state legislation in the modern period; nationalism, agrarianism, liberalism, conservatism, abolitionism, and other such movements in their intellectual and political expressions; long-term demographic trends; the process of economic growth and development; the changing occupational structure, nature of work, and labor organization; the origins and nature of black slavery in America; immigration and the history of racial and ethnic minorities; urbanization; the causes and impacts of major wars in American history; major movements and individual figures in the history of American arts and letters.

An Advanced Placement course should train students to analyze and interpret primary sources, including documentary material, maps, statistical tables, and pictorial and graphic evidence of historical events. Students should learn to take notes from both printed materials and lectures or discussions, write essay examinations, and write analytical and research papers. They should be able to express themselves with clarity and precision and know how to cite sources and credit the phrases and ideas of others.

Teacher and student access to an adequate library is essential to the success of an Advanced Placement course. Besides textbooks and standard reference works such as encyclopedias, atlases, collections of historical documents, and statistical compendia, the library should contain a wide range of scholarly works in American history, augmented annually by new book purchases and subscriptions to scholarly periodicals. The course can also make profitable use of television and audiovisual aids to instruction in the school, and also of historical exhibits in local museums, historical societies, and libraries. Anthologies and paperback editions of important works of literature are readily available for teachers wishing to stress intellectual and cultural history; so too are collections of slides illustrating changing technology, the history of art, and architecture.

Advanced Placement classes require extra time on the part of the instructor for preparation, personal consultation with students, and the reading of a much larger number of written assignments than would be given to students in regular classes. Accordingly, the Advanced Placement Development Committee for American History strongly urges that any teacher offering such a class or classes have some reduction in assigned teaching hours.

EUROPEAN HISTORY

The current Advanced Placement Program in European History corresponds to the most recent trends in history curriculums at the undergraduate level.*

In colleges and universities European history is increasingly seen in a broad perspective, with teaching methods reflecting an awareness of other disciplines and a diversity of techniques of presentation, including visual and statistical materials. These trends have led the Development Committee to divide the examination into three parts: an objective section dealing with concepts, major

*The Development Committee periodically revises the content and structure of the Advanced Placement European History course description to reflect new developments in the discipline, to aid teachers in maintaining the comprehensive quality of their courses, and to assist teachers new to the program. A revised edition of the supplementary booklet *Beginning an Advanced Placement European History Course* has been prepared and may be ordered from College Board Publication Orders, Box 2815, Princeton, N.J. 08541. There is a $1 charge for the booklet.

historical facts, and historical analysis; a thematic essay on a topic of major significance; and a document-based essay designed specifically to test students' ability to work with evidence. Together, these three parts of the examination provide students with an opportunity to demonstrate that they are qualified to pursue upper-level history studies at college.

COURSE

In addition to a basic exposure to the factual narrative, the goals of the Advanced Placement Program in European History are to develop (a) an understanding of some of the principal themes in modern European history, (b) an awareness of Europe's changing position in the world, and (c) an ability to analyze historical evidence.

THEMES IN MODERN EUROPEAN HISTORY

The themes noted below indicate some of the important areas that might be treated in an Advanced Placement course in European history. The ideas suggested do not have to be treated explicitly as topics or covered inclusively; nor should they preclude development of other themes. While for convenience a list of major categories of historical study is given here, questions on the examination will often call for students to interrelate categories or to trace developments in a particular category through several chronological periods.

1. Political and Diplomatic History

The rise and functioning of the modern state in its various forms.

The development of political parties and ideologies.

The extension and limitation of individual civil liberties.

The development and growth of nationalism.

Forms of political protest, reform, and revolution.

Colonialism and imperialism: relationship of European and non-European powers, including decolonization.

Relationship between domestic and foreign policies.

Efforts to restrain interstate conflict: treaties, balance of power diplomacy, and international organizations.

2. Intellectual and Cultural History

The secularization of learning and culture.

Changes in religious thought and organization.

The scientific revolution and its consequences.

Major trends in literature and the arts as statements of cultural values and as historical evidence.

Developments in social thought (economic and political theory).

The spread of literacy.

The diffusion of new intellectual concepts among different social groups.

Changes in popular culture such as the development of new attitudes toward religion, toward the family, toward work.

3. *Social and Economic History*

The role of the city in transforming cultural values and social relationships.

The shift in social structures from hierarchical orders to modern social classes.

Changes in the nature of elites and their interaction with the lower classes.

The development of commercial practices and their economic and social impact.

The origins, development, and consequences of industrialization.

Changes in the demographic structure of Europe.

Change and continuity in the European family structure and relationships.

The growth of competition and interdependence in national and world markets.

The relationships between private and state contributions to economic growth.

ADVANCED PLACEMENT: LATIN

Vergil and Catullus—Horace

Advanced Placement Latin comprises two courses, Vergil and Catullus—Horace, the aims of which are in general conformity with college Latin studies in the fourth through sixth semesters. As in all such courses beyond the intermediate level, their basic objective is progress in reading, understanding, and interpreting Latin in the original.

There is an Advanced Placement Latin Examination for each of these two courses; a student may elect to take either one, or both, in any given year for a single examination fee. The content of these examinations is set forth rather specifically in this booklet as a deliberate aid to teachers in planning the courses and in helping students prepare for the examinations. The works selected for emphasis are among those most frequently studied in comparable college courses. While the Development Committee in Latin recognizes variation among such courses from one American college to another, it does consider each AP Latin Examination to require and reflect one semester's study beyond the intermediate level at college. It notes that, while many colleges allot a single semester at this level to a partial reading of the *Aeneid*, others may devote an entire year to reading more.

In both courses, therefore, as in the cognate courses at colleges, students are expected to be able to translate accurately the poetry they are reading from Latin into English and to demonstrate a grasp of the grammatical structures and vocabulary the author has used. Moreover, since the appreciation of Latin literature calls for an understanding of the literary techniques used by Latin writers, stylistic analysis is also an integral part of the advanced work in both courses described here. Advanced Placement Latin courses also include the study of the political, social, and cultural background of works being read, as well as a cultivation of students' awareness of classical influences upon later literature.

Each examination has two parts: a multiple-choice section which tests students' ability to read and understand Latin literature at sight, and a free-response section which measures their ability to comprehend and interpret the material read in the specific course. The multiple-choice section of the examination is 60 minutes long and is the same for both examinations. The free-response section in each examination is also one hour long. The multiple-choice section is taken only once by candidates in any given year, whether they are taking one or both free-response sections. Thus a candidate taking only one examination is given two hours to finish, while a candidate taking both examinations is given three hours.

The description of the Vergil course is presented immediately below; the description of the Catullus—Horace course follows it [not included].

VERGIL: COURSE

The reading in Latin of Books 1, 2, 4, and 6 of the *Aeneid* is required. A knowledge of the contents of the remaining books is expected. Appreciation of the *Aeneid* as poetry implies the ability to translate accurately, to interpret critically, to read aloud with attention to pauses and phrasing, and to scan the Latin hexameter verse. Scansion includes indicating elision, marking the metrical quantities of the syllables, and dividing the syllables into feet. (The last syllable of a line may be marked long.) Students should be familiar with the figures of speech commonly used by Vergil in the *Aeneid*. They should be given extensive practice in translating accurately and in reading at sight. Familiarity with pertinent Roman cultural, social, and political history and study of the ancient epic as a literary genre are assumed. Although reading in the *Iliad* and *Odyssey* is not required, it is hoped that the teacher will point out parallels in the *Aeneid* to the works of Homer. The amount of time devoted to the AP Vergil course is flexible and depends upon such factors as the extent and character of the students' prior training, general ability, and the teacher's own background and inclinations.

ADVANCED PLACEMENT: MATHEMATICS
CALCULUS AB AND CALCULUS BC

An Advanced Placement course in mathematics consists of a full academic year of work in calculus and related topics comparable to courses in colleges and universities. Such courses differ among secondary schools, just as they do among colleges, depending upon the curriculum of the school and the preparation of its students. Recognizing this situation, the Advanced Placement Program offers descriptions of two calculus courses and an examination for each course. Each Advanced Placement candidate will write only one examination—whichever is more appropriate to the student's preparation. The two course descriptions and the two corresponding examinations are denoted Calculus AB and Calculus BC.

Calculus AB can be offered as an Advancement Placement course in the senior year by any school that is able to organize a curriculum for mathematically able students in which all of the prerequisites for a combined year's course in elementary functions and calculus are completed prior to grade 12. If students are to be adequately prepared for the Calculus AB examination, well over half of that year's course must be devoted to topics in differential and integral calculus.

Calculus BC can be offered by schools that are able to complete before grade 12 a substantial introduction to elementary functions in addition to the prerequisites for Calculus AB. Calculus BC is an intensive full-year course in the calculus of functions of a single variable. The course includes topics in infinite series and differential equations.

Both courses described here represent college-level mathematics for which most colleges grant advanced placement and credit. . . . The courses are roughly comparable to those outlined in a 1972 report entitled "Commentary on a General Curriculum in Mathematics for Colleges,"* which was prepared for the Mathematical Association of America by its Committee on the Undergraduate Program in Mathematics. Most colleges and universities offer a calculus sequence of several semester courses, and entering students are placed within this sequence according to the extent of their preparation as measured by the results of an Advanced Placement Examination or other criteria. Appropriate credit and placement are granted by each institution in accordance with local policies. At many institutions Calculus AB is given a full year's credit. In any event, the content of Calculus BC is designed to qualify the student for placement and credit one semester beyond that granted for Calculus AB. In deciding which Advanced Placement Examination a candidate should write, the student and his or her teacher should weigh carefully the extent and degree of his or her preparation in calculus and their relation to the mathematics curriculum of the college that the student plans to attend. Many colleges provide in their catalogs statements regarding their advanced placement policies.

Schools have a choice of several possible actions regarding Advanced Placement mathematics. The option that is most appropriate for a particular school depends upon local conditions and resources: school size, curriculum, the preparation of teachers, and the interest of students, teachers, and administrators.

Because of the sequential nature of mathematics, any school that offers one or both of the Advanced Placement courses in mathematics must design its mathematics curriculum carefully so that a full preparatory program can be completed by Advanced Placement candidates no later than the end of grade 11.† This can be accomplished, for example, in one or more of the following ways: starting the study of secondary school mathematics in grade 8; reorganizing the content of courses; establishing accelerated sections for the more capable students; encouraging the election of more than one mathematics course in grade 9, 10, or 11; instituting programs of summer study or guided independent study during the academic year. It is highly desirable, therefore, that potential Advanced Placement candidates be identified and placed in appropriate mathematics courses as early as possible, even in grade 7 or 8.

In redesigning a school curriculum, teachers should carefully consider not only the content but also the level of sophistication at which new concepts are introduced. Intuition is extremely important in mathematics; on the other hand, understanding of some mathematical concepts is best acquired by formal treatment. Many mathematicians attempt to achieve both of these objectives—intuition and precision—by using a spiral approach in which an idea is first intro-

---

*Copies of this report may be obtained without charge from CUPM, Box 1024, Berkeley, Calif. 94701.

†One example of such a mathematics program for grades 9, 10, 11, and the first semester of grade 12 is described in detail in the Report of the Commission on Mathematics, *Program for College Preparatory Mathematics* (New York: College Entrance Examination Board, 1959), 63 pp.

duced intuitively and later reexamined, perhaps several times, at gradually increasing levels of rigor. Both Calculus AB and Calculus BC are primarily concerned with an intuitive understanding of the concepts of calculus and experience with its methods and applications. The expanded content of Calculus BC requires some additional knowledge of the rudiments of the theoretical tools of calculus. Use of the word *intuitive* is not meant to suggest a reduction of either clarity of concept or precision of expression. Rather it attempts to distinguish between a calculus course that emphasizes precise proofs of all theorems—rigor in the formal sense—and a calculus course that states definitions and theorems correctly but that frankly defers some proofs until later. One illustration of this point of view may be found on pages 8 and 9 in the 1972 cupm report.

In deciding which course to offer, many teachers will find it helpful to seek advice from departments of mathematics in secondary schools that have had experience with the Program and from colleges in their vicinity or to which their students may be applying. There are a number of publications available that should also be of value in making a decision about which course to offer as well as in providing information for planning the teaching of the course. Two new publications that provide considerable information and resource materials for teachers became available for the first time during the 1974–75 school year. One is a report entitled "Grading the Advanced Placement Examination— 1976."* This report, prepared in alternate years by the Chief Reader at the conclusion of the reading, gives a detailed account of the standard setting, reading, and grading processes of the free-response section. The other publication is a booklet entitled "Beginning an Advanced Placement Course in Mathematics—1975,"† which provides information for teachers and school districts planning to offer an Advanced Placement course in calculus. In it Katherine P. Layton, Advanced Placement mathematics teacher and a former committee member, discusses a number of important issues relevant to beginning an Advanced Placement program in mathematics. Other features of this booklet include sample course syllabi, textbooks currently being used to teach each of the calculus courses, time frames for covering the topics found in this course description, and various other resource materials submitted by experienced Advanced Placement mathematics teachers. Two articles that appeared in the October 1971 and December 1975 issues of *The Mathematics Teacher*‡ also provide useful information. The article that appeared in 1971 contains both the objective and free-response sections of the 1969 Calculus AB and Calculus BC examinations; the 1975 article contains both the objective and free-response sections of the 1973 Calculus AB and Calculus BC examinations. Further information or assistance can be obtained by writing to the appropriate College Board regional office. . . .

ADVANCED PLACEMENT: MUSIC
Music Theory and Music Listening
and Literature

There was a time, only two hundred years ago, when those who sponsored and listened to music were themselves trained as musicians. Habsburg emperors

*Copies of these materials may be obtained from College Board Publication Orders, Box 2815, Princeton, N. J. 08540.
†Ibid.
‡Ibid.

knew enough music to compose works of their own, to conduct from time to time, and to take an active interest in the hiring of their court musicians. For several centuries, Italian and German princes competed with one another for the services of leading musicians, and, during the Renaissance, musical knowledge and skill in performance were among the principal graces expected of a courtier. Though books and treatises of a wide variety were published on music, no one conceived of writing about what to listen for in music. Such a book was unnecessary at the time, because those who listened were usually well trained as musicians.

Since the time of the Industrial Revolution, the sources for the sponsorship of music have changed, encompassing at first the box office, and then as well the colleges and universities, and more recently, at least in America, state and federal agencies. The educational preparation for those who will compose, perform, and listen to music has become almost infinitely diverse, comprising private and group instruction in performance, in theory and composition, and in history and literature, at all age levels and all over the country. The backgrounds of professional performers, of scholars and critics, of record buyers, of concertgoers, or of symphony board members reveal this diversity of education in music.

In a book entitled *The Musical Experience,* the American composer Roger Sessions asserts the importance of a common musical objective for composer, performer, and audience. A musical work, writes Sessions, is perceived most intensely by the composer, who knows it better than anyone else. Sessions believes that in most cases a performer perceives a composition with somewhat less acuity perhaps than the composer does but essentially in a manner similar to that of the composer. Sessions' principal point is that the members of a well-trained audience experience music not in a manner different from that of the composer and the performer but in a fashion that is essentially the same.

The Advanced Placement Development Committee in Music recognizes the wide variety of music courses offered in America at the secondary school and college levels, courses intended both for those who will enter the music profession and for those who will become members of a broad and discriminating musical audience. We recognize, too, that many of those most dedicated to music in high school have not yet decided whether or not they will devote their lives to careers in music. The AP Music Committee has developed two examinations in music—Music Theory and Music Listening and Literature—each of which is appropriate to the needs of future composers, performers, and listeners. Both examinations are intended for secondary school students who have completed musical studies comparable to first-year college courses for the music major or for the nonmajor with a serious interest in the field. Students may choose to take one examination or both, as their preparation warrants.

The Development Committee recommends that students who receive a grade of 3, 4, or 5 on either of these examinations be given a full year's credit for the appropriate college course.

Descriptions of the courses and of the examinations for Music Theory and Music Listening and Literature follow. Each examination includes aural materials specific to the course; the two examinations also share a common 40-minute Aural Perception Component that is taken by all candidates for advanced placement in music. . . .

Three kinds of questions are ordinarily included in the examination: multiple-choice questions based on recorded music played within the examination; multiple-choice questions based not on aural materials but on general musical knowledge; and free-response questions of various lengths, some of which are based on recorded music. . . .

MUSIC THEORY: COURSE

A major component of a college curriculum in music is a course designed for the study of musical structure. Such a course may emphasize one element of music, such as harmony, or may integrate melodic, harmonic, textural, rhythmic, and formal aspects. The student's ability to read and write musical notation is naturally fundamental to such a course. College theory courses have many titles (Basic Musicianship, Elementary Theory, Harmony and Dictation I, Structure of Music, etc.); generally the course includes analysis and some elementary composition. Aural skills, sight-singing, and keyboard harmony may be part of the theory course or may be taught in separate classes.

The ultimate goal of a music theory course is to develop a student's ability to recognize and understand the basic materials and processes in any music that is heard or read in score. This goal is perhaps best approached through the development of fundamental aural, notational, and performance skills. The course should provide a solid foundation in intervals, pitch, patterns, metric/rhythmic patterns, chords, and the terms that are part of a basic understanding of music. Generally these fundamentals are related to the major-minor tonal system. From this background a high school or college course can progress to more complicated tasks: the composition of a melody with a specific scale basis, contour, and phrase construction; the analysis and performance of a two-part contrapuntal texture, including the study of the motivic treatment and the rhythmic and melodic interaction between the voices; or the harmonic/tonal analysis and realization of a functional chordal passage.

Most first-year college courses emphasize the diatonic pitch collection, functional triadic harmony, simple meters and rhythms, two-part contrapuntal textures, and the smaller forms of music. The Advanced Placement course at the secondary school level should likewise focus on similar material. Chromatic harmony, more complicated key relationships, and the larger forms of music should generally receive less emphasis.

In an AP course in music theory, students should be required to read, notate, compose, and hear music. To the extent possible, performance—using keyboard or students' primary performance media—should also be a part of the learning process. Although sight-singing and keyboard harmony are not directly tested by the Advanced Placement Examination, training in these areas will develop those aural skills that are tested directly.

MUSIC LISTENING AND LITERATURE: COURSE

At colleges, Music Listening and Literature is frequently called Elements of Music, Music History, Music Literature, Music Application, or Masterpieces of Music. Whatever its title, the course commonly stresses (1) the development of rigorous listening techniques, (2) increasing familiarity with a variety of repertories, and (3) vocabulary appropriate for describing musical events and relationships as they are heard. It is assumed that students already possess at least a rudimentary grasp of musical notation and that it will be developed further in the course of study. Students with little performing experience are not expected to read music to the same degree of proficiency as that normally shown by music majors. Those who have some grasp of music theory will find that it aids their work in music listening and literature.

The content of the Music Listening and Literature course should normally stress varying aspects of musical coherence in a broad variety of repertories. Attention should be given both to large-scale formal design and to the syntax of musical phrases and periods. Varying uses of rhythm, melody, harmony, and texture should be addressed, as should such principles of organization as repetition, variation, departure and return, development, contrast, and symmetry.

Students should also gain some understanding of the broad outlines of music history, but the Advanced Placement course should not focus primarily upon matters of chronology, biography, and cultural context. Although the richest comprehension of music includes all of these, the primary emphasis at the secondary school level should be placed on the music itself. In an AP course, the study of cultural context is valuable insofar as it contributes to an understanding of a musical work and of the aesthetic that informs it.

The ultimate goal of Music Listening and Literature is to develop understanding listeners who respond fully to music. A work of music takes place in time and is mainly perceived through discerning attention over the span of a performance. With the aid of a relevant conceptual framework, listeners can improve their perception and memory and closely follow the course of a work in performance with something approaching the experience of the composer who conceived it. Such listeners will find their aesthetic sense sharpened and their pleasure in music enhanced.

ADVANCED PLACEMENT: PHYSICS

PHYSICS B AND PHYSICS C

Two Advanced Placement Examinations in physics, identified as Physics B and Physics C, are offered. These examinations are designed to test student achievement in the Physics B and Physics C courses. These courses are intended to be representative of courses commonly offered in colleges and universities, but they do not necessarily correspond precisely with courses at any particular institution.

An Advanced Placement secondary school course in physics should aim at developing the students' abilities to:

1. Read, understand, and interpret physical information—verbal, mathematical, and graphical.
2. Describe and explain the sequence of steps in the analysis of a particular physical phenomenon or problem; that is,
   a. Describe the idealized model to be used in the analysis, including simplifying assumptions where necessary.
   b. State the principles or definitions that are applicable.
   c. Specify relevant limitations on applications of these principles.
   d. Carry out and describe the steps of the analysis, verbally or mathematically.
   e. Interpret the results or conclusions, including discussion of particular cases of special interest.

3. Use basic mathematical reasoning—arithmetic, algebraic, geometric, trigonometric, and calculus, where appropriate in a physical situation or problem.
4. Perform experiments and interpret the results of observations, including making an assessment of experimental uncertainties.

In the achievement of these goals, concentration on basic principles of physics and their applications through careful and selective treatment of well-chosen areas is more important than superficial and encyclopedic coverage of many detailed topics. Within the general framework outlined below, teachers may exercise some freedom in the choice of topics.

In the Advanced Placement Examinations, an attempt is made through the use of multiple-choice and free-response questions to determine how well these goals have been achieved by the student either in a conventional course or through independent study. The level of the student's achievement is assigned a grade, and many colleges use this grade alone as the basis for placement and credit decisions.

Introductory college physics courses typically fall into one of three categories. In the following discussion, these categories are designated A, B, and C.

Category A includes courses in which physics is viewed primarily from a cultural or historical perspective. Emphasis is on a qualitative understanding of general principles and models and on the nature of scientific inquiry. Students in such courses are generally oriented toward the humanities and desire to develop an understanding of the historical role of science and its place in contemporary society. The level of mathematical sophistication expected may extend to simple trigonometry, but rarely beyond. These courses vary widely in content and approach, and at present there is no Advanced Placement Examination for courses in this category.

The Physics B course provides a systematic introduction to the main principles of physics and emphasizes the development of problem-solving ability. It is assumed that the student is familiar with algebra and trigonometry; calculus is seldom used, although some theoretical developments may use basic concepts of calculus. In most colleges, this is a one-year terminal course and is not the usual preparation for more advanced physics and engineering courses. However, the B course provides a foundation in physics for students in the life sciences, premedicine, and some applied sciences, as well as other fields not directly related to science.

The C course ordinarily forms the first part of the college sequence that serves as the foundation in physics for students majoring in the physical sciences or engineering. This sequence is paralleled or preceded by mathematics courses that include calculus. Methods of calculus are used wherever appropriate in formulating physical principles and in applying them to physical problems. The sequence is more intensive and analytic than the B course. Strong emphasis is placed on solving a variety of challenging problems, some requiring calculus, and there is emphasis on analysis in the laboratory as well as in the classroom. The subject matter of the C course is principally mechanics, and electricity and magnetism, with approximately equal emphasis on these two areas. The C course is the first part of a sequence which in college is sometimes a very intensive one-year course, but which usually extends over one and one-half to two years.

In certain colleges and universities, other types of unusually high-level introductory courses are taken by a few selected students. Selection of students for these courses is often based on results of Advanced Placement Examinations, other college admission information, or a college-administered examination. The Advanced Placement Examinations are not designed to test for achievement in such courses, but may facilitate admission to them.

It is important for those teaching and advising Advanced Placement students to consider the relation of Advanced Placement courses to a student's college plans. In some circumstances it is advantageous to take the Physics B Advanced Placement course. The student may be interested in studying physics as a basis for more advanced work in the life sciences, medicine, geology, and related areas, or as a component in a nonscience college program which has science requirements. Credit or advanced placement in the Physics B course provides the student with an opportunity either to accelerate and further enrich his college program or to meet a basic science requirement. It may also provide access to an intensive physics sequence for physics or science majors.

For students planning to specialize in a physical science or in engineering, most colleges require an introductory physics sequence of which the C course is the first part. Since a prior or concurrent course in calculus is often required of students taking the C course, a student who expects advanced placement or credit for Physics C should attempt advanced placement in mathematics as well; otherwise his placement in the next-in-sequence physics course may be delayed or even denied. Either of the Advanced Placement Mathematics courses, Calculus AB or Calculus BC, should provide an acceptable basis for a student preparing for a major in the physical sciences or engineering, but Calculus BC is recommended. The above considerations indicate that if such a student must make a choice between Advanced Placement Physics or Advanced Placement Mathematics, he should probably choose mathematics.

There are two separate Advanced Placement Physics Examinations, Physics B and Physics C. Both examinations contain multiple-choice and free-response questions. The Physics B Examination is for students who have taken a Physics B course or who have mastered the material of this course through independent study. The subject matter of the Physics B Examination includes mechanics, electricity and magnetism, kinetic theory and heat, waves and optics, and modern physics; a single examination grade is reported. Similarly, the Physics C Examination corresponds to the Physics C course. The subject matter of the Physics C Examination is in mechanics and in electricity and magnetism. Students are permitted to take either or both parts of this examination, and separate grades are reported for these two subject areas to provide greater flexibility in planning advanced placement courses and making advanced placement decisions. . . .

INSTRUCTIONAL APPROACHES: ALTERNATIVES

Secondary school programs for the achievement of Advanced Placement course goals can take several forms. A common format is a second-year course following the usual introductory physics course. A second possibility is an intensive first-year course. Independent study for individual students is a third possibility. The imaginative teacher can combine these and other possible approaches to fit the needs of the students.

ADVANCED PLACEMENT: SPANISH

Spanish Language and Spanish Literature

The Advanced Placement Program offers two separate, parallel courses and examinations in Spanish: Spanish Language and Spanish Literature. Each is intended for qualified students who wish to complete studies in secondary school comparable in difficulty and content to such third-year (level 3) college courses as Advanced Spanish Composition and Conversation or an Introduction to Hispanic Literature.

Students are free to take both examinations if they wish, thus demonstrating achievement in both language and literature at the third-year college level. Each examination presumes at least one academic year's special, college-level preparation, with many schools finding a two-year program more satisfactory. The description of the Spanish language program is presented first; the description of the Spanish literature program follows it.

SPANISH LANGUAGE

The Advanced Placement Program in Spanish Language is intended for those who have chosen to develop their proficiency in Spanish without special emphasis on literature.

Students who enroll should already have a basic knowledge of the language and culture of Spanish-speaking peoples and should have attained a reasonable proficiency in listening comprehension, speaking, reading, and writing. They should be familiar with the expectations of the Program.* Although these qualifications may be attained in a variety of ways, it is assumed that most students will be in the final stages of their secondary school training and will have had substantial course work in the language. To ensure that the Advanced Placement Spanish Language Examination is maintained at its intended level, a validity study has been carried out to establish the comparability of performance of college students completing a third-year Spanish language course in their institutions and Advanced Placement candidates. The results of the comparison between these two groups strongly bear out the contention of the Spanish Language Development Committee that successful performance on the examination is equivalent to the performance of students who have completed six semesters of college Spanish language courses at postsecondary institutions that admit large numbers of Advanced Placement Spanish candidates.

COURSE

A school's course in Advanced Placement Spanish Language covers the equivalent of a third-year college course in Advanced Spanish Composition and Conversation stressing oral skills, composition, and grammar. Such a course, emphasizing the use of Spanish for active communication, has the following objectives:

1. the ability to comprehend formal and informal spoken Spanish;
2. the acquisition of vocabulary and a grasp of structure to allow the easy,

---

*To assist the teacher a booklet entitled "Beginning an Advanced Placement Spanish Language Course" has been prepared and can be obtained from College Board Publication Orders, Box 2815, Princeton, N.J. 08541.

accurate reading of newspaper and magazine articles as well as of modern Hispanic literature;

3. the ability to compose expository passages;
4. the ability to express ideas orally with accuracy and fluency.

Course content might best reflect intellectual interests shared by the students and teacher (the arts, current events, literature, sports, etc.). Materials might well include recordings, films, newspapers, and magazines.

The course seeks to develop language skills that are useful in themselves and that can be applied to various activities and disciplines rather than to the mastery of any specific subject matter. The need for extensive training in the organization and writing of compositions must not be overlooked.

SPANISH LITERATURE: COURSE

Candidates for Advanced Placement Spanish Literature are expected to complete the equivalent of a college third-year Introduction to Hispanic Literature, covering selected works from the literatures of Spain and Spanish America. (Because they read and analyze Hispanic literature *in Spanish* for this purpose, the language proficiency they attain is generally well beyond that of students starting a college third-year Spanish course in Advanced Grammar and Composition.) The function of the Advanced Placement Spanish Literature course is to prepare students:

1. to understand a lecture in Spanish and to participate actively in Spanish in a discussion on a literary topic;
2. to read closely modern Hispanic literature in all genres;
3. to analyze critically, orally and in writing, the form and content of literary works.

APPENDIX A

Education of the Gifted and Talented

Report to the Congress of the United States
by the U.S. Commissioner of Education

Editor's Note: This report was prepared for the Subcommittee on Education of the Committee on Labor and Public Welfare, U.S. Senate (March 1972). This document, as it appears on the following pages, is an exact page-for-page reproduction (some introductory matter has been omitted) of the U.S. Government Printing Office Publication (Washington, D.C.: 1972). For this reason the appearance of the text does not conform to *Creating Programs for the Gifted* design and page format. The headings of the contents of this report are provided below. Volume II of this report (containing the appendixes) is not reprinted here; therefore, disregard any internal references in the report to Volume II or appendixes.

TABLE OF CONTENTS

FOREWORD

Section 806(c) of Public Law 91–230 reads as follows:
 (c) (1) The Commissioner of Education shall:
   (A) determine the extent to which special educational assistance programs are necessary or useful to meet the needs of gifted and talented children,
   (B) show which existing Federal educational assistance programs are being used to meet the needs of gifted and talented children,
   (C) evaluate how existing Federal educational assistance programs can be more effectively used to meet these needs, and
   (D) recommend which new programs, if any, are needed to meet these needs.
  (2) The Commissioner shall report his findings, together with his recommendations, to the Congress not later than one year after the enactment of this Act.

In response to the mandate of the law, the Office of Education evaluated the status of education for the nation's gifted and talented children in several ways. One of the most valuable sources of data came through public hearings held by the ten Regional Commissioners of Education at which interested educators, State educational agency administrators, parents, citizens, and gifted children from all 50 States, testified to the great importance of specialized attention to the gifted and talented child and the dearth of available resources for this purpose throughout the country. The study also included a review of the present Federal education programs, analysis of existing data bases, a review of research as it relates to critical issues in education of the gifted, and consultation with the nation's leading experts in gifted education.

This report, "Education of the Gifted and Talented", published in two volumes, has been widely acclaimed as a landmark document in the education of gifted and talented children, an area which heretofore has received scant attention in our schools. Considerable public and professional as well as Congressional interest has been manifested in the report, which now is out of print. It is highly appropriate, therefore, that the report be made more widely available through its publication and distribution as an official document of the Committee on Labor and Public Welfare.

As the author of the provision of law providing special educational assistance programs for gifted and talented children and authorizing the report, I should like to thank Senator Claiborne Pell, Chairman of the Subcommittee on Education, and Senator Harrison A. Williams, Chairman of the Committee on Labor and Public Welfare, for their interest in the education of gifted and talented children and for their cooperation in authorizing the printing of the report as a committee document.

JACOB K. JAVITS, *U.S. Senator.*

DEPARTMENT OF HEALTH, EDUCATION, AND WELFARE
OFFICE OF EDUCATION
WASHINGTON. D.C. 20202

October 6, 1971

Honorable Carl B. Albert
Speaker of the House of Representatives
Washington, D.C.

Dear Mr. Speaker:

In response to the 1970 Congressional mandate (P.L. 91-230, Section 806) for a status report on education of gifted and talented children, I am submitting ten copies of the Office of Education's Report to Congress (Volume I) and ten copies of the background papers prepared for this study (Volume 2).

In this painstaking study, the Office of Education has called on the best minds within our agency and in the field of special education. It has confirmed our impression of inadequate provisions for these students and widespread misunderstanding about their needs.

Chapter VIII of the Report outlines the immediate steps we are taking in response to some of the major deficiencies uncovered. A program group is being organized within the Office of Education for long-range comprehensive planning in cooperation with State and local educators.

We welcome your advice and assistance in improving the education of one of our most neglected and potentially productive groups of students.

Sincerely,

S. P. Marland, Jr.
U.S. Commissioner
of Education

EXECUTIVE SUMMARY

Background and Methodology of the Study

Educators, legislators, and parents have long puzzled over the problem of educating gifted students in a public educational program geared primarily to a philosophy of egalitarianism.

We know that gifted children can be identified as early as the preschool grades and that these children in later life often make outstanding contributions to our society in the arts, politics, business and the sciences. But, disturbingly, research has confirmed that many talented children perform far below their intellectual potential. We are increasingly being stripped of the comfortable notion that a bright mind will make its own way. Intellectual and creative talent cannot survive educational neglect and apathy.

This loss is particularly evident in the minority groups who have in both social and educational environments every configuration calculated to stifle potential talent.

The Congress of the United States expressed its interest and concern by passing a landmark addition to the Elementary and Secondary Education Amendments of 1969 (Public Law 91–230), section 806, "Provisions related to gifted and talented children." This amendment, unanimously passed in the House and Senate, provided for two specific changes in existing legislation. It explicated congressional intent that the gifted and talented student should benefit from Federal education legislation—notably titles III and V of the Elementary and Secondary Education Act and the teacher fellowship provisions of the Higher Education Act of 1956. Section 806 directed the Commissioner of Education to conduct a study to:

1. Determine the extent to which special educational assistance programs are necessary or useful to meet the needs of gifted and talented children.

2. Show which Federal education assistance programs are being used to meet the needs of gifted and talented children.

3. Evaluate how existing Federal educational assistance programs can be more effectively used to meet these needs.

4. Recommend new programs, if any, needed to meet these needs.

This report is the Commissioner's response to that mandate.

The study was assigned by the Acting Commissioner of Education to the then Deputy Assistant Secretary/Deputy Commissioner for Planning, Research, and Evaluation (in the Office of Education), now the Office of the Deputy Commissioner for Development. The study was planned, coordinated, and directed by Jane Case Williams.

Because this study represented an area of concern for both the Federal and non-Federal sectors, and offered the U.S. Office of Education (USOE) the opportunity to study an educational problem with nationally significant, long-term implications for society, it was determined that the study would be done directly from the Office of Education. This arrangement enabled the Office to: (1) call on its large reservoir of expertise among staff people, (2) contract for technical services as needed, (3) utilize the regional offices of USOE, and 4) draw on nationally known experts in the field.

The plan developed for the study, as accepted and amplified by the informal advisory panel, consisted of five major activities:

1. Review of research, other available literature, and expert knowledge.

2. Analysis of the educational data bases available to USOE and the development of a major data base through the "Survey of Leadership in Education of Gifted and Talented Children and Youth" (*Advocate Survey*).

3. Public hearings by the Regional Assistant Commissioners of Education in each of the 10 HEW regions to interpret regional needs.

4. Studies of programs in representative States with long-standing statewide support for education of gifted and talented children.

5. Review and analysis of the system for delivery of Office of Education programs to benefit gifted and talented children.

This study began in August 1970 with the development and acceptance of the plan and concluded in June 1971 with the preparation of the final report, which is based on the findings and documentation from the five major activities.

Public Law 91–230, Section 806, states that the Commissioner of Education shall define "gifted and talented" for purposes of Federal education programs. The definition established by the advisory panel reads:

Gifted and talented children are those identified by professionally qualified persons who by virtue of outstanding abilities, are capable of high performance. These are children who require differentiated educational programs and/or services beyond those normally provided by the regular school program in order to realize their contribution to self and society.

Children capable of high performance include those with demonstrated achievement and/or potential ability in any of the following areas, singly or in combination:

1. general intellectual ability
2. specific academic aptitude
3. creative or productive thinking
4. leadership ability
5. visual and performing arts
6. psychomotor ability.

It can be assumed that utilization of these criteria for identification of the gifted and talented will encompass a minimum of 3 to 5 percent of the school population.

Evidence of gifted and talented abilities may be determined by a multiplicity of ways. These procedures should include objective measures and professional evaluation measures which are essential components of identification.

Professionally qualified persons include such individuals as teachers, administrators, school psychologists, counselors, curriculum specialists, artists, musicians, and others with special training who are also qualified to appraise pupils' special competencies.

The advisory panel established three characteristics for a differentiated educational program:

1. A differentiated curriculum which denotes higher cognitive concepts and processes.

2. Instructional strategies which accommodate the learning styles of the gifted and talented and curriculum content.

3. Special grouping arrangements which include a variety of administrative procedures appropriate to particular children, i.e., special classes, honor classes, seminars, resource rooms, and the like.

This definition was subsequently tested through the *Advocate Survey* and in the research review.

It was determined early in the development of the study plan that inclusion in the Elementary and Secondary Amendments would delimit the study population to the elementary and secondary school age (5-17 years), although recommendations within the report have implications for early education of gifted and talented children (before age 5) and post-secondary education.

Because of the inadequacy of available data on education programs of other Federal agencies the study was limited to education programs administered by USOE.

FINDINGS AND ACTION STEPS

This study has produced recommendations on special programs and suggested priorities in planning individual programs, estimates of the professional support and teacher training required, and adjustments in legal definitions that would enhance the possibility of State and local fiscal support. Details may be found in the text and Volume II (appendixes). The major findings of the study—those with particular relevance to the future planning of the Office of Education—may be summarized as follows:

—A *conservative* estimate of the gifted and talented population ranges between 1.5 and 2.5 million children out of a total elementary and secondary school population (1970 estimate) of 51.6 million.

—Existing services to the gifted and talented do not reach large and significant subpopulations (e.g. minorities and disadvantaged) and serve only a very small percentage of the gifted and talented population generally.

—Differentiated education for the gifted and talented is presently perceived as a very low priority at Federal, State, and most local levels of government and educational administration.

—Although 21 States have legislation to provide resources to school districts for services to the gifted and talented, such legislation in many cases merely represents intent.

—Even where there is a legal or administrative basis for provision of services, funding priorities, crisis concerns, and lack of personnel cause programs for the gifted to be miniscule or theoretical.

—There is an enormous individual and social cost when talent among the Nation's children and youth goes undiscovered and undeveloped. These students cannot ordinarily excel without assistance.

—Identification of the gifted is hampered not only by costs of appropriate testing—when these methods are known and adopted—but also by apathy and even hostility among teachers, administrators, guidance counselors and psychologists.

—Gifted and talented children are, in fact, deprived and can suffer psychological damage and permanent impairment of their abilities to function well which is equal to or greater than the similar

deprivation suffered by any other population with special needs served by the Office of Education.
—Special services for the gifted (such as the disadvantaged) and talented will also serve other target populations singled out for attention and support.
—Services provided to gifted and talented children can and do produce significant and measurable outcomes.
—States and local communities look to the Federal Government for leadership in this area of education, with or without massive funding.
—The Federal role in delivery of services to the gifted and talented is presently all but nonexistent.

These findings, which are documented in Volume II, provide ample evidence of the need for action by the U.S. Office of Education to eliminate the widespread neglect of gifted and talented children. Federal leadership in this effort is required to confirm and maintain provisions for the gifted and talented as a national priority, and to encourage the States to include this priority in their own planning.

Recognizing these needs, the U.S. Office of Education is taking steps to meet them immediately. Ten major activities, under existing education legislation, will be initiated in 1971.

1. The Deputy Commissioner for School Systems will complete a planning report for the Commissioner on implementing a Federal role in education of gifted and talented children by February 1, 1972.

2. Assignment of continuing program responsibility for gifted and talented education within USOE will be made to the Deputy Commissioner for School Systems, with the expectation of further delegation to the Bureau of Education for the Handicapped. A staff program group will initially consist of three professional positions with appropriate secretarial and staff support services.

3. A nationwide field survey will obtain information on successful programs and program elements, develop more precise cost figures, improve evaluation procedures, furnish the bases for model programs, and develop a clearinghouse on gifted and talented education.

4. USOE will utilize title V, ESEA and other authorizations, to strengthen State Education Agencies capabilities for gifted and talented education.

5 USOE will support in the summer of 1972 two national leadership training institutes to upgrade supervisory personnel and program planning for the gifted at the State level.

6. USOE will support additional program activities in major research and development institutions which have the interest and capacity to work on learning problems and opportunities among minority groups.

7. USOE will build on the career education models being developed by the National Center for Educational Research and Development by including program activities specific to employer-based career education for the gifted and talented.

8. The Commissioner has requested special attention in at least one of the comprehensive experimental school projects to the individualization of programs to benefit the gifted and talented students as a component of the comprehensive design to effect educational reform.

9. USOE will continue to encourage ESEA title III activities through communication with State education agencies, issuance of program guidelines, and cooperative assignment of USOE title III program staff to the Gifted and Talented Program Group.

10. One staff member will be identified in each of the ten Regional Offices of Education as responsible, at least part time, for gifted and talented education.

11. The existing OE programs relating to higher education will be carefully studied by the Gifted and Talented Program Group in order to optimize their potential for the gifted and talented population and teachers of these students.

CHAPTER I

INTRODUCTION

For many years, interested educators, responsible legislators, and concerned parents have puzzled over the problem of educating the most gifted of our students in a public educational program geared primarily to a philosophy of egalitarianism.

We know that gifted children can be identified as early as the pre-school grades and that these children in later life often make outstanding contributions to our society in the arts, politics, business, and the sciences. But, disturbingly, research has confirmed that many talented children underachieve, performing far less than their intellectual potential might suggest. We are increasingly being stripped of the comfortable notion that a bright mind will make its own way. On the contrary, intellectual and creative talent cannot survive educational neglect and apathy.

This loss is particularly evident in the minority groups who have in both social and educational environments every configuration calculated to stifle potential talent.

The Congress of the United States expressed its interest and concern by passing a landmark addition to the Elementary and Secondary Education Amendments of 1969, section 806, "Provisions related to gifted and talented children.[1] This amendment, unanimously passed in the House and Senate, provided for two specific changes in existing legislation. It explicated congressional intent that the gifted and talented student should benefit from Federal education legislation notably from titles III and V of the Elementary and Secondary Education Act (ESEA) and teacher fellowship provisions of the Higher Education Act of 1965. Section 806 directed the Commissioner of Education to conduct a study to:

1. Determine the extent to which special educational assistance programs are necessary or useful to meet the needs of gifted and talented children.

2. Show which existing Federal education assistance programs are being used to meet the needs of gifted and talented children.

3. Evaluate how existing Federal educational assistance programs can be more effectively used to meet these needs.

4. Recommend new programs, if any, needed to meet these needs.

This report is the Commissioner's response to that mandate.

---

[1] On January 28, 1969, the proposal was jointly introduced by Congressman Erlenborn and his colleagues in House and by Senator Javits and his fellow Senators. H.R. 4807, the Gifted and Talented Children Education Assistance Act of 1969, passed the House. S. 718 was incorporated in Public Law 91–230 (the ESEA amendment of 1969), which was signed into law April 13, 1970. Minor differences in definition of gifted and talented in the two versions were resolved as "children who have outstanding intellectual ability and creative talent." Section 806 amended section 521 of the Higher Education Act of 1965 (relating to fellowships for teachers).

The study was assigned by the Acting Commissioner of Education to the Deputy Assistant Secretary/Deputy Commissioner for Planning, Research, and Evaluation (in the Office of Education), which is now the Office of the Deputy Commissioner for Development. The study was planned, coordinated, and directed by Jane Case Williams, Office of the Deputy Commissioner for Development.

Because this study represented an area of concern for both the Federal and the non-Federal sectors, and offered the U.S. Office of Education (USOE) the opportunity to study an educational problem with nationally significant long-term implications for society, it was determined that the study should be conducted directly from the Office of Education. This arrangement enabled the Office to: 1) call upon its large reservoir of expertise among staff people, 2) contract for technical services as needed, 3) utilize the regional offices of USOE, and 4) draw on nationally known experts in the field.

The plan developed for the study, as accepted and amplified by the informal advisory panel (listed in the acknowledgements section), consisted of five major activities:

1. Review of research, other available literature, and expert knowledge.

2. Analysis of the educational data bases already available to USOE and the development of a major data base through the "Survey of Leadership in Education of Gifted and Talented Children and Youth" (*Advocate Survey.*)

3. Public hearings by the Regional Assistant Commissioners of Education in each of the 10 HEW regions to interpret regional needs.

4. Studies of programs in representative States where statewide support to education programs for gifted and talented children have been conducted for several years.

5. Review and analysis of the system for delivery of Office of Education programs to benefit gifted and talented children.

The study began in August 1970 with the development and acceptance of the plan and concluded in June 1971 with the preparation of the final report, which is based on the findings and documentation from the five major activities. Throughout the study, there has been continuous interaction among the major contractors, experts on the gifted and talented, and Office of Education staff assigned to the project.

Public Law 91–230, sec. 806, directs the Commissioner of Education to define gifted and talented children for purposes of Federal education programs. The definition established by the advisory panel reads:

Gifted and talented children are those identified by professionally qualified persons who by virtue of outstanding abilities, are capable of high performance. These are children who require differentiated educational programs and/or services beyond those normally provided by the regular school program in order to realize their contribution to self and society.

Children capable of high performance include those with demonstrated achievement and/or potential ability in any of the following areas, singly or in combination:

1. general intellectual ability
2. specific academic aptitude
3. creative or productive thinking
4. leadership ability
5. visual and performing arts
6. psychomotor ability

It can be assumed that utilization of these criteria for identification of the gifted and talented will encompass a minimum of 3 to 5 percent of the school population.

Evidence of gifted and talented abilities may be determined by a multiplicity of ways. These procedures should include objective measures and professional evaluation measures which are essential components of identification.

Professionally qualified persons include such individuals as teachers, administrators, school psychologists, counselors, curriculum specialists, artists, musicians, and others with special training who are also qualified to appraise pupils' special competencies.

According to the advisory panel, a differentiated educational program has three characteristics:

1. A differentiated curriculum which denotes higher cognitive concepts and processes.

2. Instructional strategies which accommodate the learning styles of the gifted and talented and curriculum content.

3. Special grouping arrangements which include a variety of administrative procedures appropriate to particular children, i.e., special classes, honor classes, seminars, resource rooms, and the like.

This definition was subsequently tested through the *Advocate Survey* and in the research review; the question of definition is discussed in chapters II and III.

Early in the development of the study plan, it was determined that inclusion in the Elementary and Secondary Amendments would delimit the study population to the elementary and secondary school age (5–17 years), although recommendations within the report have implications for the early education of gifted and talented children (before age 5) and post-secondary education.

The study was additionally limited to education programs administered by USOE for two reasons:

(1) The Commissioner of Education is mandated to "prepare and make available in such form as he deems appropriate a catalog of all Federal education assistance programs whether or not such programs are administered by him . . ." (Public Law 91–230, title IV, sec. 413). The mandated catalog for FY 1970 was taken from the OEO Catalog of Federal Domestic Assistance and submitted to Congress with the Commissioner's annual report. Federal educational programs conducted by other agencies cannot be retrieved through use of descriptors synonymous with "gifted and talented," indicating that programs are not so classified at present. The data base is yet in an initial stage of development, with available data of questionable reliability and validity.

(2) An unpublished Federal task force study of gifted and talented education, completed in 1968, indicated problems in defining and obtaining usable data from educational programs of other Federal agencies which benefit the gifted and talented. Such an analysis would clearly be beyond the scope of the present study.

Maintenance of the catalog of Federal educational assistance programs on a current basis will provide the universe which can enable USOE to evaluate the impact of other Federal programs on the education of gifted and talented children and youth; the Office of Education recommends such an analysis.

Statistical data were collected an analyzed for the present study from four major sources:

—The *Advocate Survey* was designed to determine the current thinking of the leaders in special education for the gifted and talented, on the need and the responsiveness of education. A 26-page questionnaire was sent to 239 experts in the field.

—*The School Staffing Survey*, a pilot survey in 1969–1970 followed by a full-scale review in 1970–71, includes school data acquired from elementary and secondary school principals concerning staffing and the services to the children and youth in their schools. The survey tapped a representative sample of U.S. schools and pupils.

—*Project TALENT* is a longitudinal study of 400,000 students who were in high school (grades 9–12) in 1960. Data are available from one questionnaire administered in 1960 and two followup studies conducted 1 year and 5 years after graduation. A large number of mentally gifted participated. A broad range of data has been collected on achievement, social influences and development, intellectual ability, and other factors. (See appendix E.)

—*The State Survey* (OE Form 115) was prepared in the Office of Education and sent by the Regional Assistant Commissioners of Education to each of the 50 State Departments of Education, as part of the regional hearing procedures, to elicit information about current support for education of the gifted.

One major source of data for this report has been the research on the gifted and talented, which is summarized in appendix A. Chapter II—Profile of the Gifted and Talented Population—and chapter IV—What is a Good Program for the Gifted?—lean heavily on this research.

Another important source of data proved to be the regional hearings, which were designed to reach a broadly representative group of professionals and lay persons concerned with education for the gifted and talented. USOE's Office of Regional Office Coordination (OROC) directed each of the 10 Regional Assistant Commissioners of Education to hold hearings on the subject and provided them with appropriate background materials and survey instruments.

The hearings, though not required by the congressional amendments, were a viable way to gather information and demonstrated the role of the regional offices in the assessment of educational needs throughout the country. Both oral and written testimony far exceeded expectations; over 500 persons testified and over 400 parents wrote to state their broad support for some positive action in this area. A summary of the regional hearings, which includes many of these statements, forms appendix C. Together with material gleaned from the *Advocate Survey* (appendix B) and the research evidence (appendix A), the testimony at the regional hearings forms the basis for chapter III, which outlines the need for special programs for the gifted.

Among the issues covered by the *State Survey* were the availability of staff for gifted programs at the State level, enabling legislation for the gifted, action planning or study groups, special training provisions, major deterrents to State action, and State use of Federal funds for gifted education programs. Chapter V is based on this survey.

To complement this general data on activity at the State level, this report includes the developmental history of four strong statewide programs for the gifted—in Connecticut, California, Georgia, and Illinois. These programs are summarized in chapter VI and detailed in appendix F.

The special study made of the USOE delivery system to the gifted and talented addresses itself to the requirement in section 806 concerning the Federal role in gifted education and to recommendations for new programs or arrangements to meet the needs of the gifted and talented. This assessment, summarized in chapter VII, confirms the findings and opinions delineated throughout the Commissioner's study and proposes alternatives for action.

Chapters II through IV present the problems and needs. Chapters V through VII describe the status of State and Federal efforts. To help bridge the gap between where we are and where we should be, the final chapter of this report (VIII) summarizes the recommendations from the study and outlines action steps to be taken in 1972.

Because this whole effort is about human beings, and rather special ones, this report begins with a description of these young people.

CHAPTER II

PROFILE OF THE GIFTED AND TALENTED POPULATION

The gifted and talented: Who are they? Are they really sufficiently different from the norm to warrant special planning and attention?

One ready source of information regarding these questions—and others—can be found in the research on the gifted and talented over the past 50 years. Appendix A provides details and sources for the generalizations which follow.

From the research findings a profile emerges of a group that is distinctive in performance or potential; it is a group by no means insignificant in numbers nor limited in scope throughout our society. Here are some of the characteristics of the gifted and talented, as seen by those who have studied or worked with them over the years.

Probably the area in which the gifted and talented are recognized most frequently is achievement. Large-scale studies over the past 50 years have uniformly agreed that these individuals function at levels far in advance of their agemates. Beginning at the early primary grades and even at the time of school entry, the gifted and talented present challenging educational problems because of their deviation from the norm.

Typically, half of the gifted have taught themselves to read before school entry. Some of them learn to read as early as 2 years and appreciable numbers are reading at 4. In comparison with their classmates, these children depart increasingly from the average as they progress through the grades, *if their educational program permits.*

In one statewide study of more than 1,000 gifted children at all grade levels, the kindergarten group on the average performed at a level comparable to that of second-grade children in reading and mathematics; the average for fourth and fifth-grade gifted children in all curriculum areas was beyond that of seventh grade pupils. In another study a representative sample of gifted high school seniors took the Graduate Record Examinations in social sciences, humanities, and natural sciences—examinations normally used for admission to graduate study.

In all of the tests, the high school seniors made an average group score which surpassed the average for college seniors; in the social sciences, they surpassed the average of college seniors with majors in that field. These findings on the attainments of gifted students are typical.

WHAT ARE THEY LIKE—PSYCHOLOGICALLY AND SOCIALLY?

Early studies by Yoder in 1894, by Terman beginning in 1904, and by Katherine Dolbear in 1912 initiated our current understandings of the gifted and their behavior. These studies refuted earlier beliefs about the "mad genius" syndrome, although there are recent writings which show that giftedness may produce severe problems for certain individuals. In general, gifted children have been found to be better adjusted and more popular than the general population, although there are definite relationships between educational opportunities and adjustment.

Exceptional capacities create problems for most people, even at the earliest ages. Young gifted children encounter difficulties in attempting to manage and direct activities. Since their ideas differ, they lose the participation of others and find themselves marginal and isolated. Of all children in a large gifted popuulation, those at kindergarten level were reported by teachers to have the highest incidence of poor peer relationships. This was ascribed to the lack of experience at this age in adapting to requirements, in coping with frustrations, or in having available a repertoire of suitable substitute activities, as older pupils would.

When conditions are changed and the gifted and talented are given opportunities to satisfy their desires for knowledge and performance, their own sense of adequacy and well-being improves. Those who can function within an appropriate learning milieu also improve in their attitudes toward themselves and others. If education and life experiences for the gifted are what they should be, the likelihood that the gifted and talented will relate to the total society and work within it actually is enhanced.

The gifted explore ideas and issues earlier than their peers. While they enjoy social associations as others do, they tend early to relate to older companions and to games which involve individual skills or some intellectual pursuits. The gifted child is not necessarily a 'grind' or a 'loner,' despite the fact that he develops special interests early. Biographical data from studies of large populations reveal that these individuals characteristically perform in outstanding fashion—not only in widely varied organizations, in community groups, in student government, and in athletics. The total impression is of people who perform superbly in many fields and do so with ease.

While the academic advancement of the gifted has generally been recognized even though it has not been served, the early social and psychological development of the gifted has been less frequently noted.

Gifted pupils, even when very young, depart from self-centered concerns and values far earlier than their chronological peers. Problems of morality, religion, and world peace may be troublesome at a very early age. Interest in problems besetting society is common even in elementary-age gifted children.

The composite impression from studies ranging from childhood to adults is of a population which values independence, which is more task- and contribution-oriented than recognition-oriented, which prizes integrity and independent judgment in decision making, which rejects conformity for its own sake, and which possess unusually high social ideals and values.

Of all human groups, the gifted and talented are the least likely to form stereotypes. Their traits, interests, capacities, and alternatives present limitless possibilities for expression; the chief impression one draws from studying this group, at either the child or adult level, is of almost unlimited versatility, multiple talents, and countless ways of effective expression. Because gifted people have many options, they often also encounter problems of choice. When you do well in science but also love music, where does the energy go in a career? Again, there are numerous examples in Terman's longitudinal study of men and women who have been as productive in an avocation as in their chosen careers.

WHAT ABOUT THEIR SOCIAL AND ECONOMIC ORIGINS?

The assumption that the gifted and talented come from privileged environments is erroneous. Even in the Terman study, which made no pretense of comprehensive search and identification, some participants came from economically deprived homes while the majority came from homes with certain advantages; the Terman group included representatives of all ethnic groups and all economic levels, with 19 percent of the parents representing skilled and unskilled labor.

A later California study (a more thorough but by no means complete search for gifted children in certain rural sections) found that 30 percent of parents were in agricultural, clerical, service, semi-skilled, unskilled, semi-professional, or sales occupations. Jenkins found an incidence of nearly one percent of gifted Negroes in segregated Chicago school classes in the early 1940's, despite his extremely limited screening and referral procedures.

Even though the major studies have not employed detailed community searches, giftedness has been found in all walks of life.

CAN WE IDENTIFY THE GIFTED AND TALENTED?

Obviously, we can identify giftedness—or it identifies itself, particularly when a 2-year old begins to read or play the piano. But identification is really much more complicated. It includes many factors: 1) age of identification (given the well-known sensitivity and adjustability of the gifted, how is it identified after the child has learned to conceal it to survive happily among his peers?) ; 2) screening procedures and test accuracy; 3) the identification of children from a variety of ethnic groups and cultures; and 4) tests of creativity (before that creativity has been demonstrated in performance). What then is our capacity to locate the gifted and talented within the school population?

CAN WE IDENTIFY THE VERY YOUNG GIFTED OR TALENTED CHILD?

On the basis of both early and current studies, we *can* identify these children, quite apart from their tendency to emerge at times on their own. Attempts to identify gifted children through tests at the kindergarten level have been successful when careful preliminary search and screening have been utilized.

Although much has been said about the low relationship between infant tests and those used during the school years, infant tests are primarily motor tests; later tests emphasize verbal abilities.

Bloom, after analysis of major longitudinal studies, concluded that general intelligence develops lawfully; that the greatest impact on I.Q. from environmental factors would probably take place between ages 1 and 5, with relatively little impact after age 8. This observation is very similar to Hollingworth's observation that methods of measuring intelligence had low predictive value when applied before 7 or 8 years of age; when applied at or after 7 or 8, the methods available even in 1939 had high predictive power.

Since the gifted child is advanced beyond his age group, we may assume greater stability of intelligence than in the average or below average; young gifted children can be individually tested and accurately identified more easily than can young mentally retarded children, who are similarly deviant from the norm.

HOW ACCURATE ARE SCREENING PROCEDURES AND TESTS?

Types of screening processes commonly employed in identifying the gifted have included teacher nomination and group tests. Both means have about the same level of accuracy, and both fail to identify large numbers of gifted children.

A number of studies have shown that individual tests identify gifted children much more accurately than do group measures. *Half* of an identified gifted population remains unidentified with group tests alone. One study pointed out that group test ratings tend to be higher for the below average individual, while, for the above average, group test scores are lower than those obtained on the individually administered Binet test scale.

Data provided by a test publisher showed that the discrepancy between group scores and individual scores increased as the intelligence level increased. The most highly gifted children were penalized most by group test scores; that is, the higher the ability, the greater the probability the group test would overlook such ability.

Teachers also are able to nominate about half of the gifted. (Similar levels of accuracy occur when they attempt to nominate the creative.) It is unsafe to assume that teachers will identify even the *highly* gifted, according to one study in which 25 per cent of the most gifted were missed.

The question of test accuracy for children of varying environments is troublesome, as is the relative impact of heredity and environment on test performance. It has long been recognized that extreme environmental factors affect the performance of children in many areas, including intelligence. The measured intelligence of children declines when they are isolated or emotionally starved, as it does when verbal and nonverbal stimuli are lacking. Various estimates of the proportions of intelligence variance due to heredity and environment, based on twin studies over a 20-year period, ascribe from 60 to 88 per cent to heredity. All of the researchers agree that some part of the variance must be attributed to the effect of the environment in which children are reared.

CAN WE IDENTIFY THE GIFTED FROM MINORITIES AND DIVERGING CULTURES?

The problems of screening and identification are complicated by assumptions that talents cannot be found as abundantly in certain groups as in others—with the emphasis heavily in favor of the affluent. These assumptions may have influenced meager search and identification among other groups. There is ample evidence that highly gifted children can be identified in all groups within our society.

From a number of sources, Jenkins gathered case records on Negro children of rare ability. He found seven children whose Binet I.Q.'s were above 170, four above 180, and one above 200. (Estimates of incidence in the general population of I.Q.'s of 170 are one in 100,000, and for I.Q.'s of 180, one in a million.) Nevertheless, it has been observed that Indians and Negroes, to name two minority groups, have been insufficiently represented in the public school groups surveyed. In 1956, Ginsberg and his associates analyzed Negro potential and described it as the largest untapped talent pool.

To upgrade educational opportunities for minority groups is one thing, but to discover and to nurture the genius of the one in a million is another, and it is a more difficult task.

It is reasonably well-known that with help, young children from poverty backgrounds can improve their I.Q. levels significantly. One controversial study claimed that children gain in measured ability simply through teachers being told that they are bright, the theory being the "self-fulfilling prophecy." Evidence from various studies and reviews suggests rather that the more *specific and carefully planned* the intervention, the better the results—and the earlier the better.

Far too little attention has been given to the effect of psychological factors on the development of aptitudes and achievement among minorities and the poor. Significant here is the intellectual apathy and withdrawal in young Indians as they reach adolescence and become aware of their future possibilities. Bronfenbrenner observed that Negro boys (who are expected to earn a living) perform less well than Negro girls to a greater extent than is true in the white population, and that the difference increases with age. These problems are especially significant within minority youth of the highest capacity.

Since the full range of human talents is represented in all the races of man and in all socio-economic levels, it is unjust and unproductive to allow social or racial background to affect the treatment of an individual.

CAN WE IDENTIFY THE CREATIVE AND TALENTED?

So far, no distinction has been made between the academically, intellectually gifted and those who exhibit great prowess in the arts or who possess that quality of creativity one associates with the arts.

Complications in answering this question arose with the initiation of efforts to identify potential creativity and dormant talents through tests of various kinds. Still remaining to be settled, through longitudinal studies, is whether a test of creative process will identify the person who will later be recognized for creative production.

Initial studies to develop measures of abilities not identified by traditional group and individual intelligence tests were carried on by Guilford and his associates. These studies resulted in a number of tests designed to measure convergent and divergent thinking abilities. Many of these tests were adapted to or used directly in subsequent studies to determine creativity in children and youth, and to compare creativity and intelligence in various populations.

Controversy erupted from certain studies—notably those of Getzels, Jackson, and Torrance—which found differences between populations of high intelligence and those labeled creative. The cleavage between enthusiasts for the creativity tests and skeptics produced debate on the measurement of human abilities along with hundreds of studies on measures to identify creativity. The controversy in many respects was reminiscent of that between Terman and Stenquist in the early 1920s, when Stenquist doubted the value of the Binet test because his tests of mechanical aptitude produced results at great odds with those of the Binet. Many persons have pointed out that many of the terms used by the creativity enthusiasts, and descriptions of the creative person, are suspiciously similar to those found in the recent literature of child psychology and education—such terms as "giftedness," "discovery," "intuition," and "intelligence."

The measures developed by Guilford to identify specific traits or human abilities were combined and adapted by subsequent researchers to identify creativity. Studies of the creativity measures and their relationship to intelligence measures have produced a preponderance of evidence that the use of a common term "creativity" is misleading, since the measures bear no more relationship to one another than they do to measures of intelligence.

There are higher relationships between general intelligence and the individual tests of creativity than among the individual measures themselves. Although a few studies have supported the creativity-intelligence distinction, most have established substantial relationships between creativity and intellectual aptitude.

Greater accuracy in the use of labels has been one result of the research in creativity. The trend is away from the global use of "creativity" as a psychological concept similar to intelligence. Goldberg has suggested the use of the term "creative" be assigned to novel, reality adapted, disciplined, and fully realized products, and that "divergent thinking" be used to describe new attributes of ability.

Recent scholars have recognized the contradictory nature of timed and scheduled tests to measure creativity, and have sought conditions which will more realistically permit open and original response. Research workers have begun to develop tests to be administered under more open conditions, and to tap ideational fluency appropriate to relevant rather than whimsical productivity. These studies, and studies on qualitative values in children's products, should extend the possibilities to identify added capacities and talents.

HOW MANY GIFTED AND TALENTED STUDENTS ARE THERE?

Considering the complex profile of this group, it is no simple task to sort out the number of gifted and talented young people in our society. Some young people with potential mask their abilities in order to adapt to a more mundane group; others cannot find an outlet in the school setting for their particular talents. Many teachers and administrators turn a blind eye on the very bright child even when talent is evident. The infinite variety within the population itself is a challenge; to be gifted is to be different and unique—and, too often, invisible.

WHAT IS A GOOD OPERATIONAL DEFINITION OF "GIFTED AND TALENTED"?

This is the basic question when special education programs are being considered. Despite divergent opinions about what constitutes "giftedness" or "creativity" or "talent," workable criteria must be established to provide for the young people we know are there.

Generally, the following evidence would indicate special intellectual gifts or talent:

—Consistently very superior scores on many appropriate standardized tests.

—Judgment of teachers, pupil personnel specialists, administrators, and supervisors familiar with the abilities and potentials of the individual.

—Demonstration of advance skills, imaginative insight, and intense interest and involvement.

—Judgment of specialized teachers (including art and music), pupil personnel specialists, and experts in the arts who are qualified to evaluate the pupils demonstrated and/or potential talent.

While an operating definition is required, there are some pitfalls in describing giftedness too specifically, particularly in definitions written into law. The Special Study Project for Gifted Children in Illinois is a case in point. From the beginning of the program in 1959, planners sought to avoid placing a definition of the term "gifted children" in the legislation for two major reasons: First, specification and description of human abilties was, they thought, a problem for behavorial scientists rather than legislators. Definitions employed at the operational level in schools should be responsive to new scientific findings and response should not be delayed by legal restrictions. Second, the planners recognized that allocation of funds requires description of the special category; but they recommend that this description be made in administrative regulations and formulas for support rather than law. Thus, flexibility was retained while the need for expenditures control by the State education agency was met.

The legal definition employed in Illinois, then, is:

Gifted children are those children whose mental development is accelerated beyond the average to the extent that they need and can profit from specially planned educational services.

The administrative regulation controlling expenditures for the gifted and talented is a formula which allows the district to use 2 percent of its enrollment in applying for reimbursement; for example, Reimbursement = 2% (enrollment) × \$40. In seeking to meet a variety of special abilities, districts may involve as many as 5 percent of their pupils.

WHAT IS A GOOD ESTIMATE OF THE NUMBER OF GIFTED AND TALENTED CHILDREN?

One must project here from the studies of the gifted and at the same time consider the point that is recurrent throughout this study—that there is undiscovered genius and talent. So we are dealing with estimates. Numbers presumed to be gifted or talented have varied considerably in recent estimates. Up to the end of the 1950's, most research workers and other experts agreed that the gifted included those within the upper 2 to 3 percent of intellectual ability, defined as a Binet I.Q. of 130 or more. More variance was introduced by those wishing to include social, mechanical, and other aptitudes, and by those who saw intelligence and talent as different dimensions.

The potential numbers involved by the use of selected percentages from the total population appear in table 1. The total census projection for the 1970 United States elementary-secondary school population was 51,600,000.[1]

Table 1—*Numbers of pupils in various percentage groups to be gifted and talented*

Percent of pupils:

	Number of gifted and talented pupils
1	516,000
2	1,032,000
3	1,548,000
5	2,580,000
10	5,160,000
15	7,740,000

These numbers in table 1 would increase if the gifted at preschool levels were included. Obviously giftedness is not manifest at a set time; even though not recognized, it is present as a potential from birth. Attention to the preschool gifted population therefore merits serious consideration.

Table 2 indicates that 11,906,000 3-, 4-, and 5-year-old children in October 1968, 3,929,000 were enrolled in preschool programs outside of the regular school.[2] If a conservative 3 percent of the total were estimated to be gifted, 117,870 young children would be accessible for special early childhood programs. Another 242,310 gifted preschoolers are not in any programs! However, the proportion of children in programs has increased from 1964 to 1968, suggesting that the gifted have become more accessible.

TABLE 2.—TRENDS OF EARLY CHILDHOOD POPULATION, AGES 3 TO 5, AND SCHOOL ENROLLMENTS, OCTOBER 1964 TO OCTOBER 1968

[Numbers in thousands]

Year	3 year olds		4 year olds		5 year olds	
	Population	Enrollment	Population	Enrollment	Population	Enrollment
1964	4,238	181	4,148	617	4,110	2,389
1965	4,149	203	4,238	683	4,162	2,521
1966	4,087	248	4,155	785	4,244	[1] 2,641
1967	3,992	273	4,088	872	4,162	[1] 2,724
1968	3,811	317	4,000	911	4,095	[1] 2,701

[1] Excludes 5 year olds enrolled in primary school: 1966—505,000; 1967—444,000; 1968—444,000.

In view of what we know about early childhood learning, to be able to reach and sustain over 100,000 gifted and talented children at the beginning of their formal schooling is significant. But this is only a fraction of the whole gifted population. Some people put the figure at 3 percent of the total school population while others would range as far as 15 percent to include those children with a special talent who

[1] *Projections of Educational Statistics to 1978–79.* Washington, D.C., U.S. Department of Health, Education, and Welfare, Office of Education, National Center for Educational Statistics (OE–10030–69).
[2] Nehrt, Roy C. and Hurd, Gordon E. *Preprimary Enrollment of Children Under Six,* October 1968. U.S. Department of Health, Education, and Welfare, Office of Education, June 1969 (OE 20078–68).

may lack the full spectrum of "giftedness." This may be too broad, but even taking the very conservative estimate of 3 percent, the size of the population—1.5 million—demands attention.

EDUCATIONAL IMPLICATIONS OF RESEARCH

Gifted and talented youth are a unique population, differing markedly from their age peers in abilities, talents, interests, and psychological maturity. They are the most versatile and complex of all human groups, possibly the most neglected of all groups with special educational needs. Their sensitivity to others and insight into existing school conditions make them especially vulnerable, because of their ability to conceal their giftedness in standardized surroundings and to seek alternative outlets. The resultant waste is tragic.

Research studies on special needs of the gifted and talented demonstrate the need for special programs. Contrary to widespread belief, these students cannot ordinarily excel without assistance. The relatively few gifted students who have had the advantage of special programs have shown remarkable improvements in self-understanding and in ability to relate well to others, as well as in improved academic and creative performance. The programs have not produced arrogant, selfish snobs; special programs have extended a sense of reality, wholesome humility, self-respect, and respect for others. A good program for the gifted increases their involvement and interest in learning through the reduction of the irrelevant and redundant. These statements do not imply in any way a "track system" for the gifted and talented.

Identification of the gifted and talented in different parts of the country has been piecemeal, sporadic, and sometimes nonexistent. Very little identification has been carried on in depth, or with appropriate testing instruments. Many of the assumptions about giftedness and its incidence in various parts of the American society are based on inadequate data, partial information, and group tests of limited value. The United States has been inconsistent in seeking out the gifted and talented, finding them early in their lives, and individualizing their education. Particular injustice has occurred through apathy toward certain minorities, although neglect of the gifted in this country is a universal, increasing problem.

The next chapter discusses the typical obstacles and necessary steps in overcoming this neglect.

CHAPTER III

Special Planning Needed

Although special programs for the gifted and talented have been conducted over the last half century, the provisions have reached only a few students. Programs have never been widespread, even at periods of high interest. After a 20-year drought, efforts to provide for the gifted and talented reached a peak after the first Russian space launch. Then, during the 1960's, interest waned or was drowned out by other cries for help.

The following sections document a resurgence of concern in many quarters. Some of the queries about the need for special programs have been answered by research findings. A summary of the *Advocate Survey* discusses the views of experts in the field. And, finally, the testimony at the regional hearings expresses a need felt throughout the country. The details and documentation of these sections are found in Volume II.

RESEARCH SAYS . . .

Because many of these basic questions border on the philosophical, direct responses from research are difficult. But some clarification about oft-expressed doubts is possible.

AREN'T SPECIAL PROVISIONS UNDEMOCRATIC?

If *democratic* educational practice is interpreted as the *same* education for all, the answer is yes. If we believe that democratic education means appropriate educational opportunities and the right to education in keeping with one's ability to benefit, the answer is no. If one takes the affirmative stand, then all special educational programs would disappear, and hundreds of millions now expended by the States and the Federal Government would be diverted to other uses. Other facets of the question than the philosophical, however, have been examined in research. Among these is the waste of talent, sometimes brought on by the extra control required to adjust to pressures in the society.

In a study of 251 students of high ability Miner reported that 54.6 percent were working below a level of which they were intellectually capable. The majority were working at least four grades below that at which they could be working. The author concluded that the overall picture was one of marked wastage of intellectual ability within the school system.

In a study of Michigan high school graduates Dressel and Grabow found that gifted high school students gained satisfaction in extra-class activities and high school involvement but remained apathetic toward classwork and courses.

Approximately 3.4 percent of the dropouts in another statewide study were found to have an I.Q. of 120 or higher. On individual tests this could be appreciably higher. Almost twice as many gifted girls as boys were dropouts. The total loss represented a 17.6 percent loss through dropouts among the gifted.

Gifted women have encountered special problems. While more girls attend college and enter graduate studies, they are still penalized socially if they have interests in traditionally masculine fields. Although the gifted tend to retain their high test competence into adolescence and adulthood, girls regress toward the mean of the general college population more than boys. Five years after high school graduation about one-forth of the girls in the top 2½ percent of the Project TALENT ability range were secretaries or typists (see appendix E).

Pressey stressed the early accomplishments of Haydn, Mozart, Berlioz, Wagner, and others who played, composed and/or conducted their own compositions between the ages of 6 and 17. But he also points to others who were productive at a great age—Michelangelo was chief architect of St. Peters from age 72 until 89; Benjamin Franklin began his autobiography at 65, finished it at 82, and at 70 helped draft the Declaration of Independence.

The benefits accruing to the person who is fully educated will begin earlier if they are to begin at all—and last much longer than the formal school years.

Lifelong contributions will be advantageous to the society as a whole. Rather than argue that special planning is undemocratic, one might conclude that the special planning should be carried on for the benefit of the democracy.

WOULDN'T FUNDS BE BETTER SPENT ON THE DISADVANTAGED? THE HANDICAPPED?

Large-scale studies indicate that gifted and talented children are, in fact, disadvantaged and handicapped in the usual school siutation. Terman observed that the gifted are the most retarded group in the schools when mental age and chronological ages are compared. Great discrepancies existed during his study, and continue to persist, between what the gifted child knows and what he is offered, whether in academic or artistic areas. The ensuing boredom leads to underachievement and unworthy patterns of functioning, along with dissatisfaction with oneself and others.

Raph, Goldberg, and Passow pointed out a number of studies which indicated predisposition to underachievement in bright pupils as identifiable by the third grade. They recommended early identification in terms of cognitive as well as socio-personal factors, to permit schools to *prevent rather than have to cure* underachievement. Their own work with gifted underachievers at the high school level, as well as their evaluation of an extensive body of research literature, suggested that efforts initiated at the senior high school level had little promise of success, since underachievement at that stage became a deeply rooted way of life unamenable to change.

Some of the traits in the individual with potential for originality are both socially approved and disapproved. Those clearly disapproved are rebelliousness, disorderliness, and exhibitionism; those approved include independence of judgment, freedom of expression, and originality of construction and insight. In many school situations even the socially approved traits would be subject to censure. Much of the educational disadvantage or handicap faced by the gifted and talented lies in the external restrictions which prevent a satisfying existence.

Finally, the extension of opportunities to the gifted should increase opportunities for gifted from minorities or who are otherwise handicapped.

SHOULD CAREER EDUCATION FOR THE GIFTED BE A PRIORITY?

Evidence from school systems in which the gifted have been given opportunities to work with specialists of similar interests and to explore occupations indicates strongly that career education is of great value in allowing gifted students to assess career options and in motivating them to go to college. The gifted face career problems because of the many options available to them. Some evidence exists that opportunities to work with community specialists increases the motivation and school performance of the gifted. The early contributions of the gifted and talented made at other times in history came about through individual work affiliations and close tutorial relationships. Proper career education could contribute in similar fashion, and could be of particular significance for those with highly specialized talents. Benefits would accrue to students and for mentors who, as others have reported, develop respect for students and schools through the association.

Career education is of particular importance to minority and rural students. Assignment to a gifted adult with similar interests may profoundly affect school and career decisions.

IS A GOOD PROGRAM FOR THE GIFTED A GOOD PROGRAM FOR ALL CHILDREN?

No. If the program were good for all children, it would not be good for the gifted. Pupils who are advanced 4 or more years beyond their contemporaries need to work with content and ideas appropriate for them, but beyond the capacity of their peers. Children who have developed specialized talents, if they are truly specialized, need tutorial attention at their level of capability if they are to improve. Other children cannot compete with the highly talented, advanced performer. The highly gifted will depart increasingly from the norm in attainments if their programs are suitable; their educational experiences, while proper for them, become increasingly inappropriate for their agemates. Yet the gifted cannot usually be placed with older "normal" children who are supposedly at the same mental level but who actually differ from the gifted in their needs and mental functioning.

The program for all children is necessarily adjusted to the norm or average. The result is that those who are markedly different in potential encounter a program of limited significance.

DO SPECIAL PROGRAMS DEPRIVE REGULAR CHILDREN OF MODELS, OR
ASSOCIATION WITH THE GIFTED AND TALENTED?

The question implies that the gifted and talented are placed in completely separate programs, and that they do not associate with others during the school day. This is not the case in the vast majority of programs. One characteristic of programs for the gifted is the great variety of arrangements; in school systems with a history of consistent planning, the variety increases year by year as planning for improvement continues.

Even in programs in which highly gifted and talented students work in seminars, independent study, and individual tutorials, the gifted spend some time with other groups, and periodically bring their creative productions to classes or the entire student group in the form of creative publications, inventions, original plays, and other media.

Further evidence that special programs do not cause separation is seen in the improved social status of gifted students who have participated in special groupings. As their educational fare becomes more adequate, they apparently relate more successfully to others and actually increase in social stature.

WHAT BENEFITS WILL BE DERIVED FROM SPECIAL EDUCATION OF THE
GIFTED?

The importance to the public of educating the gifted has never been greater than at present. Conservation as a social priority includes human conservation and not solely out of respect for the individual's right to life, liberty, and the pursuit of happiness. Conservation of the gifted and talented requires that society tolerate the right of the individual with exceptional abilities and talents, even though unconventional, to attain his goals. But it means that as invention and creation are encouraged and the necessary learning is supported, increased discoveries may generate possibilities for improved conditions of life in many areas—economic as well as social. As leisure time increases, the creative and artistic will be vital to the total well-being of society, as both artists and teachers. The creatively scientific will be indispensable in efforts to cure social and human ills.

EXPERTS SAY . . .

The *Advocate Survey*, sent to 239 experts on the gifted, provided recommendations on the development of provisions for the gifted and talented. The advocates, representing various sections of the Nation, were chosen because of their specialized knowledge and experience. Many of their recommendations were virtually unanimous.[1] These expert opinions are confirmed by other data included here from the *School Staffing Survey*.[2]

---

[1] Unless otherwise noted in the text or in footnotes, the data in this section are derived from *A Survey of Leadership in Education of Gifted and Talented Children and Youth*, Silver Spring, Md.: Operations Research, Inc., 1971.

[2] *School Staffing Survey*, Spring 1970. Washington, D.C.: U.S. Department of Health, Education, and Welfare, Office of Education, National Center for Educational Statistics.

A more complete summary of both surveys may be found in appendix B of this report: *Advocate Survey and Statistical Findings*.

IDENTIFICATION OF THE GIFTED AND TALENTED

More than 80 percent of the advocate respondents agreed that the category "gifted and talented" should include those with high general intellectual ability, those with specific academic aptitude and/or those with ability in visual and performing arts. They also supported inclusion of those with underdeveloped potential. About 50 percent favored including those with social adeptness and psychomotor ability.

The general view was that the gifted and talented can be viewed and understood by the majority of educators and laymen as those of high intellectual ability, those with high creative or productive thinking ability, those with specific high academic aptitude, and/or those with high ability in the visual and performing arts. These terms are, of course, not mutually exclusive.

The definition of the talente was more inclusive. While 82 percent would confine the gifted to 5 p cent or less of the population the talented were regarded by the e. rts as 11 to 15 percent of the population. The mean percentages for each category, gifted and talented, probably are somewhat less than the percent chosen, since 38 percent favored confining the gifted to 2 percent or less, and the remainder chose the category 3 to 5 percent. Similarly, 47 percent limited the talented to 5 percent or less.

Nearly four out of five of the respondents favored continuous screening and search, or search at least annually for the gifted and talented. Two-thirds favored at least annual re-evaluation, presumably to be certain that placement and educational planning were appropriate.

The advocates favored the use of multiple means for identification of the gifted and talented, including measures of intelligence, achievement, talent, and creativity. The highest rank was accorded the individual intelligence test, a means presently not used in most States because of the cost involved. (Group measures fail to locate half of the gifted and talented in any population.)

Apparently the advocates were concerned by the failure of school personnel to identify the gifted, as well as by the well-known ability of the gifted to conceal their true abilities and to adapt themselves to school offerings and requirements. Reports, such as those of the 57.5 percent of schools nationally stating in the *School Staffing Survey* that they had *no* gifted pupils, undoubtedly led the respondents to recommend involvement of all persons in the search process. School psychologists were seen as most important, with talent specialists next. Interestingly, seven experts advocated the use of professional artists, a practice not common in schools. The relatively low ranking of school administrators and curriculum specialists may have been due to their less direct contact with children, since teachers and guidance counselors were ranked high.

The statistic, noted above, of *no* gifted pupils by 57.5 percent of all U.S. schools surveyed in 1969–70 is depressing. It may be attributed to widespread ignorance, apathy, and indifference, or outright hostility toward the notion that gifted and talented young people merit attention to their learning needs. Less effort to identify is made at the elementary level than at the secondary, although research stresses the advantages of early identification and planning. Gifted young people with the ability to invent, create, and contribute to society at an early age apparently would have little opportunity in the majority of our schools, and probably no encouragement, under present conditions.

THE STATUS OF PROVISIONS FOR THE GIFTED

The experts present a dismal view of the adequacy of programs. Nearly all communities are described as having very few provisions, or none at all. The neglect is greatest at the early school years; but even at high school level, little is done. Educational planning for the gifted has had low priority, and few persons are aware of the tragic waste of human potential. The often verbalized principle of quality education for all has only been implemented in isolated instances, often regarded as experimental, temporary programs. Most services for the gifted are reported in the cities and suburbs, although these services are meager at best.

The lack of provisions for the identified gifted is revealed in the *School Staffing Survey.* Of those recognized as gifted, the majority receive scant attention at best. One third or more of the known gifted receive no special instruction. With the exception of large cities with some grouping, the majority of gifted children are given any special attention they do receive in the regular classroom from the regular teacher. As evident in research studies, even the sympathetic and conscientious teacher in the regular classroom rarely finds time to devote to the gifted and talented pupil. Most identified gifted children therefore receive little or no attention at the elementary school level, while the programs at the secondary level consist mainly of separate part-time classes.

Lack of opportunity for the gifted secondary school student to make relevant contacts outside of the formal classroom situation is evident in the *School Staffing Survey*, where less than 2 percent were given opportunities to work with specialists or in other school settings. Yet many gifted and talented students are at a level of knowledge which requires such opportunities if they are to learn. One of the features of an excellent program is its increasing use and continuing diversification of resources.

Twenty-seven school systems, chosen from a national sample for their model programs for children with exceptional learning needs, reported only five programs for the gifted.[3] Other categories commonly had three to four times as many programs; the only exception was the multiple handicapped which is relatively new, as contrasted with the gifted, a category which has existed, though neglected, for the past half century.

Even in those local districts selected as models in their provisions for children with unusual learning needs, the gifted have the lowest priority for expenditures.[4] The average of $92 for the gifted beyond the regular per pupil expenditures, is miniscule compared to other special programs (ranging up to $1,729). However, it is considerably above amounts allocated per gifted pupil by the few States providing support.

The use of Federal funds has markedly strengthened Federal, State and local programs for the handicapped, through improved preparation of specialized personnel, quality of research, and understanding

---

[3] In *Abstracts of National Educational Finance Project Satellite Projects Reported at First National Conference,* December 7–8, 1970. See also Figure 3, appendix B of this report.

[4] Rossmiller, Richard A., Hale, James A., and Frohreich, Lloyd E., *Educational Programs for Exceptional Children: Resource Configurations and Costs.* Madison: National Educational Finance Project, Special Study No. 2, August 1970. See also Figure 4, appendix B of this report.

and support of the education profession and the public. The funds have undoubtedly improved life opportunities for thousands of the handicapped and members of their families. These programs vividly demonstrated the social benefits from a Federal investment in the education of specific target populations with needs which cannot be met by general education.

The need for funding support for the gifted and talented is critical. If funds can be devoted similarly to program improvement, personnel preparation, improved and extended research, and general support and understanding, the educational opportunities and life possibilities for this group also will improve.

Many experts in the *Advocate Survey* observed that the gifted were losing to the competition of other problems. It is seen even in States which support programs, such as California, where the allocation to State operations for the gifted in the 1971–72 budget shows a decline.

The fiscal year 1971 funds monitored by the Bureau of Education for the Handicapped, U.S. Office of Education, total $197,767,633. Several areas in which these funds are currently expended are areas in which programs for the gifted could be improved through support. Funds are allocated to the following categories relevant to the gifted: To strengthen educational and related services for preschool, elementary and secondary children; to provide grants for supplementary, innovative, or exemplary projects for educational improvement; to develop model preschool and early childhood programs; to provide vocational education and services; to improve recruitment of educational personnel and to desseminate information on educational opportunities; to provide for research, training of personnel, and to establish and operate model centers; to promote new knowledge and developments for this population; to prepare and inform teachers and others who work in the education of the target population.

The amount allocated to these categories totals $102,5888,116, of which $47,188,116, comes from title III of ESEA and the Vocational Education Act, Part B of the 1968 amendment, which earmark a percent of funds for the handicapped.

Similar categorical allocations, with specific designation of the gifted and talented, would strengthen educational efforts for this group. States have made little or no use of Federal funds for the gifted and talented. Without special definite designation of fund use for this population, it is not likely that they will.

The cost of quality educational opportunities for the gifted and talented would be relatively low, compared to other programs. Even in strictly fiscal terms, the expenditures would be returned to the Federal Government. The productivity of a well-educated, well-adjusted gifted or talented adult would be of benefit in many ways, including the monetary advantage.

Income figures for males in the United States, compiled by the U.S. Department of Commerce for the decade 1956–66, indicate that as education increases, lifetime income climbs steeply.[5] Investment in education of the gifted would be returned shortly to the Treasury through additional income tax.

---

[5] In *Digest of Educational Statistics, 1970.* U.S. Department of Health, Education and Welfare, Office of Education (OE 10024–70). See also Figure 5 in Appendix B of this report.

Categorical allocation of even 2 percent of the Federal expenditure for education would produce more than $50,000,000 from present income. The figures for 1967–68 representing 2 percent of the total expenditure were $48,000,000.[6]

VIEWS ON PROGRAMS

Some contradiction is seen in the recommendation that programs be continuous throughout the school career of the gifted child by 95 percent of the respondents, while most also responded that programs should be started in grades four to six. The item required a forced choice due to limitations of funds as to level at which a program should be started. The selection of the elementary grades also may recognize the fact that most programs still operate at the secondary level on a too-little-and-too-late basis, despite abundant knowledge from research that gifted children have the greatest adjustment problems to face at school entry and during the primary grades when patterns of under-achievement become entrenched.

The experts generally supported summer programs, the use of community resource personnel, individualized instruction, special groupings, and part-time groupings as a means toward adequate provisions. Some felt that the choices were made only as better than nothing, however.

Conventional or standardized curriculum requirements were seen as unimportant to the gifted and talented. Rather than studying grade level content required of the total group, an open curriculum based on individual interests was favored, with large blocks of independent time. The gifted and talented were seen as capable of self-management and decisionmaking for both content of study and classroom procedures.

These recommendations are compatible with the program research studies, which found that deletion of irrelevant or unnecessary content in favor of opportunities to study and learn in depth produced better achievement and better adjustment in the gifted and talented.

The need to adjust to different learning styles among the gifted was seen as essential by 89 percent of the respondents. As described by various research studies, the gifted are complex, highly diverse individuals, with an unlimited array of interests and talents. Among the gifted and talented, one may find persons who respond and function rapidly, those who are deliberate and contemplative, those who are logical and direct, or those who are exploratory and circuitous. The quality of end product may be excellent (and different) from any of these, but teaching the gifted does not comfortably permit standard rules of procedure.

The experts saw as the most important program objective the stimulation of individual interests. Next, in order of importance, were the development of student initiative, the development of self-acceptance, concept development, and recognition of the early ability to undertake comlex learning tasks.

Close to 90 percent of the advocates felt that differentiated programs for the gifted need greater resources than programs for regular students. However, adequate inservice preparation may reduce unessen-

---

[6] *Digest of Educational Statistics, 1970.* U.S. Office of Education (OE–10024–70).

tial program expenditures. Teachers with background knowledge are prone to use better existing resources, and to free students to seek needed materials or specialists personnel; they are more willing to ask for assistance from parents and consultants who can bring in necessary resources, or arrange for student contacts with them.

The need for regular teachers to carry on differentiated experiences for the gifted, whether or not they are in special programs, is a recognition of the fact that attention to the gifted in only a special program may mean neglect for the greater part of the school week, particularly if the special program is a few sessions per week or less. Liaison between regular and special teachers, and constant effort to differentiate programs in both settings, are seen as important.

THE SUCCESSFUL TEACHER OF THE GIFTED AND TALENTED

Although 15 percent of the advocates saw all teachers as teachers of the gifted, whether or not the children were found in regular classrooms without special provisions, the majority equated specialized programs or separate grouping of the gifted with recognition of the teacher as a teacher of the gifted.

Only 12 of 204 respondents felt that an adequate supply of personnel was available to teach all of the gifted within their State. The pressing need for preparation within the ranks of those teaching is seen in their recommendations for summer institutes, and inservice programs and workshops during the school year. Most of the respondents also favored the development of advanced degree programs with specialization in teaching the gifted.

To attract teachers who would specialize in the education of the gifted, the advocates recommended subsidies for training, university courses, and training centers, inservice preparation for those already in the profession, and the development of positions for those qualified. The heavy advocacy of inservice preparation is doubtless due to the knowledge that many teachers are currently working with the gifted without background, as well as knowledge of recent findings that even the best teachers can improve their skills and abilities in working with the gifted and talented through specialized preparation. (Important too is the research finding that even limited special preparation reduces hostility toward the gifted, and increases support of them as a group.)

OTHER SCHOOL PERSONNEL

Nearly all of the experts recognized the need for inservice preparation on the gifted for school administrators. Administrators affect teaching in many ways by their decisions as well as their attitudes. The administrator can encourage or discourage teacher interest through his remarks and behavior. His support must be active to encourage teachers in the extra efforts required to maintain programs of high quality.

School psychologists and guidance counselors were seen as mildly or highly positive toward the gifted by approximately two-thirds of the respondents, while social workers and tutorial workers were characterized as neutral, negative, or unknown. The need for special preparation to develop understanding of the gifted is apparent for social workers and tutors, who deal chiefly with remedial needs. A research study established school psychologists as relatively more hostile toward the gifted than other persons in education, despite their advanced preparation.

Approximately 90 percent of the experts agreed that the teacher of the gifted should have ready access to specialized consultant help and to auxiliary materials. Consultants have made appreciable improvements in the quality of programs, through inservice assistance for teachers, other school personnel, and parents, and through arranging for access to learning materials.

Experts agreed that much of the responsibility for program success and decision should be assigned to a special consultant for the gifted at the local level. The need undoubtedly is seen as one for a constant interpreter and advocate for the gifted, as well as one who would have the authority to arrange optimal learning situations and affiliations.

Only 3 percent of the experts felt that pupil personnel workers show a positive attitude toward the gifted, while 22 percent of the responses described negative attitudes, other concerns, or apathy and indifference toward the gifted.

The great majority said that pupil personnel workers are not equipped for the task of working with the gifted. The recommendation that they be given added preparation came from 85 percent of the experts, with the most important need being that of information regarding the gifted and their needs.

Studies have shown that pupil personnel workers are indifferent or hostile in their attitudes toward the gifted; it is supported as well by the general failure to seek and recognize the gifted in the schools.

RECOMMENDED PRIORITIES FOR EXPENDITURES

Priorities recommended by the experts for expenditures were 1) inservice preparation of teachers and other personnel, 2) pilot and experimental programs, and 3) direct aid to school systems.

The cost of inservice preparation of teachers apparently was interpreted as involving both part-time and full-time study. Estimates ranged widely, with 35 percent of the experts choosing a sum implying full-time fellowship study.

At the local level, the greatest need was for personnel. This category received double the number of first choices given to inservice teacher preparation.

At the State level, the experts again endorsed support of an office to coordinate and strengthen programs for the gifted. This need far outweighed others in importance.

Over 90 percent of the respondents mentioned psychological services and guidance counseling as important needs of the gifted. Their perception of need is supported by research studies in which highly gifted students have been found to require expert psychological assistance in adapting to environmental frustrations, and in understanding themselves and their relationships with others. The problems of coping with attitudes and misunderstandings of others, frequent feelings of difference and inferiority, frustrations in learning, educational choices, the development of tolerance and understanding, all require special help. Parents frequently need assistance along with their children.

SUPPORT FOR PROGRAMS

The majority of advocates felt that education for the gifted was not a continuing priority in their communities. They recommended the use of various modes for informing legislators, the general public, and educators, including media, experts, and parents of the gifted.

The opposition to special education for the gifted is seen mainly as lack of public awareness and lack of funds. The belief that the gifted can manage without provisions and that other priorities are more important were also mentioned. The major efforts of all agencies responsible for instituting programs for the gifted were described as disorganized or nonexistent. Support in rural areas was seen as the worst.

Advocacy of programs for the gifted rests primarily with those most directly concerned and affected: teachers of the gifted, parents, and children. Most others are seen as neutral.

The experts alluded to the problem of communication with others about the gifted and their needs. The most important function of a State consultant was seen as interpretation and dissemination of knowledge. Half of the respondents suggested information to the lay public as necessary to attain support for the gifted.

The present burden of education for the gifted and talented was described by one advocate as falling on parents who "weep alone for their children."

REGIONAL HEARINGS—THE PEOPLE SAY . . .

The call for oral testimony on education for the gifted by Regional Assistant Commissioners of Education in the 10 HEW regions of the country drew a surprising number and wide variety of witnesses. A total of 295 persons from diverse backgrounds delivered oral testimony: school administrators, teachers, parents, students, State legislators, school board members, etc. The results of the oral and written testimony were combined because they were so similar. In general, the testimony confirmed more eloquently and specifically the results of the State survey. Education for the gifted is seen as an important and long-term concern of educators but good intentions and plans are inundated by a flood of immediate problems. Appendix C of this report details the findings.

PERCEIVED NEEDS

Curriculum.—The testimony analysis was divided into statements of specific needs and recommendations. In the area of needs, one major theme repeatedly mentioned was the need for *curriculum flexibility* to allow talented students to move forward on their own, or to modify existing curriculum to take into account their unusual ability. The witnesses maintained that initiative and creativity were being crushed by the required conformity to an inappropriate and dull educational program.

Teachers.—A second strong need was expressed for better prepared teachers. Almost one half of the witnesses spontaneously mentioned this need, expressed as strongly by the teachers as by the other witnesses. There was a consensus that teachers are currently not prepared and cannot handle the special educational issues presented by gifted youngsters. More specific needs for better and more specific leadership at the State and Federal levels were mentioned primarily by administrators and others who know the structure of the educational system at first hand. Parents and teachers generally focused on the quality of the immediate delivery of services to the gifted student.

Special Classes.—Under organizational needs, testimony stressed the need for partial separation for a part of the educational program to allow gifted youngsters to work with one another and to allow for necessary freedom to explore. There was a general rejection of a complete separation for the entire day in either special schools or special classes.

Society's Needs.—The societal need for gifted leadership in a complex society was stressed by the witnesses. Interestingly enough, very few of the witnesses mentioned the need for the gifted to provide us with protection against hostile powers that seemed the major impetus to some educational movements, such as the NDEA in the late 1950's. The threat of a technologically superior Russia caused a great flurry to improve our educational program for talented students. Do we have to have this kind of bogeyman to thrust in front of the public in order to force it to act? Must we create a crisis, artificial or real, so that the problems of the gifted can get the same level of attention as the disadvantaged child and the handicapped child?

RECOMMENDATIONS

The recommendations for the testimony generally took the form of requests for general support for the gifted and talented rather than specific proposals. The structure and time limits of the hearings were not conducive to major innovative ideas. They did, however, underline several major points.

1. A strong need was expressed for additional funds and higher priority for gifted programs. A clear accompanying sentiment was that such funds would have to come from the Federal Government. Over 55 percent of the witnesses stressed the need for Federal funds. Those closest to the school finance position—administrators and school board members—were overwhelming in expressing need for Federal assistance.

2. Nineteen percent of the witnesses spontaneously noted that funds needed to be earmarked for specific spending on the gifted. They indicated vehemently that unless funds were earmarked for the gifted, they would be siphoned off into other problem areas.

3. Request for more training support from the Federal level follows up the need for better prepared teachers. Over 25 percent of the witnesses wished for more teacher training help in both inservice and preservice programs.

4. The major request for specific State and Federal action was maintaining a higher priority for the gifted in the State and Federal decision making channels. The Federal Government would be more of a catalyst, providing funds and such special services as training fellowships. The State would retain leadership responsibilities for the basic program and would help tailor the program to local and regional needs.

In looking at possible differences between testifiers from different regions of the country, two regions that had few developed programs for the gifted were compared with two other regions relatively far along in their developmental programs for the gifted. The former placed their primary concern on the need for teachers and supplementary personnel to deal directly with the talented student while the latter stressed the need for more State and Federal leadership.

Students expressed more interest in greater opportunities for creative work, and for partial segregation of the talented, rather than full segregation in their school program. Administrators paid more attention to administrative concerns and teachers to issues surrounding the immediate instructional program. Parents, not knowing the complexities of the school system, merely stressed their great desire to get something moving.

The most frequently mentioned specific recommendations were: 1) leadership persons in visible positions at the State and the Federal level. (Specific earmarking amendments to title V ESEA were mentioned quite often); 2) model and demonstration programs to bring greater visibility to efforts for the gifted; 3) training fellowships and scholarships to improve the educational preparation for teachers and other specialists who want to spend more time working with the gifted; 4) more research and development efforts earmarked for the gifted, particularly in specific new curriculum advances and reforms; 5) a major information exchange of program ideas and materials.

The overall portrait has been one of a great desire for educational leaders and citizens to modify somehow the 'crisis orientation' that controls educational decisionmaking today and to add some specific, definable plans and resources allocated for maximizing our societal assets—our talented children.

REPRESENTATIVE QUOTES FROM TESTIMONY—REGIONAL HEARINGS ON EDUCATION FOR THE GIFTED

With confidence that our children are our greatest single national asset, we feel that every investment in them is an investment in our national future. Without a doubt, they who will make the greatest contribution to society, they who will provide the leadership and the brainpower . . . they are the gifted. As responsible parents, educators, citizens, yes, as taxpayers, we must invest in our national future.

(Parrino—Region V)

Conformity is precisely the cross upon which special education for the gifted hangs supine.

(Beer—Region X)

One of the things that concerns me is that practically none of the teachers we have been able to hire have had any preservice experience, either in courses for the gifted or experience with talented groups.

(McGuire—Region VII)

Unless the initial development comes from the Federal Government, we cannot rely upon State and local governments to bring from their limited resources, that thrust which is necessary to get these programs off the ground.

(Weintraub—Region III)

Quality programs develop where one person, usually not a line administrator, sees it in his interest to become an advocate for the gifted program. He organizes a group of people around himself and together they forge the climate essential to the development of the program. The more outside money the advocate has, the more help he can muster from outside and inside the district, and the stronger his position, the better the program.

(House—Region V)

The neglect of the education of this gifted child, whether he or she comes from a white middle class family in Forest Hills, Queens, or from a poor black or Puerto Rican family in Harlem, is a problem as great as any of the ills facing our society.

(Feit—Region II)

Every individual is unhappy unless he can exercise his outstanding talents. He is frustrated and this is the situation, I think, with many of our children today.

(Guilford—Region IX)

CHAPTER IV

WHAT IS A GOOD PROGRAM FOR THE GIFTED?

The major thrust in American education today is to free all students to learn at their own pace—and to place on them more responsibility for their education.

Such arrangements as flexible scheduling, independence of mobility in learning decisionmaking and planning by pupils, the planning of curriculum based on pupil interests, use of community specialists, research seminars, and flexible time blocks have been successfully used. As educators study and evaluate various arrangements, they learn of their value for children with exceptional learning needs.

Information on productive approaches to gifted education is cited in several sources in Volume II of this report. The common denominators of successful programs for the gifted have been support for a given plan, inservice assistance to teachers, continuity of the program, and opportunities for the student to develop genuine relationships in the school setting.

Programs of a few weeks' duration have been less fruitful than a sustained effort. The least productive results come from regular classes, although elementary teachers and administrators initially favor this arrangement.

From all available evidence, some kind of grouping is needed for the nurture of the abilities and talents of the gifted, accompanied by quality control with well prepared teachers and staff members, consultant assistance, and careful evaluation. Special grouping and special planning, carefully conceived and executed, provide opportunities for the gifted to function at proper levels of understanding and performance. Those who oppose grouping have relied on opinion or poorly designed studies rather than available evidence. Recent studies have shown that simple administrative arrangements alone produce no change. If it is to succeed, any plan must include active and appropriate intervention.

CAN PROGRAMS FOR THE GIFTED DEMONSTRATE THEIR EFFECTIVENESS?

In all of the data gleaned from the research, from testimony at the regional hearings, and from the *State Survey*, one fact is clear. Every respondent started with the premise that special programs for the gifted and talented are *essential*. But the consideration of substantial investment in such special programs requires a closer look at this assumption. One must also ask whether special programs do, in fact, expand the child's ability to perform in accordance with his innate gifts and talents.

The four case studies in chapter VI provide a record of experience over the last 10 years for a sizable population. The following excerpt from the review of research (appendix A) presents a broader, more general law.

Special provisions, including acceleration and various special groupings, have been beneficial to gifted children. Studies have shown that gifted children can condense school requirements and cover them faster with no difficulty and with superior performance.

Followup studies of pupils who had participated in special classes have measured academic achievement, social adjustment, health, and personality factors. Clear support for special groupings was found in New York, in the Major Work Classes of Cleveland, in Los Angeles, and in numerous other locales. Participants showed improvement not only in academic areas but also in personal and social areas.

Special experimental classes have shown that gifted students can meet any standard requirements and simultaneously absorb the meaning, history, and symbols of a given discipline; study pertinent biographical data; apply principles and insights from the discipline to other fields of knowledge; and display more originality in their performance than control groups.

Interage groups have produced beneficial results when accompanied by special planning and special teacher preparation. The attitudes of teachers, administrators, pupils, and parents who have participated were generally favorable. Better teaching has produced a higher level of thinking, questioning, self-reliance, and classroom relationships.

Special adaptations to improve learning opportunities have produced favorable social results as well. Special workshop experiences helped to develop and reinforce friendships among the gifted both in and out of school. Most of the Cleveland Major Work Class pupils adjusted well and approved of their special class experiences. Pupils from rural schools who attended Saturday classes in the California State program gained significantly in social status within their regular classrooms, despite the fact that their peers were completely unaware of the special work.

This growth is true of the elementary grades and junior and senior high school levels as well. Gifted high school pupils who had participated in special programs gained in personal and social maturity, compared to equally gifted nonparticipants. All of the evidence from the assessment of personal, social, and psychological factors indicated that gifted pupils who participate in programs do so with no damage and many gains.

Recent research has concentrated on specialized studies, and intervention or analysis in areas of talent and creativity as well as academic ability.

Specialized counseling for able disadvantaged students has proved beneficial. Students were found to improve scholastically and to earn more diplomas. Students who participated in special counseling sessions for a year or more showed improvements in self-attitude, relationships with others, and achievement.

A recent study produced significant gains in tests of fluency, adaptive flexibility, and originality. The gains were in divergent response (related to creativity) rather than in convergent or cognitive areas.

The attitudes of the students toward creativity were better than controls. Art education focused on creative behavior and problem solving was determined to be important for gifted young people.

A 3-year study to test the influence of a creative-aesthetic approach to school readiness and beginning reading and arithmetic produced significantly higher scores for kindergarten children on tests of creative thinking, problem solving, and originality. Fluency, flexibility, and originality ratings were consistently around the fifth-grade level.

Programed instruction for specific skills and television instruction have been found effective with gifted students. Programs designed to use multiple resources have shown that gifted students score significantly higher than equally gifted controls in ability to learn, in motivation, in their use of abilities, and in self-indentity.

In the California State study, special arrangements for more than a thousand pupils accommodated special talents, school system philosophies, the rural gifted in remote schools as well as the full-time and part-time needs of the urban and suburban gifted; community resources were meshed with student interests. Carefully matched control groups were established. The highly significant gains of the special groups at all grade levels in academic, social, and psychological areas were attributed to careful preservice and inservice preparation of teachers; the assignment of special consultants for full-time assistance; appropriate learning opportunities (both in and out of school); a wide variety of community resources; close interschool liaison; and close collaboration with parents.

The sources and details of these studies can be found in Volume II.

CAN THE CURRENT PUBLIC SCHOOL STRUCTURE PROVIDE ADEQUATELY FOR THE GIFTED AND TALENTED?

Yes, given certain conditions. Schools which provide adequately for the gifted and talented are those in which educational plans are based on the actual needs and interests of the pupil, where freedom from the restrictions of structure requirements and schedule are possible, where pupils are given access to needed resources regardless of location, and where suitable teachers are utilized whether they possess credentials or not. Such schools have administrators who are fully aware of the gifted and their needs, and a faculty who have studied these pupils. Parents are closely involved in these programs. A special consultant assigned to the gifted is available to provide inservice and direct assistance to the adult participants.

WHAT ARE THE NECESSARY COMPONENTS OF A GOOD PROGRAM?

Do we need new buildings, libraries, and laboratories?
Is special transportation necessary?
Are there special media needs? Material needs?

Intelligent use of facilities and materials is governed by the knowledge of the users. If that knowledge is absent, capital expenditures will be wasted.

In urban communities where libraries and laboratories are available, educators have made special arrangements for individuals to use materials and to experiment under supervision. Good libraries and laboratory space in schools are highly desirable, with open areas for special projects and study. Even with good libraries and adequately stocked laboratories, it is necessary to use auxiliary resources and materials, if the special interests of the gifted are to be met. Special programs have been restricted in their success because of limited facilities. Provisions should be made so that gifted students, whether urban or rural, have access to resources and space.

Special transportation funds should be available for needed study and research opportunities. These should not be categorically limited, but should be documented and justified. These funds may be required for widely varying and sometimes unpredictable purposes, ranging from archaeological studies by special interest groups, to gathering of research specimens for marine, botanical, or geological research, to visits to specialized libraries and museums, to special contacts with artists; from individual studies of political process, to documentary studies, to recording of interview or photographic data, to acquisition of unaccessible materials.

Media and material needs are also unpredictable in advance. Funds should be made available for purchase of standard equipment and expendable supplies so that students who wish to function in areas of creative expression may do so. The young painter or musician should not be restricted by the nonavailability of supplies, equipment, musical scores, or suitable instruments. Similarly, the young person who wishes to report his research findings creatively should have access to the necessary photographic or graphic resource materials and media. Ready availability of materials and encouragement to use them enhance interest in learning and extend talents.

See Volume II for details and documentation of these generations.

WHAT KINDS OF PERSONNEL ARE NEEDED?

The teacher is the key to effective programs and the effective use of resources. Preparation of teachers to work with the gifted should precede expenditures on materials and facilities, which should be recommended by informal school personnel after careful planning for a given population of gifted and talented pupils.

The need for the special teacher preparation is apparent. Teachers with no special background have been found disinterested in and even hostile toward the gifted. They believe that the gifted will reveal themselves through academic grades, that they need all existing content plus more, and that teachers should add to existing curriculum requirements rather than delete anything.

Teachers who have worked with special programs tend to be enthusiastic, whereas those who have not are generally hostile. Opportunities for experience with programs and inservice preparation produce changes to more favorable teacher attitudes toward both gifted children and special programs.

The need for general inservice programs is evident from findings that 50 percent of public school educators opposed acceleration, despite research evidence that acceleration is beneficial at every level from kindergarten to college. Even in studies which have produced significantly favorable results, authors have commented on lack of articulation, heavy demands, evaluation problems, lack of teacher background, the inability of the school to deal with basic problems, and the unwillingness of the faculty memb rs to free gifted students for needed independent learning.

Even when teachers of the gifted are carefully selected and represent the highest levels of professional competence, their teaching performance can be significantly improved through inservice study. Highly desirable changes in the quality of learning, communication, classroom content, and diversity of classroom experiences have resulted. Other benefits reported by teachers include increase in teaching skills, knowledge of subject matter, and increased appreciation of the needs of the gifted.

Studies of successful teachers for the gifted typically have dealt with their characteristics and behavior more often than with their specific preparation. In general, the successful teachers are highly intelligent, are interested in scholarly and artistic pursuits, have wide interests, are mature and unthreatened, possess a sense of humor, are more student centered than their colleagues, and are enthusiastic about both teaching and advanced study for themselves.

The problem of credentials poses difficulty when the complexity and diversity of teaching the gifted and talented at all levels is considered. Quite evidently an array of prescribed courses typical of other credentials is inadequate; probably the credentials should be planned as an individualized program of studies. Recommendations for such a program have been outlined in a recent publication dealing with professional standards for teachers and other personnel.

School personnel other than teachers need special preparation to understand the needs of the gifted. Administrators often determine the existence of programs, decree their abolition, or deny the need for them.

Over half of a representative sample of schools in the United States reported *no* gifted students in their schools! The statement may be ascribed to apathy or hostility, but not to fact.

Even groups with special preparation which presumably should make them especially alert to individual differences are indifferent or hostile toward the gifted. Counselors in several studies were found to be more concerned with remedial problems than with the gifted. Student personnel departments in 20 western colleges and universities gave little special attention to the gifted and their problems. One study found significantly greater hostility toward the gifted among school psychologists than among other school personnel.

All of these studies indicate the need for comprehensive inservice preparation for those school personnel who contact or affect the gifted. Teachers who are prepared and interested need informed and sympathetic auxiliary support.

Volume II provides documentation of these assertions.

WHAT DOES A GOOD PROGRAM COST?

We frankly don't know because an optimal program has never been funded. Costs of programs for the gifted are frequently constrained or limited to the monies which can be made available—which in turn constrains the kinds of activities carried out with these funds. That is, limitations of expenditures to $40 per child served can scarcely do more than support a program for identification of the target population.

The "excess cost" from various programs for the gifted and talented children does increase the cost of education for these students beyond the average *per capita* expenditures in the school district. The interaction between available funds and educational responses provided makes it difficult to project costs for a national program with any degree of certainty because: (1) what would or could be provided in various areas seems to depend on amounts of funds available; and (2) there has been no evaluation of the cost effectiveness of various approaches for helping the gifted reach their maximum level of performance; cost figures for development are financially optimal programs are nonexistent.

Until basic cost data can be accumulated from a statistical search, only estimates based on local and State experience can be used. Estimates would differ markedly if existing support levels are used as a criterion, as opposed to costs documented by studies. For example, the Illinois support level is $28 per child per year; California provides $65, including identification. Administrators responsible for programs idnicate that these sums cannot be interpreted as more than token payment to encourage local effort. The California State Department of Education has for several years supported bills to increase aid to the gifted by $200 per pupil each year. In 1971, no increase is being advocated, since the department is promoting legislation to increase basic support rather than categorical aid. Funds are not allocated by local school systems for the gifted, in spite of evident need. If the California allocation were that recommended in 1961, the State expenditure for the gifted would be $32,500,000 rather than the current $7,000,000.

Since very few States have had experience with the conduct of statewide programs, and even where these exist the support figure is far from ideal, the problem of costs merits further investigation.

PRIORITIES AND RECOMMENDATIONS

Data from research studies suggest that these priorities be established:

1. Systematic inservice preparation for school personnel, including teachers and others who affect the learning opportunities of the gifted and talented.

    a. Fellowships for special preparation

    b. Support for inservice workships and course work

    c. Establishment of preparation centers for demonstration programs, experimentation, research, and teaching

2. Support of research and experimental programs.

    a. Programs to improve identification of gifted from varied backgrounds and cultures

    b. Programs to identify added human capacities and talents

    c. Programs to improve program evaluation

    d. Programs to expand learning opportunities in the arts

    e. Programs for preschool gifted and talented, including those from poor economic backgrounds

    f. Exemplary programs in school systems

3. Establishment of a Federal office for dissemination of information and improvement of efforts for the gifted

a. Use of media to improve understanding by educators and the general public

b. Dissemination of informational materials to educators

c. Provision of leadership to State and national educational agencies, to assure proper use of available and future funds.

d. Development of linkages for better understanding

4. Support for evaluation and dissemination of new findings.

5. Continuing support for exemplary programs.

Now that we have seen what the needs are, let us see what is available for the gifted and talented in the various States.

CHAPTER V

The State Survey

Because the State role is key to provision for gifted and talented students, special attention has been focused on the States in the USOE study and in this report.

As part of this study, a questionnaire prepared in the Office of Education was sent to each of the State departments of education on several major dimensions of the gifted, including the availability of staff at the State department level for gifted programs and the presence of enabling legislation for the gifted. Inquiries were made about planning or study groups active in their State, special training provisions available, major deterrents to State action, and State use of Federal funds for education of the gifted. Details and graphic presentations may be found on the *State Survey* in appendix C of this report. Appendix D, also in Volume II, summarizes State laws for gifted children.

The general definition of the gifted child used in the regional survey provided the guideline for the *State Survey:*

Gifted and talented children are those identified by professionally qualified persons who by virtue of outstanding abilities, are capable of high performance. These are children who require differentiated educational programs and/or services beyond those normally provided by the regular school program in order to realize their contribution to self and society.

The *State Survey* yielded significant information on the allocation of resources at the State level and the impact of Federal programs for supplementing those resources. The first question was: *What available personnel and legislative resources are currently available at the State level?* The breadth of interest in this problem is indicated by the fact that 21 States currently have legislation on their books that provide special resources or incentives to local school districts to increase their program efforts on education of the gifted and talented; those States that have adopted such legislation represent a broad geographic spread throughout the country. States in every HEW Region but one (Region II) have passed legislation for these purposes. Ten other States have now or have had planning commissions, but no specific legislation as yet.

STATE LEADERSHIP

Such legislation, in many cases, merely represents intent. How that intent is being implemented is of greater relevance to our current concerns. There is a consistent portrait of a shortage of available resources.

The survey asked whether there is a staff person employed at the State department level with major responsibilities for programs for the gifted in that State. Twenty-four of the States have designated such a person, including three States with no specific legislation. However, in only 10 are staff members assigned that responsibility for 50 percent or more of their time. In many instances the amount of time allocated to serving gifted students is but a small fraction of a multitude of duties and responsibilities assigned to one of the high ranking State officials.

The financial support for the State personnel assigned to the gifted almost invariably comes from the State. Twenty-one States reported their contributions as half or more of the salary of these key individuals. Only 3 States reported that a signficant proportion of a salary of a leadership person was being paid out of Federal funds, despite the clear opportunity in such programs as ESEA title V, which provides funds for strengthening State departments of education.

The thinness of the leadership staff for the gifted is even more strikingiy demonstrated by the lack of support staff or additional personnel beyond the single designated leader. Over 40 States hire no support or consultative staff or any additional personnel. The designated leader has few resources for providing technical assistance to local education programs. Only 3 States reported as many as 3 or more staff persons assigned to the specific responsibilities of education of the gifted.

The most typical personnel portrait at the State department is a single individual, with part-time responsibility for the gifted and with no support staff. Occasionally, there is someone gravitating toward this area of gifted education because no one else is there. For example, Dr. Hugh Templeton, Supervisor of Science Education in New York's State Education Department, was introduced in the oral hearings as Chief of the Bureau of Science Education, but unofficially he has been called "The supervisor for education for the gifted without portfolio."

PERSONNEL TRAINING

Key to effective services for education of gifted and talented students is the commitment to special preparation for the educational personnel to work with such students. The widespread general interest in providing some training in gifted education can be seen across the country in colleges and university programs or course work in education of gifted students, and State departments that allocate a proportion of their training resources for inservice training of teachers on education of the gifted. Only the Mountain States lack identifiable college programs or State training efforts. Inservice training activities are utilized in practically all of the regions.

PROGRAM DETERRENTS

One of the most significant survey questions dealt with the reasons for limited resources for the gifted: *What are the specific forces that the States see holding back a more extensive operation?* The differences between the various regions were not significant. The problems were seen as the same, or extremely similar, from one region to the next. The deterrents operating in one area of the country also appeared in the others.

The major deterrent, clearly, was the lack of sufficient funds to carry out significant program activity. The kinds of financial resources necessary to implement legislative intent are just not being allocated at the State level. The second, and related, deterrent is the pressure of other more crisis-oriented priorities.

In the responses to the *State Survey*, additional notes were provided on how the emphasis on children with specific education problems was using up the scarce available resources. Little or nothing was left over for significant but long-range problems that did not create immediate administrative crises—problems like education of the gifted. Of lesser concern, but still mentioned as important by a majority of the States, was the scarcity of adequate personnel. Any major move in this area would have to include substantial emphasis on the training or retraining of personnel before an educational program could become a reality.

USE OF FEDERAL LEGISLATION

The final crucial question in the *State Survey* was: *To what extent are States using the additional resources provided by Federal aid to apply to the problems of educating the gifted and talented?* The results present a discouraging story on the use of funds for the gifted under the current Federal guidelines.

Less than 15 percent of the States spent any ESEA title I funds for the identification and development of special programs for specially talented youngsters from deprived circumstances.

Title V, ESEA, which permits strengthening of State departments of education, represented one major opportunity for use of Federal funds with relatively little financial commitment. But only 9 States reported title V activities for strengthening their programs for the gifted! Only 3 of these States put funds into the support of leadership personnel, while the others spent such funds on a variety of administrative needs.

The most extensively used Federal provision was title III of ESEA, devoted to strengthening and developing innovative programs and supplementary centers. Over 20 percent of the States utilize some title III monies for the programs directed to educating the gifted. However, a closer analysis revealed a minimal effort. Only 4 of the States report 3 or more projects with this emphasis.

Other potential Federal sources to strengthen training programs were obviously doing no better. Six percent of the States use none of the available Federal legislation, while another 24 percent use only the resources of one or two acts, and these very sparingly.

The general portrait emerging from the *State Survey* is clear. Most of the States have recognized that education of the gifted is an area of substantial educational need and have tried, in a variety of ways, to put some available resources to work. These efforts have been overwhelmed by the more crisis oriented issues of the deprived child, the disruptive child, the child who cannot learn, etc. The limited resources available are absorbed by these problem areas before such long-range educational issues as gifted education are considered. Unspecified Federal aid appears to be spent in the same pattern, so that much legislation that could benefit the gifted, is not, in fact, applied to their education problems. Four States have, however, systematically attacked the problem of gifted and talented education. Let us turn now to the differing solutions they are developing for their students.

CHAPTER VI

Four Case Studies

While there are numerous programs for the gifted and talented, the experience most pertinent to this study is those cases where the planning and implementation have been statewide. Planners in other State agencies may benefit from the practical wisdom gained in Connecticut, California, Georgia, and Illinois.

These accounts are reprinted in full in appendix F. The background of each program is reported as fully as possible here to show the derivation of interest and support and how each State arrived at its own priorities.

CALIFORNIA'S PROGRAM FOR MENTALLY GIFTED MINORS (MGM)

In 1955 and 1956, personnel in the California State Department of Education participated in exploratory and planning meetings on the role of the State in encouraging school districts to make special provisions for gifted children. A California State Study conducted from 1957 to 1960 evaluated 17 different kinds of programs numbering 929 pupils; it concluded:

The special provisions made in these programs were beneficial for the gifted ... participating pupils made striking gains in achievement with accompanying personal and social benefits.

Developmental activities from 1961 to 1971 include the demonstration project, California Project Talent (1963–1966), and a title V, ESEA project (1968–1969) to prepare a statewide framework on gifted education and exemplary curriculum guides.

The types of programs which the initial State regulations identified as appropriate for mentally gifted minors were:

1. Enrichment in regular classes.
2. Correspondence courses and tutoring.
3. Placement in advanced grades or classes.
4. Attendance in college classes by high school students.
5. Special counseling or instruction outside regular classrooms.
6. Special classes organized for gifted pupils.
7. Other, or combination of programs.

Changes in the State regulations in 1969 established two general categories of programs: special services or activities and special day classes.

During the first year of the program (1961–1962), school districts spent an average of $83 extra per pupil for mentally gifted minors. A few school districts spent as much as $900 extra per pupil. The average per pupil extra expenditure for 1969–1970 was $121. Pupil participation grew from 35,164 full-time equivalent pupils (over 38,000 individuals) in 1961–1962 to approximately 112,000 full-time equivalent pupils in 1970–1971. At the present time, 250 California school districts (with about 95 percent of the statewide pupil population) make special provisions for mentally gifted minors. State money available for the Mentally Gifted Minor program in the 1970–1971 school year is approximately $8.5 million.

Ten years after the start of the program the State contributes up to $40 for identification (on a one-time basis) and up to $60 per pupil per year for the extra costs of instruction. Over the past 10 years a number of legislative bills and studies pegged the needed support level at $150 to $200 per pupil, plus funds for identification.

A report published by the California Assembly Interim Committee on Education in 1967 stated:

> 1. Contrary to some popular notions, intellectually superior children are often the most neglected children in the classroom.
>
> 2. Talent development is an important part of any growing and productive state.
>
> 3. Without the intellectual and creative skills to meet the unknown problems of tomorrow, any society will begin to stagnate and decay.

The California Assembly ended its report with seven recommendations:

1. . . . We recommend that legislation more clearly establish the objectives in existing or altered MGM programs, and that the education of gifted children be given a more prominent place within the efforts of public schools.

2. . . . We recommend that the State increase its support to a maximum of $40 for identification and $200 for programs. . . . We recommend that a sample of the existing school district programs for mentally gifted minors be audited by the Office of the Auditor General to investigate the validity of expenditures that have been claimed for excess cost reimbursement.

3. We recommend that the State establish a system of scholarships for teachers of academically talented students to provide them with advanced training in subject matter specialties or in methods of teaching gifted children. . . .

4. We recommend that school districts be encouraged to seek the best qualified teachers, both in subject matter training and demonstrated competence in teaching ability and that some of the additional salary cost be offset by State aid. . . .

5. We recommend that State teaching credential restrictions on the grade level that can be taught be suspended for MGM programs, if it is certified that a teacher who is not ordinarily authorized to teach a particular grade level is the best available teacher for the gifted program and if the State Board of Education so approves.

6. . . . We recommend that provisions of the Education Code which specify certain subject matter and hours of instruction for public schools be suspended, upon approval of the State Board of Education, for authorized programs of instruction for mentally gifted minors.

7. We recommend the creation of a "Statewide Council on Talent Development," composed of lay and professional persons from all areas of public and private life, which would serve to study methods to improve the education of mentally gifted minors, transmit innovations in curriculum and instructional techniques to the public school authorities of the State, and stimulate improvements in the quality of education offered to all of the school children. The statewide council would be charged with the responsibility of presenting to the Legislature specific and periodic proposals for the improvement in public education for the academically talented and school children as a whole.

CONNECTICUT'S COMPREHENSIVE MODEL FOR THE EDUCATION OF THE GIFTED AND TALENTED

Author John Hersey was chairman of a special study committee in 1956 which compiled a comprehensive report of the needs for programs in Connecticut for the gifted and talented. Little or no action was taken on the Roberts Report (the committee report) until a nationwide search in 1965–66 for a consultant for the gifted and talented to provide leadership for the State and its 169 school districts.

Concurrently, the State Board of Education arranged for a comprehensive study of existing legislation related to the education of exceptional children (including the handicapped and the educationally gifted and talented). The 1966 report to the State Board of Education included:

1. An analysis of procedures, policies and problems.
2. An analysis of other conditions in the State which affected the efforts of local educational agencies.
3. A synthesis of the concerns and recommendations of persons within the State interested in exceptional children.
4. Recommendations concerning legislative policies and procedures.

The study found gaps and overlaps in the existing legislation for exceptional children. Some provisions were mandatory and others were left to local initiative. Some statutes delegated insufficient authority for enforcement of the mandate and for leadership and direction by the State Department of Education.

There existed a severe shortage of professional personnel competent to diagnose, direct, experiment, evaluate, and program for exceptional children. This observation indicated that institutions of higher learning had insufficient support by legislation for such service.

One of the most serious gaps uncovered in the study was the complete absence of legislation to provide for the education of gifted and talented pupils, those who are intellectually unchallenged by regular curriculum and strategy, and those who have outstanding talents in the creative arts (music, visual, and performing arts).

The study found the limitation of financial support a major block to adequate provisions for exceptional children. None of the needs were fully met; some were much more adequately served than others. The pattern of differences in classification for State funding complicated procedures for claiming State aid. Inadequate and inequitable funding encouraged the employment of less than competent personnel, improper grouping, disproportionate pupil-teacher ratios, and inadequate identification, programing, and evaluation services.

This study pointed to an all-encompassing piece of legislation for all exceptional children. The 1966 Chubbuck Report recommended that all exceptional children be serviced under an umbrella type of State legislation.

The State Board of Education approved the Chubbuck Report in the fall of 1966 and the Legislative Commission began work almost immediately on a "special education umbrella bill," which mandated school districts to provide programs and services to its mentally retarded, physically handicapped, socially and emotionally maladjusted, neurologically impaired, and those suffering from an identifiable learning disability; and permitted school districts to provide special education to pupils with extraordinary learning ability or outstanding talent in the creative arts.

The Connecticut statute is predicated on programing rather than numbers of children. The local school district submits a prior-approval for a program; once such a program is approved by the State agency, the local district is eligible to ask for two-thirds reimbursement of the program at the close of the fiscal year.

For the gifted and talented, the most consequential aspect of the statute is the provision for adequate funding to local school districts. A large number of school districts now have the vehicle for implementing programs.

Working in cooperation with the State education agency, the State's colleges and universities have helped increasing numbers of teachers and leadership personnel to improve their skills in differentiated curriculum for the gifted and talented.

In the fall of 1966, only *one course* was being offered in the entire State on the education of the gifted and talented; now there are three graduate level programs of training and four other institutions of higher learning offering course sequences in this area of special education.

Since 1967, when efforts to activate forces on behalf of the gifted and talented were begun, the numbers of local differentiated programs have moved from 4 school districts to 62 school districts. These 62 districts are serviced by 42 operational programs to cover many types of giftedness. Among the exemplary programs are:

1. An old college campus used as a talent retrieval center for disadvantaged gifted talent.

2. A mountain top used as a site for highly gifted and talented pupils in the earth and space science.

3. A renovated synagogue to serve as a high school center for pupils with outstanding talents in the creative arts from 18 surrounding school districts.

4. A six-room regional center for gifted and talented.

In addition to the programs in operation, 20 additional school districts are planning to implement programs for reimbursement in September 1971. More than 1,500 teachers, counselors, and leadership personnel have enrolled in courses, inservice training, and workshops to prepare for impending programs, and over 2,500 professional personnel have attended short-term institutes and conferences devoted entirely to programing for gifted and talented pupils. The model to increase the quantity and quality of programs for the gifted is directly related to three basic elements:

1. A sound legal and properly funded statute to provide reimbursement to local school districts for special programs and/or services for the gifted and talented.

2. Provision of full-time consultive leadership by the State education agency to assist local school districts in programming for the gifted and talented.

3. A coordinated and articulated program for teacher training and retraining in the area of the gifted and talented.

GEORGIA'S PROGRAM FOR THE INTELLECTUALLY GIFTED

The Georgia Department of Education Program for the Intellectually Gifted is now in its 13th year. Interest within the State for such programs dates back to a 1958 House Resolution requesting the status and plans for education of Georgia's gifted children.

A small publication on education of the gifted, made available to all public school and Department personnel, began a series for school officials.

A consultant on the gifted was added to the program staff in 1958 to provide services to public school systems interested in beginning special programs for the intellectually gifted. The first years were spent in:

1. Surveying the State to determine the status of special programs for the intellectually gifted.

2. Orienting State Department of Education, university, college, and public school personnel as well as laymen to the status of programs for the intellectually gifted in the State and the Nation.

3. Providing inservice training for department personnel.

4. Developing plans for demonstration or experimental projects.

5. Providing consultive services to public school systems, colleges, and universities.

From July 1960 to July 1961, the consultant participated in the Southern Regional Education Board project, Education of the Gifted, a training program designed to place within Southern State departments of education one person informed on education of the gifted. The department accepted the responsibility for developing a 10-year plan of action. This plan was developed by the consultant working with two committees—a statewide committee of public school, State department, and university people; and a State Department of Education committee.

This plan, approved in principle by the Georgia Department of Education's Coordination Committee, recognizes the right of individuals and the need for special programs for those who differ from most children and youth. It permits a flexible State program with standards that can be adapted to metropolitan, urban or rural students' needs.

Student participants were defined as those with an I.Q. of 120 and above who could profit from unusual academic challenges.

At the April 1961 meeting of the State Board of Education, one project per congressional district was approved. Projects began in the fall of 1961 and operated through the 1963–64 school year, when they were terminated because of limited funds. According to information from the participating systems, the projects were successful and those phases which could become parts of the regular school instruction program without financial support were absorbed.

The passage of the new Minimum Foundation Program of Education Act of the 1964 General Assembly established the Governor's Honors Program. The basic plan for operating this program was developed by the consultant for the gifted, a department committee, and a statewide committee. The program is now in its 8th year of operation. A second consultant on the gifted was added to the department staff in 1967 to work with the Governor's Honors program.

Action by the 1968 General Assembly brought new emphasis to program development for the intellectually gifted. House Bill 453 mandated special programs for all exceptional children, including the intellectually gifted, by school year 1975–1976. To help implement this bill, the State Board of Education approved a new State program for the intellectually gifted. The State Superintendent of Schools asked that present State laws and operations be examined to see how special programs could be established with no additional appropriation by the General Assembly. Past experience showed that such requests were deleted from budgets prepared by the Budget Bureau for presentation to the General Assembly. The approved plan allowed one instructional person in the area of the gifted to a school system submitting an approved program plan.

The opening of the 1969–70 school year brought 20 special programs for the intellectually gifted in 20 school systems. The number of systems operating special programs grew to 44 by the 1970–71 school year.

The approved plan stipulated that the plan be evaluated each year. Since approval in 1968, Georgia's State plan has been revised so school systems may use more than one allotment in the area of the gifted, provided the personnel involved are:

1. Coordinators of programs for the gifted or consultants in the area of the gifted,
2. Resource teachers to work with all classroom teachers having intellectually gifted, or
3. Resource teachers who work part time with classroom teachers having gifted students, and part time with gifted students.

The present State program for the gifted is two-fold: (1) local schoolyear program, and (2) the Governor's Honors Program for 400 gifted high school juniors and seniors.

In 1970–71, 44 school systems were operating approved State-supported programs during the regular school year. Participating are 4,871 students in grades 1 to 12. These programs provide for those whose mental ability places them in the upper 2 to 5 percent of the general school population.

The Governor's Honors Program is an 8-week summer residential program for 400 upcoming juniors and seniors who have either high mental ability or a special talent in art, music, or drama.

Both State-operated programs are totally financed with State funds. Approximately $409,175 were spent on regular school programs and $279,566 for the Governor's Honors Programs, making a total of $688,741 spent on special programs for the gifted and talented during FY 1971.

In November 1970, the State Board of Education approved the gifted as an endorsement area for a teaching certificate. Personnel in the area of the gifted may be professionally certified in the area of the gifted if they complete 25 quarter hours of appropriate specialized study. This approval was brought about through involvement of a Georgia Teacher Education Council Committee. Through the Department's Unit Teacher Recruitment and Special Programs, a small number of grants are available for special study in the area of the gifted. The State Board of Education has named the area as a critical field of education for which special teacher preparation is necessary.

At the present time, only one graduate institution in Georgia offers a series of teacher preparation courses in gifted education. However, two other graduate institutions are planning such courses.

Since January 1958, a number of activities related to the education of the gifted have been carried out by the Georgia Department of Education. Many of the goals set forth in the 10-year plan of action have been reached, in full or in part.

ILLINOIS' SPECIAL PROGRAM FOR THE GIFTED

Out of the initial planning phase, 1959–1963, a set of principles emerged for the rationale of the Illinois Plan:

1. *Gifted children exist within all levels of society, within all racial and ethnic groups, and they come from every kind of home.* Any programs to develop their talents must be concerned with their diversity. Among the differences which vitally affect program development are the differences between elementary and secondary schools, between urban and rural setting, and between gifted children whose school achievement is high and those whose achievement is low.

2. *A State plan must take into account the ways in which innovation occurs in schools.* Brickell's study of innovation in the schools of New York State indicates that journal articles, convention speeches, and research papers are less influential in fostering change than is the onsite visit by the practitioner of a school in which the changes have been programmed and put into operation.

3. The General Assembly has delegated major responsibility for the operation of schools to local boards of education. *In recommending State action we do not intend to displace or discourage local initiative.* We would like to expand the range of possibilities open to local districts in providing for their gifted children . . .

4. Research on gifted children has gone forward for more than 40 years. We now know more than enough to support extensive, and more adequate programs for gifted children. Yet our current knowledge and our current best efforts are sure to be modified as research in this area continues at an accelerated pace. *Thus State action, while necessary, must be flexible and must not establish rigid formulas and detailed prescriptions.* Study and experimentation should continue with State support so that improvement may be continuous and responsive to new scientific findings.

The five parts of the Illinois plan are:

1. Reimbursement for Services and Materials

Any school district in Illinois may submit a plan for improving its services to gifted children. The district may employ its own definition of giftedness. State funds may be used for services such as counseling, diagnosis, and consultation on a variety of problems, for books and other materials, or for inservice teacher training.

Reimbursement funds may not be used to pay teachers' salaries, and the funds are limited in application to fewer than 5 percent of the pupils enrolled in the district. The distribution formula takes account of the wealth of the district and the number of gifted pupils served. Application procedures are simple and school districts are allowed wide latitude in expending funds. Funds provide only an average of $28 per pupil each year.

Total expenditures for reimbursement, 1963–71, are $19,450,000 or 59.8 percent of total expenditures for the Illinois Plan.

2. Demonstration Centers

Demonstration centers provide for all Illinois educators and other citizens convincing and readily accessible operating programs using particular approaches to educate gifted children.

At the outset, demonstration centers were expected to exemplify the following approaches:

a. Acceleration of highly gifted pupils.

b. Individualized instruction through such means as team teaching, nongraded plans, independent study.

c. Special classes for the highly gifted, with specially trained teachers, supervisors and consultants.

d. Special attention to gifted youth among socially and culturally underprivileged groups.

e. Curriculum improvement through programs which emphasize higher level thought processes, creativity, divergent thinking.

f. Special attention to the emotional and social adjustment of gifted pupils.

Each demonstration center is responsible for showing the program to visitors and for evaluating the program. Where possible, each demonstration center is the responsibility of at least one full-time professional staff member of the local district.

By 1970, 26 demonstration centers were in operation, employing an expanded set of functions. Total expenditures, 1963–71, are $6,300,000, or 19.4 percent of the total.

3. Experimental Projects

To advance knowledge about practical programs for the gifted, the State has provided funds for experimental projects in school districts, colleges and universities.

Total expenditures for experimental projects, 1963–71, are $2,274,000, or 7 percent of the total.

4. State Staff

To administer the program of reimbursement, demonstration, experimentation, and training, a Department of Program Development for Gifted Children was established in the Office of the Superintendent of Public Instruction.

Total expenditures for administration at the State level, 1963–71, are $21,103,900, or 6 percent of the total.

5. Training Program

To help meet the great need for specially trained personnel to carry out the other parts of the plan, State support is provided for fellowships, academic year institutes, and summer institutes.

Total expenditures 1963–71, are $2,524,000, or 7.8 percent of the total.

In evaluating the two major components, Illinois measured the effectiveness of their politics and practices.

The program of reimbursement of materials and services has successfully supported significant educational improvements based upon proven practices related to programs for gifted children. There has been an enormous increase in the number and extent of local gifted programs. Many new programs have been initiated and most students are now in districts with such programs.

The number of teachers, special personnel, and students in classes has also increased. Many districts are using special materials and methodologies.

The program has been less successful in saving talent by identification and development of pupils who, despite high ability, have not acquired the necessary knowledge and skills to fully utilize this ability.

There is considerable "spill-over" of techniques originated in gifted classes into regular classes. Many regular techers are also being trained in the inservice programs. In their effect on the regular school program, the special programs for the gifted have been highly successful.

The least successful effort has been to incorporate evaluation procedures in all phases of the program. Only 15 percent of the districts have minimally adequate evaluation.

Personnel and knowledge, rather than physical facilities, are the major limitations for future development of the individual programs.

The centers, for the most part, have excellent programs, but visitors have not adapted whole programs.

All demonstration centers were successful in establishing programs that met the requirements of the State policy: 1) internal consistency; 2) research basis; 3) educational significance; 6) exportability; 7) uniqueness; and 8) growth in quality.

These four States demonstrate the possibilities for gifted programs when commitment is evident. Each State, however, has been handicapped by the lack of Federal assistance, which chapter VII will discuss.

CHAPTER VII

The Federal Role—The USOE Delivery System

Part C, section 806 of Public Law 91–230 stipulates that the Commissioner of Education shall:

show which existing Federal educational assistance programs are being used to meet the needs of gifted and talented children, and

evaluate how existing Federal educational assistance can be more effectively used to meet these needs....

LEGAL FRAMEWORK FOR OE PROGRAMS

In response to this mandate, investigations of the legal framework within which educational programs are developed included:

titles I, II, III, V, and VIII of the Elementary and Secondary Education Act (ESEA) as amended through 1970,

the Education of the Handicapped Act, replacing title VI of ESEA as of July 1, 1971,

the Higher Education Act of 1965,

the National Defense Education Act of 1958 (NDEA),

the Cooperative Research Act,

the Economic Opportunity Act of 1964, and the

Vocational Education Act of 1963.

This review was primarily concerned with legislation which specifically mentioned the gifted and talented as recipients for program funds, and legislative restrictions that would disallow funds for this population.[1]

A review of this material indicated no restrictions within these laws that would bar funds from the gifted and talented. In most cases, however, the main thrust of the legislation is for a targeted population such as the disadvantaged or handicapped, so that gifted and talented children could only be served by these program funds if they are also disadvantaged or handicapped. Although funds could reach gifted and talented students through such legislation, it is rare to find funds being used in this way for two reasons: 1) Because the legislation does not specifically mandate programs for gifted and talented, the interpreters of the legislation do not entertain using funds this way, and 2) since gifted and talented are not an identified priority at the Federal level, program officers do not focus on this population.

Other than Public Law 91–230, the amendment of titles III and V of ESEA, and the teacher fellowship portion of the Higher Education Act, no legislation specifically mentions this population.

---

[1] Appendix G of this report provides more specific information about the population and how these data were derived, as well as other details of the assessment of the OE delivery system. Arthur D. Little, Inc. conducted the study under contract to the Office of Education.

ESEA, title III, stipulates that funds can be used for gifted and talented children. It allows funds for special instruction and equipment for students interested in advanced scientific subjects, foreign languages, and other academic areas not taught in local schools. It specifies funds can be used for modern educational equipment and qualified personnel, including artists and musicians, on a temporary basis for the benefit of children. This legislation also allows funds for testing students to identify those with outstanding aptitudes and abilities.

ESEA, title V, allows funds to be used by local (LEA) and State (SEA) agencies for consulting help and technical services in particular areas of education. Some SEA's are using title V funds for salaries for part-time consultants on the gifted and talented.

Evidence from the contracted study demonstrates that unless funds are earmarked by legislation for a targeted population, it is highly unlikely that any funds will be expended on gifted and talented youth to meet their needs, except as disadvantaged youth, handicapped youth, etc. This handicapped population was in the same situation as the gifted and talented until it became a designated population under title VI of ESEA. The development of the Education for the Handicapped Act provides an instructive model of focusing Federal funds on a targeted area of concern.

The Education Professions Development Act (EPDA) provides for funding programs or projects to prepare teachers and other educational personnel to meet the special needs of exceptionally gifted students and to prepare artists, craftsmen, scientists, artisans, etc., to teach or otherwise assist in educational programs or projects. Since the gifted and talented are not a major USOE priority and because there is not a large grassroots advocacy group, this part of the EPDA is not emphasized.

Although the National Defense Education Act of 1968 (NDEA) does not specifically mention gifted and talented children, it does fund strengthening of instruction in science, mathematics, modern foreign languages, and other subjects. By extension of the implication of NDEA, funds could be channeled for developing programs in these areas for gifted and talented children and youth. This law views top-grade instruction in these areas as critical to the protection of this country, and by implication, the development of students gifted or talented in these areas as a national resource to be developed. This act could be part of a delivery system for the gifted and talented.

The Cooperative Research Act enables the OE to conduct research, surveys, and demonstration projects, and to disseminate information derived from these activities. The Commissioner can also make grants to other agencies to assist in providing training and research in education. In situations beneficial to this country, the Commissioner can make grants to appropriate agencies to construct facilities for conducting such research.

Review of the legal framework for USOE programs indicates no direct barrier to serving gifted and talented children and youth via a USOE delivery system using Federal funds. Since the legislation does target specific populations other than gifted and talented, the gifted and talented can be served by present USOE programs if they are part of the legally specified population. ESEA, titles III and V, are the only major pieces of legislation targeted for elementary and secondary students that specifically mentioned the gifted and talented.

RELATIONSHIP BETWEEN THE OFFICE OF EDUCATION, STATE EDUCATIONAL AGENCIES, AND LOCAL EDUCATIONAL AGENCIES

In assessing the Office of Education delivery system of programs targeted for the gifted and talented, it is necessary to consider the relationships within the educational system. The smallest unit in this hierarchy is the individual school in some local educational agency. These schools are subordinate to some local governing unit such as a local school board and superintendent or a consortium. Such an LEA generally determines the policy that governs its schools. If citizens can bring enough pressure to bear at this point, they can help shape the educational priorities of their school system.

The local school board, usually through the superintendent of schools, is subject to its State Education Agency policies through the leverage of funds. In all States, money appropriated for educational purposes reaches the LEA only if the LEA complies with regulations and guidelines set by the SEA.

The SEA generally works within the framework of its State laws and Federal laws and regulations. The Federal Government also uses money leverage to affect SEA priorities, which are also subject to influence by citizens and LEA pressure. In responding to controls and guidelines from USOE, the SEA might have direct contact with a bureau, an office or a regional office.

Under the direction of the Commissioner and his deputies, the USOE interprets laws and makes them operational. The bureaus act as catalysts between the laws and the SEA's and LEA's. USOE does not dictate what happens in the schools but through its bureaus and offices set guidelines for programing that SEA's and LEA's can use in applying for funds. The SEA or LEA can alter Federal priorities to meet local needs if the use can be justified under the guidelines.

Any delivery system targeted for gifted and talented children must go through this chain before the student is finally affected.

IMPLICATIONS OF FINDINGS

Some ESEA, title III funds and title V funds are being specifically used for the gifted and talented. The amount of such funds is so low— less than $10 per treated student, that one can conclude:

There is virtually no USOE delivery system of education programs for the gifted and talented children and youth of this country.

Many factors account for this situation; but each is so closely intertwined with others that the delivery system is a package. Six major influences militate against the development of a Federal delivery system of an educational package targeted at our gifted and talented:

1. Although the need for such programs has been established in research and via some interested professional and lay groups, it has not received wide support among American educators and, hence, little public support except for parents of gifted and talented children.

2. There is no categorical Federal legislation which establishes the gifted and talented as a targeted population. This has kept the visibility of these children very low and makes it difficult to focus Federal resources on the area. (Public Law 91–230 is a recent exception.)

3. Since priorities do not focus on this population, present USOE activities do not include gifted and talented children and youth as a targeted population. Once existing funds have been disbursed to meet the priorities and crises of OE, there is little likelihood of money reaching these students.

4. The relationship of the Federal Government to State and local education agencies had traditionally been one of nonintervention. Statutory program funds have been distributed to these agencies for use as they see fit within the broad guidelines of the law. This permits general priority setting at State and local levels to meet local needs and priority concerns.

5. The expressed priority of gifted and talented children and youth is so low within USOE that although discretionary funds could be used to provide programs, this avenue is seldom used.

6. Since there is no Federal educational focus on and leadership within the area of the gifted and talented, locally funded programs targeted for this population have functioned in isolation, preventing sharing of knowledge and further development of programs nationally.

These six circumstances function as barriers against the development of a Federal educational delivery system for the gifted and talented. At the same time, unmet needs at the State and local level must be resolved if a Federal delivery system is to operate effectively in the field. Specific needs are for:

1. A national center or agency to fulfill the role of monitoring, assessing, and coordinating the present (limited) program activity for the gifted and talented to coalesce them into a significant countrywide effort.

2. Some agency or intermediate office to coordinate and disseminate research efforts which can catalyze these efforts into significant program activity at the local and State level.

3. A centralized, objective agency to evaluate which lines of program activity have been successful in delivering programs to the gifted and talented.

4. Leadership which can fulfill not only the above three needs but also, through interaction with LEA's and SEA's, assist them in setting program priorities, focusing resources, and planning program activity to meet these needs.

FRAMEWORK FOR FURTHER PROGRAMING

In order to develop within the Office of Education an effective delivery system of programing for gifted and talented children and youth, it will be necessary to remove or substantially reduce the barriers outlined above and also to develop a process that will meet the needs for leadership in developing State and local program activity for these students. The contracted study recommended the following as part of a frame work for helping this happen:

Some mechanism or agency should be set up within USOE to coordinate national activity in the area of programs for gifted and talented children and youth which can fulfill the leadership needs outlined above. In order to make this mechanism or agency most effective, a process must be developed which can remove or neutralize the barriers which at present militate against the existence of a delivery system within USOE.

Legislation should be enacted which focuses attention and priority on gifted and talented children and youth. This legislation should provide funds to assist SEA's and LEA's in developing a delivery system for their own areas. The determination to provide support by means of categorical and formula funds should be carefully weighed in order to insure that USOE can meet the needs of the leadership role. If noncategorical funds alone are provided, it is unlikely that they can be used to provide leadership and it is unlikely that they will have strong impact on the target population.

This legislation should provide for funds to be used at each level of activity within a complete delivery system. This includes activity at the teacher training level, activity at the LEA and SEA leadership level, activity at the research level, activity at the applied level for utilizing results of the research and activity and at the dissemination level for maximizing the possible return and ripple effort of successful program efforts.

The mechanism or agency set up should work very closely with many divisions and bureaus across the USOE spectrum, e.g., the Bureau of Educational Personnel Development, the National Center for Educational Research and Development, the Bureau of Higher Education, the Bureau of Elementary and Secondary Education, Experimental Schools, Office of Program Planning and Evaluation, and the National Center for Educational Communication. Failure to set up a mechanism to capitalize upon present expertise and structure within USOE will not only result in expending funds for duplicative services but it will also lessen the opportunity to focus the energies and interests of cooperative bureaus and divisions on the development of a delivery system within USOE.

Programs and project planning funded from USOE should meet stringent requirements. Any project approved for funds should declare how it is building upon the present body of knowledge regarding gifted and talented, and specify the assumptions it is predicated on and the programing built on the assumptions to produce the expected outcomes.

All programs to be funded should not only declare their evaluation plans ahead of time, they should also declare what kinds of conclusions are expected from the collected data. Failure to meet this requirement will seriously impair what can be learned from the programs.

Provisions on a national scale must be made for communicating local program results to research centers and for communicating research results to the LEA's and SEA's. The results of these efforts should, in turn, be communicated to help all educators understand the needs of gifted and talented children and youth, the ways in which these needs can be met, and how to effectively plan to meet these needs.

The framework itself, however, is not sufficient to insure a successful delivery system. It is necessary to provide for continuity of program priorities across changes in administration. For example, in the late 1950's, with the dawn of the space age, national attention was focused on the gifted through a series of NSF and NDEA programs, but those initial efforts have lost their impact because the priorities of the 1960's shifted to the problems of poverty and the disadvantaged. It is further important to maintain program continuity when a new Commissioner of Education takes office. This continuity of focus does not mean that new administrations of Commissioners of Education should not be able to set their own priorities but will insure payoffs from programs scheduled to run for several years.

STRATEGIES AND ENTRY POINTS

Given that USOE sets up an agency or mechanism as the focus for a national, coordinated delivery system, what avenues should USOE pursue in establishing this agency and what are the best entry points within the USOE for it?

Three alternative strategies to set up an agency or mechanism are:

(1) USOE could create a new bureau solely responsible for GTCY;

(2) USOE could create a new division within a bureau; or

(3) USOE could set up a GTCY Program Group with the responsibility to coordinate or orchestrate and focus resources for GTCY.

Appendix G discusses the pros and cons of each strategy, along with procedures for fitting each into the existing structure.

The final chapter summarizes the findings in this and preceding chapters and proposes some immediate steps in response to the major deficiencies uncovered.

CHAPTER VIII

Summary, Findings, and the Office of Education's Response

The Commissioner's study has produced many recommendations from various sources concerning the need for special programs, suggested priorities in planning individual programs, estimates of the professional support and teacher training required, and adjustments in legal definitions that would enhance the possibility of State and local fiscal support. Details on these recommendations may be found in the text or in the appendixes of this report.

The steps to be taken by the Office of Education in response to these recommendations are, however, the responsibility of the Commissioner of Education. These follow the summary and major findings of the study outlined below. While they reflect the needs indicated by various contributors, they are also tailored to 1) the desire for some immediate action consonant with other priorities identified within the program of the Office of Education and 2) a consistent and sustained effort over several years.

SUMMARY AND MAJOR FINDINGS

There can be few, if any, exceptions to the observations threading throughout this study that the gifted and talented youth are a unique population, differing markedly from their age peers in abilities, talents, interests, and psychological maturity. The most versatile and complex of all human groups, they suffer the neglect that is typical of all groups with special educational needs. Their sensitivity to others and insight into existing school conditions make them especially vulnerable; they frequently conceal their giftedness in standardized surroundings. The resultant waste in human terms and national resources is tragic.

The relatively few gifted students who have had the advantage of special programs have shown remarkable improvements in self-understanding and in ability to relate to others as well as in improved academic and creative performance. But many more young people go unnoticed. Very little identification has been carried on in depth, or with proper testing instruments. Many of the assumptions about giftedness and its incidence in various parts of American society are based on inadequate data, partial information, and group tests of limited value.

According to the testimony and experience of professionals and parents of gifted and talented, our educational system has been inconsistent in seeking the gifted and talented, finding them early in their lives and individualizing their education. Our educational system mirrors society's ambivalence and inconsistency toward the gifted and talented. Special injustice has occurred through apathy toward certain minorities, although neglect of the gifted in this country is a universal and increasing problem.

The major findings of the study—those with particular relevance to the future planning of the Office of Education—may be summarized as follows:

A conservative estimate of gifted and talented children ranges between 1.5 and 2.5 million out of a total elementary and secondary school population (1970 estimate) of 51.6 million.

Existing service to gifted and talented children and youth do not reach large and significant subpopulations (e.g., minorities and disadvantaged) and serve only a very small percentage of the gifted and talented elementary and secondary population generally.

Differentiated education for the gifted and talented is presently perceived as a very low priority at Federal, State, and most local levels of government and educational administration.

Although 22 States have legislation to provide resources to school districts for services to the gifted and talented, such legislation in many cases merely represents intent.

Even where there is a legal or administrative basis for provision of services, funding priorities, crisis concerns, and lack of personnel cause programs for the gifted to be miniscule or theoretical.

There is an enormous individual and social cost when talent among the Nation's children and youth goes undiscovered and undeveloped. These students cannot ordinarily excel without assistance.

Identification of the gifted is hampered not only by costs of appropriate testing—when these methods are known and adopted—but stem also from apathy and even hostility among teachers, administrators, guidance counselors, and psychologists.

Gifted and talented children are, in fact, deprived and disadvantaged, and can suffer psychological damage and permanent impairment of their abilities to function well which is equal to or greater than the similar deprivation suffered by any other population with special needs served by the Office of Education.

Special services for the gifted and talented will, in fact, also serve other target populations such as the disadvantaged singled out for attention and support.

Services provided to gifted and talented children can and do produce significant and measurable outcomes.

States (and local communities) look to the Federal Government for leadership in this area of education, with or without massive funding.

The Federal role in delivery of services to the gifted and talented is presently all but nonexistent.

These findings, which are documented in the appendixes, provide ample evidence of the need for action to eliminate the widespread neglect of this population. Federal leadership in this effort is required to confirm and establish provisions for the gifted and talented as a national priority, and to encourage the States to include this priority in their own planning. The experiences of the disadvantaged and handicapped tells us that little is done systematically for special needy groups until the Federal Government takes an interest and stimulates action.

THE OFFICE OF EDUCATION'S RESPONSE

The findings of this study are not surprising. It is obvious that the attention to the gifted which arose almost 50 years ago has waxed and waned but never reached the level of a total national commitment. The Sixties marked a reversal of the strong interest during the Fifties, originally sparked by foundation programs supporting advanced placement, early admission to college and similar changes toward individualization, and by strong government support for science programs at the end of the decade.

Commissioner S. P. Marland, Jr. has observed that a curve of funding support would show a profile of our society itself, the work of education generally, but especially the work of the Office of Education. The Office of Education is concerned about that distribution curve. There has been inadequate attention to the disadvantaged, to improved vocational education and education for the handicapped, to the thrust for equal education opportunities, to integration. All of these are massive programs to solve massive problems.

That is where our priorities have been. That is where the priorities of this Administration are. We are working hard on these problems.

But over on the other side of the curve are other neglected people. In terms of our national expenditure profile, the Commissioner has emphasized, we are not letting it be known that we are concerned about them. We are not flying the flag for those great intellects that are brighter than most of the rest of us and who, indeed, might help us to raise our sights. Thousands, tragically undiscovered, are in the very populations (such as the disadvantaged, the handicapped, and minorities) on whom we are concentrating in other ways. Adequate attention to the gifted and talented is needed to round out our educational program.

We educators need to reach these gifted young people, to encourage them, and to release them. We can do it and still work on the priorities for all of the disadvantaged minorities and others long neglected in our society. We can do it at the Federal level, the Commissioner has emphasized; it can be done at the State and local levels as well.

A single school administrator can deploy what energies he has, what energies his faculty has, what resources the Board of Education has in ways that are compatible with, but which will still not handicap the rest of his program.

None of these comments implies a "track system" for the gifted. Educators can do so much for so very little with able children simply by freeing them under teachers who recognize and respect them. There are community resources we have not begun to tap to reinforce the efforts of the schools.

It does not take a lot of money, and it does not necessarily take new laws, but it does take concern and interest and commitment.

To inject this feeling and proposition into a system ,whether a large or a small system, there has to be an individual in charge of giving complete and full-time commitment and creativity to it. There are any number of devices for structuring change in a system. But in the end it depends upon the wisdom and creativity of that person in charge and whether the chief executive officer wants to back up the person and help him or her to move.

Of the items cited in the study, other than the general neglect of the gifted and talented population, the most frequently mentioned was the need for placing leadership persons in visible positions at the State and Federal level. S. P. Marland, Jr., recently stated: "With this report, I, as Commissioner of Education, become a visible advocate for increased attention to this group of young people. Rather than proposing extensive objectives now, either in terms of money or legislation, I believe we ought to initiate those things we can realistically accomplish immediately within the Office of Education in order to meet the problems suggested in the study. The end product of this study will never be reached wholly. It will continue to grow, we hope, and remain infinite in its possibilities. But first it must begin and we believe the most appropriate way is by injecting the principle of action on behalf of the gifted into our ongoing programs."

The Office of Education will institute within its operational planning system specific goals and objectives for an increased Federal role of education for gifted and talented children. The Commissioner has announced his intention to establish a nucleus program staff under the Deputy Commissioner for School Systems; the director of this staff will, in effect, be "in charge" of the gifted and talented group on behalf of the Office of Education. The responsibilities of the program staff will be to develop viable plans for the utilization and management of various OE resources which can be committed to this effort. This is not a program with a one-year priority life. Part of the operational planning system provides for a continuum and a maintenance of national focus on this effort.

Some preliminary Federal objectives, based on the study's recommendations, are:

> To establish a working program group for gifted and talented education

> To increase the number and capability of staff responsible for gifted and talented education in the regional offices and the State education agencies

> To expand the availability of improved instruments and procedures to identify gifted and talented students and to evaluate programs for this group

> To increase the number of gifted and talented who are served by high quality programs.

Eleven action steps have been developed as feasibility or data development projects to help meet these objectives on a short-term basis while an integrated plan is devised.

The 5-year planning cycle begins with the implementation report described under action step 1 (see below). The remaining steps are concerned with immediate actions to establish the leadership function in the Office of Education and to maximize the spread of this effort to the States and local education agencies. These are immediate steps the Office of Education can and will take in 1972 to launch the Federal program for the gifted and talented. No new legislation is needed for them. These changes can be initiated while long-range planning is begun at the Federal, State, and local levels, by both the public and private sectors, to systematically ameliorate problems identified in this study.

1. *Planning Report.*—The Deputy Commissioner for School Systems will complete a planning report for the Commissioner on implementing a Federal role in education of gifted and talented children by February 1, 1972. This report will provide continuity between the study and the implementation of action steps by USOE. To be included in this report are recommendations concerning:

—quantitative objectives and goals for gifted and talented education.

—identification of and planning for public and private responsibilities in national emphasis on improving educational opportunities for gifted and talented children.

—strengthening of State-Federal relationships in education of gifted and talented.

—programmatic and administrative requirements for expansion of programs nationally.

—roles of public and private institutions for the creative and performing arts in the identification and development and operation phases.

—administrative requirements for the Office-of Education program, including regulations, guidelines, budget, staffing, and staff support.

2. *Program Responsibility.*—Assignment of continuing program responsibility for gifted and talented education within USOE will be made to the Deputy Commissioner for School Systems with the expectation of further delegation to the Bureau of Education for the Handicapped (BEH). The established BEH national structure of services, staff training programs, media development centers, research and network for dissemination, will greatly enhance the outcome of even minimal resources within USOE for gifted and talented education.

Because of the comparability of certain considerations in programming for all areas of exceptionality in education, the addition of this responsibility to the Bureau of Education for the Handicapped would be entirely consonant with existing responsibilities of this bureau. Clearly, however, program funds must be specifically separate and additional to funds appropriated for education of the handicapped or must be identified for cooperative application with BEH and other OE units.

A staff program group will initially consist of three professional positions with appropriate secretarial and staff support services. This will become the Gifted and Talented Program Group, a nucleus staff to be augmented by working relationships with staff from programs throughout the Department which have significant potential to benefit gifted and talented children (e.g., title I, title V, ESEA, Talent Search, Upward Bound and Early Childhood programs). From the elementary-secondary level, the staff will work up through higher education and down through preschool education to promote continuity throughout the school system. The program group will have line authority in administration of programs specifically for gifted and talented education. They will furnish information and seek the advice of regional, State, and local specialists as well as gifted and talented pupils and their parents.

3. *Nationwide Inventory and Assessment of Current Programs.*— The program group will supervise a field survey of programs for the gifted and talented across the country in order to:

Obtain information on successful programs and program elements—as judged by gifted and talented students themselves, and by their parents, peers, teachers, and communities.

Develop more precise cost figures on alternative approaches to education of specific groups of students.

Improve evaluation procedures and encourage their incorporation in all programs for the gifted and talented.

Furnish the bases for model programs which can be field tested for acceptability, student achievement and creative productivity, and relative costs.

Develop a clearinghouse on gifted and talented education.

Under the direction of the program group, the survey will be conducted by gifted and talented students working as summer interns in the Office of Education. The students will be encouraged to submit a report detailing their own recommendations on future directions for special programs. The Office's program planning and evaluation staff and other resources will be utilized for technical elements of this project.

4. *Strengthening State Education Agencies.*—USOE will utilize title V, ESEA and other authorizations to strengthen State education agencies. Meetings with SEA's and other means will also be planned to improve the capability of SEA's to institute or improve their programs for gifted and talented education.

5. *Leadership Development and Training.*—USOE will support in the summer of 1972 two national leadership training institutes to upgrade supervisory personnel and program planning for the gifted at the State level. This will involve cooperative arrangements, drawing on the prototype programs in several States where teachers of the gifted receive specialized training in centers attended by selected highly gifted high school juniors and seniors and recent graduates. In the national institutes, participating leaders will include the following representatives: 1) officials from a cadre of States, 2) a specialist in education for the gifted, 3) a person with legislative staff experience, and 4) gifted and talented students. The program of the institute will aim at the development of a strategic plan for the education of gifted and talented, with all participants including the students differentiating their own roles in such a process. Following services from the centralized staff of the institute are envisioned as an integral part of the program.

For these purposes, grants of approximately $100,000 each will be made to two State departments of education. Applicants for these grants will be required to identify matching or other sources of funds to support the non-training parts of the summer programs. In fiscal year 1973, USOE will also support 6 planning grants to encourage replication of the national institutes in other States.

6. *Research and Development for Minority Groups.*—USOE will support additional program activities in two major research and de velopment institutions which have the interest and capacity to work

on learning problems and opportunities among minority groups. These activities are specifically designed to call attention to the presence of numerous gifted and talented in these groups, cited in the Commissioner's study, and to provide needed research in the development of appropriate models for their education.

One contract, at about $25,000, will support an intensive search for children of high potential among its specific target population of disadvantaged preschool-aged children, and to demonstrate and evaluate differentiated education for the highly gifted and talented in this group. Another contract, at about $50,000, will develop and test an accelerated bilingual program for highly intellectually gifted children among the Mexican-Americans and other children in their schools.

A particular objective of each contract will be the development of improved instruments to detect the gifted and talented in these populations.

7. *Career Education Models.*—USOE will build on the career education models being developed by the National Center for Educational Research and Development (NCERD) by including program activities specific to employer-based career education for the gifted and talented. The career education models are designed to display the wide range of work possibilities and to provide earlier opportunities (grades one to 14) for students to explore and test out a variety of occupational fields at all levels. The employer-based model acknowledges that much learning does take place in non-academic settings and provides the opportunities for the gifted and talented to work with professionals and experts other than educators, a need cited in the Commissioner's study.

The current models under development will accommodate the needs of some gifted students by providing them with apprenticeship work experiences attached to advanced positions in management, computing, planning commissions, and the like. A plan specifically for the talented, in institutions related to the performing arts, will be developed after the general models have been tested. Approximately $200,000 will be devoted to the design and pilot testing of such a plan in 1973.

8. *Experimental Schools.*—The Commissioner has asked that at least one of the comprehensive experimental school projects devote attention to the individualization of programs to benefit the gifted and talented students as a component of the compehensive design to effect education reform. This activity is in direct response to a significant finding of the study that in early childhood, gifted and talented students are most neglected, and where special attention is provided there is inadequate and insufficient follow-through in the total educational environment.

9. *Supplementary Plans and Centers.*—Tile III, ESEA, has already been used by many States to support their program activities in gifted and talented education. In FY 1972 and FY 1973, USOE will continue to encourage these activities through communication with State education agencies, issuance of program guidelines and cooperative assignment of USOE title III program staff to the Gifted and Talented Program Group.

10. *Regional Offices.*—One staff member will be identified in each of the ten Regional Offices of Education as responsible, at least part time, for gifted and talented education. The relevant activities will include

liaison with the Office of Education national office, developmental assistance to the State education agencies, continuous dissemination of information, and management of specialized regional activities as they arise.

11. *Higher Education.*—The existing OE programs relating to higher education will be carefully studied by the Gifted and Talented Program Group in order to optimize their potential for the talented population and their teachers. The objectives of the Talent Search, Upward Bound and Student Aid programs relate to disadvantaged, low-income, and minority groups, many of them underachieving gifted and talented students. These higher education programs have as their clientele the secondary school-age group from which students of particularly high potential are identified and supported in extending their horizons to facilitate their success at institutions of higher learning. Fellowships are available for potential higher education personnel, who would educate potential teachers of the gifted and talented.

The expertise of staff personnel in the above-mentioned programs will be utilized as part of the Gifted and Talented Program Group, with the expectation of expanding the current focus and better identifying and serving the needs of the high potential disadvantaged student at the elementary and secondary level.

"Equal education is the foundation of the right to be a human being. . . . This does not mean that any gifted child or any child having a greater capability to learn may or shall be deprived of his or her opportunity of learning more. It does mean that every child shall have the equal opportunity to learn to the best of his or her ability. That opportunity must be made available to all on equal terms."— Alfred Gitelson, *Judge, County of Los Angeles, Superior Court Case 822854*

As quoted in "The Bulletin of the Gifted Children's Association, San Fernando Valley, Inc.," May 1971.

Identification and
Measurement Instruments

EXPERIENCE AND INTEREST INVENTORY*

Student _____   Grade _____

Birth date _____   Homeroom _____

Home address _____

_____

Telephone number _____

What are your hobbies?

Which school subjects do you enjoy most?   Which school subjects do you like least?

How many hours a day do you watch television? Please indicate by checking:

_____ 1 to 2 hours   _____ 3 to 4 hours   _____ more

What are your favorite television programs?

Of all the things you do, what do you enjoy most?

What are your favorite sports?

Do you enjoy reading magazines? _____ YES   _____ NO

Which magazines do you read regularly?

Would you be interested in any of the following activities? Indicate by writing YES or NO in the blank before the activity:

_____ Planning assembly programs

_____ Introducing guest speakers in an assembly program

_____ Writing news items for a GATE newspaper

_____ Writing news items for the Northland Public Library newspaper

_____ Making announcements over the intercom

_____ Learning to operate the television camera

*North Hills School District Elementary GATE Program.

EXPERIENCE AND INTEREST INVENTORY (cont.)

_____ Learning to design and conduct an opinion poll
_____ Learning to square dance
_____ Serving as chairman of a GATE learning project
_____ Organizing learning centers for the classroom
Which careers interest you?

_____   _____
_____   _____
_____   _____

Do you enjoy reading for pleasure _____ YES _____ NO
Please identify the *five* kinds of fiction you would enjoy most:

_____ Adventure	_____ Pirates
_____ Animal	_____ School
_____ Biographical	_____ Science
_____ Family	_____ Sea
_____ Fantasy	_____ Social problems
_____ Historical	_____ Sports
_____ Humorous	_____ Supernatural
_____ Hunting	_____ Teenage
_____ Knights	_____ Underwater exploration
_____ Minorities	_____ War
_____ Mystery	_____ Western

Please list below other kinds of fiction you would enjoy:

_____   _____
_____   _____

Please identify the *five* kinds of nonfiction you would enjoy most:

_____ American history	_____ Hobbies
_____ Ancient history	_____ Hockey
_____ Animals	_____ Horses
_____ Anthropology	_____ House plants
_____ Aquariums	_____ Jokes and riddles
_____ Archaeology	_____ Legends
_____ Astronomy	_____ Magic
_____ Aviation	_____ Mathematics
_____ Babysitting	_____ Medicine
_____ Ballet	_____ Middle Ages
_____ Baseball	_____ Minorities
_____ Biography	_____ Model making
_____ Biology	_____ Music
_____ Boating	_____ Mythology
_____ Bowling	_____ Nature study
_____ Camping	_____ Needlework
_____ Careers	_____ Painting
_____ Cartooning	_____ Pets
_____ Caves	_____ Phenomena
_____ Chemistry	_____ Photography
_____ Coin collecting	_____ Plays
_____ Computers	_____ Poetry
_____ Cooking	_____ Radio (CB)
_____ Crafts	_____ Science
_____ Crime	_____ Scouting
_____ Drawing	_____ Scuba diving
_____ Ecology	_____ Skiing
_____ Electronics	_____ Skydiving
_____ Fashions	_____ Space
_____ Fishing	_____ Stamp collecting
_____ Folklore	_____ Supernatural
_____ Football	_____ Tennis
_____ Geology	_____ Witchcraft
_____ Golf	_____ Women's rights

SELECTED MEASURES OF CREATIVE PROCESS, POTENTIAL ATTITUDES, AND PRODUCTS*

NAME OF TEST	AUTHORS	TYPE OF MEASURE	SOURCE FROM WHICH MEASURE MAY BE OBTAINED	AGE OR GRADE
Bugart Symbol Test of Originality	Herbert J. Bugart	Visual-written test of originality	Bugart, H. J.*The development of a visual-verbal measure of general creativity.* ERIC Document No. 019801	Reading young through adult
Carlson Analytical Originality Scoring Scale	Ruth K. Carlson	Rating scale of originality of children's stories	*Sparking words: 200 Creative and practical writing ideas*	Elementary and intermediate grades
Children's Individual Test of Creativity	N. S. Mettfessel, Marilyn Burns, and J. T. Foster	Individual test of creativity	Marilyn Burns, 3858 Buena Park Drive, Studio City CA 91604	Preschool through elementary grades
Classroom Creativity Observation Schedule	David A. Denny	Observation schedule of classroom behaviors fostering pupil creativity	David A. Denny, State University College, Oneonta NY 13820	Kindergarten to 9 years
Cognitive Orientation Questionnaire of Creativity	Schulamith Kreitler and Hans Kreitler	Questionnaire referring to beliefs about curiosity	Schulamith Kreitler, Department of Psychology, Tel Aviv University Tel Aviv, Israel	4 to 8 years
Creative Writing Rating Scale	Jack R. McClellan	Rating scale	McClellan, J. R. *Creative writing characteristics of children.* Doctoral Dissertation, University of Southern California, Los Angeles, 1956	8 to 12 years
Creative Attitude Survey	Charles E. Schaefer	Self report questionnaire	Psychologists and Educators, Inc., Suite 212, 211 West State Street, Jacksonville IL 62650	8 to 12 years
Creativity Self-Report Scale	John F. Feldhusen	Self report questionnaire on creative and divergent thinking	John F. Feldhusen, Educational Psychology Section, SCC-G Purdue University, West Lafayette IN 47906	Junior high through adult
Drawing Completion Test	Helen H. Davidson and Judith W. Greenberg	Divergent production in figural materials	Judith W. Greenberg, The City College, Convent Avenue, New York NY 10031	8 years to adult

Instrument	Author	Description	Source	Age range
Drawing Completion Task (DCT)	David Schulman	Drawing rating scale	Schulman, D. Openness of perception as a condition for creativity. *Exceptional Children*, 1966, 33, 89–94	Elementary and junior high
Gross Geometric Forms	Ruth B. Gross	Visual-pictorial rating scale of drawings	Ruth B. Gross, Department of Psychology, Xavier University, Cincinnati OH 45229	3 to 10 years
Instances, Alternate Uses, Similarities, Pattern Meanings, Line Meaning	Michael A. Wallach and Nathan Kogan	Paper and pencil measure of ideational fluency	Wallach, M. A., and Kogan, N., *Modes of thinking in young children.* New York: Holt, 1965	8 years and older
Maws' About Myself Scale	Wallace H. Maw and Ethel W. Maw	Curiosity rating scale	Maw, W. H., and Maw, E. W. Self-appraisal of curiosity. *Journal of Educational Research,* 1968, 61, 462–466	Grades 4 through 6
Pennsylvania Assessment of Creative Thinking	Thomas J. Rookey	Attitude inventory	Thomas J. Rookey, Educational Development Center, East Stroudsberg State College, East Stroudsberg PA 18301	9 to 14 years
Scale for Rating Behavioral Characteristics of Superior Students (SRBCSS)	Joseph S. Renzulli et al.	Rating scale of student characteristics including creativity	Creative Learning	Elementary to high school
Something About Myself (SAM)	Joe Khatena	Self report checklist	Joe Khatena, Department of Educational Foundations, Marshall University, Huntington WV 25701	Adolescent to adult
Starkweather Originality Test for Young Children	Elizabeth K. Starkweather	Fluency	E. K. Starkweather, Family Relations and Child Development Dept. Oklahoma State University, Stillwater OK 74074	3½ to 6½ years

*Carolyn M. Callahan, *Developing Creativity in the Gifted and Talented* (Reston, Va.: Council for Exceptional Children, 1978), pp. 83–85.

WHO ARE THE GIFTED?*

Who are the gifted and talented? Some say they are the top 2% of the population, the top 5%, the top 10%; those with IQs over 140, over 135, over 130, over 120; those scoring in the top 5% on tests of creativity; and so on. The definitions are as varied as the educational programs serving them. For our purposes, let's say that gifted and talented children are those who are clearly superior to their peers in academic excellence, creative talent, or both.

Specific tests of intelligence, creativity, and achievement are frequently used for identification purposes. However, you can identify gifted kids without formalized testing by using a talent behavior checklist. The one below will not only help you identify the gifted in your class, but also will give you a better understanding of what giftedness and talent is all about.

IDENTIFYING CHARACTERISTICS

These are the common identification methods most schools use. Past and present performance is also carefully considered.

_____ Consultants on the gifted/creative
_____ Report card grades
_____ Teacher judgment
_____ Self-identification
_____ Peer identification
_____ Parent identification
_____ Psychological evaluation, individual IQ, Stanford Binet, or Wechsler

_____ Achievement tests scores, two years or more above chronological age
_____ Early school entrance
_____ Grade skipping
_____ Honors classes eligibility
_____ Community agency recommendations: YMCA, scouts, religious education classes

In addition, the following characteristics are normally evident. Gifted children . . .

_____ Are curious
_____ Have a large vocabulary
_____ Have long memories
_____ Sometimes learn to read alone
_____ Have a keen sense of humor
_____ Are persistent
_____ Like to collect things
_____ Are creative and imaginative
_____ Are healthy and well coordinated, but some may be delicate
_____ May be bigger and stronger than average
_____ Sustain interest in one or more fields over the years
_____ Initiate their own activities
_____ Develop earlier
_____ Learn easily
_____ Have a keen sense of humor
_____ Enjoy complicated games
_____ Are interested and concerned about world problems
_____ Analyze themselves, are often self-critical
_____ Like older children when very young

_____ Are original
_____ Set high goals and ideals
_____ Are leaders
_____ Have talent(s) in art, music, writing, drama, dance
_____ Use scientific methods of research
_____ See relationships and draw sound generalizations
_____ Produce work which is fresh, vital, and unique
_____ Create new ideas, substances, and processes
_____ Invent and build new mechanical devices
_____ Often run counter to tradition
_____ Continually question the status quo
_____ Do the unexpected
_____ Apply learning from one situation to different ones
_____ Solve problems on a superior level, divergently, innovatively
_____ May appear different

*The checklist is reprinted from The National Association for Creative Children and Adults, Copyright © 1976 by Ann Fabe Isaacs. Used by permission.

U.S. Office of Gifted
and Talented Fact Sheets

These fact sheets (produced for the Office of Gifted and Talented, U.S. Office of Education, Department of Health, Education, and Welfare, by The Council for Exceptional Children) are available free of charge on request from:

> Ms. Martha Bokee
> U.S. Office of Gifted and Talented
> Donahue Buliding, Rm. 3538
> Sixth and D Streets S.W.
> Washington, D.C. 20202
> 202-245-2481

For fact sheets "Characteristics of the Gifted and Talented" and "Identification of the Gifted and Talented," see Chapter 2. For fact sheets "Curriculum for the Gifted and Talented" and "Developing Programs for the Gifted and Talented," see Chapter 3.

CAREER AWARENESS FOR THE GIFTED
AND TALENTED FACT SHEET

Career awareness, a component of career education, is a relatively new but increasingly strong emphasis in American education. More and more, teaching and learning is directed toward the acquisition of basic skills directly related to students' futures in the "world of work."

The specific relevance of career awareness for the gifted and talented student has been acknowledged by the federal government, which has stated that career education should be a priority for all students. Gifted and talented programing in career awareness is a means to increase the motivation and school performance of these students as well as to help bring their abilities into full use for the good of the students themselves and for that of society.

Career awareness in education may be described as those educational activities which are geared to building a bridge between school and work. The Career Awareness Division of the National Institute of Education outlines four major areas through which this goal may be accomplished:

Knowledge which includes factual information about the job and self.

Values which include the individual's reasons for judging the value of routines, requirements, purposes, and rewards of work and values of self.

Preference which relates to the feelings of attraction an individual may have for a particular career and preparing for it.

Self concept which relates to an individual's perceptions of his or her specific abilities and capacities as they may be challenged and fulfilled by a particular career.

These areas are particularly relevant to programs for gifted and talented students, who are often able to learn and perform at levels of sophistication earlier and more fully than their peers. Recent studies of career education programs have found that gifted and talented students are able to learn highly sophisticated skills in computer science, statistics and probability, journalism, advertising, architecture, gerontology, and marine biology. While it is easy to see the application of scientific and mathematical skills to careers, the arts and humanities should not be overlooked since they are most often the sources for the values and perspectives which will guide not only career choice but also career performance as an adult.

In conducting career awareness through education, it is best to have professionals in the field serve as instructors and/or consultants. Although some classroom teachers may have training in the conduct of career awareness classes, the cooperation of several individuals and institutions from the business and labor community will lend credibility. The novelty of interaction with different career professionals also tends to make students more aware of the uniqueness of the program itself in comparison with regular parts of the curriculum.

Two of the greatest advantages of career awareness courses also contain the kernel of serious problems which must receive attention. First, a career awareness emphasis can often be important for economically and culturally isolated children, but it should present career alternatives not generally considered while at the same time indicating realistic channels through which these alternatives can be exercised. Second, in designing career awareness programs, precautions should be taken that sex role, race, and other stereotyping is eliminated. Often boys are encouraged in scientific and mathematical areas and girls are encouraged toward humanities and arts. These approaches, in addition to being sexist, can generate unnecessary conflicts for a child who possesses gifts or talents in an area outside the boundaries of the stereotype. Well planned career awareness programs can help break down stereotype barriers.

Career awareness programs should be designed primarily with the needs and interests of individuals in mind. Approaches which simply hand out information on a potpourri of careers should be avoided in favor of allowing individual students to pursue their interest in a career area. This interest may then be supplemented and enriched through interaction with a career professional who can answer questions and offer guidance. Career awareness program planners should also be aware of the educational possibilities offered to gifted and talented students by combining career awareness programs with community based mentorship approaches.

RESOURCES

Fox, Lynn H. Career education for gifted pre-adolescents. *The Gifted Child Quarterly.* Fall, 1976, *20*(3), 262–273.

Gourley, Theodore J. *Programs for gifted students: A national survey.* Pitman, NJ: Educational Improvement Center, 1975.

Hoyt, Kenneth B., and Hebeler, Jean R. *Career education for gifted and talented students.* Salt Lake City, UT: Olympus Publishing Company, 1974.

Lake, Thomas P. The arts and humanities come alive for gifted and talented. *Exceptional Children.* January, 1975, *41*, 261–264.

Riessman, Frank. *The culturally different child.* New York: Harper and Row, 1962.

Sato, Irving S. The culturally deprived gifted child: The dawning of his day. *Exceptional Children.* May, 1974, *40*, 572.

US General Accounting Office. *Career education: Status and needed improvements.* Washington, DC: General Accounting Office, 1977.

Wise, R., Charmer. I., and Randour, M. *A conceptual framework for career awareness.* Washington, DC: National Institute of Education, 1976.

CREATIVE THINKING TECHNIQUES FACT SHEET

Creativity can be fostered in connection with subject oriented curriculum, can be linked to higher levels of thinking skills, and can be the basis for both inquiry and critical thinking activities.

It is helpful to remember, however, that creativity is a form of divergent thinking, i.e., creative thought does not necessarily "fit" into set patterns and does not necessarily generate "correct" answers. The very nature of creativity demands fluency and flexibility in processes which require a nonrestrictive, accepting, and open ended atmosphere to flourish. See the fact sheet "What Is Creativity?" for a brief discussion of these terms.

There are four basic rules that apply to most activities designed to encourage creative thinking:

Defer judgment. When generating ideas or problem solving, it is inhibiting both to students and to the process itself to impose evaluative or negative judgments on any given idea. Evaluation comes later, when it is necessary to choose among several alternatives in order to actually solve the problem, or to verify the acceptability of an alternative which has been implemented in a solution strategy.

Generate many ideas for any given situation, both in number (fluency) and in kind (flexibility). The more ideas generated, the larger the base for finding the best solution strategy. In this stage of creative thinking, quantity surpasses quality.

Solicit free thinking. Unusual ideas, bizarre notions, and outlandish scenarios are acceptable and welcome. Any idea that seems implausible may spark a workable one, or one that can be modified into a solution or strategy. Originality and elaboration often surface here as integral components of the creative process.

Combine ideas. When experiencing a creative thinking activity, it is not unusual for one idea to spawn another; group work often excites such combinations. By joining unlikely ideas, utterly new and original solutions can be brought into being.

These four general rules apply to all idea generating and creative thinking activities. Evaluation, verification, and implementation occur once a substantial idea pool has been established. There are a variety of techniques and methods which have been published and practiced in both education and industry to enhance creative thinking abilities. Some of these are described below. Others may be found among the resources listed at the end of the fact sheet.

CREATIVE THINKING EXERCISES

BRAINSTORMING

Generating ideas and alternatives to a situation. An example is: "Think of all the uses for a tin can, a screwdriver, or an acorn." Another example is the "just suppose activity": "Just suppose all the rivers became salty. What would happen?"

ATTRIBUTE LISTING

Given a problem, list all its components or elements in one column. List all the attributes or characteristics of each component in a second column. Generate ideas for improvement in a third, and positive and negative features in a fourth. The problem should be stated in how-to fashion: "How to improve the playground."

ELEMENT	ATTRIBUTE	IDEAS FOR IMPROVEMENT	POSITIVE FEATURES	NEGATIVE FEATURES
1. Swings	Too high	Lower them	Small kids can swing easier	If too low, little kids could get hurt
2. Ground	Blacktop	Soften with mats, artificial turf	Increases # of games playable	−Cost −Effect of weather on mats

On this model, each positive and negative feature can then be translated into a new element of the problem to be run through the entire process again, making the creative activity self perpetuating.

MORPHOLOGICAL ANALYSIS (CHECKERBOARD)

Given a problem, make a grid. List the elements of the problem across the top and attributes down the side. Force combinations to fill in the squares of the grid. Example: Invent a new type of candy.

	CHEWY	HARD	GUM
Nut	Cashew	Walnut	Peanut butter
	Toffee	Lifesaver	Chewing gum
Fruit	Apple	Peach	Mango
	Taffy	Lifesaver	Chewing gum

SYNECTICS

Given a problem, use analogies and opposites to associate comparable responses. Then force fit generated responses into realistic solution/strategies. The most common types of analogies are fantasy, direct parallel/opposite, and personal. Example: How to move heavy objects in a factory.

Analogy #1—*Fantasy:* Use levitation to move the objects. *Force Fit:* Use air currents to levitate the objects.

Analogy #2—*Direct Parallel:* What natural forces move heavy objects? *Brainstorm:* earthquakes, floods, geothermal pressure. *Force Fit:* Use geothermal geysers to power flotation devices to move the objects.

Analogy #3—*Personal:* How would I like to be moved if I were a heavy object? *Brainstorm:* on a soft cloud, on a mattress, on a waterbed. *Force Fit:* On a foam covered conveyor belt.

RESOURCES

Biondi, A. M. (Ed.). *The journal of creative behavior.* Buffalo, NY: Creative Education Foundation.

Creativity general/classroom/problem solving. *Exceptional child bibliography series #667.* Reston, VA: The Council for Exceptional Children, 1976.

Creativity—Research/tests and measurements/intelligence. *Exceptional child bibliography series #639.* Reston, VA: The Council for Exceptional Children, 1976.

Davis, G.A. *The psychology of problem solving: Theory and practice.* New York: Basic Books, 1973.

Davis, G.A., and Scott, J.A. *Training creative thinking.* New York: Holt, Rinehart, and Winston, 1971.

Feldhusen, J. F., and Treffinger, D. J. *Teaching creative thinking and problem solving.* Dubuque, IA: Kendall/Hunt Publishing Co., 1977.

Feldhusen, J. F., Treffinger, D. J., Pine, P. A., et al. *Teaching children how to think.* West Lafayette, IN: Purdue University, 1975.

Gordon, W. J. *Synectics: The development of creative capacity.* New York: Harper Brothers, 1961.

Osborn, A. F. *Applied imagination.* New York: Charles Scribner's Sons, 1963.

Parnes, S. J., Noller, R. B., and Biondi, A.M. *Guide to creative action.* New York: Charles Scribner's Sons, 1976.

Torrance, E. P., and Myers, R. *Creative learning and teaching.* New York: Dodd, Mead, 1970.

THE CULTURALLY DIVERSE GIFTED
AND TALENTED CHILD FACT SHEET

The culturally diverse gifted and talented are generally those children from Black, American Indian, Mexican American, Asian American, and Puerto Rican populations. The designation "culturally diverse" is used because their behavior patterns and responses often vary from the typical indicators of giftedness and talent observed in the dominant culture, e.g., high IQ scores or proficiency in the dominant language. The term has also gained currency because previous designations implied the superiority of the dominant culture, and that differences are somehow deficits requiring remediation.

What are some problems in identifying gifts and talents among the culturally diverse?

Often these children are overlooked in the identification process. While particular talents may be observable, their intellectual ability and potential may be neglected, obscured by a cultural veil, or dismissed. These children are often penalized when assessed by instruments normed on the dominant culture.

We often mistakenly assume that culturally diverse children are alike; since they belong to an identifiable group, we assume they must all share the same characteristics. They should be seen as individuals.

When the behavior of culturally diverse gifted and talented children is interpreted, their boredom with already learned or irrelevant material is often interpreted as antiintellectual. Dissatisfaction expressed as disruptive or impulsive behavior reinforces misperceptions. The desire to accept challenges may be seen as aggressive or unrealistic.

Preoccupation with the ethnicity or social characteristics of the group from which the child comes may blind us to potential. Attention is diverted from the variation in ability among individuals (especially at the upper end of the performance scale) and the characteristics of low achievers are applied to the group as a whole, including its gifted and talented members.

How can culturally diverse gifted and talented children be identified?

In settings where the home and school environment is a barrio, ghetto, or reservation, and access to the dominant culture is restricted, specialized testing measures must be developed because the language, cultural norms, and content of the test may be beyond the experience of the testee. To compensate for these factors, potential may be assessed using one or more of the following resources.

1. *Interpreting results from standardized measures.*

Meeker suggests relating IQ test responses to the various abilities set forth in Guilford's Structure of Intellect model to make these instruments more diagnostically useful for designing instructional strategies. Contact: Dr. Mary Meeker, SOI Institute, 214 Main Street, El Segundo, CA 90245.

Bruch has suggested that traditional instruments (e.g., Binet, WISC-R) be scored to highlight specific strengths among culturally diverse groups. She has developed an abbreviated method of scoring the Binet which has been used to identify the strengths of Black school children. Contact: Dr. Catherine Bruch, Department of Educational Psychology, University of Georgia, Athens, GA 30602.

Mercer's System of Multi-Cultural Pluralistic Assessment (SOMPA) provides a means to compare a culturally diverse child's performance with standard norms by a system of differential weightings of behaviors and performances. Contact Dr. Jane Mercer, Department of Sociology, University of California at Riverside, Riverside, CA 92502.

2. Tests which may be used with the culturally diverse to identify particular gifts. *
The following tests may be used with culturally diverse children who might be penalized
by traditional formal methods.

Torrance Tests of Creative Thinking. Contact: Personnel Press, 191 Spring Street,
Lexington, MA 02173.

Raven's Progressive Matrices Tests. Contact: Psychological Corp., 304 E. 45th
Street, New York, NY 10017.

Arthur Point Scale of Performance. Available through Stoelting Company, 434
N. Holman Avenue, Chicago, IL 60624.

Leiter International Performance Scale. Available from Stoelting Company, 434
N. Holman Avenue, Chicago, IL 60624.

Test of General Ability. Contact: Science Research Associates, 259 Erie Street,
Chicago, IL 60611.

3. Inventories and questionaires that tap the potential of the culturally diverse child. †
The following are designed for use with elementary and secondary school students.
They allow the student to describe himself and his background.

Alpha Biographical Inventory. Available from Institute for Behavioral Research
in Creativity, University of Utah, Salt Lake City, UT 84112.

Relevant Aspects of Potential (RAP). Contact: RAP Researchers, Sandy Lane,
Marlborough, CT 06424.

Behavioral Identification of Giftedness Questionnaire (BIG). Contact: Western
Behavioral Science Institute, 1150 Silverado, La Jolla, CA 92037.

*4. Examples of procedures suggested to select the culturally diverse gifted and tal-
ented.* ‡

A method advanced by Stallings includes environmental testing, teacher observa-
tion, and peer evaluation, the Stallings Environmentally Based Screen (SEBS).
Contact: Dr. Clifford Stallings, United States International University, 10455
Pomerado Road, San Diego, CA 92131.

Fitzgibbon (1975) reports identifying the top 2% in ability among eighth graders
in an inner city school using a combination of the California Test of Mental
Maturity, Ravens Matrices, and the California Achievement Test.

*What steps must be taken to create effective learning environments for the culturally
diverse gifted and talented?*

Accept the fact that children from culturally diverse backgrounds are not innately
deficient, and that they do deviate upward from the norm.

Recognize that all programs for the gifted and talented should provide both
in-school and out-of-school opportunities, and that program success depends on
focusing attention on developing potential.

Plan program opportunities which encourage the expression of abilities within the
context of cultural diversity.

Develop inservice programs which concentrate on developing curricula that capitalize on the potential of the culturally diverse.

Interpret to parents and the community a commitment to finding and developing
the potential of the culturally diverse.

Note: Instruments and methods listed here are for informational purposes only. No endorsement
by either The Council for Exceptional Children or the U.S. Office of Education is intended or
implied.
†Ibid.
‡Ibid.

Be sensitive to the needs of culturally diverse youngsters and *reinforce* their achievements.

Use the potential of divergent cultural expression to instill pride and a sense of appreciation for the values of diversity and pluralism.

RESOURCES

Bernal, E. M., Jr. Gifted programs for the culturally different. *NASSP Bulletin,* 1976, *60,* (398) 67–76.

Bruch, C. B. Modification of procedures for identification of the disadvantaged gifted. *Gifted Child Quarterly,* 1971, *15,* 267–72.

Cross, D. E., Baker, G., and Stiles, L. J. (Eds.). *Teaching in a multicultural society.* New York: The Free Press, 1977.

Gold, M., Grand, C. A., and Rivlin, H. N. (Eds.). *In praise of diversity: A resource book for multicultural education.* Washington DC: Association of Teacher Educators, 1977.

Sato, I. S. The culturally different gifted child: The dawning of his day. *Exceptional Children,* 1974, *40,* 572–580.

Torrance, E. P. *Discovery and nurturance of giftedness in the culturally different.* Reston, VA: The Council for Exceptional Children, 1977.

DEVELOPING A COMMUNITY BASED MENTORSHIP PROGRAM FOR THE GIFTED AND TALENTED FACT SHEET

What is a mentor?

A mentor is one who already stands within the context of a particular tradition, discipline, profession, or craft and who serves as an advisor, guide, teacher, and role model to those who seek access to the mentor's world and skills.

What characteristics should a mentor have?

There are no set rules, especially since the mentorship plays such a highly individualized educational role. In general, however, the mentor:

Is usually but not always an adult.

Has a special skill, interest, or activity which engages the learner's interest.

Is able to guide the learner toward personally rewarding experiences where challenges can be met, skills developed, problems solved, and relationships established.

Is flexible, helping the learner review and revise activities and, when necessary, goals.

Is often a role model for the learner. The mentor can impart an understanding of life style and attitudes different from those the student might ordinarily meet.

Is, above all, interested in the student as a learner and as an individual.

Why are mentors good people to work with gifted and talented students?

Mentors are particularly valuable to the development of the gifted and talented student because they provide models of competency, exploration, commitment to a field or discipline, and caring. Mentors can be found in all occupations and endeavors.

How can mentors be identified?

As a first step, those developing community based mentorship programs should conduct a critical assessment of both their program's goals and the resources of the community in which it will operate. Community agencies, e.g., governmental, educational, and service, are usually excellent places to start. These agencies often compile lists of individuals who act as resources in their particular occupational areas. Many of these people are delighted to serve as mentors to gifted and talented students who express similar interests. Labor, business, industrial, and professional groups can be approached as well as individual artists, doctors, lawyers, and craftsmen.

Are mentorship programs good for all gifted and talented students?

No. Mentorships are usually inappropriate for elementary school age students. Secondary students who are beginning to explore vocational and career interests or who have consuming hobbies are often good candidates for mentorship programs. Candidates should be sufficiently mature to be able to benefit from a one to one relationship with an adult, be able to take both guidance and criticism well, and should show evidence of ability in independent study situations.

What is required of those involved in mentorships?

The most important quality of mentorship is a shared understanding of the tasks, responsibilities, and functions to be performed by both the mentor and student. This requirement is best met through a careful matching of student and mentor by the program coordinator, director, or liaison person.

What is the role of the director of the program?

The most effective director or intermediary is one familiar with the community, its institutions, and its human resources. The intermediary should conduct interviews to ascertain students' goals and interests and to help students clearly define their objectives in becoming involved with a mentor. The intermediary will also interview prospective mentors, assessing not only their ability to relate to young people but also their goals for the mentorship, to narrow the range of possible placements. The major purpose of both sets of interviews is to clarify expectations. The intermediary will then combine objective data, such as learner interests and abilities, schedule and transportation problems, and mentor skills and resources, with subjective factors, such as personality traits. Placement can then be proposed.

How do I start a mentorship program for gifted and talented students?

There is no ideal formula. To a large extent, the nature of the community and the resources within it will determine how a given program will be developed. However diverse, all mentorship programs should provide opportunities for gifted and talented students to:

Pursue their interest at an appropriate level of difficulty.

Explore career options through the real world of work experiences.

Determine which of many talents and abilities holds the most promise for developing a career or life interest.

Interact with other highly talented peers and adults.

To gather support for these goals, you may want to speak to community groups, parents, school personnel, and likely sources for mentors. Inform them that mentorship services need not be secured through a programmatic approach but can be established on an individual basis. When gathering support, it is important to remember that:

A mentorship program can help bring the school and the community together.

Student work habits will be developed and strengthened.

The innovative nature of the program can be used to generate educator interest.

The program is not unstructured; rather it seeks to restructure the educational context.

The program will be carefully evaluated.

What features of community based mentorship programs make them attractive?

Gifted and talented students often need a latitude and depth of involvement that is not always available within the framework of the normal classroom.

Gifted and talented students need settings where their curiosity can thrive among adults who can respond to it wholeheartedly.

Gifted and talented students need to test the limits of their understanding, skills, and expression in the real world and to have the opportunity to create, examine, and test the products of their special vision with adults who can challenge them.

Gifted and talented students of ethnic and racial minorities and lower socioeconomic environments often go unrecognized because the schools to which they are assigned lack appropriate resources.

How do I evaluate a community based mentorship program?

Like all educational programs, community based mentorship programs should be evaluated for their effectiveness and for the sake of improving them. Planning for evaluation of the program should begin at the same time as planning for the program itself. Evaluation as an afterthought is usually too little and too late and seldom provides the opportunity to make timely adjustment during the course of a program's life. If you are unfamiliar with how to approach an evaluation, the basic resources by Worthen and Saunders (1972) or Renzulli (1975) provide a survey of basic evaluation principles.

RESOURCES

For more information on community based mentorship programs write to your state education agency's consultant for gifted and talented programs or to:

> The Council for Exceptional Children
> 1920 Association Drive
> Reston, VA 22091

Readings in the area which may be helpful are:

Boston, Bruce. *The sorcerer's apprentice: A course study in the role of the mentor.* Reston, VA: The Council for Exceptional Children, 1976.
Campbell, F. P., Dunette, M. D., Lawler, E. E., and Weick, K. E. *Managerial behavior, performance and effectiveness.* New York: McGraw Hill, 1970.
National Commission on Resources for Youth. *In-service training manual for developing community based mentorships for gifted and talented.* Unpublished manuscript, 1977.
Renzulli, Joseph. *A guidebook for evaluating programs for the gifted and talented.* Ventura, CA: Office of the Ventura County Superintendent of Schools, 1975.
Worthen, B., and Saunders, J. *Educational evaluation: Theory and practice.* Worthington, OH: Charles A. Jones, 1972.

DEVELOPING INDIVIDUALIZED EDUCATION PROGRAMS (IEPs) FOR THE GIFTED AND TALENTED FACT SHEET

Historically, the fact that individual children possess certain physical, emotional, and learning characteristics which distinguish them from other children has led educators to realize the importance and desirability of developing educational programs which meet the individual needs of their students. More recently, considerable legislation and litigation, at both state and federal levels, have been interpreted as establishing the need for individualized education programs (IEPs) for all children. To date, largely because of semantic restrictions in much of the current law, gifted and talented children are not usually included in most IEP mandates. Nevertheless, growing numbers of educators and policy makers at state and local levels are rapidly realizing that the unique needs of this population justify their inclusion in the development and implementation of such mandates.

What is an IEP?

An IEP is a written document, developed and revised annually in a conference involving the child's parents and teacher(s), a qualified special education representative of the education agency (other than the teacher), and where appropriate, the child. The program must be a realistic assessment of the child's present level of performance, and should present a reasonable expectation of what the child can learn over the course of one year, as well as the identification of appropriate evaluation strategies to determine the student's progress.

What should the IEP include?

A child's IEP should include at least the following:

A written statement of the child's present levels of educational performance. Before an IEP planning team can determine the child's needs, a survey of all relevant formal and informal information should be made. This information can be acquired from current school files and personnel, and from people, e.g., parents, who have contact with the child in informal settings. This information will provide a more balanced picture for determining the most appropriate instructional environment for the child.

A statement of annual goals to be achieved by the child. Annual goals are written statements of what the child can be expected to learn in the educational program, as well as the targets toward which the child's learning is to be directed in specific instructional areas. Identification of annual goals must begin by assessing the child's present levels of functioning to determine the content and skills which need emphasis. IEP planners for gifted and talented children should consider factors such as the areas and degree of giftedness, special abilities, learning rates, and behavioral factors. Reasonable goals for gifted and talented children should challenge their abilities without frustrating them, be broad enough to allow for unexpected gains, and enhance those that are expected.

Short term objectives to be realized in the achievement of each annual goal. Short term objectives are specific units of learning which serve annual goals within instructional areas. They should be mastered in relatively short time periods, depending on learning characteristics and their specificity. Short term objectives may be derived from published curricula, collections of objectives for specific instructional areas, and from teacher written objectives. Objectives should also include a method for evaluating the child's program.

A statement of appropriate objectives, criteria, evaluation procedures, and schedules for determining whether the instructional objectives are being achieved. Procedures for evaluating student mastery of objectives should be decided on by the team.

A statement of the extent to which the student will be able to benefit from participation in a regular education program, and for what purposes. Like other exceptional children, gifted and talented children should participate in educational programs in the least restrictive environment, in order to optimize the student's educational and social growth in consonance with his or her ability to benefit.

A description of all special education and related services required to meet the student's need. Both special and related services should be stipulated in the IEP. A description of special requirements should include the type of classroom services (resource room, self contained class, etc.), the number of times per week the student is to be in a special setting, length of attendance, and a specific statement of what related services are to be delivered, why, by whom, and for how long.

The projected starting dates for, and duration of, these services. The date for service delivery should be specified in the IEP. Actual placement occurs following the development of the IEP. Services should continue for one year and the termination date should be stated. Changes in the IEP can be made during the year and should be recorded.

These steps encompass the basics of an IEP for a gifted and talented student. Because the program is individualized, variations can and will occur within these guidelines. For more information concerning the development of IEPs for gifted and talented children, write your state department of education consultant for gifted and talented education, or The Council for Exceptional Children, 1920 Association Drive, Reston, VA 22091, 800/336-3728.

Resources

Boston, B. O. *A resource directory on P.L. 94-142.* Washington, D.C.: Institute for Educational Leadership, 1977.
Mager, R. F. *Preparing instructional objectives.* Belmont, CA: Fearon Publishers, 1972.
Pennsylvania Department of Education. *An introduction to individualized education programs in Pennsylvania: Guidelines for school age IEP development.* Harrisburg, PA: Author, 1977.
Saunders, N. M. *Classroom questions: What kinds?* New York: Harper and Row, 1966.
Torres, S. (Ed.). *A primer on individualized education programs for handicapped children.* Reston, VA: The Council for Exceptional Children, 1977.

EVALUATION OF PROGRAMS FOR THE GIFTED AND TALENTED FACT SHEET

What is educational evaluation?

Educational evaluation is a tool for determining if the goals and objectives of an educational program are being met and the reasons for success or failure in meeting them. An evaluator makes this determination by gathering data about all aspects of the program: its procedures, practices, methods, innovations, materials, and personnel.

There are two general types of evaluation, each with its own purpose. *Summative evaluation* can be used to judge the overall impact and effectiveness of an entire program, or part of a program, after a specified period of time. *Formative evaluation* can be used to provide feedback while the program is still going on, so those aspects of the program which impede the achievement of goals and objectives can be modified.

Evaluation should not just provide judgments. It should also offer alternative approaches and suggestions for improvement.

Why do we need to evaluate programs for the gifted and talented?

As interest in gifted and talented education has grown, there has been a proliferation of programs to serve these students. In order to make reasonable judgments about the effectiveness of various identification procedures, curriculum designs, teaching strategies, and administrative arrangements, their impact has to be carefully assessed. Too often those things which look good on paper or in textbooks turn out to be unsatisfactory in specific situations or with specific children. The positive and negative effects of various program features must be evaluated in order to guide local decision makers toward appropriate modifications.

Accountability also demands evaluation. As competition for the educational dollar becomes more intense, programs for the gifted and talented will be scrutinized more carefully. It will not be possible to rely on conjecture or feelings to persuade public agencies to commit funds for gifted and talented students. Educators will need convincing evidence on the effectiveness of programs for developing the potential of these students.

How can I develop an effective evaluation design?

Begin at the beginning. Planning for evaluation should begin at the same time as planning for the program itself. Evaluations as afterthoughts, used in an attempt to rescue the floundering program, are usually too little and too late. Overall surveys of some basic educational evaluation designs, including first steps, are provided by Worthen and Saunders (1972) and Renzulli (1975).

Identify decision makers. Evaluation designs should identify the administrative decision makers who can use the evaluation data to improve program functioning. Together with these decision makers, the evaluators should plan a design that will provide useful information on the degree to which program goals are being met. Factors contributing to or inhibiting the success should also be identified.

Specify goals and objectives. Being specific about goals and objectives is crucial to evaluation planning. These may be gleaned from statements of philosophy, curriculum guides, project proposals, interviews, and from other sources. It is essential that both cognitive and affective components of student development be examined. The evaluator may also choose to look into other effects not specifically noted as goals and objectives, such as the effect of removing a gifted child from the classroom on peer relations. All factors to be evaluated should be listed, including outcomes for students, impact on school and community, communication, management, attitudes, and finances.

Identify sources of information. Once basic concerns have been isolated, identify the sources of information on each and construct a timetable for collecting the data. Student performance and progress may best be measured by a pretest and posttest design, but students themselves are probably the best source of information about student growth. If the evaluation design compares experimental and control groups, the selection of students for both groups should be made early so that baseline data can be appropriately gathered prior to program implementation.

How can I select evaluation instruments which will meet the needs of my program?

After determining the best sources of information and a timetable for gathering it, data gathering instruments must be selected. Because inappropriate instruments produce worthless evaluations, this task is extremely important. A first step is to consult *The Sixth Mental Measurements Yearbook* (Buros, 1965) for reviews of published tests and instruments which can measure the goals and objectives specified in the program. If you are unsure about the choice of a test, seek the guidance of a consultant. If no existing instruments suit your precise needs, one must be constructed. Since instrument construction is a highly specialized, complex, and time consuming activity, it must be done expertly. If you have no expertise in this area, a consultant should be brought in.

What do I do with the information once it is collected?

If you have carefully specified the questions which were asked when collecting the data, analysis can proceed by grouping the data relevant to a particular question. If statistical analysis is necessary and you do not have this skill, seek the advice of a statistician *before* collecting the data.

How should I report my findings?

The major consideration in reporting evaluation findings is to tailor the report to its audience. If changes must be made in the program, the language of the evaluation report should be one that decision makers understand. If more expensive activities must be undertaken, the report should make sense to a budget committee. Avoid technical statistical discussions. School boards generally do not respond well to the subtleties of covariant analysis and multiple regression equations. Whenever possible, use charts, graphs, and illustrations to make your results clear.

RESOURCES

Buros, O. K. (Ed.). *The sixth mental measurements yearbook.* Highland Park, NJ: The Gryphon Press, 1965.

Caro, F. G. (Ed.). *Readings in evaluation research.* New York: Russell Sage Foundation, 1971.

Eash, M. *Issues in evaluation and accountability in special programs for gifted and talented children.* Chicago Circle, IL: University of Illinois, 1971.

Furst, E. G. *Constructing evaluation instruments.* New York: McKay, 1958.

Gottman, J. M., and Clasen, R. E. *Evaluation in education: A practitioner's guide.* Itaska, IL: F. E. Peacock, 1972.

Hyman, H. *Survey design and analysis.* New York: The Free Press, 1955.

Hyman, H., Hopkins, T., and Wright, C. *Applications of methods of evaluation.* Berkeley: University of California Press, 1962.

Mager, R. F. *Preparing instructional objectives.* Palo Alto, CA: Fearon Publishers, 1975.

Renzulli, Joseph S. *A guidebook for evaluating programs for the gifted and talented.* Ventura, CA: Office of the Ventura County Superintendent of Schools, 1975.

Worthen, B., and Saunders, J. *Educational evaluation: Theory and practice.* Worthington, OH: Charles A. Jones, 1972.

FINDING FUNDS FOR GIFTED PROGRAMS FACT SHEET

In a nation sold on the idea that equal education means the same education for all students, advocates of special education for any exceptional group must work to convince the rest of the community of the need for different educational programs.

Advocates of programs for the gifted and talented frequently must act as persuasive salesmen in communities that spend their money on other "products." This includes convincing them to pay the bill for services.

Sprucing up the idea

Right now you probably have an idea either to begin, continue, or expand a program for the gifted and talented. A number of other people support this idea and are willing to work with you. Together your group must start selling the idea to others. This requires expanding the idea and developing it into a written program proposal which should clearly and concisely explain what is to be accomplished, who expects to accomplish it, how much it will cost, and how long the program will last. Below are some features which you should consider in your written program proposal:

Description of the program. This should contain an objective assessment of the need for such a program with a defense of why *this* program is needed, clearly stated goals and objectives, and major features of the proposed program and how these will meet the stated objectives.

Staffing. This section should give brief explanations of positions and duties, the biography or vita of key individuals who have already been selected and the qualifications required for selection of the other positions, as well as establish that the staff can accomplish the job.

Budget. This should present a clear delineation of costs including rationale for figures. The figures should be realistic not "padded" to allow room for bargaining.

History of your organization, if applicable. This should describe the objectives of your group and give an explanation of your past achievements and resources.

Other materials. Some that you may want to include in your program proposal are letters of endorsement or any other materials you think are relevant, such as reports of previous projects or activities.

Who might buy it

Pull the program supporters together and outline a strategy for obtaining the necessary funds. Such a strategy should probably focus first on local sources for support. When these are exhausted and you have not obtained the needed funds, then consider state level sources. National level sources, such as the federal government and foundations, should probably be solicited last as these sources often require a great deal of competitive effort to locate and to meet their requirements. Also, waiting for approval of your program and the actual receipt of the first check may take too much time.

Your group may want to "brainstorm" local sources that should be considered. Remember to include your school district, local business and industry, local branches of nationwide companies, civic organizations, and local philanthropists. Often the key to receiving money is a personal contact within an organization, so as you brainstorm find out who has any special contact with the possible source. Use these contacts when approaching the sources to request funding. For example, the proposal could be sent along with a letter introducing the program and expressing personal support from an influential friend of your group.

If you also need to solicit from statewide sources, you may wish to contact the consultant for gifted and talented in your state's department of education as well as resources familiar with business and industry in your state.

Your strategy should be flexible so that a refusal from one organization does not halt your efforts. You may only get a portion of your funding from one source and it may take the contributions of several organizations or agencies to yield your total budget.

How to sell it

You have written your proposal and identified sources which may be interested in funding it. Now comes the selling part of the process when you convince enough of those sources to buy your program. This may require considerable flexibility as you emphasize some aspects of your program and deemphasize others in order to match the funding priorities of different potential supporters.

Before you approach an organization, investigate their objectives, their interests, and the nature of their past and present contributions. Tailor your proposal and presentation to appeal to their unique pattern of involvement.

After you have decided on your approach to a given organization, you should initiate the first contact by telephone or letter. Make sure that your first contact, particularly if it is a letter, is directed to the proper person. The purpose of this contact is to ascertain if the organization is interested in hearing more about your program. It probably will be better to wait before mailing or taking the full proposal to them until after they have shown an interest. They will respond by indicating the criteria or specifications which should be used to amend the proposal to make it acceptable.

When the organization expresses a further interest in examining your program, respond quickly with the proposal and a cover letter. If possible this letter should be written by a person who has a contact in the organization. The spokesperson for the proposal may wish to include the key individual(s) of the program when visiting an interested source of funding.

Finally, when you have sold your program to enough organizations to achieve your funding goal, don't forget "the hand that feeds you." Keep up the contacts and advise them of your progress. If you have to go through another round of selling, you will probably already have developed a core of convinced listeners.

RESOURCES

The bread game: The realities of foundation fundraising. San Francisco: Glide Publications, 1972.

The foundation directory (6th ed.). New York: The Foundation Center, 1977. (Available through your public library. The introduction provides helpful information on structuring a foundation proposal.)

You may also want to write to the following organizations:

The Foundation Center
888 Seventh Avenue
New York, NY 10019

Office of Gifted and Talented
U.S. Office of Education
400 6th Street, S.W., Room 3835
Washington, D.C. 20202

For listings of businesses and industries, write to your local or state chamber of commerce or:

U.S. Chamber of Commerce
1615 H Street, N.W.
Washington, D.C. 20062

Discuss your program with the consultant for gifted and talented in your state education agency.

GIFTED AND TALENTED HANDICAPPED FACT SHEET

Who are the gifted and talented handicapped?

The gifted and talented handicapped are those people who by virtue of outstanding abilities are capable of high performance in spite of a handicapping condition such as visual, hearing, or orthopedic impairments, emotional disturbances, or learning disabilities. These are people who require special educational programs and/or services beyond those normally provided by the regular school program in order to realize their contribution to themselves and society. So often persons only think of the gifted in terms of intellectual talents, but special abilities may occur in the areas of psychomotor skills, social (leadership) skills, performing arts, or creativity.

How can people be both gifted and handicapped?

Even though it may seem incongruous for handicapped people to also be gifted or talented, the fact remains that people with handicaps can function at a gifted level in society or in school. Some examples of well known gifted handicapped people are writer, lecturer, and humanitarian Helen Keller (deaf, blind, and mute), inventor Thomas Edison (deaf), painter-sculptor Leonardo da Vinci (learning disabled), President Franklin Roosevelt (orthopedically impaired), and singer-composer Ray Charles (blind).

Do they need special programs?

Special programs for the gifted and talented handicapped are necessary because the unique physical and intellectual needs of this group require that special attention be given to both their handicap and their giftedness. Historically, special consideration has most often been given to a handicapped person's disability, while intellectual development has not received a high priority. Those celebrated gifted handicapped people, while certainly noteworthy for achieving greatness in spite of a handicapping condition, are unfortunately the exception rather than the rule.

How can we identify the gifted and talented handicapped?

Identification of the gifted and talented handicapped is often difficult. Caution must be taken not to overlook the potential hidden beneath the handicapping condition. Talent may be present but not functional. How does one calculate the intellectual ability of a deaf child who has not yet learned to use language effectively enough to communicate what is locked up in his bright mind? How can one estimate the potential of a physically handicapped child who cannot even respond by pointing to a chosen answer? Standardized intelligence tests are commonly used to identify gifted children but such tests cannot be considered reliable measures of the gifted handicapped child's potential. Identification is an ongoing process that must be conducted within the context of a program that encourages and nourishes the development of talent.

Other forms of assessment that may be used to identify talents and abilities are:

1. *Biographical information forms,* which combine information obtained from a number of sources such as parents, teachers, friends, and self reports by using behavioral characteristics as predictors of future performance.

2. *Behavioral checklists,* which may be used in indicating a person's potential to develop certain talents and abilities if given the opportunity.

3. *Play observation records,* which gather a sampling of information about individual children in less structured play situations where leadership abilities and creativity may be more readily observable.

4. *Peer evaluation forms,* which may be used to obtain children's perceptions of their peers which may be a revealing source of information about a particular child.

What can be done to promote services for gifted and talented handicapped?

Help the public become aware of the existence and potential of gifted and talented handicapped children.

Support research in the field of gifted and talented handicapped.

Encourage the development of programs and more appropriate curriculum and materials for this special group.

Establish advocate groups in both the private and public sectors of society.

Encourage the development of better methods of identifying the gifted and talented handicapped including referral, diagnostic, and placement strategies.

If you are interested in programs for the gifted handicapped, you may want to write the state consultant for the gifted in your state office of education or you may find out about special federally funded projects for the gifted and talented handicapped by writing:

> The Office of Gifted and Talented
> United States Office of Education
> 6th and D Streets, S.W.
> Washington, D.C. 20202

> National Association for Creative Children and Adults
> 8080 Springvalley Drive
> Cincinnati, OH 45236

> American Association for Gifted Children
> 15 Gramercy Park
> New York, NY 10003

ADDITIONAL READINGS

Baker, H. J. *Biographical sagas of willpower.* New York: Vantage Press, 1970.
Goertzel, V., and Goertzel, M. G. *Cradles of eminence.* Boston: Little Brown, 1962.
Keller, H. *The story of my life.* Garden City, NY: Doubleday, 1954.
Maker, J. C. *Providing programs for the gifted handicapped.* Reston, VA: The Council for Exceptional Children, 1977.
Meeker, M. N. *The structure of the intellect: Its implications and uses.* Columbus, OH: Charles E. Merrill, 1969.

MATH AND SCIENCE FOR THE GIFTED AND TALENTED CHILD FACT SHEET

Who are the mathematically gifted and talented?

Mathematical talent is probably best described as precocious development in both reasoning and achievement. The student who at age 12 or 13, for example, scores as well as or better than high school seniors on difficult tests of mathematical reasoning ability, such as the Scholastic Aptitude Test—Mathematics or a similar test, could best be described as gifted in that particular aptitude. A third or fourth grader who has already mastered the mathematics curriculum through the sixth grade level, and who scores very high on measures of abstract reasoning ability, may also be precocious.

Abstract reasoning ability and mathematical talent are not synonymous, however. Sometimes a good reasoner in math is not ahead in knowledge of specific mathematical concepts or computational skills. Although mathematical ability is different from verbal ability, the two are probably not totally independent. Thus, a student who is a good mathematical reasoner is likely to be above average for his/her age group on verbal reasoning tests.

Scientific talent is more difficult to describe. Some areas of science require mathematical reasoning ability, while others may require qualitative rather than quantitative skills. A precocious math student is likely to be good in quantitative science subjects such as physics or chemistry, but may show little talent or interest in biology or botany.

One indication of an aptitude for science is a strong knowledge of and interest in it. The seventh grade student who possesses a great deal of general science knowledge may be very talented in this area. If the same student is relatively better at verbal than quantitative tasks, he or she will probably be more interested and successful in the biological and descriptive sciences than in the physical sciences.

How can talented students be identified?

A great deal is known about identifying mathematically gifted students in the middle school years, less in other age groups. An initial screening can look for students in grades sixth through ninth who score at or above the 95th percentile on the mathematical concepts portion of in-grade standardized achievement tests. This should be supplemented with teacher nominations. The initial pool of students can then be tested on a more difficult test intended for higher age groups.

Such tests as the Academic Promise Tests (APT) or the appropriate level of the School and College Abilities Test (SCAT) could also be used to identify students in the upper elementary grades. It is much more difficult to identify children below grade five because, typically, they have not yet developed their full potential beyond basic arithmetic skills. Facility at computation alone is not generally a good indication of superior mathematical reasoning ability.

Scientifically gifted secondary level students can be identified by looking at projects entered in science fairs or by screening for scores at the 95th and higher percentiles on verbal and mathematics tests at their grade level. These high scorers can then be retested on more advanced measures of science achievement such as the STEP Science Test.

Although children with IQ scores of 130 and above have often been identified for special programs in mathematics or science, it is important to remember that IQs are generally a better indicator of learning rate than of specific aptitude; they are not synonymous with mathematical or scientific talent.

Parents and teachers should ask three questions: (1) Is the child bored by in-grade science and math material? (2) Does the child score at or above the 95th percentile on standardized tests, such as the Iowa Test of Basic Skills? and (3) Does the child seem eager to learn more and at a faster pace? If all three questions can be answered "Yes," the child should be tested to determine his or her readiness to accelerate in science and/or math.

Do girls achieve as well as boys in math and science?

More boys than girls exhibit talent and interest in math and science in the secondary school years. This appears to result, in part, from the differential encouragement of males and females, as well as from the students' own culturally conditioned perceptions of math and science as male domains, reinforced by both parents and schools. Additionally, gifted boys tend to be more career oriented than most gifted girls, although this has been changing in recent years. Girls may need special encouragement to overcome the stereotypic view that math and science are unimportant for their futures.

How can mathematics and science talents be facilitated?

Although some would argue that new or special curricula need to be developed for gifted math and science students, research does not support this view. What the gifted student needs most is to be given the opportunity to study these subjects at an appropriately fast pace, with the help of a knowledgeable and enthusiastic teacher.

College level math and/or science courses are sometimes available for 11th and 12th graders. In some areas special Advanced Placement Program (AP) courses are available. Some students may need special facilitation at younger ages when their interests and talents have begun to blossom. They may be ready to begin more abstract mathematics such as algebra and plane geometry as early as the higher elementary grades, or simply starting the traditional math or science sequence at grade six or seven may provide sufficient enrichment to meet their needs.

If a sizable number of gifted students can be identified at grades six, seven, or eight, a special enriched and accelerated math or science program can be formed for them. The key to these programs is fast pacing through the skills acquisition stage and in-depth treatment of the subject matter. Such classes need not meet daily; once a week for 2 hours is generally enough. Students selected should be highly motivated and capable of independent study.

A well trained teacher is crucial. Regrettably, many elementary school teachers lack the necessary training in math or science to work successfully with the highly gifted student. In such cases a junior or senior high school teacher, or a college student tutor, might be recruited to conduct special classes. The tutorial model should be one of diagnostic testing and prescriptive teaching, moving the student along at his or her natural learning rate.

The sequential nature of mathematics and much science makes acceleration a necessary component of gifted programs. Basic curriculum enrichment is also needed, however, and can be provided through courses in computer programing, statistics and probability, astronomy, and other areas of applied science and mathematics.

RESOURCES

Fox, L. H. Women and the career relevance of mathematics and science. *School Science and Mathematics,* 1976, *76,* 347–353.

Fox, L. H., and Stanley, J. C. A university responds to the plight of intellectually talented youths. *MAHE Journal,* 1977, *1* (2), 12–15.

George, W. C. Accelerating mathematics instruction for the mathematically talented. *The Gifted Child Quarterly,* 1976, *20* (3), 246–261.

Keating, D.P. *Intellectual talent: Research and development.* Baltimore: The Johns Hopkins University Press, 1976.

Solano, C. H., and George, W. C. College courses and educational facilitation of the gifted. *The Gifted Child Quarterly,* 1976, *20* (3), 274–285.

Stanley, J. C. The case for extreme educational acceleration of intellectually brilliant youths. *The Gifted Child Quarterly,* 1976, *20* (1), 66–75; 41.

Stanley, J. C., George, W. C., and Solano, C. H. (Eds.). *The gifted and the creative: Fifty-year perspective.* Baltimore: The Johns Hopkins University Press, 1977.

Stanley, J. C., Keating, D. P., and Fox, L. H. (Eds.). *Mathematical talent: Discovery, description and development.* Baltimore: The Johns Hopkins University Press, 1974.

PARENTS OF GIFTED AND TALENTED CHILDREN FACT SHEET

What is a good working definition of gifted and talented?

The U.S. Office of Education has identified six areas in which children may demonstrate capabilities of high performance or giftedness:

General intellectual ability—the all around bright child.

Specific academic aptitude—the math or science whiz.

Creative or productive thinking—the child who comes up with novel solutions to problems.

Leadership ability—initiates and leads games and groups.

Ability in the visual or performing arts—painting, music, drama, and sculpture.

Psychomotor ability—athletic ability and mechanical skills.

A gifted child may have one or more of these abilities. One leading educator defines gifted and talented children as those who have learned to use the symbol systems of our society at a much higher and more effective rate than other children. However, a parent leader offers a less technical definition, saying gifted and talented children do things a little earlier, a little better, a little more quickly, and a little bit differently from other children. Parents also gather much useful information by observing the behavior of their children.

What are some behaviors or characteristics to look for?

Gifted children learn to read earlier often before entering school and sometimes on their own and with a greater comprehension of the nuances of language.

They usually have large vocabularies for their age.

They learn basic skills more quickly and need less practice.

They display an ability for abstract thinking in advance of their peers.

Their concentration and attention spans are longer.

They often have a wide variety of interests and experiment with them.

They have a highly developed sense of curiosity and a limitless supply of questions.

They are good guessers.

They can construct relationships between things that are not readily obvious.

They can retain a lot of information.

They usually relate well to peers and adults.

Many behavioral checklists (see Appendix B) for gifted and talented children are available. Check with your school system or with one of the resources listed in this fact sheet for assistance in securing a checklist.

How is a gifted and talented child identified?

Several sources of information should be used to identify gifted and talented children, such as reports from teachers, parental observations, pupil products, school achievement, standardized tests of intelligence and creativity, case studies, and other measures.

My children have been identified as gifted and talented. What can I do at home to encourage them?

It is important to provide a variety of stimuli and experience geared to the child's natural interests. Books, toys, stories, puzzles, and games are obviously helpful, but you should also take care to provide materials and experiences that enrich imagery, challenge the child's abilities, and encourage the development of perceptual and motor skills.

Encourage your children to record their ideas in some way. Parents can sometimes play secretary.

Permit ample time for thinking and daydreaming. These are the child's equivalent to a full time job.

Assign household tasks that coincide with interests.

Encourage your children to translate their interests into specific products, e.g., stories, pictures, collections, inventions, tools. Be a cautious editor. Budding creativity does not stand up well to stifling in the name of correctness.

Accept and use the tendency to see things differently.

Encourage active rather than passive learning.

Play word games. Common settings like shopping and shared chores provide occasions for all kinds of word play.

Do not be anxious about single mindedness—"All she cares about is horses!" This, too, shall pass.

Develop the habit of asking your children as many questions as you are asked. For example, "What would happen if . . . ?" "How does it work?" "How would you change it?" "What else can you do with that?" "Why?" "What will it be like a (week, month, year) from now?"

My children are gifted and talented but they seem turned off and tuned out. What's going on?

A gifted and talented child is a child first and gifted and talented second. Like all children, they need and respond to the love, caring, interest, and guidance of their parents. Sometimes, however, being gifted and talented becomes a burden, especially if the children's environment does not meet their needs and expectations or if peers react negatively to their abilities. They may act out frustrations in the form of disruptive behavior, become insecure, or withdraw. It is not uncommon for gifted and talented children to achieve at levels lower than their capabilities if lack of a challenge in school produces disinterest. Meeting these problems will require a cooperative effort between parents, school officials, and in some cases, a professional counselor.

What about programs in the schools?

Many schools have programs for gifted and talented children, but they are not always appropriate for every gifted and talented child. Program administrators and teachers can help you decide. If no program exists, you may want to think about helping to start one or consult with teachers to see what can be done to meet your child's special needs within the regular class.

Is there an association or group I can join?

There is probably a state level association for parents of gifted and talented children in your state or in a large city near you. Address inquiries to your state education agency's consultant for the gifted and talented. You may also want to join one of these national associations which welcome parents:

> The Association for the Gifted
> The Council for Exceptional Children
> 1920 Association Drive
> Reston, VA 22091

> The American Association for Gifted Children
> 15 Gramercy Park
> New York, NY 10003

> The National Association for Gifted Children
> 217 Gregory Drive
> Hot Springs, AR 71901

RESOURCES

Barbe, W., and Renzulli, J. *Psychology and education of the gifted* (2nd ed.). New York: Halsted Press, 1975.

Delp, J., and Martinson, R. *The gifted and talented: A handbook for parents*. Ventura, CA: The Ventura County Superintendent of Schools, 1975.

Eberle, R. *Scamper: Games for imagination development*. Buffalo, NY: D.O.K. Publishers, 1971.

Fine, B. *Stretching their minds*. New York: E. P. Dutton, 1964.

Ginsberg, G. *Is your child gifted?* New York: Simon and Schuster, 1976.

Gowan, J. C., and Bruch, C. *The academically talented student and guidance.* Boston: Houghton Mifflin, 1971.

Gowan, J., and Torrance, E. P. (Eds.). *Educating the ablest.* Itasca, IL: P. E. Peacock Publishers, 1971.

Kaufman, Felice. *Your gifted child and you.* Reston, VA: The Council for Exceptional Children, 1976.

Martinson, R. *Identification of the gifted and talented.* Reston, VA: The Council for Exceptional Children, 1976.

Maynard, F. *Guiding your child to a more creative life.* Garden City, NY: Doubleday, 1973.

Parnes, S. J. *Creative behavior guidebook.* New York: Charles Scribner's Sons, 1967.

Parnes, S. J. *Creative behavior workbook.* New York: Charles Scribner's Sons, 1967.

Renzulli, J. S. *New directions in creativity.* New York: Harper and Row, 1973.

Weinlander, A. *Your child in a scientific world.* Garden City, NY: Doubleday, 1959.

THE PRESCHOOL GIFTED AND TALENTED CHILD FACT SHEET

Who is the preschool gifted and talented child?

The preschool child, ages 2–5, who functions significantly above age level in language development, cognitive and social skills, physical adaptability, creativity, or leadership may in fact be gifted and talented. Criteria for identifying preschool gifted and talented children may be specifically defined by state or local guidelines.

Is early identification and education of value to the preschool gifted and talented child?

There are strong indications that much of a person's mature intelligence is developed between conception and 4 years of age. Therefore, it is important that the young gifted and talented child be exposed to a high quality learning environment as soon as possible. Learning environments should be designed to meet the unique needs of each child, and the child's indication of readiness to learn should be a determining factor in the type of challenge presented. It is important to remember that demonstration of advanced ability in one area does not necessarily mean similar levels of competence in all areas.

How can a preschool gifted and talented child be identified?

If a standardized intelligence test is to be used as a part of the identification process, it should be administered by a professional who is experienced in working with preschool children. A child with advanced skills may not have been exposed to the types of experiences necessary for superior performance on a standardized IQ test.

Tests should never be used exclusively to determine children's potential ability for assessing cognitive development. Techniques such as those developed by Piaget may effectively supplement standardized measures. Teacher checklists, parent observations, and peer nomination procedures are all helpful in identifying gifted and talented children.

What are teacher checklists?

If a child is enrolled in a preschool program, the teacher will have many opportunities to observe those characteristics and behaviors that may indicate exceptional ability. Some of the characteristics that a teacher could observe in gifted and talented preschool children are:

The use of advanced vocabulary for their age.

Employment of spontaneous verbal elaboration with new experiences.

The ability to construct interesting or unusual shapes or patterns through various media, such as blocks, play dough, and crayons.

The ability to assemble puzzles designed for older children.

A sense of humor used in general conversation.

An understanding of abstract concepts, such as death and time.

Mastery of new skills with little repetition.

Demonstration of advanced physical skills.

Demonstration of advanced reasoning skills through the explanation of occurrences.

The use of a checklist (see Appendix B) that includes these and other characteristics can be of great help in alerting teachers to potentially gifted and talented children.

What should parents be looking for in observing their children?

Parent observations can assist in the identification of preschool gifted children. Parents are able to supply developmental information and other data not readily observable in more structured situations. A child's approach to dramatic play, constructive play, and humor can provide a great deal of information regarding the child's level of cognitive development. Intensive interaction among young children takes place during less supervised and less structured play situations and therefore should be included as part of a comprehensive identification process. Observations should take place when children are free to choose activities either alone or with others and when they have access to a variety of materials. Free play behavior should be observed for periods of approximately 15 minutes. Include at least one indoor and one outdoor observation. Make observations for several days and record them for future reference.

Some questions which may guide parent observation are:

Dramatic play. Do your children ever engage in make believe play in which they pretend or simulate situations and people? Which best describes the variety in your children's dramatic play? (a) have one favorite theme which they use almost all of the time, (b) have two or three favorite themes which they like to vary but generally stick with, or (c) have a wide range of themes and enjoy variety.

Constructive play. Do your children ever engage in play in which they make things, build things, or draw? When they are free to build or make things, what do they make? Which statement best applies to the products of your children's constructive play? (a) attempt to make products as representative of reality as possible, (b) products have some representation to reality but have some unique aspects as well, or (c) draw or make up things as they remember them or as they would like for them to be with little attention to perspective, proportion, or relationships.

Humor. Which statement best describes your children's ability to perceive humor? (a) make little or no attempt to do or say funny things, (b) attempt to do or say some funny things primarily to imitate what they have seen others do, or (c) can take information and use it to produce creative humor which is new for them.

Why should information from a child's peers be considered?

Children's perceptions of their peers can be a revealing source of information. Therefore, nominations of children by their peers should be included in the identification process, especially at the preschool level. To find out how children who possess unique abilities are perceived by their peers, the following types of questions can be asked:

Which child in class can make a broken toy work?

Who in the class can make up the best new game?

Who is the very best at following directions?

Who asks the most questions?

How can parents help meet the needs of the preschool gifted and talented child?

Parents can help meet the needs of their preschool gifted and talented children by providing them with a wide variety of experiences. Take children to museums, airports, and the library. Play new games, do experiments, engage in sports, together. If your child is enrolled in a structured educational or enrichment program, parent participation, input, and support are vital to ensure that the program is meeting the needs of the child. Parents are their child's first teachers and, therefore, have a responsibility to provide that child with secure, quality, learning environments.

Where can I get more information about preschool gifted and talented children?

If you are interested in more information on preschool gifted and talented children, you may wish to contact the state consultant for the gifted in your state department of education or write:

> Information Services for the Gifted and Talented
> The Council for Exceptional Children
> 1920 Association Drive
> Reston, VA 22091

RESOURCES

Delp, J., and Martinson, R. *The gifted and talented: A handbook for parents.* Ventura, CA: Office of the Ventura County Superintendent of Schools, 1975.

Eberle, R. *Scamper: Games for imagination and development.* Buffalo, NY: D.O.K. Publishers, 1971.

Fine, B. *Stretching their minds.* New York: E. P. Dutton, 1964.

Kaufman, Felice. *Your gifted child and you.* Reston, VA: The Council for Exceptional Children, 1976.

Maynard, F. *Guiding your child to a more creative life.* Garden City, NY: Doubleday and Co., 1973.

Renzulli, J. S. *New directions in creativity.* New York: Harper and Row, 1973.

Sharp, D. *Thinking is child's play.* New York: E. P. Dutton, 1969.

READING FOR THE GIFTED AND TALENTED FACT SHEET

Most reading programs devote a great deal of time to decoding and basic comprehension skills. Because many gifted children master these skills at earlier ages, subjecting them to the regular readiness, decoding, and simple comprehension exercises of the primary grades often wastes time and frustrates the child. It would be far more valuable to move on to skills of critical reading, i.e., the development of logical thinking processes and the abilities to apply those processes to informative and literary material.

Although some researchers have listed as many as 186 individual critical reading skills, most can be grouped into six basic areas:

Inference

Assumption

Deduction

Interpretation

Prediction

Evaluation

Reading programs for gifted children should concentrate on these general areas. The level of sophistication on which a child can work will necessarily depend upon age, ability and experiential background. Even very young gifted children, however, will be able to perform at advanced levels, if instruction is geared toward them. The teacher must be concerned about aiding the thought processses in the child that will facilitate this development.

Commonly, gifted students are simply directed to read more books. While this "instructional strategy" may broaden their experiential background, it does not necessarily provide for needed skill development. Critical thinking and reading do not occur automatically.

The types of material used can help to vary a critical reading program. While fiction is often analyzed in the upper grades, there is a notable lack of evaluation of more expository material, such as newspapers, popular magazines, textbooks, government reports, research findings, etc. Since these materials are necessary for efficient, informed living, they should be included along with the appreciation and analysis of literature. The combination will offer the gifted child variety as well as the opportunity to transfer learned skills from one type of material to another.

The gifted child may also begin school with well developed writing skills or develop them at a much more rapid rate than their age-mates. Many of these children already have, or will quickly gain, the understanding of grammar and composition necessary to express themselves in a creative, well organized manner. On the other hand, there are also children who possess a talent for creative ideas but lack the writing skills, i.e., their verbal skills lag behind their creative abilities. Here instruction must maintain a careful balance. While the child needs to develop structure and organization, the teacher must be careful not to discourage or inhibit the child's creativity. Constant reassurance as to the worth of the child's ideas, as well as reinforcement of basic language skills become the primary goals for teachers of gifted children whose abilities are unevenly developed.

It is often assumed, mistakenly, that *all* gifted students should be developing these creative writing techniques. While these may be valuable and relevant for some children, others will find a far greater need to develop their ability in expository writing and research skills. Creative works can bring a great deal of personal satisfaction, but skill development for written reports and research studies is also vital. Since many gifted programs are based on independent study, a weakness in this area of writing could cause failure in such a program. Teachers must, therefore, look at each individual child's talents, interests and plans before arbitrarily assigning one writing program for all.

Instruction and related projects in journalism, advertising and other topics of student interests can integrate all of the language arts with critical reading skills, yet still provide ample opportunity for creative expression. An integrated language arts program that stresses the application of many writing skills to numerous content areas is recommended.

RESOURCES

Cheyney, A. B., *Teaching reading skills through the newspaper*. Newark DE: International Reading Association, 1971.
Dawson, M. A. (Ed.). *Developing comprehension including critical reading*. Newark DE: International Reading Association, 1971.
Eller, A., and Wolf, J. G. (Ed.). *Critical reading: A broader view*. Newark DE: International Reading Association, 1971.
Herber, H. L. (Ed.). *Developing study skills in secondary schools*. Newark DE: International Reading Association, 1974.
Labuda, M. (Ed.). *Creative reading for gifted learners: A design for excellence*. Newark DE: International Reading Association, 1974.
Witty, P. A. (Ed.). *Reading for the gifted and the creative student*. Newark DE: International Reading Association, 1971.

WHAT IS CREATIVITY FACT SHEET?

It has been said that the ordinary man looks at the world and sees what everyone else sees, but the creative man looks at the world and thinks what no one else has thought. A fairly good thumbnail definition of creativity, then, is that it is the process of combining what exists into something new, whether in the form of an idea, a procedure, or a product.

Some people are better at doing this than others, and this ability manifests itself in children as well as adults. Each of us has had what might be called an "Aha!" experience, and all of us can learn to foster our creativity by developing the necessary abilities, if we better understand the process of creative thinking.

What is creative thinking?

The creative process can be understood best by looking at the stages involved in finding a creative solution to a particular problem. Although experts have differing ways of explaining exactly what happens, most agree that a four stage process takes place.

The first stage may be called the *definition* of the problem. Many refer to it as "statement" or "fact finding." But the basic idea is to gather together as much information as possible about the problem—its extent, nature, and qualities. Most important to this stage is to keep an open mind, to state the problem in as many different ways as possible, and to have as much information as is available. The search for facts and information may, however, become so self perpetuating that it never ends. It is necessary, at some point, to call a halt, usually when one feels that further defining activity has reached the level of diminishing returns.

After the problem has been defined, the second stage of *brainstorming,* or idea finding begins. Here problem solvers engage in free association techniques of various kinds to jolt their minds out of conventional tracks and into unconventional areas. Word play, extravagant wishes, scenarios, and way out ideas are all actively encouraged. During this phase it is crucial that all ideas be accepted, and that the quality of ideas not be judged. The emphasis is on quantity, not quality. Something that seems silly may trigger a solution from another quarter.

The next stage in the process is the most mysterious and ill-defined. Although this stage is not well understood, most experts agree it is crucial to creative problem solving. It can be described as a *pause,* or as some call it, a fallow period in which the previous activities of definition and brainstorming are allowed to cook. Sometimes it is helpful to leave the problem solving altogether and turn attention to an unrelated activity. Many creative problem solving techniques have this down time as a formally structured component. The result is often that a solution leaps unbidden to the consciousness, almost as a bolt from the blue. This result is well documented in the writings of creative individuals.

Solution finding is the final stage, and it frequently receives less than its fair share of attention. It is a dependent activity which requires accurate definitions, brainstorming, a creative pause, and the selection of the best alternative for implementing a solution. During the idea finding stage, it is best to suspend judgment about the ideas generated; during this stage, alternatives must be evaluated according to carefully chosen criteria.

When using creative problem solving processes it is very important to remember that idea finding and solution finding are distinct and separate stages. Deferring judgment until the final stage will encourage the development of more and better ideas.

What abilities are necessary to be creative?

There are four basic abilities necessary to creativity and problem solving operations: fluency, flexibility, originality, and elaboration.

Fluency is part of the information retrieval process. A person gathers information and stores it until needed in the mind. The ability to retrieve it quickly and in quantity is called fluency, which is generally measured by the number of different ideas an individual generates in response to a specific problem. A student may be asked, for example, to list all the possible uses for a brick. If the student lists: "paperweight, anchor, doorstop, breaking a window, crushing nuts," and so on for several more ideas, the student is demonstrating fluency. This trait may also be observed in class discussions when a student offers many ideas on one topic, or generates several ways to implement an idea.

Flexibility is the ability to switch from one *kind* of thought to another. In problem solving and other creative activities people must be able to generate a variety of applications of a particular principle or concept. In the above example, the possibilities cited for using the brick demonstrate flexibility, since both the weight of the brick (as an anchor or doorstop) and its potential as an implement of destruction (breaking windows) were considered. If the list should include "build a house" and "make book-shelves," other properties of the brick would be brought into play and, hence, other kinds of uses. Flexibility, then, is the ability to transcend the boundaries of a given context when solving problems. It can be demonstrated in the classroom when a student switches easily from one topic to another, or generates several different kinds of alternatives in problem solving situations.

Originality, often assumed to be the same as creativity, is really the ability to come up with unique or unusual ideas, concepts, or alternatives. To continue our example for a moment, using a brick to build buildings is not very original; however, using it as a pencil holder or grinding it up to use the dust as a bird cage liner are unusual responses.

Elaboration is the ability to embellish and/or complete an idea. The student who suggests using a brick as a pencil holder may demonstrate elaborative thinking by covering the bottom with felt, painting the brick, modifying the sizes of the holes in the brick to accommodate different sizes of pencils.

The Council for Exceptional Children and ERIC Clearinghouse on Handicapped and Gifted Children

THE COUNCIL FOR EXCEPTIONAL CHILDREN: AN OVERVIEW

The Council for Exceptional Children (CEC) has as its principle purpose the advancement of the education of exceptional children and youth, both handicapped and gifted.

CEC is a membership organization; however, any interested individual, lay or professional, may request information from CEC. Researchers, graduate students, parents, and special education professionals all use the services regularly. Any interested person may become a member of CEC.

ACTIVITIES AND SERVICES COORDINATED BY THE CEC CENTER ON TECHNICAL ASSISTANCE, TRAINING, AND INFORMATION ON THE EXCEPTIONAL PERSON

INFORMATION

Major activities of The Council for Exceptional Children include operation of the CEC Information Center and the ERIC Clearinghouse on Handicapped and Gifted Children. The Information Center and Clearinghouse serve as a comprehensive information center identifying and collecting English language literature on the education of handicapped and gifted children, much of which is unavailable from commercial sources. The collection currently includes over 29,000 books, journal articles, curriculum guides, conference reports, research reports, guidelines, etc. Citations and abstracts for these documents are prepared by CEC/ERIC staff and are computer stored for rapid retrieval.

CEC's Information Center provides customized computer searches of literature in the Exceptional Child and ERIC data bases and provides topical bibliographies on popular topics. A new service, Selective Dissemination of Information, automatically and regularly provides current awareness of all literature acquired by the Center on the most frequently requested topics.

Other services of the Center include: (1) answering phone or mail inquiries; (2) referring inquirers to other organizations or information centers; (3) sending brochures, pamphlets, and fact sheets; and (4) permitting on-site use of its holdings, including the collection of literature on the exceptional child and the entire collection of documents in *Resources in Education* (ERIC) on microfiche.

PUBLICATIONS

Publications of The Council for Exceptional Children include the following periodicals: (1) *Exceptional Child Education Resources,* which contains citations of all publications stored in the CEC Information Center; (2) *TEACHING Exceptional Children,* which includes information on instructional methods and learning materials designed or adapted for use with handicapped or gifted children, educational diagnostic techniques and evaluation of instructional materials; (3) *Exceptional Children,* the official journal of CEC, which emphasizes current issues, research, and trends in special education and has a selection of articles on a broad range of educational topics; and (4) *Insight,* the CEC monthly governmental newspaper which contains information on state and federal legislation, programs, and services for handicapped and gifted children.

A wide range of other CEC publications—books, monographs, and nonprint media—offer resources for continuing growth and practical assistance in many areas such as early childhood education, delivery of services, assessment and placement, research, children's rights, career education, cultural diversity, and the gifted.

TRAINING

Other new CEC services include CEC Training Institutes which offer intensive study and instruction for developing skills and techniques in delivering services to exceptional children. Institutes are delivered by CEC trainers and are available for replication. Examples of current institute topics include "Placement of Exceptional Children" and "Due Process."

GOVERNMENTAL RELATIONS

CEC's Governmental Relations Unit is composed of two principal parts. The Policy Implementation Section attempts to effectively monitor, coordinate, and implement the variety of federal, state, and local public policy that directly or indirectly influences the education of exceptional children. The unit's Policy Research Section maintains a comprehensive data bank on state and federal legislation, regulations and litigation involving the education of handicapped and gifted and talented children as well as providing information, products, and technical assistance in this area.

CONVENTIONS AND CONFERENCES

A major function of CEC is the sponsoring of an annual international convention. Recent conventions have been attended by over 12,000 participants and have included features such as job opportunity notices, over 390 professional program sessions, and over 300 exhibitors.

Regional and topical conferences have been sponsored by CEC on topics such as early childhood, individualized education program planning, and instructional technology.

MEMBERSHIP AND DIVISIONS

The Council for Exceptional Children was founded in 1922 and currently has over 60,000 members (including over 17,000 student members). There are 54 state and provincial federations and over 950 local CEC chapters throughout the U.S., Canada, and their territories, which conduct their own professional programs and produce publications. The Council has 12 membership divisions: (1) Association for the Gifted; (2) Council for Administrators of Special Education; (3) Council for Children with Behavioral Disorders; (4) Council for Educational Diagnostic Services; (5) Division for Children with Learning Disabilities; (6) Division of Mental Retardation; (7) Division of Early Childhood Education; (8) Division of Children with Communication Disorders; (9) Division on the Physically Handicapped, Homebound, Hospitalized; (10) Division for the Visually Impaired, Partially Seeing and Blind; (11) Teacher Education Division; and (12) Division on Career Development.

For more information, write or call:

John Grossi, Director, Gifted and Talented Information Project
The Council for Exceptional Children

1920 Association Drive
Reston, Virginia 22091
800-336-3728 (Toll free number for continental U.S. only.
Virginia residents call collect 703-620-3660.)

ERIC CLEARINGHOUSE ON HANDICAPPED AND GIFTED CHILDREN

INFORMATION AND SERVICES

ERIC, the Educational Resources Information Center, is a national information system designed to put people in touch with literature in the field of education. ERIC is funded by the National Institute of Education and consists of a network of 16 clearinghouses that gather literature in special fields.

The ERIC Clearinghouse on Handicapped and Gifted Children is a comprehensive information center on research, programs, evaluation methods, administration, services, teacher education, and curricula related to handicapped and gifted children and youth. The clearinghouse acquires, abstracts, and indexes literature for inclusion in the ERIC reference publications; publishes synthesis papers, monographs, newsletters, bibliographies, and fact sheets on topics of current interest; and assists anyone in search of education literature.

The ERIC Clearinghouse on Handicapped and Gifted Children is located at the Council for Exceptional Children, 1920 Association Drive, Reston, Va. 22091. Toll free telephone number: 800-336-3728.

Services offered by the ERIC Clearinghouse on Handicapped and Gifted Children include:

Responding to mail and telephone inquiries with fact sheets, spot bibliographies, information packets, form letters, publication lists, referrals, or personal letters.

Conducting individualized computer searches of the ERIC data base.

Providing public access to the ERIC Reading Room (open 8:00–4:30 Monday through Friday). The Reading Room contains the ERIC microfiche collection and the clearinghouse journal collection.

Questions and Answers about the Advanced Placement Program*

1. What is the Advanced Placement (AP) Program?

A program of college-level courses and exams for secondary school students. Over 90 percent of the nation's colleges that most AP candidates attend give credit and/or advanced placement to students whose AP examination grades are considered acceptable.

2. What courses are offered in the AP Program?

English†	Music (two courses)
American History	Studio Art†
European History	History of Art
Calculus (two courses)	Classics (two courses)
Biology	French (two courses)
Chemistry	German†
Physics (three courses)	Spanish (two courses)

Individual Course Description booklets describing the essential content of each course are prepared by committees of college professors and AP teachers. These booklets also contain sample exam questions.

3. Does every secondary school offer all these courses?

No. But about 1 in 5 of the nation's 22,000 secondary schools has college-level AP course work. They offer those AP classes most appropriate for their college preparatory students; the average is three or four courses. Ask your counselor which courses are available at your school.

4. What is an AP course like?

It is a special college-level learning experience that most often takes a full academic year. It may not be called an "AP course," and it may not even be a course. It can take the form of an honors class, a strong regular course, a tutorial, or independent study. It is usually challenging and thought-provoking and—compared to other high school courses—it often takes more time, requires more work, gives greater opportunity for individual progress and accomplishment, goes into greater depth, and is more stimulating.

---

*Some Questions and Answers about the Advanced Placement Program, Item No. 273654, free from College Board Publication Orders, Box 2815, Princeton, N.J. 08541.
†Second course planned for 1980.

In a study of 400 former AP students interviewed at their colleges, more than 90 percent ranked their AP experiences as the most valuable of their high school studies. As one student said: "I wasn't just learning facts and more facts . . . he [the AP teacher] taught us the tools and techniques of scholarship so you could see what facts you need and how to get them. . . ." To get your own idea, ask other students about their experiences with AP.

5. *What are AP Exams like? When are they given?*

In all subjects except Art, the exams contain both multiple-choice questions and free-response questions that require essay writing, problem solving, and so forth. In History of Art there are only essay questions—some based on projected color slides—and there is an option between an essay based on a required text and an individual study. In Studio Art there is no exam; rather, students submit portfolios of their work. Tape recordings are used with certain portions of the Music and foreign language exams.

Most of the examinations are three hours long, but some take only an hour and a half or two hours. They are given every year in the third week of May, at your school or one nearby.

6. *Are the exams hard? How are they graded?*

Probably the best way to describe the exams is "tough but fair." Each one is carefully developed to match the AP course description by a committee of examiners made up of college professors and AP teachers who specialize in that field. It ordinarily takes between one and two years to develop a single AP Examination.

The multiple-choice answer sheets are scored by special scoring equipment. The essays are evaluated by more than 700 carefully selected professors and AP teachers who spend a week each June grading answers in the more than 120,000 essay booklets. No matter how many answers there may be in a booklet, each is graded by a different person who has been especially trained to assess this question; the typical booklet is evaluated by four professors and teachers. No grader ever knows the scores given by another grader.

Every examination receives an overall grade on a five-point scale: 5 (extremely well qualified), 4 (well qualified), 3 (qualified), 2 (possibly qualified), and 1 (no recommendation). An AP Grade Report is sent in early July to each student at his or her home address, school, and, if the student requested it, to his or her college.

7. *How many students pass the AP Exams each year?*

That depends on what is meant by "pass." Each college decides what AP Examination grades it will accept for credit and/or advanced placement. The great majority of college and universities accept grades of 3 and above, and there are quite a few that will consider grades of 2. If you wish to know what AP grades are considered acceptable by the colleges you are interested in, write to the Director of Admissions of the college or ask your AP Coordinator to let you see the latest edition of *College Placement and Credit by Examination.* (You can also purchase this publication by writing to the AP address given at the end of this appendix.)

More than 93,000 students take the AP Exams each year, and while the percentages vary from subject to subject, a rough breakdown of the grades received is as follows:

93 percent of AP students get a grade of 2 or higher

73 percent of AP students get a grade of 3 or higher

36 percent of AP students get a grade of 4 or higher

15 percent of AP students get a grade of 5

To obtain a score comparable to a grade of 3 on the multiple-choice section of the typical exam, a student needs to answer about half the questions correctly. Of course, he or she also must do acceptable work on the broader questions in the free-response section to get a grade of 3 or higher.

8. *What do AP Exams cost?*

The fee is $32 for each exam taken. (A limited number of fee reductions that reduce the cost to as little as $15 per exam are available to students with financial need.)

9. *That's a lot. What do I get out of it?*

The benefits that go with advanced placement and credit are numerous. Advanced placement means that in college you can avoid the boredom of repeating work you've already done. You can also take advanced courses in your AP subject, explore other subjects that interest you, and join honors and other special programs. If you earn the required grade on an AP Exam, you may receive the equivalent of 6–8 semester hours or 10–12 quarter hours of credit, probably worth between $300 and $700. If you're granted a full year of college credit, the savings could be anywhere from $2,500 to $8,000.

10. *Can I really get a year of college credit for AP work?*

Definitely. Some of the most selective colleges are among the approximately 650 institutions that consider acceptable grades on three or more AP Exams as evidence that the student has done work comparable to a year's academic program at college. More than 10,000 AP students are potentially eligible for sophomore standing each year.

11. *Why are colleges interested in AP candidates?*

Studies undertaken by individual colleges have shown repeatedly that AP students who take advanced courses in their first year of college do as well as or better than upperclassmen. Most AP students do extremely well throughout their college careers, and a good number graduate with honors.

12. *If I take AP, am I going to hurt my chances of being admitted to college?*

It's unlikely that an AP course or an AP Exam could work against you—regardless of the grade you get in either—for the following reasons:

At many secondary schools the grades received in AP courses are weighted to reflect the quality of work undertaken; for example, a "B" in an AP or honors course counts for more in a student's grade point average than the same grade in a regular course.

Even if no adjustment is made to a grade, college admissions officials know the value of AP-level work and judge students accordingly.

Remember, too, that if you take an AP Exam, your AP Grade Report is usually sent to a college *after* you are admitted, and *only* if you request it. Even so, it is improbable that you would be disadvantaged by having any AP grade, no matter how low, reported to the college you plan to attend.

Finally, it is generally to your benefit to submit all evidence of your college-level work to the colleges you're interested in.

13. *Why bother with AP Exams if my college doesn't grant recognition for AP grades in my subject?*

For two reasons: The college may change its mind, or you may change yours. Colleges continually update their policies, or you may decide to attend a different college. It is generally in your interest to accumulate all the academic credentials you can. Because AP grades are always kept on file by the College Board you can use them not only now but also in the future—for example, if you transfer to another college.

Also, although it may be hard to believe, some students have found taking an AP Exam in a subject they've studied in depth to be a worthwhile experience in itself.

14. *Why take AP Exams rather than other college placement tests?*

While several studies show that AP Exams are the most generally accepted college-level examinations, they are not the only good tests around. Certain colleges have their own placement tests, and the College-Level Examination Program (CLEP) of the College Board offers a number of tests, many covering subjects not included in AP.

AP Exams differ from these other tests in two major ways: (1) They are based on the content of specific courses, and (2) they offer essay components that are graded under controlled conditions. Further, AP Examination grades are nationally recognized and are, therefore, widely transferable among institutions.

If you decide to explore alternatives to the AP Exams, the first thing to do is ask the colleges you're interested in about their placement and credit-by-examination policies. (Your counselor or AP Coordinator can give you an idea of the kinds of questions to ask.) After you have the facts, compare the various options and choose the one that offers the best credit and placement opportunities. Whatever test you choose, you should plan to take it as close to the end of your course as possible. Remember, however, that you have only one chance at the AP Exams each year.

15. *How can I get involved in AP?*

Talk to your principal, department chairman, teacher, counselor, AP Coordinator—whoever knows about AP at your school. He or she can fill you in on the AP Program and help you decide which AP courses may be for you. It's a good idea to plan ahead—even in the ninth or tenth grade—so you will have the appropriate background courses for the AP experience in your junior or senior year. You don't have to take an AP course to be able to take an AP Exam, but—however you prepare—you should be sure your study fits the appropriate AP course description.

If you want further information about AP, request a free copy of the *Guide to the Advanced Placement Program* from College Board Publication Orders, Box 2815, Princeton, NJ 08541.

Thinking-Learning-Communicating Skills Continuum, K–12

This skill continuum is a basic multipurpose instructional planning and implementation tool. It provides an articulation framework for a school district's skill development program, K–12, pinpointing where within the program of studies each thinking-learning-communicating skill can be appropriately introduced, reinforced, and/or extended. This continuum is also an invaluable instructional planning guide for classroom teachers and school library media specialists to use when determining specific thinking-learning-communicating skills to be integrated within a teaching or learning program.

For each skill listed indicate the appropriate grade level for that skill to be introduced, reinforced, or extended.

PART ONE: THINKING SKILLS

	Introduce	Reinforce	Extend
I. THINKING PROCESSES			

A. Make effective use of perceptive thinking
    1. Visualizing mentally
    2. Discriminating properties of objects
    3. Discriminating among events
    4. Perceiving relationships
    5. Interpreting meanings
B. Make effective use of associative thinking
    1. Linking and matching similar ideas, events, and problems
    2. Relating terms and meanings
    3. Translating signs and symbols
    4. Relating behavior traits and actions
C. Make effective use of conceptual thinking
    1. Classifying data into groups
    2. Listing, grouping, and labeling data
    3. Generalizing common elements
    4. Comparing and contrasting categories of data
    5. Organizing data under specific headings such as: desirable, undesirable, feasible, infeasible
D. Make effective use of problem solving
    1. Defining the problem
      a. Encountering the problem
      b. Selecting the problem

PART ONE: THINKING SKILLS

	Introduce	Reinforce	Extend

I. THINKING PROCESSES (cont.)

  c. Stating the problem
  d. Framing tentative solutions
 2. Working on the problem
  a. Recalling known information and past experience
  b. Locating information
  c. Appraising, organizing, and interpreting information
 3. Drawing conclusions
  a. Stating possible conclusions
  b. Determining the most logical conclusion
  c. Reaching a conclusion
 4. Carrying out a conclusion
  a. Acting on a conclusion
  b. Reconsidering the conclusion

E. Make effective use of critical thinking
 1. Defining the problem
  a. Becoming aware of a problem
  b. Making it meaningful
  c. Making it manageable
 2. Developing a tentative answer; hypothesizing
  a. Examining and classifying available data
  b. Seeking relationships, drawing logical inferences
  c. Stating the hypothesis
 3. Testing the tentative answer
  a. Assembling evidence
   –Identifying the needed evidence
   –Collecting the needed evidence
   –Evaluating the needed evidence
  b. Arranging evidence
   –Translating evidence
   –Interpreting evidence
   –Classifying evidence
  c. Analyzing evidence
   –Seeking relationships
   –Noting similarities and differences
   –Identifying trends, sequences, and regularities
 4. Developing a conclusion
  a. Finding meaningful patterns or relationships
  b. Stating the conclusion
 5. Applying the conclusion
  a. Testing against new evidence
  b. Generalizing the results

F. Make effective use of creative thinking
 1. Wondering why not, what if, just suppose
 2. Recalling past experiences*
 3. Gathering facts and seeking answers (PREPARATION)
 4. Observing the odd and the unusual
 5. Formulating new interpretations

---

*"Experience is one of the most important sources of raw material for creativity." From Jacolyn A. Mott, *Creativity and Imagination* (Mankato, Minn.: Creative Education, 1973), p. 26.

PART ONE: THINKING SKILLS

	Introduce	Reinforce	Extend

I.   THINKING PROCESSES (cont.)

    6. Grasping new relationships
    7. Incubating ideas (INCUBATION)
    8. Generating solutions spontaneously (IN-
       SPIRATION)
    9. Testing and proving validity of solutions
       (VERIFICATION)

G. Make effective use of adventurous thinking
    1. Thinking bold, new thoughts
    2. Projecting beyond what is
    3. Risking defeat by attempting the impossible
    4. "Manipulating complexity, incompleteness,
       and imperfections to achieve break-
       throughs and genuine innovations"*

II.   THINKING IN THE COGNITIVE AREA

A. Make effective use of knowledge building skills
    1. Building knowledge of specifics
    2. Building knowledge of ways and means of
       dealing with specifics; organizing
    3. Building knowledge of universals and ab-
       stractions

B. Make effective use of comprehension skills
    1. Relating knowledge to other material; see-
       ing the full implication
    2. Translating, paraphrasing, or restructuring
       ideas
    3. Interpreting, summarizing, reorganizing
    4. Extrapolating; extending trends beyond
       given data

C. Make effective use of application skills
    1. Using abstractions in concrete situations
    2. Restructuring situations so the abstraction
       applies

D. Make effective use of analysis skills
    1. Analyzing elements; distinguishing facts
       from hypotheses
    2. Analyzing relationships; connections and
       interactions
    3. Analyzing organizational principles; system-
       atic arrangement

E. Make effective use of synthesis skills
    1. Producing unique communication
    2. Producing a plan or proposed set of opera-
       tions
    3. Formulating hypotheses or propositions
    4. Recombining of parts of previous experi-
       ence with new material; reconstructing into
       a new order or pattern
    5. Producing a product that did not exist be-
       fore

F. Make effective use of evaluation skills

---

*E. Paul Torrance, "What It Means to Become Human" in *To Nurture Humaneness,* ed. by Mary-Margaret Scobey and Grace Graham (Washington, D.C.: Association for Supervision and Curriculum Development, NEA, 1970), p. 7.

PART ONE: THINKING SKILLS

	Introduce	Reinforce	Extend
II. THINKING IN THE COGNITIVE AREA (cont.)			

1. Making judgments in terms of internal evidence
2. Making judgments in terms of external criteria

III. THINKING IN THE AFFECTIVE AREA			

A. Make effective use of receiving (attending) skills
   1. Developing awareness; being conscious of a situation, object, or state of affairs
   2. Willing to receive; giving attention but remaining neutral
   3. Controlling or selecting focus of attention; selecting stimuli to attend to; attention controlled by learner
B. Make effective use of responding skills
   1. Acquiescing in response; compliance or obedience
   2. Willing to respond; voluntary response; proceeding from one's own choice
   3. Deriving satisfaction in response; behavior accompanied by a feeling of pleasure, zest, or enjoyment
C. Make effective use of valuing skills
   1. Accepting a value; showing consistency of response to the class of phenomena with which a belief or an attitude is identified
   2. Preferring a value; sufficient commitment to a value that the individual will pursue, seek out, or want it
   3. Committing one's self; belief involving a high degree of certainty bordering on faith; includes loyalty to a position, group, or cause
D. Make effective use of organizing skills
   1. Conceptualizing a value; shown by attempts to identify characteristics of an object or position valued and by expression of judgments about a value
   2. Organizing a value system; bringing together a complex of values into an ordered relationship
E. Make effective use of characterizing valuing skills
   1. Acting consistently in accordance with internalized values
   2. Developing a consistent philosophy of life or a code of behavior which becomes characteristic of the person

PART TWO: LEARNING SKILLS

	Introduce	Reinforce	Extend
I. LOCATING INFORMATION			

A. Make effective use of libraries
   1. Valuing a library as a learning laboratory

PART TWO: LEARNING SKILLS

	Introduce	Reinforce	Extend

I.   LOCATING INFORMATION (cont.)

    a. A means of becoming a participant in all that mankind has ever thought, questioned, dreamed, created, achieved, and valued

    b. A basic resource for building self-awareness and achieving self-realization

    c. A source and a force for lifelong learning

2. Respecting information retrieval as a basic learning skill

3. Respecting the librarian as a teacher whose subject is learning itself

    a. A source of concerned, informed, and competent guidance in how to locate, organize, use, and evaluate information

    b. A concerned counselor to be consulted when searching for answers to personal problems or questing for advice or reassurance

4. Respecting all media—print and nonprint—as carriers of knowledge worthy of exploration

5. Using the Dewey Decimal Classification System as a guide for locating books in the school library

    000   General works
    100   Philosophy
    200   Religion
    300   Social science
    400   Language
    500   Pure science
    600   Technology
    700   The arts
    800   Literature
    900   History

6. Using the Library of Congress Classification System as a guide for locating books in public, college, university, and special libraries

    A   General works—polygraphy
    B   Philosophy—religion
    C   History—auxiliary sciences
    D   History and topography (except America)
    E–F America
    G   Geography—anthropology
    H   Social sciences
    J   Political science
    K   Law
    L   Education
    M   Music
    N   Fine arts
    P   Language and literature
    Q   Science
    R   Medicine

PART TWO: LEARNING SKILLS

	Introduce	Reinforce	Extend
I. LOCATING INFORMATION (cont.)			

      S Agriculture—plant and animal indus-
         try
      T Technology
      U Military service
      V Naval science
      Z Bibliography and library science

  7. Using card catalog as the key to the holdings of the library
    a. Books are indexed in card catalog by
      –Author
      –Title
      –Subject
    b. Author card contains most information
      –Author(s)
      –Editor(s)
      –Compiler(s)
      –Illustrator(s)
      –Full title and subtitle
      –Edition
      –Imprint—place of publication, publisher, date of publication
      –Copyright date
      –Collation—number of pages, number of volumes, illustrations, size of book

B. Make effective use of books
  1. Using title and subtitle of book as guide to contents
  2. Using blurb on book jacket as indication of contents
  3. Using title page to identify
    a. Author(s)
    b. Editor(s)
    c. Compiler(s)
    d. Illustrator(s)
    e. Edition
    f. Abridgement
    g. Translation
    h. Imprint information
      –Place of publication
      –Publisher
      –Imprint date
  4. Using back (verso) of title page
    a. Date of first and subsequent copyright dates
    b. Owner(s) of copyright
    c. Place of copyright registration
  5. Using table of contents to identify
    a. Titles of chapters
    b. Sequence of chapters
    c. Pages of chapters, appendices, lists of maps, lists of illustrations, glossary, bibliography, and index
  6. Using preliminary information (front matter)
    a. End papers

PART TWO: LEARNING SKILLS

	Introduce	Reinforce	Extend
I. LOCATING INFORMATION (cont.)			

       b. Frontispiece
       c. Dedication
       d. Preface
       e. Foreword
       f. Introduction
       g. Acknowledgments
       h. Contributors
       i. Usage notes
    7. Using the index to discover
       a. Subjects or topics included in the book: persons, places, things, events, processes
       b. Main subjects and topics listed in alphabetical order; subtopics listed after main topics
       c. Page numbers after main subjects, main topics, and subtopics
       d. Inclusive paging indicated by hyphen between the first and last page
       e. Poetry uses separate indexes for poet, title of poem, and first line of poem
       f. Cross references to key topics
    8. Using bibliography to identify
       a. Depth and breadth of information beyond content of book used
       b. Verification of sources cited; means of placing paraphrased information in context
    9. Using glossary and terminology list
       a. Discover special meaning of words
       b. Discover translation of foreign words
    10. Using illustrations—pictures, charts, graphs, maps—to heighten meaning of text
  C. Make effective use of dictionaries
    1. Using dictionaries as data sources for
       a. Definitions of words
       b. Spelling of words
       c. Pronunciation of words
       d. History of words
       e. Synonyms
       f. Abbreviations
       g. Signs and symbols
       h. Foreign terms
       i. Diagrams
       j. Tables
    2. Recognizing the distinguishing characteristics of
       a. Abridged language dictionaries
       b. Unabridged language dictionaries
    3. Recognizing the useful features of a dictionary
       a. Alphabetical arrangement
       b. Guide words
       c. Thumb index
       d. Hints on dictionary use
       e. Abbreviations

PART TWO: LEARNING SKILLS

	Introduce	Reinforce	Extend

I.   LOCATING INFORMATION (cont.)

      f. Illustrations
      g. Diagrams
      h. Tables
      i. List of important people, places, and
         events
      j. Common given names
   4. Recognizing the distinguishing characteris-
     tics of
      a. Language dictionaries
      b. Specialized dictionaries
   5. Realizing the value of having a dictionary
     readily at hand when studying; developing
     the dictionary habit

D. Make effective use of encyclopedias
   1. Using encyclopedias as data sources for
     brief information about
      a. Persons
      b. Places
      c. Things
      d. Events
      e. Processes
   2. Recognizing the distinguishing characteris-
     tics of
      a. General encyclopedias
      b. Special encyclopedias
   3. Gaining facility in using
      a. Key words
      b. Guide words
      c. Cross references
      d. Indexes
      e. Reference outlines and study
         guides
      f. Illustrations
   4. Updating encyclopedias by checking annu-
     als and yearbooks for
      a. Art
      b. Business
      c. Chronologies
      d. Drama
      e. Education
      f. Fashion
      g. International affairs
      h. Legislation
      i. Literature
      j. Medicine
      k. Motion pictures
      l. Necrologies
      m.Politics
      n. Radio and television
      o. Science
      p. Special reports on major issues
      q. Sports
      r. Transportation
      s. Urban problems and development
      t. Year in review

PART TWO: LEARNING SKILLS

	Introduce	Reinforce	Extend

I.   LOCATING INFORMATION (cont.)

    5. Recognizing limitations of encyclopedic information
       a. Serves as an introduction; provides an overview of skeletal facts
       b. Serves as an outline identifying main topics to be researched further in other sources

E. Make effective use of other basic reference tools

    1. Recognizing distinguishing characteristics and informational value of abstracts
       a. List new literature in a specialized field
       b. Give brief abstracts of books and periodical articles listed

    2. Recognizing distinguishing characteristics and informational value of almanacs and fact books
       a. Contain statistical information on all topics of universal interest
       b. Published each year
       c. Charts, tables, and graphs used for clarity and brevity
       d. General almanacs and fact books cover universal topics in limited detail
       e. Specialized almanacs and fact books provide in depth statistical analysis of a specific area

    3. Recognizing distinguishing characteristics and informational value of atlases and gazetteers
       a. Atlases are books of maps
       b. Gazetteers are books of places: names, location, description
       c. Interpreting maps requires use of longitude, latitude, scale, key, legend, symbols

    4. Recognizing distinguishing characteristics and informational value of bibliographies
       a. Bibliographies are lists of books and/or articles about a particular subject, a particular person, a particular author, a particular collection
       b. Bibliographies are used
         –To find out something about a given book: author's name, title, edition, publisher, date, cost
         –To find out what has been written on a given subject
         –To choose a book for a certain purpose
       c. Bibliographies of bibliographies are tools to be used in identifying special or general bibliographies

    5. Recognizing distinguishing characteristics and informational value of handbooks and manuals

PART TWO: LEARNING SKILLS

	Introduce	Reinforce	Extend

I.   Locating Information (cont.)

      a. The terms *handbook* and *manual* are used interchangeably

      b. Handbooks and/or manuals are reference books designed to help their readers to understand or use something

      c. Style manuals are basic guides to the mechanics of writing; an invaluable tool to be kept readily at hand and consulted when undertaking a writing assignment

   6. Recognizing distinguishing characteristics and informational value of indexes other than indexes to periodicals

      a. Indexes are location keys to anthologies of poetry, plays, essays, short stories, fairy tales, and general literature

      b. Concordances show in context each use of all important words used by an author of exceptional note or as found in the Bible

      c. Indexes to quotations may also include a concordance of key words

F. Make effective use of periodicals and periodical indexes

   1. Realizing that magazines are called periodicals

      a. A periodical is a publication issued periodically, or at stated intervals

      b. Journals are periodicals issued by professional organizations and learned societies

   2. Valuing periodicals as rich sources of information especially useful for

      a. Subjects requiring latest information available in print

      b. Subjects for which books are not available

      c. Contemporary opinion on a given subject, person, happening

      d. Current editorial comment

      e. Current bibliographies

   3. Valuing periodical indexes as effective tools for locating information in periodicals

      a. Periodical indexes cover the period from 1802 to date

      b. *Readers' Guide to Periodical Literature* indexes articles within two weeks of publication date

   4. Valuing microreproductions as ready reference sources for periodical information, past and present

      a. Microcard

      b. Microfiche

      c. Microfilm

   5. Guarding against the threat of bias in periodical articles

PART TWO: LEARNING SKILLS

	Introduce	Reinforce	Extend

I.   LOCATING INFORMATION (cont.)

    6. Being aware of propaganda techniques
       a. Name calling
       b. Glittering generalities
       c. Transfer
       d. Testimonial
       e. Plain folks
       f. Card stacking
       g. Bandwagon

G. Make effective use of newspapers and newspaper indexes

    1. Becoming acquainted with organization patterns of newspapers; the purposes of various sections

    2. Perceiving the reasons for article placement

    3. Perceiving the dangers of news that is slanted, biased, sensationalized

    4. Realizing the distinguishing features and significance of the front page
       a. Headline
       b. Banner
       c. Streamer
       d. Subhead
       e. Masthead
       f. Nameplate
       g. Flag
       h. Edition
       i. Motto
       j. Lead story
       k. News feature
       l. Index
       m. Byline
       n. Dateline
       o. Publisher
       p. Correspondent
       q. Weather ear

    5. Realizing the distinguishing features and significance of news stories
       a. Lead paragraph
       b. Summary lead
       c. Copy editor
       d. Reporter
       e. News service
       f. Interpretive stories
       g. Investigative stories
       h. Editorializing

    6. Realizing the distinguishing features and significance of the editorial page
       a. Syndicated column
       b. Syndication service
       c. Editorial
       d. Editorial cartoon
       e. Letters to the editor
       f. Opinion
       g. Viewpoint

PART TWO: LEARNING SKILLS

	Introduce	Reinforce	Extend

I. LOCATING INFORMATION (cont.)

  h. Editorial board

  i. Editorial policy

 7. Judging reliability of a news report

  a. Comparing reports on the same event as found in several newspapers

  b. Comparing newspaper reports with news magazine reports

  c. Comparing reports in newspapers with those given by radio and television reporters

 8. Valuing the *New York Times Index* as an excellent reference tool

  a. Best quick source of information on events since 1851

  b. Indexing is thorough

  c. Use the index to find exact date of an event, to check proper names, and to discover cross references

 9. Valuing microreproductions of newspapers as research treasure troves

H. Make effective use of U.S. government documents, publications, and indexes

 1. Recognizing the distinguishing characteristics and informational value of federal documents

  a. Congressional documents

   –The *Congressional Record*

   –House and Senate Reports and Documents

   –Bills, resolutions, acts, statutes, laws

   –Hearings and Committee Prints

  b. Judicial documents

  c. Executive documents

   –Federal regulations

   –Departmental documents

   –Presidential documents

 2. Recognizing the distinguishing characteristics and informational value of indexes to U.S. government publications

  a. *Monthly Catalog* is the only comprehensive, current listing

  b. *Selected U.S. Government Publications* is issued biweekly

  c. *Price Lists* are issued by 80 departments and agencies

 3. Realizing that the Superintendent of Documents, U.S. Government Printing Office, Washington, D.C. 20402, is the information source and the sales agent for government publications

I. Make effective use of pamphlets

 1. Recognizing the distinguishing characteristics and informational value of pamphlets

  a. Unbound publication

  b. Fewer than 100 pages

PART TWO: LEARNING SKILLS

Introduce   Reinforce   Extend

I.   LOCATING INFORMATION (cont.)

    c. Complete in itself
    d. Excellent sources on current topics not
      available in book form

  2. Recognizing that unbound pamphlets are
    usually not filed with books
    a. Usually filed in filing cabinets (vertical
      files); arranged alphabetically by topic
      or subject
    b. Most important pamphlets are usually
      listed in the card catalog

  3. Recognizing that the following are prolific
    sources of pamphlet material
    a. Local, state, and national governments
    b. The United Nations
    c. Associations
    d. Business and industry

J.   Make effective use of primary source materials

  1. Learning the essentials of historical
    method*
    a. Collection of objects and of printed,
      written, and oral materials that may be
      relevant
    b. Exclusion of materials (or parts thereof)
      that are unauthentic
    c. Extraction from the authentic material
      of testimony that is credible
    d. Organizing of that reliable testimony
      into a meaningful narrative or exposition

  2. Determining the authenticity and signifi-
    cance of primary source materials†
    a. Who is the authority?
    b. What is his background?
    c. What is the purpose of the material?
    d. When and under what circumstances
      was the information recorded?
    e. Was the information written from mem-
      ory or was it a direct account of what
      happened?
    f. Is there corroboration of the facts from
      other sources?
    g. Is the authority objective in the treat-
      ment of the material?
    h. Is the material pertinent?
    i. Is there mention in this source of other
      documents, people, or events that
      should be researched?

  3. Validating and utilizing information gained
    from

---

*Louis Gottschalk, *Understanding History: A Primer of Historical Method* (New York: Alfred A. Knopf, 1950), p. 28.

†Adapted from Alice Elkenberry and Ruth Ellsworth, "Organizing and Evaluating Information," in *Skill Development in Social Studies,* ed. by Helen McCracken Carpenter (Washington, D.C.: National Council for the Social Studies, NEA, 1963), p. 89.

PART TWO: LEARNING SKILLS

	Introduce	Reinforce	Extend

I.   LOCATING INFORMATION (cont.)

        a. Written or printed sources; reprints, fac-
           similes, and microreproductions
          –Account books
          –Bills of sale
          –Charters
          –Cookbooks
          –Court records
          –Deeds
          –Diaries
          –Eyewitness accounts
          –Handbills
          –Handbooks
          –Indenture papers
          –Journals
          –Legislative records
          –Letters
          –Memoirs
          –Military records
          –Newspapers
          –Pamphlets
          –Periodicals
          –Speeches
          –Tax records

        b. Disc and tape recorded materials
          –Debates
          –Hearings
          –Interviews
          –Newscasts
          –Plays
          –Poems
          –Songs
          –Speeches

        c. Artifacts; realia, museum replicas
          –Banners
          –Buildings
          –Buttons
          –Cemeteries
          –Ceramics
          –Clothing
          –Currency
          –Flags
          –Furniture
          –Jewelry
          –Machines
          –Musical instruments
          –Paintings
          –Photographs
          –Religious articles
          –Sculptures
          –Stamps
          –Textiles
          –Tools
          –Vehicles
          –Weapons

K. Make effective use of audiovisual media
    1. Developing audiovisual literacy

PART TWO: LEARNING SKILLS

	Introduce	Reinforce	Extend
I. LOCATING INFORMATION (cont.)			

    a. Preplan the purpose for using nonprint
       media

    b. Study carefully the guides and usage
       notes accompanying the various media

    c. Develop the habit of concentrated view-
       ing, observing, and listening

    d. Link ideas gained from viewing, observ-
       ing, and listening with previously gained
       understanding

    e. Take careful notes
       –Identify type of media, title, producer,
        series, and copyright or issuing date
       –For filmstrips, note specific frame or
        frames where information was found
       –For art prints and study prints, note
        specific print or prints where informa-
        tion was found
       –List those topics introduced in each
        filmstrip, tape, record, motion picture,
        etc., worthy of further research

    f. Following the first viewing, observing,
       and listening, review notes
       –Determine adequacy of notes; clear?
        complete?
       –Re-view, re-observe, or re-listen to
        check and/or revise notes

    g. Search for additional information in
       other print and/or audiovisual media

  2. Valuing nonprint media as authentic car-
    riers of knowledge—rich data banks for in-
    formation retrieval

II. ACQUIRING INFORMATION THROUGH PURPOSEFUL AND APPRECIATIVE READING			

A. Develop reading competence

  1. Decoding the meaning from the printed
    word

  2. Grasping, translating, inferring the intent,
    selecting, organizing, and expressing ideas

  3. Thinking, feeling, and imagining within the
    frame of reference being read

  4. Analyzing and appraising what is being
    read both critically and objectively

  5. Interacting intellectually and emotionally
    with what is being read

  6. Responding to the imagery, the beauty,
    and the power of words

  7. Synthesizing ideas gleaned from current
    reading with previous understandings

  8. Going beyond literal meaning to discover
    and savor hidden meaning

  9. Interpreting allusions and figures of speech

  10. Reading between, behind, and beyond the
     words

  11. Finding the facts, filtering the facts, facing
     the facts, and following the facts

PART TWO: LEARNING SKILLS

	Introduce	Reinforce	Extend
II. ACQUIRING INFORMATION THROUGH PURPOSEFUL AND APPRECIATIVE READING (cont.)			

12. Developing the habit of reading with a dictionary readily at hand
13. Linking ideas gained from reading with those gained from viewing, observing, and listening
14. Valuing books as carriers of knowledge—rich data banks for informational retrieval
15. Valuing reading as a basic tool for life-long learning
16. Valuing reading as an art as well as a science

B. Adjust reading rate to purpose
  1. Skimming
    a. Reading rapidly to discover topic inclusion and arrangement of content
    b. Reading here and there, looking for signal phrases
    c. Determining relevance and/or significance of information
    d. Verifying statements, quotations, dates, spellings, statistics
    e. Locating tables, graphs, charts, illustrations, maps
    f. Pinpointing where best to begin to read for specific information
  2. Cursory reading
    a. Reading rapidly
    b. Skipping unknown words and puzzling ideas
    c. Reviewing previously read material
      –Making a summary
      –Generalizing
      –Validating
      –Formulating questions
      –Identifying topics (persons, places, things, events, processes, opinions) requiring further study
  3. Study reading
    a. Reading deliberately with optimum concentration and understanding
    b. Using the SQ4R method*
      –Based on research on the college level: how to read college textbooks effectively
      –Study time can be reduced 25 percent without reducing comprehension
      –Comprised of six basic steps
      S—SURVEYING a chapter to determine author's outline
      Q—Developing QUESTIONS (developing topic headings into questions)

*Kenneth H. Hoover, *The Professional Teacher's Handbook: A Guide for Improving Instruction in Today's Middle and Secondary Schools* (Boston: Allyn and Bacon, 1976), sec. II, pp. 135–136.

PART TWO: LEARNING SKILLS

Introduce   Reinforce   Extend

II.   ACQUIRING INFORMATION THROUGH
PURPOSEFUL AND APPRECIATIVE READING (cont.)

R—READING; skimming for main ideas; scanning to discover signal or flag words

R—RECITING; when an answer is found stop and recite answer in own words

R—WRITING key words (permanent study notes) that serve as cues to answers

R—REVIEWING by concentrating on key questions; review immediately following completion of the assignment; repeat at least once weekly to minimize forgetting

4. Critical reading
   a. Pausing to recall and associate what is being read with past experience
   b. Pausing to reflect, compare, and validate
   c. Savoring what is said and how it is said
   d. Noting and evaluating the style of writing
   e. Delving deeply to uncover hidden meanings
   f. Comparing information from several sources noting similarities, differences, and omissions
   g. Noting relationships, images, allusions, implied meanings, emotional tones, biases, and prejudices

5. Creative reading
   a. Reading with the heart, the imagination, and the soul as well as with the intellect
   b. Developing a mind-set for using information that is read
   c. Generating ideas uniquely different but supportive to what is being read
   d. Internalizing what is read; having a dialogue with the author
   e. Reacting creatively to what is read
      –Drawing a cartoon, poster, picture
      –Composing music, writing a song, matching music to mood, time period, or event
      –Writing a poem, play, short story, biography, scenario
   f. Weaving into the tapestry of thoughts and feelings the various attitudes, values, commitments, and insights gained from reading

C. Read to form relationships
   1. Perceiving chronological and time relationships
      a. Developing an understanding of
         –How centuries are numbered
         –How historical periods are designated

PART TWO: LEARNING SKILLS

	Introduce	Reinforce	Extend

II. ACQUIRING INFORMATION THROUGH
PURPOSEFUL AND APPRECIATIVE READING (cont.)

–How geological time is designated
–How time lines sequentialize and link
events
b. Interpreting and comparing the Julian
and Gregorian calendars
c. Interpreting dates using the perpetual
calendar
d. Developing a vocabulary of definite and
indefinite time expressions
e. Interpreting charts, graphs, and tables
f. Perceiving the distinguishing characteristics of chronologies and their informational value
2. Perceiving cause and effect relationships
a. Seeing the influence of human behavior
on historical and contemporary events
b. Seeing the influence of attitudes, values,
and commitments on behavior
c. Seeing the effect of geography on historical, social, cultural, industrial, economic, and political developments
d. Seeing the relationship between various
forms of government and standards of
living and levels of expectation
e. Seeing the relationship between adventurous thinking and human progress
3. Perceiving space and distance relationships
a. Recognizing the distinguishing characteristics and informational value of maps
and globes
b. Using cardinal and intermediate directions
c. Using parallels and meridians when determining directions
d. Using a highway map to locate places by
using number-and-key
e. Using distance, direction, and location
when planning a trip
f. Using tour guides and atlases to locate
places and determine distances
g. Comparing routes and distances for alternative means of travel
4. Perceiving the relative importance of ideas
a. Identifying inherent properties of things
b. Identifying, grouping, and interpreting
ideas in order of significance
c. Reading accounts from several sources
and noting those events always, seldom,
never mentioned
d. Sequentializing ideas in priority order
e. Using chronologies to identify significant
events and people
f. Using time lines to highlight the interplay of people and events

PART TWO: LEARNING SKILLS

	Introduce	Reinforce	Extend

II. ACQUIRING INFORMATION THROUGH
     PURPOSEFUL AND APPRECIATIVE READING (cont.)

    5. Perceiving analogous relationships
      a. Discerning similarities and likenesses
      b. Avoiding the mistaken idea that if two
        things are alike in certain characteristics
        they are alike in all characteristics
      c. Realizing that the strength of an analogy
        depends on whether or not similarities
        are noteworthy or trivial
      d. Using analogies for clarification; pre-
        senting the unfamiliar in terms of the fa-
        miliar as a means of explanation
    6. Applying what is read to personal experi-
      ence
      a. Relating what is read to own experience
        for validation, assimilation, comparison,
        and utilization
      b. Relating what is read to own beliefs, at-
        titudes, commitments, and values

D. Read literature with perception and appreciation
    1. Recognizing and enjoying effective literary
      style
    2. Identifying the essential or basic character-
      istics of effective literary expression
    3. Identifying the distinguishing characteris-
      tics of the various literary genres
      –Autobiography
      –Biography
      –Drama
      –Essay
      –Fable
      –Folklore
      –History
      –Legend
      –Myth
      –Novel
      –Personal narrative
      –Poem
      –Short story
    4. Distinguishing between fact and fiction,
      realism and fantasy
    5. Understanding the characteristics and pur-
      poses of figural and idiomatic expression
    6. Visualizing described settings and actions
    7. Responding to mood, tone, and imagery of
      a literary work
    8. Reading literature with the imagination;
      sharing vicariously the action; interacting
      with the ongoing drama of events
    9. Responding creatively to what has been
      read
   10. Interpreting literary criticism to mean en-
      deavoring "to find, to know, to love, to
      recommend not only the best, but all the

PART TWO: LEARNING SKILLS

	Introduce	Reinforce	Extend

II. ACQUIRING INFORMATION THROUGH
   PURPOSEFUL AND APPRECIATIVE READING (cont.)

    good that has been known and written in
    the world."*

11. Identifying the distinguishing characteristics of the various literary awards such as
    −Caldecott Medal
    −John Newbery Award
    −Nobel Awards
    −Pulitzer Awards
12. Using literary handbooks for overview and insight
13. Developing an ever-widening interest in and an ever-deepening appreciation of literature

III. ACQUIRING INFORMATION THROUGH
    PURPOSEFUL AND APPRECIATIVE LISTENING

A. Develop listening competence
   1. Decoding the meaning from the spoken word
   2. Grasping, translating, inferring the intent of the spoken word
   3. Selecting, organizing, and expressing ideas gained from listening
   4. Analyzing and appraising what is being said both critically and objectively
   5. Interacting intellectually and emotionally with what is being said
   6. Responding to the imagery, the beauty, and the power of the spoken word
   7. Thinking, feeling, and imagining within the spoken frame of reference
   8. Synthesizing ideas gained from listening with previous understandings
   9. Going beyond the literal meaning of the spoken word; discovering and savoring implied meanings
  10. Listening to find the facts, filter the facts, face the facts, and follow the facts
  11. Linking ideas gained from listening with those gained from reading, viewing, and observing
  12. Valuing recordings—disc and tape—as carriers of knowledge—rich data banks for informational retrieval

B. Make effective use of critical listening
   1. Applying critical thinking skills when listening
   2. Using the TA2R formula when listening for information
     T—TUNE IN: preset your mind to listen attentively
     A—ANALYZE what is being said; take notes

---

*William H. Burton et al., *Education for Effective Thinking* (New York: Appleton-Century-Crofts, 1960), p. 350.

PART TWO: LEARNING SKILLS

	Introduce	Reinforce	Extend

III. ACQUIRING INFORMATION THROUGH
PURPOSEFUL AND APPRECIATIVE LISTENING (cont.)

in jot form; main ideas, supporting details,
unfamiliar words, statistics, authorities
cited

R—RESPOND: questioning; evaluating;
forming associations; noting discrepancies
and gaps in information; being sensitive to
bias, prejudice, emotion laden words, un-
warranted conclusions, sweeping generali-
ties, intonation, facial expression and gestures; making value judgments about what
is being said

R—REVIEW notes; incubating ideas gained
and formulating afterthoughts; validating
questioned statements and statistics; linking what has been learned with previous
knowledge

C. Make effective use of appreciative listening

1. Being alive, open, and responsive to the
   beauty, power, and imagery of sound
2. Listening with the heart, soul, imagination,
   and spirit
3. Exploring the artistic, technical, biographical, psychological, and historical components of music
4. Experiencing music; responding to melody,
   tone, harmony, rhythm, and pattern
5. Coexisting with a composer in "a moment
   of mutuality"*
6. Responding to music in own "inner time"†
7. Building an ever expanding repertoire of
   treasured listening experiences
8. Acquiring the habit of checking commercial catalogs to identify new disc and tape
   recordings
9. Furnishing own "house of intellect" with
   memories of listening experiences of limitless delight
10. Becoming acquainted with the musical
    greats (composers and performers), past
    and present, who have left an imprint on
    the development of music
11. Experimenting with a variety of musical
    forms and techniques
12. Selecting and taping mood music as back-
    ground for a play, poem, or dramatic reading

IV. ACQUIRING INFORMATION THROUGH
PURPOSEFUL VIEWING AND OBSERVING

A. Recognize that viewing is visual inspection; a
critical assessment with a definite purpose in
mind

*Gerard L. Knieter, "The Nature of Aesthetic Education" in *Toward an Aesthetic Education*
(Washington, D.C.: Music Educators National Conference, 1971), pp. 3–19.

†Maxine Greene, "Teaching for Aesthetic Experience" in *Toward an Aesthetic Education* (Washington, D.C.: Music Educators National Conference, 1971), pp. 21–24.

PART TWO: LEARNING SKILLS

	Introduce	Reinforce	Extend

IV. ACQUIRING INFORMATION THROUGH
PURPOSEFUL VIEWING AND OBSERVING (cont.)

B. Recognize that observing goes beyond viewing and stresses adherence to criteria or following a scientific model

C. Recognize that viewing is purposeful looking and that observing is carefully and scientifically studying and interpreting what is seen

D. Apply critical thinking skills when "reading" visual media such as
   1. Art prints and art objects
   2. Cartoons, drawings, and photographs
   3. Charts, graphs, and tables
   4. Diagrams
   5. Filmstrips, motion pictures, and videotapes
   6. Maps
   7. Mock-ups and models
   8. Realia and museum objects
   9. Slides
   10. Specimens
   11. Study prints
   12. Television programs
   13. Transparencies for overhead projection

E. "Read" visual media and employ the inquiry processes in communicating understanding
   1. Analyzing data
   2. Describing data
   3. Explaining data
   4. Classifying data
   5. Categorizing data
   6. Evaluating data
   7. Predicting from data

F. Study teacher-constructed and commercially prepared learning guides (which accompany many visual media), before attempting to "read" the visual medium
   1. Identifying the purpose
   2. Obtaining an introduction to and an overview of the contents

G. Organize and consolidate the ideas gained from viewing with ideas gained from other print and nonprint sources as well as from own past experience

H. Explore the artistic, technical, psychological, biographical, and historical components of the fine arts
   1. Responding to the imagery, the beauty, the form, and power of the work of art
   2. Viewing from the heart, soul, imagination, and spirit

I. Become acquainted with the great artists, past and present, and their works
   1. Visiting museums and becoming acquainted with the permanent art collection and special loan collections

PART TWO: LEARNING SKILLS

Introduce   Reinforce   Extend

IV. ACQUIRING INFORMATION THROUGH
    PURPOSEFUL VIEWING AND OBSERVING (cont.)

    a. Studying the catalog before the visit to
    become familiar with the holdings

    b. Using the catalog as a guide while tour-
    ing the galleries

    c. Checking events calendars in the news
    media for notice of special exhibitions

  2. Visiting art galleries

    a. Studying the catalogs before you visit

    b. Using the catalogs as guides while tour-
    ing the galleries

J. "Read" the record of man's historical past

  1. Visiting museums of natural history

  2. Searching for evidence of the historical
    past in the community

K. Recognize that essential to effective observa-
    tion are the abilities to

  1. Identify a focus, purpose, problem, or con-
    cern

  2. Establish criteria to guide observation

  3. Be objective; keep biases and prejudices
    under control

  4. Identify appropriate data sources

  5. Select relevant data

  6. Use all the senses

  7. Use appropriate instruments

  8. Control the variables

  9. Make necessary records

  10. Check observations for accuracy and com-
    pleteness

  11. Use scientific terminology (classification
    nomenclature, instruments, measurement,
    and processes) when reporting findings

V. CONSTRUCTING AND INTERPRETING SURVEYS
    AND OPINION POLLS

A. Recognize that a survey is an investigation of
   things as existing or of events past, to gain information or to test hypotheses

B. Recognize that a poll is a type of survey

C. Recognize that an opinion is an answer that is
   given to a question in a given situation

D. Recognize that a poll is a sampling or collection of opinions on a subject; the accuracy of
   the sample is based on three different factors

  1. The size of the sample

    a. The bigger the sample, the more accu-
    rate the poll

    b. The bigger the sample, the smaller the
    difference between the sample answer
    and the true population answer

  2. The answers people give

    a. How accurate a particular percentage is
    depends on the extent to which the re-
    spondents agree or disagree

    b. The more people disagree, the larger

PART TWO: LEARNING SKILLS

	Introduce	Reinforce	Extend

V. CONSTRUCTING AND INTERPRETING SURVEYS
AND OPINION POLLS (cont.)

      the sample has to be to represent all attitudes

  3. How the sample is picked
    a. All the different groups in the unit being surveyed must be represented
    b. For a nationwide survey, the sample must include people from different parts of the nation, from cities and towns, from different ages, religions, races, and incomes, both men and women

E. Recognize the basic steps employed when conducting an opinion poll
  1. Designing the overall plan
    a. Defining the issue or the question to be examined
    b. Deciding the procedure to follow
  2. Selecting the population sample
    a. Deciding type of people to interview
    b. Deciding how they are to be selected
  3. Designing the questionnaires
    a. Wording the questions
    b. Placing the questions in order
  4. Conducting the interviews
    a. Contacting the respondents
    b. Choosing one of three methods
      –By mail
      –By telephone
      –In person
  5. Processing the questionnaires
    a. Checking all questionnaires for accuracy
    b. Counting, cross-tabulating, and analyzing the answers
  6. Analyzing the findings
    a. Converting the figures into percentages
    b. Analyzing the data and drawing carefully reasoned conclusions

F. Recognize various data collecting techniques employed in conducting surveys
  1. Self-report techniques
    a. Using summary rating scales
    b. Inventorying attitudes
  2. Observational techniques
    a. Measuring specific behaviors requiring minimum inferences
    b. Inventorying social and emotional behavior
  3. Projective techniques
    a. Using sentence completion, essays, and ambiguous drawings for attitude measurement
    b. Inventorying social values, propaganda, and media content

G. Analyze nationally recognized surveys such as
  1. Gallup Polls
  2. Harris Polls
  3. Purdue University Polls

PART TWO: LEARNING SKILLS

	Introduce	Reinforce	Extend

V.   CONSTRUCTING AND INTERPRETING SURVEYS
     AND OPINION POLLS (cont.)

H. Design and field test a survey employing the
six basic steps outlined in E above
1. Summarizing the findings in chart or graph
form
2. Interpreting the significance of the findings
in paragraph form

VI. LEARNING THROUGH GROUP AND SOCIAL
     INTERACTION

A. Recognize that excellence in interpersonal relationships is based on psychological maturity
B. Recognize that a psychologically mature person
is one who*
1. Is secure within himself/herself
2. Has the capacity to give as well as receive
genuine affection
3. Has the ability to feel with others and see
things from their point of view
4. Is objective about himself/herself, recognizing own limitations
5. Is comparatively unselfish in demands on
others, willingly shares ideas, responsibility, time, and energy
6. Is self-reliant and independent in thinking
and actions
7. Has inner resources for living and working
alone without shunning others
8. Selects worthwhile long-term goals and
strives to attain them
9. Has the capacity to size up a situation
10. Has a sense of justice; takes a stand for
what he/she believes to be right
11. Is respectful toward authority
12. Recognizes that the real substance of a
person is much more than the outer, observable dimension
13. Recognizes that all human problems cannot be solved scientifically
14. Takes the long view in solving human-rela-
tions problems; makes intelligent and sensitive choices
15. Is sufficiently flexible to adjust to or cope
with various types of situations
16. Meets unexpected stresses and disappoint-
ments without going to pieces
17. Has a basic set of values that guide his/her
decisions
18. Has self-confidence but knows the virtue
of doubt
19. Forms and defends opinions on the basis
of reasoning

*Adapted from Victor E. Pitkin, "Youth Development and Democratic Citizenship Education" in
Citizenship and a Free Society: Education for the Future, ed. by Franklin Patterson (Washington,
D.C.: National Council for the Social Studies, NEA, 1960), pp. 37–38.

PART TWO: LEARNING SKILLS

	Introduce	Reinforce	Extend

VI. LEARNING THROUGH GROUP AND SOCIAL
INTERACTION (cont.)

20. Accepts such compromises as do not violate his/her fundamental convictions
21. Appreciates that it is mete and right to march to a different drumbeat just so long as one keeps in tune with his/her fellowman and in step with his/her own best self

C. Perceive that an effective group member is one who*
1. Recognizes and utilizes the contributions of others, making them feel that their efforts are appreciated and needed
2. Learns to preserve his/her individuality, uniqueness, and personal creativity within a group setting
3. Is both a good follower and a competent leader at appropriate times; learns how to complement the efforts of another leader; how to organize, plan, draw out others, listen carefully; move the group toward a course of action
4. Enjoys sharing objects, ideas, and knowledge without always seeking credit, aggrandizement, or glory
5. Abides by the rules and regulations created and enforced by mutual consent and does not seek special privileges or feel that guidelines are only for others
6. Initiates changes in laws and standards that he/she feels are unfair to individuals or groups

D. Recognize the function of a committee as a small group endeavor requiring adherence to basic ground rules
1. Establishing the purpose for forming the committee as the first step
2. Selecting members to serve on the committee who are willing to work congenially and see that the job is done
3. Selecting the chairperson on the basis of leadership qualifications; one who will
   a. Focus the attention of the committee on the purpose for which it has been created
   b. Solicit ideas from the group; have the group reach a consensus on procedure
   c. Establish target dates and keep the group on schedule
   d. Be a facilitator, not a dictator
4. Being an effective committee member requires
   a. Staying open to suggestions from other members

*Raymond H. Muessig and Vincent R. Rogers, "Developing Competence in Group Participation and Human Relations; in *Skill Development in Social Studies,* ed. by Helen McCracken Carpenter (Washington, D.C.: National Council for the Social Studies, NEA, 1963), p. 246.

PART TWO: LEARNING SKILLS

Introduce   Reinforce   Extend

VI. LEARNING THROUGH GROUP AND SOCIAL INTERACTION (cont.)			

    b. Feeding in ideas for group consideration

    c. Fulfilling commitments accepted

    d. Sharing the responsibility of the chairperson and the group to complete the committee's assignment

E. Perceive the function of a panel as an information generating group

    1. Discovering that a panel is usually composed of five to eight members seeking agreement on a problem

    2. Discovering that the panel group is usually selected because of interest

    3. Discovering that in an initial planning session a leader is chosen; the problem is defined, then subdivided into subtopics for individual panelists to research

    4. Discovering the responsibilities of the panel leader to include

       a. Guiding the panelists in their research

       b. Preparing a list of guide questions to be answered by the panelists in their presentation

       c. Keeping the panel discussion moving

       d. Inviting questions from the audience; directing the questions to various members of the panel

       e. Summarizing the main points of the discussion

F. Perceive the buzz group as an effective alternative to large group discussions

    1. Recognizing that the buzz group is commonly referred to as the "six-six" procedure; groups of six consult for six minutes

    2. Realizing that there are serious drawbacks to large group discussions

       a. Some individuals hesitate to speak before a large group

       b. The problem often is not clearly defined; purpose of the discussion becomes submerged in extraneous comment

       c. All too frequently, discussion drags; extent of agreement or disagreement not easily assessed

    3. Realizing that buzz groups may be formed at random or by choice of topic being discussed

    4. Realizing that "buzzing" can be

       a. Informal, without even a chairperson or

       b. Carefully structured with an outline, chairperson, recorder, observer, and even a resource person

    5. Realizing that reporting to the large group can be oral or written

G. Appreciate the value of parliamentary procedure being carefully followed in formal group meetings

PART TWO: LEARNING SKILLS

	Introduce	Reinforce	Extend

VI. LEARNING THROUGH GROUP AND SOCIAL INTERACTION (cont.)

1. Using the standard handbook of parliamentary law, *Robert's Rules of Order,* to determine correct procedure for conducting business, making motions, and voting
2. Perceiving the wisdom of having a parliamentarian settle questions of procedure

VII. ORGANIZING INFORMATION

A. Make effective use of outlining techniques
   1. Realizing the value of the outline for organizing ideas
   2. Realizing the function of the outline as a blueprint to follow in writing a paper; a skeletal framework for organizing information
   3. Realizing that the framework of the outline is a hierarchy of logically related items
      a. Broken into major divisions (headings), subdivisions, and sub-subdivisions
      b. Each division is subordinate to the item on the level immediately above
      c. All items within a division are of equal importance
      d. Minimum of two major divisions; maximum of six
      e. Balance within all divisions is the goal
      f. Main headings can stand alone or be subdivided
      g. May be in topic or sentence form; one or the other; cannot alternate or mix forms
B. Recognize the distinguishing characteristics and mechanics of the two basic outlining systems
   1. Understanding the notation system employed in the classic, standard, or Harvard form of outlining
      a. Use Roman numerals for main topics
      b. Use capital letters for subtopics
      c. Use Arabic numerals for points under each subtopic
      d. Use lower case letters for points under each sub-subtopic
      e. Put a period after each numeral and letter
      f. Indent topics under each division; indent subtopics under each topic; indent each point under subtopics
   2. Matching the following sample standard outline form to above explanation
      I. First main topic _____
         A. First subtopic _____
            1. First point _____
            2. Second point _____
         B. Second subtopic _____
            1. First point _____

PART TWO: LEARNING SKILLS

Introduce   Reinforce   Extend

VII. Organizing Information (cont.)

   2. Second point
    a. First subpoint
    b. Second subpoint

  3. Understanding the decimal system of outlining
   a. Use Arabic numerals only
   b. Each main topic is numbered in se-
    quence beginning with 1
   c. Each subtopic is numbered in sequence
    following a decimal point
  4. Matching the following sample decimal
   outline form to above explanation
   1. First main topic

    1.1 First subtopic

    1.2 Second subtopic

   2. Second main topic

    2.1 First subtopic

    2.2 Second subtopic

    2.3 Third subtopic

   3. Third main topic

    3.1 First subtopic

    3.2 Second subtopic

    3.3 Third subtopic

  5. Perceiving the value of using the decimal
   system of outlining for scientific and technical reports and for business and industrial reports
C. Make effective use of note-taking techniques
  1. Establishing a definite procedure for note-
   taking
   a. Write notes in ink
   b. Use either 4x6 or 3x5 index cards for
    taking notes
   c. Place only one item of information on a
    card
   d. Each card should contain
    –The source and paging
    –The topic, heading, or"slug"
    –The note itself
   e. Enclose quotations in quotation marks
   f. Reduce paragraphs to a few sentences
   g. Write only on one side of card; if addi-
    tional cards are needed, staple them to-
    gether
   h. Avoid copying verbatim information;
    write note in own words
  2. Establishing a definite procedure for writing bibliography cards or bibliography
   notebook entries
   a. Note on bibliography cards
    –Library call number for the source
    –Author's full name, last name first

PART TWO: LEARNING SKILLS

	Introduce	Reinforce	Extend

VII. ORGANIZING INFORMATION (cont.)

      –Title of book, underlined
      –Imprint data; place of publication, publisher
      –Copyright date
      –Code designation to be used on note cards to indicate this book as the source of the note
   b. Encyclopedia notation on bibliography cards
      –Author of article, if signed
      –Title of article, in quotes
      –Name of encyclopedia, underlined
      –Copyright date
      –Volume number in Roman numerals
      –Page numbers of article
   c. Periodical notation on bibliography cards
      –Author of article, if signed
      –Title of article, in quotes
      –Name of periodical, underlined
      –Volume and number of issue, if given
      –Date of issue
      –Pages of the article, also section for newspaper article
      –Code designation to be used on note cards to indicate this source
   d. Bibliography notebook entries
      –Use 8½x11 inch, 3 ring notebook paper
      –Write, type, or photocopy information
      –Written or typed bibliography data follows exactly the procedure outlined above for bibliography cards; only one source on each page
      –Photocopy technique saves time, gives additional information
      –Photocopy title page on 8½x11 inch paper
      –Write copyright date under imprint
      –Write library call number upper left-hand corner
      –Write code designation on upper right-hand corner
      –Photocopy the table of contents
         Data bank for review of book chapter coverage
         Quick source to consult for information on new topics in an expanded search
      –Notebook convenient to carry to library when working on research
      –Note-taking can still be on cards using bibliography code for reference to source
      –Notebook permits photocopying of charts, graphs, tables, lengthy

PART TWO: LEARNING SKILLS

	Introduce	Reinforce	Extend

VII. ORGANIZING INFORMATION (cont.)

    quotations, diagrams for information retrieval

  3. Sorting note cards preparatory to writing a paper
    a. Sort note cards by topic or "slug"
    b. Arrange note cards for each topic in sequence matching topic placement in outline for writing the paper
  4. Matching the notes to each topic in the outline, read notes in sequence, decide
    a. Adequacy of information
    b. Need to delete, keep, or search for additional information

PART THREE: COMMUNICATING SKILLS

	Introduce	Reinforce	Extend

I. WRITING AS A COMMUNICATION TOOL

A. Perceive the significance of writing
  1. Realizing that writing is a tool of thinking
    a. Clarity of written expression is evidence of clarity of thought
    b. Writing and reason are interdependent and inseparable
  2. Realizing that writing is a learned process
    a. Requires concentration
    b. Requires a disciplined will
    c. Requires craftsmanship
  3. Realizing that there are two basic requirements for effective writing
    a. Have something significant to say
    b. Say it skillfully with clarity, precision, and style
B. Perceive the significance of functional literacy
  1. Realizing that functional literacy means being able to read, to write, to think, and to act with competence
  2. Realizing that functional literacy is a basic requirement for*
    a. Holding a decent job
    b. Supporting self and family
    c. Leading a life of dignity and pride
C. Perceive the hallmarks of excellence in written communication to be
  1. Honest, concise, and effective use of language
  2. Significant ideas organized in a clear, coherent, precise, and persuasive way

II. WRITING THE ESSAY

A. Perceive the distinguishing characteristics of the essay form
  1. Recognizing that the essay is a composition expressing a point of view

---

*David Harmon, "Illiteracy: An Overview," in *Harvard Educational Review* 40, no. 2, May 1970, p. 227.

PART THREE: COMMUNICATING SKILLS

	Introduce	Reinforce	Extend
II. WRITING THE ESSAY (cont.)			

   2. Recognizing that the basic components of the essay are
     a. A significant thesis
     b. Accurate, adequate information
     c. Compelling writing style
   3. Recognizing that the basic types of the essay are
     a. Narrative
     b. Descriptive
     c. Expository
     d. Argumentative
   4. Realizing that ideas for the essay come from
     a. Reading
     b. Observing
     c. Remembering
     d. Reflective reasoning
     e. Creative thinking

B. Become aware of the techniques employed in designing and structuring the essay
   1. Focusing on a subject of personal interest or concern
     a. Narrow the subject to a manageable thesis or theme
        –Avoid the trite, the commonplace, the "same old thing"
        –Search for a thought-provoking thesis; an attention grabber
     b. Be sure that sufficient information is available
   2. Designing the essay
     a. Use the thesis as the internal organizer
     b. Organize ideas in jot outline form
     c. Gather information
        –Sift it, evaluate it
        –Relate it to jot outline
   3. Prewriting the essay
     a. Use the jot outline as the blueprint
     b. Build the essay in three main parts
        –The beginning
        –The middle
        –The end
     c. State the thesis in the beginning paragraph
        –In opening sentence introduce the thesis in broad, general terms
        –State the thesis in the *last* sentence; set the stage for successive paragraphs
     d. Develop the thesis in the middle paragraphs
        –Arrange points in order of increasing interest
        –Save the most interesting or convincing until last

PART THREE: COMMUNICATING SKILLS

	Introduce	Reinforce	Extend

II.   WRITING THE ESSAY (cont.)

    e. Reword the thesis in the concluding
      paragraph
      –Drive home the main point or
       points
      –Make final sentence the clincher

  4. Reading the essay critically
    a. Determine if
      –Sentences are sharp and clear
      –Paragraphs are related to thesis
      –Topic sentences are strong and precise
      –The thought is developed logically and
       smoothly
      –Unnecessary phrases need to be de-
       leted
      –Punctuation and spelling are correct
    b. Answer the questions
      –Are you satisfied with the content and
       the organization?
      –Have you said what you wanted to
       say?
      –Is it the best you can do?

  5. Revising the essay
    a. Rewrite until the thought comes clear
    b. Read the final draft aloud once or
      twice
      –Does it read smoothly?
      –Does it still need to be pared or
       pruned?
      –Is it convincing?
    c. Make all corrections

  6. Typing the essay in final form
    a. Type finished essay on white paper
      8½x11 inches
    b. Proofread carefully

III.   WRITING THE RESEARCH PAPER

A. Recognize the purpose and value of the research paper
  1. Perceiving research to mean
    –The careful, critical, disciplined process
     of inquiry
  2. Perceiving the research paper to be
    –The organized, documented communica-
     tion of information gained through re-
     search in support of the paper's thesis
  3. Perceiving the value of the research paper
    to be
    –Learning the basic techniques, proce-
     dures, and mechanics of research writing
    –Learning to identify, refine, and state a
     research problem or thesis
    –Learning to use library resources effi-
     ciently and effectively
    –Learning disciplined working habits; to
     follow the rules and procedures of stan-
     dard research methodology

PART THREE: COMMUNICATING SKILLS

	Introduce	Reinforce	Extend

III. WRITING THE RESEARCH PAPER (cont.)

–Learning to complete a time-consuming and demanding task in a craftsmanlike manner

–Learning to think analytically and critically and to find challenge and satisfaction in doing so

–Learning to communicate thought in a clear, concise, direct, and lively style

B. Study the procedure to follow as outlined in a basic style manual or research guide*

   1. Discerning established procedure for preparing the research paper

   2. Following the established procedure from first to last step in

     a. Choosing a topic

     b. Preliminary reading

     c. Narrowing the topic

     d. Stating the thesis

     e. Gathering information

     f. Preparing a working bibliography

     g. Preparing a preliminary outline

     h. Taking notes

     i. Preparing final outline

     j. Writing first draft

     k. Footnoting

     l. Reading first draft and revising it

     m. Writing the final draft

     n. Preparing the bibliography

     o. Proofreading

IV. SPEAKING AS A COMMUNICATION TOOL

A. Perceive that speech is a vehicle for conveying thought and emotion

   1. What is said and how it is said is evidence of mental and emotion processes

   2. Speech mirrors personality

B. Perceive that effective speaking is a learned process

   1. Requiring training and practice

   2. Requiring understanding and mastery of basic techniques, procedures, and mechanics of speaking

   3. Requiring the ability to communicate thought orally in a clear, concise, direct, and convincing style

C. Perceive the requirements for a speech of quality and effectiveness

   1. Seeing the similarity between the process of designing and structuring the essay and the process of designing and structuring the speech

   2. Viewing the speech as a spoken essay

*James D. Lester, *Writing Research Papers: A Complete Guide,* 2nd ed. (Glenview, Ill.: Scott, Foresman, 1976) and Kate L. Turabian, *Student's Guide for Writing College Papers,* 3rd ed. (Chicago: University of Chicago Press, 1976).

PART THREE: COMMUNICATING SKILLS

	Introduce	Reinforce	Extend

IV. SPEAKING AS A COMMUNICATION TOOL (cont.)

    3. Recognizing that as an essay expresses a point of view, so does a speech

    4. Recognizing that the basic components of a speech are
       a. A significant thesis
       b. Accurate, adequate, thought-provoking information logically presented
       c. Compelling speaking style

    5. Recognizing that the basic types of speeches are
       a. To entertain or amuse
       b. To inform or instruct
       c. To stimulate or actuate through emotion
       d. To convince or move to action

D. Perceive the distinguishing characteristics of the speech designed to entertain or amuse
    1. Recognizing the typical situations calling for this type of speech
       a. Parties
       b. Dinners
       c. Club meetings
    2. Recognizing the main purpose is to entertain or amuse plus
       a. Something of substance
       b. Something with appeal for the audience
    3. Recognizing the essentials of delivery and content
       a. Keep the speech moving
       b. Show that you are enjoying yourself
       c. Don't be sarcastic, rude, or degrading
       d. Don't use "tired" jokes
       e. Laugh at yourself
       f. Let one incident, story, or anecdote lead smoothly to the next
       g. Trigger humor by
         –Exaggeration
         –Puns
         –Poking fun at authority
         –Irony
         –Absurdities
       h. Don't talk too long

E. Perceive the distinguishing characteristics of the speech designed to inform or instruct
    1. Seeing the similarity between the process of designing and structuring the research paper and the process of designing and structuring an informational speech
    2. Recognizing the typical situations calling for this type of speech
       a. Reports of a scientific or scholarly nature
       b. Lectures by teacher, lawyer, traveler, writer, etc.
    3. Recognizing the main purpose to be
       a. Building understanding

PART THREE: COMMUNICATING SKILLS

	Introduce	Reinforce	Extend

IV. SPEAKING AS A COMMUNICATION TOOL (cont.)

    b. Helping audience grasp certain fundamental facts

    c. Creating interest in the subject

  4. Recognizing the essentials of delivery and content

    a. Speak distinctly with a well modulated voice

    b. Speak slowly enough for the audience to grasp the meaning; rapidly enough to hold the attention of the audience

    c. Establish rapport with the audience; let your delivery convince the audience of your sincerity

    d. Don't alienate the audience by talking over the heads of the listeners

    e. Limit the main points to no more than four

    f. Logically develop each point; don't digress

    g. Use concrete data; avoid abstractions

    h. Use appropriate gestures

    i. Know your speech; convince the audience that you know what you are talking about and that you believe in what you are saying

    j. Don't exceed the time allotted for the speech

F. Perceive the distinguishing characteristics of the speech designed to stimulate or actuate through emotion

  1. Recognizing the typical situations calling for this type of speech

    a. Commencement exercises

    b. Dedications

    c. Eulogies

    d. Patriotic celebrations

  2. Recognizing the main purpose to be

    a. Stimulating listeners to greater devotion to a cause

    b. Inspiring listeners to greater effort coupled with lasting enthusiasm

  3. Recognizing the essentials of delivery and content

    a. Speak distinctly with a well modulated voice

    b. Speak slowly enough for the audience to grasp the meaning; rapidly enough to hold the attention of the audience

    c. Establish rapport with the audience; let your delivery convince the audience of your sincerity and depth of feeling

    d. Don't use notes; don't hesitate; keep your ideas moving

    e. Use a slogan or an apt phrase to stimulate interest

PART THREE: COMMUNICATING SKILLS

Introduce   Reinforce   Extend

IV. SPEAKING AS A COMMUNICATION TOOL (cont.)

    f. Be concrete and specific

    g. Use vivid examples, anecdotes, or incidents

    h. Build upon fact and common beliefs in fundamental human desires

    i. Use vivid imagery

    j. Use appropriate gestures

    k. Know your speech; convince the audience that you know what you are talking about and that you believe wholeheartedly in what you are saying

    l. Don't exceed the time allotted for the speech

G. Perceive the distinguishing characteristics of the speech designed to convince or move to action

    1. Recognizing the typical situations calling for this type of speech

        a. Political meetings

        b. Civic mass meetings

        c. Corporate business meetings

        d. Legislative hearings

    2. Recognizing the main purpose to be

        a. Convincing the audience of the logic of your argument

        b. Committing the audience to action in support of your beliefs, proposals, or recommendations

    3. Recognizing the essentials of delivery and content

        a. Speak distinctly with a well modulated voice

        b. Speak slowly enough for the audience to grasp the meaning; rapidly enough to hold the attention of the audience

        c. Establish rapport with the audience; let your delivery convince the audience of your sincerity

        d. Appeal to the common sense of the audience

        e. Use concrete facts, sound, logical reasoning

        f. Define the criteria or standards upon which your proposals or recommendations are made

        g. Stick to the point; don't introduce extraneous matter

        h. Make the conclusion a summation of both the thesis and substantiating arguments, proposals, or recommendations

        i. Know your speech; convince the audience that you know what you are talking about and that you believe wholeheartedly in what you are saying

        j. Don't exceed the time allotted for the speech

PART THREE: COMMUNICATING SKILLS

	Introduce	Reinforce	Extend
IV. SPEAKING AS A COMMUNICATION TOOL (cont.)			

H. Perceive the distinguishing characteristics of debate
   1. Recognizing that debate is a type of argumentative speaking regulated by
     a. Time limitations
     b. Parliamentary or forensic rules
   2. Recognizing that the purpose of debate is for
     a. Arguing a proposition pro and con
     b. Arriving at and recording a decision
   3. Recognizing the rules and regulations of formal debate
     a. Time limits are imposed on debaters; typical distribution of time for each of four speakers as follows
       Constructive speeches:
       –First affirmative—10 minutes
       –First negative—10 minutes
       –Second affirmative—10 minutes
       –Second negative—10 minutes
       Rebuttal speeches:
       –First negative—5 minutes
       –First affirmative—5 minutes
       –Second negative—5 minutes
       –Second affirmative—5 minutes
     b. The argument is conducted according to parliamentary rules
       Each side receives equal treatment
     c. The subject is phrased in resolution form
       The decision is based on the "merits of the question"

Basic Reference Tools

Reference books are those books that are designed and arranged for rapid information retrieval. The purpose of this bibliography is to identify those reference tools that should be the intellectually gifted student's first port of call when searching for information. This bibliography is introduced to the students in the 12th-grade seminar, Revving Up for College, and is included in the student-compiled *Practical Scholar's Handbook for Lifelong Learning* (see Model 43).

Joseph S. Renzulli, in *The Enrichment Triad Model: A Guide for Developing Defensible Programs for the Gifted and Talented* (Mansfield Center, Conn.: Creative Learning Press, 1977), strongly recommends providing the gifted students with *advanced* library skills. He advocates that gifted students have access to the full range of information, for it is important "that they learn about the existence, nature and function of each of the following types of reference materials" (pp. 59–60):

TYPES OF REFERENCE BOOKS

Bibliographies	Reviews	Histories and Chronicles
Encyclopedias	Reader's Guides	of Particular Fields,
Dictionaries and	Abstracts	Organizations
Glossaries	Diaries	Concordances
Annuals	Catalogues	Data Tables
Handbooks	Books of Quotations,	Digests
Directories and Registers	Proverbs, Maxims, and	Record Books
Indexes	Familiar Phrases	Surveys
Atlases	Source Books	Almanacs
Yearbooks	Periodicals	Anthologies
Manuals		

TYPES OF NONBOOK REFERENCE MATERIALS

Art Prints	Transparencies	Records
Talking Books	Globes	Slides
Videotapes	Kits	Charts
Microforms	Maps	Films
Filmstrips	Film Loops	Study Prints
Realia	Pictures	Models

Renzulli cautions that it will take several years to cover these reference materials "in an efficient and meaningful manner. Nevertheless, a systematic plan should be developed so that youngsters who are being encouraged to become investigators will also be continuously learning where and how information is stored. . . . If we want gifted students to do *advanced* work in particular areas, then it is important for them to learn about, and have access to, *advanced* kinds of information."

The reference tools cited in this bibliography are the *basic* tools essential for advanced investigation by gifted students in high school, college, and specialized libraries.

GENERAL REFERENCE

ALMANACS, FACT BOOKS, YEARBOOKS

(Note: Encyclopedia yearbooks are listed under the general heading *Encyclopedias.*)

CBS News Almanac. 1975 to date. Maplewood, N.J.: Hammond, current edition. Annual. Comprehensive almanac comparable in organization and coverage to the *Information Please Almanac* and *The World Almanac.* Special features include: a "Year in Review" series of articles written by CBS news commentators, accounts of each presidential election, and historical summaries of the nations of the world.

Historical Statistics of the United States, Colonial Times to 1970. Washington, D.C. Government Printing Office, 1975. Overview and summary of the statistical history of the United States from 1610 through 1970. The current edition of the *Statistical Almanac* brings this tool up-to-date.

*Information Please Almanac. 1947 to date. New York: Information Please Publication, current edition. Annual. Comprehensive compilation of facts that supplements *The World Almanac.* Includes: descriptive articles on the year's developments in certain fields; a statistical profile of the United States; historical and scientific chronologies; news and views about people and places; statistical analysis of business, education, communication, industry, transportation, energy, taxes, medicine, etc.; and an atlas of colored maps.

Reader's Digest Almanac. 1966 to date. New York: Funk and Wagnalls, current edition. Annual. Encyclopedic yearbook similar in format and coverage to the *Information Please Almanac.* Includes: official results of elections, the year's events in every field, a college guide for students, and the results of Olympic Games.

Statesman's Year-Book. 1864 to date. London: Macmillan, current edition. Annual. Manual of concise, reliable data about the governments of the world. Includes: the constitution, government, diplomatic representatives, economic conditions, defenses, agriculture, commerce, and extensive statistical information on a variety of topics.

Statistical Abstract of the United States. 1879 to date. U.S. Bureau of the Census. Washington D.C.: Government Printing Office, current edition. Annual. Digest of data collected by all the statistical agencies of the United States as well as statistics gathered by a number of private agencies. Contains more than 1,500 tables and charts. Specific headnote references link many tables to earlier data shown in *Historical Statistics of the United States, Colonial Times to 1970. The U.S. Fact Book* (see below) is a reprint edition of the *Statistical Abstract of the United States.*

Statistical Yearbook. 1948 to date. New York: UNESCO, distributed by UNIPUB, current edition. Annual. Includes data for over 150 countries and territories. Major sections provide world summaries for broad areas such as population, education, libraries and museums, newspapers, film and cinema, and radio and television broadcasting.

---

*Asterisk indicates reference book recommended for inclusion in a home reference library.

*U.S. Fact Book: The American Almanac. New York: Grosset and Dunlap, current edition. Annual. Paperbound reprint of the *Statistical Abstract of the United States* as prepared by the U.S. Bureau of the Census.

*World Almanac and Book of Facts. 1868 to date. New York: Newspaper Enterprise Association and Doubleday, current edition. Annual. Compendium of universal knowledge; world's best-selling book after the Bible. Contains facts and statistics on social, industrial, political, financial, religious, scientific, educational, and historical subjects; 1,000 years of memorable events; awards, medals, prizes; flags of the world; consumer affairs; laws and documents; personalities; theater, recordings, films; United Nations; women; and world facts.

Yearbook of the United Nations. 1947 to date. New York: United Nations, Office of Public Information, current edition. Annual. Excellent source of information on all activities of the United Nations and its related agencies. Divided into two main sections: (1) political, economic, and social questions of recent concern and (2) international organizations related to the United Nations.

ATLASES AND GAZETTEERS

International Atlas rev. 2nd ed. Chicago: Rand McNally, 1976. Contains a 16,000-word introductory essay, "Patterns and Imprints of Mankind." Includes maps for each major geographic area, features 60 maps of major metropolitan regions, and indexes 160,000 place names.

Medallion World Atlas. Maplewood, N.J.: Hammond, 1975. Over 600 maps provide physical, political, and special subject information on every country of the world plus each of the 50 states. Contains a world index of over 100,000 place names. Special sections are devoted to ecology and to biblical as well as world and U.S. history.

National Atlas of the United States of America. Washington, D.C.: U.S. Geological Survey, 1970. Comprehensive atlas presenting nearly 800 political, social, physical, economic, agricultural, and historical maps of the United States. Indexes more than 41,000 place names.

*National Geographic Atlas of the World, 4th ed. Washington, D.C.: National Geographic Society, 1975. Contains 380 up-to-date maps of the countries of the world. Emphasis of coverage is on the United States. Index provides references to over 130,000 entries.

Oxford Economic Atlas of the World 4th ed. New York: Oxford University Press, 1972. Provides 89 pages of maps showing population distribution, political structures, defense and economic alliances, world commodities, etc. Numerous tables and graphs supplement the maps.

Shepherd's Historical Atlas, 9th ed. New York: Barnes and Noble, 1973. Standard historical atlas covering the period from 2000 B.C. to 1955. Maps highlight historical events and developments such as commercial routes, war campaigns, territorial boundaries, and treaties.

Times Atlas of the World ed. by John Barthalomew, 5 vols. London: London Times, 1955–1959. New edition of one of the most comprehensive world atlases. Volume 1 includes the world, Australasia and East Asia; Volume 2, Southwest Asia and Russia; Volume 3, Northern Europe; Volume 4, Southern Europe and Africa; Volume 5, The Americas. Each volume contains detailed index.

Times Atlas of the World: Comprehensive Edition, 5th ed. London: London Times, distributed in the United States by Quadrangle/New York Times, 1975. One-volume

*Asterisk indicates reference book recommended for inclusion in a home reference library.

edition reflects contemporary world changes including those brought about by space exploration; includes an expanded coverage of city maps and an index-gazetteer of some 200,000 place names.

Webster's New Geographical Dictionary. Springfield, Mass.: Merriam, 1972. More than 47,000 entries plus 217 maps provide information on the world's countries, regions, cities, and natural features; 15,000 cross references facilitate fact identification and location.

BIOGRAPHICAL DICTIONARIES AND INDEXES

(*Note:* Biographical dictionaries and indexes for special fields such as art, literature, music, and science are listed under the heading designating the special field.)

Biography Index: A Cumulative Index to Biographical Material in Books and Magazines. 1946 to date. New York: Wilson, current edition. Quarterly, annual, 3-year cumulations. Covers biographical material in approximately 1,900 periodicals, current books of individual and collective biography in the English language, and obituaries including those in the *New York Times.* Includes an index by professions and occupations.

Current Biography. 1940 to date. New York: Wilson, current edition. Monthly, annual. Essay-length biographies of persons of many nationalities prominent in the day's news. As many as 350 biographies included in each annual.

Dictionary of American Biography, 15 vols., 6 supplements. 1935–1979. New York: Scribner, 1928–1979. Most comprehensive biographical dictionary, contains 16,004 scholarly biographies of Americans who have made a significant contribution to American life. Limited to deceased Americans only. The abridgment, *Concise Dictionary of American Biography* (New York: Scribner, 1977) summarizes all of the biographies in the original work and supplements.

Dictionary of National Biography, 21 vols., 2nd to 7th supplements. London: Oxford University Press, 1912–1971. Monumental, scholarly reference set containing over 32,000 essay-length biographies of noteworthy inhabitants of the British Isles and its colonies, excluding living persons. The abridgment, *Concise Dictionary of National Biography* (London: Oxford University Press, vol. I, 1952, vol. II, 1961) summarizes all of the biographies of the original work and supplements.

McGraw-Hill Encyclopedia of World Biography. 12 vols. New York: McGraw-Hill, 1972. Contains essay-length biographies of famous, deceased figures, from all periods of history and from all countries. Articles are by scholars and stress commentary and evaluation as much as facts. Over 6,000 illustrations; classified index identifies persons, places, events, treaties, pictures, styles, ideas, etc.

Notable American Women, 1607–1950: A Biographical Dictionary, 3 vols. Cambridge, Mass.: Harvard University Press, Belknap Press, 1972. Scholarly dictionary, comparable in format and style to the *Dictionary of American Biography;* contains biographies of 1,359 deceased American women, whose lives and careers have had significant impact on American life. Volume 3 includes a "selected" list of names arranged in 82 vocational categories.

Webster's American Biographies. Springfield, Mass.: Merriam, 1974. Basic one-volume reference tool providing brief biographical accounts of over 3,000 men and women, past and present, who have made significant contributions to American life. Offers both a geographical and an occupational index.

Webster's Biographical Dictionary: A Dictionary of Names and Noteworthy Persons with Pronunciation and Concise Biographies. Springfield, Mass.: Merriam, 1974. Contains

*Asterisk indicates reference book recommended for inclusion in a home reference library.

40,000 concise biographies of persons from all nations and all periods of time including some living today. Contains many charts, tables, lists of government officials, heads of foreign states, popes, and other important kinds of information.

Who's Who. 1849 to date. London: Black, current edition. Annual. Concise biographical information about prominent living English men and women and a few distinguished citizens of other countries, with addresses.

Who's Who in America. 1899 to date. Chicago: Marquis, current edition. Biennial. Basic current reference tool listing over 64,000 names of living Americans and some few world notables. Entries are factual and brief; addresses are included with the biography.

Who's Who of American Women. 1959 to date. Chicago: Marquis, current edition. Biennial. Contains biographical sketches of over 21,000 American women of current interest because of their contributions to society, their significant accomplishments in a special field of endeavor, or their holding elected or appointed government offices.

ENCYCLOPEDIAS

Collier's Encyclopedia, 24 vols. 1949 to date. New York: Macmillan Educational Corp., current edition. Comprehensive, constantly updated. Contains about 25,000 articles, 17,000 illustrations (more than 1,400 in color), 1,450 maps, and a separate index volume, which includes a bibliography of 12,000 titles. Issues *Collier's Encyclopedia Yearbook,* an excellent survey of national and international events.

Encyclopedia Americana, 30 vols. 1829 to date. New York: Grolier, current edition. Comprehensive, constantly updated. Contains about 56,000 articles, over 19,000 illustrations, and a detailed index volume with 350,000 entries. Among its many useful features are its histories of the different centuries; glossaries of technical terms; texts of documents; articles on American places, biography, and events; definitive articles on World Wars I and II; and bibliographies at the end of most of the articles. Issues *Americana Annual,* an excellent survey of national and international events.

New Columbia Encyclopedia. 4th ed. New York: Columbia University Press, 1975. One-volume, quick-reference work containing 75,000 brief entries plus some 80,000 cross references. An excellent tool for quick identification of persons, places, things, events, documents, and ideas.

New Encyclopaedia Britannica, 15th ed., 30 vols. 1768 to date. Chicago: Encyclopaedia Britannica, 1976. Standard, scholarly encyclopedia providing both alphabetical and topical approaches to knowledge. Revised edition is divided into three separate parts. The one-volume *Propaedia* is an "Outline of Knowledge"; notations following each entry in the outline identify articles where information can be found in the *Macropaedia,* 19 volumes containing in-depth articles on all areas of knowledge. The 10-volume *Micropaedia* serves as a ready reference guide and alphabetical index to the contents of the *Macropaedia.* More than 102,000 entries are included in this revised edition. Issues *Britannica Book of the Year,* an excellent survey of national and international events.

World Book Encyclopedia, 22 vols. 1917 to date. Chicago: Field Enterprises, current edition. Comprehensive, popular general encyclopedia containing more than 19,000 articles, over 29,000 illustrations (more than 10,000 in color), more than 2,200 maps, an elaborate system of cross references, and study outlines and bibliographies for all major topics. Volume 22, Research Guide/Index contains a 32-page section, "How to Do Research." Issues *World Book Year Book,* an excellent survey of national and international events.

ENGLISH-LANGUAGE DICTIONARIES

American Heritage Dictionary of the English Language. New York: American Heritage, 1975. Contains more than 155,000 entries and more than 5,000 illustrations. Single

*Asterisk indicates reference book recommended for inclusion in a home reference library.

alphabetical listing includes 6,000 geographical entries, 3,000 abbreviations, 6,000 idiomatic entries, 800 usage notes, 20,000 sample sentences, 6,000 illustrative quotations, and 40,000 etymologies; emphasizes scientific and technical terms.

Funk and Wagnalls New Standard Dictionary. New York: Funk and Wagnalls, 1964. Contains more than 450,000 entries, includes over 65,000 proper names. Emphasizes present-day meanings, pronunciation, and spelling. Antonyms as well as synonyms are given; geographical and biographical names are included in the main alphabetical listing.

Oxford English Dictionary, 13 vols. Oxford: Clarendon Press, 1933. *Supplement . . . ,* vol. 1: A–G, 1972; vol. 2: H–N, 1976; vol. 3 in preparation. Scholarly, authoritative, historical dictionary of the English language first published by the London Philological Society in 1857. Gives the history of every word used in England since A.D. 1150; shows when, how, and in what form each word entered the language and the changes that have taken place in spelling, meaning, and usage. The *Shorter Oxford English Dictionary,* 2 vols. (Oxford: Clarendon Press, 1973) is an authorized abridgment of the 13-volume publication. It lists almost two-thirds of the words in the original edition, but limits the extent of the coverage offered for each word.

*Random House Dictionary of the English Language. New York: Random House, 1966. Contains 260,000 words, emphasis on current usage. All words, place names, proper names, literary characters, titles of literary works, scientific and technical terms, etc., are given in straight alphabetical order.

*Roget's International Thesaurus, 4th ed. New York: Crowell, 1977. Based on the original *Roget* published in 1852, enlarged in 1879 and in 1911. Contains about 240,000 words and phrases, a glossary of foreign words and phrases, and 45,000 words in science and technology. An extensive index facilitates usage.

*Webster's New Collegiate Dictionary, 8th ed. Springfield, Mass.: Merriam, 1976. Basic desk dictionary containing 150,000 entries; 191,000 definitions; 22,000 new words from sports, business, science, and other fields; 24,000 usage examples, 3,000 illustrative quotations; a handbook of style; foreign words and phrases; and thousands of biographical and geographical names.

Webster's New International Dictionary of the English Language, 2nd ed. Springfield, Mass.: Merriam, 1960. The authority for questions of good usage and the status of words. Includes over 600,000 words; antonyms as well as synonyms; supplementary lists of abbreviations, signs, and symbols; forms of address; pronouncing gazetteer; and pronouncing biographical dictionary.

Webster's Third New International Dictionary. Springfield, Mass.: Merriam, 1971. Revision of *Webster's New International . . . ,* 2nd ed. Contains 450,000 words, including 100,000 additional new words or new meanings for words in the original edition. Over 200,000 quotations, mostly from current sources, illustrate word usage and meaning. Omits status labels for slang, colloquialisms, etc.

INDEXES TO NEWSPAPERS, PERIODICALS, AND BOOKS

(Note: Indexes pertaining to but one field such as art, literature, music, or science are listed under the heading designating that special field.)

Bibliographic Index. 1938 to date. New York: Wilson, current edition. Triannual, annual. Indexes by subject bibliographies in English and foreign languages published separately or included in books, pamphlets, and over 1,900 periodicals. Entries are limited to bibliographies containing 40 or more citations.

Book Review Digest. 1905 to date. New York: Wilson, current edition. Monthly, annual. Index to reviews of current books appearing in more than 70 periodicals and

---

*Asterisk indicates reference book recommended for inclusion in a home reference library.

journals; lists over 6,000 books a year. Full references to magazines are given; a subject and title index appears in each volume and cumulates every five years.

Cumulative Book Index. 1898 to date. New York: Wilson, current edition. Monthly, annual. Author, title, and subject index to current books published in the English language in all countries excluding government publications and pamphlets. Price, publisher, paging, edition, date of publication, and International Standard Book Number given for each book. Directory of publishers and distributors included in each issue and annual.

Essay and General Literature Index. 1900 to date. New York: Wilson, current edition. Semiannual, annual. Author, subject, and, in case of documents, title index in a single alphabet to miscellaneous collections of articles. Every field of knowledge is covered.

Guide to Microforms in Print. 1961 to date. Weston, Conn.: Microform Review, current edition. Annual. Guide to books, periodicals, and newspapers on microfilm from U.S. and foreign publishers. *Subject Guide to Microforms in Print* (Weston, Conn.: Microform Review), published annually, provides a subject index to microforms.

Humanities Index. 1974 to date. New York: Wilson, current edition. Formerly published as part of *Social Sciences and Humanities Index* (New York: Wilson, 1907–1974). Author and subject index to articles in scholarly journals pertaining to archaeology, folklore, history, literature, philosophy, and related subjects.

National Geographic Index, 2 vols. Washington: National Geographic Society, 1967, 1970. Biennial cumulations. Handy key to articles and illustrations—photographs, drawings, charts, graphs, and maps—found in the *National Geographic.* Volume 1 covers the period 1888–1946, and Volume 2, 1947–1969.

New York Times Index. 1851 to date. New York: *The New York Times Company,* current edition. Semimonthly, annual. Indispensable, comprehensive subject index to the *Times.* Brief synopses of articles answer many queries without further reference to the newspaper itself. The *Personal Name Index to the New York Times Index* (Succasunna, N.J.: Roxbury Data Interface, 1976–   ), in preparation and to be completed in 22 volumes, will be an invaluable companion to the *New York Times Index.*

Readers' Guide to Periodical Literature. 1900 to date. New York: Wilson, current edition. Bimonthly, quarterly, annual. Index to the contents of over 160 general and nontechnical periodicals. Each article is entered under author and subject; title entries are limited to short stories and plays. Complete citations including volume number and paging are given under each entry.

Social Sciences Index. 1974 to date. New York: Wilson, current edition. Quarterly, annual. Formerly published as *Social Sciences and Humanities Index* (New York: Wilson, 1907–1974). Author and subject index to scholarly journals in the fields of anthropology, economics, geography, political science, sociology, and related subjects.

RESEARCH AND STYLE MANUALS

Handbook for Scholars by Mary-Claire van Leunen. New York: Knopf, 1978. Complete guide to the mechanics of scholarly writing: citation, references, footnotes, bibliographies, format, styling, text preparation, and related matters. Includes two appendixes of special value: The Vita, and Federal Documents of the United States.

*Manual for Writers of Term Papers, Theses, and Dissertations by Kate L. Turabian, 4th ed. Chicago: University of Chicago Press, 1973. Guide to the accepted style for the typewritten presentation of formal papers in both scientific and nonscientific fields; provides instructions and examples of all parts of the paper; abbreviations and numbers;

*Asterisk indicates reference book recommended for inclusion in a home reference library.

spelling and punctuation; capitalizing, underlining, and other matters of style; quotations; footnotes; bibliographies; public documents; tables; illustrations; scientific papers; and typing the paper.

Manual of Style, 12th ed. Chicago: University of Chicago Press, 1969. Standard working tool of editors, authors, advertisers, typographers, proofreaders, and printers. Provides clear and simple guidelines for preparing and editing copy. Includes a glossary of technical terms.

MLA Handbook for Writers of Research Papers, Theses, and Dissertations. New York: Modern Language Association, 1977 (new ed. forthcoming). Contains information ranging from the elementary to the esoteric; covers selecting the topic, using the library, preparing a bibliography, taking notes, outlining, and writing. Contains over 100 examples of citation forms for both print and nonprint media.

Modern Researcher by Jacques Barzun and Henry F. Graff, 3rd ed. New York: Harcourt, 1977. Classic manual on all aspects of research and writing, including: research and report as historian's work, ABC of technique, searchers mind and virtues, finding the facts, verification, handling ideas, truth and causation, organizing, plain words, clear sentences, arts of quoting and translating, rules of citing, revising, and discipline for work.

*Practical Stylist by Sheridan Baker, 3rd ed. New York: Crowell, 1973. Basic handbook providing essential information on form and style. Invaluable for guidance in essay writing as well as in selecting and researching topics, mastering the art of written communication, and documenting a research paper.

*Student's Guide for Writing College Papers by Kate L. Turabian, 3rd ed. Chicago: University of Chicago Press, 1976. Basic, introductory handbook giving step-by-step directions for all aspects of research from choosing the topic to writing the paper in its final form. Appendix A presents a sample research paper.

Style Guide for Writers of Term Papers, Masters' Theses, and Doctoral Dissertations by Janice L. Gorn. New York: Monarch Press, 1973. Readable, easy-to-follow directions for writing research papers. Includes how to take notes; usage; format; documentation; bibliography; tables, figures, charts, graphs, and illustrations; foreign words and abbreviations; foreword, acknowledgments; tables of contents; and sample title pages.

10 Steps in Writing the Research Paper by Roberta H. Markman and Marie L. Waddell. Woodbury, N.Y.: Barron's Educational Series, 1971. Arranged to lead the student step-by-step through the writing of a research paper from finding a suitable subject to checking the final copy. Excellent examples including a sample thesis outline and research paper.

Writer's Guide and Index to English by Porter G. Perrin, rev. by Wilma R. Ebbitt, 5th ed. Glenview, Ill.: Scott, Foresman, 1972. Basic textbook and reference tool on the art and techniques of good writing. Discusses the writer's resources, developing ideas, persuading and proving, finding structure, elements of style, special projects, and a model research paper. The final section, Index to English, contains articles in alphabetical arrangement on basic terminology, language, and language usage.

Writer's Manual. Palm Springs, Calif.: ETC Publications, 1977. Comprehensive, technical handbook covering all major areas of professional writing, editing, and publishing. Includes how to write scripts for the theater, television, and film; how to write term papers, theses, dissertations; how to write for academic publication; how to style manuscripts for articles and books; and a writer's handbook of basic composition.

Writing Research Papers: A Complete Guide by James D. Lester, 2nd ed. Glenview, Ill.: Scott, Foresman, 1975. Comprehensive step-by-step guide to research and research

**Asterisk indicates reference book recommended for inclusion in a home reference library.

paper writing. Unique features include documentation of science papers and a list of reference books and journals for each of the academic areas.

U.S. Government Publications, Documents, and Records

Catalog of the Public Documents . . . March 4, 1893–December 31, 1940, issued by the U.S. Superintendent of Documents, 25 vols. Washington, D.C.: Government Printing Office, 1896–1945. Comprehensive bibliography listing authors, subjects, and sometimes titles in one alphabet. For documents since 1940, one must use the *Monthly Catalog of United States Government Publications* and the *Cumulative Subject Index to the Monthly Catalog,* listed below.

Comprehensive Index to the Publications of the United States Government, 1881–1893, comp. by John Griffith Ames, 2 vols. Washington, D.C.: Government Printing Office, 1905. Bridges the 12-year gap between Poore's *Descriptive Catalogue of the Government Publications of the United States* and *Catalog of the Public Documents.*

Congressional Quarterly Almanac. 1945 to date. Washington, D.C.: Congressional Quarterly Service, current edition. Annual. Annual cumulative volume of *Congressional Quarterly Weekly Report* (Washington, D.C.: Congressional Quarterly Service, 1945 to date). Includes information on all major legislation, voting record of members of Congress, Supreme Court decisions, presidential messages, etc. Excellent graphs and charts.

Cumulative Subject Index to the Monthly Catalog of United States Government Publications, 1900–1971, comp. by William Buchanan and Edna A. Kanely, 15 vols. Washington, D.C.: Carrollton Press, 1973–1975. Comprehensive index covering the first 71 years of government publications in the twentieth century.

Descriptive Catalogue of the Government Publications of the United States . . . 1774–1881, comp. by Benjamin Poore. Washington, D.C.: Government Printing Office, 1885. Standard key to the publications of the U.S. government during its first century. Arranged chronologically, with general index. Gives title, author, date, and brief abstract for each document. Updated by Ames's *Comprehensive Index to the Publications of the United States Government,* 1881–1893, the *Catalog of Public Documents . . .* 1893–1940, and the *Cumulative Subject Index to the Monthly Catalog of United States Government Publications,* 1900–1971. The *Index to Publications of the United States Congress,* 1970 to date, listed below, provides a monthly index to current government publications.

Index to Publications of the United States Congress. 1970 to date. Washington, D.C.: Congressional Information Service, current edition. Monthly, annual. Comprehensive index to all congressional hearings, reports, committee prints, House and Senate documents; an abstract is given for each entry. Annual edition issued in two parts: Part 1 gives abstracts, bibliographic descriptions, and contents summary for each publication; also legislative history of each law passed within the year; Part 2 provides a subject and name index to documents, testimonies, witnesses, committees, as well as indexes to title, bill, document and report numbers, and the names of committee and subcommittee chairpersons.

Index to U.S. Government Periodicals. 1974 to date. Chicago: Infordata International, current edition. Quarterly, annual. Computer-produced, comprehensive index to some 150 government periodicals. Identifies articles by subject and author.

Monthly Catalog of United States Government Publications, issued by the U.S. Superintendent of Documents. 1895 to date. Washington, D.C.: Government Printing Office, current edition. Monthly, semiannual, annual. Basic bibliographic guide for identification and verification of approximately 20,000 documents issued annually by government departments, agencies, and bureaus. Contains a list of documents published during the month, with full title, date, paging, issuing agency, and price for each publication.

United States Government Organization Manual, issued by the U.S. National Archives and Records Service. 1935 to date. Washington, D.C.: Government Printing Office, current edition. Annual. Official organization handbook of the federal government. Contains sections describing the agencies of the legislative, judicial, and executive branches and independent agencies. Includes lists of current officials, organization charts for large departments, and a complete name index and subject/departmental index. Government publications are listed with the discussion of each agency.

AREAS OF SPECIALIZED KNOWLEDGE

Art, Architecture, and Minor Arts

American Art Museums: An Introduction to Looking by Eloise Spaeth, 3rd ed. New York: Harper. 1975. Provides information on American museums in all areas of the nation including museum collections in colleges and universities. Gives specific directions on how to get to the museum, any admission charges, hours open to the public, and special collections and publications.

Art Index. 1929 to date. New York: Wilson, current edition. Quarterly, annual. Author/subject index to 156 periodicals and museum bulletins, including foreign journals. Subjects included are archaeology, architecture, art history, arts and crafts, fine arts, graphic arts, industrial design, interior decorating, photography and films, and landscape design.

*Art through the Ages by Helen Gardner, rev. by Horst de la Croix and Richard G. Tansey, 6th ed. New York: Harcourt, 1975. Standard one-volume history of art in all parts of the world from ancient to modern times. Includes glossary of technical terms.

Britannica Encyclopaedia of American Art. Chicago: Encyclopaedia Britannica, 1973. Beautifully illustrated introduction to the study of American art. Broad subject coverage includes folk art, handicrafts, photography, and printmaking.

Dictionary of Architecture and Construction, ed. by Cyril M. Harris. New York: McGraw-Hill, 1975. Practical dictionary of current everyday words used in architecture and construction fields; includes more than 1,700 illustrations.

History of Art by H. W. Janson, 2nd rev. ed. New York: Abrams, 1977. Survey of the major visual arts from the dawn of history to the present day; profusely and beautifully illustrated. Includes pre-Columbian and Oriental art.

McGraw-Hill Dictionary of Art, ed. by Bernard S. Myers, 5 vols. New York: McGraw-Hill, 1969. Contains approximately 15,000 entries covering all countries, periods, and developments in architecture, painting, sculpture, and decorative and graphic arts. Includes biographies, definitions, concepts, schools, trends, monuments, museums, and individual works of art.

McGraw-Hill Encyclopedia of World Art, 15 vols. New York: McGraw-Hill, 1967. Comprehensive, authoritative encyclopedia containing more than 1,000 major entries, including over 200 historical articles and 550 biographical articles. Covers every culture, every period, movement, and form of artistic expression including painting, sculpture, architecture, ceramics, glassware, furniture, armor, fashions, toys, photography, and many more. Extensive bibliography accompanies major articles; colored plates take up about half of each volume. Last volume serves as index to the set.

Praeger Encyclopedia of Art, 5 vols. New York: Praeger, 1973. Based on the French encyclopedia *Dictionnaire Universel de L'Art et des Artistes* (Paris: Fernand Hazan,

*Asterisk indicates reference book recommended for inclusion in a home reference library.

1967). Includes 4,000 entries covering periods, styles, schools, and movements; 3,000 articles on individual artists from all nations and all periods; approximately 1,000 pictures integrated with articles in each of the five volumes.

HISTORY: UNITED STATES

Album of American History, ed. by James Truslow Adams, 6 vols. New York: Scribner, 1969. Record of American history from colonial times to 1968 presented in more than 6,000 black-and-white illustrations. Last volume contains a general index making it possible to locate pictures of persons, places, things, and events.

Annals of America, ed. by Mortimer J. Adler et al., 20 vols. Chicago: Encyclopaedia Britannica, 1969. Chronological record of American life from 1492 to 1968 as revealed in more than 2,200 original writings including: laws, speeches, diaries, journals, transcriptions of dialogues, on-the-scene reports, and reminiscences and other primary sources. Documents are indexed in the two-volume Conspectus, which breaks down U.S. history into 25 "Great Issues" and 501 major topics.

Congress Investigates: A Documentary History 1792–1974, ed. by Arthur M. Schlesinger, Jr., and Roger Burns, 5 vols. New York: Chelsea House, distributed by Bowker, 1975. In-depth study of 29 of the most important investigations conducted by the U.S. Congress including: Harper's Ferry Inquiry, 1859; Impeachment Investigation of Andrew Johnson, 1867; Teapot Dome Investigation, 1924; and the Watergate Investigation, 1973. Each investigation is introduced by an interpretive essay followed by the original documents.

Dictionary of American History, ed. by Louise B. Ketz, rev. ed., 7 vols. New York: Scribner, 1976. Comprehensive encyclopedia covering great variety of topics connected with American history, encompassing nearly all political, social, economic, and cultural aspects. Does not include biography since it is a companion set to the *Dictionary of American Biography* (see Basic Reference Tools, General Reference, Biographical Dictionaries and Indexes).

Documents Illustrative of the Formation of the Union of the United States. Washington, D.C.: Government Printing Office, 1927; reprinted 1965. Collection of reprints of documents on the formation of the United States including: Declaration of Independence; Constitution of the United States; the first 19 Amendments; notes and papers of Alexander Hamilton, James Madison, Rufus King, and others; resolutions, declarations, and reports that played a part in the preparation of the documents.

Encyclopedia of American History, ed. by Richard B. Morris and Jeffrey B. Morris. Bicentennial 5th ed. New York: Harper, 1976. Valuable one-volume reference work divided into three main parts: basic chronology of major political and military events; presidents and their cabinets; 400 notable Americans.

Guide to the Study of the United States of America, issued by the General Reference and Bibliography Division of the Library of Congress. Washington, D.C.: Superintendent of Documents, 1960. Supplement 1956–1965. Washington, D.C.: Superintendent of Documents, 1976. Supplement 1966–1975 currently being compiled. Basic guide to materials covering every phase of American life—literature, language, biography, periodicals, geography, American Indian, diplomatic history, intellectual history, local history, minorities, society, science, entertainment, sports, art, economic life, politics, books and libraries, etc. There is an author, title, and subject index.

Harvard Guide to American History, ed. by Frank Freidel, rev. ed., 2 vols. Cambridge, Mass.: Harvard University Press, 1974. Valuable compilation of references to materials on all phases and periods of American history. Volume 1 contains topical entries arranged chronologically; volume 2 contains indexes by subject and name.

Makers of America, 10 vols. Chicago: Encyclopaedia Britannica, 1971. Chronological arrangement of 731 primary sources—letters, diaries, newspaper editorials, etc.—describing activities of minority groups, their organizations, hopes, experiences, beliefs, and accomplishments. Contains excellent indexes such as: ethnic index, proper name index, topical index, author-source index, and illustration index.

Negro in American History, ed. by Mortimer Adler, 3 vols. Chicago: Encyclopaedia Britannica, 1972. Sourcebook of 195 selections drawn from *Annals of America* cited above. Volumes are arranged in reverse chronological order: Volume 1, Black Americans 1928–1971; Volume 2, A Taste of Freedom, 1854–1927; Volume 3, Slaves and Masters, 1567–1854.

*Webster's Guide to American History: A Chronological, Geographical, and Biographical Survey and Compendium, ed. by Charles Van Doren and Robert McHenry. Springfield, Mass.: Merriam, 1971. Reading reference compendium of basic information. Divided into three main sections. Section 1 presents a chronology from 1492 to the end of 1969. Alongside the chronology of events, quotations from primary sources are given. Section 2 consists of a collection of maps and tables. Section 3 includes 1,035 biographical sketches of notable Americans.

HISTORY: WORLD

Cambridge Ancient History, 3rd ed., 12 vols., 5 vols. of plates. Cambridge: Cambridge University Press, 1970–1977. Basic reference set, a complete revision of the original set published between 1923 and 1939. This scholarly work is the recognized authoritative source for in-depth study of all aspects of ancient history—social, economic, political, and cultural. This revision incorporates knowledge gained from important archaeological discoveries. Detailed chronologies and documentation via footnotes are two valuable features.

Cambridge Medieval History, 2nd ed., 8 vols. in 9. Cambridge: Cambridge University Press, 1966– in process. First edition of this scholarly reference set was published from 1911 to 1936 in eight volumes and serves as the basic reference tool for the medieval period while the second edition is in progress. All aspects of the medieval period are covered in depth—social, economic, political, and cultural. The third title in the Cambridge History series is the *New Cambridge Modern History,* which covers the period 1493 through 1945, listed below.

Concise Encyclopedia of Archaeology, ed. by Leonard Cottrell, 2nd ed., New York: Hawthorn Books, 1971. Contains a wealth of information on all aspects of archaeology. Each article written by a British scholar recognized as an authority in the field. Covers places and peoples, cities and civilizations, trends and techniques, and ancient languages. Includes 10 regional maps of archaeological sites and a number of illustrations.

*Encyclopedia of World History, ed. by William L. Langer, 5th ed., Boston: Houghton, 1972. Standard one-volume compendium of historical events arranged in outline form, covering human history from prehistoric times to 1970. Broad periods are subdivided geographically and the events are described in a concise manner. Excellent for information on new techniques for determining historical dates; lists of popes, emperors, and rulers; and genealogical tables.

Harper Encyclopedia of the Modern World: A Concise Reference History from 1760 to the Present, ed. by Richard B. Morris and Graham W. Irwin. New York: Harper, 1970. Excellent one-volume reference tool divided into two main parts: Part 1, Basic Chronology of political and military history; Part 2, Topical Chronology highlighting the social, cultural, scientific, and intellectual developments of each period. The history of Asia, Africa, Latin America, Europe, and North America is well covered.

*Asterisk indicates reference book recommended for inclusion in a home reference library.

New Cambridge Modern History, 13 vols. and Atlas. Cambridge: Cambridge University Press, 1957–1970. Complete revision of the *Cambridge Modern History* published from 1902 to 1926. This edition covers the period from 1493 through 1945. Each volume is edited by a scholar who specializes in that period and each article is written by a recognized authority. No bibliographies in the revised edition; a separate publication, *A Bibliography of Modern History,* ed. by John Roach (Cambridge: Cambridge University Press, 1968), supplements this current set.

Oxford Classical Dictionary, ed. by G. L. Hammond and H. H. Scullard, 2nd ed., Oxford: Oxford University Press, 1970. Scholarly, comprehensive basic reference tool providing information on Greek and Roman history, biography, geography, religion, literature, mythology, etc. Includes an index to all names not listed as main entries.

Timetables of History: A Horizontal Linkage of People and Events by Bernard Grun. New York: Simon and Schuster, 1975. Encyclopedic chronology identifying what has happened concurrently in all parts of the world throughout human history. The chronology is divided into the following categories: history and politics; literature and the theater; religion; philosophy; learning; visual arts; music; science, technology,·and growth; and daily life. This work is a direct translation of the German masterpiece *Kultur-Fahr Plan* (the culture timetables) published in Germany in 1946. This edition is greatly enlarged and updated to include the events of the year 1974.

LITERATURE, FOLKLORE, MYTHOLOGY, and THEATER

American Authors 1600–1900: A Biographical Dictionary of American Literature, ed. by Stanley J. Kunitz and Howard Haycraft. New York: Wilson, 1938. Standard one-volume biographical dictionary covering the first 300 years of America's literary history. Contains biographies of 1,300 authors; nearly every American who has written anything of value during the 300-year period is included; also contains 400 black-and-white portraits, which accompany the biographical sketches of major literary figures. Each sketch is followed by a list of principal works with original dates of publication; also gives a list of works about the author.

Brewer's Dictionary of Phrase and Fable, ed. by Ivor H. Evans, centenary edition. New York: Harper, 1971. Standard handbook of curious facts first compiled by Ebenezer Brewer in 1870, and revised a number of times. This revised and greatly expanded edition contains over 20,000 entries including: a history of gods and goddesses; a record of superstitions and customs; names of saints and giants; real and fictitious names from history, literature, and the arts; and colloquial and proverbial phrases.

British Authors Before 1800: A Biographical Dictionary, ed. by Stanley J. Kunitz and Howard Haycraft. New York: Wilson, 1952. Standard biographical dictionary containing concise biographies of 650 British authors living before 1800. Biographies are arranged alphabetically, with cross-references from variant name forms. Following each sketch is a list of the principal works of the author with dates of original publication. Contains 220 black-and-white portraits.

British Authors of the Nineteenth Century, ed. by Stanley J. Kunitz and Howard Haycraft. New York: Wilson, 1936. Standard biographical dictionary containing 1,000 biographies and 350 black-and-white portraits of major and minor authors of the British Empire, including Canada, Australia, South Africa, and New Zealand, who have published between 1800 and 1900. Biographies are arranged alphabetically with cross-references from variant name forms. Following each sketch is a list of the principal works of the author with dates of original publication.

British Writers, ed. under the auspices of the British Council, 7 vols. New York: Scribner, 1979–1981. A complete survey of the works of the major British writers from 1332 to today. Originally published as a series of individual works, all articles in this reference set have been revised, brought up-to-date, and completely re-edited for publication in this multi-volume format. *British Writers* is an essential, comprehensive source for the study of British literary history.

Cassell's Encyclopedia of World Literature, ed. by J. Buchanan-Brown, rev. and enl. ed., 3 vols. New York: Morrow, 1973. Comprehensive literature handbook providing articles on literary genres, schools and movements, national literatures, and biographies of authors.

Concise Cambridge History of English Literature, 3rd rev. and enl. ed. Cambridge: Cambridge University Press, 1973. Based on the *Cambridge History of English Literature* (1907–1929, 15 vols.), the first *Concise* edition was published in 1941; thoroughly updated and expanded. Covers the literary history of the United States as well as literature in English of Ireland, Pakistan, Ceylon, Malaysia, Canada, Australia, New Zealand, West Indies, and South Africa.

Contemporary Authors: A Bio-Bibliographical Guide to Current Writers, ed. by Jane Bowden and Christine Nasso. 1962 to date. Detroit: Gale, current edition. Semiannual. Guide to writers in fiction, general nonfiction, poetry, journalism, drama, motion pictures, television, and other fields. These sketches, prepared by the individual author, include personal facts, career summaries, and lists of writings.

Crowell's Handbook of Classical Drama by Richmond Y. Hathorn. New York: Crowell, 1967. Standard dictionary giving definitions of terms, digests of plays, notes on costume, identification of characters, and biographical data on playwrights.

Crowell's Handbook of Classical Mythology by Edward Tripp. New York: Crowell, 1970. Comprehensive handbook of Greek and Roman mythology. Includes information on characters, place names, events, as well as a retelling of the myths themselves. Genealogical trees and maps are also given.

Dictionary of Literary Biography. 1978 to date. Detroit: Gale, current edition. Contains definitive essays on literary figures of major importance. Each entry divided into three parts: brief career chronology and list of publications; personal and career summary; and a bibliography of works by and about the subject. Provides literary assessment and examines the author's relation to the social and literary concerns of his or her time.

Encyclopedia of World Literature in the 20th Century, ed. by Wolfgang B. Fleischman, 3 vols. New York: Ungar, 1967–1971. Supplement vol. 4, 1975. Enlarged and updated edition of the German encyclopedia *Herder Lexicon der Weltliteratur im 20. Jahrbundert* (Freeberg: Herder, 1960–1961, 2 vols.). Includes articles on writers, literary movements, genres, and national literatures. Valuable for facts about foreign authors.

European Authors 1000–1900: A Biographical Dictionary of European Literature, ed. by Stanley J. Kunitz and Vineta Colby. New York: Wilson, 1967. Standard biographical dictionary containing 967 biographies of continental European writers born after 1000 A.D. and dead prior to 1925. Covers writers in 31 languages; French, German, and Russian writers predominate. Includes bibliographies of books by and about each author.

*Familiar Quotations by John Bartlett, 14th rev. and enl. ed. Boston: Little, 1968. Standard handbook of quotations from English and American writing with special sections for biblical and historical quotes. Contains a detailed index of over 117,000 entries; arranged chronologically by author, the index is the key to locating each quotation.

Funk and Wagnalls Standard Dictionary of Folklore, Mythology and Legend, ed. by Maria Leach. New York: Funk and Wagnalls, 1972. Dictionary of topics such as gods and goddesses, legendary and folk heroes, demons and ogres, signs and symbols, plant

---

*Asterisk indicates reference book recommended for inclusion in a home reference library.

and animal folklore, festivals, customs, and many more. Contains index to over 2,400 countries, regions, cultures, tribes, and ethnic groups.

*Good Reading, ed. by J. Sherwood Weber, 21st ed. New York: Bowker, 1978. Classic guide that lists, annotates, evaluates, and provides full bibliographic data on over 2,500 carefully selected books. Titles are arranged by subject areas covering virtually every area of inquiry and endeavor. Includes a "100 Significant Books" section. Provides author, title, and subject index.

Great Books of the Western World, ed. by Robert M. Hutchins and Mortimer J. Adler, 54 vols. Chicago: Encyclopaedia Britannica, 1952. Includes 443 works by 74 of the greatest thinkers in Western civilization during the past 3,000 years. All books in the set relate to the continuity of the discussion of common themes and problems down through the centuries. Authors and titles are arranged chronologically within four categories: poetry, fiction, and drama; science and mathematics; history and social sciences; and philosophy and religion. The Syntopicon is a two-volume topical index in which the writings in the *Great Books* are indexed in terms of 102 great ideas.

Great Treasury of Western Thought: A Compendium of Important Statements on Man and His Institutions by the Great Thinkers in Western History, ed. by Mortimer J. Adler and Charles Van Doren. New York: Bowker, 1977. Encyclopedic in scope, this anthology contains over 8,800 quotations from Homer to Santayana. Explanatory headnotes provide background information. Provides both an author and a key word index.

Home Book of Quotations, Classical and Modern by Burton E. Stevenson, 10th ed. New York: Dodd, 1967. Comprehensive handbook to more than 50,000 quotations from writers of all periods of history and from all countries. Arranged alphabetically by subject. Includes an index of authors, giving full name, dates of birth and death, with reference to all quotations cited; a word index identifies the quotations under key words.

Literary History of the United States, ed. by Robert E. Spiller et al., 4th ed. rev., 2 vols. New York: Macmillan, 1974. Survey history of American literature as seen through the eyes of modern literary critics. Each chapter written by a literary authority. Influences that have shaped the development of literature in America are traced throughout the survey. Volume 2 contains an extensive bibliography.

McGraw-Hill Encyclopedia of World Drama, 4 vols. New York: McGraw-Hill, 1972. Comprehensive reference work on drama as literature. Covers all types of drama, national theater, synopses of plays, and detailed biographies of 300 major dramatists. Contains an index of plays with over 30,000 entries.

New Larousse Encyclopedia of Mythology. New York: Putnam, 1969. Profusely illustrated survey of world mythology arranged topically and by regions and countries. Includes Egyptian, classical, Teutonic, Celtic, Persian, Indian, Chinese, Japanese, African, and American folklore, legend, and religious customs.

New York Theatre, ed. by Catherine R. Hughes. 1978 to date. Detroit: Gale, current edition. Annual. Covers all Broadway and off-Broadway productions. Gives a synopsis of the play, full production and cast listings, plot summary, extracts from major reviews, opening and closing dates, and photographs.

Notable Names in the American Theatre, 2nd ed. Detroit: James T. White, distributed by Gale, 1976. Contains over 2,600 biographies of leading theatrical figures, including performers, producers, playwrights, stage and costume designers, choreographers, composers, educators, authors, historians, archivists, administrators, and publicists. Necrology provides vital statistics for more than 8,000 theater greats from 526 B.C. to today.

*Asterisk indicates reference book recommended for inclusion in a home reference library.

Gives a list of New York productions, premieres in America, premieres of American plays abroad, theater group biographies, and theater building biographies.

Oxford Dictionary of English Proverbs, rev. by F. P. Wilson, 3rd ed., rev. Oxford: Clarendon Press, 1970. Over 10,000 proverbs arranged alphabetically by key word, with numerous cross-references from other words. Gives the date of the earliest use and source where found; also identifies subsequent variant uses and sources.

Reader's Adviser: A Layman's Guide to Literature, ed. by Sarah L. Prakken, 12th ed., 3 vols. New York: Bowker, 1974–1977. Standard reference tool giving background information pertaining to literature; nearly every subject, every type of book, every period and literary form, and every noted writer from antiquity to today.

Something about the Author, ed. by Anne Commire. 1971 to date. Detroit: Gale, current edition. Biannual. Information on the lives, careers, and works of the most popular modern authors and illustrators of books for young people. Each volume contains over 200 biographical entries of authors and illustrators of young people's fiction, nonfiction, poetry, and drama. Cumulative index of authors and an index of illustrators included in each volume.

Twentieth Century Authors: A Biographical Dictionary of Modern Literature, ed. by Stanley J. Kunitz and Howard Haycraft. New York: Wilson, 1942. First supplement, 1955. Standard biographical dictionary. Main volume contains 1,850 biographies and 1,700 black-and-white portraits of writers of all nations. The supplement brings the original sketches up to date and adds 700 new biographies, 670 with black-and-white portraits. The index lists biographies of 2,500 writers contained in both volumes.

World Authors 1950–1970: A Companion Volume to Twentieth Century Authors, ed. by John Wakeman. New York: Wilson, 1975. Standard biographical dictionary updating *Twentieth Century Authors* main volume and supplement. Includes 959 additional biographies.

MATHEMATICS

Barlow's Tables of Squares, Cubes, Square Roots, Cube Roots, and Reciprocals of all Integers, Up to 12,500 by Peter Barlow, 4th ed. New York: Halsted Press, 1965. Standard handbook for statisticians, engineers, physicists, and chemists.

*Handbook of Mathematical Functions: With Formulas, Graphs and Tables, rev. ed. Washington, D.C.: Government Printing Office, 1971. Basic handbook including every special function normally needed by anyone using mathematical tables in his or her work. Over 1,046 pages devoted to numerical tables and special mathematical functions.

Handbook of Mathematical Tables and Formulas by Richard S. Burington, 5th ed. New York: McGraw-Hill, 1973. Designed as a ready reference tool for engineers, physicists, chemists, and workers in other related fields. Includes formulas and theorems of algebra, trigonometry, calculus, and vector analysis; numerical tables; glossary of symbols; index of numerical tables; and subject index.

James and James Mathematics Dictionary by Glenn James, 3rd ed. New York: Van Nostrand, 1968. Basic dictionary containing 8,000 mathematical terms used in engineering, physics, and chemistry. Also includes numerous illustrations, tables, symbols, abbreviations, and formulas.

Universal Encyclopedia of Mathematics. New York: Simon and Schuster, 1964. Translation of the German handbook *Meyers Rechenduden* (1960). Covers all major mathematical functions including arithmetic, algebra, applications, geometry, trigonometry, differential calculus, and integral calculus.

*Asterisk indicates reference book recommended for inclusion in a home reference library.

World of Mathematics, ed. by James R. Newman, 4 vols. New York: Simon and Schuster, 1956–1960. Anthology of original documents setting forth the history of mathematics from the ancient Egyptians to the time of Einstein. Volume 1, Men and Numbers; Volume 2, World of Laws and the World of Chance; Volume 3, Mathematical Way of Thinking; and Volume 4, Machines, Music, and Puzzles.

MUSIC

American Music Handbook by Christopher Pavlakis. New York: Free Press, 1974. Comprehensive handbook containing a wealth of information on music in America. Typical categories are: Over 160 symphony orchestras with auditorium seating capacity, season, budget, recordings; university bands, tours, and recordings; opera companies; music festivals and camps; record companies; and music publishers.

American Popular Songs: From the Revolutionary War to the Present, ed. by David Ewen. New York: Random House, 1966. Contains about 3,600 title entries listing names of lyricists, composers, and singer who introduced the song or made it popular, and anecdotes about the song's popularity or how it came to be written. Excellent coverage of Broadway musicals and Tin Pan Alley.

Baker's Biographical Dictionary of Musicians, rev. by Nicolas Slonimsky, 5th ed. New York: Schirmer, 1958. Supplement, 1971. Standard biographical dictionary of musicians of all periods and all countries. Lists musician's own works as well as titles about him or her. Indicates pronunciation of foreign names.

Book of World-Famous Music: Classical, Popular and Folk by James J. Fuld, rev. and enl. ed. New York: Crown, 1971. Approximately 1,000 compositions from various countries spanning 500 years of music are traced to their first appearance in print. Each entry gives the title of the song, historical background, location of the earliest known printed copy, biographical note on the composer and lyricist, and a musical rendition of the opening line.

Complete Book of Classical Music, ed. by David Ewen. Englewood Cliffs, N.J.: Prentice-Hall, 1965. Chronological guide to 1,000 works by over 100 composers from 1300 to 1900. Includes identification, description, commentary, and critical evaluation of each work.

Complete Encyclopedia of Popular Music and Jazz, 1900–1950 by Roger D. Kinkle, 4 vols. New Rochelle, N.Y.: Arlington House, 1974. Comprehensive coverage of contributors to popular music and jazz during the 50-year period. Volume 1 lists Broadway musicals, popular songs, movie musicals, and recordings of popular music and jazz for each year. Volumes 2 and 3 contain biographies of singers, musicians, composers, bandleaders, etc., and list their songs and recordings. Volume 4 contains awards, principal recording labels, and indexes to personal names, popular songs, musicals, and major recordings.

Complete Guide to Modern Dance by Don McDonagh. New York: Doubleday, 1976. Covers more than 100 American choreographers from the pioneers in the nineteenth century to contemporary artists. Brief biographical sketch of each choreographer is followed by an analytical description of his or her major dances and a chronological list of all known works. Includes a modern dance chronology, 1862–1975.

Composers of Tomorrow's Music: A Non-Technical Introduction to the Musical Avant-Garde Movement by David Ewen. New York: Dodd, 1971. Introduction to avant-garde music via 10 in-depth studies of notable composers such as Ives and Schoenberg. Topics such as the 12-tone system, electronic music, noise, chance music, and synthesizers are discussed. Comprehensive index.

Composers Since 1900: A Biographical and Critical Guide, ed. by David Ewen. New York: Wilson, 1969. Basic biographical dictionary containing 220 biographies of twentieth-century composers from Europe and the United States. A companion volume to *Great Composers, 1300–1900,* listed below.

Dance Encyclopedia, comp. by Anatole Chujoy and P. W. Manchester, rev. and enl. ed. New York: Simon and Schuster, 1967. Comprehensive encyclopedia containing 5,000 entries and 274 illustrations covering all aspects of the dance: History, biography, terminology, choreography, music, stage design, instruction, and criticism. Emphasis on ethnic and folk dances.

Encyclopedia of Folk, Country and Western Music by Irwin Stambler and Grelun Landon. New York: St. Martin's Press, 1969. Biographical dictionary including 500 entries for classical folk and country performers, as well as folk rock and country blues artists. Groups as well as individual performers are included. Appendixes provide list of awards, discography, and bibliography.

Encyclopedia of Jazz in the Sixties by Leonard Feather. New York: Horizon, 1966. Contains 1,100 biographical sketches plus a number of articles on jazz. Includes a list of recordings, bibliography, and many illustrations.

Great Composers, 1300–1900: A Biographical and Critical Guide, ed. by David Ewen. New York: Wilson, 1966. Basic biographical dictionary containing biographical sketches of over 200 composers. Each sketch discusses the musical significance of the composer, provides critical and historical commentary, and lists major works. Provides a chronological list of composers and a list by nationality.

Harvard Dictionary of Music by Willi Apel, 2nd ed., rev. and enl. Cambridge, Mass.: Harvard University Press, 1969. Standard authoritative dictionary including music history, forms, instruments, notation, performance, and theory; omits biography. Profusely illustrated. Contains list of music libraries.

International Cyclopedia of Music and Musicians, ed. by Oscar Thompson. 10th ed., ed. by Bruce Bohle. New York: Dodd, 1975. Basic one-volume musical encyclopedia covering a wide range of topics such as composers, musicians, terms, tables of notation, instruments, opera, folk music, libraries of music, and music criticism.

Literature of Jazz: A Critical Guide by Donald Kennington. Chicago: American Library Association, 1971. Critical narrative bibliography covering all significant works in English about jazz as well as essential books in foreign languages published through 1969. Covers general works, histories, biographies, technical and critical works, reference books, and periodicals. Contains title index and index of authors and subjects.

Music Index. 1949 to date. Detroit: Coordinators, current edition. Monthly, annual. Subject and author index to over 300 periodicals, including some foreign titles. Includes book reviews of current music titles.

Music of Black Americans: A History by Eileen Southern. New York: Norton, 1971. Comprehensive, scholarly history of black American music from 1619 to the present. Arrangement is chronological; topics cover the African heritage, musical instruments, musicians, religious music, songs, dances, folk music, musical organizations, ragtime, blues, jazz, the black renaissance, and black symphony and concert artists.

Music Reference and Research Materials: An Annotated Bibliography, comp. by Vincent Duckles, 2nd ed. New York: Free press, 1967. Basic music bibliography arranged by type of material such as dictionaries, histories, bibliographies, catalogs, discographies, etc. Complete bibliographic information for each of the 1,382 entries. Index of authors, editors, and reviewers, index of subjects, and one of titles.

New Complete Book of the American Musical Theater by David Ewen. New York: Holt, 1970. Comprehensive handbook listing over 500 shows; gives plot, leading performers, production history, and hit songs. Separate section gives brief biographies of composers, librettists, and lyricists. An appendix contains a chronology of shows and a list of hit songs and singers

New Encyclopedia of the Opera by David Ewen. New York: Hill and Wang, 1971. Contains 1,500 entries covering stories of operas, characters, arias, biographies, terminology, histories of opera houses, conductors, and critics.

New Grove Dictionary of Music and Musicians, 6th ed., 20 vols. Washington, D.C. Grove's Dictionaries of Music, Inc., 1979. Standard music encyclopedia in the English language. Comprehensive in scope, includes articles on music history, biographies of composers and musicians, theory and practice, musical terms and instruments, individual compositions, songs, operas, etc.

New Kobbe's Complete Opera Book, rev. by the Earl of Harewood. New York: Putnam, 1976. Standard opera guide providing comprehensive and highly technical coverage of standard repertoire and opera history. Synopses of over 300 operas; lists major performances, characters, plots, and music.

New Oxford History of Music. Oxford: Oxford University Press, 1954, in process. Scholarly history of music to be completed in 11 volumes. The following have been published to date: Volume 1, Ancient and Oriental Music, 1957; Volume 2, Early Medieval Music Up to 1300, 1954; Volume 3, Art Nova and the Renaissance, 1300–1540, 1960; Volume 4, Age of Humanism, 1540–1630, 1968; Volume 5, Opera and Church Music, 1630–1750, 1975; Volume 7, Age of Enlightenment, 1745–1790, 1973; Volume 10, Modern Age, 1890–1960, 1974.

Popular American Composers, from Revolutionary Times to the Present: A Biographical and Critical Guide. New York: Wilson, 1962. First Supplement, 1972. Biographical dictionary containing 130 sketches of American composers; sketches emphasize personal information rather than critical appraisal. Provides a chronological list of composers and an index of songs. The first supplement updates the main volume and adds 31 new biographies.

Popular Song Index by Patricia P. Havlice. Metuchen, N.J.: Scarecrow, 1975. Indexes 300 songbooks published or reprinted between 1940 and 1972; identifies folk songs, blues, popular tunes, spirituals, hymns, children's songs, and sea songs. Entries under the first line of the song and the first line of the chorus; index of composers and lyricists is included.

Record and Tape Reviews Index by Antoinette C. Maleady. 1971 to date. Metuchen, N.J.: Scarecrow, latest edition. Annual. Reviews of classical music on records and tapes from 19 periodicals. Divided into three sections: Composers, Music in collections, and Spoken recordings.

Records in Review: The High Fidelity Annual. 1955 to date. Great Barrington, Mass.: Wyeth Press, current edition. Annual. Annual cumulation of the reviews published in *High Fidelity;* covers classical and semiclassical music. Separate section lists recitals and miscellany. Arranged alphabetically by composer; provides index of performers.

World of Twentieth-Century Music by David Ewen. Englewood Cliffs, N.J.: Prentice-Hall, 1969. Biographical dictionary containing 149 biographical sketches of twentieth-century composers. Following each sketch is a chronological list of the composer's works.

OCCUPATIONS

Dictionary of Occupational Titles, prepared by the U.S. Department of Labor, Bureau of Employment Security, 4th ed. Washington, D.C.: Government Printing Office, 1977. Basic handbook providing standard job titles and descriptions for 20,000 occupations. Completely updated; over 3,500 occupations listed in the 3rd edition have been deleted.

Encyclopedia of Careers and Vocational Guidance, ed. by William E. Hopke, 3rd ed., 2 vols. New York: Doubleday, 1975. Volume 1 covers planning a career, including advantages and requirements for career fields. Volume 2 provides information on specific jobs, trades, occupations, and professions, including job descriptions, history, nature of work, requirements, advancement, outlook, earnings, working conditions, and social and psychological factors.

Occupational Outlook Handbook, prepared by the Division of Manpower and Occupational Outlook. 1949 to date. Washington, D.C.: Government Printing Office, current edition. Biennial. Handbook containing accurate career information; provides specific information about education and training requirements, employment outlook, places of employment, earnings, and working conditions for over 700 occupations. *Occupational Outlook Quarterly* (Government Printing Office) updates the handbook between editions.

PHILOSOPHY AND RELIGION

Archaeological Encyclopedia of the Holy Land, ed. by Avraham Negev. New York: Putnam, 1972. Authoritative sourcebook prepared by 20 specialists providing information on over 600 topics, including articles on archaeological methods of research, agriculture, places, peoples, manners and customs, history, architecture, commerce, etc. Includes maps and chronological tables as well as a glossary.

Cambridge History of Later Greek and Early Medieval Philosophy, ed. by Arthur H. Armstrong. Cambridge: Cambridge University Press, 1967. Scholarly, historical study of the development of philosophy from the later Greek period down through the Early Middle Ages. Each period is treated in depth. Includes bibliography and index.

Concise Encyclopedia of Western Philosophy and Philosophers, ed. by J. O. Urmson. New York: Hawthorn Books, 1960. Handbook of brief articles on persons and ideas of all times that have shaped the thinking of people in the Western world.

Dictionary of Comparative Religion, ed. by S. G. F. Brandon. New York: Scribner, 1970. Comprehensive dictionary covering iconography, philosophy, anthropology, and the psychology of Asian, Western, ancient, and primitive religions. Includes articles on doctrines, rituals, scriptures, theological trends, music, and religious leaders. A Synoptic Index lists all entries that pertain to each major religion.

Dictionary of Liturgy and Worship, ed. by J. G. Davies. New York: Macmillan, 1972. Comprehensive dictionary covering all major denominations. Each sect or rite is presented in a separate article; includes articles on liturgical books, rituals, prayers, and sacraments. Includes illustrations for many of the topics.

Dictionary of the History of Ideas: Studies of Selected Pivotal Ideas, ed. by Philip P. Wiener, 4 vols. and index. New York: Scribner, 1973–1974. Scholarly encyclopedic dictionary presenting an interdisciplinary, cross-cultural, historical approach to the study of ideas. Articles are of three different kinds: cross-cultural studies limited to a given century or period; studies that trace an idea down through history; and studies that show how ideas have been developed in the minds of the world's great thinkers.

Encyclopaedia of Religion and Ethics, ed. by James Hastings, 13 vols. New York: Scribner, 1908–1927. Comprehensive encyclopedia including topics on all religions, ethical systems, and movements. Subjects covered include anthropology, mythology, folklore, biography, psychology, and sociology in relation to religion.

Encyclopedia of Philosophy, ed. by Paul Edwards, 8 vols. New York: Macmillan, 1967. Comprehensive, authoritative encyclopedia, international in scope; covers Eastern and Western philosophy as well as ancient, medieval, and modern philosophers. Contains 1,450 signed articles varying in length from 40 to 60 pages. Provides many cross references and analytical subject index.

Encyclopedic Dictionary of Judaica, ed. by Geoffrey Wigoder. New York: Leon Amiel, 1974. Distillation of topics covered in detail in the 16-volume *Encyclopaedia Judaica* (New York: Macmillan 1972). Excellent quick reference source for information on Jewish history, customs, writings, religious rites and observances, and biography.

Exhaustive Concordance of the Bible by James Strong. New York: Abingdon, 1961. Reprint of the 1894 edition. Comprehensive, standard concordance for the King James version of the Bible. Exhaustive in coverage, this tool is basic for quick identification of any biblical passage. Provides a dictionary of Hebrew and Greek words.

Guide to Philosophical Bibliography and Research by Richard T. DeGeorge. New York: Appleton-Century-Crofts, 1971. Comprehensive bibliographic reference tool citing encyclopedias, dictionaries, handbooks, histories, bibliographies, and journals. Annotations given for each entry highlight scope and special value of the title.

Handbook of Denominations in the United States by Frank S. Mead, 6th ed. Nashville, Tenn.: Abingdon, 1975. Presents history, doctrines, organization, and present status in the United States of over 250 religious denominations. Includes directory of administrative denominational headquarters, glossary of terms, classified bibliography, and proper name index.

Interpreter's Dictionary of the Bible, ed. by George Arthur Buttrick et al., 4 vols. New York: Abingdon, 1962. Supplement 1976. Scholarly, comprehensive, basic reference tool based on the Revised Standard Version of the Bible. Includes articles on all biblical names of people, places, things, and events. Highlights archaeological findings; includes the Apocrypha.

New Standard Jewish Encyclopedia, ed. by Cecil Roth and Geoffrey Wigoder, rev. ed. New York: Doubleday, 1970. Concise presentation of the history of the Jewish people as well as their manners and customs, literature, holidays and festivals, religious beliefs and teachings, and place in the contemporary world. Contains biographies of Jewish leaders past and present. Comprehensive articles on the establishment of the state of Israel, on the Holocaust, and on the emergence of the United States as the Diaspora community.

Oxford Dictionary of the Christian Church, ed. by F. L. Cross and E. A. Livingstone, 2nd ed. Oxford: Oxford University Press, 1974. Scholarly compendium of over 6,000 entries covering all aspects of the Christian church. Includes biographies, terminology, literature, art, history, theology, ritual, geography, and various religious beliefs and practices.

Philosopher's Index: An International Index to Philosophical Periodicals. 1967 to date. Bowling Green, Ohio: Bowling Green University, current edition. Quarterly, annual. Computer-compiled index to over 250 American and British periodicals with a selection from other countries. Provides subject and author listings, with abstracts entered under the author listing. Separate list of book reviews.

Religions of America by Leo Rosten. New York: Simon and Schuster, 1975. Readable, fact-filled accounts of the major and minor religions in America, their beliefs, leaders, historical and social significance, and contemporary status.

Shorter Encyclopaedia of Islam, ed. by H. A. R. Gibb and J. H. Kramers. Ithaca, N.Y.: Cornell University Press, 1957. Condensation of the multivolume *Encyclopaedia of Islam* (Leiden: Brill). Scholarly, authoritative articles on the religion, history, manners and customs, and biography.

Yearbook of American and Canadian Churches. 1915 to date. Nashville, Tenn.: Abingdon, current edition. Provides current information for all American and Canadian churches, such as membership statistics, organizations, seminaries, clergy, etc.

POLITICAL SCIENCE

All about Politics: Questions and Answers on the U.S. Political Parties by Paul A. Theis and William P. Steponkus. New York: Bowker, 1972. Provides concrete information about the history and future of American politics. Divided into three main sections: Politics: Everyone's Business; Politics: Campaigning for Office; and Politics: Checks and Balances.

Almanac of American Politics: The Senators, The Representatives, Their Records, States, and Districts ed. by Michael Barone et al. New York: Dutton. Encyclopedic almanac providing biographical data and voting record of each member of Congress. Concise descriptions of the political, economic, and social makeup of each congressional district.

American Poltical Terms by Hans Sperber and Travis Tritschuh. Detroit: Wayne State University Press, 1962. Historical dictionary providing not only definitions of political terms but also the history of each term. Carefully documented quotations given for each term.

Book of the States. 1935 to date. Lexington, Ky.: Council of State Governments, current edition. Biennial. Standard reference tool giving information on officials, agencies, taxation, finance, health and welfare, transportation, education, business and industry, and natural resources for each of the 50 states. Supplements between issues keep this source up-to-date.

Dictionary of American Politics ed. by Edward C. Smith and Arnold J. Zurcher, 2nd ed. New York: Barnes and Noble, 1968. Provides concise definitions for over 3,800 political science terms. Includes nicknames and political slogans; gives definitions, applications, and etymology of terms.

Dictionary of Politics ed. by Walter Laqueur, rev. ed. New York: Free Press, 1974. Comprehensive dictionary providing 3,000 brief articles on important political events, changes in terminology, historical background of contemporary political happenings and developments, and biographical sketches of prominent political leaders.

Encyclopaedia of Parliament by Norman Wilding and Philip Laundy, 4th ed., rev. New York: St. Martin's, 1971. Comprehensive handbook providing background information on virtually all aspects of the history, procedures, ceremony, officials, and laws of the English Parliament and of the various parliamentary institutions throughout the Commonwealth. Appendix includes lists such as the Parliaments of England from 1213 to 1955, the Lord Chancellors and Keepers of the Great Seal, Presiding Officers and Speakers of the House of Commons, and Secretaries of State for Air, the Colonies, and War.

Glossary of Political Ideas ed. by Maurice Cranston and Sanford A. Lakoff. New York: Basic Books, 1969. Compendium of articles on 51 basic political ideas. Provides historical background as well as current usage. Short bibliographies for each entry.

History of U.S. Political Parties, ed. by Arthur M. Schlesinger, Jr., 4 vols. New York: Chelsea House, dist. by Bowker, 1973. Scholarly, comprehensive, in-depth information on all American parties from 1789 to 1972. Arranged chronologically; documents printed at the end of each article. Includes index to topics and documents.

International Relations Dictionary by Jack C. Plano and Roy Olton. New York: Holt, 1969. Classified dictionary grouping terms under 12 subject headings. Entries are concise; terms are defined in clear and straightforward manner. Detailed index provides quick identification of the location of each term defined.

Municipal Year Book. 1934 to date. Washington, D.C.: International City Management Association, current edition. Annual. Provides up-to-date information on local governments. Divided into nine sections: City and the Community; Science, Technology, and the City; Public Safety; City Functions; Public Manpower; Municipal Finance; Small City Data; References; Directories.

Political Handbook and Atlas of the World: Governments and Intergovernmental Organizations, ed. by Richard P. Stebbins and Alba Amoia. 1927 to date. New York: Council on Foreign Relations, dist. by Simon and Schuster, current edition. Annual. Basic handbook providing data for all of the world's sovereign states and certain territories, such as area, population, political history, constitutional structure, foreign relations, governmental personnel, communication media, party programs, and leaders. Contains a separate section of maps.

Treaties and Alliances of the World: An International Survey Covering Treaties in Force and Communities of States. New York: Scribner, 1974. Analysis of treaty agreements giving names of the parties to the treaty, date of signature, date of entry into force, and provisions and stipulations.

Yearbook of the United Nations. 1946 to date. New York: United Nations, Office of Public Information, current edition. Annual. Annual summary of the activities of the United Nations and its specialized agencies. Includes subject and name index.

SCIENCE AND TECHNOLOGY

American Men and Women of Science, ed. by Jaques Cattell Press, 13th ed., 6 vols. and index. New York: Bowker, 1978. Comprehensive biographical reference containing profiles of almost 110,000 U.S. and Canadian scientists working in agriculture, biochemistry, botany, geology, medicine, nucleonics, zoology, and other physical and biological sciences. Index volume lists biographies under two separate categories: Geography and Discipline.

Applied Science and Technology Index. 1958 to date. New York: Wilson, current edition. Monthly, annual. Subject index to some 225 engineering and technical periodicals in aeronautics, automation, chemistry, construction, metallurgy, industrial and mechanical arts, transportation, and other areas.

*Asimov's Biographical Encyclopedia of Science and Technology by Isaac Asimov. New York: Doubleday, 1972. Lives and achievements of 1,195 great scientists from ancient to contemporary times presented in brief, readable style. Provides a history of science through the chronology of biographies. Excellent for an orientation and overview of scientific greats.

Biological Abstracts. 1926 to date. Philadelphia: BioSciences Information Services, current edition. Semimonthly, semiannual cumulation. Abstract index covering the fields of general biology, basic medical sciences, microbiology, immunology, public health and parasitology, plant sciences, animal sciences, and many related subjects. Provides five separate indexes: author, systematic, cross, generic, and a computer-made subject index.

Biological and Agricultural Index. 1916 to date. New York: Wilson, current edition. Monthly, annual. Cumulative subject index to 189 periodicals in the fields of biology, agriculture, and related subjects such as chemicals, economics, engineering, animal husbandry, soil science, forestry, veterinary medicine, nutrition, bacteriology, ecology, genetics, and zoology.

Biology Data Book, ed. by Philip L. Altman and D. S. Dittmer, 3 vols. Bethesda, Md.: Federation of American Societies for Experimental Biology, 1972–1974. Basic handbook of tables providing data on all aspects of biology such as anticoagulants, biocides, life spans for animals and seeds, temperature tolerance, and humans. Each table is followed by a full list of references.

*Asterisk indicates reference book recommended for inclusion in a home reference library.

Britannica Yearbook of Science and the Future. 1969 to date. Chicago: Encyclopaedia Britannica, current edition. Annual. Half of the yearbook is devoted to a review of developments in the field of science during the year. The second half provides survey articles on a wide spectrum of contemporary developments in the field of science. Profusely illustrated.

*Chambers Dictionary of Science and Technology, ed. by T. C. Collocott. New York: Barnes and Noble, 1972. Comprehensive, up-to-date, one-volume dictionary arranged alphabetically and covering all aspects of science and technology. Each definition identifies the specific scientific field to which it applies. Appendixes include Table of Chemical Elements, Periodic Table, Igneous Rock, Sedimentary Rocks, The Plant Kingdom, The Animal Kingdom, and the New International Metric System.

Chemical Abstracts. 1907 to date. Columbus, Ohio: American Chemical Society, current edition. Weekly, annual. Basic guide to current articles pertaining to chemistry and allied fields. Each citation is accompanied by an abstract of its contents. Weekly issue is arranged by topic and includes an author index, patent number index, and key word index.

Chemical Formulary, ed. by Harry Bennett, 17 vols. Brooklyn, N.Y.: Chemical Publishing, 1933–1973. Unique reference set providing recipes and formulas for making myriad home and industrial products. Directions are given in concise, easy-to-follow manner.

Condensed Chemical Dictionary, 8th ed. New York: Van Nostrand, 1971. Comprehensive dictionary giving physical properties, uses, sources, values, grades, hazardous nature, and shipping regulations for each chemical listed. Chemical processes are well covered.

Current Physics Index. 1975 to date. New York: American Institute of Physics, current edition. Quarterly, annual cumulative indexes. Quarterly issues provide approximately 4,000 abstracts of journal articles. Abstracts arranged by subject; author index included. Cumulative author and subject indexes issued annually.

Dictionary of Geology by John Challinor, 5th ed. Oxford: Oxford University Press, 1978. Contains 1,500 terms and names; quotations from geological literature illustrate the usage of a given term.

Dictionary of Scientific Biography, ed. by Charles C. Gillispie, 14 vols. New York: Scribner, 1970–1976. Comprehensive, scholarly reference tool published under the auspices of the American Council of Learned Societies. Deceased scientists who have made a significant contribution to the history of science are included. Among these represented are mathematicians, astronomers, physicists, chemists, biologists, metallurgists, pathologists, and earth scientists of all regions and all periods of history.

Encyclopedia of Biochemistry, ed. by Roger J. Williams and E. M. Lansford, Jr. New York: Reinhold, 1967. Designed for use by both lay people and scientists. Provides extensive coverage of biology and chemistry, including biography, definition of terms, and research procedures and findings. Contains analytical index.

Encyclopedia of Physics by Robert M. Besancon, 2nd ed. New York: Van Nostrand, 1974. Covers all phases of the study of physics and allied fields. Includes terminology, processes, formulas, methodology, measurement, etc. Contains detailed index.

Encyclopedia of the Biological Sciences, ed. by Peter Gray, 2nd ed. New York: Van Nostrand, 1970. Standard, scholarly reference tool covering basic aspects of biology— developmental, functional, genetic, structural, and taxonomic. Includes biographies, bibliographies, and illustrations.

---

*Asterisk indicates reference book recommended for inclusion in a home reference library.

Engineering Index. 1884 to date. New York: Engineering Index, current edition. Annual. International in scope, this index analyzes articles in over 3,500 technical journals. Includes abstracts of the articles cited. *Engineering Index Monthly* (New York: Engineering Index, 1962 to date) provides current identification of articles.

General Science Index. 1978 to date. New York: Wilson, current edition. Monthly, annual. Subject index to 90 English-language periodicals. Indexes articles in the fields of astronomy, atmospheric science, biology, botany, chemistry, earth science, environment and conservation, food and nutrition, genetics, mathematics, medicine and health, microbiology, oceanography, physics, physiology, psychology, and zoology. Following the main index is an author listing of citations to book reviews.

Grzimek's Animal Life Encyclopedia, ed. by Bernhard Grzimek, 13 vols. New York: Van Nostrand, 1972–1975. Comprehensive encyclopedia covering all kinds of animal life from the amoeba to the mammals. Chapters are devoted to a specific order or family, giving the characteristics and habits of each. Each volume includes classification outlines, animal name dictionaries, and reading lists. Profusely illustrated.

Handbook of Chemistry and Physics. 1919 to date. Cleveland: Chemical Rubber Co. Press, current edition. Annual. Standard handbook revised annually, giving the constants and formulas used in chemistry and physics, including mathematical and conversion tables.

History of Technology, ed. by Trevor I. Williams, rev. ed. Oxford: Oxford University Press, in process. Complete revision and enlargement of the 1954–1958 edition, edited by Charles Singer et al. Will cover the period from ancient times to today, stressing both the development of technology and the development of society.

McGraw-Hill Encyclopedia of Science and Technology, 3rd ed., 15 vols. New York: McGraw-Hill, 1971. Basic, comprehensive reference tool containing more than 7,600 articles covering all natural and applied sciences. Biographical and historical articles are excluded. Includes many diagrams, charts, and illustrations.

McGraw-Hill Yearbook of Science and Technology. 1966 to date. McGraw-Hill, current edition. Annual. Updates the *McGraw-Hill Encyclopedia of Science and Technology.* Includes three main sections: articles of current concern, photo highlights, and alphabetically arranged articles on new scientific and technological developments.

Mammals of the World by Ernest Pillsbury Walker, 3rd ed., 2 vols. Baltimore: Johns Hopkins Press, 1975. Basic reference tool covering every living genus. Includes a bibliography of some 4,500 titles listed under zoological groups, geographical areas, and general subjects.

Science Year: The World Book Science Annual. 1965 to date. Chicago: Field Enterprises, current edition. Annual. Provides special reports on current scientific breakthroughs and developments as well as special reports on the year's major advances in various fields of science and technology.

A Selected Guide to Information on the Gifted and Talented

NATIONAL INFORMATION SOURCES

The American Association for the Gifted
15 Gramercy Pk.
New York, N.Y. 10003
(212) 473-4266

The Association for the Gifted (TAG)
The Council for Exceptional Children
1920 Association Dr.
Reston, Va. 22091
(800) 336-3728 (toll free)

National Association for Gifted Children
Rte. 5, Box 630A
Hot Springs, Ark. 71901
(501) 767-2669

National Clearing House for the Gifted
and Talented (CEC)
1920 Association Dr.
Reston, Va. 22091
(800) 336-3728 (toll free)

National/State Leadership Training Institute on the Gifted and Talented
316 W. Second St., Suite 708
Los Angeles, Calif. 90012
(213) 489-7470

Office of Gifted and Talented
U.S. Office of Education
Donahue Bldg., Rm. 3538
Sixth and D Sts. S.W.
Washington, D.C. 20202
(202) 245-2481

STATE INFORMATION SOURCES

ALABAMA

Program for Exceptional Children and
Youth
Alabama State Dept. of Education
State Office Bldg., Rm. 416
Montgomery 36130
Cynthia Aguero, Consultant
(205) 832-3230

ALASKA

Office for Exceptional Children
State Dept. of Education
Pouch F
Alaska Office Bldg.
Juneau 99801
Diane Le Resche, Consultant
(907) 465-2970

ARIZONA

Division for Special Education
Arizona Dept. of Education
1535 W. Jefferson
Phoenix 85005
Eleanor Teselle, Coordinator
(602) 255-5009

ARKANSAS

Division of Special Education
Arch Ford Education Bldg.
Little Rock 72201
Clifford Curl, Coordinator
(501) 371-2161

CALIFORNIA

Gifted and Talented Team
California State Dept. of Education
721 Capital Mall
Sacramento 95814
Dr. Paul Plowman, Consultant
(916) 322-3776

COLORADO

Development and Demonstration Unit
Colorado State Dept. of Education
Denver 80203
Jerry Villers, Consultant
(303) 892-2111

CONNECTICUT

Gifted and Talented
State Dept. of Education
Box 2219
Hartford 06115
William G. Vassar, Consultant
(203) 566-3444

DELAWARE

Program for Exceptional Children
State Dept. of Public Instruction
Townsent Bldg.
Dover 19901
Thomas Pledgie, Supervisor
(302) 678-4667

DISTRICT OF COLUMBIA

Gifted and Talented Program
Seaton Elementary School, Rm. 311A
Tenth and Rhode Island Ave. N.W.
Washington, D.C. 20001
Patsy Baker Blackshear, Coordinator
(202) 673-7054

FLORIDA

Gifted and Talented
State Dept. of Education
319 Knott Bldg.
Tallahassee 32304
Joyce Runyon, Consultant
(904) 488-3103

GEORGIA

Program for the Gifted
State Dept. of Education
State Office Bldg.
Atlanta 30334
Margaret O. Bynum, Consultant
(404) 656-2578

HAWAII

Gifted and Talented
State Dept. of Education
1270 Queen Emma St., Rm. 1206
Honolulu 96813
Thomas Hale, Program Specialist
(808) 548-2474

IDAHO

Gifted and Talented
State Dept. of Education
Len B. Jordan Bldg.
Boise 83720
Genelle Christensen, Consultant
(208) 384-2203

ILLINOIS

Gifted Program
Office of Superintendent of Public Instruction
100 N. First St.
Springfield 62777
Linda Avery, Consultant
(217) 782-6601

INDIANA

Curriculum
Dept. of Public Instruction
229 State House
Indianapolis 46204
John A. Harrold, Director
(317) 927-0111

IOWA

Dept. of Public Instruction
Grimes State Office Bldg.
Fourteenth and Grand Ave.
Des Moines 50319
Shirley Perkins, Consultant
(515) 281-3264

KANSAS

Special Education
State Dept. of Education
120 E. Tenth St.
Topeka 66612
James E. Marshall, Director
(913) 296-3866

KENTUCKY

Gifted and Talented
1827 Capitol Plaza Tower
Frankfort 40601
Joseph T. Clark, Coordinator
(502) 564-4774

LOUISIANA

Gifted and Talented
State Dept. of Education
Box 44064, Capital Sta.
Baton Rouge 70804
Ruth Castille, Consultant
(504) 342-3636

MAINE

Special Education Div.
Dept. of Education
Augusta 04333
Patricia O'Connell, Consultant
(207) 289-2033

MARYLAND

Gifted and Talented Education
Box 8717
B.W.I. Airport
Baltimore 02116
Dr. Janice Wickless, Senior Staff Special-
ist
(301) 796-8300

MASSACHUSETTS

Div. of Curriculum and Instruction
31 St. James Ave.
Boston 02116
Roselyn Frank, Consultant
(617) 727-7934

MICHIGAN

Gifted and Talented
Michigan Dept. of Education
Box 30008
Lansing 48909
Nancy Mencemoyer, Consultant
(517) 373-8793

MINNESOTA

Gifted Education
State Dept. of Education
641 Capitol Sq.
St. Paul 55101
Lorraine Hertz, Coordinator
(612) 296-4072

MISSISSIPPI

Div. of Special Education
State Dept. of Education
Box 771
Jackson 39205
Betty Walker, Assistant Director
(601) 354-6950

MISSOURI

Gifted and Talented, Special Education
Dept. of Elementary and Secondary Edu-
cation
Box 480
Jefferson City 65101
Mel Sanders, Consultant
(314) 751-2453

MONTANA

Gifted and Talented
Office of Public Instruction
State Capitol
Helena 59601
Judy Senton, Consultant
(406) 449-3116

NEBRASKA

Gifted and Talented
301 Centennial Mall S.
Lincoln 68509
Ann Crabbe, Consultant
(402) 471-2446

NEVADA

Gifted and Talented
State Dept. of Education
400 W. King St.
Carson City 89701
Jane Early, Consultant
(702) 885-5700

NEW HAMPSHIRE

Dept. of Special Education
State Dept. of Education
105 Loudon Rd., Bldg. 3
Concord 03301
Harvey Harkness, Consultant
(603) 271-3741

NEW JERSEY

Div. of Special Education
State Dept. of Education
225 W. State St.
Trenton 08625
Dr. Ted Gourley, Consultant
(609) 292-7602

NEW MEXICO

Special Education
State Dept. of Education
Education Bldg.
Santa Fe 87503
Elie Gutierrez, Director
(505) 827-2793

NEW YORK

Education for the Gifted
State Education Dept.
Albany 12234
Roger Ming, Supervisor
(518) 474-4973

NORTH CAROLINA

Div. for Exceptional Children
Gifted and Talented
State Dept. of Public Instruction
Education Bldg.
Raleigh 27611
Cornelia Tongue, Coordinator
(919) 829-7931

NORTH DAKOTA

Gifted and Talented Program
Dept. of Public Instruction
Div. of Special Education
State Capitol
Bismarck 58505
LaDonna Whitmore, Coordinator
(701) 224-2277

OHIO

Program for Gifted and Talented
Dept. of Education
922 High St.
Worthington 43085
George Fichter, Educational Consultant
(614) 466-8854

OKLAHOMA

Gifted and Talented
State Dept. of Education
Hodge Bldg.
2500 N. Lincoln Blvd.
Oklahoma City 73105
Renee Amonson, Consultant
(405) 521-3353

OREGON

Gifted and Talented
State Dept. of Education
942 Lancaster Dr. N.E.
Salem 97310
Robert J. Sievert, Specialist
(503) 378-3702

PENNSYLVANIA

Right to Education for Gifted and Talented
500 Valley Forge Pl.
1150 First Ave.
King of Prussia 19406
Jean Farr, Program Director
(215) 265-3706

RHODE ISLAND

Roger Williams Bldg.
22 Hayes St.
Providence 02908
Carolyn Hazard
(401) 277-2821

SOUTH CAROLINA

Program for the Gifted and Talented
Rm. 803, Rutledge Bldg.
State Dept. of Education
Columbia 29201
James Turner, Coordinator
(803) 758-2652

SOUTH DAKOTA

Gifted and Talented
Section for Special Education
Div. of Elementary and Secondary Education
New State Office Bldg.
Pierre 57501
Robert R. Geigle, Consultant
(605) 773-3678

TENNESSEE

State Dept. of Education
103 Cardell Hull Bldg.
Nashville 37219
Dr. Joel Walton, Consultant
(615) 741-2851

TEXAS

Gifted and Talented
Texas Education Agency
201 E. Eleventh St.
Austin 78701
Ann G. Shaw, Program Director
(512) 475-6582

UTAH

Gifted and Talented
250 E. Fifth S.
Salt Lake City 84111
Jewel Bindrup, Consultant
(801) 533-5061

VERMONT

Special Education
State Dept. of Education
Montpelier 05602
Dr. Herb Tilley, Consultant
(802) 828-3161

VIRGINIA

Special Programs for the Gifted
State Dept. of Education
Richmond 23216

Dr. Joseph R. White, Director
(804) 786-3317

WASHINGTON

Gifted and Talented
Dept. of Public Instruction
Old Capital Bldg.
Olympia 98504
Mary Henri Fisher, Director
(206) 753-1140

WEST VIRGINIA

Program Development
Div. of Special Education
Dept. of Education
Capital Complex, Bldg. B, Rm. 315
Charleston 25305
Dr. Barbara Jones, Coordinator
(304) 348-2034

WISCONSIN

Gifted and Talented Program
Dept. of Public Instruction
126 Langdon St.
Madison 53702
Thomas F. Diener, Supervisor
(608) 266-2658

WYOMING

Language Arts and Gifted and Talented
　Education
State Dept. of Education
Hathaway Bldg. W., Rm. 250
Cheyenne 82002
Sue Holt, Coordinator
(307) 777-7411

OTHER INFORMATION SOURCES

AMERICAN SAMOA

Gifted and Talented
Dept. of Special Education
Pago Pago 96799
Dennis McCray, Program Director
Overseas Operator 633-2435

GUAM

Special Education
Dept. of Education
Box DE
Agana 96910
Victoria T. Harper, Associate Superintendent
Overseas Operator 772-8418

PUERTO RICO

Special Education
Dept. of Education
Hato Rey 00924
Maria L. de Jesus, Director
(809) 765-1475

TRUST TERRITORY

Leadership Training Center for Gifted
　and Talented Education
Trust Territory of the Pacific Islands
`Ebeye, Marshall Islands
Box 1748
A.P.O. San Francisco 96555
Carol Shulkind, Director

JOURNALS AND NEWSLETTERS

*Bulletin of the National/State Leadership
　Training Institute on the Gifted and
　Talented*
Civic Center Tower Bldg.
316 W. Second St., Suite PH-C
Los Angeles, Calif. 90012 (monthly $11)

G/C/T (Gifted/Creative/Talented Children)
G/C/T Publishing Co.
Box 66654
Mobile, Ala. 36606 (5 times a year
　$12.50)

The Gifted Child Quarterly
The National Association for Gifted Children
217 Gregory Dr.
Hot Springs, Ark. 71901 (quarterly $20,
　includes membership in NAGC)

Gifted/Talented Education Newsletter
Box 533
Branford, Conn. 06405 (monthly $12.50)

ITYB (Intellectually Talented Youth Bulletin)
Box 1360
Johns Hopkins Univ.
Baltimore, Md. 21218 (10 issues a year
　$6)

Journal for the Education of the Gifted
The Association for the Gifted
Council for Exceptional Children
Editorial Office
School of Education
University of Virginia
Charlottesville 22903 (quarterly $12)

Journal of Creative Behavior
State University College at Buffalo
1300 Elmwood Ave.
Buffalo, N.Y. 14222 (quarterly $9)

Teaching Gifted Children: Methods, Motivation and Materials
Croft-NEI Publications
24 Rope Ferry Rd.
Waterford, Conn. 06386 (9 issues a year,
  $2 per issue)

Publisher/Producer/Distributor Directory

Abingdon Press
201 Eighth Ave. S.
Nashville, Tenn. 37202

Harry N. Abrams, Inc.
110 E. 59 St.
New York, N.Y. 10022

Activa Products, Inc.
582 Market St.
San Francisco, Calif. 94104

Addison-Wesley Publishing Co., Inc.
Jacob Way
Reading, Mass. 01867

Advanced Placement
College Board
Box 2815
Princeton, N.J. 08541

Aldine Publishing Co.
529 S. Wabash Ave.
Chicago, Ill. 60605

Allyn and Bacon, Inc.
470 Atlantic Ave.
Boston, Mass. 02210

American Automobile Association
8111 Gatehouse Rd.
Falls Church, Va. 22042

American Chemical Society
1155 16 St. N.W.
Washington, D.C. 20036

American Heritage Press
1221 Ave. of the Americas
New York, N.Y. 10036

American Institute of Physics
335 E. 45 St.
New York, N.Y. 10017

American Library Assn.
50 E. Huron St.
Chicago, Ill. 60611

American Pageant
Produced by Media Systems
Consultants for the Perfection
Form Co.
Logan, Iowa 51546

Leon Amiel Publishing
31 W. 46 St.
New York, N.Y. 10036

Animal Protection Institute of America
Box 22505
Sacramento, Calif. 95822

Appleton-Century-Crofts
(see Prentice-Hall, Inc.)

Applied Arts Publishers
Box 479
Lebanon, Pa. 17042

Arlington House Publishers
165 Huguenot St.
New Rochelle, N.Y. 10801

Associated Press
(see Pathescope Educational Media, Inc.)

Atheneum Publishers
122 E. 42 St.
New York, N.Y. 10017

BFA Educational Media
Bailey Film Associates
Box 1795
2211 Michigan Ave.
Santa Monica, Calif. 90406

Ballinger Publishing Co.
17 Dunster St., Harvard Sq.
Cambridge, Mass. 02138

Bantam Books, Inc.
666 Fifth Ave.
New York, N.Y. 10019

Barnes & Noble, Inc.
10 E. 53 St.
New York, N.Y. 10022

Barron's Educational Series, Inc.
113 Crossways Park Dr.
Woodbury, N.Y. 11797

Basic Books, Inc.
10 E. 53 St.
New York, N.Y. 10022

Becky Thatcher Gift Shop
Hannibal, Mo. 63857

Belknap Press
(see Harvard University Press)

Benefic Press
10300 W. Roosevelt Rd.
Westchester, Ill. 60153

Benziger, Bruce & Glencoe, Inc.
866 Third Ave.
New York, N.Y. 10022

Beswick
Doulton and Co., Inc.
400 Paterson Plank Rd.
Carlstadt, N.J. 07072

Channing L. Bete Co.
Greenfield, Mass.

Books for Libraries, Inc.
One Dupont St.
Plainview, N.Y. 11803

R. R. Bowker Co.
1180 Ave. of the Americas
New York, N.Y. 10036

Bowling Green University
Popular Press
101 University Hall
Bowling Green, Ohio 43403

Bowmar Publishing Corp.
4563 Colorado Blvd.
Los Angeles, Calif. 90039

Boy Scouts of America
North Brunswick, N.J. 08902

George Braziller, Inc.
One Park Ave.
New York, N.Y. 10016

Herbert E. Budek
Box 307
Santa Barbara, Calif. 93102

Cambridge University Press
32 E. 57 St.
New York, N.Y. 10022

Capitol Records
1750 N. Vine St.
Hollywood, Calif. 90028

Carrollton Press
19-11 Fort Myer Dr.
Arlington, Va. 22209

Cathedral Films, Inc.
2921 W. Alameda Ave.
Burbank, Calif. 91905

Center for Humanities, Inc.
Communications Pk.
Box 100
White Plains, N.Y. 10602

Center for Short-Lived Phenomena
138 Mt. Auburn St.
Cambridge, Mass. 02138

Centron Films
1621 W. Ninth St.
Box 687
Lawrence, Kans. 66044

Chelsea House Publishers
70 W. 40 St.
New York, N.Y. 10018

Chemical Publishing Co., Inc.
200 Park Ave. S.
New York, N.Y. 10003

Children's Book Council
67 Irving Pl.
New York, N.Y. 10003

Childrens Press, Inc.
1224 W. Van Buren St.
Chicago, Ill. 60607

College Board Publications
Box 2815
Princeton, N.J. 08541

Collier Macmillan, Inc.
866 Third Ave.
New York, N.Y. 10022

Collins & World
2080 W. 117 St.
Cleveland, Ohio 44111

Columbia Records
51 W. 52 St.
New York, N.Y. 10020

Columbia University Press
562 W. 113 St.
New York, N.Y. 10025

Congressional Information Service
7101 Wisconsin Ave.
Washington, D.C. 20014

Cooper Square Publishers, Inc.
59 Fourth Ave.
New York, N.Y. 10003

Cornell University Press
124 Roberts Pl.
Ithaca, N.Y. 14850

Coronet Instructional Media
65 E. South Water St.
Chicago, Ill. 60601

Council for Exceptional Children
1920 Association Dr.
Reston, Va. 22091

Council of State Governments
Box 11910
Lexington, Ky. 40511

Council on Foreign Relations
58 E. 68 St.
New York, N.Y. 10020

Coward, McCann and Geoghegan, Inc.
200 Madison Ave.
New York, N.Y. 10016

Creative Educational Society, Inc.
123 S. Broad St.
Mankato, Minn. 56001

Creative Learning Press, Inc.
Box 320
Mansfield Center, Conn. 06250

Thomas Y. Crowell Co.
666 Fifth Ave.
New York, N.Y. 10003

Crown Publishers, Inc.
419 Park Ave. S.
New York, N.Y. 10016

DOK Publishers
71 Radcliffe Rd.
Buffalo, N.Y. 14214

Da Capo Press, Inc.
227 W. 17 St.
New York, N.Y. 10011

Dana Productions
6249 Babcock Ave.
North Hollywood, Calif. 91696

Marcel Dekker, Inc.
270 Madison Ave.
New York, N.Y. 10016

Dekor Shop
(no address available)

Dell Publishing Co.
One Dag Hammarskjold Pl.
New York, N.Y. 10017

Disney Educational Media. Inc.
500 S. Buena Vista St.
Burbank, Calif. 91521

Dodd, Mead, & Co.
79 Madison Ave.
New York, N.Y. 10016

Doubleday & Co., Inc.
245 Park Ave.
New York, N.Y. 10017

Dover Publications, Inc.
180 Varick St.
New York, N.Y. 10014

Dutch Inn Gift Shop
211 N. Water St.
Mill Hall, Pa. 17751

E. P. Dutton & Co., Inc.
201 Park Ave. S.
New York, N.Y. 10003

ERIC Clearinghouse on Handicapped &
Gifted Children
1920 Association Dr.
Reston, Va. 22091

ETC Publications
18512 Pierce Terr.
Homewood, Ill. 60430

Educational Dimensions Group
Box 126
Stamford, Conn. 06904

Educational Enrichment Materials
110 S. Bedford Rd.
Mt. Kisco, N.Y. 10549

Educational Reading Service
(see Troll Associates)

Educational Records, Inc.
157 Chambers St.
New York, N.Y. 10007

Educational Technology Publications,
Inc.
140 Sylvan Ave.
Englewood Cliffs, N.J. 07632

Encyclopaedia Britannica Educational
Corp.
425 N. Michigan Ave.
Chicago, Ill. 60611

Engineering Index, Inc.
345 E. 47 St.
New York, N.Y. 10017

Enrichment Records
(see Educational Enrichment Materials)

Eye Gate Media
146-01 Archer Ave.
Jamaica, N.Y. 11435

Federation of American Societies for Experimental Biology
9650 Rockville Pike
Bethesda, Md. 20014

Field Enterprises Educational Corp.
510 Merchandise Mart Pl.
Chicago, Ill. 60654

Films, Inc.
1144 Wilmette Ave.
Wilmette, Ill. 60091

Follett Publishing Co.
1010 W. Washington Blvd.
Chicago, Ill. 60607

Free Press
(see Macmillan, Inc.)

Funk & Wagnalls Co.
(Dist. by Thomas Y. Crowell, Co.)

Gakken Publishing Co.
(see Japan Publications Trading Co.)

Gale Research Co.
Book Tower
Detroit, Mich. 48226

Garrard Publishing Co.
Champaign, Ill. 61820

Glencoe Press, Inc.
(see Benziger, Bruce & Glencoe, Inc.)

Globe Book Co., Inc.
175 Fifth Ave.
New York, N.Y. 10010

Globe Filmstrips, Inc.
175 Fifth Ave.
New York, N.Y. 10010

Golden Press
(see Western Publishing Co., Inc.)

Gordon & Breach Science Publishers
One Park Ave.
New York, N.Y. 10016

William Greaves Productions, Inc.
254 W. 54 St.
New York, N.Y. 10019

Greenwood Press, Inc.
51 Riverside Ave.
Westport, Conn. 06880

Grolier, Inc.
575 Lexington Ave.
New York, N.Y. 10022

Grosset & Dunlap
51 Madison Ave.
New York, N.Y. 10010

Guidance Associates
757 Third Ave.
New York, N.Y. 10017

E. M. Hale & Co.
1201 S. Hastings Way
Eau Claire, Wis. 54701

Halsted Press
(see John Wiley & Sons, Inc.)

Hammond, Inc.
515 Valley St.
Maplewood, N.J. 07040

Handel Film Corp.
8730 Sunset Blvd.
Los Angeles, Calif. 90069

Harcourt Brace Jovanovich, Inc.
757 Third Ave.
New York, N.Y. 10017

Harper & Row Publishers, Inc.
10 E. 53 St.
New York, N.Y. 10022

Harvard University Press
79 Garden St.
Cambridge, Mass. 02138

Harvey House, Inc.
(see E.M. Hale & Co.)

Hastings House Publishers, Inc.
10 E. 40 St.
New York, N.Y. 10016

Hawthorn Books, Inc.
260 Madison Ave.
New York, N.Y. 10016

Heritage Press
170 Franklin St.
Buffalo, N.Y. 14202

Hill & Wang, Inc.
19 Union Sq.
New York, N.Y. 10003

Holiday House, Inc.
18 E. 53 St.
New York, N.Y. 10022

Holt, Rinehart, & Winston, Inc.
383 Madison Ave.
New York, N.Y. 10017

Horn Book, Inc.
585 Boylston St.
Boston, Mass. 02116

Houghton Mifflin Co.
2 Park St.
Boston, Mass. 02107

Imperial Productions, Inc.
Educational Division
Kankakee, Ill. 60901

Institute of Electrical & Electronics Engineers
445 Hoes Lane
Piscataway, N.J. 08854

Institute of General Semantics
Lakeville, Conn. 06039

International City Management Assn.
1140 Connecticut Ave. N.W.
Washington, D.C. 20036

International Society for General Semantics
Box 2469
San Francisco, Calif. 94126

International Society for the Protection of Mustangs & Burros
140 Greenstone Dr.
Reno, Nev. 89502

Japan Publications Trading Co.
1255 Howard St.
San Francisco, Calif. 94103

Johns Hopkins Press
Baltimore, Md. 21218

Kendall Hunt Publishing Co.
2460 Kerper Blvd.
Dubuque, Iowa 52001

Alfred A. Knopf, Inc.
201 E. 50 St.
New York, N.Y. 10022

Larlin Corp.
Box 1523
Marietta, Ga. 30061

Lerner Publications Co.
241 First Ave. N.
Minneapolis, Minn. 55401

Library Products
Box 130
Sturgis, Mich. 49091

J. B. Lippincott Co.
E. Washington Sq.
Philadelphia, Pa. 19105

Listening Library, Inc.
One Park Ave.
Old Greenwich, Conn. 06870

Little, Brown & Co.
34 Beacon St.
Boston, Mass. 02106

Lothrop, Lee & Shepard Co.
105 Madison Ave.
New York, N.Y. 10016

McGraw-Hill Book Co.
1221 Ave. of the Americas
New York, N.Y. 10036

David McKay Co., Inc.
750 Third Ave.
New York, N.Y. 10017

Macmillan, Inc.
866 Third Ave.
New York, N.Y. 10022

Macmillan Educational Corp.
(see Macmillan, Inc.)

Marquis–Who's Who Books
200 E. Ohio St.
Chicago, Ill. 60611

Media Systems, Inc.
3637 E. 7800, S.
Salt Lake City, Utah 84121

G. & C. Merriam Co.
47 Federal St.
Box 281
Springfield, Mass. 01101

Julian Messner, Inc.
One W. 39 St.
New York, N.Y. 10018

Miller-Brody Productions, Inc.
342 Madison Ave.
New York, N.Y. 10017

Modern Language Association of America
62 Fifth Ave.
New York, N.Y. 10011

Monarch Press
One W. 39 St.
New York, N.Y. 10018

William Morrow & Co., Inc.
105 Madison Ave.
New York, N.Y. 10016

NASA Publications
National Aeronautics & Space Administration
Washington, D.C. 20546

National Association for Creative Children & Adults
8080 Springvalley Dr.
Cincinnati, Ohio 45236

National Broadcasting Co.
30 Rockefeller Center
New York, N.Y. 10020

National Council for the Social Studies
2030 M St. N.W.
Suite 400
Washington, D.C. 20036

National Council of Teachers of English
1111 Kenyon Rd.
Urbana, Ill. 61801

National Education Association
1201 16th St. N.W.
Washington, D.C. 20036

National Film Board of Canada
680 Fifth Ave.
New York, N.Y. 10019

National Geographic Society
17th & M Sts. N.W.
Washington, D.C. 20036

New American Library
1301 Ave. of the Americas
New York, N.Y. 10019

New York Graphic Society, Ltd.
11 Beacon St.
Boston, Mass. 02108

New York Times Co.
Book Div.
330 Madison Ave.
New York, N.Y. 10017

North Hills School District
Administrative Offices
50 Rochester Rd.
Pittsburgh, Pa. 15229

W. W. Norton & Co., Inc.
500 Fifth Ave.
New York, N.Y. 10036

Ortho Books
575 Market St.
San Francisco, Calif. 94105

Outdoor Pictures
Box 277
Anacortes, Wash. 98221

Oxford University Press, Inc.
200 Madison Ave.
New York, N.Y. 10016

Pantheon Books
201 E. 50 St.
New York, N.Y. 10022

Parents Magazine Press
52 Vanderbilt Ave.
New York, N.Y. 10017

Pathescope Educational Media, Inc.
71 Weyman Ave.
New Rochelle, N.Y. 10802

Patterson Smith Publishing Co.
23 Prospect Terr.
Montclair, N.J. 07042

Pennsylvania Department of Education
Box 911
Harrisburg, Pa. 17126

Peter Smith Publisher, Inc.
6 Lexington Ave.
Gloucester, Mass. 01930

Pflaum Publishing Co.
2285 Arbor Blvd.
Dayton, Ohio 45402

Phi Delta Kappa, Inc.
Eighth & Union
Box 789
Bloomington, Ind. 47401

Pied Piper Productions
Box 320
Verdugo City, Calif. 91046

Platt & Munk Publishers
1055 Bronx River Ave.
Bronx, N.Y. 10472

Praeger Publishers
111 Fifth Ave.
New York, N.Y. 10003

Prentice-Hall, Inc.
Englewood Cliffs, N.J. 07632

G. P. Putnam's Sons
200 Madison Ave.
New York, N.Y. 10016

Quadrangle/New York Times Co.
10 E. 53 St.
New York, N.Y. 10022

Rand McNally & Co.
Box 7600
Chicago, Ill. 60680

Random House, Inc.
201 E. 50 St.
New York, N.Y. 10022

Reader's Digest Press
10 E. 53 St.
New York, N.Y. 10022

Ronald Press Co.
79 Madison Ave.
New York, N.Y. 10016

Routledge & Kegan Paul, Ltd.
9 Park St.
Boston, Mass. 02108

Running Press
38 S. 19 St.
Philadelphia, Pa. 19103

Russell Sage Foundation
230 Park Ave.
New York, N.Y. 10017

SVE
(see Society for Visual Education, Inc.)

St. Martin's Press, Inc.
175 Fifth Ave.
New York, N.Y. 10010

Sandler Institutional Films
1001 N. Poinsettia
Hollywood, Calif. 90046

Scarecrow Press, Inc.
52 Liberty St.
Box 656
Metuchen, N.J. 08840

Schirmer Books
866 Third Ave.
New York, N.Y. 10022

Scholastic Book Services
906 Sylvan Ave.
Englewood Cliffs, N.J. 07632

Scott, Foresman & Co.
1900 E. Lake Ave.
Glenview, Ill. 60025

Charles Scribner's Sons
597 Fifth Ave.
New York, N.Y. 10020

Seabury Press, Inc.
815 Second Ave.
New York, N.Y. 10017

Sears Roebuck & Co.
925 Hohman Ave.
Chicago, Ill. 60607

Silver Burdett Co.
250 James St.
Morristown, N.J. 07960

Simon & Schuster, Inc.
630 Fifth Ave.
New York, N.Y. 10020

Smithsonian Institution Press
Washington, D.C. 20560

Society for Visual Education (SVE), Inc.
1345 Diversey Pkwy.
Chicago, Ill. 60614

Somerset
(Reprinted by) Burt Franklin & Co., Inc.
235 E. 44 St.
New York, N.Y. 10017

Spoken Arts, Inc.
310 North Ave.
New Rochelle, N.Y. 10801

Stackpole Books
Cameron & Keller Sts.
Harrisburg, Pa. 17105

Steck-Vaughn Co.
Box 2028
Austin, Tex. 78767

Sterling Publishing Co., Inc.
419 Park Ave.
New York, N.Y. 10016

Superintendent of Documents
U.S. Government Printing Office
Washington, D.C. 20402

Swallow Press, Inc.
811 W. Junior Terr.
Chicago, Ill. 60613

Teaching Resources Films, Inc.
Station Plaza
Bedford Hills, N.Y. 10507

Troll Associates
320 Rte. 17
Mahwah, N.J. 07430

Frederick Ungar Publishing Co., Inc.
250 Park Ave. S.
New York, N.Y. 10003

UNIPUB
Xerox Publishing Co.
Box 433
Murray Hill Sta.
New York, N.Y. 10016

United Learning
6633 Howard St.
Niles, Ill. 60648

United Nations
Office of Public Information
New York, N.Y. 10017

U.S. Government Printing Office
(see Superintendent of Documents)

U.S. Office of Gifted & Talented
Donahue Building, Rm. 3538
Sixth & D Sts. S.W.
Washington, D.C. 20202

Universe Books, Inc.
381 Park Ave. S.
New York, N.Y. 10016

University Microfilms International
300 N. Zeeb Rd.
Ann Arbor, Mich. 48106

D. Van Nostrand Co.
450 W. 33 St.
New York, N.Y. 10001

Viking Press
625 Madison Ave.
New York, N.Y. 10022

Henry Z. Walck, Inc.
750 Third Ave.
New York, N.Y. 10017

Walker & Co.
720 Fifth Ave.
New York, N.Y. 10019

Frederick Warne & Co.
101 Fifth Ave.
New York, N.Y. 10003

Warner Books, Inc.
75 Rockefeller Pl.
New York, N.Y. 10019

Washburn, Ives, Inc.
750 Third Ave.
New York, N.Y. 10017

Watson-Guptill
2160 Patterson St.
Cincinnati, Ohio 45214

Franklin Watts, Inc.
730 Fifth Ave.
New York, N.Y. 10019

Wayne State University Press
5980 Cass Ave.
Detroit, Mich. 48202

John Weatherhill, Inc.
149 Madison Ave.
New York, N.Y. 10016

Weise Winkler Bindery,
   Inc.
631 North St.
Cincinnati, Ohio 45202

Western Publishing Co.,
   Inc.
150 Parish Dr.
Wayne, N.J. 07470

Weston Woods Studios
Weston, Conn. 06883

James T. White Co.
1700 State Highway 3
Clifton, N.J. 07013

Albert Whitman & Co.
560 W. Lake St.
Chicago, Ill. 60606

John Wiley & Sons, Inc.
605 Third Ave.
New York, N.Y. 10016

H. W. Wilson
950 University Ave.
Bronx, N.Y. 10452

World Book–Childcraft International,
   Inc.
Box 3565
Merchandise Mart Pl.
Chicago, Ill. 60654

World Book Encyclopedia,
   Inc.
510 Merchandise Mart Pl.
Chicago, Ill. 60654

World Publishing Co., Inc.
2080 W. 117 St.
Cleveland, Ohio 44111

Wyeth Press
Great Barrington, Mass. 02130

Bibliography

Barzun, Jacques. *House of Intellect*. New York: Harper, 1959.

Bloom, Benjamin S., ed. *Taxonomy of Educational Objectives: The Classification of Educational Goals—Handbook I, Cognitive Domain*. New York: David McKay, 1956.

Bruner, Jerome S. *The Process of Education*. Cambridge, Mass.: Harvard University Press, 1960.

Burton, William H. *The Guidance of Learning Activities: A Summary of the Principles of Teaching Based on the Growth of the Learner*, 3rd ed. New York: Appleton, 1962.

———, Kimball, Roland B., and Wing, Richard L. *Education for Effective Thinking*. New York: Appleton, 1960.

Callahan, Carolyn M. *Developing Creativity in the Gifted and Talented*. Reston, VA: Council for Exceptional Children, 1978.

Correll, Marsha M. *Teaching the Gifted and Talented*. Bloomington, Ind.: Phi Delta Kappa, 1978.

Council for Exceptional Children. *The Nation's Commitment to the Education of Gifted and Talented Children and Youth: Summary of Findings from a 1977 Survey of States and Territories*.

Dale, Edgar. *Building a Learning Environment*. Bloomington, Ind.: Phi Delta Kappa, 1972.

Davies, Ruth Ann. *The School Library Media Program: Instructional Force for Excellence*, 3rd ed. New York: R. R. Bowker, 1979.

Drews, Elizabeth M. *Learning Together: How to Foster Creativity, Self-Fulfillment, and Social Awareness in Today's Students and Teachers*. Englewood Cliffs, N.J.: Prentice-Hall, 1972.

Feldhusen, J. F., and Treffinger, D. J. *Teaching Creative Thinking and Problem-Solving*. Dubuque, Iowa: Kendall/Hunt, 1977.

Fortna, Richard O., and Boston, Bruce O. *Testing the Gifted Child: An Interpretation in Lay Language*. Reston, VA: Council for Exceptional Children, 1976.

Gallagher, James J. *Teaching the Gifted Child*, 2nd ed. Boston: Allyn and Bacon, 1975.

General Education in a Free Society: A Report of the Harvard Committee. Cambridge, Mass.: Harvard University Press, 1945.

Getzels, Jacob W., and Jackson, Philip W. *Creativity and Intelligence*. New York: Wiley, 1962.

Gowan, John C., Demos, George D., and Torrance, E. Paul. *Creativity: Its Educational Implications*. New York: Wiley, 1967.

Guilford, J. P. *The Nature of Human Intelligence*. New York: McGraw-Hill, 1967.

Jones, T. P. *Creative Learning in Perspective*. New York: Wiley, 1972.

Kagan, Jerome, ed. *Creativity and Learning*. Boston: Houghton, 1967.

Kaplan, Sandra N. *Providing Programs for the Gifted and Talented: A Handbook.* Reston, VA: Council for Exceptional Children, 1975.

Krathwohl, David R., et al. *Taxonomy of Educational Objectives: The Classification of Educational Goals—Handbook II, Affective Domain.* New York: David McKay, 1964.

Lewy, Arieh, ed. *Handbook of Curriculum Evaluation.* Institute for Educational Planning. Paris. UNESCO and New York: Longman, 1977.

Lyon, Harold C. *Learning to Feel, Feeling to Learn: Studies of the Person.* Columbus, Ohio: Charles E. Merrill, 1971.

Marland, Sidney P., Jr. *Education of the Gifted and Talented, Report to the Congress of the United States by the U.S. Commissioner of Education,* 2 vols. Washington, D.C.: U.S. Government Printing Office, 1972.

Martinson, Ruth A. *The Identification of the Gifted and Talented.* Reston, VA: Council for Exceptional Children, 1975.

Mott, Jacolyn A. *Creativity and Imagination.* Basic Student Orientation Reference. Mankato, Minn.: Creative Education, 1973.

Parnes, Sidney J. *Creativity: Unlocking Human Potential.* Buffalo, N.Y.: D.O.K., 1972.

Passow, A. Harry, ed. *The Gifted and the Talented: Their Education and Development.* The Seventy-Eighth Yearbook of the National Society for the Study of Education, Part I. Chicago: National Society for the Study of Education, 1979.

The Pursuit of Excellence: Education and the Future of America. America at Mid-Century Series, Special Studies Project Report V, Rockefeller Brothers Fund. New York: Doubleday, 1958.

Renzulli, Joseph S. *The Enrichment Triad Model: A Guide for Developing Defensible Programs for the Gifted and Talented.* Mansfield Center, Conn.: Creative Learning Press, 1977.

————. *New Directions in Creativity, Mark 1, Mark 2,. Mark 3,* 3 vols. New York: Harper, 1973, 1976.

The Report of the President's Commission on National Goals. *Goals for Americans.* The American Assembly, Columbia University, New York. Englewood Cliffs, N.J.: Prentice-Hall, 1960.

Shane, Harold G. *Curriculum Change Toward the 21st Century.* Curriculum series. Washington, D.C.: National Education Association, 1977.

Taylor, Calvin W., ed. *Creativity across Education.* Ogden: University of Utah Press, 1968.

————, ed. *Creativity: Progress and Potential.* New York: McGraw-Hill, 1964.

Taylor, Irving A., and Getzels, Jacob W., eds. *Perspectives in Creativity.* Chicago: Aldine, 1975.

Tickton, Sidney G., ed. *To Improve Learning: An Evaluation of Instructional Technology,* 2 vols. New York: R. R. Bowker, 1971.

Torrance, E. Paul. *Creativity in the Classroom.* What Research Says to the Teacher series. Washington, D.C.: National Education Association, 1977.

————, *Education and the Creative Potential.* Minneapolis: University of Minnesota Press, 1963.

Travers, Robert M. W., ed. *Second Handbook of Research on Teaching.* A Project of the American Educational Research Association. Chicago: Rand McNally, 1973.

Tuttle, Frederick B., Jr. *Gifted and Talented Students.* What Research Says to the Teacher series. Washington, D.C.: National Education Association, 1978.

Williams, Frank E. *Classroom Ideas for Encouraging Thinking and Feeling,* 2nd ed. Buffalo, N.Y.: D.O.K., 1970.

————. *Total Creativity Program for Individualizing and Humanizing the Learning Process.* Englewood Cliffs, N.J.: Educational Technology Publications, 1972.

Index